Ric   s'®

D0379122

AMSTERDAM
BRUGES & BRUSSELS

Rick Steves & Gene Openshaw

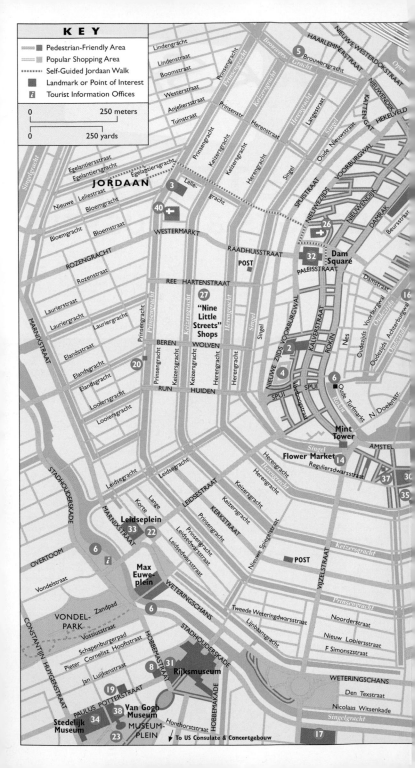

KEY

- Pedestrian-Friendly Area
- Popular Shopping Area
- Self-Guided Jordaan Walk
- Landmark or Point of Interest
- **i** Tourist Information Offices

0 ——— 250 meters
0 ——— 250 yards

Lindengracht
Lindenstraat
Boomstraat
Westerstraat
Anjeliersstraat
Tuinstraat

NIEUWE WESTERDOKSTRAAT
HAARLEMMERSTRAAT
Brouwersgracht
5
Brouwersgracht

Prinsengracht
Keizersgracht
Herengracht
Prinsenstr
Herenstraat
Singel
Langestraat
Oude Nieuwezijds
NIEUWENDIJK
KATTENGAT
HEKELVELD

Egelantiersstraat
Egelantiersgracht
Egelaptiersgracht
JORDAAN
3
Lelie-gracht
SPUISTRAAT
NIEUWEZIJDS
NIEUWENDIJK
DAMRAK

Nieuwe Leliestraat
Bloemgracht
Bloemgracht
Bloemstraat
40 ✚
WESTERMARKT
RAADHUISSTRAAT
POST
26 ✇
32
Dam Square
PALEISSTRAAT
Damstraat
Beursstr

ROZENGRACHT
Rozenstraat
REE HARTENSTRAAT
27
"Nine Little Streets" Shops
NIEUWE ZIJDS VOORBURGWAL
Voorburgwal
Oudezijds
Oudezijds Achterburgwal
16
Omtmegp

MARNIXSTRAAT
Lauriergracht
Laurierstraat
Lauriergracht
Elandsstraat
Elandsgracht
Looiersgracht
Looiersgracht
20
Prinsengracht
Prinsengracht
Keizersgracht
Keizersgracht
Herengracht
Herengracht
BEREN
WOLVEN
RUN
HUIDEN
Singel
Singel
2
4
6
SPUI
SPUI
Spuistraat
Nes
Oude Turfmarkt
N. Doelenstr.

Mint Tower
AMSTEL
Flower Market
14
Reguliersdwarsstraat
37
30
35

STADHOUDERSKADE
Leidsegracht
Leidsegracht
Korte
Lange
Leidsestraat
KERKSTRAAT
Herengracht
Herengracht
Keizersgracht
Keizersgracht
Prinsengracht
Prinsengracht
Nieuwe Spiegelstraat
Leidsedwarsstraat
Leidsedwarsstraat
Singel
VIJZELSTRAAT
Keizersgracht

Leidseplein
33
22
6
i
OVERTOOM
Vondelstraat

Max Euwe-plein
WETERINGSCHANS
POST
Prinsengracht

VONDEL-PARK
6
Vossiusstraat
Schapenburgerpad
Pieter Cornelisz Hooftstraat
Jan Luijkenstraat
CONSTANTIJN HUYGENSSTRAAT
Zandpad
Tweede Weteringdwarsstraat
Lijnbaansgracht
Noorderstraat
Nieuw Looiersstraat
F Simonszstraat

STADHOUDERSKADE
HOBBEMASTRAAT
31
8
Rijksmuseum
HOBBEKADE
Honthorststraat
WETERINGSCHANS
Den Texstraat
Nicolaas Witsenkade
Singelgracht

19
PAULUS POTTERSTRAAT
38
Van Gogh Museum
34
Stedelijk Museum
23
MUSEUM-PLEIN
To US Consulate & Concertgebouw
17

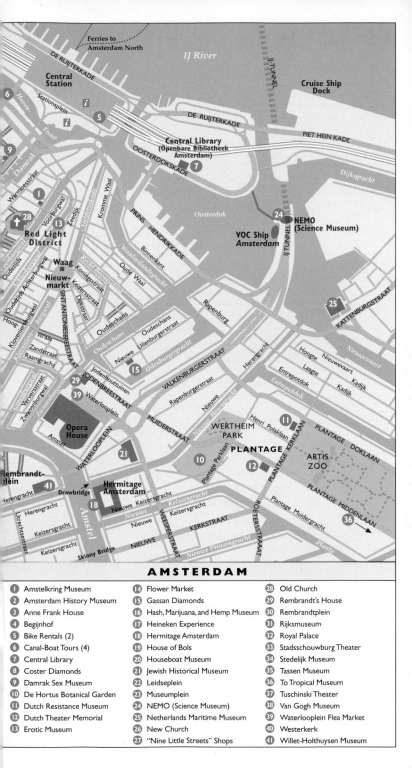

AMSTERDAM

1. Amstelkring Museum
2. Amsterdam History Museum
3. Anne Frank House
4. Begijnhof
5. Bike Rentals (2)
6. Canal-Boat Tours (4)
7. Central Library
8. Coster Diamonds
9. Damrak Sex Museum
10. De Hortus Botanical Garden
11. Dutch Resistance Museum
12. Dutch Theater Memorial
13. Erotic Museum
14. Flower Market
15. Gassan Diamonds
16. Hash, Marijuana, and Hemp Museum
17. Heineken Experience
18. Hermitage Amsterdam
19. House of Bols
20. Houseboat Museum
21. Jewish Historical Museum
22. Leidseplein
23. Museumplein
24. NEMO (Science Museum)
25. Netherlands Maritime Museum
26. New Church
27. "Nine Little Streets" Shops
28. Old Church
29. Rembrandt's House
30. Rembrandtplein
31. Rijksmuseum
32. Royal Palace
33. Stadsschouwburg Theater
34. Stedelijk Museum
35. Tassen Museum
36. To Tropical Museum
37. Tuschinski Theater
38. Van Gogh Museum
39. Waterlooplein Flea Market
40. Westerkerk
41. Willet-Holthuysen Museum

KEY

═══ A7 ═══	Freeway
———	Major Rail Line
·············	Ferry Lines
✈	Airport
Haarlem	Recommended Location*
Nijmegen	Just Passing Through**
■	Ruin, Museum, Other Point of Interest

* Black locations are places of interest to tourists, sized by importance. Many are covered in this guidebook.

** Gray locations are places of little or no interest to tourists and are sized by population.

0 km	50 km	100 km

0 mi		50 mi

North

Sea

Wadden Islands

Emden

Waddenzee

Groningen

Leeuwarden

A7

A28

Den Helder

Afsluitdijk

• Hindeloopen

A31

NETHERLANDS

Medemblik •■

■ *Zuiderzee Museum*

Alkmaar •

Enkhuizen ■ *Schokland*

Zaanse Schans ■

Hoorn

Lelystad

Haarlem ■

Edam

Zandvoort •

• Marken

Flevoland

Keukenhof ■

✈ **Amsterdam**

Aalsmeer •

✈ *Schiphol*

A1

Bad Bentheim

Scheveningen •

Leiden

HOGUE VELUWE NATIONAL PARK

Hengelo • A30

The Hague •

Utrecht

A2

A12

Open-Air Museum ■

• **Delft**

Hoek van Holland •

Rotterdam

A15

A16 A27

Waal

Arnhem

Emmerich

Nijmegen

Rhine

To Harwich, England

A3

Maas

A2

A57

Middelburg •

A58

✈

Eindhoven •

A73

Duisburg

Essen

Zeebrugge

A67

Venlo •

✈

Ostende •

■ **Bruges**

F L A N D E R S

• **Antwerp**

E313

Düsseldorf

A1

E40

Flanders Fields Museum

Ghent

✈

Hasselt •

GERMANY

■ *Ieper*

E17

Brussels

Leuven •

• **Maastricht**

Köln •

Waterloo ■

E40

Tournai •

BELGIUM

• Aachen

Remagen •

Lille

A26

E40

Líege

E42

A1

A6

E42

Namur

Meuse

Mons •

E25

Zel

Arras •

Cambrai •

W A L L O N I E

Cochem •

Dinant •

• La Roche

A1

Aulnoye •

Bastogne

A R D E N N E S

• Vianden

FRANCE

St. Quentin

LUXEMBOURG

• Trier

Charleville Mézières •

Laon

Longwy

Mosel

Soissons

A26

Luxembourg City

• Senlis

Thionville •

✈ *Charles de Gaulle*

A4

A4

Verdun Battlefield

Saarbrücken

▲ To Paris

• **Reims**

A4

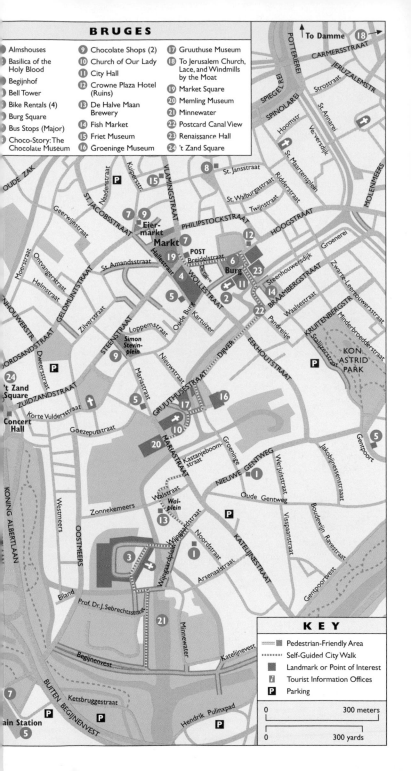

BRUGES

- Almshouses
- Basilica of the Holy Blood
- Begijnhof
- Bell Tower
- Bike Rentals (4)
- Burg Square
- Bus Stops (Major)
- Choco-Story: The Chocolate Museum
- 9 Chocolate Shops (2)
- 10 Church of Our Lady
- 11 City Hall
- 12 Crowne Plaza Hotel (Ruins)
- 13 De Halve Maan Brewery
- 14 Fish Market
- 15 Friet Museum
- 16 Groeninge Museum
- 17 Gruuthuse Museum
- 18 To Jerusalem Church, Lace, and Windmills by the Moat
- 19 Market Square
- 20 Memling Museum
- 21 Minnewater
- 22 Postcard Canal View
- 23 Renaissance Hall
- 24 't Zand Square

KEY

- ▬▬▬ Pedestrian-Friendly Area
- ••••••• Self-Guided City Walk
- ■ Landmark or Point of Interest
- 𝒊 Tourist Information Offices
- P Parking

0 — 300 meters
0 — 300 yards

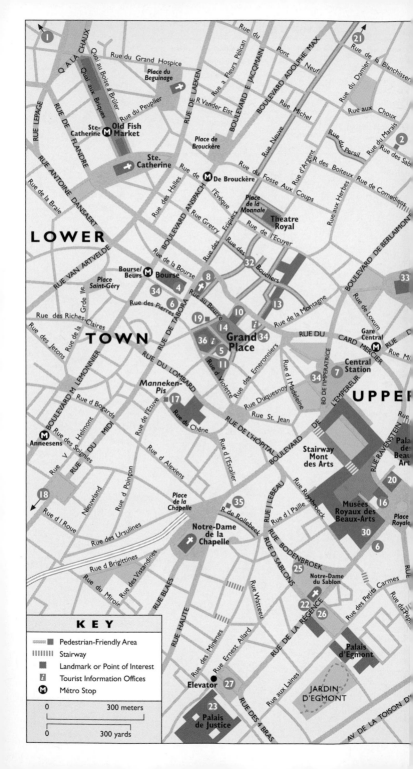

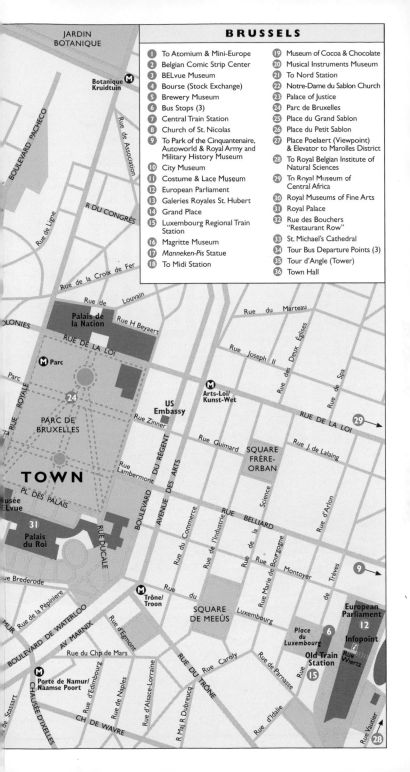

BRUSSELS

1. To Atomium & Mini-Europe
2. Belgian Comic Strip Center
3. BELvue Museum
4. Bourse (Stock Exchange)
5. Brewery Museum
6. Bus Stops (3)
7. Central Train Station
8. Church of St. Nicolas
9. To Park of the Cinquantenaire, Autoworld & Royal Army and Military History Museum
10. City Museum
11. Costume & Lace Museum
12. European Parliament
13. Galeries Royales St. Hubert
14. Grand Place
15. Luxembourg Regional Train Station
16. Magritte Museum
17. *Manneken-Pis* Statue
18. To Midi Station
19. Museum of Cocoa & Chocolate
20. Musical Instruments Museum
21. To Nord Station
22. Notre-Dame du Sablon Church
23. Palace of Justice
24. Parc de Bruxelles
25. Place du Grand Sablon
26. Place du Petit Sablon
27. Place Poelaert (Viewpoint) & Elevator to Marolles District
28. To Royal Belgian Institute of Natural Sciences
29. To Royal Museum of Central Africa
30. Royal Museums of Fine Arts
31. Royal Palace
32. Rue des Bouchers "Restaurant Row"
33. St. Michael's Cathedral
34. Tour Bus Departure Points (3)
35. Tour d'Angle (Tower)
36. Town Hall

Rick Steves'

AMSTERDAM
BRUGES & BRUSSELS

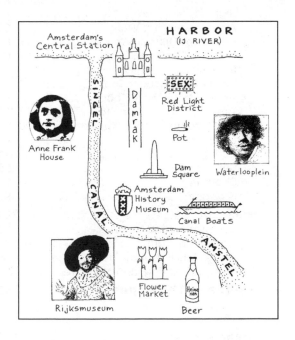

AVALON
TRAVEL

CONTENTS

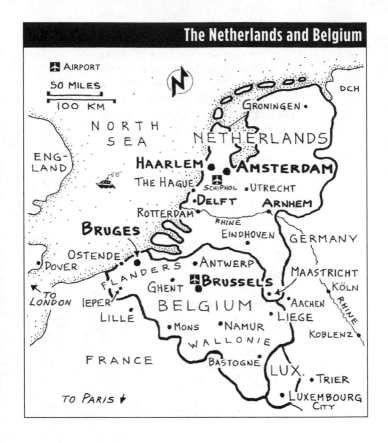

The Netherlands and Belgium

✈ AIRPORT

50 MILES
100 KM

NORTH SEA

ENG-LAND

NETHERLANDS

GRONINGEN

DCH

HAARLEM

AMSTERDAM

THE HAGUE

SCHIPHOL

UTRECHT

DELFT

ARNHEM

ROTTERDAM

RHINE

EINDHOVEN

GERMANY

BRUGES

OSTENDE

DOVER

FLANDERS

ANTWERP

MAASTRICHT

KÖLN

GHENT

BRUSSELS

AACHEN

TO LONDON

IEPER

BELGIUM

LILLE

MONS

NAMUR

LIEGE

RHINE

KOBLENZ

WALLONIE

FRANCE

BASTOGNE

LUX.

TRIER

TO PARIS

LUXEMBOURG CITY

INTRODUCTION

Amsterdam, Bruges, and Brussels—the three greatest cities of the Low Countries—are a delight to experience. Rattling on your bike over the cobbles, savoring fresh pralines, lingering in flower-carpeted squares, you'll find a slow-down-and-smell-the-tulips world that enchants. Any time of year, you can enjoy the intimate charms of these cities.

Amsterdam is called "the Venice of the North," both for its canals and for its past position as an economic powerhouse. Bruges—once mighty, now mighty cute—comes with fancy beers in fancy glasses, lilting carillons, and lacy Gothic souvenirs of a long-gone greatness. Brussels—the capital of Europe, with a low-rise Parisian ambience—exudes a joie de vivre, from its famous cuisine to its love of comic books and chocolate.

Belgium and the Netherlands are called the Low Countries because nearly half their land is below sea level. Surrounded by mega-Europe, the Low Countries are easy to overlook. But travel here is a snap, the area is steeped in history, and all the charming icons of the region—whirring windmills, Dutch Masters, dike hikes, one-speed bikes, and ladies tossing bobbins to make fine lace—line up for you to enjoy. If ever an area were a travel cliché come true, it's the Low Countries.

This book covers the predictable biggies in and around Amsterdam, Bruges, and Brussels—and mixes in a healthy dose of Back Door intimacy. In Amsterdam, you can see Vincent van Gogh's *Sunflowers*...and climb through Captain Vincent's tiny houseboat museum. You'll tour Brussels' ultramodern European Parliament and enjoy a Michelangelo statue in small-town Bruges. And you'll meet intriguing people, who will show you how to swallow pickled herring, paddle you in a canoe through the *polderland* to a stuck-in-the-mud (and stuck-in-the-past) village, and pop a

INTRODUCTION

taste of the latest chocolate into your mouth.

This book is selective, including only the top sights in these three great cities in hopes that you'll enjoy the trip of a lifetime. The best is, of course, only my opinion. But after spending more than half of my adult life exploring and researching Europe, I've developed a sixth sense for what travelers enjoy.

About This Book

Rick Steves' Amsterdam, Bruges & Brussels is a personal tour guide in your pocket. Better yet, it's actually two tour guides in your pocket: The co-author of this book is Gene Openshaw. Since our first "Europe through the gutter" trip together as high-school buddies in the 1970s, Gene and I have been exploring the wonders of the Old World. An inquisitive historian and lover of European culture, Gene wrote most of this book's self-guided museum tours and neighborhood walks. Together, Gene and I will keep this book up-to-date and accurate (though for simplicity, from this point "we" will shed our respective egos and become "I").

In this book, you'll find the following chapters:

Orientation includes tourist information, specifics on public transportation, local tour options, helpful hints, and an easy-to-read map designed to make the text clear and your arrival smooth. The "Planning Your Time" section suggests a schedule for how to best use your limited time.

Sights provides a succinct overview of the most important sights, arranged by neighborhood, and rated:

▲▲▲—Don't miss.

▲▲—Try hard to see.

▲—Worthwhile if you can make it.

No rating—Worth knowing about.

The **Self-Guided Walks and Tours** take you through the must-see attractions in Amsterdam (Rijksmuseum, Van Gogh Museum, Anne Frank House, a city walk, the Jordaan neighborhood, the Red Light District, and more), nearby Haarlem (the Grote Kerk and the Frans Hals Museum), Bruges (a city walk, Groeninge Museum, and Memling Museum), and Brussels (a city walk, an Upper Town walk, and the Royal Museums of Fine Arts of Belgium).

Sleeping describes my favorite hotels, from budget deals to cushy splurges.

Eating serves up a range of options, from inexpensive pubs to fancier restaurants.

Smoking covers Amsterdam's best "coffeeshops," which openly sell marijuana.

Shopping gives you tips for shopping painlessly and enjoyably, without letting it overwhelm your vacation or ruin your budget.

Nightlife is your guide to Amsterdam's evening fun, including music, comedy, movies, and cruises.

Chapters such as **Delft and The Hague, Near Arnhem,** and **Dutch Day Trips** covers small towns and destinations (such as Dutch open-air folk museums) in the Netherlands.

Transportation Connections covers how to get to nearby destinations by train and bus, and includes information on getting to and from the airports.

The **History** chapter gives you a quick overview of Dutch and Belgian history and a timeline of major events.

The **appendix** is a traveler's tool kit, with a handy packing checklist, recommended books and films, instructions on how to use the telephone, and useful phone numbers. You'll also find detailed information on driving and public transportation, as well as a climate chart, festival list, a hotel reservation form, and Dutch and French survival phrases.

Throughout this book, when you see a ✪ in a listing, it means that the sight is covered in much more depth in a self-guided walk or one of my museum tours—a page number will tell you just where to look to find more information.

Browse through this book and select your favorite sights. Then have a great trip! Traveling like a temporary local and taking advantage of the information here, you'll get the absolute most out of every mile, minute, and euro. As you visit places I know and love, I'm happy you'll be meeting some of my favorite Europeans.

PLANNING

Trip Costs

Five components make up your trip cost: airfare, surface transportation, room and board, sightseeing and entertainment, and shopping and miscellany.

Airfare: A basic, round-trip, US-to-Amsterdam flight costs $750–1,400 (cheaper in winter), depending on where you fly from and when. While you can often save time in Europe by flying "open jaw" (into one city and out of another), if you're sticking to the Low Countries, you're never more than about three hours from Amsterdam's or Brussels' international airports.

Surface Transportation: If you're just touring Amsterdam, Bruges, Brussels, and nearby day-trip destinations, you're best off enjoying the region's excellent and affordable train system. Trains leave at least hourly between each of the cities. It costs about $55 for a ticket from Amsterdam to Brussels or to Bruges. If you plan to venture farther afield, you may want a rental car. Driving in the Low Countries is flat-out easy (figure $750 per person—based on two people sharing—for a three-week car rental, gas, and insurance).

Major Holidays and Weekends

Popular places are even busier on weekends...and can be inundated on three-day weekends. Plan ahead and reserve your accommodations and transportation well in advance.

The big holidays in the Netherlands are the Easter weekend (Fri–Sun: April 2–4 in 2010), Queen's Day (Koninginnedag, April 30), May 4 (Remembrance of the WWII Dead), May 5 (Liberation Day), Ascension (May 13 in 2010), Pentecost (May 23 in 2010), December 5 (St. Nicholas' Eve), Christmas (celebrated on December 25 and 26), and New Year's Day.

Belgium's major holidays include New Year's, Easter, Ascension, Pentecost, and Christmas, plus Labor Day (May 1), Belgian Independence Day (July 21), Assumption (Aug 15), All Saints' Day (Nov 1), and Armistice Day (Nov 11).

For a more complete list of festivals and holidays, see page 465 in the appendix.

Room and Board: You can thrive in the Low Countries on $120 a day per person for room and board (less for Bruges and Brussels, more for Amsterdam). That allows $20 for lunch, $30 for dinner, and $70 for lodging (based on two people splitting the cost of a $140 double room that includes breakfast). To live and sleep more elegantly, I'd propose a budget of $140 per day per person ($20 for lunch, $40 for dinner, and $80 each for a $160 hotel double with breakfast). Students and tightwads eat and sleep for $60 a day ($30 per bed, $30 for meals and snacks).

Sightseeing and Entertainment: In big cities, figure $12–18 per major sight (Rijks, Memling, and Van Gogh museums); $3–5 for minor ones (climbing church towers or windmills); $10–18 for guided walks, boat tours, and bike rentals; and $30–60 for splurge experiences such as concerts, special art exhibits, big-bus tours, and guided canoe trips. An overall average of $20 a day works for most. Don't skimp here. After all, this category is the driving force behind your trip—you came to sightsee, enjoy, and experience the Low Countries.

Shopping and Miscellany: Figure $1–2 per postcard, tea, or ice-cream cone, and $5 per beer. Shopping can vary in cost from nearly nothing to a small fortune. Good budget travelers find that this category has little to do with assembling a trip full of lifelong and wonderful memories.

When to Go

Although Bruges and Amsterdam can be plagued by crowds, the long days, lively festivals, and sunny weather make summer a great time to visit. It's rarely too hot for comfort. Brussels' fancy business-class hotels are also deeply discounted in the summer.

Peak Season: Amsterdam is surprisingly crowded—and hotel prices can be correspondingly high—in late March, April, and May, because of the tulip fields flowering in full glory. Seasonal conferences can also drive up prices in September in Amsterdam. July and August have the typical summer crowds.

Shoulder Season: Late spring and fall are also pleasant, with generally mild weather and lighter crowds (except during holiday weekends—see opposite page).

Winter Season: Travel from late October through mid-March is cold and wet in this region, as coastal winds whip through these low, flat countries. It's fine for visiting Amsterdam, Bruges, and Brussels, but smaller towns and countryside sights feel dreary and lifeless. Some sights close for lunch, tourist information offices keep shorter hours, and some tourist activities (like English-language windmill tours) vanish altogether.

Sightseeing Priorities

With affordable flights from the US, minimal culture shock, almost no language barrier, and a well-organized tourist trade, the Low Countries are a good place to start a European trip. Depending on the length of your trip, and taking geographic proximity into account, the following are my recommended priorities.

2 days:	Amsterdam, Haarlem
3–4 days, add:	Bruges
5–6 days, add:	Brussels and another day in Amsterdam
7 days, add:	Side-trips from Amsterdam (e.g., Edam, Arnhem, Delft, the Historic Triangle, and more)

Travel Smart

Your trip to Europe is like a complex play—easier to follow and really appreciate on a second viewing. While no one does the same trip twice to gain that advantage, reading this book's chapters on your intended destinations before your trip accomplishes much the same thing. The Rijksmuseum is much more entertaining if you've boned up on ruffs and Dutch Masters the night before.

Design an itinerary that enables you to visit the various sights at the best possible times. Make note of festival weekends and days when sights are closed. For example, on Mondays nearly all the museums are closed in Bruges. Sundays have the same pros and cons as they do for travelers in the US—sights are generally open but may have limited hours, shops and banks are closed, city traffic is light, and public transportation options are limited. Popular destinations are even more crowded on weekends. Rowdy evenings are rare on Sundays.

Know Before You Go

Your trip is more likely to go smoothly if you plan ahead. Check this list of things to arrange while you're still at home.

Be sure that your **passport** is valid at least six months after your ticketed date of return to the US. If you need to get or renew a passport, it can take up to two months (for more on passports, see www.travel.state.gov).

Book your rooms in advance if you'll be traveling during any major **holidays** (see "Major Holidays and Weekends," page 4). It's smart to reserve rooms in peak season if you'd like to stay in my lead listings, and definitely reserve for your first night.

Call your **debit and credit card companies** to let them know the countries you'll be visiting, so they'll accept (and not deny) your international charges. Confirm your daily withdrawal limit; consider asking to have it raised so you can take out more cash at each ATM stop. Ask about international transaction fees.

The big three **museums** in Amsterdam—Rijks, Van Gogh, and Anne Frank—can come with long lines during high season. Consider buying tickets online from home (for details, see page 34).

If you plan on **renting a car** in the Low Countries, you'll need your driver's license, and it's recommended—but not required—that you carry an International Driving Permit (IDP), available at your local AAA office ($15 plus two passport photos, www.aaa.com). Confirm pickup hours—many car-rental offices close Saturday afternoon and all day Sunday.

Since **airline carry-on restrictions** are always changing, visit the Transportation Security Administration's website (www.tsa.gov/travelers) for an up-to-date list of what you can bring on the plane with you...and what you have to check. Remember to arrive with plenty of time to get through security.

To give yourself a little rootedness, minimize one-night stands. It's worth a post-dinner drive or train ride to be settled into a town for two nights. B&Bs are also more likely to give a good price to someone staying more than one night.

Be sure to mix intense and relaxed periods in your itinerary. Every trip (and every traveler) needs at least a few slack days. Pace yourself. Assume you will return.

Reread this book as you travel, and visit local tourist information offices. Upon arrival in a new town, lay the groundwork for a smooth departure; write down the schedule for the train or bus you'll take when you depart.

Plan ahead for laundry and picnics. Get online at Internet

cafés or your hotel to research transportation connections, confirm events, check the weather, and get directions to your next hotel. Buy a phone card (or carry a mobile phone) and use it to make reservations, reconfirm hotels, book tours, and double-check hours of sights.

Connect with the culture. Set up your own quest to find the best salted herring or canal boat ride. Slow down and be open to unexpected experiences. Ask questions—most locals are eager to point you in their idea of the right direction. Keep a notepad in your pocket for organizing your thoughts. Wear your money belt, and learn the local currency and how to estimate prices in dollars. Those who expect to travel smart, do.

PRACTICALITIES

Red Tape: You need a passport—but no visa or shots—to travel in the Netherlands and Belgium. Your passport must be valid for at least six months beyond the time you leave. Pack a photocopy of your passport in your luggage in case the original is lost or stolen.

Borders: There are no border checks between the Low Countries, but when you change countries, you must still change telephone cards and postage stamps.

Time: In Europe—and in this book—you'll use the 24-hour clock. It's the same through 12:00 noon, then keep going: 13:00, 14:00, and so on. For anything over 12, subtract 12 and add p.m. (14:00 is 2:00 p.m.).

The Low Countries, like most of continental Europe, are generally six/nine hours ahead of the East/West Coasts of the US. The exceptions are the beginning and end of Daylight Saving Time: Europe "springs forward" the last Sunday in March (two weeks after most of North America) and "falls back" the last Sunday in October (one week before North America). For a handy online time converter, try www.timeanddate.com/worldclock.

Business Hours: Most stores throughout the Low Countries are open from about 9:00 until 18:00–20:00 on weekdays, but close early on Saturday (generally between 12:00 and 17:00, depending on whether you're in a town or a big city), and they are often closed on Sunday. Many museums and sights are closed on Monday.

Watt's Up? Europe's electrical system is different from North America's in two ways: the shape of the plug (two round prongs) and the voltage of the current (220 volts instead of 110 volts). For your North American plug to work in Europe, you'll need an adapter, sold inexpensively at travel stores in the US. As for the voltage, most newer electronics or travel appliances (such as hair dryers, laptops, and battery chargers) automatically convert the voltage. If you see a range of voltages printed on the item or its

Just the FAQs, Please

Whom do I call in case of emergency?
Dial 112 for police or medical emergencies in both the Netherlands and Belgium.

What if my credit card is stolen?
Act immediately. See "Damage Control for Lost Cards," page 10, for instructions.

How do I make a phone call to, within, and from the Netherlands and Belgium?
For detailed dialing instructions, refer to page 458.

How can I get tourist information about my destination?
Both countries have national tourist information offices in the US (see page 453) and offices in virtually every destination covered in this book. Note that Tourist Information is abbreviated "TI" in this book.

What's the best way to pack?
Light. For a recommended packing list, see page 469.

Does Rick have other resources that could help me?
For info on Rick's guidebooks, public television series, free audiotours, public radio show, website, guided tours, travel bags, accessories, and railpasses, see page 454.

Are there any updates to this guidebook?
Check www.ricksteves.com/update for changes to the most recent edition of this book.

Can you recommend any good books or movies for my trip?
For suggestions, see pages 456–458.

Do you have information on driving, train travel, and flights?
See "Transportation" on page 14.

How much do I tip?
Relatively little. For tips on tipping, see page 11.

Will I get a student or senior discount?
While discounts are not listed in this book, some sights are discounted for seniors (loosely defined as those who are retired or willing to call themselves seniors), youths (ages 8–18), students, groups of 10 or more, and families. To get a teacher or student ID card, visit www.statravel.com or www.isic.org.

How can I get a VAT refund on major purchases?
See the details on page 11.

Do the Low Countries use the metric system?
Yes. A liter is about a quart, four to a gallon. A kilometer is six-tenths of a mile. I figure kilometers to miles by cutting them in half and adding back 10 percent of the original (120 km: 60 + 12 = 72 miles, 300 km: 150 + 30 = 180 miles). For more metric conversions, see page 467.

plug (such as "110–220"), it'll work in Europe. Otherwise, you can buy a converter separately in the US (about $20).

News: Americans keep in touch via the *International Herald Tribune* (published almost daily throughout Europe). Every Tuesday, the European editions of *Time* and *Newsweek* hit the stands with articles of particular interest to European travelers. Sports addicts can get their daily fix from *USA Today*. Good websites include www.iht.com, http://news.bbc.co.uk, and www.europeantimes.com. Many hotels have CNN or BBC television channels available.

MONEY

Cash from ATMs

Throughout Europe, cash machines (ATMs) are the standard way for travelers to get local currency. As an emergency backup, bring several hundred US dollars in cash. Avoid using currency exchange booths (lousy rates and/or outrageous fees); if you have currency to exchange, take it to a bank. Also avoid traveler's checks, which are a waste of time (long waits at banks) and a waste of money (in fees).

To use an ATM to withdraw money from your account, you'll need a debit card (ideally with a Visa or MasterCard logo for maximum usability), plus a PIN code. Know your PIN code in numbers; there are only numbers—no letters—on European key-pads. It's smart to bring two cards, in case one gets demagnetized or eaten by a temperamental machine.

Before you go, verify with your bank that your cards will work overseas, and alert them that you'll be making withdrawals in Europe; otherwise, the bank may not approve transactions if it perceives unusual spending patterns. Also ask about international fees; see "Credit and Debit Cards," below.

Try to take out large sums of money to reduce your per-transaction bank fees. If the machine refuses your request, try again and select a smaller amount (some cash machines limit the amount you can withdraw—don't take it personally). If that doesn't work, try a different machine.

Keep your cash safe. Use a money belt—a pouch with a strap that you buckle around your waist like a belt and wear under your clothes. Thieves target tourists. A money belt provides peace of mind, allowing you to carry lots of cash safely. Don't waste time every few days tracking down a cash machine—withdraw a week's worth of money, stuff it in your money belt, and travel!

Credit and Debit Cards

For purchases, Visa and MasterCard are more commonly accepted than American Express. Just like at home, credit or debit cards

Exchange Rate

I list prices in euros for the Netherlands and Belgium.

1 euro (€) = about $1.40

To convert prices in euros to dollars, add about 40 percent: €20 = about $28, €50 = about $70. Just like the dollar, the euro is broken into 100 cents. You'll find coins ranging from 5 cents to 2 euros, and bills from 5 euros to 50 euros. (To get the latest rates and print a cheat sheet, see www.oanda .com.)

So those €65 wooden clogs are about $100, and the €90 taxi ride through Brussels is…uh-oh.

work easily at larger hotels, restaurants, and shops, but smaller businesses prefer payment in local currency (in small bills—break large bills at a bank or larger store). If receipts show your credit-card number, don't toss these thoughtlessly.

Fees: Credit and debit cards—whether used for purchases or ATM withdrawals—now charge additional, tacked-on "international transaction" fees of up to 3 percent; some also take an extra $5 per transaction. To avoid unpleasant surprises, call your bank or credit-card company before your trip to ask about these fees. If the fees are too high, consider getting a card just for your trip: Capital One (www.capitalone.com) and most credit unions have low-to-no international transaction fees.

If merchants offer to convert your purchase price into dollars (called dynamic currency conversion), refuse this "service." You'll pay even more in fees for the expensive convenience of seeing your charge in dollars.

Damage Control for Lost Cards

If you lose your credit, debit, or ATM card, you can stop people from using it by reporting the loss immediately to the respective global customer-assistance centers. Call these 24-hour US numbers collect: Visa (410/581-9994), MasterCard (636/722-7111), and American Express (623/492-8427).

At a minimum, you'll need to know the name of the financial institution that issued you the card, along with the type of card (classic, platinum, or whatever). Providing the following information will allow for a quicker cancellation of your missing card: full card number, whether you are the primary or secondary cardholder, the cardholder's name exactly as printed on the card, billing address, home phone number, circumstances of the loss or theft, and identification verification (your birth date, your mother's maiden name, or your Social Security number—memorize this, don't carry a copy). If you are the secondary cardholder, you'll also need to provide the primary cardholder's identification-verification details. You can generally receive a temporary card within two or three business days in Europe.

If you promptly report your card lost or stolen, you typically won't be responsible for any unauthorized transactions on your account, although many banks charge a liability fee of $50.

Tipping

Tipping in Europe isn't as automatic and generous as it is in the US, but for special service, tips are appreciated, if not expected. As in the US, the proper amount depends on your resources, tipping philosophy, and the circumstances, but some general guidelines apply.

Restaurants: Tipping is an issue only at restaurants that have table service. If you order your food at a counter, don't tip.

At Dutch and Belgian restaurants that have wait staff, service is included, although it's common to round up the bill after a good meal (usually 5–10 percent; so, for an €18.50 meal, pay €20).

Taxis: To tip the cabbie, round up. For a typical ride, round up about 5–10 percent (to pay a €4.50 fare, give €5; or for a €28 fare, give €30). If the cabbie hauls your bags and zips you to the airport to help you catch your flight, you might want to toss in a little more. But if you feel like you're being driven in circles or otherwise ripped off, skip the tip.

Special Services: It's thoughtful to tip a euro to someone who shows you a special sight and who is paid in no other way. Tour guides at public sites often hold out their hands for tips after they give their spiel; if I've already paid for the tour, I don't tip extra, though some tourists do give a euro, particularly for a job well done. I don't tip at hotels, but if you do, give the porter about a euro for carrying bags and leave a couple of euros in your room at the end of your stay for the maid if the room was kept clean. In general, if someone in the service industry does a super job for you, a tip of a euro or two is appropriate...but not required.

When in doubt, ask. If you're not sure whether (or how much) to tip for a service, ask your hotelier or the tourist information office; they'll fill you in on how it's done on their turf.

Getting a VAT Refund

Wrapped into the purchase price of your souvenirs is a Value Added Tax (VAT) of about 19 percent in the Netherlands and 21 percent in Belgium. If you make a purchase of more than a certain amount (€50 in the Netherlands, €125.01 in Belgium) at a store that participates in the VAT-refund scheme, you're entitled to get most of that tax back. Getting your refund is usually straight-forward and, if you buy a substantial amount of souvenirs, well worth the hassle.

If you're lucky, the merchant will subtract the tax when you make your purchase. (This is more likely to occur if the store ships the goods to your home.) Otherwise, you'll need to:

Get the paperwork. Have the merchant completely fill out the necessary refund document, called a "Tax-Free Shopping Cheque." You'll have to present your passport at the store.

Get your stamp at the border or airport. Process your cheque(s) at your last stop in the EU (e.g., at the airport) with the customs agent who deals with VAT refunds. It's best to keep your purchases in your carry-on for viewing, but if they're too large or dangerous (such as knives) to carry on, track down the proper customs agent to inspect them before you check your bag. You're not supposed to use your purchased goods before you leave. If you show up at customs wearing your new Belgian lace, officials might look the other way—or deny you a refund.

Collect your refund. You'll need to return your stamped document to the retailer or its representative. Many merchants work with a service, such as Global Refund (www.globalrefund.com) or Premier Tax Free (www.premiertaxfree.com), which have offices at major airports, ports, or border crossings. These services, which extract a 4 percent fee, can refund your money immediately in your currency of choice or credit your card (within two billing cycles). If the retailer handles VAT refunds directly, it's up to you to contact the merchant for your refund. You can mail the documents from home, or quicker, from your point of departure (using a stamped, addressed envelope you've prepared or one that's been provided by the merchant)—and then wait. It could take months.

Customs for American Shoppers

You are allowed to take home $800 worth of items per person duty-free, once every 30 days. The next $1,000 is taxed at a flat 3 percent. After that, you pay the individual item's duty rate. You can also bring in duty-free a liter of alcohol (slightly more than a standard-size bottle of wine; you must be at least 21), 200 cigarettes, and up to 100 non-Cuban cigars. You may take home vacuum-packed cheeses; dried herbs, spices, or mushrooms; and canned fruits or vegetables, including jams and vegetable spreads. Meats (even vacuum-packed or canned) and fresh fruits and vegetables are not permitted. Note that you'll need to carefully pack any bottles of wine and other liquid-containing items in your checked luggage, due to limits on liquids in carry-ons. To check customs rules and duty rates before you go, visit www.cbp.gov, and click on "Travel," then "Know Before You Go."

SIGHTSEEING

Sightseeing can be hard work. Use these tips to make your visits to the Low Countries' finest sights meaningful, fun, fast, and painless.

Plan Ahead

Set up an itinerary that allows you to fit in all your must-see sights. For a one-stop look at opening hours in Amsterdam, Bruges, and Brussels, see the "At a Glance" sidebars for each destination. Most sights keep stable hours, but you can easily confirm the latest by checking with the local TI.

Don't put off visiting a must-see sight—you never know when a place will close unexpectedly for a holiday, strike, or restoration. If you'll be visiting during a holiday, find out if a particular sight will be open by phoning ahead or visiting its website.

When possible, visit major sights first thing (when your energy is best), and save other activities for the afternoon. Hit the museum highlights first, then go back to other things if you have the stamina and time.

Going at the right time can also help you avoid crowds. This book offers tips on specific sights. Try visiting very early, at lunch, or very late. Evening visits (when possible) are usually peaceful, with fewer crowds.

At Sights

All sights have rules, and if you know about these in advance, they're no big deal.

Some important sights have metal detectors or conduct bag searches that will slow your entry.

Major museums and sights require you to check daypacks and coats. They'll be kept safely. If you have something you can't bear to part with, stash it in a pocket or purse. If you don't want to check a small backpack, carry it under your arm like a purse as you enter. From a guard's point of view, a backpack is generally a problem, while a purse is not.

Photography is sometimes banned at major sights. Look for signs or ask. If cameras are allowed, flashes or tripods are usually not. Flashes damage oil paintings and distract others in the room. Even without a flash, a handheld camera will take a decent picture (or buy postcards or posters at the museum bookstore). Video cameras are generally allowed.

Some museums have special exhibits in addition to their permanent collection. Some exhibits are included in the entry price; others come at an extra cost (which you may have to pay even if you don't want to see the exhibit).

Many sights rent audioguides, which generally offer excellent recorded descriptions of the art. If you bring along your own pair of headphones and a Y-jack, two people can sometimes share one audioguide and save. Guided tours (widely ranging in quality) are most likely to occur during peak season.

Expect changes—paintings can be on tour, on loan, out sick, or shifted at the whim of the curator. To adapt, pick up any available free floor plans as you enter, and ask museum staff if you can't find a particular painting.

Most important sights have an on-site café or cafeteria (usually a good place to rest and have a snack or light meal). The WCs are free and generally clean.

Key sights and museums have bookstores selling postcards and souvenirs. Before you leave, scan the postcards and thumb through the biggest guidebook (or skim its index) to be sure you haven't overlooked something that you'd like to see.

Most sights stop admitting people 30–60 minutes before closing time, and some rooms close early (generally about 45 minutes before the actual closing time). Guards usher people out, so don't save the best for last.

Every sight or museum offers more than what is covered in this book. Use the information in this book as an introduction— not the final word.

TRANSPORTATION

By Car or Train?

Because of the short distances and excellent public transportation systems in the Low Countries, and the fact that this book covers three big cities, I recommend connecting Amsterdam, Bruges, and Brussels by train, not by car. You absolutely do not want or need a car in any of these cities.

Hourly trains connect each of these towns faster and easier than you could by driving. Just buy tickets as you go. You don't need advance reservations to ride a train between these cities, unless you take the pricey Amsterdam–Brussels Thalys train (it's avoidable; plenty of regular trains make this run). For specifics on transportation in the Netherlands, see page 301; for Belgium, see page 437. For more extensive travels beyond the Low Countries, you may want to study your railpass options (see www.ricksteves.com/rail).

SLEEPING

I favor accommodations (and restaurants) handy to your sight-seeing activities. Rather than list hotels scattered throughout a city, I choose two or three favorite neighborhoods and recommend

the best accommodations values in each, from $30 bunk beds to fancy-for-my-book $300 doubles.

I look for places that are friendly; clean; a good value; located in a central, safe, quiet neighborhood; English-speaking; and not mentioned in other guidebooks. I'm more impressed by a handy location and a fun-loving philosophy than hair dryers and shoeshine machines. I also like local character and simple facilities that don't cater to American "needs." Obviously, a place meeting every criterion is rare, and all of my recommendations fall short of perfection—sometimes miserably. But I've listed the best values for each price category, given the above criteria. I've also thrown in a few hostels, private rooms, and other cheap options for budget travelers.

The prices listed in this book are generally valid for peak season, but may go up during major holidays and festivals (see page 465). Prices can soften off-season, for stays of two nights or longer, or for payment in cash (rather than by credit card). Always mention that you found the place through this book—many of the hotels listed offer special deals to my readers.

For environmental reasons, towels are often replaced in hotels only when you leave them on the floor. In cheaper places, they aren't replaced at all, so hang them up to dry and reuse.

Before accepting a room, confirm your understanding of the complete price. The only tip my recommended hotels would like is a friendly, easygoing guest. And, as always, I appreciate feedback on your accommodation experiences.

Types of Accommodations
Hotels
In this book, the price for a double room ranges from $70 (very simple, toilet and shower down the hall) to $300 (maximum plumbing and more), with most clustering at about $140. You'll pay more at Amsterdam hotels, less at Brussels hotels and Bruges B&Bs.

Most hotels have lots of doubles and a few singles, triples, and quads. While groups sleep cheap, traveling alone can be expensive. Singles (except for the rare closet-type rooms that fit only a twin bed) are simply doubles used by one person, so they often cost nearly the same as a double.

A hearty breakfast with cereal, meats, local cheeses, fresh bread, yogurt, juice, and coffee or tea is standard in hotels.

Sleep Code

(€1 = about $1.40)
To help you sort easily through these listings, I've divided the rooms into three categories based on the price for a standard double room with bath:

$$$ **Higher Priced**
$$ **Moderately Priced**
$ **Lower Priced**

To give maximum information in a minimum of space, I use the following code to describe the accommodations. Prices listed are per room, not per person. When a price range is given for a type of room (such as "Db-€80–120"), it means the price fluctuates with the season, size of room, or length of stay.

S = Single room (or price for one person in a double).
D = Double or twin. Double beds are usually big enough for nonromantic couples.
T = Triple (generally a double bed with a single).
Q = Quad (usually two double beds).
b = Private bathroom with toilet and shower or tub.
s = Private shower or tub only (the toilet is down the hall).

According to this code, a couple staying at a "Db-€85" hotel would pay a total of €85 (about $130) for a double room with a private bathroom. Unless otherwise noted, English is spoken, breakfast is included, and credit cards are accepted.

Bed-and-Breakfasts

B&Bs offer double the cultural intimacy and—often—nicer rooms for a good deal less than most hotel rooms. Hosts usually speak English and are interesting conversationalists.

In the Low Countries, B&Bs are common in well-touristed areas outside the big cities. There are plenty to choose from in Haarlem, and especially in Bruges. Amsterdam also has B&Bs, though they tend to be more expensive and not as good a value as those in small towns (I've listed the better-value B&Bs in Amsterdam). Urban Brussels has no recommended B&Bs. Local TIs have lists of B&Bs and can book a room for you, but you'll save money by booking direct with the B&Bs listed in this book.

Hostels

For $30 a night, you can stay at a youth hostel. Travelers of any age are welcome, if they don't mind dorm-style accommodations or meeting other travelers. Cheap meals are sometimes available, and kitchen facilities are usually provided. Hostels are also a tremendous source of local and budget travel information. Expect crowds in the summer, snoring, and lots of youth groups giggling and making rude noises while you try to sleep.

If you're serious about traveling cheaply, get a membership card (www.hihostels.com), carry your own sheets, and cook in the members' kitchens. Travelers without a hostel card can generally spend the night for a small, extra "one-night membership" fee. In official IYHF-member hostels, family rooms are sometimes available on request, but it's basically boys' dorms and girls' dorms. You usually can't check in before 17:00 and must be out by 10:00. There's often a 23:00 curfew. Official hostels are marked with a triangular sign that shows a house and a tree.

The Low Countries also have plenty of private hostels, where you'll find no midday lockout, no curfew, no membership requirement, co-ed dorms, simple double rooms, a more easygoing staff, and a rowdy atmosphere.

Making Reservations

Given the quality of the places I've found for this book, I'd recommend that you reserve your rooms in advance, particularly if you'll be traveling during peak season. Book several weeks ahead, or as soon as you've pinned down your travel dates. Note that some holidays merit your making reservations far in advance (see "Major Holidays and Weekends" sidebar on page 4).

To make a reservation, contact hotels directly by email, phone, or fax. Email is the clearest and most economical way to make a reservation. In addition, many hotel websites now have online reservation forms. If phoning from the US, be mindful of time zones (see page 7). Most hotels listed are accustomed to English-only speakers. To ensure you have all the information you need for your reservation, use the form in this book's appendix (also at www .ricksteves.com/reservation). If you don't get a response within a few days, call to follow up.

When you request a room for a certain time period, use the European style for writing dates: day/month/year. Hoteliers need to know your arrival and departure dates. For example, for a two-night stay in July, I would request: "2 nights, arrive 16/07/10, depart 18/07/10." Consider carefully how long you'll stay; don't just assume you can extend your reservation for extra days once you arrive.

If the response from the hotel tells you its room availability and rates, it's not a confirmation. You must tell them that you want that room at the given rate.

For more spontaneity, you can make reservations as you travel, calling hotels or B&Bs a few days to a week before your visit. If

How Was Your Trip?

Were your travels fun, smooth, and meaningful? If you'd like to share your tips, concerns, and discoveries, please fill out the survey at www.ricksteves.com/feedback. I value your feedback. Thanks in advance—it helps a lot.

you prefer the flexibility of traveling without any reservations at all, you'll have greater success snaring rooms if you arrive at your destination early in the day. If you anticipate crowds, call hotels around 9:00 on the day you plan to arrive, when the hotel clerk knows who'll be checking out and just which rooms will be available.

Whether you reserve from home or on the road, the hotelier will sometimes request your credit-card number for a one-night deposit. While you can email your credit-card information (I do), some people prefer to share that personal info via phone call, fax, or secure online reservation form (if the hotel has one on its website).

If you must cancel your reservation, it's courteous to do so with as much advance notice as possible (at least three days; simply make a quick phone call or send an email). Family-run hotels and B&Bs lose money if they turn away customers while holding a room for someone who doesn't show up.

Understandably, most hoteliers bill no-shows for one night. Hotels in larger cities sometimes have strict cancellation policies (for example, you might lose a deposit if you cancel within two weeks of your reserved stay, or you might be billed for the entire visit if you leave early). Ask about cancellation policies before you book.

Always reconfirm your room reservation a few days in advance from the road. If you'll be arriving after 17:00, let them know.

On the small chance that a hotel loses track of your reservation, bring along a hard copy of their emailed or faxed confirmation.

TRAVELING AS A TEMPORARY LOCAL

We travel all the way to Europe to enjoy differences—to become temporary locals. You'll experience frustrations. Certain truths that we find "God-given" or "self-evident," such as cold beer, ice in drinks, bottomless cups of coffee, hot showers, and bigger being better, are suddenly not so true. One of the benefits of travel is the eye-opening realization that there are logical, civil, and even better alternatives.

If there is a negative aspect to the image Europeans have of Americans, it's that we are big, loud, aggressive, impolite, rich, superficially friendly, and a bit naive.

My Dutch and Belgian friends place a high value on speaking quietly in restaurants and on trains. Listen while on the bus or in a restaurant—the place can be packed, but the decibel level is low. Try to adjust your volume accordingly to show respect for their culture.

While Europeans look bemusedly at some of our Yankee excesses—and worriedly at others—they nearly always afford individual travelers all the warmth we deserve. Judging from all the happy feedback I receive from travelers who have used this book, it's safe to assume you'll enjoy a great, affordable vacation—with the finesse of an independent, experienced traveler.

Thanks, and have a *goede vakantie!*

BACK DOOR TRAVEL PHILOSOPHY
From Rick Steves' Europe Through the Back Door

Travel is intensified living—maximum thrills per minute and one of the last great sources of legal adventure. Travel is freedom. It's recess, and we need it.

Experiencing the real Europe requires catching it by surprise, going casual..."Through the Back Door."

Affording travel is a matter of priorities. (Make do with the old car.) You can travel—simply, safely, and comfortably—nearly anywhere in Europe for $120 a day plus transportation costs (allow more in big cities). In many ways, spending more money only builds a thicker wall between you and what you came to see. Europe is a cultural carnival, and, time after time, you'll find that its best acts are free and the best seats are the cheap ones.

A tight budget forces you to travel close to the ground, meeting and communicating with the people, not relying on service with a purchased smile. Never sacrifice sleep, nutrition, safety, or cleanliness in the name of budget. Simply enjoy the local-style alternatives to expensive hotels and restaurants.

Extroverts have more fun. If your trip is low on magic moments, kick yourself and make things happen. If you don't enjoy a place, maybe you don't know enough about it. Seek the truth. Recognize tourist traps. Give a culture the benefit of your open mind. See things as different but not better or worse. Any culture has much to share.

Of course, travel, like the world, is a series of hills and valleys. Be fanatically positive and militantly optimistic. If something's not to your liking, change your liking. Travel is addictive. It can make you a happier American as well as a citizen of the world. Our Earth is home to six and a half billion equally important people. It's humbling to travel and find that people don't envy Americans. Europeans like us, but, with all due respect, they wouldn't trade passports.

Globe-trotting destroys ethnocentricity. It helps you understand and appreciate different cultures. Regrettably, there are forces in our society that want you dumbed down for their convenience. Don't let it happen. Thoughtful travel engages you with the world—more important than ever these days. Travel changes people. It broadens perspectives and teaches new ways to measure quality of life. Rather than fear the diversity on this planet, travelers celebrate it. Many travelers toss aside their hometown blinders. Their prized souvenirs are the strands of different cultures they decide to knit into their own character. The world is a cultural yarn shop, and Back Door travelers are weaving the ultimate tapestry. Join in!

THE NETHERLANDS

THE NETHERLANDS

Holland: windmills, wooden shoes, cheese, tulips, and tranquility. In its 17th-century glory days, tiny Holland was a world power—politically, economically, and culturally—with more great artists per square mile than any other country.

Today, the Netherlands is Europe's most densely populated country and also one of its wealthiest and best organized. In 1944, the neighboring countries of Belgium, the Netherlands, and Luxembourg became the nucleus of a united Europe when they joined economically to form Benelux.

The average income in the Netherlands is higher than in the United States. Though only 8 percent of the labor force is made up of farmers, 70 percent of the land is cultivated, and—if you venture outside of Amsterdam—you'll travel through vast fields of barley, wheat, sugar beets, potatoes, and flowers.

"Holland" is just a nickname for the Netherlands. North Holland and South Holland are the largest of the 12 provinces that make up the Netherlands. The word Netherlands means "lowlands," and the country is so named because half of it is below sea level, reclaimed from the sea (or rivers or lakes). That's why the locals say, "God made the Earth, but the Dutch made Holland." Modern technology and plenty of Dutch elbow grease have turned much of the sea into fertile farmland. Though a new province—Flevoland, near Amsterdam—has been drained, dried, and populated in the last 100 years, Dutch reclamation projects are essentially finished. But in this era of global warming and rising sea levels, the Dutch are developing plans to upgrade their dikes and bulk up their beaches to hold back the sea. They also continue to be innovative, building floatable homes and greenhouses (which rise with the tides) and relocating dikes farther back from the rivers (to create wider floodplains).

All of that flat, reclaimed land makes the Netherlands a biker's dream. The Dutch, who average four bikes per family, have put small bike roads (with their own traffic lights) beside nearly every major highway. You can rent bikes at most train stations and drop them off at most others. And you can take bikes on trains, outside of rush hour, for €6 per day.

The Dutch can generally speak English, pride themselves on their frankness, and like to split the bill. Thriftiness, efficiency, and a dislike of wastefulness are longstanding Dutch traits. Traditionally, Dutch cities have been open-minded, loose, and liberal (to attract sailors in the days of Henry Hudson). And today, Amsterdam is a capital of alternative lifestyles—a city where nothing's illegal as long as nobody gets hurt. While freewheeling Amsterdam does have a quiet side (particularly in West Amsterdam, which contains the pleasant Jordaan neighborhood), travelers who prefer more small-town Dutch evenings sleep in a small town nearby, such as Haarlem, and side-trip into the big city.

Of course, Amsterdam and Haarlem are just the beginning. To get a complete taste of the Netherlands, venture beyond these

THE NETHERLANDS

Netherlands Almanac

Official Name: Koninkrijk der Nederlanden (Kingdom of the Netherlands), or simply Nederland.

Population: 16.5 million people (1,023 people per square mile; 15 times the population density of the US). About 80 percent are Dutch, 5 percent hail from other EU countries, and the rest are Indonesian, Turkish, Surinamese, and Moroccan. About a third are Catholic, 20 percent are Protestant, and 6 percent are Muslim. About 40 percent have no religious affiliation.

Latitude and Longitude: 52°N and 5°E. The latitude is similar to Alberta, Canada.

Area: 16,000 square miles—about twice the size of New Jersey.

Geography: The Netherlands is located at the mouths of three major European rivers: the Rhine, the Waal, and the Meuse. It shares borders with Belgium, Germany, and the North Sea, which the Dutch have been beating back for centuries, forming *polders*—flat, low-lying lands reclaimed from the sea. The Netherlands has a mild marine climate.

Biggest Cities: Amsterdam is the largest city, with about 750,000 people, followed by Rotterdam (580,000) and The Hague (480,000).

Economy: The Netherlands is prosperous, with the planet's 16th-largest economy ($645 billion), a per capita GDP in the world's top 10 ($39,000), and one of Europe's lowest unemployment rates. Its port at Rotterdam is Europe's largest, and the country relies heavily on foreign trade. The nation's highly mechanized farms produce huge quantities of flowers, bulbs, and produce for export. The economy has also benefited from its large natural gas field—one of the world's biggest—located in the north.

Government: The Netherlands is a parliamentary democracy, with its seat of government at The Hague, although the country's official capital is Amsterdam. The ceremonial head of state is Queen Beatrix, whose ascension to the throne on April 30, 1980 (also the birthday of her mother, Juliana) is celebrated each spring on Queen's Day. The Dutch parliament consists of two houses: the 150-member, directly elected Second Chamber (or Lower House), and the 75-member First Chamber (or Upper House), elected by provincial assemblies. The government is led by a prime minister.

Flag: The Netherlands' flag is composed of three horizontal bands of red (top), white, and blue.

The Dutch: They're among the world's tallest people—the average height for a man is 6'1" and for a woman, 5'6". The average age for both men and women is around 40 years old, and they'll live to be 79. They ride their bikes about 1.5 miles a day and smoke half as much marijuana as their American friends.

cities. Combining Delft (Vermeer's hometown, laced with canals) with the neighboring city, The Hague, makes a rewarding day of sightseeing. Two impressive sights near the city of Arnhem—the Arnhem Open-Air Folk Museum and the Kröller-Müller Museum of modern art (in Hogue Veluwe National Park)—also merit the trip. And there are several other easy and fun side-trips from the Amsterdam/Haarlem area, including the Historic Triangle (a nostalgic loop trip on a steam train and boat), Keukenhof's flower garden (one of the world's best, open in spring only), Edam (an adorable village), Alkmaar (Holland's cheese mecca), Aalsmeer (a bustling modern flower auction), Schokland (for a chance to walk on what was the bottom of the sea at this village/museum), more open-air folk museums (Enkhuizen and Zaanse Schans), and so on. Your options are described in the "Dutch Day Trips at a Glance" sidebar on page 272.

AMSTERDAM

ORIENTATION

Amsterdam is a progressive way of life housed in Europe's most 17th-century city. Physically, it's built upon millions of pilings. But more than that, it's built on good living, cozy cafés, great art, street-corner jazz, stately history, and a spirit of live-and-let-live. It has 750,000 people and almost as many bikes. It also has more canals than Venice...and about as many tourists.

During its Golden Age in the 1600s, Amsterdam was the world's richest city, an international sea-trading port, and the cradle of capitalism. Wealthy, democratic burghers built a planned city of canals lined with trees and townhouses topped with fancy gables. Immigrants, Jews, outcasts, and political rebels were drawn here by its tolerant atmosphere, while painters such as young Rembrandt captured that atmosphere on canvas.

The Dutch are unique. They are among the world's most handsome people—tall, healthy, and with good posture—and the most open, honest, and refreshingly blunt. They like to laugh. As connoisseurs of world culture, they appreciate Rembrandt paintings, Indonesian food, and the latest French film—but with an unsnooty, blue-jeans attitude.

Approach Amsterdam as an ethnologist observing a strange culture. Stroll through any neighborhood and see things that are commonplace here but rarely found elsewhere. Carillons chime quaintly in neighborhoods selling sex, as young professionals smoke pot with impunity next to old ladies in bonnets selling flowers. Observe the neighborhood's "social control," where an elderly man feels safe in his home knowing he's being watched by the prostitutes next door.

Be warned: Amsterdam, a bold experiment in freedom, may box your Puritan ears. Take it all in, then pause to watch the clouds blow past stately old gables—and see the Golden Age reflected in a quiet canal.

Amsterdam: A Verbal Map

Amsterdam's Central Train Station (Amsterdam Centraal), on the north edge of the city, is your starting point, with the TI, bike rental, and trams branching out to all points. Damrak is the main north–south axis, connecting Central Station with Dam Square (people-watching and hangout center) and its Royal Palace. From this main street, the city spreads out like a fan, with 90 islands, hundreds of bridges, and a series of concentric canals—named Herengracht (Gentleman's Canal), Keizersgracht (Emperor's Canal), and Prinsengracht (Prince's Canal)—that were laid out in the 17th century, Holland's Golden Age. Amsterdam's major sights are within walking distance of Dam Square.

To the east of Damrak is the oldest part of the city (today's Red Light District), and to the west is the newer part, where you'll find the Anne Frank House and the Jordaan neighborhood. Museums and Leidseplein nightlife cluster at the southern edge of the city center.

Amsterdam by Neighborhood

Amsterdam can feel like a big, sprawling city, but its major sights cluster in convenient zones. Grouping your sightseeing, walks, dining, and shopping thoughtfully can save you time.

Central Amsterdam—the historic core—runs north–south from Central Station along Damrak, passing through two major city squares (Dam and Spui) and ending at the Mint Tower. The central spine of streets (Damrak, Kalverstraat, Rokin) has some of the city's main department, chain, and tourist stores. Flanking Damrak on the east is the city's oldest area (today's Red Light District) and the revitalized waterfront around the train station.

West Amsterdam lies west of Damrak—from Dam Square to the Anne Frank House. This pleasant area is famous for its four grand canals (Singel, Herengracht, Keizersgracht, and Prinsengracht) that circle the historic core. West Amsterdam has tree-lined canals fronted by old, gabled mansions, as well as many of my recommended accommodations and restaurants. Within West Amsterdam is the boutique shopping district known as the Nine Little Streets. Farther west is the quieter, cozier Jordaan neighborhood, which is good for a stroll, though it's mostly residential.

Southwest Amsterdam is defined by two main features: museums and a city park. The city's major art museums (Rijksmuseum, Van Gogh) and other sights cluster together on an expansive square, Museumplein. The museums are just a short

AMSTERDAM ORIENTATION

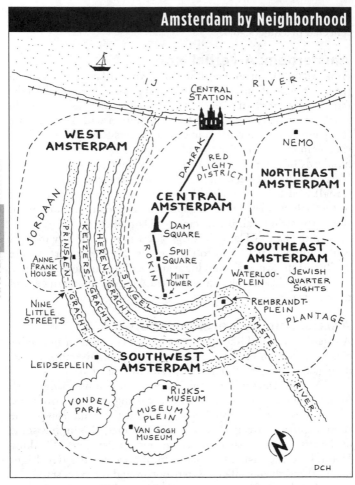

Amsterdam by Neighborhood

walk from Vondelpark, Amsterdam's version of a central park. The lively Leidseplein (a small square that's home to nightlife and restaurants) and the Spiegelkwartier (classy antique-shopping district) are nearby. While it's less central to stay in Southwest Amsterdam, I've recommended accommodations that are a quick, convenient walk to the area's tram lines.

Northeast Amsterdam has a children's science museum (NEMO) and nautical sights.

Southeast Amsterdam contains the former Jewish Quarter and the Jewish Historical Museum. Several sights can be found around the square known as Waterlooplein (Rembrandt's House and a flea market). Additional sights are gathered in a park-dotted area called the Plantage (Dutch Resistance Museum, a theater

Daily Reminder

The biggest Amsterdam sights—the Rijksmuseum, the Van Gogh Museum, and the Anne Frank House—are open daily year-round. The city's naughty sights stay open late every day (Erotic Museum until 24:00, Damrak Sex Museum until 23:00, and the Hash, Marijuana, and Hemp Museum until 22:00).

Sunday: These sights have limited, afternoon-only hours today—the Amstelkring Museum (13:00–17:00) and Old Church (13:00–17:00). The Westerkerk church and tower are closed, as is the Waterlooplein flea market.

Monday: The Houseboat Museum is closed today. From September through May, NEMO is closed today (but open in peak season). Many businesses are closed Monday morning.

Tuesday: The House of Bols is closed.

Wednesday–Thursday: All recommended sights are open. The Hermitage Amsterdam is open until 20:00.

Friday: Rijksmuseum and Van Gogh Museum are open late (until 20:30 and 22:00, respectively).

Saturday: All recommended sights are open.

turned Holocaust memorial, a zoo, and a botanical garden). Rembrandtplein, another nightlife center, is a five-minute walk away.

Planning Your Time

Amsterdam is worth a full day of sightseeing on even the busiest itinerary. While the city has a couple of must-see museums, its best attraction is its own carefree ambience. The city's a joy on foot—and a breezier and faster delight by bike.

Amsterdam in One Day

9:00   Follow my self-guided Amsterdam City Walk, which takes you from the train station to the Rijksmuseum, with stops at the peaceful Begijnhof, the Amsterdam History Museum, and the flower market. Break up the walk with a relaxing hour-long canal cruise (departs from Spui dock or from near Leidseplein).

14:00   Visit Amsterdam's two great art museums, located side by side: the Van Gogh and the Rijksmuseum.

18:30   Tour the Anne Frank House. (Consider ordering tickets online to skip long lines at sight.) Arrive earlier off-season, when it closes at 19:00.

19:30   Wander the Jordaan neighborhood, enjoying dinner by a canal or on a cobbled, quiet street.

21:30   Stroll the Red Light District for some of Europe's most fascinating window-shopping.

Amsterdam Landmarks

Dam (pronounced dahm)	Amsterdam's main square
Damrak (DAHM-rock)	main street between Central Station and Dam Square
Spui (spow, rhymes with cow)	both a street and square
Rokin (roh-KEEN)	street connecting Dam Square and Spui
Kalverstraat (KAL-ver-straht)	pedestrian street
Leidseplein (LIDE-zuh-pline)	lively square
Jordaan (yor-DAHN)	neighborhood in southwest Amsterdam
Museumplein (myoo-ZAY-um-pline)	square with Rijks and Van Gogh museums
gracht (khrockt, pron. gutturally)	canal
straat (straht)	street
plein (pline)	public square
huis (house)	house
kerk (kerk)	church

Amsterdam in Two or More Days

Day 1

9:00   Follow my self-guided Amsterdam City Walk, leading from the train station to the Rijksmuseum, via the quiet Begijnhof, the Amsterdam History Museum (make time to tour this), and the flower market.

12:00   Stop for lunch in the Spui neighborhood before completing the walk.

14:00   Visit Amsterdam's two outstanding art museums, located next to each other: the Van Gogh and the Rijksmuseum.

18:00   Dinner.

20:00   Stroll the Red Light District for some memorable window-shopping.

Day 2

10:00   Start your day with a one-hour canal boat tour (boats leave across from train station).

11:00   Visit the sights of your choice around Rembrandtplein (Rembrandt's House, Waterlooplein flea market, Gassan Diamonds polishing demo, Dutch Resistance Museum), breaking for lunch at one of the recommended

restaurants (Plancius or Café Koosje) near the Dutch
Resistance Museum.

14:30   Free time to shop and explore.

17:00   Tour the Anne Frank House. (Consider booking tickets
online to avoid long lines.)

18:30   Take my self-guided Jordaan Walk.

20:00   Dinner in the Jordaan neighborhood.

Day 3

Visit the nearby town of Haarlem (see page 201).

Day 4

Side-trip by train to one folk museum; choose among Arnhem's,
Enkhuizen's, or Zaandijk's (Zaanse Schans museum). Unless
you're visiting far-flung Arnhem, you could also easily fit in a short
visit to one of these towns: Edam, Delft, or The Hague.

OVERVIEW

(area code: 020)

Tourist Information

"VVV" (pronounced "vay vay vay") is Dutch for "TI," a tourist
information office. Amsterdam's tourist offices are crowded and
inefficient—avoid them if you can. For €0.60 a minute, you can
save yourself a trip by calling the TI toll line from within the
Netherlands at 0900-400-4040 (Mon–Fri 9:00–17:00, from the
US dial 011-31-20-551-2525). The TI at Schiphol Airport (offering
all the information found at the offices in the city center) and the
TI in Haarlem (offering the Amsterdam basics; see page 202) are
much friendlier and less crowded.

If you want to visit an Amsterdam TI in person, here are the
locations of the four offices:

• inside Central Station at track 2b (summer: Sat–Thu
8:00–20:00, Fri 8:00–21:00; winter: Mon–Sat 8:00–20:00, Sun
9:00–17:00; may move to ground floor as part of ongoing train
station construction)

• in front of Central Station (daily July–Aug 8:00–20:00,
Sept–June 9:00–17:00, most crowded)

• on the Singel Canal, in a kiosk at Stadhouderskade 1 (daily
9:30–17:00, less crowded)

• at the airport (daily 7:00–22:00)

Amsterdam's TIs sell tickets to the Anne Frank House (for
€0.50 extra per ticket, same-day tickets available), allowing you
to skip the line at the sight (though it's quicker to order tickets
online—see next page). The TIs also sell tickets (without a fee) to

the Rijks and Van Gogh museums.

At Amsterdam's TIs, consider buying a city map (€2) and any of the walking-tour brochures (€2 each, including *Discovery Tour Through the Center*, *The Former Jewish Quarter*, and *Walks Through Jordaan*). For entertainment, pick up the €2 *Day by Day* calendar; for additional entertainment ideas, see the free papers listed later in this chapter (under "Helpful Hints") and in the Nightlife chapter.

At Amsterdam's Central Station, GWK Change has hotel reservation windows whose clerks sell local and international phone cards, mobile-phone SIM cards, and city maps (€2), and can answer basic tourist questions, with shorter lines (in west tunnel, at right end of station as you leave platform, tel. 020/627-2731).

Don't use the TI or GWK to book a room; you'll pay €5 per person and your host loses 13 percent—meaning you'll likely be charged a higher rate. The phone system is easy, everyone speaks English, and the listings in this book are a better value than the potluck booking you'd get from the TI.

Advance Tickets and Sightseeing Cards

Buying Tickets in Advance for the Major Sights: If you'll be visiting Amsterdam in high season (late March through September) and want to avoid standing in long ticket-buying lines, it's smart to book your tickets online for the Anne Frank House, Rijksmuseum, and Van Gogh Museum.

It's easy to buy tickets through each museum's website: www.annefrank.org (€0.50 surcharge per ticket, but worth it), www.rijksmuseum.nl, and www.vangoghmuseum.com (no extra fee for the Rijks or Van Gogh). For the Rijks and Van Gogh museums, print out your reservation and bring it with you to the ticket-holder's line for a quick entry. For the Anne Frank House (if you don't have access to a printer), simply bring your confirmation number.

You can also buy tickets for these sights in advance at Amsterdam's TIs (see "Tourist Information," previous page), but the lines at the TIs seem as long as the ones you're trying to avoid at the sights.

Tips if You Don't Have Advance Tickets: If you haven't booked ahead, here are a few tips for beating the lines. Going to the Anne Frank House late in the day can help trim your wait in line; this works better in early spring and fall than in summer, when even after-dinner lines can be long. The Museumkaart pass can get you in quickly at the Van Gogh Museum (details in "Sightseeing Cards," next). Or visit the Van Gogh and Rijks museums on a Friday evening, when they're open late (until 22:00 and 20:30, respectively), with no lines and few crowds, even in peak season.

Sightseeing Cards: There are two cards for heavy-duty

sightseers to consider. You're more likely to save money by purchasing the Museumkaart, which covers many sights throughout the Netherlands, than the overpriced *I amsterdam* Card, which is valid only in Amsterdam. (There's no reason to buy both.) Both cards allow free entry to most of the sights in Amsterdam (including the Rijks and Van Gogh museums), but neither card covers the Anne Frank House, Heineken Brewery, Westerkerk tower, NEMO science center, or any sights dealing with diamonds, sex, or marijuana.

The **Museumkaart,** which costs €39.95 and is valid for a year throughout the Netherlands, can save you money if you're planning on seeing six or more museums during your trip (for example, an itinerary that includes these museums, for a total of €52.50: Rijksmuseum-€10, Van Gogh Museum-€12.50, Amsterdam History Museum-€8, Amstelkring Museum-€7, Jewish Historical Museum-€7.50, and Haarlem's Frans Hals Museum-€7.50). The Museumkaart is sold at all participating museums, and you can use it to skip the line everywhere but the Rijksmuseum (which doesn't provide a passholders' line). If you plan to buy a Museumkaart, get it at a smaller, less-crowded museum (such as the Amsterdam History Museum), and flash the pass to skip the long ticket-buying line at the Van Gogh Museum. Note that *museumkaart* translates as "a ticket to a museum" in Dutch. To avoid confusion, ask for the one-year Museumkaart pass.

The *I amsterdam* **Card,** which focuses on Amsterdam and includes most transportation, is not worth the money unless you're planning on a day or two of absolutely non-stop sightseeing. You'll have a set number of consecutive hours to use it (for example: Visit your first museum at 14:00 Mon with a 24-hour pass, and it's good until 13:59 on Tue). Along with many sights and discounts, the pass includes two free canal boat tours and unlimited use of the trams, buses, and metro, but not the trains. This pass does not allow you to skip lines at the major sights (€33/24 hrs, €43/48 hrs, or €53/72 hrs; cards sold at major museums, TIs, and with shorter lines at the GVB transit office across from Central Station, next to TI; www.iamsterdamcard.com).

Arrival in Amsterdam

By Train: Amsterdam swings, and the hinge that connects it to the world is its aptly named Central Station (Amsterdam Centraal). Through 2012, expect a chaotic construction zone due to renovations. The international ticket office should be at track 2. Luggage lockers are at the eastern end of the building—but during busy summer weekends, they can fill up fast, causing a line to form (€4–6/24 hrs, depending on size of bag, daily 7:00–23:00, ID required).

Walk out the door of the station, and you're in the heart of the city. You'll nearly trip over trams ready to take you anywhere your feet won't. Straight ahead is Damrak street, leading to Dam Square. With your back to the entrance of the station, the TI and GVB public-transit offices are just ahead to your left. On your right is a vast, multistory bike garage, and bike rentals are to the far left as you exit.

By Plane: For details on getting from Schiphol Airport into downtown Amsterdam, see page 306.

Helpful Hints

Theft Alert: Tourists are considered green and rich, and the city has more than its share of hungry thieves—especially on trams and at the many hostels. Wear your money belt.

Emergency Telephone Number: Throughout the Netherlands, dial 112.

Street Smarts: Most canals are lined by streets with the same name. When walking around town, beware of the silent transportation—trams and bicycles. (Don't walk on tram tracks or pink/maroon bicycle paths.)

Sightseeing Strategies: To beat the lines at Amsterdam's most popular sights, plan ahead. You can bypass the main ticket-buyers' line at the Anne Frank House, Rijksmuseum, and Van Gogh Museum by buying online tickets before you go (see page 34 for details). Remember, Friday night is a great time to visit the Van Gogh and the Rijks, which are both open late (until 22:00 and 20:30, respectively) to far smaller crowds.

Cash Only: Thrifty Dutch merchants hate paying fees to the credit-card companies; expect to pay cash in unexpected places, including post offices, grocery stores, train station windows, and some museums.

Shop Hours: Most shops are open Tuesday through Saturday 10:00–18:00, and Sunday and Monday 12:00–18:00. Some shops stay open later (21:00) on Thursdays. Supermarkets are generally open Monday through Saturday 8:00–20:00 and are closed on Sundays.

Internet Access: It's easy at cafés all over town, but the best place for serious surfing and email is the towering **Central Library,** which has hundreds of fast, free terminals (Openbare Bibliotheek Amsterdam, daily 10:00–22:00, free Wi-Fi, a 5-min walk from train station, described on page 58). "Coffeeshops," which sell marijuana, usually also offer Internet access—letting you surf the Net with a special bravado.

English Bookstores: For fiction and guidebooks—including mine—try the **American Book Center** at Spui 12, right on the square (Mon–Sat 10:00–20:00, Thu until 21:00, Sun

11:00–18:30, tel. 020/625-5537, www.abc.nl). The huge and helpful **Selexyz Scheltema** is at Koningsplein 20 near the Leidsestraat (included in Amsterdam City Walk—see page 83; store open Mon–Sat 10:00–18:00, Thu until 21:00, Sun 12:00–18:00; lots of English novels, guidebooks, and maps; tel. 020/523-1411). **Waterstone's Booksellers,** a UK chain, also sells British newspapers (152 Kalverstraat, Mon–Sat 10:00–18:00, Thu until 21:00, Sun 11:00–18:00, tel. 020/638-3821).

Free Papers: If you're interested in cutting-edge art, movies, and concerts (hip-hop, jazz, classical), pick up the *Amsterdam Weekly,* a free local English-language paper that's published every Wednesday. It's available at the bookstores listed above (www.amsterdamweekly.nl).

Entertainment: Pick up the *Day by Day* calendar at any TI (€2), check out this book's Nightlife chapter, and call the **Last Minute Ticket Shop** (theater, classical music, and major rock shows, tickets sold only at shop, Leidseplein 26, tel. 0900-0191, calls costs €0.40/min, www.lastminuteticketshop.nl).

Maps: The free and cheap tourist maps can be confusing, except for *Amsterdam Museums: Guide to 37 Museums* (includes tram info and stops, ask for it at the info desk at the big museums, such as the Van Gogh). If you want a top-notch map, buy one (about €2.50). I like the *Carto Studio Centrumkaart Amsterdam* or, better yet, *Amsterdam: Go Where the Locals Go* by Amsterdam Anything.

Pharmacy: The shop named **DA** (Dienstdoende Apotheek) has all the basics—shampoo and toothpaste—as well as a pharmacy counter hidden in the back (Mon–Sat 9:00–22:00, Sun 11:00–22:00, Leidsestraat 74–76 near where it meets Keizersgracht, tel. 020/627-5351).

Laundry: Try **Clean Brothers Wasserij** in the Jordaan (daily 8:00–20:00 for €7 self-service, €9 drop-off—ready in an hour—Mon–Fri 9:00–17:00, Sat 9:00–12:00, no drop-off Sun, Westerstraat 26, one block from Prinsengracht, tel. 020/627-9888) or **Powders** near Leidseplein (daily 8:00–22:00, €6.50 self-service, €8.50 drop-off, Kerkstraat 56, one block south of Leidsestraat).

Holidays: Every year, **Queen's Day** (Koninginnedag, April 30) and **Gay Pride** (Aug 5–8 in 2010) bring crowds, fuller hotels, and higher room prices.

Best Views: While the **Westerkerk** offers fine views from its tower (and is convenient if you're visiting the Anne Frank House), the best city views are from the new **Central Library,** Openbare Bibliotheek Amsterdam (see page 58).

Strip Tickets *(Strippenkaart)*

Within Amsterdam and throughout the Netherlands, the bus, tram, and metro network uses a uniform system of strip tickets, or *strippenkaart*. Although buying individual tickets is sometimes possible, they often cost more. You'll save money and feel like a local by taking advantage of the easy *strippenkaart* system.

A standard *strippenkaart* ticket has 15 strips and costs €6.90. You can buy them all over the country—at newsstands, tobacco shops, post offices, Amsterdam's GVB public-transit office, and machines at the train station. Stock up to avoid having to buy more expensive *strippenkaarts* on board—you can sometimes buy shorter strip tickets (2, 3, and 8) from the driver or conductor, but the per-strip cost is about double. With any *strippenkaart,* you can share strips with your travel partner.

Armed with your *strippenkaart,* board the tram or bus. Typically you'll present your *strippenkaart* to the driver or conductor (on Amsterdam trams, the conductor is stationed in a little booth about halfway back). Tell her your final destination (e.g., "Museumplein"), place your *strippenkaart* on the counter, and she'll stamp the appropriate number of strips.

If there's no conductor, you'll need to stamp the *strippenkaart* yourself. First figure out how many strips the journey costs (for example, two strips for rides in central Amsterdam; other amounts listed in this book—if you're not sure, ask the driver or a fellow passenger). Then fold your *strippenkaart* back the appropriate number of strips (if the trip costs two strips, fold the ticket so the second vacant strip is showing). Insert the folded *strippenkaart* into the orange machine, which stamps it...and—bam—you're legal. To transfer (possible for one hour within central Amsterdam), just show the driver or conductor your stamped *strippenkaart*.

The farther you go, the more strips you'll use: A trip within Amsterdam's city center costs two strips (€0.92); a bus to a nearby town might cost four strips (€1.84); while a bus to a more distant town, such as Edam, runs seven strips (€3.22).

Getting Around Amsterdam

Amsterdam is big, and you'll likely find the trams handy (see below). The longest walk a tourist would make is an hour from Central Station to the Rijksmuseum. When you're on foot, watch out for silent but potentially painful bikes, trams, and crotch-high curb posts.

If you've got a car, park it—all you'll find are frustrating one-way streets, terrible parking, and meter maids with a passion for booting cars parked incorrectly.

By Tram, Bus, and Metro

The helpful GVB public-transit information office is in front of the Central Train Station (next to TI, Mon–Fri 7:00–21:00, Sat–Sun

10:00–18:00, good detailed info on www.gvb.nl). Its free, multilingual *Public Transport Amsterdam Tourist Guide* includes a transit map and explains ticket options and tram connections to all the sights. In keeping with the Dutch mission to automate life, they'll tack on a €0.50 penalty if you buy your transit tickets from a human ticket seller, rather than from a machine. If you're stressed, jetlagged, or otherwise cranky, it's worth the fee for the personal assistance.

You have various ticket options:

• **Individual tickets** cost €1.60 and give you an hour on the buses, trams, and metro system (on trams and buses, pay as you board; for the metro, buy tickets from machines).

• The **24-hour** (€7), **48-hour** (€11.50), or **72-hour** (€14.50) **tickets** give you unlimited transportation on Amsterdam's public-transit network. Buy them at the GVB public-transit office (all versions available), at any TI, or as you board (24-hour version only costs €0.50 extra).

• **Strip tickets** *(strippenkaart),* nearly half the cost of individual tickets, are good on buses, trams, and the metro in Amsterdam. A strip of 15 shareable strips costs €6.90. Any downtown ride in Amsterdam uses two strips (worth €0.92, good for one hour of transfers). For more on buying and using strip tickets, see the sidebar on the opposite page.

• Along with its sightseeing perks, the *I amsterdam* **Card** offers unlimited use of the tram, bus, and metro for its duration (24, 48, or 72 hours—see page 35).

Trams: While buses and the metro can be handy for connecting some points in Amsterdam, travelers find the trams most useful. Trams #2 *(Nieuw Sloten)* and #5 *(A'veen Binnenhof)* travel the north–south axis from Central Station to Dam Square to Leidseplein to Museumplein (Van Gogh and Rijks museums). Tram #1 (marked *Osdorp*) also runs to Leidseplein. At Central Station, these three trams depart from the west side of the Stationsplein (with the station behind you, the shelters for these lines are in front of a row of shops).

Tram #14—which doesn't connect to Central Station—goes east–west (Westerkerk–Dam Square–Muntplein–Waterlooplein–Plantage). If you get lost in Amsterdam, 10 of the city's 17 trams take you back to Central Station. Note that you may have to press a button to open the door to get off.

Metro: The metro (underground train) is used mostly for commuting to the suburbs, but it does connect Central Station with some sights east of Damrak (Nieuwmarkt–Waterlooplein–Weesperplein).

By Bike

Everyone—bank managers, students, pizza delivery boys, and police—uses this mode of transport. It's *the* smart way to travel in a city where 40 percent of all traffic rolls on two wheels. You'll get around town by bike faster than you can by taxi. On my last visit, I rented a bike for five days, chained it up outside my hotel at night, and enjoyed wonderful mobility. I highly encourage this for anyone who wants to get maximum fun per hour in Amsterdam. One-speed bikes, with *"brrringing"* bells,

rent for about €10 per day (cheaper for longer periods) at any number of places—hotels can send you to the nearest spot.

Rental Shops: MacBike, with 900 bikes and counting, is the bike-rental powerhouse. It has a huge and efficient outlet at Central Station (€7/3 hrs, €9.50/24 hrs, €14/48 hrs, €19/72 hrs, more for 3 gears, 25 percent discount with *I amsterdam* Card, €50 deposit plus passport or credit-card imprint, no helmets, daily 9:00–17:45; at east end of station—on the left as you're leaving, by the buses; tel. 020/624-8391, www.macbike.nl). They have two smaller, satellite stations at Leidseplein (Weteringschans 2, tel. 020/528-7688) and Waterlooplein (Mr. Visserplein 2, tel. 020/620-0985). Return your bike to the station where you rented it. MacBike sells several pamphlets outlining bike tours in and around Amsterdam for €1.

Frederic Rent-a-Bike, near Central Station, has quality bikes and a helpful staff (€10/24 hrs, €16/48 hrs, €40/week, 10 percent discount on multi-day rental with this book, daily 9:00–17:30,

Bike Theft

Bike thieves are bold and brazen in Amsterdam. Bikes come with two locks and stern instructions to use both. The wimpy  ones go through the spokes, and the industrial-strength chains are meant to be wrapped around the actual body of the bike and connected to something stronger than any human. Do this diligently. Once, I used both locks, but my chain wasn't around the main bar of my bike's body. In the morning, I found only my front tire (still safely chained to the metal fence). If you're sloppy, it's an expensive mistake and one that any "included" theft insurance won't cover.

Brouwersgracht 78, tel. 020/624-5509, www.frederic.nl).

Tips: No one wears a helmet. For safety, use arm signals, follow the bike-only traffic signals, stay in the obvious and omnipresent bike lanes, and yield to traffic on the right. Fear oncoming trams and tram tracks. Carefully cross tram tracks at a perpendicular angle to avoid catching your tire in the rut. Warning: Police ticket bikers the same as they do drivers. Obey all traffic signals, and walk your bike through pedestrian zones. Fines for biking through pedestrian zones are reportedly €300. A handy bicycle route-planner can be found at www.routecraft.com (select "bike-planner" and click British flag for English). For a "Do-It-Yourself Bike Tour of Amsterdam" and for bike tours, see page 44.

By Boat

While the city is great on foot, bike, or tram, another option is the **Museum Boat,** which shuttles tourists from sight to sight on an all-day ticket. Tickets cost €19, include museum discounts, and are good for 24 hours. Sales booths in front of Central Station (and the boats) offer free brochures with museum times and admission prices. The boat ride comes with recorded narration and takes two hours if you don't get off (about hourly, fewer in winter, 12 stops, recorded narration, departures daily 10:00–17:00, tel. 020/530-1090, www.lovers.nl).

The similar **Canal Company Bus** is actually a boat, offering 14 stops on three different boat routes (€20, ticket is valid until 12:00 the following day, departures daily 10:00–18:00, until 22:00 in summer, leaves near Central Station and Museum Boat dock, tel. 020/623-9886, www.canal.nl). They also run smaller tour boats with live commentary (see next page).

If you're simply looking for a floating, nonstop tour, the regular canal tour boats (without the stops) give more information, cover more ground, and cost less (see "Tours," below).

For do-it-yourself canal tours and lots of exercise, Canal Bus also rents "canal bikes" (a.k.a. paddleboats) near the Anne Frank House and Rijksmuseum (€8/hr per person, daily July–Aug 10:00–21:30, Sept–June 10:00–18:00).

By Taxi

For short rides, Amsterdam is a bad town for taxis. The city's taxis have a high drop charge (€7.50) for the first two kilometers, after which it's €2 per kilometer. You can wave them down, find a rare taxi stand, or call one (tel. 020/677-7777). Given the fine tram system and the wonders of biking the city, I use taxis less in Amsterdam than just about any city in Europe. You'll also see **bike taxis,** particularly near Dam Square and Leidseplein. Negotiate a rate for the trip before you board (no meter), and they'll wheel you wherever you want to go (€10/30 min, no surcharge for baggage or extra weight, sample fare from Leidseplein to Anne Frank House: about €6).

TOURS

By Boat

▲▲Canal Boat Tours—These long, low, tourist-laden boats leave continually from several docks around town for a relaxing, if unin-

spiring, one-hour introduction to the city (with recorded headphone commentary). Select a boat tour for convenience based on the starting point, or if a particular tour is free and included with the *I amsterdam* Card (which covers Rederij Noord-Zuid and Holland International boats).

Tip: Boats leave only when full. Jump on a full boat to avoid sitting at the dock waiting. Choose from one of these three companies:

Rondvaart Kooij is cheapest (€8, 3/hr in summer 10:00–22:00, 2/hr in winter 10:00–17:00, at corner of Spui and Rokin streets, about 10 min from Dam Square, tel. 020/623-3810, www.rederijkooij.nl).

Rederij Noord-Zuid departs from near Leidseplein (€10, 2/hr April–Oct 10:00–18:00, hourly Nov–March 10:00–17:00, tel. 020/679-1370, www.blueboat.nl).

Holland International offers a standard one-hour trip and a variety of longer tours (€12, 60-min "100 highlights" tour with recorded commentary, runs about every 15 min daily 9:00–22:00, tel. 020/625-3035, www.hir.nl). Their €18, 90-minute "ultimate" tour with a live guide leaves twice daily (at 11:00 and 13:00).

No fishing allowed—but bring your camera. Some prefer to cruise at night, when the bridges are illuminated.

Hop-On, Hop-Off Canal Boats—Small, 12-person electric Canal Hopper boats leave every 25–35 minutes with live commentary on two different hop-on, hop-off routes (€20 day-pass, runs Sat–Mon 2/hr 9:30–17:30, none Tue–Fri, west route includes Anne Frank House, less-frequent east route includes Rembrandt's House, tel. 020/623-9886, www.canal.nl).

Wetlands Safari, Nature Canoe Tours near Amsterdam—If you'd like to get some exercise and a dose of the *polder* country and village life, consider this five-hour tour. Majel Tromp, a friendly villager who speaks great English, takes groups limited to 15 people. The program: Meet at the VVV tourist information office outside Central Station at 9:30, catch a public bus, stop for coffee, take a 3.5-hour canoe trip (2–3 people per canoe) with several stops, tour a village by canoe, munch a rural canalside picnic lunch (included), then canoe and bus back into the big city by 15:00 (€38, €3 discount with this book, May–mid-Sept Sun–Fri, reservations required, tel. 020/686-3445, mobile 06-5355-2669, www.wetlands safari.nl, info@wetlandssafari.nl).

On Foot

Red Light District Tours—For a stroll through Amsterdam's most infamous neighborhood, consider my self-guided Red Light District Walk on page 88. But if you'd be more comfortable exploring with a group, a guided tour is a good way to go. **Randy Roy's Red Light Tours** consists of one expat American woman, Kimberley. She lived in the Red Light District for years and gives fun, casual, yet informative 90-minute walks through this fascinating and eye-popping neighborhood. While the actual information is light, you'll walk through various porn and drug shops and have an expert to answer your questions. Call or email to reserve (€12.50 includes a drink in a colorful bar at the end, nightly at 20:00, Fri and Sat 22:00, tours meet in front of Victoria Hotel—in front of Central Station, mobile 06-4185-3288, www.randyroysredlight tours.com, kimberley@randyroysredlighttours.com).

Free City Walk—**New Europe Tours** "employs" native, English-speaking students to give these irreverent and entertaining three-hour walks (using the same "free tour, ask for tips, sell their other tours" formula popular in so many great European cities). This long walk covers a lot of the city with an enthusiasm for the contemporary pot-and-prostitution scene (free, daily at 11:15 and 13:15, just show up at the National Monument on Dam Square, www.neweurope tours.eu).

Adam's Apple Tours—This walking tour offers a two-hour, English-only look at the historic roots of Amsterdam. You'll have a small group of generally 5–6 people and a caring guide, starting off at Central Station and ending up at Dam Square (€25; May–Sept daily at 10:00, 12:30, and 15:00 based on demand; call 020/616-7867 to confirm times and book, www.adamsapple.nl, Frank).

Private Guide—**Albert Walet** is a likeable, hardworking, and knowledgeable local guide who enjoys personalizing tours for Americans interested in knowing his city. "Ab" specializes in history and architecture, and exudes a passion for Amsterdam (€49/2 hrs, €89/4 hrs, small groups, on foot or by bike, mobile 06-2069-7882, abwalet@yahoo.com). Ab also takes travelers to nearby towns, including Haarlem, Leiden, and Delft.

By Bike

The **Yellow Bike Guided Tours** company offers a three-hour city tour (€20, April–Oct Sun–Fri at 9:30 and 13:00, Sat at 9:30 and 14:00) and a six-hour, 22-mile tour of the dikes and green pastures of the countryside (€28, lunch extra, April–Oct daily at 11:00). Both tours leave from Nieuwezijds Kolk 29, three blocks from Central Station (reservations smart, tel. 020/620-6940, www.yellowbike .nl). If you take one of their tours, you can rent the bike for the rest of the day at a 50 percent discount (€10/24 hrs, €100 deposit and ID required). If you'd prefer a private guide, see Albert Walet, above.

Do-It-Yourself Bike Tour of Amsterdam—A day enjoying the bridges, bike lanes, and sleepy, off-the-beaten-path canals on your own one-speed is an essential Amsterdam experience. The real joys of Europe's best-preserved 17th-century city are the count-

less intimate glimpses it offers: the laid-back locals sunning on their porches under elegant gables, rusted bikes that look as if they've been lashed to the same lamppost since the 1960s, wasted hedonists planted on canalside benches, and happy sailors permanently moored, but still manning the deck.

For a good day trip, rent a bike at Central Station (see "By Bike" on page 40). Head west down Haarlemmerstraat, working your wide-eyed way down the Prinsengracht (drop into Café 't Papeneiland at Prinsengracht 2) and detouring through the small, gentrified streets of the Jordaan neighborhood before popping out at Westerkerk under the tallest spire in the city.

Pedal south to the lush and peaceful Vondelpark, then cut back through the center of town (Leidseplein to the Mint Tower, along Rokin street to Dam Square). From there, cruise the Red Light District, following Oudezijds Voorburgwal past the Old Church (Oude Kerk) to Zeedijk street, and return to the train station.

Then, you can escape into the countryside by hopping on the free ferry behind Central Station (see below). In five minutes, Amsterdam will be gone, and you'll be rolling through your very own Dutch painting.

Taking Bikes Across the Harbor on a Free Ferry—Behind Central Station is a little commuter port where four ferries come and go constantly (free, bikes welcome, signs count down the minutes until the next departure), offering two quick little excursions. The middle two ferries run immediately across the harbor (3-min ride). Bring your bike and ride two kilometers (1.25 miles) along the canal, through suburbs, and then into the *polderland* and villages.

Ferries leaving from the far-left "NDSM" wharf cruise 10 minutes across the North Sea Canal (2/hr, generally departing at :15 and :45). This gives a fun look at the fifth-biggest harbor in Europe (Rotterdam is number one), old wheat silos now renovated into upscale condos, and the shoreline of north Amsterdam, where the planned metro connection to the center is bringing growth, with lots of new apartments under construction. The ferry deposits you in an industrial wasteland (a vacant old warehouse just past the modern MTV headquarters building is filled with artist studios, wacky ventures, and a noisy skateboard hall). **IJ-Kantine** is a fine modern restaurant/café 30 yards from the ferry landing (daily from 9:00, tel. 020/633-7162).

By Public Minibus

For a quick, do-it-yourself public bus tour along scenic Prinsengracht (Prince's Canal), catch Amsterdam's cute little Stop/Go minibus. It arcs along the city's longest canal, offering clever budget travelers a very cheap and fun 20-minute experience that's faster than a touristy canal tour. The scenic bus ride goes where normal big buses can't fit (along the bumpy and cobbled canal-side lanes), giving you a delightful look at the workaday city—without a tourist in sight. The high ride, comfortable seats, and big windows show you Amsterdam well.

The Stop/Go route follows the outside of the canal counter-clockwise and returns clockwise along the inside. The buses have no set stops—just wave them down. Grab a seat in the back for the best view. If you see something fun, just jump out—there's another bus in 12 minutes (2 strips or €1, tickets valid one hour, daily 9:00–17:30, 8 seats, can be muggy on hot days; departs from train station, **Central Library,** and more; www.gvb.nl).

For this short tour, catch the bus at the train station. From the station, the minibus passes characteristic cafés in the Jordaan district, countless houseboats, and the whole gamut of gables (under a parade of leaning, Golden Age buildings complete with all the hooks and pulleys). Rolling along the Prinsengracht, you'll see the long line at the Anne Frank House just before the towering Westerkerk. You'll pass within a block of the thriving Leidseplein and Rijksmuseum (look to the right at Spiegelgracht) before passing Rembrandtplein (with its fun 3-D *Night Watch* statues) and crossing the Amstel River to finish at the Waterlooplein flea market, near Rembrandt's House, Gassan Diamonds, and the metro station (subway trains run every 2 min, returning you to Central Station in 3 min).

From the bus, watch for these little bits of Amsterdam:
- green, metal public urinals
- late 19th-century lamp poles
- bikes chained to anything unmovable (including the practical new "staple" design bike racks)
- *amsterdammertjes* (literally "little one from Amsterdam," referring to the countless, little, dark-red bollards—bearing the city's emblem of three diagonal crosses—that protect walkers from passing traffic)
- underground recycling and garbage bins designed to keep workers from having to dump out bins into trucks (a new law prohibits employees from lifting anything over 25 kilos— about 55 pounds)
- and "*ja*" and "*nee*" stickers on mail slots, indicating whether residents accept junk mail and advertising. (The cool people of the Jordaan are mostly "*nee nee.*")

SIGHTS

One of Amsterdam's delights is that it has perhaps more small specialty museums than any other city its size. From houseboats to sex, from marijuana to Old Masters, you can find a museum to suit your interests.

For tips on how to save time otherwise spent in the long lines of the big three museums—the Anne Frank House, Van Gogh Museum, and Rijksmuseum—see "Advance Tickets and Sightseeing Cards" on page 34.

Note that most museums require baggage check (usually free, often in coin-op lockers where you get your coin back).

The following sights are arranged by neighborhood for handy sightseeing. When you see a ✪ in a listing, it means the sight is covered in much more depth in one of my walks or self-guided tours. This is why Amsterdam's most important attractions get the least coverage in this chapter—we'll explore them later in the book.

Southwest Amsterdam

▲▲▲Rijksmuseum—Built to house the nation's great art, the Rijksmuseum owns several thousand paintings, including an incomparable collection of Dutch Masters: Rembrandt, Vermeer, Hals, and Steen. The museum has made it easy for you to focus on the highlights, because that's all that is on display while most of the building undergoes several years of renovation (due to wrap up in 2013). You'll be able to wander through a wonderful, concentrated dose of 17th-century Dutch masterpieces (€10, audioguide-€4, daily 9:00–18:00, Fri until 20:30, tram #2 or #5 from Central Station to Hobbemastraat, tel. 020/674-7047 for automated info or tel. 020/674-7000 for main number, www.rijksmuseum.nl). The Philips Wing entrance is near the corner of Hobbemastraat and

AMSTERDAM SIGHTS

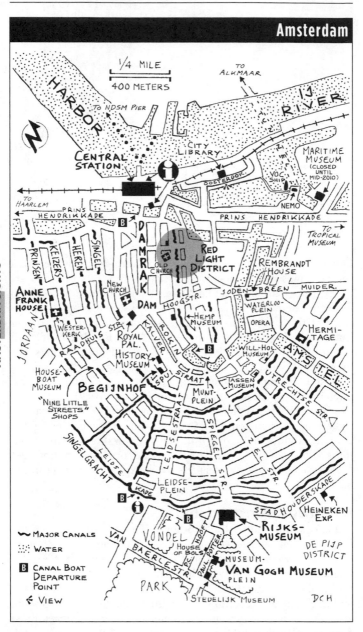

Amsterdam

1/4 MILE
400 METERS

TO ALKMAAR

HARBOR

TO NDSM PIER

IJ RIVER

CITY LIBRARY

CENTRAL STATION

MARITIME MUSEUM (CLOSED UNTIL MID-2010)

VOC SHIP

OOSTERDOK

NEMO

TO HAARLEM

PRINS HENDRIKKADE

PRINS HENDRIKKADE

TO TROPICAL MUSEUM

PRINSEN

KEIZERS

HEREN

SINGEL

DAMRAK

OLD CHURCH

RED LIGHT DISTRICT

REMBRANDT HOUSE

MUIDER.

NEW CHURCH

ANNE FRANK HOUSE

JORDAAN

WESTER-KERK

RAADHUIS

HOUSE-BOAT MUSEUM

DAM

HOOGSTR.

JODEN-BREEN

HEMP MUSEUM

WATERLOO-PLEIN

OPERA

HERMI-TAGE

ROYAL PAL.

HISTORY MUSEUM

KALVER

ROKIN

STR.

WILL-HOL MUSEUM

AMSTEL

BEGIJNHOF

SPUI STRAAT

TASSEN MUSEUM

MUNT-PLEIN

UTRECHTSE STR.

"NINE LITTLE STREETS" SHOPS

LEIDSESTRAAT

SPIEGEL STR.

NGEL STR.

SINGELGRACHT

LEIDSE KADE

LEIDSE-PLEIN

STADHOUDERSKADE

HEINEKEN EXP.

VONDEL

VAN

BAERLESTR.

HOUSE OF BOLS

HOOFT

PAUL POTTER

RIJKS-MUSEUM

DE PIJP DISTRICT

MUSEUM-PLEIN

VAN GOGH MUSEUM

PARK

STEDELIJK MUSEUM

DCH

~ MAJOR CANALS

⋮⋮⋮ WATER

🅱 CANAL BOAT DEPARTURE POINT

← VIEW

Jan Luijkenstraat, on the south side of the Rijks—the part of the huge building nearest the Van Gogh Museum.

○ See Rijksmuseum Tour, page 113.

▲▲▲**Van Gogh Museum**—Near the Rijksmuseum, this remark-

able museum features works by the troubled Dutch artist whose art seemed to mirror his life. Vincent, who killed himself in 1890 at age 37, is best known for sunny, Impressionist canvases that vibrate and pulse with life. The museum's 200 paintings, a stroll through the artist's work and life, were owned by Theo, Vincent's younger, art-dealer brother. Highlights include *Sunflowers*, *The Bedroom*, *The Potato Eaters*, and many brooding self-portraits. The third floor shows works that influenced Vincent, from Monet and Pissarro to Gauguin, Cézanne, and Toulouse-Lautrec. The worthwhile audioguide includes insightful commentaries and quotes from Vincent himself. Temporary exhibitions fill the new wing, down the escalator from the ground floor lobby (€12.50, audioguide-€4, daily 10:00–18:00, Fri until 22:00—with no crowds in evening, Paulus Potterstraat 7, tel. 020/570-5200, www.vangoghmuseum.nl).

○ See Van Gogh Museum Tour, page 132.

▲**Museumplein**—Bordered by the Rijks and Van Gogh museums and the Concertgebouw (classical music hall), this park-like square is interesting even to art-haters. Amsterdam's best acoustics are found underneath the Rijksmuseum, where street musicians perform everything from chamber music to Mongolian throat singing. Mimes, human statues, and crafts booths dot the square. Skateboarders careen across a concrete tube, while locals enjoy a park bench or a coffee at the Cobra Café.

Nearby is **Coster Diamonds,** a handy place to see a diamond-cutting and polishing demo (free and interesting 30-min tours on request followed by sales pitch, popular for decades with tour groups, prices marked up to include tour guide kickbacks, daily 9:00–17:00, Paulus Potterstraat 2, tel. 020/305-5555, www.costerdiamonds.com). The tour at Gassan Diamonds is better (see "Southeast Amsterdam," later in this chapter), but Coster is convenient to the Museumplein scene.

House of Bols: Cocktail & Genever Experience—This leading Dutch distillery has opened a pricey and slick little museum

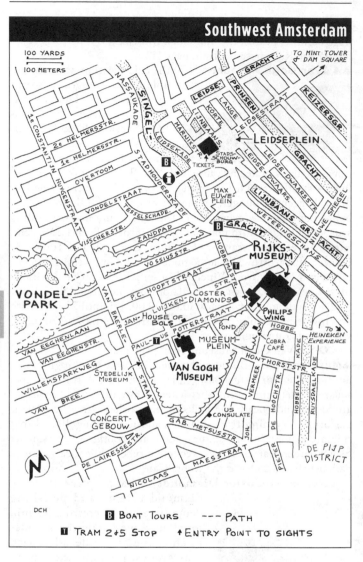

across the street from the Van Gogh Museum. The "experience" is a self-guided walk through what is essentially an ad for Bols—"four hundred years of working on the art of mixing and blending…a celebration of gin"—with some fun sniffing opportunities and a drink at a modern cocktail bar for a finale. The highlight is a chance to taste up to five different local gins with a talkative expert guiding you. Then have your barista mix up the cocktail of your dreams—based on what you learned during your sniffing (€10, Wed–Mon 10:00–18:00, closed Tue, must be 18, Paulus

Potterstraat 14, tel. 020/570-8575, www.houseofbols.com). If you like the booze and hang out and talk, this can be a good deal (but do it after the Van Gogh Museum).

Stedelijk Museum—This modern-art museum is expected to reopen in 2010 in its spiffed-up original Stedelijk Museum building, located near the Rijksmuseum. Its fun, far-out, and refreshing collection includes post-1945 experimental and conceptual art and works by Picasso, Chagall, Cézanne, Kandinsky, and Mondrian (check www.stedelijk.nl for updates).

Heineken Experience—This famous old brewery—modernized and enlarged—welcomes visitors to a slick and entertaining beer-appreciation fest (€15, includes two drinks, daily 11:00–19:00, last entry at 17:30; tram #16, #24, or #25 to Heinekenplein; an easy walk from Rijksmuseum, tel. 020/523-9222, www.heineken experience.com).

De Pijp District—This former working-class industrial and residential zone (behind the Heineken Experience, near the Rijksmuseum) is emerging as a colorful, vibrant district. Its spine is Albert Cuypstraat, a street taken over by a long, sprawling produce market packed with interesting people. The centerpiece is **Restaurant Bazar** (marked by a roof-capping golden angel), a church turned into a Middle Eastern food circus (see listing on page 189).

▲**Leidseplein**—Brimming with cafés, this people-watching mecca is an impromptu stage for street artists, accordionists, jugglers, and unicyclists. Sunny afternoons are liveliest. The Boom Chicago theater fronts this square (see Nightlife chapter, page 199). Stroll nearby Lange Leidsedwarsstraat (one block north) for a taste-bud tour of ethnic eateries, from Greek to Indonesian.

▲▲**Vondelpark**—This huge and lively city park is popular with the Dutch—families with little kids, romantic couples, strolling seniors, and hippies sharing blankets and beers. It's a favored venue for free summer concerts. On a sunny afternoon, it's a hedonistic scene that seems to say, "Parents...relax."

Rembrandtplein and Tuschinski Theater—One of the city's premier nightlife spots is the leafy Rembrandtplein (the artist's statue stands here, along with a jaunty new group of statues giving us *The Night Watch* in 3-D) and the adjoining Thorbeckeplein.

Amsterdam at a Glance

▲▲▲**Rijksmuseum** Best collection anywhere of the Dutch Masters: Rembrandt, Hals, Vermeer, and Steen. **Hours:** Daily 9:00–18:00, Fri until 20:30. See page 47.

▲▲▲**Van Gogh Museum** 200 paintings by the angst-ridden artist. **Hours:** Daily 10:00–18:00, Fri until 22:00. See page 49.

▲▲▲**Anne Frank House** Young Anne's hideaway during the Nazi occupation. **Hours:** Daily March 15–Sept 14 9:00–21:00, July–Aug until 22:00, Sept 15–March 14 9:00–19:00. See page 54.

▲▲**Vondelpark** City park and concert venue. **Hours:** Always open. See page 51.

▲▲**Amsterdam History Museum** City's growth from fishing village to trading capital to today, including some Rembrandts and a playable carillon. **Hours:** Mon–Fri 10:00–17:00, Sat–Sun 11:00–17:00. See page 55.

▲▲**Dutch Resistance Museum** History of the Dutch struggle against the Nazis. **Hours:** Tue–Fri 10:00–17:00, Sat–Mon 11:00–17:00. See page 67.

▲▲**Amstelkring Museum** Catholic church hidden in the attic of a 17th-century merchant's house. **Hours:** Mon–Sat 10:00–17:00, Sun 13:00–17:00. See page 57.

▲▲**Red Light District** Women of the world's oldest profession on the job. **Hours:** Best from noon into the evening; avoid late at night. See page 57.

▲**Museumplein** Square with art museums, street musicians, crafts, and nearby diamond demos. **Hours:** Always open. See page 49.

▲**Leidseplein** Lively square with cafés and street musicians. **Hours:** Always open, best on sunny afternoons. See page 51.

Several late-night dance clubs keep the area lively into the wee hours. Utrechtsestraat is lined with upscale shops and restaurants. Nearby Reguliersdwarsstraat (a street one block south of Rembrandtplein) is a center for gay and lesbian nightclubs in the city.

The **Tuschinski Theater,** a movie palace from the 1920s (a half-block from Rembrandtplein down Reguliersbreestraat), glitters inside and out. Still a working theater, it's a delightful

▲**Begijnhof** Quiet courtyard lined with picturesque houses. **Hours:** Daily 8:00–17:00. See page 55.

▲**Rembrandt's House** The master's reconstructed house, displaying his etchings. **Hours:** Daily 10:00–17:00. See page 62.

▲**Diamond Tours** Offered at shops throughout the city. **Hours:** Generally daily 9:00–17:00. See page 62.

▲**Willet-Holthuysen Museum (a.k.a. Herengracht Canal Mansion)** Elegant 17th-century house. **Hours:** Mon–Fri 10:00–17:00, Sat–Sun 11:00–17:00. See page 63.

▲**Hermitage Amsterdam** Russia's Tsarist treasures, on loan from St. Petersburg. **Hours:** Daily 10:00–17:00, Wed until 20:00. See page 64.

▲**Jewish Historical Museum** The Great Synagogue and exhibits on Judaism and culture. **Hours:** Daily 11:00–17:00. See page 65.

▲**Dutch Theater** Moving memorial in former Jewish detention center. **Hours:** Daily 11:00–16:00. See page 65.

▲**Tropical Museum** Re-creations of tropical-life scenes. **Hours:** Daily 10:00–17:00. See page 68.

▲**Hash, Marijuana, and Hemp Museum** All the dope, from history and science to memorabilia. **Hours:** Daily 10:00–22:00. See page 58.

Heineken Experience Mini-brewery and tasting bar. **Hours:** Daily 11:00–19:00. See page 51.

House of Bols: The Cocktail & Genever Experience Gin museum culminating in a cocktail bar. Hours: Wed-Mon 10:00–18:00, closed Tue. See page 49.

old place to see first-run movies. The exterior is an interesting hybrid of styles, forcing the round peg of Art Nouveau into the square hole of Art Deco. The stone-and-tile facade features stripped-down, functional Art Deco squares and rectangles, but is ornamented with Art Nouveau elements—Tiffany-style windows, garlands, curvy iron

lamps, Egyptian pharaohs, and exotic gold lettering over the door. Inside (lobby is free), the sumptuous decor features red carpets, nymphs on the walls, and semi-abstract designs. Grab a seat in the lobby and watch the ceiling morph (Reguliersbreestraat 26–28).

Houseboat Museum (Woonbootmuseum)—In the 1930s, modern cargo ships came into widespread use—making small, sail-powered cargo boats obsolete. In danger of extinction, these little vessels found new life as houseboats lining the canals of Amsterdam. Today, 2,500 such boats—their cargo holds turned into classy, comfortable living rooms—are called home by locals. For a peek into this *gezellig* (cozy) world, visit this tiny museum. Captain Vincent enjoys showing visitors around the houseboat, which feels lived-in because, until 1997, it was (€3.25, March–Oct Tue–Sun 11:00–17:00, closed Mon; Nov–Feb Fri–Sun 11:00–17:00, closed Mon–Thu; on Prinsengracht, opposite #296 facing Elandsgracht, tel. 020/427-0750, www.houseboatmuseum.nl).

West Amsterdam

▲▲▲Anne Frank House—A pilgrimage for many, this house offers a fascinating look at the hideaway of young Anne during the Nazi occupation of the Netherlands. Anne, her parents, an older sister, and four others spent a little more than two years in a "Secret Annex" behind her father's business. While in hiding, 13-year-old Anne kept a diary chronicling her extraordinary experience. Acting on a tip, the Nazis arrested the group in August 1944 and sent them to concentration camps in Poland and Germany. Anne and her sister died of typhus in March 1945, only weeks before their camp was liberated. Of the eight inhabitants of the Secret Annex, only Anne's father, Otto Frank, survived. He returned to Amsterdam and arranged for his daughter's diary to be published in 1947. It was followed by many translations, a play, and a movie.

Pick up the English pamphlet at the door. The thoughtfully designed exhibit offers thorough coverage of the Frank family, the diary, the stories of others who hid, and the Holocaust. It may be less crowded after 18:00 (€8.50, not covered by any sightseeing passes, daily March 15–Sept 14 9:00–21:00, July–Aug until 22:00, Sept 15–March 14 9:00–19:00, last entry 30 min before closing, no baggage check, no large bags allowed inside, Prinsengracht 267, near Westerkerk, tel. 020/556-7100, www.annefrank.org). For information on buying advance tickets, see page 34.

✪ See Anne Frank House Tour, page 145.

Westerkerk—Located near the Anne Frank House, this landmark church (free, generally open April–Sept Mon–Sat 11:00–15:00, closed Sun) has a barren interior, Rembrandt's body buried somewhere under the pews, and Amsterdam's tallest steeple.

The tower is open only for tours and offers a grand city view.

The tour guide, who speaks in English and Dutch, tells of the church and its carillon. Only six people are allowed at a time (it's first-come, first-served), so lines can be long (€6, 30 min, departures on the half hour, April–Oct Mon–Sat 10:00–17:30, last tour leaves at 17:30, closed Sun and Nov–March, call 020/689-2565 for info and to arrange private tour).

Central Amsterdam, near Dam Square

Royal Palace (Koninklijk Huis)—The palace, reopening to the public in June of 2009, is right on Dam Square. It was built as a lavish City Hall for Amsterdam, when the country was a proud new republic and Amsterdam was the richest city on the planet—awash in profit from trade. When constructed in 1648, this building was one of Europe's finest, with a sumptuous interior. Today, it's the official (but not actual) residence of the queen (€7.50, Tue–Sun 12:00–17:00, closed Mon, tel. 020/620-4060, www.paleisamsterdam.nl).

○ See Amsterdam City Walk, page 69.

New Church (Nieuwe Kerk)—Barely newer than the "Old" Church (located in the Red Light District), this 15th-century sanctuary has an intentionally dull interior, after the decoration was removed by 16th-century iconoclastic Protestants seeking to unclutter their communion with God. This is where many Dutch royal weddings and all coronations take place. There's a steep entrance fee to see the rotating, temporary exhibitions, but you can pop in to look at the vast interior if no exhibitions are going on (€10; May–July daily 10:00–17:00—sometimes until 18:00 for exhibitions; Aug–April daily 10:00–18:00, Thu until 22:00; on Dam Square, info tel. 020/353-8168, tel. 020/638-6909, www .nieuwekerk.nl).

○ See Amsterdam City Walk, page 69.

▲**Begijnhof**—Stepping into this tiny, idyllic courtyard in the city center, you escape into the charm of old Amsterdam. Notice house #34, a 500-year-old wooden structure (rare, since repeated fires taught city fathers a trick called brick). Peek into the hidden Catholic church, dating from the time when post-Reformation Dutch Catholics couldn't worship in public. It's opposite the English Reformed church, where the Pilgrims worshipped while waiting for their voyage to the New World (marked by a plaque near the door). Be considerate of the people who live around the courtyard (free, daily 8:00–17:00, on Begijnensteeg lane, just off Kalverstraat between #130 and #132, pick up flier at office near entrance, for more details, see Amsterdam City Walk, page 69).

▲▲**Amsterdam History Museum (Amsterdams Historisch Museum)**—Follow the city's growth from fishing village to world trade center to hippie haven. Housed in a 500-year-old former orphanage, this creative and hardworking museum features

AMSTERDAM SIGHTS

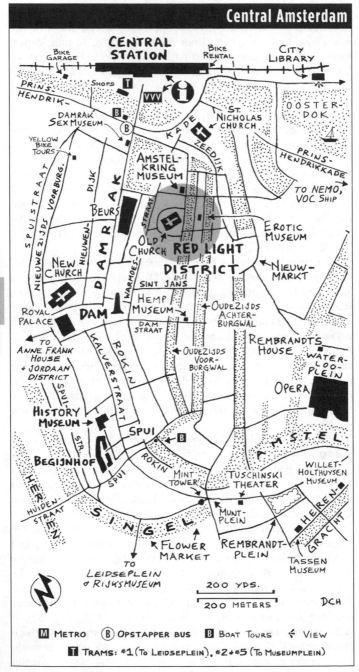

Central Amsterdam

CENTRAL STATION

BIKE GARAGE

BIKE RENTAL

CITY LIBRARY

PRINS-HENDRIK-

Shops

VVV

OOSTER-DOK

DAMRAK SEX MUSEUM

YELLOW BIKE TOURS

ST. NICHOLAS CHURCH

KADE ZEEDIJK

PRINS-HENDRIKKADE

TO NEMO, VOC SHIP

AMSTEL-KRING MUSEUM

SPUISTRAAT

NIEUWEZIJDS VOORBURG.

DIJK

BEURS

STRAAT

NIEUWEN-

DAMRAK

NEW CHURCH

Old Church

RED LIGHT DISTRICT

EROTIC MUSEUM

NIEUW-MARKT

ROYAL PALACE

WARMOES-

SINT JANS

HEMP MUSEUM

DAM STRAAT

OUDEZIJDS ACHTER-BURGWAL

OUDEZIJDS VOOR-BURGWAL

REMBRANDT'S HOUSE

WATER-LOO-PLEIN

DAM

TO ANNE FRANK HOUSE & JORDAAN DISTRICT

ROKIN

KALVERSTRAAT

SPUI

SPUI STR.

HISTORY MUSEUM

BEGIJNHOF

SPUI

ROKIN

AMSTEL-

OPERA

HEREN-

HUIDEN-STRAAT

SINGEL

MINT TOWER

MUNT-PLEIN

TUSCHINSKI THEATER

WILLET-HOLTHUYSEN MUSEUM

HEREN-GRACHT

FLOWER MARKET

REMBRANDT-PLEIN

TASSEN MUSEUM

TO LEIDSEPLEIN & RIJKSMUSEUM

200 YDS.

200 METERS

DCH

M METRO   (B) OPSTAPPER BUS   **B** BOAT TOURS   ↰ VIEW

T TRAMS: #1 (To LEIDSEPLEIN), #2 & #5 (To MUSEUMPLEIN)

Rembrandt's paintings, fine English descriptions, and a carillon loft. The loft comes with push-button recordings of the town bell tower's greatest hits and a self-serve carillon "keyboard" that lets you ring a few bells yourself (€8, Mon–Fri 10:00–17:00, Sat–Sun 11:00–17:00, pleasant restaurant, next to Begijnhof, Kalverstraat 92, tel. 020/523-1822, www.ahm.nl). The museum's free pedestrian corridor—lined with old-time group portraits—is a powerful teaser. The Amsterdam History Museum is a fine place to buy the Museumkaart, and then use it to skip long lines at the Van Gogh Museum (for details, see page 35).

O See Amsterdam History Museum Tour, page 161.

Red Light District

▲▲Amstelkring Museum (Our Lord in the Attic/Museum Ons' Lieve Heer op Solder)—While Amsterdam has long been known for its tolerant attitudes, 16th-century politics forced Dutch Catholics to worship discreetly. Near the train station in the Red Light District, you'll find a fascinating hidden Catholic church filling the attic of three 17th-century merchants' houses. Don't miss the silver collection and other exhibits of daily life from 300 years ago (€7, Mon–Sat 10:00–17:00, Sun and holidays 13:00–17:00, closed Jan 1 and April 30, no photos, Oudezijds Voorburgwal 40, tel. 020/624-6604, www.museumamstelkring.nl).

O See Amstelkring Museum Tour, page 153.

▲▲Red Light District—Europe's most touristed ladies of the night tease and tempt here, as they have for centuries, in 400 display-case windows around Oudezijds Achterburgwal and Oudezijds Voorburgwal, surrounding the Old Church (Oude Kerk, see next page). Drunks and druggies make the streets uncomfortable late at night after the gawking tour groups leave (about 22:30), but it's a fascinating walk earlier in the evening.

The neighborhood, one of Amsterdam's oldest, has hosted prostitutes since 1200. Prostitution is entirely legal here, and the prostitutes are generally entrepreneurs, renting space and running their own businesses, as well as filling out tax returns and even paying union dues. Popular prostitutes net about €500 a day (for what's called "S&F" in its abbreviated, printable form, costing €25–50 per customer).

O See Red Light District Walk, page 88.

The **Prostitution Information Center,** open to the public, offers a small €1.50 booklet that answers most of the questions tourists have about the Red Light District (free, Tue–Sat 12:00–19:00, closed Sun–Mon, tours on Sat—check website for details, facing Old Church at Enge Kerksteeg 3, tel. 020/420-7328, www.pic-amsterdam.com).

Sex Museums—Amsterdam has two sex museums: one in the Red Light District and another a block in front of Central Station on Damrak street. While visiting one can be called sightseeing, visiting both is hard to explain. The one on Damrak is cheaper and more interesting. Here's a comparison:

The **Erotic Museum** in the Red Light District is five floors of uninspired paintings, videos, old photos, and sculpture (€5, daily 11:00–24:00, along the canal at Oudezijds Achterburgwal 54, tel. 020/624-7303; see page 99).

The **Damrak Sex Museum** tells the story of pornography from Roman times through 1960. Every sexual deviation is revealed in various displays. The museum includes early French pornographic photos; memorabilia from Europe, India, and Asia; a Marilyn Monroe tribute; and some S&M displays (€3, daily 9:30–23:00, Damrak 18, a block in front of Central Station, tel. 020/622-8376).

Old Church (Oude Kerk)—This 14th-century landmark—the needle around which the Red Light District spins—has served as a reassuring welcome-home symbol to sailors, a refuge to the downtrodden, an ideological battlefield of the Counter-Reformation, and today, a tourist sight with a dull interior (€5, Mon–Sat 11:00–17:00, Sun 13:00–17:00, tel. 020/625-8284, www.oudekerk.nl).

○ See Red Light District Walk, page 88.

▲**Hash, Marijuana, and Hemp Museum**—This is a collection of dope facts, history, science, and memorabilia (€9, daily 10:00–23:00, Oudezijds Achterburgwal 148, tel. 020/623-5961, www.hashmuseum.com). While small, it has a very memorable finale: the high-tech grow room, in which dozens of varieties of marijuana are grown in optimal hydroponic (among other) environments. Some plants stand five feet tall and shine under the intense grow lamps. The view is actually through glass walls into the neighboring Sensi Seed Bank Grow Shop (at #150), which sells carefully cultivated seeds and all the gear needed to grow them. (Both the museum and the Seed Bank may move in 2010.)

The nearby **Cannabis College** is "dedicated to ending the global war against the cannabis plant through public education" (free, daily 11:00–19:00, Oudezijds Achterburgwal 124, tel. 020/423-4420, www.cannabiscollege.com). For more, ○ see Red Light District Walk (page 88) and the Smoking chapter (page 190).

Northeast Amsterdam

Central Library (Openbare Bibliotheek Amsterdam)—This huge, multistory glass building holds almost 1,400 seats—many with wraparound views of the city—and hundreds of free Internet terminals. It's the classiest possible place to check email. This library, which opened in 2007, demonstrates the Dutch people's dedication to a freely educated populace (the right to information, they point out, is enshrined in the UN's Universal Declaration of Human Rights). This being Amsterdam, the library has almost twice as many bike racks as parking places. Everything's relaxed and inviting, from the fun kids' zone and international magazine and newspaper section on the ground floor to the cafeteria with its dramatic view-terrace dining on the top (La Place, €10 meals, salad bar, daily 10:00–21:00). The library is a three-minute walk from Central Station (daily 10:00–22:00, tel. 020/523-0900, www.oba.nl).

NEMO (National Center for Science and Technology)—This

kid-friendly science museum is a city landmark. Its distinctive copper-green building, jutting up from the water like a sinking ship, has prompted critics to nickname it the *Titanic*. Designed by Italian architect Renzo Piano (known for Paris' Pompidou Center and Berlin's Potsdamer Platz complex), the building's shape reflects its nautical surroundings as well as the curve of the underwater tunnel it straddles.

Several floors feature permanent and rotating exhibits that allow kids (and adults) to explore topics such as light, sound, and gravity, and play with bubbles, topple giant dominoes, and draw with lasers. Whirring, room-size pinball machines reputedly teach kids about physics. English explanations are available. Up top is a restaurant with a great city view, as well as a sloping terrace that becomes a popular "beach" in summer, complete with lounge chairs, a sandbox, and a lively bar. On the bottom floor is an inexpensive cafeteria offering €3 sandwiches (€11.50, includes rooftop beach in July–Aug, €2.50—beach only July–Aug, combo-ticket with VOC Ship *Amsterdam*–€13.50; Tue–Sun 10:00–17:00, generally closed Mon but open daily June–Aug; Oosterdok 2, above entrance to IJ tunnel, tel. 0900-919-1100—€0.35/min, www .e-nemo.nl). It's a 15-minute walk from Central Station or bus #22, #42, or #43 to Kadijksplein stop. The roof terrace—which is open later than the museum in the summer—is generally free.

VOC Ship *Amsterdam*—While the nearby Maritime Museum is closed (see next page), the good ship *Amsterdam* moors near the NEMO, welcoming kids (and kids at heart) to join its crew.

The *Amsterdam* is a replica of a type of ship called an East Indiaman, which had its heyday during the 17th and 18th centuries, sailing for the Dutch East India Company (abbreviated VOC, for Vereenigde Oostindische Compagnie—you'll see it on insignias throughout the boat). Even though trade was the name of the game, with scurvy thieves in the waters, ships such as the

Amsterdam had to be prepared to defend themselves. You'll see plenty of muskets, as well as cannons and gunpowder kegs.

Wander the decks, then duck your head and check out the captain's and surgeon's quarters, packed with items they would have used. While the ship is a little light on good historical information (be sure to pick up the free flier, which explains terminology like the difference between the poop deck and the quarterdeck), it's still a shipshape sight that entertains naval history buffs as well as fans of *Pirates of the Caribbean* films (€4, combo-ticket with NEMO—€13.50, same hours as NEMO, docked just to the west of NEMO at Oosterdok 2, tel. 020/523-2222, www .scheepvaartmuseum.nl).

Netherlands Maritime Museum (Nederlands Scheepvaart-museum)—This huge collection of model ships, maps, and sea-battle paintings—which will be closed through mid-2010 for major renovations—fills the 300-year-old Dutch Navy Arsenal. Given the Dutch seafaring heritage, I expected a more interesting museum; let's hope the renovations perk up the place (€9; mid-June–mid-Sept daily 10:00–17:00; mid-Sept–mid-June Tue–Sun 10:00–17:00, closed Mon; English explanations, bus #22 or #42 to Kattenburgerplein 1, tel. 020/523-2222, www.scheepvaart museum.nl).

Southeast Amsterdam

To reach the following sights from the train station, take tram #9 or #14. All of these sights (except the Tropical Museum) are close to each other and can easily be connected into an interesting walk, or better yet, a bike ride. Several of the sights in southeast Amsterdam cluster near the large square, Waterlooplein, dominated by the modern opera house.

For an orientation, survey the neighborhood from the lamp-lined Blauwbrug ("Blue Bridge")—a modest, modern version of Paris' Pont Alexandre III. The bridge crosses the Amstel River. From this point, the river is channeled to form the city's canals.

Scan clockwise. The big, curved modern facade belongs to the opera house, commonly called the "Stopera," as it's the combo City Hall *(stadshuis)* and opera. Behind the Stopera are these sights (not visible from here, but described next): the Waterlooplein flea market, Rembrandt's House, and Gassan Diamonds. To the right of the Stopera are the twin gray steeples of the Moses and Aaron Church, which sits roughly in the center of the former Jewish Quarter.

Several Jewish sights cluster to the right of the Moses and Aaron Church: the Jewish Historical Museum, the Portuguese Synagogue, and the dockworker statue, a Holocaust memorial. Just east of those is the De Hortus Botanical Garden.

Southeast Amsterdam

TO NEMO, VOC SHIP, MARITIME MUSEUM & IJ TUNNEL

↖ TO RED LIGHT DISTRICT

REMBRANDT'S HOUSE

GASSAN DIAMONDS

UILENBURGERGRACHT

VALKENBURGERSTRAAT

ENTREPOTDOK

MOSES & AARON CHURCH

FLEA MARKET

WATERLOO-PLEIN

TO

①

OPERA

Ⓜ Ⓑ

MR. VISSER-PLEIN

MUIDERSTRAAT

HERENGRACHT

WERT-HEIM PARK

RESISTANCE MUSEUM

③

VERKLAAN

JEWISH HISTORY MUSEUM

Ⓜ

DOCK-WORKER STATUE

PLANTAGE-MIDDEN

PLANTAGE

④

ARTIS ZOO

A M S

BLAUWBRUG

DRAW-BRIDGE

WEESPERSTRAAT

NIEUWE

HORTUS BOTANICAL GARDEN

DUTCH THEATER MEMORIAL

PLANTAGE LAAN

⑤

TO REMBRANDT-PLEIN

HERMITAGE AMSTERDAM

NIEUWE KEIZERSGR.

TO TROPICAL MUSEUM & **②**

200 YARDS

200 METERS

Ⓜ METRO   Ⓑ STOP/GO BUS

↟ ENTRY POINT TO SIGHTS

TO MAGERE (SKINNY) BRIDGE

DCH

① To Stayokay Stadsdoelen Hostel   **④** Café Koosje
② To Stayokay Zeeburg Hostel   **⑤** Taman Sari Restaurant
③ Restaurant Plancius

The cute little drawbridge, while not famous, is photogenic. (Its traditional counterbalance design is so effective that even a child can lift the bridge.) Beyond that is the Hermitage Amsterdam (the new, much-expanded site takes up an entire city block—see page 64). Crossing the Amstel upstream is one of the city's romantic spots, the Magere Brug ("Skinny Bridge"). A block away is the city's best look at a Golden Age mansion, the Willet-Holthuysen Museum (a.k.a. Herengracht Canal Mansion).

Waterlooplein Flea Market—For more than a hundred years,
the Jewish Quarter flea market has raged daily except Sunday (at the Waterlooplein metro station, behind Rembrandt's House). The long, narrow park is filled with stalls selling cheap clothes, hippie stuff, old records, tourist knickknacks, and garage-sale junk.

▲Rembrandt's House (Museum Het Rembrandthuis)—A middle-aged Rembrandt lived here from 1639 to 1658 after his wife's death, as his popularity and wealth dwindled down to obscurity and bankruptcy. As you enter, ask when the next etching demonstration is scheduled and pick up the fine, included audioguide. Tour the place this way: Explore Rembrandt's reconstructed house (filled with exactly what his bankruptcy inventory of 1656 said he owned); imagine him at work in his reconstructed studio; marvel at his personal collection of exotic objects, many of which he included in paintings; attend the etch-

ing demonstration and ask the printer to explain the etching process (drawing in soft wax on a metal plate that's then dipped in acid, inked up, and printed); and then, for the finale, enjoy several rooms of original Rembrandt etchings. You're not likely to see a single painting, but the master's etchings are marvelous and well-described. I came away wanting to know more about the man and his art (€8 includes audioguide, daily 10:00–17:00, Jodenbreestraat 4, tel. 020/520-0400, www .rembrandthuis.nl).

▲Diamonds—Many shops in this "city of diamonds" offer tours. These tours come with two parts: a chance to see experts behind magnifying glasses polishing the facets of precious diamonds, fol-lowed by a visit to an intimate sales room to see (and perhaps buy) a mighty shiny yet very tiny souvenir.

The handy and professional **Gassan Diamonds** facility fills

a huge warehouse a block from Rembrandt's House. A visit here plops you in the big-tour-group fray (notice how each tour group has a color-coded sticker so they know which guide gets the commis-sion on what they buy). You'll get a sticker, join a free 15-minute tour to see a polisher at work, and hear a general explanation of the process. Then you'll have an opportunity to sit down and have color and clarity described and illustrated with diamonds ranging in value from $100 to $30,000. Before or after, you can have a free cup of cof-fee in the waiting room across the parking lot (daily 9:00–17:00, Nieuwe Uilenburgerstraat 173, tel. 020/622-5333, www.gassan diamonds.com, handy WC). Another company, Coster, also offers diamond demos, not as good as Gassan's, but convenient if you're near the Rijksmuseum (see page 49).

▲Willet-Holthuysen Museum (a.k.a. Herengracht Canal Mansion)—This 1687 townhouse is a must for devotees of Hummel-topped sugar bowls and Louis XVI–style wainscoting. For others, it's a pleasant look inside a typical (rich) home with much of the original furniture and decor. Forget the history and just browse through a dozen rooms of beautiful and saccharine objects from the 19th century.

Upon entering (through the servants' door under the grand entry), see photos of the owners during the house's heyday in the 1860s. The 15-minute video explains how the wealthy heiress Louise Holthuysen and the art-collecting bon vivant Abraham Willet got married and became joined at the hyphen, then set out to make their home the social hub of Amsterdam.

Picture the couple's servants in the kitchen—before electricity and running water—turning meat on the spit at the fireplace or filtering rainwater. Upstairs, where the Willet-Holthuysens entertained, wall paintings introduce you to Abraham's artistic tastes, showing scenes of happy French peasants and nobles frolicking in the countryside. Several rooms are done in the Louis XVI style, featuring chairs with straight, tapering legs (not the heavy, curving, animal-claw feet of earlier styles); blue, yellow, and purple-themed rooms; wainscoting ("wallpaper" covering only the lower part of walls); and mythological paintings on the ceiling.

The impressive gilded ballroom contains a painting showing the room in its prime—and how little it's changed. Imagine Abraham, Louise, and 22 guests retiring to the Dining Room, dining off the 275-piece Meissen porcelain set; chatting with friends in the Blue Room by the canal; or sipping tea in the Garden Room, gazing out at symmetrically curved hedges and classical statues. Up another flight is the bedroom, with a canopy bed and matching oak washstand and makeup table (and a chamber pot tucked under the bed).

When the widow Louise died in 1895, she bequeathed the house to the city, along with its collection of candelabras, snuff boxes, and puppy paintings (€5, Mon–Fri 10:00–17:00, Sat–Sun 11:00–17:00; take tram #4, #9, or #14 to Rembrandtplein—it's a 2-min walk southeast to Herengracht 605; tel. 020/523-1870, www.willetholthuysen.nl). The museum lacks audioguides, but you can request a free blue notebook to learn more about the house's history.

Tassen Museum (Hendrikje Museum of Bags and Purses)— This hardworking little museum fills an elegant 1664 canal house with 500 years of bag and purse history—from before the invention of pockets through the 20th century. The collection, with lots of artifacts, is well-described in English and gives a fascinating insight into fashion through the ages that fans of handbags will love, and their partners might even enjoy. The creative and surreal bag styles of the 1920s and 1930s are particularly interesting (€6.50, daily 10:00–17:00, three floors—one houses temporary exhibits and two hold the permanent collection, behind Rembrandtplein at Herengracht 573, tel. 020/524-6452, www.tassenmuseum.nl).

▲Hermitage Amsterdam—The famous Hermitage Museum in St. Petersburg, Russia, loans art to Amsterdam for display in the Amstelhof, a 17th-century former nursing home that takes up a whole city block along the Amstel River.

Why is there Russian-owned art in Amsterdam? The Hermitage collection in St. Petersburg is so vast that they can only show about 5 percent of it at any one time. Therefore, the Hermitage is establishing satellite collections around the world. The one here in Amsterdam is the biggest, and it grew considerably in spring of 2009 when the museum took over even more of the Amstelhof. By law, the great Russian collection can only be out of the country for six months at a time, so the collection is always rotating. Curators in Amsterdam make a point to display art that complements—rather than just repeats—what the city's other museums show so well (€15, daily 10:00–17:00, Wed until 20:00, Nieuwe Herengracht 14, tram #4 to Rembrandtplein or #9 or #14 to Waterlooplein, recorded info tel. 020/530-8751, www .hermitage.nl).

De Hortus Botanical Garden—This is a unique oasis of tranquility within the city (no mobile phones are allowed, because "our collection of plants is a precious community—treat it with respect"). One of the oldest botanical gardens in the world, it dates from 1638, when medicinal herbs were grown here. Today, among its 6,000 different kinds of plants—most of which were collected by the Dutch East India Company in the 17th and 18th centuries— you'll find medicinal herbs, cacti, several greenhouses (one with a fluttery butterfly house—a hit with kids), and a tropical palm house. Much of it is described in English: "A Dutch merchant snuck a coffee plant out of Ethiopia, which ended up in this garden in 1706. This first coffee plant in Europe was the literal grand-daddy of the coffee cultures of Brazil—long the world's biggest coffee producer" (€7; Mon–Fri 9:00–17:00, Sat–Sun 10:00–17:00, July–Aug until 19:00, Dec–Jan until 16:00; Plantage Middenlaan

2A, tel. 020/625-9021, www.dehortus.nl). The inviting Orangery Café serves tapas.

▲Jewish Historical Museum (Joods Historisch Museum)—This interesting museum tells the story of the Netherlands' Jews

through three centuries, serving as a good introduction to Judaism and educating visitors on Jewish customs and religious traditions.

Originally opened in 1932, the museum was forced to close during the Nazi years. Recent renovations have brought it into the 21st century. Its current location comprises four historic former synagogues that have been joined by steel and glass to make one modern complex.

The highlight is the Great Synagogue. Have a seat in the high-ceilinged synagogue, surrounded by religious objects, and picture it during its prime (1671–1943). The hall would be full for a service—men downstairs, women above in the gallery. On the east wall (the symbolic direction of Jerusalem) is the Ark, where they keep the scrolls of the Torah (the Jewish scriptures, including the first five books of the Christian Bible). The rabbi and other men, wearing thigh-length prayer shawls, would approach the Ark and carry the Torah to the raised platform in the center of the room. After unwrapping it from its drapery and silver cap, a man would use a *yad* (ceremonial pointer) to follow along while singing the text aloud.

Video displays around the room explain Jewish customs, from birth (circumcision) to puberty (the bar/bat mitzvah, celebrating the entry into adulthood) to marriage—culminating in the groom stomping on a glass while everyone shouts "Mazel tov!"

From the upper level, a skyway leads to the 20th century. The new, worthwhile exhibit on the Jews of the Netherlands uses personal artifacts and touch-screen computers to tell the devastating history of the Nazi occupation. By purposefully showing mundane daily objects, the museum helps make an inconceivable period of time meaningful and real.

The museum has a modern, minimalist, kosher café, as well as temporary exhibition space, generally showing the work of Jewish artists (€7.50, daily 11:00–17:00, free audioguide but displays all have English explanations, Jonas Daniel Meijerplein 2, tel. 020/531-0310, www.jhm.nl).

▲Dutch Theater (Hollandsche Schouwburg)—Once a lively theater in the Jewish neighborhood, and today a moving memorial, this building was used as an assembly hall for local Jews destined

Jews in Amsterdam

In 1940, one in ten Amsterdammers was Jewish, and most lived in the neighborhood behind Waterlooplein. Jewish traders had long been welcome in a city that cared more about business than religion. In the late 1500s, many Sephardic Jews from Spain and Portugal immigrated, fleeing persecution. (The philosopher Baruch Spinoza's ancestors were among them.) In the 1630s, Yiddish-speaking Eastern European Jews (Ashkenazi) poured in. By 1700, the Jewish Quarter was a bustling, exotic, multicultural world, with more people speaking Portuguese, German, and Yiddish than Dutch.

However, Jews were not first-class citizens. They needed the city's permission to settle here, and they couldn't hold public office (but then, neither could Catholics under Calvinist rule). Still, the Jewish Quarter was not a ghetto (enforced segregation), there were no special taxes, and cosmopolitan Amsterdam was well-acquainted with all types of beliefs and customs.

In 1796, Jews were given full citizenship. In exchange, they were required to learn the Dutch language and submit to the city's legal system...and the Jewish culture began assimilating into the Dutch.

In 1940, Nazi Germany occupied the Netherlands. On February 22, 1941, the Nazis began rounding up Jews and shipping them to extermination camps in Eastern Europe. By war's end, more than 100,000 of the city's 130,000 Jews had died.

Today, about 25,000 Jews live in Amsterdam, and the Jewish Quarter has blended with the modern city. For more information on Amsterdam's many Jewish sights, see www .jhm.nl.

for Nazi concentration camps. On the wall, 6,700 family names pay tribute to the 104,000 Jews deported and killed by the Nazis. Some 70,000 victims spent time here, awaiting transfer to concentration camps. Upstairs is a small history exhibit with photos and memorabilia of some victims, putting a human face on the staggering numbers. Television monitors show actual footage of the rounding-up of Amsterdam's Jews by the Nazis. The ruined theater offers relatively little to see but plenty to think about. Back on the ground floor, notice the hopeful messages that visiting school groups attach to the wooden tulips (free, daily 11:00–16:00, Plantage Middenlaan 24, tel. 020/531-0340, www .hollandscheschouwburg.nl).

▲▲Dutch Resistance Museum (Verzetsmuseum)—This is an impressive look at how the Dutch resisted their Nazi occupiers from 1940 to 1945. You'll see propa-

ganda movie clips, study forged ID cards under a magnifying glass, and read about ingenious and courageous efforts—big and small—to hide local Jews from the Germans and undermine the Nazi regime.

The first dozen displays set the stage, showing peaceful, upright Dutch people of the 1930s living oblivious to the rise of fascism. Then—bam—it's May of 1940 and the Germans invade the Netherlands, pummel Rotterdam, send Queen Wilhelmina into exile, and—in four short days of fighting—hammer home the message that resistance is futile. The Germans install local Dutch Nazis in power (the "NSB"), led by Anton Mussert.

Next, in the corner of the exhibition area, push a button to see photos of the event that first mobilized organized resistance. In February of 1941, Nazis start rounding up Jews from the neighborhood, killing nine protesters. Amsterdammers respond by shutting down the trams, schools, and businesses in a massive two-day strike. (This heroic gesture is honored today with a statue of a striking dockworker on the square called Jonas Daniel Meyerplein, where Jews were rounded up.) The next display makes it clear that this brave strike did little to save 100,000 Jews from extermination.

Turning the corner into the main room, you'll see numerous exhibits on Nazi rule and the many forms of Dutch resistance: vandals turning Nazi V-for-Victory posters into W-for-Wilhelmina, preachers giving pointed sermons, schoolkids telling "Kraut jokes," printers distributing underground newspapers (such as *Het Parool*, which became a major daily paper), counterfeiters forging documents, and ordinary people hiding radios under floorboards and Jews inside closets. As the war progresses, the armed Dutch Resistance becomes bolder and more violent, killing German occupiers and Dutch collaborators. In September of 1944, the Allies liberate Antwerp, and the Netherlands starts celebrating...too soon. The Nazis dig in and punish the country by cutting off rations, plunging West Holland into the "Hunger Winter" of 1944 to 1945 in which 20,000 die. Finally, it's springtime. The Allies liberate the country, and at war's end, Nazi helmets are turned into Dutch bedpans (€6.50, Tue–Fri 10:00–17:00, Sat–Mon 11:00–17:00, well-described in English, no flash photos, tram #9 from station or #14 from Dam Square, Plantage Kerklaan 61, tel. 020/620-2535, www.verzetsmuseum.org).

Two recommended eateries—Restaurant Plancius and Café Koosje—are adjacent to the museum (see listings on page 189), and Amsterdam's famous zoo is just across the street.

▲Tropical Museum (Tropenmuseum)—As close to the Third World as you'll get without lots of vaccinations, this imaginative museum offers wonderful re-creations of tropical life and explanations of Third World problems (largely created by Dutch colonialism and the slave trade). Ride the elevator to the top floor, and circle your way down through this immense collection, opened in 1926 to give the Dutch people a peek at their vast colonial holdings. Don't miss the display case where you can see and hear the world's most exotic musical instruments. The Ekeko cafeteria serves tropical food (€7.50, daily 10:00–17:00, tram #9 to Linnaeusstraat 2, tel. 020/568-8215, www.tropenmuseum.nl).

AMSTERDAM CITY WALK

From Central Station to the Rijksmuseum

Amsterdam today looks much as it did in its Golden Age, the 1600s. It's a retired sea captain of a city, still in love with life, with a broad outlook and a salty story to tell.

Take a Dutch sampler walk from one end of the old center to the other, tasting all that Amsterdam has to offer along the way. It's your best single stroll through Dutch clichés, hidden churches, surprising shops, thriving happy-hour hangouts, and eight centuries of history.

ORIENTATION

Length of This Walk: Allow three hours.

Bike Rental: If you'd like to make this "walk" a much faster "roll," there's a handy bike rental place in Central Station (MacBike, daily 9:00–17:45, at left side of station as you leave it, on right side if you're facing it, tel. 020/624-8391, www.macbike.nl).

Tips: You can find public toilets at fast-food places (generally €0.30) and near the entrance to the Amsterdam History Museum. Beware of silent transport—trams and bikes. Stay off the tram tracks and bike paths, and yield to bell-ringing bikers.

Amsterdam History Museum: €8, Mon–Fri 10:00–17:00, Sat–Sun 11:00–17:00, Kalverstraat 92, tel. 020/523-1822, www.ahm.nl.

Begijnhof: Free, daily 8:00–17:00 for "tourist visits" (groups and guided tours). At other times, be quiet and stick to the area near the churches. Don't photograph homes or their residents, and remember that these are private dwellings (on Begijnensteeg lane, just off Kalverstraat between #130 and #132). The English Church is sometimes open for tourists (free, open about four days a week 10:00–14:00 and always for

English-speaking worshippers at Sun service at 10:30).

Rijksmuseum: €10, audioguide-€4, daily 9:00–18:00, Fri until 20:30, tel. 020/674-7047 for automated info or tel. 020/674-7000 for main number, www.rijksmuseum.nl.

Van Gogh Museum: €12.50, audioguide-€4, special kids' audioguide-€2.50, daily 10:00–18:00, Fri until 22:00, Paulus Potterstraat 7, tel. 020/570-5200, www .vangoghmuseum.nl.

OVERVIEW

The walk starts at the central-as-can-be Central Station. You'll walk about three miles, heading down Damrak to Dam Square, continuing south down Kalverstraat to the Mint Tower (Munttoren), then wafting through the flower market (Bloemenmarkt), before continuing south to Leidseplein and jogging left to the Rijksmuseum. To return to Central Station, catch tram #2 or #5 from the southwest corner of the Rijksmuseum.

THE WALK BEGINS

Central Station

Here, where today's train travelers enter the city, sailors of yore disembarked from seagoing ships to be met by street musicians,

pickpockets, hotel-runners, and ladies carrying red lanterns. When the station was built (on reclaimed land) at the former harbor mouth, Amsterdam lost some of its harbor feel, but it's still a bustling port of entry.

Central Station, with warm red brick and prickly spires, is the first of several Neo-Gothic buildings we'll see from the late 1800s, built during Amsterdam's economic revival. One of the towers has a clock dial; the other tower's dial is a weathervane. Watch the hand twitch as the wind gusts—N, Z, O, and W.

As you emerge from the train station, you'll immediately see a mess. The construction is for a new office and condo zone (left of station as you leave it) and subway line (in front of station). The new north–south metro line (to open in 2013) will complement the existing one. While it sounds like a fine idea, the project has been riddled with delays.

Beyond the construction, the city spreads out before you in

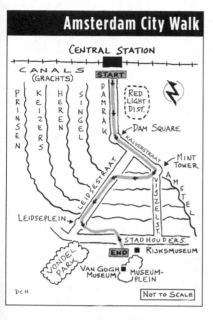

Amsterdam City Walk

CENTRAL STATION

CANALS (GRACHTS)

PRINSEN
KEIZERS
HEREN
SINGEL
DAMRAK

START

RED LIGHT DIST.

DAM SQUARE

KALVERSTRAAT

LEIDSESTRAAT

MINT TOWER

AMSTEL

VIJZELST.

LEIDSEPLEIN

STADHOUDERS.

END ■ RIJKSMUSEUM

VONDEL PARK

Van Gogh Museum

MUSEUMPLEIN

DCH

NOT TO SCALE

a series of concentric canals. Ahead of you stretches the street called Damrak, which leads to Dam Square a half mile away. To the left of Damrak is the city's old *(oude)* side; to the right is the new *(nieuwe)*.

The big church towering above the old side (at about 10 o'clock) is St. Nicholas Church, built in the 1880s when Catholics—after about three centuries of oppression—were finally free to worship in public. The church marks the beginning of the Red Light District (for a tour of that neighborhood, ✪ see my Red Light District Walk on page 88). The city's biggest bike garage, a multistory wonder, is on your right in front of the Ibis Hotel. Parking your bike in the garage is free—courtesy of the government (they want to encourage biking).

• *We'll basically walk south from here to the Rijksmuseum. The art museum and the train station—designed by the same architect—stand like bookends holding the old town together. Follow the crowds south on Damrak, walking along the right side of the street.*

Damrak

Stroll past every Dutch cliché at the tourist shops: wooden shoes, plastic tulips, Heineken fridge magnets, and windmill salt-shakers. Listen to a hand-cranked barrel organ. Order french fries (called *Vlaamse frites,* or Flemish fries, since they were invented in the Low Countries), and dip them in mayonnaise, not ketchup. Eating international cuisine (Indonesian rijsttafel, Argentine steak, Middle Eastern *shoarma*—pronounced SHWAHR-mah) is going local in cosmopolitan Amsterdam. And you'll find the city's most notorious commodity displayed at the Damrak Sex Museum (see page 58).

This street was once a riverbed, where the Amstel River flowed north into the IJ (eye) River behind today's train station. Both rivers then emptied into a vast inlet of the North Sea (the Zuiderzee), unique geography that turned Amsterdam into a major seaport. Today, the Amstel is channeled into canals, its former mouth covered by Central Station, and the North Sea inlet has been diked off to make an inland lake. More than 100,000 ships a year reach the open waters by sailing west through the North Sea Canal, making Amsterdam Europe's fifth-busiest seaport.

Local landowners are concerned that the tunneling for the new subway line will cause their buildings to settle. The snoopy-looking white cameras mounted on various building corners (such as the Beurs) are monitoring buildings to check for settling.

• *The long brick building with the square clock tower, along the left side of Damrak, is the...*

Stock Exchange (Beurs)

Built with nine million bricks on about 5,000 tree trunks hammered into the marshy soil, the Beurs stands as a symbol of the city's long tradition as a trading town.

Back when "stock" meant whatever could be loaded and unloaded onto a boat, Amsterdammers gathered to trade. Soon, rather than trading goats, chickens, and kegs of beer, they were exchanging slips of paper and "futures" at one of the world's first stock exchanges. Traders needed moneychangers, who needed bankers, who made money by lending money...and Amsterdam of the 1600s became one of the world's first great capitalist cities, loaning money to free-spending kings, dukes, and bishops.

This impressive building, built in 1903 in a geometric, minimal, no-frills style, is one of the world's first "modern" (i.e., 20th-century-style) buildings, emphasizing function over looks. In 1984, the stock exchange moved next door (see the stock prices readout) to the Euronext complex—a joint, if overly optimistic, attempt by France, Belgium, and the Netherlands to compete with the power of Britain's stock exchange. The old Beurs building now hosts concerts and a museum for temporary exhibits.

Amsterdam still thrives as the center of Dutch business and is home to Heineken, Shell Oil, Philips Electronics, and Unilever. Amsterdammers have always had a reputation for putting business above ideological differences, staying neutral while trading with both sides.

• *Damrak opens into...*

Dam Square

The city got its start right here in about 1250, when fishermen in this marshy delta settled along the built-up banks of the Amstel River. They blocked the river with a *damme* and created a small village called "Amstel-damme." With access to the sea, the fishermen were soon trading with German riverboats traveling downstream and with seafaring boats from Stockholm, Hamburg, and London. Dam Square was the center of it all.

The dam on the Amstel divided the *damrak* (meaning "outer

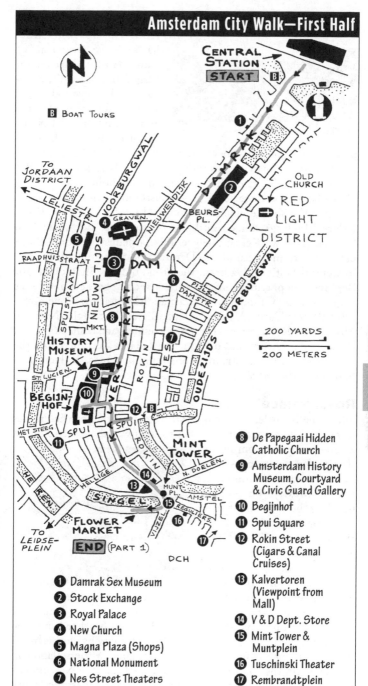

Amsterdam City Walk—First Half

N

B BOAT TOURS

CENTRAL STATION **START** **B**

TO JORDAAN DISTRICT

LELIESTR.

VOORBURGWAL

NIEUWENDIJK

DAMRAK

OLD CHURCH

RED LIGHT DISTRICT

GRAVEN.

BEURS-PL.

RAADHUISSTRAAT

SPUISTRAAT

NIEUWEZIJDS

DAM

VOORBURGWAL

PIJLS.

DAM STR.

200 YARDS

200 METERS

HISTORY MUSEUM

MKT.

ROKIN

NES

OUDEZIJDS

ST. LUCIEN.

BEGIJN-HOF

KALVER STRAAT

HET STEEG

SPUI

SPUI

B

MINT TOWER

HEI REN

HELLIGE

ROKIN

N. DOELEN.

MUNT PL.

AMSTEL

REGULIERS

TO LEIDSE-PLEIN

SINGEL

FLOWER MARKET

VIJZEL

END (PART 1)

DCH

AMSTERDAM CITY WALK

1 Damrak Sex Museum
2 Stock Exchange
3 Royal Palace
4 New Church
5 Magna Plaza (Shops)
6 National Monument
7 Nes Street Theaters

8 De Papegaai Hidden Catholic Church
9 Amsterdam History Museum, Courtyard & Civic Guard Gallery
10 Begijnhof
11 Spui Square
12 Rokin Street (Cigars & Canal Cruises)
13 Kalvertoren (Viewpoint from Mall)
14 V & D Dept. Store
15 Mint Tower & Muntplein
16 Tuschinski Theater
17 Rembrandtplein

harbor"—for sea traffic) from the *rokin* ("inner harbor"—for river traffic). Land trade routes converged here as well, and a customs house stood in this spot. Today, the Damrak and Rokin (roh-KEEN) are major roads, and the city's palace and major department stores face the square, where mimes, jugglers, and human statues mingle with locals and tourists. This is the historic heart of the city. As the symbolic center of the Netherlands, it's where political demonstrations begin and end.

Pan the square clockwise to see the following: the Royal Palace (the large domed building on the west side), the New Church (Nieuwe Kerk), Nieuwendijk (a pedestrian-only shopping street running parallel to Damrak and stretching all the way to Central Station), Damrak, the proud old De Bijenkorf ("The Beehive") department store (with a recommended café—see page 186), the Grand Hotel Krasnapolsky (with its fine circa-1900 Winter Garden), the white phallic obelisk of the National Monument, Rokin street (Damrak's counterpart, continuing past the square), touristy and overpriced Madame Tussauds, and the entrance to the pedestrian-only shopping street, Kalverstraat (look for *Rabobank* sign).

Royal Palace

The name is misleading, since Amsterdam is one of the cradles of modern democracy. For centuries, this was the Town Hall of

a self-governing community that prided itself on its independence and thumbed its nose at royalty. The current building, built in about 1650, is appropriately classical (like the democratic Greeks), with a triangular pediment featuring—fittingly for Amsterdam—denizens of the sea cavorting with Neptune (with his green copper trident).

After the city was conquered by the French, Napoleon imposed a monarchy on Holland, making his brother Louis the king of the Netherlands (1808). Louis used the city hall as his "royal palace," giving the building its current name. When Napoleon was defeated, the victorious powers dictated that the Netherlands remain a monarchy, under a noble Dutch family called the House of Orange. If the current Queen Beatrix is in town, this is, technically, her residence. The Royal Palace reopened to the public in 2009 after a lengthy renovation. Amsterdam is the nominal capital of the Netherlands, but all governing activity—and the queen's actual permanent home—are in The Hague (a city 30 miles southwest).

• *A few paces away, to the right as you're facing the Royal Palace, is the...*

New Church (Nieuwe Kerk)

The "New" Church is 600 years old (newer than the 700-year-old "Old" Church in the Red Light District). The sundial above the entrance once served as the city's official timepiece.

The church's bare, spacious, well-lit interior (occupied by a new art exhibit every three months) looks quite different from the Baroque-encrusted churches found in the rest of Europe. In 1566, clear-eyed Protestant extremists throughout Holland marched into Catholic churches (like this once was), lopped off the heads of holy statues, stripped gold-leaf angels from the walls, urinated on Virgin Marys, and shattered stained-glass windows in a wave of anti-Catholic vandalism.

This iconoclasm (icon-breaking) of 1566 started an 80-year war against Spain and the Habsburgs, leading finally to Dutch independence in 1648. Catholic churches like this one were converted to the new dominant religion, Calvinist Protestantism (today's Dutch Reformed Church). From then on, Dutch churches downplayed the "graven images" and "idols" of ornate religious art.

From just inside the door, you can get a free look at the 1655 organ (far left end, often played for midday concerts); the stained-glass window (opposite entrance) showing Count William IV giving the city its "XXX" coat of arms (symbolism described on page 77); and the window (over entrance) showing the inauguration of Queen Wilhelmina. She eventually became the steadfast center of Dutch Resistance during World War II.

This church is where many of the Netherlands' monarchs are married and all are crowned. In 1980, Queen Beatrix—Wilhelmina's granddaughter—held her coronation in the New Church. When Beatrix dies or retires (her mother and grandmother both abdicated late in life), her son, Crown Prince Willem-Alexander, will parade to the center of the church, sit in front of

---

City on a Sandbar

Amsterdam is built upon millions of wooden pilings. The city was founded on unstable mud, which sits on stable sand. In the Middle Ages, buildings were made of wood, which rests lightly and easily on mud. But devastating fires repeatedly wiped out entire neighborhoods, so stone became the building material of choice. Stone is fire resistant, but was too heavy for a mud foundation, so for more support, pilings were driven 30 feet through the mud and into the sand. The Royal Palace sits upon 13,000 such pilings—still solid after 350 years. (The wood survives if kept wet and out of the air.) Since World War II, concrete, rather than wood, has been used for the pilings, with foundations driven 60 feet deep through the first layer of sand, through more mud, and into a second layer of sand. And today's biggest buildings have foundations sinking as much as 120 feet deep.

---

the golden choir screen, and—with TV lights glaring and cameras flashing—be crowned the next sovereign.

• *Looking between the Royal Palace and the New Church, you'll see the fanciful brick facade of the Magna Plaza shopping center.*

National Monument

The obelisk, which depicts a crucified Christ, men in chains, and howling dogs, was built in 1956 as a WWII memorial. Now it's considered a monument for peace.

The Nazis occupied Holland from 1940–1945. They deported 100,000 Amsterdam Jews, driving many—including young Anne Frank and her family—into hiding. Near the end of the war, the "Hunger Winter" of 1944–1945 killed thousands and forced many to survive on tulip bulbs. Today, Dutch people in their mid-70s—whose growth-spurt years coincided with the Hunger Winter—are easy to identify, because they are uniformly short.

Circling the Square

You're at the center of Amsterdam. A few blocks to the east is the top of the Red Light District. Amsterdam is a world center for experimental theater, and several edgy theaters line the street called the Nes (stretching south from Grand Hotel Krasnapolsky).

• *From Dam Square, head south (at* Rabobank *sign) on...*

Kalverstraat

This pedestrian-only street is lined with many familiar franchise stores and record shops. (If you're on a bike, you must dismount and walk it.) This has been a shopping street for centuries, and today it's notorious among locals as *the* place for cheesy, crass materialism. For smaller and more elegant stores, try the adjacent district called De Negen Straatjes ("The Nine Little Streets"), where 190 shops mingle by the canals (about four blocks west of Kalverstraat).

• *About 120 yards along (just before and across from the McDonald's), pop into...*

De Papegaai Hidden Catholic Church (Petrus en Paulus Kerk)

This Catholic church, while not exactly hidden (after all, you found it), keeps a low profile, even now that Catholicism has been legalized in Amsterdam. In the late 1500s, with Protestants fighting Catholics and the Dutch fighting Spanish invaders, Amsterdam tried to stay neutral, doing business with all parties. Finally, in 1578, Protestant extremists (following the teachings of Reformer John Calvin) took political control of the city. They expelled Catholic leaders and bishops, outlawed the religion, and allied Amsterdam with anti-Spanish forces in an action known to historians as the Alteration.

For the next two centuries, Amsterdam's Catholics were driven underground. Catholicism was illegal but tolerated, as long as it was practiced not in public, but in humble, unadvertised places like this. (The stuffed parrot—*papegaai*—hanging in the nave refers to the house formerly on this site, which had a carving of a parrot in its gable stone.)

Today, the church, which asks for a mere "15 minutes for God" *(een kwartier voor God)*, stands as a metaphor for how religion has long been a marginal part of highly commercial and secular Amsterdam (free, daily 10:00–16:00).

• *Farther along (about 75 yards) at #92, where Kalverstraat crosses Wijde Kapel Steeg, look to the right at an archway leading to the...*

Entrance and Courtyard of the Amsterdam History Museum

On the arch is Amsterdam's coat of arms—a red shield with three Xs and a crown. Not a reference to the city's sex trade, the X-shaped crosses (which appear everywhere in town) symbolize

heroism, determination, and mercy; they represent the crucifixion of St. Andrew, the patron saint of fishermen. The crown dates to 1489, when Maximilian I (the Low Countries' first Habsburg ruler and later Holy Roman Emperor) paid off a big loan from city bankers and, as thanks for the cash, gave the city permission to use his prestigious trademark, the Habsburg crown, atop its shield. The relief above the door (see photo), dated 1581, shows boys around a dove, reminding all who pass that this was an orphanage and asking for charity.

Go inside. The pleasant David & Goliath café (with a shady courtyard) is watched over by a giant statue of Goliath and a knee-high David (from 1650). In the courtyard are the old lockers for the orphans' uniforms, and a pay toilet.

• *The courtyard leads to another courtyard with the best city history museum in town, the ✪ Amsterdam History Museum (see page 161). Between the two courtyards (on the left) is a free, glassed-in passageway lined with paintings, called the...*

Civic Guard Gallery (Schuttersgalerij)

In these group portraits from Amsterdam's Golden Age (early 1600s), look into the eyes of the frank, dignified men (and some women) with ruffs and lace collars, who made Amsterdam the most prosperous city in Europe, sending trading ships to distant colonies and pocketing interest from loans. The weapons they carry are mostly symbolic, since these "Civic Guards," who once protected the town (fighting the Spanish), had become more like fraternal organizations of business bigwigs.

Many paintings look the same in this highly stylized genre. Military companies often sit in two rows. Someone holds the company flag. Rank is indicated by the weapons they hold: Captains wield pikes (axe-like weapons topped with spearhead-shaped tips); lieutenants hold partisans (pikes with sword-like tips); and privates wield hatchet-headed halberds or muskets. Later group portraits showed "captains" of industry going about their work, dressed in suits, along with the tools of their trade—ledger books, quill pens, and money.

Everyone looks straight out, and every face is lit perfectly. Each paid for his own portrait and wanted it right. It took masters like Rembrandt and Frans Hals to take the starch out of the collars and compose more natural scenes.

• *The gallery offers a shortcut to the Begijnhof, 75 yards farther south. But if the gallery is closed, backtrack to Kalverstraat, continue south, then turn right on Begijnensteeg. Either route leads to the entrance of the walled courtyard called the...*

Begijnhof

This quiet courtyard (pronounced gutturally: buh-HHHINE-hof), lined with houses around a church, has sheltered women since 1346.

This was for centuries the home of Beguines—women who removed themselves from the world at large to dedicate their lives to God. It literally was a "woman's island"—a circle of houses facing a peaceful courtyard, surrounded by water. (To ensure a pleasant visit, see "Begijnhof," in the "Orientation" section at the beginning of this chapter.)

The Beguines' ranks swelled during the Crusades, when so many men took off, never to return, leaving society with an abundance of single women. Later, women widowed by the hazards of overseas trade lived out their days as Beguines. Poor and rich women alike turned their backs on materialism and marriage to live here in Christian poverty. While obedient to a mother superior, members of the lay order of Beguines were not nuns. The Beguines were very popular in their communities for the unpretentious, simple, and Christ-like lives they led. They spent their days deep in prayer and busy with daily tasks—spinning wool, making lace, teaching, and caring for the sick and poor. In quiet seclusion, they inspired each other as well as their neighbors.

In 1578, when Catholicism was outlawed, the Dutch Reformed Church (and the city) took over many Catholic charities like this place. The last Beguine died in 1971, but this Begijnhof still provides subsidized housing to about 100 needy single women (mostly Catholic seniors and students). The Begijnhof is just one of about 75 *hofjes* (little housing projects surrounding courtyards) that dot Amsterdam.

Begin your visit at the statue of one of these charitable sisters. She faces the **wooden house** *(houten huys)* at #34. The city's oldest, it dates from 1477. Originally, the whole city consisted of wooden

houses like this one. To the left of the house is a display of carved gable stones that once adorned housefronts and served as street numbers (and still do at #19 and #26, the former mother superior's house).

The brick-faced **English Church** (Engelse Kerk, from 1420) was the Beguine church until 1607, when it became Anglican. The Pilgrims (strict Protestants), fleeing persecution in England, stopped here in tolerant Amsterdam and prayed in this church before the *Mayflower* carried them to religious freedom at Plymouth Rock in America. If the church is open (its hours are sporadic), step inside to see a stained-glass window of the Pilgrims praying before boarding the *Mayflower* (far end), an old pew they may have sat on (right wall), and a 1763 Bible (on the altar) with lot∫ of old-∫tyle ∫'s.

The "hidden" **Catholic Church** (notice the painted-out windows, second and third floors) faces the English Church. Amsterdam's oppressed 17th-century Catholics, who refused to worship as Protestants, must have eagerly awaited the day when, in the 19th century, they were legally allowed to say Mass. Step inside (through the low-profile doorway), pick up an English brochure near the entry, and tap softly on a "marble" column.

Today, Holland still has a religious divide, but not a bitter one. Roughly a third of the population is Catholic, a fifth is Protestant...and two-fifths list themselves as "unchurched."

• *Backtrack to busy Kalverstraat, turn right, and continue south. Pause at the intersection with Spuistraat and look to the right.*

Spui and Rokin

A block to the right is the square called **Spui** (spow, rhymes with cow). Lined with cafés and bars, it's one of the city's more popular spots for nightlife and sunny afternoon people-watching.

A block to the left is the busy street called **Rokin**. A statue of Queen Wilhelmina (1880–1962) on the Rokin shows her riding

daintily sidesaddle. Remember that in real life, she was the iron-willed inspiration for the Dutch Resistance against the Nazis.

• *Walk toward the statue and pause at the canal dock.*

Canal cruises depart from the Rondvaart Kooij dock (€8, 3/hr in summer 10:00–22:00,

Amsterdam City Walk—Second Half

200 YARDS
200 METERS

B BOAT TOURS

MINT TOWER
& MUNTPLEIN

18 Flower Market
19 Koningsplein
20 Selexyz Scheltema
Bookstore
21 Metz & Co. (View)
22 Smartshop
23 The Delft Shop
24 Pipe Museum
25 Stadsschouwburg
26 Last Minute
Ticket Shop
27 Melkweg
28 Boom Chicago
29 "Restaurant Row"
30 Bulldog Café &
Coffeeshop
31 Max Euweplein
32 Paradiso
33 Rijksmuseum
34 Trams #2 & #5

AMSTERDAM CITY WALK

2/hr in winter 10:00–17:00, yellow canal house—for more info see
"Canal Boat Tours," page 42).

The **House of Hajenius,** at Rokin 92 (50 yards left of the
canal dock, toward Central Station), is a temple of cigars, a
"paradise for the connoisseur" showing "175 years of tradition and
good taste." To enter this sumptuous Art Nouveau building with
painted leather ceilings is to step back into 1910 (free, Tue–Sat
9:30–18:00, Sun 12:00–17:00, Mon 12:00–18:00). Don't be shy—
the place is as much a free museum for visitors as it is a store for
paying customers. The brown-capped canisters (under the wall
of pipes, to the right) are for smelling fine pipe tobacco. Take a
whiff. The personal humidifiers (read the explanation) allow locals
(famous local names are on the cupboard doors) to call in an order
and have their cigars waiting for them at just the right humidity.
Look up at the humidifier pipes pumping moisture into the room.

Upstairs in back is a small, free museum.

• *Head back toward the pedestrian street, Kalverstraat, and turn left when you get there. You'll pass various department stores with cafeterias.*

At the end of Kalverstraat, the **Kalvertoren** shopping complex offers a top-floor viewpoint and café (walk straight into the mall atrium and go past the escalators to ride the slanting glass elevator, Mon 11:00–18:30, Tue–Sat 10:00–18:30, Thu until 21:00, Sun 12:00–18:30). Across Kalverstraat, the **Vroom & Dreesman (V&D)** department store (at #200) is one of Holland's oldest chains. Inside, La Place is a sprawling self-service cafeteria—handy for a quick and healthy lunch (see the "Near the Mint Tower" section of the Eating chapter, page 185).

• *Continue on Kalverstraat, which dead-ends at the...*

Mint Tower (Munttoren)

This tower, which marked the limit of the medieval walled city, served as one of the original gates (the steeple was added later, in 1620).

The city walls were girdled by a moat—the Singel canal. Until about 1500, the area beyond here was nothing but marshy fields and a few farms on reclaimed land.

From the busy intersection at Muntplein, look left (at about 10 o'clock) down Reguliersbreestraat. A long block east of here (where you see trees) is Rembrandtplein, another major center for nightlife (and site of the fun statue nicknamed "*The Night Watch* in 3-D"). Halfway down the block, the twin green domes mark the exotic **Tuschinski Theater,** where you can see current movies in a sumptuous Art Deco setting (see page 51). Take a seat in the lobby and stare at the ever-changing ceiling, imagining this place during the Roaring '20s.

• *Just past the Mint Tower, turn right and walk west along the south bank of the Singel, which is lined with the greenhouse shops of the...*

Flower Market (Bloemenmarkt)

This busy block of cut flowers, plants, bulbs, seeds, and garden supplies attests to Holland's reputation for growing flowers. Tulips, imported from Turkey in the 1600s, grew well in the sandy soil of the dunes and reclaimed land. By the 1630s, the country was in the grip of a full-blown tulip mania, when a single bulb sold for as much as a house, and fortunes were won and lost. Finally, in 1637, the market plummeted, and the tulip became just one of many beauties in the country's flower arsenal. Today, Holland is a major exporter of flowers. Certain seeds are certified and OK to bring back into the United States (merchants have the details).

• *The long Flower Market ends at the next bridge, where you'll see a square named...*

Koningsplein

Choke down a raw herring—the commodity that first put Amsterdam on the trading map—with locals who flock to this popular outdoor herring stand. (*Hollandse nieuwe* means the herring are in season.)

• *From Koningsplein, turn left, heading straight to Leidseplein. At first, the street southward is just labeled Koningsplein (*Selexyz Scheltema, *Amsterdam's leading bookstore, is at Koningsplein 20). Soon, Koningsplein becomes...*

Leidsestraat

Between here and Leidseplein, you'll cross several grand canals, following a street lined with fashion and tourist shops, and

crowded with shoppers, tourists, bicycles, and trams. Trams must wait their turn to share a single track as the street narrows.

The once grand, now frumpy **Metz & Co.** department store (where Leidsestraat crosses Herengracht) offers a rare above-the-rooftops panorama of the city from its sixth-floor café.

Looking left down Herengracht, you'll see the **"Golden Curve"** of the canal, lined with grand, classical-style gables.

• *Past the posh stores, find the humble When Nature Calls Smartshop, located where Leidsestraat crosses Keizersgracht (at Keizersgracht 508, open daily until 22:00).*

When Nature Calls Smartshop

"Smartshops" like this one are clean, well-lighted, fully professional retail outlets that sell powerful drugs, many of which are illegal in America. Their "natural" drugs include harmless nutrition

boosters (royal jelly), harmful but
familiar tobacco, and herbal versions
of popular dance-club drugs (herbal
Ecstasy). The big item: marijuana
seeds.

Prices are clearly marked, with
brief descriptions of the drugs, their
ingredients, and effects. The knowledgeable salespeople can give more
information on their "100 percent
natural products that play with the
human senses."

Still, my fellow Americans, *caveat emptor!* We've grown used
to thinking, "If it's legal, it must be safe. If it's not, I'll sue." While
perfectly legal and aboveboard in the Netherlands, some of these
substances can cause powerful, often unpleasant reactions.

• *Where Leidsestraat crosses Prinsengracht, just over the bridge on the
right (at Prinsengracht 440), you'll find...*

The Delft Shop

The distinctive blue-and-white design characterizes glazed ceram-
ics made in Delft (30 miles southwest of here and covered later in
this book; for info on the pottery, see "Delft Blue Manufacturing
Process," page 245). Dutch traders learned the technique from the
Chinese of the Ming dynasty, and many pieces have an Oriental
look. The doodads with arms branching off a trunk are popular
"flower pagodas," vases for displaying tulips.

• *Head back toward where you came, and with the Prinsengracht on
your left, cross over Leidsestraat and walk half a block until you reach
Prinsengracht 488, home to the...*

Pipe Museum (Pijpenkabinet)

This small, funky museum holds 300 years of pipes in a 17th-
century canal house. (It's almost worth the price just to see the
inside of one of these elegant homes.) Once upstairs, a docent
guides you through a 30-minute tour of smoking history. You
begin with some pre-Columbian terra-cotta pipes (from the dis-
coverers of tobacco, dating from 500 B.C.). You'll see plenty of
intricate, finely decorated Baroque and Victorian curiosities. Ask
questions—your guide is happy to explain why the opium pipes
have their bowls in the center of the stem, or why some white clay
pipes are a foot long. The shop downstairs, Smokiana, sells antique
pipes and curiosities related to smoking (€5, Wed–Sat 12:00–18:00,
closed Sun–Tue, tel. 020/421-1779, www.pijpenkabinet.nl).

• *Return once again to Leidsestraat, which empties into the square
called...*

Leidseplein

Filled with outdoor tables under trees, ringed with cafés, theaters, and nightclubs, bustling with tourists, diners, trams, mimes, and

fire-eaters, and lit by sun- or lantern-light, Leidseplein is Amsterdam's liveliest square.

Do a 360-degree spin: Leidseplein's south side is bordered by the city's main serious theater, the **Stadsschouwburg,** which dates back to the 17th-century Golden Age (present

building from 1890). Tucked into the far corner of the theater is the **Last Minute Ticket Shop,** which sells tickets to all the shows in town, including half-price, same-day tickets (after 12:00) to select shows (Leidseplein 26, see map on page 81). To the right of the Stadsschouwburg, down a lane behind the big theater, stands the **Melkweg** ("Milky Way"), the once revolutionary, now institutional entertainment complex housing all things youth-oriented under one roof (Lijnbaansgracht 234a). Step into the lobby or check out posters plastered on the walls to find out who's playing tonight. On Leidseplein's west side, at #12, is the **Boom Chicago** nightclub theater, presenting English-language spoofs of politics, Amsterdam, and tourists (see page 199; pick up their free, informative intro-to-Amsterdam magazine at the door; see if any tickets are discounted and on the push list for tonight). The neighborhood beyond Burger King is **"Restaurant Row,"** featuring countless Thai, Brazilian, Indian, Italian, Indonesian, and even a few Dutch eateries. Next, on the east end of Leidseplein, is the **Bulldog Café and Coffeeshop,** the flagship of several café/bar/coffeeshops in town with that name. (Notice the sign above the door: It once housed the police bureau.) A small green-and-white decal in the window indicates that it's a city-licensed "coffeeshop," where marijuana is sold and smoked

legally. There's a proposal to close the Bulldog by 2011, because it's located too close to a school. Nearby are Rederij Noord-Zuid **canal boats,** offering one-hour tours (€10, 2/hr April–Oct 10:00–18:00, hourly Nov–March 10:00–17:00—for more info see "Canal Boat Tours," page 42).

• *From Leidseplein, turn left and head along the taxi stand down the broad, busy, tram-filled boulevard called Kleine-Gartman Plantsoen, which becomes Weteringschans. At the triangular garden,*

Canals

Amsterdam's canals tamed the flow of the Amstel River, creating pockets of dry land to build on. The city's 100 canals are about 10 feet deep, crossed by some 1,200 bridges, fringed with 100,000 Dutch elm and lime trees, and bedecked with 2,500 houseboats. A system of locks (back near the Central Station) controls the flow outward to (eventually) the North Sea and inward to the Amstel River. The locks are opened periodically to flush out the system.

Some of the boats in the canals look pretty funky by day, but Amsterdam is an unpretentious, anti-status city. When the sun goes down and the lights come on, people cruise the sparkling canals with an on-board hibachi and a bottle of wine, and even scows can become chick-magnets.

AMSTERDAM CITY WALK

cross the street and pass under a row of tall, gray, Greek-style columns, entering...

Max Euweplein

The Latin inscription above the colonnade—*Homo Sapiens non urinat in ventum*—means "People, don't pee into the wind." Pass between the columns and through a passageway to reach a pleasant interior courtyard with cafés and a large chessboard with knee-high kings. (Max Euwe was a Dutch world chess champion.) The square gives you access to the Casino, and just over the small bridge is the entrance to **Vondelpark.**

• *Return to Weteringschans street. Turn right and continue 75 yards east to a squat, red-brick building called...*

Paradiso

Back when rock-and-roll was a religion, this former church staged intimate concerts by big-name acts such as the Rolling Stones. In the late 1960s, when city fathers were trying hard to tolerate hordes of young pot-smokers, this building was redecorated with psychedelic colors and opened up as the first place where marijuana could be smoked—not legally yet, but it was tolerated. Today, the club hosts live bands and DJs and sells pot legally (for current shows, see www.paradiso.nl).

• *Continue down Weteringschans to the first bridge, where you'll see the Rijksmuseum across the canal.*

The Rijksmuseum and Beyond

The best visual chronicle of the Golden Age is found in the Rijksmuseum's portraits and slice-of-life scenes.

For a tour of the Rembrandts, Vermeers, and others, ✪ see the Rijksmuseum Tour on page 113.

On this walk, we've seen landmarks built during the city's late-19th-century revival: Central Station, the Stadsschouwburg, and now the Rijksmuseum. They're all similar, with red-brick and Gothic-style motifs (clock towers, steeples, prickly spires, and stained glass). Petrus Cuypers (1827–1921), who designed the train station and the Rijksmuseum, was extremely influential. Mainly a builder of Catholic churches, he made the Rijksmuseum, with its stained-glass windows, a temple to art. Most of the building is currently closed for renovation through 2013, with the highlights of the collection beautifully displayed in its Philips Wing (around back, on the right). Next to the Philips Wing, a small, free exhibit describes the exciting renovation project.

Behind the Rijksmuseum are the Museumplein (always entertaining) and the Van Gogh Museum (✪ see tour on page 132). The Heineken Experience (beer tour) is a half mile east of the Rijks on Heinekenplein (see page 51), and the Albert Cuypstraat street market is a block south of the Heineken Experience.

To return to Central Station (or to nearly anyplace along this walk), catch tram #2 or #5 from the southwest corner of the Rijks. Or walk north on Nieuwe Spiegelstraat, which leads (with a little detour) back to the Mint Tower.

RED LIGHT DISTRICT WALK

Amsterdam's oldest neighborhood has hosted the world's oldest profession since 1200. The Red Light District lies between Damrak and Nieuwmarkt. Amsterdammers call it De Wallen, or "The Walls," after the old city walls that once stood here. On your walk, you'll see history, sleaze, and cheese—chickens in Chinatown windows, drunks in doorways, cruising packs of foreign twenty-somethings, cannabis in windows, and sex for sale.

The sex trade runs the gamut from sex shops selling porn and accessories to blue video arcades, from glitzy nightclub sex shows featuring strippers and sex acts to the real deal—prostitutes in bras, thongs, and high heels, standing in window displays, offering their bodies. Amsterdam keeps several thousand prostitutes employed—and it's all legal.

Amsterdam's current city government is trying to rein in the sex trade by limiting it to De Wallen. It's also hoping to splice other commerce into a district that for centuries has had variations on basically only one product. As many as half of the sex businesses may close over the next few years—not because of prudishness, but to limit the encroachment of organized crime. A major Red Light District landlord was essentially given the option either to lease many of his booths to the city or be zoned out of business. The city picked up the leases, and windows that once showcased "girls for rent" now showcase mannequins wearing the latest fashions—lit by lights that aren't red.

Not for Everyone: The Red Light District has something offensive for everyone. Whether it's in-your-face images of graphic sex, exploited immigrant women, whips and chains, passed-out drug addicts, the pungent smells of pot smoke and urine, or just the shameless commercialism of it all, it's not everyone's cup of tea. While I encourage people to expand their horizons—that's a great thing about travel—it's perfectly OK to say, "No, thank you."

ORIENTATION

Length of This Walk: Allow two hours.

Photography: Consider leaving your camera in your bag. Absolutely avoid taking photos of ladies in windows—even with a nobody-will-notice camera phone—or a snarling bouncer may appear from out of nowhere to forcibly rip it from your hands. Taking even seemingly harmless pictures of ordinary people is frowned upon by privacy-loving locals. Photos of landmarks like the Old Church (Oude Kerk) and wide shots of distant red lights from the bridges are certainly OK, but remember that a camera is a prime target in this high-theft area.

When to Go: Mornings are quiet, but also when you see more passed-out-drunk-in-a-doorway scenes. Afternoons bring out more prostitutes, and evenings (starting at about 20:00) are actually quite festive, with many tourists and out-of-towners. Avoid late nights (after about 22:30), when the tourists disappear.

Safety: Coming here is asking for trouble, but if you're on the ball and smart, it's perfectly safe. While there are plenty of police on horseback keeping things orderly, there are also plenty of rowdy drunks, drug-pushing lowlifes, con artists, and pickpockets (not to mention extremely persuasive women in windows). Assume any fight or commotion in the streets is a ploy to distract innocent victims who are about to lose their wallets. As always, wear your money belt and keep a low profile.

Tours: This walk is enough for most visitors, but if you want a more in-depth visit with a guide and a group, consider Randy Roy's Red Light Tours (described on page 43). The Prostitution Information Center offers tours only on Saturday (see page 94).

Old Church (Oude Kerk): €5, Mon–Sat 11:00–17:00, Sun 13:00–17:00, tel. 020/625-8284, www.oudekerk.nl.

Amstelkring Museum (Our Lord in the Attic): €7, Mon–Sat 10:00–17:00, Sun and holidays 13:00–17:00, no photos, Oudezijds Voorburgwal 40, tel. 020/624-6604, www.museum amstelkring.nl.

OVERVIEW

The walk starts at the centrally located Dam Square. Two parallel streets with similar names—Oudezijds Voorburgwal and Oudezijds Achterburgwal—run north–south through the heart of De Wallen. You'll walk a big, long loop: north on Voorburgwal past the Old Church, hook around on Zeedijk street, and return on Achterburgwal, ending two blocks from Dam Square.

THE WALK BEGINS

• *From Dam Square, head down Warmoesstraat (to the left as you face the big, fancy Grand Hotel Krasnapolsky). A long block ahead, you'll see a small shop on the right...*

Condomerie

This condom shop has a knack for entertainment. Inside is a small glass case displaying a condom museum. On the counter is a three-ring notebook displaying all of the inventory (Mon–Sat 11:00–18:00, closed Sun, Warmoesstraat 141, tel. 020/627-4174, www.condomerie.com).

• *From here, pass the two little phallic street barricades with cute red lights around them and enter the traffic-free world of...*

De Wallen

Dildos, dirty playing cards, penis-headed lipsticks, S&M starter kits, kinky magazines, and blue videos—welcome to De Wallen. While the Red Light District is notorious throughout the Netherlands, even small rural towns often have **sex shops** like these to satisfy their citizens' needs. Browsers are welcome inside the sex shops. Video arcades—giving access to dozens of porn films—charge by the minute.

According to legend, Quentin Tarantino holed up at the Winston Hotel for three months in 1993 to write *Pulp Fiction*. Farther down, you come to an intersection with the Old Church down the street on the right (you'll go to the church in a moment). Standing here, note the gay rainbow flags and the S&M flags (black and blue with a heart). Also notice the security cameras and modern lighting. While freedom reigns here, everything is kept under a watchful eye by the two neighborhood police departments.

Along this street and throughout the Red Light District, you'll see bars displaying advertisements for football (soccer) games, as

Red Light District Walk

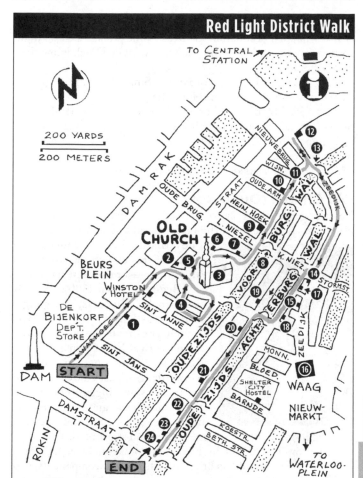

1. Condomerie & Museum
2. Sex Shops, S&M Flags & Mr. B's
3. Old Church
4. Prostitutes in Narrow Alleyways
5. Cheaper Prostitutes
6. Prostitution Info Center & Room-Rental Office
7. Princess Juliana Daycare
8. Pill Bridge
9. Amstelkring Museum
10. Historic Building (1580)
11. View of Little Venice
12. Old Wooden House
13. Zeedijk Street & Locks
14. Police Station
15. Buddhist Temple & Chinatown
16. The Waag & Nieuwmarkt
17. S.M. Sign
18. Banana Bar
19. Erotic Museum
20. Absolute Danny Shop
21. Theatre Casa Rosso
22. Cannabis College
23. Hash, Marijuana & Hemp Museum
24. Sensi Seed Bank Store

well as British, Scottish, and Irish flags. The Red Light District is a very popular destination for Brits—who are just a cheap flight away from Amsterdam—and the money-savvy Dutch know their best customers.

At #97 is the Elements of Nature Smartshop, a little grocery store of mind-bending natural ingredients.

At #89, Mr. B's Leather and Rubber Land, marked by the S&M flag, takes macho to painful and what seems like anatomically impossible extremes. Downstairs you'll find great deals on whips and masks.

• *Now, backtrack a few steps, and head down to the church.*

Old Church (Oude Kerk)

Returning from a long sea voyage, sailors of yore would spy the steeple of the Old Church on the horizon and know they were home.

They thanked St. Nicholas—the patron of this church, seafarers, and Amsterdam—for their safe return.

Begun in about 1300 and dedicated to St. Nicholas, the gangly church was built in fits and starts during the next 300 years. Even when the rival New Church (Nieuwe Kerk) was built on Dam Square, Amsterdam's oldest church still had the tallest spire, biggest organ, and most side-altars, and remained the neighborhood's center of activity, bustling inside and out with merchants and street markets.

The tower (290 feet high, with an octagonal steeple atop a bell tower), which still has original 14th-century components, was updated in the 18th century and served as a model for many other Dutch churches. The carillon's 47 bells chime mechanically or can be played by one of Amsterdam's three official carillonneurs.

Today, there's not much to see inside (but if you're interested and don't mind paying the €5 entry fee, you can reach the entrance by going around the right side of the church, circling it counterclockwise). Of the 2,500 gravestones in the floor, the most famous is opposite the entrance: "Saskia 19 Juni 1642," the grave of Rembrandt's wife. The church is spacious and stripped-down, due to iconoclastic vandals. In the 16th century, rioting anti-Spanish Protestants gutted the church, smashed windows, and removed politically incorrect "graven images" (religious statues). One renowned girl threw her shoe at the Virgin statue. (Strict Calvinists at one point even removed the organ as a senseless luxury, until they found they couldn't stay on key singing hymns without it.) Atop the brass choir screen, an inscription *('t misbruyk in Godes...)* commemorates the iconoclasm: "The false practices introduced into God's church were undone here in 1578."

The church, permanently stripped of "pope-ish" decoration, was transformed from Catholic to Dutch Reformed, the name St. Nicholas' Church was dropped, and it became known by the nickname everyone called it anyway—the Old Church.

Around the Old Church

The church is surrounded by prostitution, yes, but there are other things as well—namely, everyday life. Attached to the Old Church like barnacles are small buildings, originally homes for priests, church offices, or rental units. The house to the right of the entrance (at #25), inhabited by an elderly woman, is very tiny—32 feet by 8 feet. Remember, someone lives here—be discreet.

• *Walk along the church to the right, heading toward the canal. Passing* Belle, *a monument to "sex workers around the world," and a bronze breast in the pavement, you reach a green metal urinal that gets a lot of use. From the urinal by the canal, go half a block down the canal to just before the first intricately painted Bulldog Café (coffeeshop), and turn right at a narrow alleyway. Take a deep breath and squeeze into this tight opening.*

Prostitutes in Narrow Alleyways

You're right in the thick of high-density sleaze. Several narrow streets are lined with panty-and-bra-clad women in the windows winking at horny men, rapping on the window to attract atten-

tion, or looking disdainfully at sightseers. You may notice that different zones feature prostitutes from different lands—Asia, Africa, Eastern Europe. This is to cater to customer tastes, as regulars know what they want.

The area sure looks rough, but, aside from tricky pickpockets, these streets are actually very safe. The entire Red Light District is dotted with teeny-tiny video surveillance cameras, located above doorways and in narrow alleys. If prostitutes have or notice any trouble, they press a buzzer that swiftly unleashes a burly, angry bouncer or the police.

There are other pockets of prostitution around, but this is one of the most concentrated. Explore.

• *Double-back to the Old Church on Sint Annendwarsstraat. Now start to circle the church clockwise. Around the back (on Oudekerksplein), you'll see older, plumper (and cheaper) prostitutes.*

Prostitution

Prostitution has been legal here since the 1980s. The women are often entrepreneurs, renting space and running their own businesses. Women usually rent their space for eight-hour shifts. A good spot costs €100 for a half-day shift and €150 for an evening. Amsterdam's mayor recently engineered a deal to close about 50 of the city's prostitution windows; prices—what the women pay and what they charge their customers—may go up as a result.

The rooms look tiny from the street ("Do they have to do it standing up?"), but most are just display windows, opening onto a room behind or upstairs with a bed, a sink, and little else.

Prostitutes have to keep their premises hygienic, make sure their clients use condoms, and avoid minors. Most prostitutes opposed legalization, not wanting taxes and bureaucratic regulations.

Popular prostitutes charge €25–50 for a 20-minute visit and make about €500 a day. They fill out tax returns, and many belong to a loose union called the Red Thread. The law, not pimps, protects prostitutes. If a prostitute is diagnosed with AIDS, she gets a subsidized apartment to encourage her to quit the business. As shocking as this may seem to some, it's a good example of a pragmatic Dutch solution to a problem—getting the most dangerous prostitutes off the streets to combat the spread of AIDS.

RED LIGHT DISTRICT WALK

While many women choose prostitution as a lucrative career, many others are forced into it by circumstance—poverty, drug addiction, abusive men, and immigration scams. Since the fall of the Iron Curtain, many Eastern Europeans have flocked here for the high wages. Russian and East European crime syndicates have muscled in. The line between victim and entrepreneur grows finer and less clear.

• *Around the back of the Old Church is the...*

Prostitution Information Center (at #3)

Doling out information, books, condoms, and souvenir T-shirts, the PIC welcomes visitors. They have a €1.50 map showing exactly where prostitution is legal and offer a small, frank €1.50 booklet answering the most common questions tourists have about Amsterdam's Red Light District (free, Tue–Sat 12:00–19:00,

closed Sun–Mon, facing the Old Church at Enge Kerksteeg 3, www.pic-amsterdam.com).
• *Next door is a...*

Room-Rental Office (Kamerverhuurbedrijf)

Women come here to rent window-space and bedrooms to use for prostitution. Several of the available rooms are just next door. In return for their 8-, 12-, or 24-hour rental, they get security—the man at the desk keeps an eye on them via video surveillance. (See the monitors inside, and the small cameras and orange alarm lights above the doors.) The office also sells supplies (condoms by the case, lubricants, Coca-Cola).

This man does not arrange sex. The women who rent space from this business are self-employed. Customers negotiate directly with a woman at her door.

How does it work? A customer browses around. A prostitute catches his eye. If the prostitute is interested in his business (they are selective for their own safety), she winks him over. They talk at the door as she explains her price. Many are very aggressive at getting the man inside, where the temptation game revs up. A price is agreed and paid in advance.

Are there male prostitutes? Certainly, anything you might want is available somewhere in the Red Light District, but an experiment in the 1990s to put male prostitutes in windows didn't stand up. There are, however, "reconstructed women"—gorgeous transvestites who may (or may not) warn customers, to ward off any rude surprises.
• *Continue circling clockwise around the church. Amid prostitutes in windows and just past the "sex-cinema," the orange brick building on the left is the...*

Princess Juliana Daycare

Life goes on, and locals need someplace to send their kids. This school was built in the 1970s, when the idea was to mix all dimensions of society together, absorbing the seedy into the decent. The location of this daycare center (for kids from newborn to 4 years old) would be a tough sell where I come from. (If you're having trouble finding this discreet building—which is sealed up tight—look for the black-and-white photo of the princess near a gunmetal-gray door.)
• *Turn left at the canal and continue north on Oudezijds Voorburgwal to the end of the canal. Along the way, you'll pass...*

Pill Bridge and Little Venice

The first bridge you pass is nicknamed "Pill Bridge" for the retail items sold by the seedy guys who hang out here. Beyond

that, on the left, is the fascinating Amstelkring Museum, in the Our Lord in the Attic Church (at #40, one of the city's most visit-worthy museums—see Amstelkring Museum Tour, page 153).

Near the next bridge (at #14) is a historic building from 1580 (two years after Amsterdam's Protestants booted out their Spanish rulers, and two decades before the Dutch East India Company formed, but built during a time of increasing overseas trade).

On the right, farther down the canal, a view of "Little Venice" shows houses rising directly from the water (no quays or streets). Like Venice, the city was built in a marshy delta area, on millions of pilings. And, like Venice, it grew rich on sea trade.

• *From here, passing a collection of fine gable stones embedded in the wall, continue straight up a small lane called Sint Olofssteeg to Zeedijk street. Turn left and walk along Zeedijk street to where it dead-ends at a viewpoint overlooking the marina, Damrak, and Central Station. On the corner, at Zeedijk 1, you'll find an...*

Old Wooden House

Picture the scene in the 1600s, when this café was a tavern, sitting right at what was then the water's edge. (Central Station sits on reclaimed land at the former mouth of the harbor.) Sailors tied up in today's marina, arriving from, say, a two-year voyage to Bali, bringing home fabulous wealth. They spilled into Zeedijk street, were greeted by swinging ladies swinging red lanterns, stopped by St. Olaf's chapel to say a prayer of thanks, then anchored in this tavern for a good Dutch beer.

• *Turn around and backtrack, heading up Zeedijk street, to the crest of a bridge, to see...*

The Zeedijk and the Locks

The street called Zeedijk runs along the top of the "sea dike" that historically protected sea-level Amsterdam from North Sea tides. Once a day, a city worker unlocks the green box (by the railing) and presses a button, the locks open, and the tides flush out the city's canals. If the gate is open, you might see water flowing in or out.

In the 1970s and 1980s, this street was unbelievably sleazy (I live to tell)—a no-man's-land of junkies fighting amongst themselves. Today, it's increasingly trendy and upscale, fast becoming a vibrant neighborhood of urban diversity.

The street is a mix of ethnic restaurants (Thai and Portuguese) and bars, like the gay-oriented Queen's Head (at #20). The new building at #30, built in "MIIM" (1998), offers apartments for rent and sale to the neighborhood's new, upscale inhabitants.

The former Café 't Mandje (at #63) was perhaps Europe's first gay bar (opened in 1927 and closed in 1985). It stands as a memorial to owner Bet van Beeren (1907–1967), "Queen of the Zeedijk." The original Zee-dyke, Bet cruised the street in leather on her motorcycle. The café's interior has been rebuilt as an exhibit in the Amsterdam History Museum (see page 161).

Amsterdam's Chinatown is just around the corner, featuring chickens in windows, some of the city's best Chinese restaurants (such as Nam Kee at #113), and Asian gift shops.

It's easy to miss the **police station** (at #80, marked *Steunpunt Zeedijk*), which is deliberately low-profile. In addition to patrolmen on foot, the neighborhood is peppered with plainclothes cops.

• *Making a right before the police station, this walk heads onto Korte Stormsteeg street, back to the canalside red lights. But first, you may wish to venture a block or two farther south, where you'll find a temple and a prison...*

The Lotus Flower Chinese Buddhist Temple

Enter this colorful, red-and-yellow, open-air temple by climbing the stairs, passing through one of three entry arches represent-

ing the Buddhist Threefold Path (clean living, meditation, and wisdom). Under the roof, on lotus flowers, sits a statue of Guan Yin, whose thousand hands are always busy helping Buddha.

Three nuns (who live in the convent) and Chinatown's faithful kneel before the goddess, burn incense, and offer her fruit and flowers. The walls hold terra-cotta panels bearing the names of donors to this new addition to the neighborhood (free, Tue–Sat 12:00–17:00, Sun 10:00–17:00, closed Mon, Zeedijk street).

The Waag and Nieuwmarkt

In 1488, this octagonal tower was the main gate of the city's eastern wall. Later, it became a weighing house *(Waag)*, then a prison. In the 1600s, the tower was an operating theater for med students,

Social Control

The buzzword in Holland is "social control," meaning that neighborhood security comes not from iron shutters, heavily armed cops, and gated communities, but from neighbors looking out for each other. Everyone knows everyone in this tight-knit neighborhood. If Magreet doesn't buy bread for two days, the baker asks around. Unlike in many big cities, there's no chance that anyone here could lie dead in his house unnoticed for weeks. Video surveillance cameras watch prostitutes, while prostitutes survey the streets, buzzing for help if they spot trouble. Watch the men who watch the women who watch out for their neighbors across the street who watch the flower shop on the corner—"social control."

where Rembrandt sat, sketchpad in hand, to see a criminal's body dissected. The painting that resulted *(The Anatomy Lesson of Dr. Jan Deijman)* now hangs in the Amsterdam History Museum (see page 161).

Today, the Waag is a café, sitting in the middle of Nieuwmarkt Square (which sports a modern public urinal)—a scene that is somewhat seedy, but hip, bar-filled, and very local.

• *From the square, go back on Zeedijk street to the police station, head west a few steps down Korte Stormsteeg, then go left along the canal.*

Oudezijds Achterburgwal

This beautiful, tree-lined canal is the heart of Red Light District nightlife, playing host to most of the main nightclubs. The majority of the sights are along the right-hand side of the street.

• *But first, on the left-hand side, find...*

S.M. Sign (at #11)

The *S.M.* signs in the windows advertise prostitutes specializing in sadomasochistic sex. Formerly, the international code for rough sex was "Russian Massage." ("French" meant oral, "Greek" meant anal, and "British," I believe, meant sharing tea.)

Banana Bar (Bananenbar, at #37)

The facade of this nightclub is decorated with Art Nouveau eroticism classier than what's offered inside. For €45, you get admission for an hour, with drinks included. Undressed ladies serve the drinks, perched atop the bar. Touching is not allowed, but you can order a banana, and the lady will serve it to you any way you like... For a full description, step into the lobby (open nightly until 2:00 in the morning, Oudezijds Achterburgwal 37, tel. 020/622-4670).

• *On side streets around here, you'll notice blue lights—these mark the transvestites. At Molensteeg, cross the bridge to head to the right side of Oudezijds Achterburgwal. A few paces to the right from the bridge is the...*

Erotic Museum (at #54)

"Wot a rip-off!" said a drunk British lout to his mates as he emerged from the Erotic Museum. If it's graphic sex you seek, this is not the place. To put it bluntly, this museum is not very good.

What you will see, besides the self-pleasuring bicycle girl in the lobby, is erotic statuettes from Asian cultures and some mildly risqué John Lennon sketches of him and Yoko Ono (on the first floor); a collection of racy comic books, photos, and old French literature (on the second floor); reconstructions of what you see in today's Red Light District, including a prostitute's chambers, sex-shop window displays, and videos of nightclub sex shows (on the third floor); and finally, the S&M room, where you're greeted by a mannequin urinating on you (on the top floor). S-mannequins torment M-mannequins for their mutual pleasure, and there are photos of America's raunchy 1950s pinup girl, Bettie Page, in black hair, stockings, garters, and high heels (€5, daily 11:00–24:00, Zeedijk street, tel. 020/624-7303). Note that Amsterdam has another, more entertaining sex museum—the Damrak Sex Museum (see page 58).

Absolute Danny (at #76)

This shop "for all your sensual clothing" sells leather and rubber outfits with dog collars suggesting bondage scenarios, in a full array of colors from red to black to...well, that's about it.

• *Continuing south on Oudezijds Achterburgwal, on the right (lined by pink elephants) you'll find...*

Theatre Casa Rosso

This is the area's best-known nightclub for live sex shows. Unlike some sex shows that draw you in to rip you off with hidden charges, the Casa Rosso is a legitimate operation. Fixed-price tickets offer evening performances featuring strippers and live sex acts—some simulated, some real (€30, €45 includes drinks, nightly until 2:00 in the morning, Oudezijds Achterburgwal 106–108, tel. 020/627-8954).

• *Along the right side of the next block, you'll find three cannabis sights, starting with the...*

Cannabis College (at #124)

This free, public study center explains the positive industrial, medicinal, and recreational uses of cannabis. Books and newspaper clippings tell about practical hemp products, the medical uses of marijuana, and police prosecution/persecution of cannabis users. The pride and joy of the college is downstairs—the organic flowering cannabis garden, "where you can admire the plant in all her beauty." The garden (access by €3 donation) happens to fit the Dutch legal limit of three plants per person or five per household (free, daily 11:00–19:00, Oudezijds Achterburgwal 124, tel. 020/423-4420, www.cannabiscollege.com).

The Hash, Marijuana, and Hemp Museum (at #148)

Though informative and educational, this earnest museum is small and somewhat overpriced. If you patiently read the displays, you'll

learn plenty about cannabis and its various uses through history. (Note: the museum may relocate in 2010.)

The leafy, green cannabis plant was grown on large plantations by (among others) Golden Age Dutch merchants. They turned the fibrous stalks (hemp) into rope and canvas for ships, and used it to make clothing and lace.

Some cannabis plants—particularly mature females of the *sativa* and *indica* species—contain the psychoactive alkaloid tetrahydrocannabinol (THC) that makes you high. The buds, flowers, and leaves of the plant (marijuana) and the brown sap/resin/pitch that oozes out of the leaves (hashish, or hash) can be dried and smoked to produce effects ranging from euphoria to paranoia to the munchies.

Some peoples, from ancient Scythians and Hindus to modern Nepalis and Afghanis, have used cannabis as a sacred ritual drug. Modern Rastafarians, following a Bible-based religion centered in Jamaica, smoke cannabis, bob to reggae music, and praise God for creating "every herb" and calling them all "good" (Genesis 1:11–12).

The museum's highlight is the grow room, where you look through windows at real, live cannabis plants in various stages of growth, some as tall as my mom. Grown hydroponically (in water, no soil) under grow lights, at a certain stage they're "sexed" to weed out the boring males and "selected" to produce the most powerful strains (€6, daily 10:00–22:00, tel. 020/623-5961, www.hash museum.com).

Sensi Seed Bank Store

Also known as the Cannabis Connoisseurs Club, this shop is geared toward cannabis growers. They sell seeds, grow lights, climate-control devices, bug sprays, how-to books, and CDs of music to grow dope by (free, daily 10:00–22:00, Oudezijds Achterburgwal 150, tel. 020/624-0386, www.sensiseeds.com). They may relocate in 2010.

• *Where Oudezijds Achterburgwal intersects Oude Doelen street, look to the right to see the Royal Palace on Dam Square, two blocks away.*

Congratulations

You've peeked at locals—from prostitutes to drug pushers to Buddhists to politically active heads with green thumbs—and survived. Now, go back to your hotel and take a shower.

JORDAAN WALK

This walk takes you from Dam Square—the Times Square of Amsterdam—to the Anne Frank House, and then deep into the characteristic Jordaan neighborhood. It's a cultural scavenger hunt, offering you a chance to experience the laid-back Dutch lifestyle and catch a few intimate details that most busy tourists never appreciate. In the Jordaan (yor-DAHN), you'll see things that are commonplace in Amsterdam, but that you won't find in any other city in the world.

This is a short and easygoing walk—nice in the sleepy morning or en route to a Jordaan dinner in the evening. Bring your camera, as you'll enjoy some of Amsterdam's most charming canal scenes.

ORIENTATION

Length of This Walk: Allow 90 minutes.

St. Andrew's Hof: Free, Mon–Sat 9:00–18:00, closed Sun, Egelantiersgracht 107.

Electric Ladyland: €5, Tue–Sat 13:00–18:00, closed Sun–Mon, Tweede Leliedwarsstraat 5-HS, tel. 020/420-3776, www.electric-lady-land.com.

Noordermarkt: This square at the end of Westerstraat is lively and colorful during the Monday morning flea market.

OVERVIEW

The walk begins at Dam Square and ends at the center of the Jordaan by Egelantiers canal. From there, it's just a short and scenic walk back to your starting point.

THE WALK BEGINS

• *From Dam Square, leave the McDonald's, the mimes, and the tourists behind, and head to the place where real Amsterdammers live. Face the palace. Slip (to the right) between the palace and the New Church (Nieuwe Kerk), and you'll see the facade of the red brick...*

Magna Plaza Shopping Center

Built in 1899 on top of 4,560 pilings, this "modern"-looking building symbolized the city's economic revival after two centuries of

decline. The revival was brought on by the opening of the North Sea Canal and increased industrialization, capped by a World's Fair in 1883. The shopping center, originally the main post office, now houses 40 stores. On the ground floor (on the left), the cheery cheese ladies (Diane and her mom, Coby) would love for you to try their Gouda—free and generous samples of three or four kinds, with explanations.

• *Exiting Magna Plaza, go left—walking 50 yards on busy Nieuwezijds Voorburgwal,*

then left again on tiny Molsteeg. (Like bike lanes all over town, the pink/maroon pavement alerts you that this stretch of street is actually a bike path—keep to the sides.) From here, it's a straight shot west (though the street changes names along the way) past the Anne Frank House and into the Jordaan.

Bicycles

At the intersection with Spuistraat, with its pink-paved bike path, see the rows of bicycles parked along the street. Amsterdam's 750,000 residents own nearly that many bikes. The Netherlands' 16.5 million people own 16.5 million bikes, with many people owning two—a long-distance racing bike and a junky in-city bike, often deliberately kept in poor maintenance, so it's less enticing to the many bike thieves. Locals are diligent about locking their bikes twice: They lock the spokes and then use a heavy chain to attach the bike to something immovable.

The efficient Dutch appreciate a self-propelled machine that travels five times faster than walking, without pollution, noise, parking problems, or high fuel costs. On a *fiets* (bicycle), a speedy local can traverse the historic center in 10 minutes. As you explore, enjoy the quiet of a people-friendly town where bikes outnumber cars. Notice how 100 bikes might be parked along the road, yet they blend right in. Then imagine if each bike were a car. Notice

Jordaan Walk

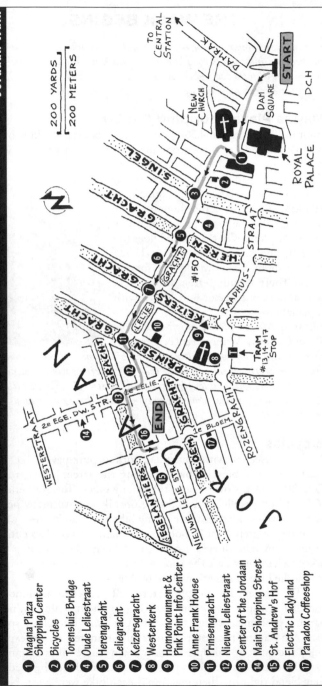

1 Magna Plaza
   Shopping Center
2 Bicycles
3 Torensluis Bridge
4 Oude Leliestraat
5 Herengracht
6 Leliegracht
7 Keizersgracht
8 Westerkerk
9 Homomonument &
   Pink Point Info Center
10 Anne Frank House
11 Prinsengracht
12 Nieuwe Leliestraat
13 Center of the Jordaan
14 Main Shopping Street
15 St. Andrew's Hof
16 Electric Ladyland
17 Paradox Coffeeshop

also how biking seems to keep the populace fit and good-looking. Locals say Amsterdam's athletic clubs are more for networking than for working out.

• *After another block, the street opens onto a small square (understandably nicknamed "Big Head" square), with fine benches for picnics. It's actually a bridge, straddling the Singel canal.*

Torensluis Bridge

With cafés and art galleries, this quiet neighborhood seems farther than just three blocks from busy Dam Square. The canal today looks much as it might have during the Golden Age of the 1600s, when the city quickly became a major urban center. Pan 360 degrees and take in the variety of buildings.

The so-called **skinniest house in Amsterdam** is the red house

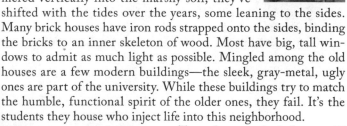

at #166. In fact, it's just the entryway to a normal house that opens up farther back. Most Amsterdam buildings extend far back, with interiors looking quite different from what you might expect from the facade. Real estate has always been expensive on this canal, and owners were taxed by the amount of street frontage. A local saying at the time was, "Only the wealthy can live on the inside of a canal's curve" (where they would have maximum taxable frontage with a minimum of usable space).

The houses crowd together, shoulder to shoulder. Built on top of thousands of logs hammered vertically into the marshy soil, they've shifted with the tides over the years, some leaning to the sides. Many brick houses have iron rods strapped onto the sides, binding the bricks to an inner skeleton of wood. Most have big, tall windows to admit as much light as possible. Mingled among the old houses are a few modern buildings—the sleek, gray-metal, ugly ones are part of the university. While these buildings try to match the humble, functional spirit of the older ones, they fail. It's the students they house who inject life into this neighborhood.

Two **characteristic bars** spill out onto the bridge. Van Zuylen is famous for its variety of beers, and Villa Zeezicht is popular for its sandwiches and apple pie. Both are great for their canal setting.

The "big head" statue of **Multatuli** (1820–1887) honors the "Dutch Rudyard Kipling," whose real name was Eduard Douwes

Dekker. His autobiographical novel, *Max Havelaar* (1860), follows a progressive bureaucrat's fight to improve the lives of Javanese natives slaving away on Dutch-owned plantations. He was the first author to criticize Dutch colonial practices—very bold back then.

Amsterdam's **canals** (roughly 50 miles of them) are about 10 feet deep. Back when the canals also functioned as sewers, they were flushed daily by opening the locks as the North Sea tides came in and out. You can glimpse the locks in the distance at the north end of the Singel canal—the white flagpole thingies sprouting at 45-degree angles (beyond the dome) are part of the apparatus to open and shut the gates. The Dutch are credited with inventing locks in the 1300s. This single greatest invention in canal-building allows ships to pass from higher to lower water levels.

The historic Singel canal was originally the moat running around the medieval walled city. The green copper dome in the distance marks the Lutheran church. Left of that is the new city—reclaimed in the 1600s and destined to be the high-rent district. To the right is the old town.

• *Continue west on...*

Oude Leliestraat

Consumers will find plenty to consume on this block of shops and cafés that runs Amsterdam's gamut—Puccini's bonbons, Grey Area's marijuana, Foodism's vegetarian fare, Zool's traditional café fare, Cafeteria's lamb *shoarmas,* and more.

Grey Area bucks the trend of typical coffeeshops. While most cultivate a dark, exotic, opium-den atmosphere, this is small, clean, and well-lit. The green-and-white decal in the window identifies it as #092 in the city's licensing program. This esteemed coffeeshop was a recent winner of Amsterdam's Cannabis Cup, a high honor. (For more on this and other coffeeshops, see page 190.)

• *The next canal is the...*

Herengracht

During the Golden Age boom in the 1600s, Amsterdam expanded, adding this fine canal named for the *Heren,* or wealthy city merchants who lined it with their mansions. As the city was anti-royalty, there was no blue-blooded

JORDAAN WALK

Gables

Along the rooftops, Amsterdam's famous gables are false fronts to enhance roofs that are, generally, sharply pitched. Gables come in all shapes and sizes, sometimes decorated with animal and human heads, garlands, urns, scrolls, and curlicues. Despite the infinite variety, you can recognize several generic types.

A simple point gable just follows the triangular shape of a normal pitched roof. A bell gable—there's one two doors to the right of the skinny house—is shaped like (duh) a bell. Step gables, triangular in shape and lined with steps, are especially popular in Belgium. Spout gables have a rectangular protrusion at the peak. Neck gables rise up vertically from a pair of sloping "shoulders." Cornice gables make pointed roofs look classically horizontal. (There's probably even a clark gable, but frankly, I don't give a damn.)

POINT   BELL   STEP

SPOUT   NECK   CORNICE

class; these *Heren* functioned as the town's aristocracy. Even today, the Herengracht is a high-rent district. (Notice that zoning here forbids houseboats.) The house that's kitty-corner across the bridge (Herengracht 150) fronts the canal, giving us a cutaway of its entire depth—the long white side. Most Amsterdam buildings are much bigger than they appear from the front. On the roof, rods support the false-front gable (which originally supported a rich merchant's ego).

Parking is a problem in a city designed for boats, not cars.

Parking signs (there's one along Herengracht—on the left) warn you to put money in the meter at the end of the block, or have your wheels shackled with "the boot," which stays on until you pay your fine. Parking in the center runs about €27 for a "day ticket," and parking fees and fines fund a substantial portion of the city's transportation budget.

• *Continue west, walking along...*

Leliegracht

This is one of the city's prettiest small canals, lined with trees and crossed by a series of arched bridges (some of the city's 400). Notice that several of the buildings—furniture stores and bookstores—have staircases leading down below the street level to residences.

Many buildings have a beam jutting out from the top with a hook on the end. Attach a pulley to that, and you can lift up a sofa and send it through a big upper-story window—much easier than lugging it up a narrow staircase.

• *The next canal you cross is...*

Keizersgracht

The **Westerkerk** tower rises above the rooftops, capped with a golden crown and the Amsterdam coat of arms. The crown

shape was a gift of the Habsburg Maximilian I, as thanks for a big loan. Rembrandt is buried under the floor of this "Western Church," which dates from 1631. Its carillons toll every 15 minutes, a sound that reminded Anne Frank—who hid out just down the street—that there was, indeed, an outside world.

Detour 100 yards left (south) along the Keizers canal, where a triangular pink dock juts into the canal—the **Homomonument** (it's three small triangles within one large one). There are often flowers on the dock, remembering another AIDS victim. The pink-triangle design reclaims the Nazi concentration-camp symbol for gay men (lesbians had black triangles) and is a reminder of the persecution homosexuals still experience today.

For information on gay and lesbian Amsterdam, there's a colorful nearby kiosk called Pink Point, staffed by volunteers, on Westermarkt square (daily 10:00–18:00, www.pinkpoint.org).

The green metal structure near the Homomonument is a public urinal (called a *pissoir*) that offers only minimal privacy. But for

Dutch men who are usually ignored by worldly Dutch women, it's no problem.

The busy street just beyond the Homomonument is Raadhuisstraat, where there's a taxi stand; the handy east–west trams #13, #14, and #17 and a french-fry stand featuring art with the lowly fried potato worked into some famous paintings.

• *Backtrack to Leliegracht and continue west...*

More on Leliegracht

Things that would seem odd elsewhere in the world are common-place in Amsterdam. The mail slots on several doors have stickers saying *Nee* or *Ja* (no or yes), telling the postman what types of junk mail they'll accept or refuse. At #52, a handy bike ramp slants down the steps to a home below street level. And at

#62, glance up to the first story to see a rearview mirror. Why go way down steep stairs to see who's at the door when you can just check the well-positioned mirror?

• *At the Prinsengracht, the **Anne Frank House** (❂ see Anne Frank House Tour, page 145) is 100 yards to the left, and the Westerkerk and its tower is another 50 yards beyond that.*

Prinsengracht

One of the most livable canals in town is lined with several of the city's estimated 2,500 houseboats. When small, sail-powered cargo ships became uneconomical with the advent of modern cargo boats in the 1930s, they found a new use—as houseboats lining the canals of Amsterdam, where land was so limited and pricey. Today, their cargo holds are fashioned into elegant, cozy living rooms. Moorage spots are prized and grandfathered in, making some of the junky old boats worth more than you'd think. Boaters can plug hoses and cables into outlets along the side of this canal to get water and electricity. (To learn more about houseboats, visit the charming Houseboat Museum, described on page 54.)

Notice the canal traffic. The official speed limit on canals is four miles per hour. At night, boats must have running lights on the top, side, and stern. Most boats are small and low to glide under the city's bridges. The Prinsengracht bridge is average size, with less than seven feet of headroom (it varies with the water level); some bridges have less than six feet. Good maps indicate the critical height of the bridges.

Just across the bridge are several typical cafés. The relaxed Café de Prins serves food and drink both day and night. The old-timey De 2 Zwaantjes occasionally features the mournful songs of the late local legend Johnny Jordaan. And the Café 't Smalle (not visible from here, a half block to the right) has a deck where you can drink outside along a quiet canal (for details, see "Hungry?" on the next page).

• *Once you cross the Prinsengracht, you enter the Jordaan. Facing west (toward Café de Prins), cross the bridge and veer left down...*

Nieuwe Leliestraat

Here the buildings are smaller, the ground-level apartments are remarkably open to the street, signs warn speeding drivers to *Let op!* (Watch out!) for the speed bumps *(drempels),* and the mail slots sport more *Nees* than *Jas* (no junk mail, please). Welcome to the quiet Jordaan. Built in the 1600s as a working-class housing area, it's now home to artists and yuppies. Though many apartments have windows right on the street, the neighbors don't stare and the residents don't care. They even invite their friends for candlelit dinners right by the front window. The name Jordaan probably wasn't derived from the French *jardin*—but given the neighborhood's garden-like ambience, it seems like it should have been.

• *At the first intersection, Eerste (1E) Leliedwarsstraat, turn right and go one block to Egelantiers canal. The bridge over the canal is what I think of as...*

The Center of the Jordaan

This place—with its bookstores, small cafés full of rickety tables, art galleries, and working artists' studios—sums up the Jordaan.

Look down the quiet Egelantiers canal, lined with trees and old, narrow, gabled buildings, and scattered with funky scows by day that become cruising *Love Boat*s by night.

Look south at the Westerkerk, and see a completely different view from the one the tourists in line at the Anne Frank

House get. Framed by narrow streets, crossed with street-lamp wires, and looming over shoppers on bicycles, this is the church in its best light.

With your back to the church, look north down the street called Tweede (2E) Egelantiers Dwarsstraat, the laid-back neighborhood's main shopping and people street, lined with boutiques, galleries, antiques stores, hair salons, restaurants, and cafés. A few blocks down (but don't go there now), the street changes names a few times before it intersects Westerstraat, a wide, east–west boulevard with more everyday businesses. A

Monday street market fills the street all the way to Noordermarkt at Westerstraat's western end.

• *Just past the next bridge going west along Egelantiers canal, on the left at #107, is the entrance to...*

St. Andrew's Hof (Sint-Andrieshof)

Enter—quietly—through the black door marked *Sint-Andrieshof 107 t/m 145* (open Mon–Sat until 18:00, closed Sun, push hard on door) and encounter a slice of Vermeer—a tiny courtyard surrounded by a dozen or so residences. Take a seat on a bench and immerse yourself in this still world. This small-scale version of the Begijnhof is one of scores of *hofjes* (subsidized residences built around a courtyard) funded by churches, charities, and the city for low-income widows and pensioners.

Hungry?

There are several recommended restaurants in the area. Especially good are **Café Restaurant de Reiger** and **Café 't Smalle.** For full descriptions of these and more Jordaan eateries, see the Eating chapter, page 179.

• *Your tour's over. It's a short walk back to Dam Square. But old hippies have two more stops: Heading back toward the center of town along Egelantiers canal, make a right turn on Tweede (2E) Leliedwarsstraat, where you'll find...*

Hippie Highlights

A small shop with a flowery window display, **Electric Ladyland: The First Museum of Fluorescent Art,** hides a fluorescent won-

derland. It's the creation of Nick Padalino...one cool cat who really found his black-light niche in life. Downstairs, under Nick's shop, is a unique and tiny museum featuring fluorescent black-light art. Nick lovingly guides you, demonstrating fluorescent minerals from all over the world and fluorescence in everyday objects (stamps, candy, and so on). He seems to get a bigger kick out of it than even his customers. You can see the historic first fluorescent crayon from San Francisco in the 1950s. Wow. The label says, "Use with black light for church groups." Wow. (€5, Tue–Sat 13:00–18:00, closed Sun–Mon, Tweede Leliedwarsstraat 5-HS, tel. 020/420-3776, www.electric-lady-land.com.)

The nearby **Paradox Coffeeshop** is the perfect coffeeshop for the nervous American who wants a mellow place to go local and friendly service to help out (light meals, fresh juice, easy music, daily 10:00–20:00, Eerste Bloemdwarsstraat 2, see listing in Smoking chapter, page 193).

RIJKSMUSEUM TOUR

At Amsterdam's Rijksmuseum ("Rijks" sounds like "bikes"), Holland's Golden Age shines with the best collection anywhere of the Dutch Masters—from Vermeer's quiet domestic scenes, to Steen's raucous family meals, to Hals' snapshot portraits, to Rembrandt's moody brilliance.

The 17th century saw the Netherlands at the pinnacle of its power. The Dutch had won their independence from Spain, trade and shipping boomed, the wealth poured in, the people were understandably proud, and the arts flourished. For the Dutch, this was

their Golden Age. With no local church or royalty to commission big canvases in the Protestant Dutch republic, artists had to find different patrons—the upper-middle-class businessmen who fueled Holland's capitalist economy. Artists painted their portraits and decorated their homes with pretty still lifes and non-preachy, slice-of-life art.

The main core of the Rijksmuseum is closed until 2013 for a massive renovation. Thankfully, the most famous masterpieces—nearly everything on the typical tourist's hit list—are on display in the wonderful and easy-on-the-feet Philips Wing (southwest corner of the Rijks, the part of the building nearest the Van Gogh Museum). This delightful exhibit offers one of the most exciting and enjoyable art experiences in Europe.

ORIENTATION

Cost: €10.

Hours: Daily 9:00–18:00, Fri until 20:30, closed only on Jan 1.

Sightseeing Strategies: Friday evening is a relatively crowd-free time to visit. If you plan to visit during the day in peak season, you can buy an online ticket—for no extra cost—ahead of time in order to skip the long ticket-buying line (www.rijksmuseum.nl). For more information on various options, see "Advance Tickets and Sightseeing Cards" on page 34.

Getting There: The entrance to the Philips Wing is clearly marked near the corner of Jan Luijkenstraat and Hobbemastraat. From Central Station, catch tram #2 or #5 (get out at Hobbemastraat, directly at the Philips Wing).

Information: The helpful information booth inside the museum has free maps and a good guidebook, *The Masterpieces* (€5, €7.50 combo with audioguide). An information center outside in the garden explains the renovation (on Jan Luijkenstraat, to the left as you enter). Tel. 020/674-7047 for automated info, or tel. 020/674-7000 for main number, www.rijksmuseum.nl.

Audioguide Tour: The excellent €4 audioguide gives two tours— a "highlights" tour, and a more quirky and intimate tour narrated by a popular local artist.

Length of This Tour: Allow one hour.

Checkrooms: Leave your bag at the free checkrooms.

Cuisine Art: In the summer the museum has a fun "lunch-box-with-a-blanket-in-the-park" deal (€13 with museum entry or €4 for just the boxed lunch and a loaner blanket, Mon–Fri 12:00–14:00). There are plenty of picnic spots on the museum grounds.

Just a short walk away you'll find the Leidseplein (a lively square with cafés) and Vondelpark (a picnic-perfect park with the delightful Café Vertigo). Even closer is Cobra Café on Museumplein (toward the Van Gogh Museum, daily 10:00–18:00, tel. 020/470-0111). For good pancakes, try the untouristy Le Soleil (€4–8, daily 10:00–18:00, share a big table with other guests, Nieuwe Spiegelstraat 56, tel. 020/622-7147).

Photography: Not allowed.

Starring: Rembrandt van Rijn, Frans Hals, Johannes Vermeer, Jan Steen.

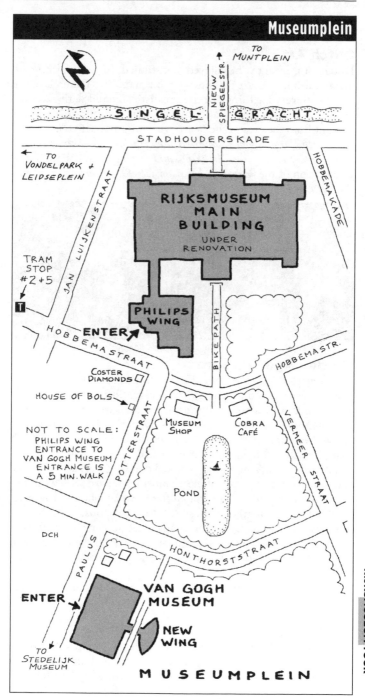

Museumplein

TO
MUNTPLEIN

NIEUW SPIEGEL STR.

SINGEL-GRACHT

STADHOUDERSKADE

HOBBEMAKADE

TO
VONDELPARK +
LEIDSEPLEIN

JAN LUIJKENSTRAAT

RIJKSMUSEUM
MAIN
BUILDING
UNDER
RENOVATION

TRAM
STOP
#2+5

T

HOBBEMASTRAAT

PHILIPS
WING

ENTER

BIKE PATH

HOBBEMA STR.

COSTER
DIAMONDS

HOUSE OF BOLS

POTTERSTRAAT

MUSEUM
SHOP

COBRA
CAFÉ

VERMEER STRAAT

NOT TO SCALE:
PHILIPS WING
ENTRANCE TO
VAN GOGH MUSEUM
ENTRANCE IS
A 5 MIN. WALK

POND

DCH

PAULUS

HONTHORSTSTRAAT

ENTER

VAN GOGH
MUSEUM

NEW
WING

TO
STEDELIJK
MUSEUM

MUSEUMPLEIN

RIJKSMUSEUM TOUR

THE TOUR BEGINS

Dutch Art

Dutch art is meant to be enjoyed, not studied. It's straightforward, meat-and-potatoes art for the common man. The Dutch love the beauty of everyday things painted realistically and with exquisite detail. So, set your cerebral cortex on "low" and let this art pass straight from the eyes to the heart, with minimal detours.

• *Enter the large Room 1, dominated by the large, colorful painting of a group of men eating, drinking, and staring at you,* Banquet in Celebration of the Treaty of Münster *(1648), by Bartholomeus van der Helst.*

Golden Age Treasures

Welcome to the Golden Age. Gaze into the eyes of the men who made Amsterdam the richest city on earth in the 1600s. Though shown in their military uniforms, these men were really captains of industry—shipbuilders, seamen, salesmen, spice-tasters, bankers, and venture capitalists—all part of the complex economic web that planned and financed overseas trade. Also in Room 1, find a ship's cannon and a big wooden model of a 74-gun Dutch man-of-war that escorted convoys of merchant ships loaded with wealth.

The five rooms on the ground floor display objects that bring Holland's Golden Age to life, including weapons, dolls' houses (*poppenhuizen*, Room 3), and precious objects (especially Delftware, inspired by Chinese porcelain, Room 5). Soak up the ambience to prepare for the paintings that the Golden Age generation produced and enjoyed.

• *Ride the spacey elevator upstairs to Room 6 (Floor 1). Head into the first room on the left.*

New Genres

Rather than religious art, Dutch painters portrayed small-scale, down-home, happy subjects, such as portraits, landscapes, still lifes, and so-called "genre scenes" (snapshots of everyday life).

Hendrick Avercamp (1585–1634)—*Winter Landscape with Ice Skaters*

The village stream has frozen over, and the people all come out to play. (Even today, tiny Holland's speed-skating teams routinely beat those from much larger nations.) In the center, a guy falls

flat on his face. A couple makes out in the hay-tower silo. There's a "bad moon on the rise" in the broken-down outhouse at left, and another nearby. We see the scene from above (the horizon line is high), making it seem as if the fun goes on forever.

A song or a play is revealed to the audience at the writer's pace. But in a painting, we set the tempo, choosing where to look and how long to linger. Exercise your right to loiter. Avercamp, who was deaf and mute, presents a visual symphony of small scenes. Just skate among these Dutch people—rich, poor, lovers hand-in-hand, kids, and moms—and appreciate the silent beauty of this intimate look at old Holland.
• *Enter Room 7.*

Frans Hals (c. 1581–1666)—*The Merry Drinker* (1627)

You're greeted by a jovial man in a black hat, capturing the earthy, exuberant spirit of the Golden Age. Notice the details—the happy red face of the man offering us a glass of wine, the sparkle in his eyes, the lacy collar, the decorative belt buckle, and so on.

Now move in closer. All these meticulous details are accomplished with a few quick, thick, and messy brushstrokes. The beard is a tangle of brown worms, the belt buckle a yellow blur. His hand is a study in smudges. Even the expressive face is done with a few well-chosen patches of color. Unlike the still-life scenes, this canvas is meant to be viewed from a distance, where the colors and brushstrokes blend together.

Frans Hals was the premier Golden Age portrait painter. Merchants hired him the way we'd hire a wedding photographer. With a few quick strokes, Hals captured not only the features, but also the personality.

Rather than posing his subject, making him stand for hours saying "cheese," Hals tried to catch him at a candid moment. He often painted common people, fishermen, and

Rijksmuseum—Philips Wing

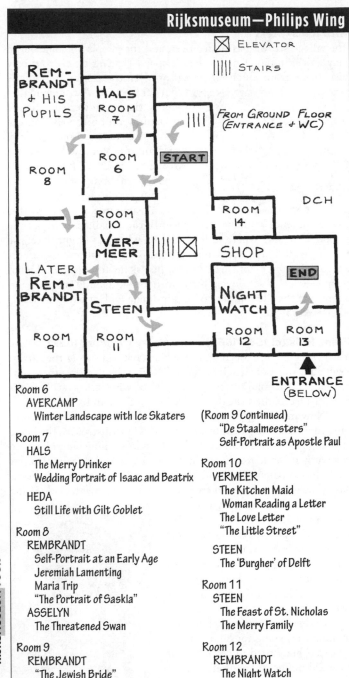

⊠ ELEVATOR

||||| STAIRS

REM-BRANDT + HIS PUPILS

HALS
ROOM 7

FROM GROUND FLOOR
(ENTRANCE & WC)

ROOM 8

ROOM 6

START

DCH

ROOM 10
VER-MEER

ROOM 14

SHOP

END

LATER REM-BRANDT

STEEN

NIGHT WATCH

ROOM 9

ROOM 11

ROOM 12

ROOM 13

ENTRANCE
(BELOW)

Room 6
AVERCAMP
Winter Landscape with Ice Skaters

Room 7
HALS
The Merry Drinker
Wedding Portrait of Isaac and Beatrix

HEDA
Still Life with Gilt Goblet

Room 8
REMBRANDT
Self-Portrait at an Early Age
Jeremiah Lamenting
Maria Trip
"The Portrait of Saskia"
ASSELYN
The Threatened Swan

Room 9
REMBRANDT
"The Jewish Bride"

(Room 9 Continued)
"De Staalmeesters"
Self-Portrait as Apostle Paul

Room 10
VERMEER
The Kitchen Maid
Woman Reading a Letter
The Love Letter
"The Little Street"

STEEN
The 'Burgher' of Delft

Room 11
STEEN
The Feast of St. Nicholas
The Merry Family

Room 12
REMBRANDT
The Night Watch

barflies, such as this one. He had to work quickly to capture the serendipity of the moment. Hals used a stop-action technique, freezing the man in mid-gesture, where the rough brushwork creates a blur that suggests the man is still moving.

Two centuries later, the Impressionists learned from Hals' messy brushwork. In the Van Gogh Museum, you'll see how Van Gogh painted, say, a brown beard by using thick dabs of green, yellow, and red that blend at a distance to make brown.

Frans Hals—*Wedding Portrait of Isaac Abrahamsz Massa and Beatrix van der Laen* (1622)

This wedding portrait of a chubby, pleasant merchant and his bride sums up the story of the Golden Age. Because this overseas trader

was away from home for years at a time on business, Hals makes a special effort to point out his patron's commitment to marriage. Isaac pledges allegiance to his wife, putting his hand on his heart. Beatrix's wedding ring is prominently displayed dead center between them (on her right-hand forefinger, Protestant-style). The vine clinging to a tree is a symbol of man's support and woman's dependence. And in the distance at right, in the classical love garden, are other happy couples strolling arm-in-arm amid peacocks, a symbol of fertility.

In earlier times, marriage portraits put the man and wife in separate canvases, staring out grimly. Hals' jolly couple reflects a societal shift from marriage as business partnership to an arrangement that's more friendly and intimate.

Hals didn't need symbolism to tell us that these two are prepared for their long-distance relationship—they seem relaxed together, but they each look at us directly, with a strong, individual identity. Good as gold, these are the type of people who propelled this soggy little country into its glorious Golden Age.

Various Still Lifes (c. 1630)

Savor the fruits of Holland's rich overseas trade—lemons from the south, pitchers from Germany, and spices from Asia, including those most exotic of spices...salt and pepper. These carefully composed, photo-realistic still lifes reflect the same sense of pride the Dutch have for their homes, cultivating them like gardens until they're immaculate, decorative, and well-ordered.

Pick one, such as *Still Life with Gilt Goblet* (by Willem Claesz Heda, 1635). Get so close that the guard joins you. Linger over

The Golden Age
(1600s)

Who bought this art? Look around at the Rijksmuseum's many portraits, and you'll see ordinary middle-class people, merchants, and traders. Even in their Sunday best, you can tell that these are hardworking, businesslike, friendly, simple people (with a penchant for ruffled lace collars).

Dutch fishermen sold their surplus catch in distant areas of Europe, importing goods from these far lands. In time, fishermen became traders, and by 1600, Holland's merchant fleets ruled the waves with colonies as far away as India, Indonesia, and America (New York was originally "Nieuw Amsterdam"). The Dutch slave trade—selling Africans to Americans—generated a lot of profit for luxuries such as the art you're viewing. Back home, these traders were financed by shrewd Amsterdam businessmen on the new frontiers of capitalism.

Look around again. Is there even one crucifixion? One saint? One Madonna? OK, maybe one. But this art is made for the people, not for the church. In most countries, Catholic bishops and rich kings supported the arts. But the Republic of the Netherlands, recently free of Spanish rule and Vatican domination, was independent, democratic, and largely Protestant, with no taste for saints and Madonnas.

Instead, Dutch burghers bought portraits of themselves, and pretty, unpreachy, unpretentious works for their homes. Even poor people bought smaller canvases painted by "no-name" artists and designed to fit the budgets and lifestyles of this less-than-rich-and-famous crowd. We'll see examples of their four favorite subjects—still lifes (of food and mundane objects), landscapes, portraits (often of groups), and scenes from everyday life.

the little things: the pewter-ware, the seafood, the lemon peels, the rolls, and the glowing goblets that cast a warm reflection on the tablecloth. You'd swear you could see yourself reflected in the pewter vessels. At least, you can see the faint reflections of the food and even of surrounding windows. The closer you get, the better it looks.

• *Enter Room 8.*

Rembrandt van Rijn (1606–1669)— Early Works

Rembrandt van Rijn is the greatest of all Dutch painters. Whereas most painters specialized in one field—portraits, landscapes, still lifes—Rembrandt excelled in them all.

Rembrandt—*Self-Portrait at an Early Age*

Here we see the young, small-town boy about to launch himself into whatever life has to offer. Rembrandt was a precocious kid.

His father, a miller, insisted that he become a lawyer. His mother hoped he'd be a preacher (look for a portrait of her reading the Bible, nearby). Rembrandt combined the secular and religious worlds by becoming an artist, someone who can hint at the spiritual by showing us the beauty of the created world.

He moved to Amsterdam and entered the highly competitive art world. Amsterdam was a booming town and, like today, a hip and cosmopolitan city. Rembrandt portrays himself at age 22 as being divided—half in light, half hidden by hair and shadows—open-eyed, but wary of an uncertain future. As we'll see, Rembrandt's paintings are often light-and-dark, both in color and in subject, exploring the "darker" side of human experience.

Rembrandt—*Jeremiah Lamenting the Destruction of Jerusalem* (1630)

The Babylonians have sacked and burned Jerusalem, but Rembrandt leaves the pyrotechnics (in the murky background at left) to Spielberg and the big screen. Instead, he tells the story of Israel's destruction in the face of the prophet who predicted the disaster. Jeremiah slumps in defeat, deep in thought, confused and despondent, trying to understand why this evil had to happen. Rembrandt turns his floodlight of truth on the prophet's deeply lined forehead.

Rembrandt wasn't satisfied to crank out portraits of fat merchants in frilly bibs, no matter what they paid him. He wanted to experiment, trying new techniques and more probing subjects. Many of his paintings weren't commissioned and were never even intended for sale. His subjects could be brooding and melancholy, a bit dark for the public's taste. So was his technique.

You can recognize a Rembrandt canvas by his play of light and dark. Most of his paintings are a deep brown tone, with only a few bright spots glowing from the darkness. This allows Rembrandt to highlight the details he thinks are most important and express moody emotions.

Light has a primal appeal to humans. (Dig deep into your DNA and remember the time when fire was not tamed. Light! In the middle of the night! This miracle separated us from our fellow animals.) Rembrandt strikes at that instinctive level.

Rembrandt—*Maria Trip* (1639)

This debutante daughter of a wealthy citizen is shy and reserved—

maybe a bit awkward in her new dress and adult role, but still self-assured. When he chose to, Rembrandt could dash off a commissioned portrait like nobody's business. The details are immaculate—the lace and shiny satin, the pearls behind the veil, the subtle face and hands. Rembrandt gives us not just a person, but a personality.

Look at the red rings around her eyes, a detail a lesser painter would have airbrushed out. Rembrandt takes this feature, unique to her, and uses it as a setting for her luminous, jewel-like eyes. Without being prettified, she's beautiful.

Rembrandt—*A Young Woman* (a.k.a. *The Portrait of Saskia,* 1633)

It didn't take long for Amsterdam to recognize Rembrandt's great talent. Everyone wanted a portrait done by the young master, and

he became wealthy and famous. He fell in love with and married the rich, beautiful, and cultured Saskia. By all accounts, the two were enormously happy, entertaining friends, decorating their house with fine furniture, raising a family, and living the high life. In this wedding portrait, thought to be of Saskia, the bride's face literally glows. A dash of white paint puts a sparkle in her eye. Barely 30 years old, Rembrandt was the most successful painter in Holland. He had it all.

Other "Rembrandts"

The Rijksmuseum displays real Rembrandts, paintings by others that look like his, portraits of Rembrandt by his students, and

Rembrandt van Rijn
(1606–1669)

The son of a Leiden miller who owned a waterwheel on the Rhine ("van Rijn"), Rembrandt took Amsterdam by storm with his famous painting of *The Anatomy Lesson* (1632, currently in the Mauritshuis museum in The Hague). The commissions poured in for official portraits, and he was soon wealthy and married (1634) to Saskia van Uylenburgh. They moved to an expensive home in the Jewish Quarter (today's Rembrandt's House museum), and decorated it with their collection of art and exotic furniture. His portraits were dutifully  detailed, but other paintings explored strong contrasts of light and dark, with dramatic composition.

In 1642, Saskia died, and his fortunes changed, as the public's taste shifted and commissions dried up. In 1649, he hired an 18-year-old model named Hendrickje Stoffels, and she soon moved in with him and gave birth to their illegitimate daughter. Holland's war with England (1652–1654) devastated the art market, and Rembrandt's free-spending ways forced him to declare bankruptcy (1656)—the ultimate humiliation in success-oriented Amsterdam. He moved to more humble lodgings on Rozengracht Straat.

In his last years, his greatest works were his self-portraits, showing a tired, wrinkled man stoically enduring life's misfortunes. Rembrandt piled on layers of paint and glaze to capture increasingly subtle effects.

In 1668, his lone surviving son, Titus, died, and Rembrandt passed away the next year. His death effectively marked the end of the Dutch Golden Age.

one or two "Rembrandts" that may not be his. A century ago, there were 1,000 so-called Rembrandt paintings in existence. Since then, a five-man panel of art scholars has declared most of those to be by someone else, winnowing the number of authentic Rembrandts to 300, with some 50 more that may one day be "audited" by the Internal Rembrandt Service. Most of the fakes are not out-and-out forgeries, but works by admirers of his distinctive style. So be careful the next time you plunk down $15 million for a "Rembrandt."

• *In Room 9, you'll find...*

Rembrandt's Later Works

Enjoying fame, wealth, and happiness, Rembrandt may have had it all, but not for long. His wife, Saskia, died. The commissions came more slowly. The money ran out. His mother died. One by one, his sons died. He had to auction off his paintings and furniture to pay debts. He moved out of his fine house to a cheaper place. His bitter losses added a new wisdom to his work.

Rembrandt—*Isaac and Rebecca* (a.k.a. *The Jewish Bride*, 1667)

The man gently draws the woman toward him. She's comfortable enough with him to sink into thought, and she reaches up uncon-

sciously to return the gentle touch. They're young but wizened. This uncommissioned portrait (known as *The Jewish Bride*, though the subject is unknown) is a truly human look at the relationship between two people in love. They form a protective pyramid of love amid a gloomy background. The touching hands form the center of this somewhat sad but peaceful work. Van Gogh said, "Rembrandt alone has that tenderness—the heartbroken tenderness."

Rembrandt was a master of oil painting. In his later years, he rendered details with a messier, more Impressionistic style. The red-brown-gold of their clothes is a patchwork of oil laid on thick with a palette knife.

Rembrandt—*The Syndics of the Amsterdam Drapers' Guild (De Staalmeesters*, 1662)

While commissions were rarer, Rembrandt could still paint an official group portrait better than anyone. In the painting made

famous by Dutch Masters cigars, he catches the Drapers Guild in a natural but digni-fied pose (dignified, at least, until the guy on the left sits down in his friend's lap).

It's a business meeting, and they're all dressed in black with black hats—the standard power suit of the Golden Age. They gather around a table examining the company's books. Suddenly, someone walks in (us), and they look up. It's as natural as a snapshot, though X-rays show Rembrandt made many changes in posing them perfectly.

The figures are "framed" by the table beneath them and the top of the wood paneling above their heads, making a three-part composition that brings this band of colleagues together. Even in this simple portrait, we feel we can read the guild members' personalities in their faces. (If the table in the painting looks like it's sloping a bit unnaturally, lie on the floor to view it at Rembrandt's intended angle.)

Rembrandt—*Self-Portrait as the Apostle Paul* (1661)

Rembrandt's many self-portraits show us the evolution of a great painter's style, as well as the progress of a genius' life. For

Rembrandt, the two were intertwined.

Compare this later self-portrait (he's 55 but looks 70) with the youthful, curious Rembrandt of age 22 we saw earlier. With lined forehead, bulbous nose, and messy hair, he peers out from under several coats of glazing, holding old, wrinkled pages. His look is...skeptical? Weary? Resigned to life's misfortunes? Or amused? (He's looking at us, but remember that a self-portrait is done staring into a mirror.)

This man has seen it all—success, love, money, fatherhood, loss, poverty, death. He took these experiences and wove them into his art. Rembrandt died poor and misunderstood, but he remained very much his own man to the end.

• *Enter Room 10.*

Johannes Vermeer (1632–1675)

Vermeer is the master of tranquility and stillness. He creates a clear and silent pool that is a world in itself. Most of his canvases show interiors of Dutch homes, where Dutch women engage in everyday activities, lit by a side window.

Vermeer's father, an art dealer, gave Johannes a passion for painting. Late in the artist's career, with Holland fighting draining wars against England, the demand for art and luxuries went sour in the Netherlands, forcing Vermeer to downsize—he sold his big home, packed up his wife and 14 children, and moved in with his mother-in-law. He died two years later, and his works fell into centuries of obscurity.

The Rijksmuseum has the best collection of Vermeers in the world—all four of them. (There are only some 30 in captivity.) But each is a small jewel worth lingering over.

Shhh...Dutch Art

You're sitting at home late one night, and it's perfectly calm. Not a sound, very peaceful. And then...the refrigerator motor turns off, and it's really quiet.

Dutch art is really quiet art. It silences our busy world, so that every sound, every motion is noticeable. You can hear cows tearing off grass 50 yards away. Dutch art is still. It slows our fast-lane world, so we notice the motion of birds. We notice how the cold night air makes the stars sharp. We notice that the undersides of leaves and cats are always a lighter shade than the tops. Dutch art stills the world so we can hear our own heartbeat and reflect upon that most noble muscle that, without thinking, gives us life.

To see how subtle Dutch art is, realize that one of the museum's most exciting, dramatic, emotional, and extravagant Dutch paintings is probably *The Threatened Swan* (in Room 8). It's quite a contrast to the rape scenes and visions of heaven of Italian Baroque paintings from the same time period.

Vermeer—*The Kitchen Maid* (c. 1658)

It's so quiet...you can practically hear the milk pouring into the bowl.

Vermeer brings out the beauty in everyday things. The subject is ordinary—a kitchen maid—but you could look for hours

at the tiny details and rich color tones. These are everyday objects, but they glow in a diffused light: the crunchy crust, the hanging basket, even the rusty nail in the wall with its tiny shadow. Vermeer had a unique ability with surface texture, to show how things feel when you touch them.

The maid is alive with Vermeer's distinctive yellow and blue—the colors of many traditional Dutch homes—against a white backdrop. She is content, solid, and sturdy, performing this simple task as if it's the most important thing in the world. Her full arms are built with patches of reflected light. Vermeer squares off a little world in itself (framed by the table in the foreground, the wall in back, the window to the left, and the footstool at right), then fills this space with objects for our perusal.

Vermeer—*Woman Reading a Letter* (c. 1662–1663)

Vermeer's placid scenes often have an air of mystery. The woman is reading a letter. From whom? A lover? A father on a two-year business trip to Indonesia? Not even taking time to sit down, she reads it intently, with parted lips and a bowed head. It must be important. (She looks pregnant, adding to the mystery, but that may just be the cut of her clothes.)

Again, Vermeer has framed a moment of everyday life. But within this small world are hints of a wider, wilder world—the light coming from the left is obviously from a large window, giving us a whiff of the life going on outside. The map hangs prominently, reminding us of travel, and perhaps of where the letter is from.

Vermeer—*The Love Letter* (c. 1669–1670)

There's a similar theme here. The curtain parts, and we see

through the doorway into a dollhouse world, then through the seascape on the back wall to the wide ocean. A woman is playing a lute when she's interrupted by a servant bringing a letter. The mysterious letter stops the music, intruding like a pebble dropped into the pool of Vermeer's quiet world. The floor tiles create a strong 3-D perspective that sucks us straight into the center of the painting—the woman's heart.

Vermeer—*View of Houses in Delft* (a.k.a. *The Little Street*, c. 1658)

Vermeer was born in the picturesque town of Delft, grew up near its Market Square, and set a number of his paintings there. This may be the view from his front door.

In *The Little Street*, the details actually aren't very detailed—the cobblestone street doesn't have a single individual stone in it. But Vermeer shows the beautiful interplay of colored rectangles on the buildings. Our eye moves back and forth from shutter to gable to window...and then from front to back, as we notice the woman deep in the alleyway.

Jan Steen—*The Burgher of Delft and His Daughter* (1655)

This painting is the latest major acquisition of the Rijksmuseum and another star in its lineup. In August of 2004, they paid $15 million for it...and figured they got a  great deal. While the rest of the Steen collection is in the next room (see below), the curators often display this one with Vermeer's works because it's pristine and peaceful—more like an exquisite Vermeer than a raucous Steen.

Steen's well-dressed burgher sits on his front porch, when a poor woman and child approach to beg, putting him squarely between the horns of a moral dilemma. On the one hand, we see his rich home, well-dressed daughter, and a vase of flowers—actually a symbol that his money came from morally suspect capitalism (the kind that produced the folly of 1637's "tulipmania"). On the other hand, there are his poor fellow citizens and the church steeple, reminding him of his Christian duty. The man's daughter avoids the confrontation. Will the burgher set the right Christian example? The moral dilemma perplexed many nouveau-riche Dutch Calvinists of Steen's day.

This early painting by Steen demonstrates his mastery of several popular genres: portrait, still life (the flowers and fabrics), cityscape, and moral instruction.

• *Enter Room 11.*

Jan Steen (1626–1679)

Not everyone could afford a masterpiece, but even poorer people wanted works of art for their own homes (like a landscape from Sears for over the sofa). Jan Steen (pronounced "yahn stain"), the Norman Rockwell of his day, painted humorous scenes from the lives of the lower classes. As a tavern owner, he observed society firsthand.

Jan Steen—*The Feast of St. Nicholas*

It's Christmas time, and the kids have been given their gifts. A little girl got a doll. The mother says, "Let me see it," but the girl turns away playfully.

Everyone is happy except...the boy who's crying. His Christ-

Ruffs

I cannot tell you why Dutch men and women of the Golden Age found these ruffled, fanlike collars attractive, but they were the rage here and elsewhere in Europe. Ruffled collars and sleeves were first popular in Spain in the 1540s, but the style really took off with a marvelous discovery in 1565—starch. Within decades, Europe's wealthy merchant class was wearing nine-inch collars made from 18 yards of material.

The ruffs were detachable and made from a long, pleated strip of linen set into a neck (or wrist) band. You tied it in front with strings. Big ones required that you wear a wire frame underneath for support. There were various types—the "cartwheel" was the biggest, a "double ruff" had two layers of pleats, and a "cabbage" was somewhat asymmetrical.

Ruffs required elaborate maintenance. First, you washed and starched the linen. While the cloth was still wet, hot metal pokers were inserted into the folds to form the characteristic figure-eight pattern. The ruffs were stored in special round boxes to hold their shape.

By 1630, Holland had come to its senses, and the fad faded.

mas present is only a branch in his shoe—like coal in your stocking, the gift for bad boys. His sister gloats and passes it around. The kids laugh at him. But wait—it turns out the family is just

playing a trick. In the background, the grandmother beckons to him, saying, "Look, I have your real present in here." Out of the limelight, but smack in the middle, sits the father providing ballast to this family scene and clearly enjoying his children's pleasure.

Steen has frozen the moment, sliced off a piece, and laid it on a canvas. He's told a story with a past, present, and future. These are real people in a real scene.

Steen's fun art reminds us that museums aren't mausoleums.

Jan Steen—*The Merry Family* (1668)

This family—three generations living happily under one roof—is eating, drinking, and singing like there's no tomorrow. The

broken eggshells and scattered cookware symbolize waste and extravagance. The neglected proverb tacked to the fireplace reminds us that children will follow in the footsteps of their parents. The father in this jolly scene is very drunk—ready to topple over—while in the foreground his mischievous daughter is feeding her brother wine straight from the flask. Mom and grandma join the artist himself (playing the bagpipes) in a lively sing-along, but the child learning to smoke would rather follow dad's lead.

Golden Age Dutch families were notoriously lenient with their kids. Even today, the Dutch describe a rowdy family as a "Jan Steen household."

• Room 12 is dominated by...

Rembrandt—*The Company of Frans Banning Cocq* (a.k.a. *The Night Watch,* 1642)

• *The best viewing spot is to the right of center—the angle Rembrandt had in mind when he designed it for its original location.*

This is Rembrandt's most famous—though not necessarily greatest—painting. Done in 1642 when he was 36, it was one of his most important commissions: a group portrait of a company of Amsterdam's civic guards to hang in their meeting hall.

It's an action shot. With flags waving and drums beating, the guardsmen (who, by the 1640s, were really only an honorary militia of rich bigwigs) spill into the street from under an arch in the back. It's "all for one and one for all" as they rush to the rescue of

Amsterdam. The soldiers grab lances and load their muskets. In the center, the commander (in black, with a red sash) strides forward energetically with a hand gesture that seems to say, "What are we waiting for? Let's move out!" His lieutenant focuses on his every order.

Rembrandt caught the optimistic spirit of Holland in the 1600s. Its war of independence from Spain was heading to victory and the economy was booming. These guardsmen on the move epitomize the proud, independent, upwardly mobile Dutch.

Why is *The Night Watch* so famous? Compare it with other,

less famous group portraits, where every face is visible, and everyone is well-lit, flat, and flashbulb-perfect. These people paid good money to have their mugs preserved for posterity, and they wanted it right up front. Other group portraits may be colorful, dignified, works by a master...but not quite masterpieces.

By contrast, Rembrandt rousted the civic guards off their fat duffs. By adding movement and depth to an otherwise static scene, he took posers and turned them into warriors. He turned a simple portrait into great art.

OK, some *Night Watch* scuttlebutt: First off, *"Night Watch"* is a misnomer. It's a daytime scene, but over the years, as the preserving varnish darkened and layers of dirt built up, the sun set on this painting, and it got its popular title. When the painting was moved to a smaller room, the sides were lopped off (and the pieces lost), putting the two main characters in the center and causing the work to become more static than intended. During World War II, the painting was rolled up and hidden for five years. More recently, a madman attacked the painting, slicing the captain's legs (now skillfully repaired).

The Night Watch, contrary to popular myth, was a smashing success in its day. However, there are elements in it that show why Rembrandt soon fell out of favor as a portrait painter. He seemed to spend as much time painting the dwarf and the mysterious glowing girl with a chicken (the very appropriate mascot of this "militia" of shopkeepers) as he did the faces of his employers.

Rembrandt's life darkened long before his *Night Watch* did. This work marks the peak of Rembrandt's popularity...and the beginning of his fall from grace. He continued to paint masterpieces. Free from the dictates of employers whose taste was in their mouths, he painted what he wanted, how he wanted it. Rembrandt goes beyond mere craftsmanship to probe into, and draw life from, the deepest wells of the human soul.

VAN GOGH MUSEUM TOUR

The Van Gogh Museum (we say "van GO," the Dutch say "van HHHOCK") is a cultural high even for those not into art. Located near the Rijksmuseum, the museum houses the 200 paintings owned by Vincent's younger brother, Theo. It's a user-friendly stroll through the work and life of one enigmatic man. If you like brightly colored landscapes in the Impressionist style, you'll like this museum. If you enjoy finding deeper meaning in works of art, you'll really love it. The mix of Van Gogh's creative genius, his tumultuous life, and the traveler's determination to connect to it makes this museum as much a walk with Vincent as with his art.

ORIENTATION

Cost: €12.50, free for those under 12 and for those with one ear.

Hours: Daily 10:00–18:00, Fri until 22:00, closed only on Jan 1.

Sightseeing Strategies: Visit on Friday evening (when crowds are sparse and sometimes there are musicians or a DJ and a wine bar in the lobby). During the day, the lines move fairly quickly (with wait times of just 15–30 minutes if all cashiers are working); you'll be herded into a line based on whether you're buying a ticket (slowest line, which also includes the *I amsterdam* Card crowd) or if you have a ticket in hand or a Museumkaart (fastest line). It's easy to buy your ticket online (no extra charge, www.vangoghmuseum.nl). For information on various options, see "Advance Tickets and Sightseeing Cards" on page 34.

Getting There: It's the big, modern, gray-and-beige place behind the Rijksmuseum at Paulus Potterstraat 7. From Central Station, catch tram #2 or #5 to Hobbemastraat.

Information: At the information desk, pick up a free floor plan (containing a brief history of the artist's brief life). The bookstore is understandably popular, with several good basic "Vincent" guidebooks and lots of posters (with mailing tubes). A fine 15-minute video with a basic introduction to Van Gogh plays continuously in the downstairs auditorium. Tel. 020/570-5200, www.vangoghmuseum.nl.

Audioguide Tour: The €4 audioguide includes 90 creatively produced minutes of insightful commentaries about Van Gogh's paintings, along with related quotations from Vincent himself.

Length of This Tour: Allow one hour.

Checkroom: Free and mandatory.

Cuisine Art: The terrace cafeteria (soup, salads, sandwiches) is OK. Recommended eateries are nearby: Cobra Café on Museumplein, and Café Vertigo in Vondelpark.

Photography: No photos allowed.

OVERVIEW

The core of the museum and this entire tour is on the first floor (one flight up from the ground floor). The bookstore, stairs to the auditorium, and cafeteria are on the ground floor, along with

paintings by artists who preceded and influenced Van Gogh's generation. The second floor has a study area and more paintings (including Van Gogh's smaller-scale works). The third floor shows works by his friends and colleagues, from smooth-surfaced Academy art, to Impressionists Claude Monet and Camille Pissarro, to fellow post-Impressionists Paul Gauguin, Paul Cézanne, and Henri de Toulouse-Lautrec. These are painters who influenced and were influenced by Van Gogh. The exhibition wing (accessed from the ground floor by going down the escalator) showcases temporary exhibitions.

The main collection of Van Gogh paintings on the first floor is arranged chronologically, taking you through the changes in Vincent van Gogh's life and styles. The paintings are divided into five periods of Vincent's life—the Netherlands, Paris, Arles, St. Rémy, and Auvers-sur-Oise—proceeding clockwise around the floor. (Although the busy curators frequently move the paintings around, they *usually* keep them within the same room, so look around; some may even be upstairs.) Some background on

Vincent's star-crossed life makes the museum even better, so I've included doses of biographical material for each painting.

THE TOUR BEGINS

• *Climb the stairs to the first floor. The first room—often displaying self-portraits—introduces you to the artist.*

Vincent van Gogh (1853–1890)

"I am a man of passions..."

—Vincent van Gogh

You could see Vincent van Gogh's canvases as a series of suicide notes—or as the record of a life full of beauty...too full of beauty. He attacked life with a passion, experiencing highs and lows more intensely than the average person. The beauty of the world overwhelmed him, and its ugliness struck him as only another dimension of beauty. He tried to absorb all of life, good and bad, and channel it onto a canvas, and the frustration of this overwhelming task drove him to madness. If all this is a bit overstated—and I guess it is—it's an attempt to show the emotional impact that Van Gogh's works have had on many people, me included.

Vincent, a pastor's son from a small Dutch town, started working at age 16 as a clerk for an art dealership. But his two interests, art and religion, distracted him from his dreary work, and after several years, he was finally fired.

The next 10 years were a collage of dead ends as he traveled northern Europe pursuing one path after another. He launched into each project with incredible energy, then became disillusioned and moved on to something else: teacher at a boarding school, assistant preacher, bookstore apprentice, preacher again, theology student, English student, literature student, art student. He bounced around England, France, Belgium, and the Netherlands. He fell in love, but was rejected for someone more respectable. He quarreled with his family and was estranged. He lived with a prostitute and her daughter, offending the few friends he had. Finally, in his late 20s, worn out, flat broke, and in poor health, he returned to his family in Nuenen and made peace. He started to paint.

• *For his stark early work, enter the next room.*

The Netherlands (1880–1885): Poverty and Religion

These dark gray canvases show us the hard, plain existence of the people and town of Nuenen, in the rural southern Netherlands. We see simple buildings, bare or autumnal

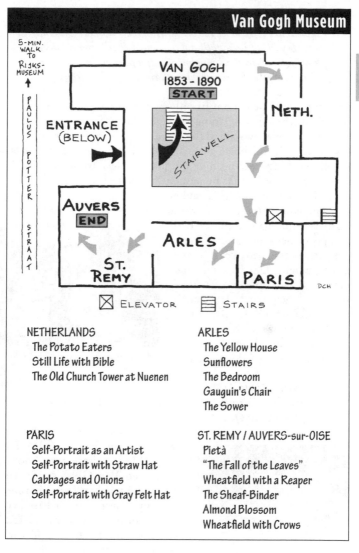

Van Gogh Museum

5-MIN. WALK TO RIJKS-MUSEUM ↑

PAULUS POTTER STRAAT

VAN GOGH
1853 – 1890
START

ENTRANCE (BELOW) ➤

STAIRWELL

NETH.

AUVERS END

ARLES

ST. REMY

PARIS

DCH

☒ ELEVATOR   ▤ STAIRS

NETHERLANDS
The Potato Eaters
Still Life with Bible
The Old Church Tower at Nuenen

ARLES
The Yellow House
Sunflowers
The Bedroom
Gauguin's Chair
The Sower

PARIS
Self-Portrait as an Artist
Self-Portrait with Straw Hat
Cabbages and Onions
Self-Portrait with Gray Felt Hat

ST. REMY / AUVERS-sur-OISE
Pietà
"The Fall of the Leaves"
Wheatfield with a Reaper
The Sheaf-Binder
Almond Blossom
Wheatfield with Crows

trees, and overcast skies—a world where it seems spring will never arrive. What warmth there is comes from the sturdy, gentle people themselves.

The style is crude—Van Gogh couldn't draw very well and would never become a great technician. The paint is laid on thick, as though painted with Nuenen mud. The main subject is almost always dead center, with little or no background, so there's a claustrophobic feeling. We are unable to see anything but the immediate surroundings.

The Potato Eaters (1885)

> *"Those that prefer to see the peasants in their Sunday-best may do as they like. I personally am convinced I get better results by painting them in their roughness.... If a peasant picture smells of bacon, smoke, potato steam—all right, that's healthy."*
>
> —Vincent van Gogh

In a dark, cramped room lit only by a dim lamp, poor workers help themselves to a steaming plate of potatoes. They've earned it. Vincent deliberately wanted the canvas to be potato-colored.

Vincent had dabbled as an artist during his wandering years, sketching things around him and taking a few art classes, but it wasn't until age 29 that he painted his first oil canvas. He soon threw himself into it with abandon.

He painted the poor working peasants. He worked as a lay minister among the poorest of the poor, peasants and miners. He joined them at work in the mines, taught their children, and even gave away his own few possessions to help them. The church authorities finally dismissed him for "excessive zeal," but he came away understanding the poor's harsh existence and the dignity with which they bore it.

Still Life with Bible (1885)

> *"I have a terrible need of—shall I say the word?—religion. Then I go out and paint the stars."*
>
> —Vincent van Gogh

The Bible and Emile Zola's *La Joie de Vivre*—these two books dominated Van Gogh's life. In his art, he tried to fuse his religious upbringing with his love of the world's beauty. He lusted after life with a religious fervor. The burned-out candle tells us of the recent death of his father. The Bible is open to Isaiah 53: "He was despised and rejected of men, a man of sorrows...."

The Old Church Tower at Nuenen (1885)

The crows circle above the local cemetery of Nuenen. Soon after his father's death, Vincent—in poor health and depressed—moved briefly to Antwerp. He then decided to visit his brother Theo, an art dealer living in Paris, the art capital of the world.

Theo's support—financial and emotional—allowed Vincent to spend the rest of his short life painting.

Vincent moved from rural, religious, poor Holland to Paris, the City of Light. Vincent van Gone.

• *Continue to...*

Paris (March 1886–Feb 1888): Impressionism

The sun begins to break through, lighting up everything he paints. His canvases are more colorful and the landscapes more spacious, with plenty of open sky, giving a feeling of exhilaration after the closed, dark world of Nuenen.

In the cafés and bars of Paris' bohemian Montmartre district, Vincent met the revolutionary Impressionists. He roomed with Theo and became friends with other struggling young painters, such as Paul Gauguin and Henri de Toulouse-Lautrec. His health improved, he became more sociable, had an affair with an older woman, and was generally happy.

He signed up to study under a well-known classical teacher but quit after only a few classes. He couldn't afford to hire models, so he roamed the streets, sketch pad in hand, and learned from his Impressionist friends.

The Impressionists emphasized getting out of the stuffy studio and setting up canvases outside on the street or in the countryside to paint the play of sunlight off the trees, buildings, and water.

As you see in this room, at first, Vincent copied from the Impressionist masters. He painted garden scenes like Claude Monet, café snapshots like Edgar Degas, "block prints" like the Japanese masters, and self-portraits...like nobody else.

Self-Portrait as an Artist (1888)

"I am now living with my brother Vincent, who is studying the art of painting with indefatigable zeal."

—Theo van Gogh to a friend

Here, the budding young artist proudly displays his new palette full of bright new colors, trying his hand at the Impressionist technique of building a scene using dabs of different-colored paint. A whole new world of art—and life—opened up to him in Paris.

Self-Portrait with Straw Hat (1887)

*"You wouldn't recognize Vincent, he has changed so much....
The doctor says that he is now perfectly fit again. He is making
tremendous strides with his work....He is also far livelier than
he used to be and is popular with people."*

— Theo van Gogh to their mother

In Paris, Vincent learned the Impressionist
painting technique. The shimmering effect
comes from placing dabs of different colors
side by side on the canvas. At a distance, the
two colors blend in the eye of the viewer to
become a third color. Here, Vincent uses
separate strokes of blue, yellow, green, and
red to create a brown beard—but a brown
that throbs with excitement.

Still Lifes, such as Cabbages and Onions (1887)

Vincent quickly developed his own style—thicker paint, broad,

swirling brushstrokes, and
brighter, clashing colors that
make even inanimate objects
seem to pulsate with life.
The many different colors are
supposed to blend together,
but you'd have to back up to
Belgium before these colors
resolve into focus.

Self-Portrait with Gray Felt Hat (1887–1888)

*"He has painted one or two portraits which have turned out
well, but he insists on working for nothing. It is a pity that he
shows no desire to earn some money because he could easily do
so here. But you can't change people."*

— Theo van Gogh to their mother

Despite his new sociability, Vincent never
quite fit in with his Impressionist friends.
As he developed into a good painter, he
became anxious to strike out on his own.
Also, he thought the social life of the big
city was distracting him from serious work.
In this painting, his face screams out from a
swirling background of molecular activity.
He wanted peace and quiet, a place where
he could throw himself into his work completely. He headed for the sunny south of
France.

VAN GOGH MUSEUM TOUR

• *Travel to the next room to reach...*

Arles (Feb 1888–May 1889): Sunlight, Beauty, and Madness

Winter was just turning to spring when Vincent arrived in Arles, near the French Riviera. After the dreary Paris winter, the colors of springtime overwhelmed him. The blossoming trees inspired him to paint canvas after canvas, drenched in sunlight.

The Yellow House (a.k.a. The Street, 1888)

"It is my intention...to go temporarily to the South, where there is even more color, even more sun."

—Vincent van Gogh

Vincent rented this house with the green shutters. (He ate at the pink café next door.) Look at that blue sky! He painted in a frenzy,

working feverishly to try and take it all in. For the next nine months, he produced an explosion of canvases, working very quickly when the mood possessed him. His unique style evolved beyond the Impressionists'—thicker paint, stronger outlines, brighter colors (often applied right from the paint tube), and swirling brushwork that makes even inanimate objects pulse and vibrate with life.

Sunflowers (1889)

"The worse I get along with people, the more I learn to have faith in Nature and concentrate on her."

—Vincent van Gogh

Vincent saw sunflowers as his signature subject, and he painted a half-dozen versions of them, each a study in intense yellow. If he signed the work (look on the vase), it means he was proud of it.

Even a simple work like these Sunflowers bursts with life. Different people see different things in *Sunflowers*. Is it a happy painting, or is it a melancholy one? Take your own emotional temperature and see.

The Bedroom (1888)

"I am a man of passions, capable of and subject to doing more or less foolish things—which I happen to regret, more or less, afterwards."

—Vincent van Gogh

Vincent was alone, a Dutchman in Provence. And that had its downside. Vincent swung from flurries of ecstatic activity to bouts

of great loneliness. Like anyone traveling alone, he experienced those high highs and low lows. This narrow, trapezoid-shaped, single-room apartment (less than 200 square feet) must have seemed like a prison cell at times. (Psychologists point out that most everything in this painting comes in pairs—two chairs, two paintings, a double bed squeezed down to a single—indicating his desire for a mate. Hmm.)

He invited his friend Paul Gauguin to join him, envisioning a sort of artists' colony in Arles. He spent months preparing a room upstairs for Gauguin's arrival.

Gauguin's Chair (1888)

"Empty chairs—there are many of them, there will be even more, and sooner or later, there will be nothing but empty chairs."

—Vincent van Gogh

Gauguin arrived. At first, they got along great, painting and carousing. But then things went bad. They clashed over art, life, and personalities. On Christmas Eve 1888, Vincent went ballistic. Enraged during an alcohol-fueled argument, he pulled out a knife and waved it in Gauguin's face. Gauguin took the hint and quickly left town. Vincent was horrified at himself. In a fit of remorse and madness, he mutilated his own ear and presented it to a prostitute.

The Sower (1888)

A dark, silhouetted figure sows seeds in the burning sun. It's late in the day. The heat from the sun, the source of all life, radiates out in thick swirls of paint. The sower must be a hopeful man, because the field looks slanted and barren.

Someday, he thinks, the seeds he's planting will grow into something great, like the tree that slashes diagonally across the scene—tough and craggy, but with small, optimistic blossoms.

In his younger years, Vincent had worked in Belgium sowing the Christian gospel in a harsh environment (see Mark 4:1–9). Now in Arles, ignited by the sun, he cast his artistic seeds to the wind, hoping.

• *Continue into the next room. Note that paintings featured in the rest of this tour are shifted around a lot. They'll probably be displayed...but likely in a different order.*

St. Rémy (May 1889–1890): The Mental Hospital

The people of Arles realized they had a madman on their hands. A doctor diagnosed "acute mania with hallucinations," and the local vicar talked Vincent into admitting himself to a mental hospital. Vincent wrote to Theo: "Temporarily I wish to remain shut up, as much for my own peace of mind as for other people's."

In the mental hospital, Vincent continued to paint whenever he was well enough. He often couldn't go out, so he copied from books, making his own distinctive versions of works by Rembrandt, Delacroix, Millet, and others.

We see a change from bright, happy landscapes to more introspective subjects. The colors are less bright and more surreal, the brushwork even more furious. The strong outlines of figures are twisted and tortured.

Pietà, after Delacroix (1889)

It's evening after a thunderstorm. Jesus has been crucified, and the corpse lies at the mouth of a tomb. Mary, whipped by the cold wind, holds her empty arms out in despair and confusion. She is the tender mother who receives us all in death, as though saying, "My child, you've been away so long—rest in my arms." Christ has a Vincent-esque red beard.

At first, the peace and quiet of the asylum did Vincent good, and his health improved. Occasionally, he was allowed outside to paint the gardens and landscapes. Meanwhile, the paintings he had sent to Theo began to attract attention in Paris for the first time. A woman in Brussels bought one of his canvases—the only painting he ever sold during his lifetime. In 1987, a *Sunflowers* sold for $40 million. Three years later a portrait of Vincent's doctor sold for more than $80 million.

The Garden of Saint Paul's Hospital (a.k.a. The Fall of the Leaves, 1889)

"...a traveler going to a destination that does not exist...."
—Vincent van Gogh

The stark brown trees are blown by the wind. A solitary figure (Vincent?) winds along a narrow, snaky path as the wind blows leaves on him. The colors are surreal—blue, green, and red tree trunks with heavy black outlines. A road runs away from us, heading nowhere.

Wheatfield with a Reaper (1889)

"I have been working hard and fast in the last few days. This is how I try to express how desperately fast things pass in modern life."
—Vincent van Gogh

The harvest is here. The time is short. There's much work to be done. A lone reaper works uphill, scything through a swirling wheat field, cutting slender paths of calm.

The Sheaf-Binder, after Millet (1889)

"I want to paint men and women with that something of the eternal which the halo used to symbolize...."
—Vincent van Gogh

Vincent's compassion for honest laborers remained constant fol-

lowing his work with Belgian miners. These sturdy folk, with their curving bodies, wrestle as one with their curving wheat. The world Vincent sees is charged from within by spiritual fires, twisting and turning matter into energy, and vice versa.

The fits of madness returned. During these spells, he lost all sense of his own actions. He couldn't paint, the one thing he felt driven to do. He wrote to Theo, "My surroundings here begin to weigh on me more than I can say—I need air. I feel overwhelmed by boredom and grief."

Auvers-sur-Oise (May–July 1890): Flying Away

"The bird looks through the bars at the overcast sky where a thunderstorm is gathering, and inwardly he rebels against his fate. 'I am caged, I am caged, and you tell me I have everything I need! Oh! I beg you, give me liberty, that I may be a bird like other birds.' A certain idle man resembles this idle bird...."

—Vincent van Gogh

Almond Blossom (1890)

Vincent moved north to Auvers, a small town near Paris where he could stay at a hotel under a doctor friend's supervision. On the

way there, he visited Theo. Theo's wife had just had a baby, whom they named Vincent. Brother Vincent showed up with this painting under his arm as a birthday gift. Theo's wife later recalled, "I had expected a sick man, but here was a sturdy, broad-shouldered man with a healthy color, a smile on his face, and a very resolute appearance."

In his new surroundings, he continued painting, averaging a canvas a day, but was interrupted by spells that swung from boredom to madness. His letters to Theo were generally optimistic, but he worried that he'd soon succumb completely to insanity and never paint again. The final landscapes are walls of bright, thick paint.

Wheatfield with Crows (1890)

"This new attack...came on me in the fields, on a windy day, when I was busy painting."

—Vincent van Gogh

On July 27, 1890, Vincent left his hotel, walked out to a nearby field and put a bullet through his chest.

This is the last painting Vincent finished. We can try to search the wreckage of his life for the black box explaining what happened, but there's not much there. His life was sad and tragic, but the record he left is one not of sadness, but of beauty. Intense beauty.

The windblown wheat field is a nest of restless energy. Scenes like this must have overwhelmed Vincent with their incredible beauty—too much, too fast, with no release. The sky is stormy and dark blue, almost nighttime, barely lit by two suns boiling through the deep ocean of blue. The road starts nowhere, leads nowhere, disappearing into the burning wheat field. Above all of this swirling beauty fly the crows, the dark ghosts that had hovered over his life since the cemetery in Nuenen.

ANNE FRANK HOUSE TOUR

ANNE FRANK TAGEBUCH

On May 10, 1940, Germany's Luftwaffe began bombing Schiphol Airport, preparing to invade the Netherlands. The Dutch army fought back, and the Nazis responded by leveling Rotterdam. Within a week, the Netherlands surrendered, Queen Wilhelmina fled to Britain, and Nazi soldiers goose-stepped past the Westerkerk and into Dam Square, where they draped huge swastikas on the Royal Palace. A five-year occupation began. The Netherlands had been neutral in World War I, and Amsterdam—progressive and modern, but a bit naive—was in for a rude shock.

The Anne Frank House immerses you, in a very immediate way, in the struggles and pains of the war years. Walk through rooms where, for two years, eight Amsterdam Jews hid from Nazi persecution. Though they were eventually discovered, and seven of the eight died in concentration camps, their story has an uplifting twist—the diary of Anne Frank, which bolsters the human spirit, affirming it cannot be crushed.

ORIENTATION

Cost: €8.50. (The Anne Frank House is not covered by any sightseeing pass.)

Hours: Daily March 15–Sept 14 9:00–21:00, July–Aug until 22:00, Sept 15–March 14 9:00–19:00, last entry 30 min before closing.

Avoiding Lines: The Anne Frank House is plagued by long lines—especially in the daytime during the summer. You can sometimes avoid the wait by arriving after 18:00 (last entry July–Aug is 21:30), or—the more foolproof option—buy a ticket online ahead of time (€0.50/ticket fee, www.annefrank.org; you can also buy tickets at Amsterdam's TIs, but

they often have long lines). If you've booked a ticket online, you can skip the line: During your allotted one-hour entry window, take your printed confirmation to the door to the left of the main entrance, and press the buzzer to enter.

Getting There: It's at Prinsengracht 267, near Westerkerk and about a 20-minute walk from Central Station. Or take tram #13, #14, or #17 or bus #170 or #172 to the Westermarkt stop, about a block from the museum's entrance. From the tram stop, head north along the canal, past the church.

Information: The museum has excellent information in English—a pamphlet at the door and fine descriptions with quotes from the diary throughout. Use this chapter as background, and then let the displays and videos tell you more. Tel. 020/556-7100, www.annefrank.org. Note that the house has many steep, narrow stairways.

Length of This Tour: Allow one hour.

Baggage Check: The museum has a strict, no big bags policy and has no place to check them.

Services: The bookshop at the end sells a great little pamphlet, *Persecution and Resistance in Amsterdam* (€0.50), which will lead you on a guided walk from here to the Dutch Resistance Museum across town (see page 67).

OVERVIEW

We'll walk through the rooms where Anne Frank's family and four other Jews hid for 25 months. The front half of the building, facing the canal, remained the offices and warehouses of an operating business. The back half, where the Franks and others lived, was the Secret Annex, its entrance concealed by a bookcase.

THE TOUR BEGINS

• *Buy your ticket and enter the ground-floor exhibit.*

Models of the Secret Annex

Two models—of the two floors where Anne's family lived with the rest—use dollhouse furniture to help you envision life in the now bare living quarters. In the first model, find the swinging bookcase that hid the secret entrance leading to Anne's parents' room (with wood stove). Anne's room is next to it, with a blue bed, a brown sofa, a table/chair/bookcase ensemble, and photos on the wall. On the upper floor (the next model) was the living room and the Van Pels' rooms. All told, eight people lived in a tiny apartment smaller than 1,000 square feet.

• *After viewing the important five-minute video, go upstairs to the offices/warehouses of the front half of the building.*

First Floor: Offices

From these offices, Otto Frank ran a successful business called Opekta, selling spices and pectin for making jelly. When the Nazis gained power in Germany in 1933, Otto had moved his family from Frankfurt to tolerant Amsterdam, hoping for a better life.

Photos and displays show Otto with some of his colleagues. During the Nazi occupation, while the Frank family hid in the back of the building, these brave people kept Otto's business running, while secretly bringing supplies to the Franks. Miep Gies, Otto's secretary (see her in the video), brought food every few days, while bookkeeper Victor Kugler cheered up Anne with the latest movie magazines.

• *Go upstairs to the...*

Second Floor: Warehouse

At first, the Nazi overlords were tolerant of, and even friendly with, the vanquished Dutch. But soon they imposed restrictions that affected one in ten Amsterdammers—that is, Jews. Jews had to wear yellow-star patches and register with the police. They were forbidden in movie theaters and on trams, and even forbidden to ride bikes.

In February of 1941, the Nazis started rounding up Jews, shipping them by train to "work camps," which, in reality, were transit stations on the way to death camps in the east. Outraged, the people of Amsterdam called a general strike that shut down the city for two days...but the Nazis responded with even harsher laws.

In July of 1942, Anne's sister Margot got her **call-up notice** for a "work-force project." Otto handed over the keys to the business to his Aryan colleagues, sent a final postcard to relatives, gave the family cat to a neighbor, spread rumors they were fleeing to Switzerland, and prepared his family to "dive under" (*onderduik*, as it was called) into hiding.

Life in the Annex

By day, it's enforced silence, so no one can hear them in the offices. They whisper, tiptoe, and step around squeaky places in the floor. The windows are blacked out, so they can't even look outside. They read or study, and Anne writes in her diary.

At night and on weekends, when the offices close, one or two might sneak downstairs to listen to Winston Churchill's BBC broadcasts on the office radio. Everyone's spirits rise and sink with news of Allied victories and setbacks.

Anne's diaries make clear the tensions, petty quarrels, and domestic politics of eight people living under pressure. Mr. Van Pels annoys Anne, but he gets along well with Margot. Anne never gets used to Mr. Pfeffer, who is literally invading her space. And, most of all, pubescent Anne is often striking sparks with her German mom. (Anne's angriest comments about her mom were deleted from early editions of the published diary.)

Despite their hardships, the group feels guilty—they have shelter, while so many other Jews are rounded up and sent off.

As the war progresses, they endure long nights when the house shakes from Allied air raids, and Anne cuddles up in her dad's bed.

Boredom tinged with fear—existentialist hell.

Photos of *The People in Hiding* put faces on the eight people—all Jewish—who eventually inhabited the Secret Annex. First was the Frank family—Otto and Edith and their daughters, 13-year-old Anne and 16-year-old Margot. A week later, they were joined by the Van Pels (called the "Van Daans" in the *Diary*), with their teenage son, Peter. A few months later, Fritz Pfeffer (called "Mr. Dussel" in the *Diary*) was invited in.

• *At the back of the third floor warehouse is...*

The Bookcase Entrance

On a rainy Monday morning, July 6, 1942, the Frank family—wearing extra clothes to avoid carrying suspicious suitcases—breathed their last fresh air, took a long look at the Prinsengracht canal, and disappeared into the back part of the building, where they spent the next two years. Victor Kugler concealed the entrance to the annex with this swinging bookcase, stacked with business files.

Though not exactly a secret (since it's hard to hide an entire building), the annex was just one of thousands of back-houses *(achterhuis)*, a common feature in Amsterdam, and the Nazis had no reason to suspect anything on the premises of the legitimate Opekta business.

• *Pass through the bookcase entrance into the Secret Annex into...*

Otto, Edith, and Margot's Room

The family carried on life as usual. Otto read Dickens' **Sketches by Boz,** Edith read from a **prayer book** in their native German, and the children continued their studies, with Margot taking **Latin lessons** by correspondence course. They avidly followed the course of the war by radio broadcasts and news from their helpers. As the tides of war slowly turned and it appeared they might one day be saved from the Nazis, Otto tracked the Allied advance on a **map** of Normandy.

The room is very small, even without the furniture. Imagine yourself and two fellow tourists confined here for two years....

Pencil lines on the wall track Margot's and Anne's heights, marking the point at which these growing lives were cut short.

Anne Frank's Room

Pan the room clockwise to see some of the young girl's idols in photos and clippings she pasted there herself: American actor Robert Stack, the future Queen Elizabeth II as a child, matinee idol Rudy Vallee, figure-skating actress Sonja Henie, and on the other wall, actress Greta Garbo, actor Ray Milland, Renaissance man Leonardo da Vinci, and actress Ginger Rogers.

Out the window (which had to be blacked out) is the back courtyard—a chestnut tree and a few buildings. These things, along with the Westerkerk bell chiming every 15 minutes, represented the borders of Anne's "outside world."

Picture Anne at her small desk, writing in her diary.

In November of 1942, they invited a Jewish neighbor to join them, and Anne was forced to share the tiny room. Fritz Pfeffer (known in the *Diary* as "Mr. Dussel") was a middle-aged dentist with whom Anne didn't get along. Pfeffer wrote a farewell letter to his non-Jewish fiancée, who continued to live nearby and receive news of him from Miep Gies without knowing his whereabouts.

The Bathroom

The eight inhabitants shared this bathroom. During the day, they didn't dare flush the toilet.

• *Ascend the steep staircase—silently—to the...*

Common Living Room

This was also the kitchen and dining room. Otto Frank was well off, and early on, the annex was well-stocked with food. Miep Gies would dutifully take their shopping list, buy food for her "family" of eight, and secretly lug it up to them. Buying such large quantities in a coupon-rationed economy was highly suspect, but she knew a sympathetic grocer (a block away on Leliegracht) who was part of a ring of Amsterdammers risking their lives to help the Jews.

The **menu** for a special dinner lists soup, roast beef, salad, potatoes, rice, dessert, and coffee. Later, as war and German restrictions plunged Holland into poverty and famine, they survived on canned foods and dried kidney beans.

At night, the living room became sleeping quarters for Hermann and Auguste van Pels.

Peter van Pels' Room

On Peter's 16th birthday, he got a Monopoly-like board game called "The Broker" as a present.

Initially, Anne was cool toward Peter, but after two years together, a courtship developed, and their flirtation culminated in a kiss.

The staircase (no visitor access) leads up to where they stored their food. Anne loved to steal away here for a bit of privacy. At night, they'd open a hatch to let in fresh air.

One hot August day, Otto was in this room helping Peter learn English, when they looked up to see a man with a gun. The hiding was over.

• *From here, we leave the Secret Annex, returning to the Opekta store-room and offices in the front house. As you work your way downstairs, you'll see a number of exhibits on the aftermath of this story.*

Front House: The Arrest, Deportation, and Auschwitz Exhibits

They went quietly. On August 4, 1944, a German policeman accompanied by three Dutch Nazis pulled up in a car, politely entered the Opekta office, and went straight to the bookcase entrance. No one knows who tipped them off. The police gave the surprised hiders time to pack. They demanded their valuables and stuffed them into Anne's briefcase...after dumping her diaries onto the floor.

Taken in a van to Gestapo headquarters, the eight were pro-cessed in an efficient, bureaucratic manner, then placed on a train to Westerbork, a concentration camp northeast of the city (see their 3-inch-by-5-inch **registration cards**).

From there, they were locked in a car on a normal passenger train and sent to Auschwitz, a Nazi extermination camp in Poland (see the **transport list,** which includes "Anneliese Frank"). On the platform at Auschwitz, they were "forcibly separated from each other" (as Otto later reported) and sent to different camps. Anne and Margot were sent to Bergen-Belsen.

Don't miss the **video** of one of Anne's former neighbors who, by chance, ended up at Bergen-Belsen with Anne. In English, she describes their reunion as they talked through a barbed wire fence shortly before Anne died. She says of Anne, "She didn't have any more tears."

Anne and Margot both died of typhus in March of 1945, only weeks before the camp was liberated. Five of the other original eight were either gassed or died of disease. Only Otto survived.

The Franks' story was that of Holland's Jews. The seven who died were among 100,000 Dutch Jews killed during the war years. (Before the war, 135,000 Jews lived in the Netherlands.) Of Anne's school class of 87 Jews, only 20 survived.

• *The next room is devoted to Anne's father.*

The Otto Frank Room

Listen to a 1967 video of Anne's father talking about how he discovered her diary. In a case are a few notebooks that Otto kept during the hiding period.

• *Downstairs you come to the...*

Videos and the Diaries

See Anne's three diaries, which were discovered and published after the war. (Sometimes a reproduction of the fragile original

is on display.) Anne received the first diary as a birthday present when she turned 13, shortly before the family went into hiding. She wrote it in the form of a letter to an imaginary friend named Kitty.

The video of Miep Gies, who is still living, describes how she found Anne's diaries in the Secret Annex after the arrest and gave them to Otto when he returned. Another video shows Otto's reaction. Though the annex's furniture had been ransacked during the arrest, afterward the rooms remained virtually untouched, and we see them today much as they were.

Otto decided to have the diaries published, and in 1947, *De Achterhuis (The Back-House)* appeared in Dutch, soon followed by many translations, a play, and a movie. While she was alive, Anne herself had recognized the uniqueness of her situation and had been in the process of revising her diaries, preparing them to one day be published.

• *Continue downstairs to the ground floor and enter the theater.*

Series of Videos

The Anne Frank Foundation is obviously concerned that we learn from Europe's Nazi nightmare. The thinking that made the Holocaust possible still survives. Even today, some groups promote the notion that the Holocaust never occurred and contend that stories like Anne Frank's are only a hoax. After watching a series of videos, you'll leave the Anne Frank House with an indelible impression—and a better ability to apply these lessons to our contemporary challenges.

ANNE FRANK HOUSE

AMSTELKRING MUSEUM TOUR

Our Lord in the Attic—
A Hidden Catholic Church

For two centuries (1578–1795), Catholicism in Amsterdam was illegal, but tolerated (like pot in the 1970s). When hard-line Protestants took power in 1578, Catholic churches were vandalized and shut down, priests and monks were rounded up and kicked out of town, and Catholic kids were razzed on their way to school. The city's Catholics were forbidden to worship openly, so they gathered secretly to say Mass in homes and offices. In 1663, a wealthy merchant built Our Lord in the Attic (Museum Ons' Lieve Heer op Solder), one of a handful of places in Amsterdam that served as a secret parish church until Catholics were once again allowed to worship in public. This unique church—embedded within a townhouse in the middle of the Red Light District—comes with a little bonus: a rare glimpse inside a historic Amsterdam home straight out of a Vermeer painting.

ORIENTATION

Cost: €7.

Hours: Mon–Sat 10:00–17:00, Sun and holidays 13:00–17:00, closed Jan 1 and April 30.

Getting There: It's at Oudezijds Voorburgwal 40, a seven-minute walk from either Central Station or Dam Square.

Information: Tel. 020/624-6604, www.museumamstelkring.nl. Note that the museum has several steep, narrow staircases.

Photography: No photos allowed.

Length of This Tour: Allow one hour.

THE TOUR BEGINS

Exterior

Behind the attic windows of this narrow townhouse sits a 150-

seat, three-story church the size of a four-lane bowling alley. Below it is the home of the wealthy businessman who built the church. This 17th-century townhouse, like many in the city, also has a back-house *(achterhuis)* that was rented out to another family. On this tour, we'll visit the front house, then the church, then the back-house. Before entering, notice the emergency-exit door in the alley. This was once the hidden church's main entrance.

• *Step inside. Buy your ticket and climb the stairs to the first floor, where we begin touring the front house. The first stop is a room with a big fireplace, the...*

Parlor

By humble Dutch standards, this is an enormous, highly ornate room. Here, in the largest room of the house, the family received guests and hosted parties. The decor is the Dutch version of classical, where everything comes in symmetrical pairs—corkscrew columns flank the fireplace, the coffered ceiling mirrors the patterned black-and-white marble floor, and a fake exit door balances the real entrance door.

Over the fireplace is the coat of arms of Jan Hartman (1619–1668), a rich Catholic businessman who built this house for his family and built the church for his fellow Catholics in the neighborhood. The family symbol, the crouching hart (deer), became the nickname of the church—*Het Hert.*

The painting over the fireplace *(The Presentation in the Temple)* has hung here since Hartman's time and shows his taste for Italian, Catholic, Baroque-style beauty. On the wall opposite the windows, the family portrait is right out of the Dutch Golden Age, showing a rich Catholic businessman and his family of four...but it's not Hartman.

• *Now ascend the small spiral staircase that leads to a room facing the canal, called the...*

Canal Room

Unlike the rather formal parlor, this was where the family just hung out, staring out the windows or warming themselves at the stove. The furnishings are typical of a wealthy merchant's home of the time. The wood stove and the textiles on the walls are re-creations but look like the originals. In the Dutch custom (still occasionally seen today), the family covered tables with exotic Turkish rugs imported by traders of the Dutch East India Company. The Delftware vase would have been filled with tulips, back then still an exotic and expensive transplant from the East. The tall ceramic doodad is a multi-armed tulip vase. Its pagoda shape reminds us that Delftware originally came from China.

Despite the family's wealth, space was tight. In the 1600s, entire families would often sleep together in small bed cabinets. They sat up to sleep, because they believed if they lay down, the blood would pool in their heads and kill them.

The black ebony knickknack cabinet is painted with a scene right out of the 1600s Red Light District. On the right door, the Prodigal Son spends his inheritance, making merry with bare-breasted, scarlet-clothed courtesans—high-rent prostitutes who could also entertain educated, cello-loving clients. On the left door, the Prodigal Son has spent it all. He can't pay his bill, and is kicked out of a cheap tavern—still half-dressed—by a pair of short-changed prostitutes.

• *As you climb the staircase up to the church, you can look through a window into the small...*

Chaplain's Room

Originally the maid's room, this humble bedroom is now furnished to look as it did in the 1800s, when the church chaplain lived here. See the tiny bed cabinet decorated with a tiny skull—a reminder of mortality—and a pipe on the table. Next to the room is the font used by worshippers to wet their fingers and cross themselves upon entering the church.

• *Continue up to the church.*

Our Lord in the Attic Church—Nave and Altar

The church is long and narrow, with an altar at one end, an organ at the other, and two balconies overhead to maximize the seat-

ing in this relatively small space. Compared with Amsterdam's whitewashed Protestant churches, this Catholic church has touches of elaborate Baroque decor, with statues of saints, garlands, and baby angels. The balconies are suspended from the ceiling and held in place by metal rods.

This attic church is certainly hidden, but everyone knew it was here. In tolerant (and largely Catholic) Amsterdam, it was rare for Catholics to actually be arrested or punished (after the Protestants' initial anger of 1578), but they were socially unacceptable. Hartman was a respected businessman who used his wealth and influence to convince the city fathers to look the other way as the church was built. Imagine the jubilation when the church opened its doors in 1663, and Catholics could finally gather together and worship in this fine space without feeling like two-bit criminals.

The altar is flanked by classical columns and topped with an arch featuring a stucco God the Father, a dove of the Holy Spirit, and trumpeting angels.

The **base of the left column**—made of wood painted to look like marble—is hollow. Inside is a fold-out wooden pulpit that could be pulled out for the priest to preach from—as explained with photos on the wall opposite.

The altarpiece painting (Jacob de Wit's *Baptism of Jesus*) is one of three that could be rotated with the feast days. Step into the room behind the altar to see the two spares. In a glass case on the back side of the altar, squint at the ship-in-a-bottle miniature home devotionals.

• *Behind the altar is a room called the...*

Lady Chapel

An altar dedicated to Our Lady—the Virgin Mary, the mother of Christ—contains more of the images that so offended and out-raged hard-line Protestants. See her statue with baby Jesus and find her symbols, the rose and crown, in the blue damask altar cloth.

Catholics have traditionally honored Mary, addressing prayers to her or to other saints, asking them to intercede with God on their behalf. To Calvinist extrem-ists, this was like bowing down to a false goddess. They considered statues of the Virgin to be among the "graven images" forbidden by the Ten Commandments (Exodus 20:4).

The **collection box** (*voor St. Pieter*, on the wall by the stair-case down) was for donations sent to fund that most Catholic of monuments, the pope's own church, the Basilica of St. Peter

Anti-Catholic = Anti-Spanish

The anti-Catholic laws imposed by Protestants were partly retribution for the Catholics' own oppressive rule, partly a desire to reform what was seen as a corrupted religion... but mostly they were political. By a quirk of royal marriage, Holland was ruled from afar by Spain—Europe's most militantly Catholic country, home of the Inquisition, the Jesuits, and the pope's own Counter-Reformation army.

In 1578, Amsterdam's hard-line Protestants staged the "Alteration"—a coup kicking out their Spanish oppressors and allying the city with the Prince of Orange's rebels. Catholics in the city—probably a majority of the population—were considered guilty by association. They were potential enemies, suspected as puppets of the pope, spies for Spanish kings, or subverters of the social order. In addition, Catholics were considered immoral worshippers of false idols, bowing down to graven images of saints and the Virgin Mary.

Catholic churches were seized and looted, and prominent Catholics were dragged to Dam Square by a lynch mob, before being freed unharmed outside the city gates. Laws were passed prohibiting open Catholic worship. For two centuries, Protestant extremists gave Catholics a taste of their own repressive medicine. However, Amsterdam's long tradition of tolerance meant that Catholics were not actually arrested or prosecuted under these laws. Still, many families over many generations were torn apart by the religious and political strife of the Reformation.

in Rome—to Calvinists, the center of corruption, the "whore of Babylon."

• *Later, we'll head down the stairs here, but first climb the stairs to the first balcony above the church.*

Lower Balcony

The window to the left of the altar (as you face it) looks south across ramshackle rooftops (note the complex townhouse-with-back-house design of so many Amsterdam buildings) to the steeple of the Old Church (Oude Kerk). The Old Church was the main Catholic church until 1578, when it was rededicated as Dutch Reformed (Protestant), the new official religion of the Netherlands. For the next hundred years, Catholics had no large venue to gather in until Our Lord in the Attic opened in 1663.

The 1749 organ is small, but more than adequate. These days, music-lovers flock here on special evenings for a *Vondelkonzert* (wandering concert). They listen to a few tunes here, have a drink, then move on to hear more music at, say, the Old Church or the Royal Palace.

Calvinism

Holland's Protestant movement followed the stern reformer John Calvin more than the beer-drinking German Martin Luther. Calvin's French followers, called Huguenots, fled religious persecution in the 1500s, finding refuge in tolerant Amsterdam. When Catholic Spain began persecuting them in Holland, they entered politics and fought back.

Calvin wanted to reform the Catholic faith by condemning corruption, simplifying rituals, and returning the faith to its biblical roots. Like other Protestants, Calvinists emphasized that only God's grace—and not our good works—can get us to heaven.

He went so far as to say that God predestined some for heaven, some for hell. Later, some overly pious Calvinists even claimed to be able to pick out the lucky winners from the unlucky, sinful losers. Today, the Dutch Reformed Church (and some other Reformed and Presbyterian churches) carries on Calvin's brand of Christianity.

Next to the organ, the painting *Evangelist Matthew with an Angel* (*De Evangelist Mattheus*, c. 1625, by Jan Lievens) features the wrinkled forehead and high-contrast shadings used by Lievens' more famous colleague, Rembrandt.

• *Stairs next to the organ lead to the...*

Upper Balcony

Looking down from this angle, the small church really looks small. It can accommodate 150 seated worshippers. From here, the tapering roofline creates the "attic" feel that gives the church its nickname.

• *At the back of the upper balcony is the...*

Canalside Room—Religious Art

This kind of religious hardware is standard in Catholic church services—elaborate silver and gold monstrances (ornamental holders in which the Communion wafer is displayed), chalices (for the Communion wine), ciboria (chalices with lids for holding consecrated wafers), pyxes (for storing unconsecrated wafers), candlesticks, and incense burners. "Holy earth boxes" were used for Catholics denied burial in consecrated ground. Instead, they put a little consecrated dirt in the box, and placed it in the coffin.

Admiring these beautiful pieces, remember that it was this

kind of luxury, ostentation, and Catholic mumbo-jumbo that drove thrifty Calvinists nuts.

Looking out the window, you can see that you're literally in the attic. Straight across the canal is a house with an ornate gable featuring dolphins. This street was once the city's best address.

• *Back down on the lower balcony, circle around to the window just to the right of the altar for a...*

Northern View

Look north across modern junk on rooftops to the impressive dome and twin steeples of St. Nicholas Church, near Central Station. This is the third Amsterdam church to be dedicated to the patron saint of seafarers and of the city. The first was the Old Church (until 1578), then Our Lord in the Attic (1663). Finally, after the last anti-Catholic laws were repealed (1821), St. Nicholas was built as a symbol of the faith's revival.

When St. Nicholas Church was dedicated in 1887, Our Lord in the Attic closed up shop. The next year, wealthy Catholics saved it from the wrecking ball, turning it into one of Amsterdam's first museums.

• *Head back downstairs, passing through the room behind the altar with the Lady Chapel and taking the stairs (past the offering box) down to the...*

Confessional

The confessional dates from 1740. The priest sat in the left half, while parishioners knelt in the right to confess their sins through a grilled window. Catholic priests have church authority to forgive sins, while Protestants take their troubles directly to God.

(The sociologist Max Weber theorized that frequently forgiven Catholics more easily accept the status quo, while guilt-ridden Protestants are driven to prove their worth by making money. Hence, northern Protestant countries—like the Netherlands— became capitalist powerhouses, while southern Catholic countries remained feudal and backward. Hmm.)

• *Go down another flight and turn right, into the...*

Jaap Leeuwenberg Room (Room 10)

We've now left the church premises and moved to the back-house rooms that were rented out to other families. This room's colors are seen in countless old homes—white walls, ochre-yellow beamed ceiling, oxblood-red landing, and black floor tiles. The simple colors, lit here by a light shaft, make small rooms seem bright and spacious.

• *Some very steep stairs lead down to the...*

17th-Century Kitchen

This reconstructed room was inhabited as-is until 1952. Blue-tiled walls show playful scenes of kids and animals. Step into the small pantry, then open a door to see the toilet.

• *Climb the rope back up the stairs and turn left to find exhibits on Amsterdam's other Catholic churches and the "Miracle of Amsterdam." Then descend a different set of stairs into the...*

19th-Century Kitchen

This just looks so Dutch, with blue tiles, yellow walls, and Vermeer-esque lighting from a skylight. The portrait opposite the fireplace depicts the last resident of this house on her First Communion day. When she died in 1953, her house became part of this museum.

Think of how her age overlaps our age...of all the change since she was born. Consider the contrast of this serene space with the wild world that awaits just outside the door of this hidden church. And plunge back into today's Amsterdam.

AMSTELKRING MUSEUM

AMSTERDAM HISTORY MUSEUM TOUR

Amsterdam Historisch Museum

Dozens of rooms (with great English explanations) take you creatively through Amsterdam's story, from fishing village, to sea-trading superpower, to hippie haven, to city of immigrants. Simply follow the *Grand Tour* signs, and you'll see every room on your hike through 1,000 years of Amsterdam history. I've highlighted a few stops worth checking out.

ORIENTATION

Cost: €8, covered by Museumkaart and *I amsterdam* Card.

Hours: Mon–Fri 10:00–17:00, Sat–Sun 11:00–17:00.

Getting There: It's on Kalverstraat 92, next to the Begijnhof, in downtown Amsterdam.

Information: Tel. 020/523-1822, www.ahm.nl.

Length of This Tour: Allow one hour.

Cuisine Art: The museum has the classy David & Goliath café and restaurant—peek inside to see the huge 17th-century Goliath statue (€8–9 salads and sandwiches, daily 9:30–18:00, until 17:00 in winter).

THE TOUR BEGINS

Ground Floor Entrance Hall: Growth of the City

Take time to watch the entire sequence as the computer-generated growth screen ("The Growth of Amsterdam," at the far end of the room) takes you through the city's rise. Watch the population go from zero to 750,000 in 1,000 years. Witness the birth of the city—the damming of the Amstel, which created Dam Square, the commercial zone where the Damrak's sea harbor met the Rokin's river port. Then follow the subsequent canalization as the city fills in its fortified center and continues to expand outward in rings.

• *Go through the glass doors and up the first set of stairs. Enter the room with the sign above that says* Start/Rondgang 1350–2000 Grand Tour.

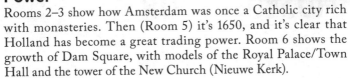

Rooms 2–7: From a City of Monasteries to a Trading Power

Rooms 2–3 show how Amsterdam was once a Catholic city rich with monasteries. Then (Room 5) it's 1650, and it's clear that Holland has become a great trading power. Room 6 shows the growth of Dam Square, with models of the Royal Palace/Town Hall and the tower of the New Church (Nieuwe Kerk).

• *Climb the stairs.*

Rooms 8–9: Amsterdam's Harbor and Medieval Justice

Look for the interesting model (in the stairwell) showing how ships got in and out of the city's shallow harbor. Ingenious 150-foot wooden pontoons, pumped full of air, were attached to the sides of ships to float them high over sandbars. The next room (Room 9, with the tough-sounding title "Social Care, Stern Discipline") displays instruments of medieval-style justice and paintings of great faces, from the big shots to the orphans who used to inhabit this building. This room provides a handy opportunity to study the paintings hanging in the atrium outside this wing, called the Shooting Gallery. There are several 17th-century group portraits of shooting club members, including fine English descriptions.

• *In Room 10, find a staircase up to...*

Carillon Lessons

Invented by Dutch bellmakers in the 1400s and perfected in the 1600s, this musical instrument is a Flemish specialty. The carillon player (called a "carillonneur"), seated at his keyboard up in the tower, presses keys with his fists and feet, jerking wires that swing clappers against tuned bells. The bells range in size from 20-pound high notes to 8-ton low notes, struck by 100-pound clappers. These days, some carillons have electric actions to make the carillonneur's job easier, plus player-piano mechanisms to automate the playing.

Mozart, Vivaldi, Handel, and Bach—all of whom lived during the carillon's heyday—wrote Baroque music that sounds beautiful on bells.

Sit down and pound your fists on the keys (that's why they're there). Hitting the red-marked keys, play a chromatic scale (successive keys) as fast as you can. Hit 'em hard. Try to pound out "Louie Louie" (Hint: The notes are "C," "F," and "G"). Then push the buttons on the walls to hear recordings of actual Amsterdam carillons in action—and imagine the fists flying.

• *Cross the skybridge (over the Civic Guard's Gallery) into Room 11, where you'll find...*

Rembrandt's *The Anatomy Lesson of Dr. Jan Deijman*

His famous *Anatomy Lesson of Dr. Tulp* (1632) put young Rembrandt on Amsterdam's artistic map two decades earlier. Now, in 1656, Rembrandt returned to the dissection room for another anatomy lesson—this time from Dr. Jan Deijman.

A fire in 1732 damaged this group portrait, incinerating the surrounding spectators and leaving us with just the stars of the

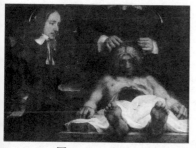

scene—Dr. Deijman and the corpse. The body of this recently hanged thief ("Black Jack" Fonteijn) was donated to the surgery theater in the Waag (today's Red Light District), where Dr. D. held a dissecting demonstration for med students and the paying public. Rembrandt attended, sketch pad in hand.

The corpse's feet are right in our face (similar to Mantegna's famous *Dead Christ*), a masterpiece of foreshortening. We stare into the gaping hole of his disemboweled stomach. The doctor (his head was burned off in the fire) does the work, opening the head and exposing the brain, while the assistant looks on calmly, hand on hip.

• *Enjoy the rest of the paintings here. Return to Room 10, pass directly through it, and continue through Rooms 12–16 until you reach Room 17. Hop on the bike—that's what it's for—and take a ride through Amsterdam in the 1920s. The next few rooms, "Modern City," give you a sense of...*

Rooms 17–21: 20th-Century Sociology

Room 19 shows housing in contemporary Amsterdam. Many residents are crammed into small apartments, either in historic

AMST. HISTORY MUSEUM

Amsterdam's Story

Visualize the physical layout of this man-made city: built on trees, protected by dikes, and laced with canals in the marshy delta at the mouth of the Amstel River. Location, location, location. Boats could arrive here from Germany by riverboat down the Rhine, from England across the Channel and down the IJ River, and from Denmark by entering the Zuiderzee inlet of the North Sea. No wonder that St. Nicholas, protector of water travelers, was the city's patron saint.

As early as 1300, Amsterdam was already an international trade center of German beer, locally caught herring, cloth, bacon, salt, and wine. Having dammed and canalized the Amstel and diked out the sea tides, the Dutch drained land, sunk pilings, and built a city from scratch. When the region's leading bishop granted the town a charter (1300), Amsterdammers could then set up their own law courts, judge their own matters, and be essentially autonomous. The town thrived.

By 1500, Amsterdam was a walled city of 12,000, with the Singel canal serving as the moat. Midcentury, the city had a growth spurt when its trading rival Antwerp fell to Spanish troops, and a flood of fellow Flemish headed north, fleeing chaos and religious persecution.

In 1602, hardy Dutch sailors (and the Englishman Henry Hudson) tried their hand at trade with the Far East. When they returned, they brought with them valuable spices, jewels, luxury goods...and the Golden Age.

The Dutch East India Company (abbreviated as "VOC" in Dutch), a state-subsidized import/export business, combined nautical skills with capitalist investing. With 500 or so 150-foot ships cruising in and out of Amsterdam's harbor, it was the first great multinational corporation. Amsterdam's Golden Age (c. 1600-1650) rode the wave of hard work and good fortune. Over the next two centuries, the VOC would send a half million Dutch people on business trips to Asia, broadening their horizons. (If you're interested in the history of the Dutch East India Company, walk the planks of the VOC Ship *Amsterdam*, a recreated trading ship docked near the NEMO science museum; see the listing on page 59.)

buildings or in developments of city-built housing. Recently, many Indonesians, Surinamese, and Muslims have immigrated here (see sidebar on "Islam and the Netherlands Today," page 444). Tracing the evolution of housing in Amsterdam in the 20th century, you study typical apartments from aerial views and dollhouses. The big blue board of doorbells represents the residents who live in a suburban apartment complex (in a district called Fleerde, which has probably never seen a tourist). Hit the red

This city of the Golden Age was perhaps the wealthiest on earth, thriving as the "warehouse of the world." Goods came from everywhere. The VOC's specialties were spices (pepper and cinnamon), coffee and tea, Chinese porcelain (Delftware's Eastern inspiration), and silk. Meanwhile, the Dutch West India Company concentrated on the New World, trading African slaves for South American sugar. With its wealth, Amsterdam built in grand style, erecting the gabled townhouses we see today. The city expanded west and south, adding new neighborhoods.

But by 1650, Amsterdam's overseas trade was being eclipsed by new superpowers England and France. Inconclusive wars with Louis XIV and England drained the economy, destroyed the trading fleet, and demoralized the people. Throughout the 1700s, Amsterdam was a city of backwater bankers rather than international traders, although it remained the cultural center of Holland. In early 1795, Napoleon's French troops occupied the country, and the economy was dismal.

A revival in the 1800s was spurred by technological achievements. The Dutch built a canal reconnecting Amsterdam directly with the North Sea (1824–1876), railroads laced the small country, and the city expanded southward by draining new land. The Rijksmuseum, Central Station, and Magna Plaza were built as proud monuments to the economic upswing.

The 1930s Depression hit hard, followed by four years of occupation under the Nazis, aided by pro-Nazi Dutch. The city's large Jewish population was decimated by Nazi deportations and extermination (falling from about 80,000 Jews in 1940 to just 16,000 in 1945).

With postwar prosperity, 1960s Amsterdam again became a world cultural capital as the center for Europe's hippies, who came here to smoke marijuana. Grassroots campaigns by young, artistic, politically active people promoted free sex and free bikes.

Today, Amsterdam is a city of 750,000 people jammed into small apartments (often with the same floor plan as their neighbors'). Since the 1970s, many immigrants have become locals. One in 10 Amsterdammers is Surinamese, and one in 10 bows toward Mecca.

buzzers to meet the residents and tour their homes.
• *Head upstairs to the second floor.*

Rooms 22–24: World War II to the Hippie Age

Don't miss the color footage of Liberation Day in 1945 (Room 23). In the 1960s, hippies from around the world were drawn to freewheeling Amsterdam. A socialist group called the Provos provoked the Establishment by publishing an outrageous magazine (the first issue contained a page of smokable paper made from marijuana), staging pro-pot events, and promoting innovative (but ultimately unsuccessful) campaigns to provide free white bicycles and white electric-powered cars to city commuters. You can trace the evolution of Amsterdam's "no war on drugs" and even listen to a Ted Koppel interview of former New York mayor Ed Koch

and his Dutch counterparts on the pros and cons of legalizing marijuana.

In Room 24, you enter a reconstruction of the famous Café 't Mandje from 1967, a gay bar on Zeedijk street. See a photo of owner Bet van Beeren and her motorcycle in the window, then step inside to see her hanging collection of neckties, which she cut off delighted customers with a butcher knife. (For more details on the café, see page 97.)

• *Go down the stairs, and as you leave the museum, don't miss the room opposite the ticket desk (between the WC and the exit door)...*

Former Orphanage and Regents' Chamber

The first small room tells of the former orphanage located here. Originally a cloister, it became an orphanage in 1570 and took in kids until the 1960s.

Finally, you enter a stately Regents' Room (for the orphanage's board of directors), where you'll see grand, ego-elevating paintings honoring big shots. Many of the Dutch Masters' paintings you'll see in the Netherlands' museums were commissioned to decorate rooms like this.

SLEEPING

Greeting a new day by descending steep stairs and stepping into a leafy canalside scene—graceful bridges, historic gables, and bikes clattering on cobbles—is a fun part of experiencing Amsterdam. But Amsterdam is a tough city for budget accommodations, and any room under €140 will have rough edges. Still, you can sleep well and safely in a great location for €100 per double.

I've grouped my hotel listings into three neighborhoods, each of which has its own character. Staying in **Central Amsterdam** is ideal for people who like shopping, tourist sights, and easy access to public transportation (including Central Station). On the downside, the area has traffic noise, concrete, and urban grittiness, and the hotels can lack character.

West Amsterdam (which includes the Jordaan) has Old World ambience, with quiet canals, old gabled buildings, and candlelit restaurants. It's also just minutes on foot to Dam Square. Many of my hotels are charming, friendly, gabled mansions. The downside here is that you'll pay more.

Southwest Amsterdam has two main areas for accommodations: near Leidseplein (more central) and near Vondelpark (farther away). The streets near the bustling Leidseplein have restaurants, tourist buzz, nightlife, canalside charm, B&B coziness, and walkable (or easy tram) access to the center of town. Farther afield is the quieter semi-suburban neighborhood around Vondelpark and Museumplein, close to the Rijks and Van Gogh museums. You'll find good hotel values and ready access to Vondelpark and the art museums, but you're a half-hour walk (or 10-minute tram ride) to Dam Square.

Note that some national holidays merit your making reservations far in advance (see "Major Holidays and Weekends" on page 4). Amsterdam is jammed during tulip season (late

Sleep Code

(€1 = about $1.40, country code: 31, area code: 020)
S = Single, **D** = Double/Twin, **T** = Triple, **Q** = Quad, **b** = bathroom, **s** = shower only. Nearly everyone speaks English in the Netherlands. Credit cards are accepted, and prices include breakfast and tax unless otherwise noted.

To help you easily sort through these listings, I've divided the rooms into three categories, based on the price for a standard double room with bath:

$$$ **Higher Priced**—Most rooms €140 or more.
$$ **Moderately Priced**—Most rooms between €80–140.
$ **Lower Priced**—Most rooms €80 or less.

March–mid-May), conventions, festivals, and on summer weekends. During peak season, some hoteliers will not take weekend bookings for people staying fewer than two or three nights.

Around just about every corner in downtown Amsterdam, you'll see construction: cranes for big transportation projects and small crews of bricklayers repairing the wobbly, cobbled streets that line the canals. Canalside rooms can come with great views—and early-morning construction-crew noise. If you're a light sleeper, ask the hotelier for a quiet room in the back. Smoking is illegal in hotel rooms throughout the Netherlands.

Parking in Amsterdam is even worse than driving. You'll pay €32 a day to park safely in a garage—and then have to hike to your hotel.

If you'd rather trade big-city action for small-town coziness, consider sleeping in Haarlem, 15 minutes away by train (see page 201).

IN WEST AMSTERDAM

Stately Canalside Hotels

These hotels, a half-mile apart, both face historic canals. They come with fine lobbies (some more ornate than others) and rooms that can feel like they're from another century. This area oozes elegance and class, and it is fairly quiet at night.

$$$ **The Toren** is a chandeliered, historic mansion with a pleasant, canalside setting and a peaceful garden out back for guests. Run by Eric and Petra Toren, this recently renovated, super-romantic hotel is classy yet friendly, with 38 rooms in a great location on a quiet street two blocks northeast of the Anne Frank House. The capable staff is a great source of local advice. The gilt-

frame, velvet-curtained rooms are an opulent splurge (tiny Sb-€115, Db-€200, deluxe Db-€250, third person-€40, prices bump way up during conferences and decrease in winter, rates do not include 5 percent tax, breakfast buffet-€12, air-con, elevator, Internet access and Wi-Fi, Keizersgracht 164, tel. 020/622-6352, fax 020/626-9705, www.thetoren.nl, info@thetoren.nl). To get the best prices, check their website for their "daily rate," and in the "remarks" field, ask for the 10 percent Rick Steves cash discount.

$$$ **Hotel Ambassade,** lacing together 59 rooms in 10 adjacent houses, is elegant and fresh, sitting aristocratically on the Herengracht. The staff is top-notch, and the public areas (including a library and breakfast room) are palatial, with antique furnishings and modern art (Sb-€195, Db-€195–235, spacious "deluxe" Db with canal view-€250–275, Db suite-€275–375, Tb-€235–275, extra bed-€40, see website for specials, rates do not include 5 percent tax, breakfast-€16—and actually worth it, air-con, elevator, Internet access and Wi-Fi, Herengracht 341, for location see map on page 176, tel. 020/555-0222, www.ambassade-hotel.nl, info @ambassade-hotel.nl, Roos).

Simpler Canalside Hotels

$$ **Hotel Brouwer** is a woody and homey old-time place. It's situated tranquilly yet centrally on the Singel canal and rents eight rooms with old furniture and soulful throw rugs (Sb-€60, Db-€95, Tb-€120, cash only, small elevator, Internet access, located between Central Station and Dam Square, near Lijnbaanssteeg at Singel 83, tel. 020/624-6358, fax 020/520-6264, www.hotelbrouwer.nl, akita@hotelbrouwer.nl).

$$ **Hotel Hegra** is cozy, affordable, and inviting, with 11 rooms filling a 17th-century merchant's house overlooking the canal (S-€50, Ds-€70, Db-€105, Ts-€115, Tb-€145, breakfast-€5, Wi-Fi, just north of Wolvenstraat at Herengracht 269, tel. 020/623-7877, www.hotelhegra.nl, Robert).

$$ **Hotel Hoksbergen** is a welcoming, well-run place with a peaceful location where hands-on owners Tony and Bert rent 19 rooms (Db-€98, Tb-€143, 5 apartments-€165–198, fans, Wi-Fi, Singel 301, tel. 020/626-6043, www.hotelhoksbergen.com, info @hotelhoksbergen.nl).

$$ **Hotel Chic & Basic Amsterdam** has a boutique-hotel feel, even though it's part of a Spanish chain. With its mod utilitarian design and younger clientele, it provides a break from all the lace curtains. Located near Central Station, it offers 25 minimalist, bathed-in-white rooms (you can change the color based on your mood). Rooms with canal views are pricier and breezier (Sb-€95–130, Db-€120–155, €20 more on holiday weekends, always free coffee, fans on request, tangled floor plan connecting

Hotels and Restaurants in West Amsterdam

AMSTERDAM SLEEPING

T TRAM #13, 14 & 17 STOP

❶ The Toren	⓮ Restaurant de Luwte
❷ Hotel Brouwer	⓯ De Bolhoed
❸ Hotel Hegra	⓰ Café Restaurant de Reiger
❹ Hotel Hoksbergen	⓱ Café 't Smalle
❺ Hotel Chic & Basic Amsterdam	⓲ Restaurant Vliegende Schotel
❻ Hotel Van Onna	⓳ Top Thai
❼ Boogaard's B&B	⓴ Toscana Italian Restaurant
❽ Herengracht 21 B&B	㉑ To Bistro 't Stuivertje
❾ Truelove Antiek & Guesthouse	㉒ Ristorante Toscanini
❿ Frederic Rent-a-Bike Guestrooms	㉓ Café 't Papeneiland
⓫ Hotel Pax & Sara's Pancake House	㉔ Stubbe's Haring (Fish Stand)
⓬ Hotel Aspen	㉕ Albert Heijn Grocery
⓭ To The Shelter Jordan	㉖ Paradox Coffeeshop
	㉗ The Grey Area Coffeeshop
	㉘ Siberië Coffeeshop
	㉙ Launderette

three canalside buildings, Internet access and Wi-Fi, Herengracht 13, tel. 020/522-2345, fax 020/522-2389, www.chicandbasic.com, amsterdam@chicandbasic.com, manager Bernardo Campo).

In the Jordaan Neighborhood

The quiet, flower-filled Jordaan neighborhood feels like the Red Light District's complete opposite. While it's not central for tram lines and other connections, it's got plenty of restaurants nearby. (For more on the Jordaan, see my self-guided walk on page 102.)

$$ Hotel Van Onna, very European and professional-feeling, has 41 simple, industrial-strength rooms. The price is right, and the leafy location makes you want to crack out your easel. Loek van Onna, who has slept in the building all his life, runs the hotel. The popular top-floor attic rooms are cozy hideaways (Sb-€45, Db-€90, Tb-€135, cash only, cot-like beds seem sufficient, in the Jordaan at Bloemgracht 104, tel. 020/626-5801, www.hotelvanonna.nl, info @hotelvanonna.nl, Leon).

Private-Room Rentals

B&Bs offer a chance to feel like a local during your visit. The first two listings here are perfectly located—a short walk from Central Station, but in a residential and peaceful neighborhood. The next two listings are services that manage and rent many apartments and rooms in West Amsterdam.

$$ Boogaard's B&B is a delightful pad on a cozy lane right out of Mister Rogers' neighborhood. The B&B, which has four comfortable rooms and an inviting public living room, is run by Peter, an American expat opera singer. Peter, who clearly enjoys hosting Americans in his home, serves his fresh-baked goodies at breakfast and offers one of the best values in town (Db-€100, 2-night minimum; furnished family apartment with kitchen-€220 for 4 people, 3-night minimum; air-con, DVD library, Wi-Fi, loaner cell phones and laptops, Langestraat 34, tel. 064/358-6835, www.boogaardsbnb.com, info@boogaardsbnb.com).

$$ Herengracht 21 B&B is a tiny, intimate two-room place run by Loes Olden (Db-€125, near Central Station, Herengracht 21, tel. 020/625-6305, mobile 06-2812-0962, www.herengracht21 .nl, loes@herengracht21.nl).

$$ At Truelove Antiek & Guesthouse, a room-rental service, you'll feel like you're staying at your Dutch friends' house while they're out of town. Sean, Paul, and Nellson—whose tiny antique store on Prinsenstraat doubles as the reception desk for their rental service—have 15 rooms and apartments in houses sprinkled throughout the northern end of the Jordaan neighborhood. The apartments are stylish and come with kitchens and pull-out beds (Db-€80–90, Db apartment-€100, Qb apartments-€150, prices soft in winter and midweek, 2-night minimum on weekends, pick up keys in store at Prinsenstraat 4 or—if arriving after 17:00—call ahead and they'll meet you at Central Station with keys and a map, store tel. 020/320-2500, mobile 06-2480-5672, fax 084-711-4950, www.truelove.be, trueloveantiek@zonnet.nl).

$ Frederic Rent-a-Bike Guestrooms, with a bike-rental shop as the reception, is a collection of private rooms on a gorgeous canal just outside the Jordaan, a five-minute walk from Central Station. Frederic has amassed about 100 beds, ranging from dumpy €70 doubles to spacious and elegant apartments (from €46 per person). Some places are ideal for families and groups of up to six. He also rents houseboat apartments. All are displayed on his website (phone bookings preferred, book with credit card but pay with cash, 2-night minimum, no breakfast, Brouwersgracht 78, tel. 020/624-5509, www.frederic.nl, Sebastian and Frederic). His excellent bike shop is open daily 9:00–17:30 (€10/24 hrs).

IN SOUTHWEST AMSTERDAM

Charming B&Bs near Leidseplein

The area around Amsterdam's rip-roaring nightlife center (Leidseplein) is colorful, comfortable, and convenient. These canalside mom-and-pop places are within a five-minute walk of rowdy Leidseplein, but are in generally quiet and typically Dutch settings.

$$ Hotel de Leydsche Hof is a hidden gem located on a canal. Its two large rooms are a symphony in white, overlooking a tree-filled backyard. Frits and Loes give their big, elegant, old building a stylish air (Db-€120, includes breakfast, cash only, 2-night minimum, Internet access and Wi-Fi, Leidsegracht 14, tel. 020/638-2327, mobile 06-5125-8588, www.freewebs.com /leydschehof, loespiller@planet.nl).

$$ Wildervanck B&B, run by Helene and Sjoerd Wildervanck, offers two rooms in an elegant, 17th-century canal house (big Db on first floor-€130, Db with twin beds on ground floor-€110, extra bed-€30, breakfast in their pleasant dining room, 2-night minimum, Wi-Fi, family has three little girls, Keizersgracht 498, on Keizersgracht canal just west of Leidsestraat, tel. 020/623-3846, fax 020/421-6575, www.wildervanck.com, info@wildervanck.com). As it's in a busy area, you may get some bar noise at night.

$$ Hotel Keizershof is wonderfully Dutch, with six bright, airy rooms in a 17th-century canal house with a lush garden and a fine living room. A very steep spiral staircase leads to rooms named after old-time Hollywood stars. The enthusiastic hospitality of Mrs. de Vries and her daughter, Hanneke, give this place a friendly, almost small-town charm (S-€70, D-€75–90, Ds-€100, Db-€115,

AMSTERDAM SLEEPING

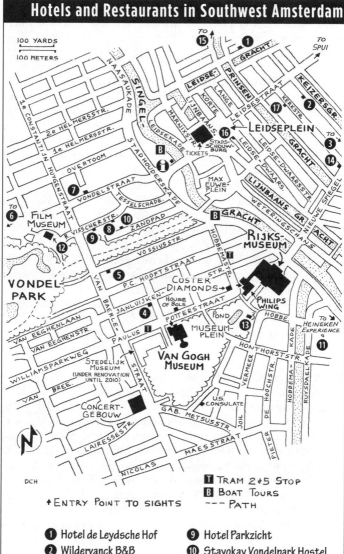

Hotels and Restaurants in Southwest Amsterdam

100 YARDS
100 METERS

▲ ENTRY POINT TO SIGHTS
T TRAM 2 & 5 STOP
B BOAT TOURS
--- PATH

DCH

1 Hotel de Leydsche Hof
2 Wildervanck B&B
3 To Hotel Keizershof
4 Hotel Fita
5 Hotel Piet Hein
6 To Hotel Filosoof & Tulips B&B
7 Hotel Alexander
8 Hotel Hestia

9 Hotel Parkzicht
10 Stayokay Vondelpark Hostel
11 To Restaurant Bazar
12 Café Vertigo
13 Cobra Café
14 Le Soleil
15 To La Tertulia Coffeeshop
16 The Bulldog Coffeeshop
17 Launderette

AMSTERDAM SLEEPING

2-night minimum, reserve with credit card but pay with cash; tram
#16, #24, or #25 from Central Station, Keizersgracht 618, where
Keizers canal crosses Nieuwe Spiegelstraat; tel. 020/622-2855,
www.hotelkeizershof.nl, info@hotelkeizershof.nl).

Near Vondelpark and Museumplein

These options cluster around Vondelpark in a safe neighborhood.
Though they don't have a hint of Old Dutch or romantic canalside
flavor, they're reasonable values and only a short walk from the
action. Many are in a pleasant nook between rollicking Leidseplein
and the park, and most are a 5- to 15-minute walk to the Rijks
and Van Gogh museums. They are easily connected with Central
Station by trams #1, #2, and #5.

$$$ Hotel Fita has 16 bright, fresh rooms located 100 yards
from the Van Gogh Museum (Sb-€100, two small ground-floor
Db-€135, Db-€145–165, Tb-€195, discounts for multiple nights—
ask when you book, free laundry service, free Wi-Fi and Internet
access in lobby, elevator, Jan Luijkenstraat 37, tel. 020/679-0976,
fax 020/664-3969, www.fita.nl, info@fita.nl, joking and colorful
owner Hans).

$$$ Hotel Piet Hein offers 81 comfortable renovated rooms
with a swanky nautical atmosphere (Sb-€105, Db-€165, extra bed-
€30, specials on website, quiet garden, air-con, Wi-Fi, Vossiusstraat
52–53, tel. 020/662-7205, www.hotelpiethein.nl, info@hotelpiet
hein.nl).

$$$ Hotel Filosoof greets you with Aristotle and Plato in the
foyer and classical music in its generous lobby. Its 38 rooms are deco-
rated with themes; the Egyptian room has a frieze of hieroglyphics.
Philosophers' sayings hang on the walls, and thoughtful travelers
wander down the halls or sit in the garden, rooted in deep discus-
sion. The rooms are small, but the hotel is endearing (Db-€130
weeknights, €150 Fri–Sat; elevator, 3-min walk from tram line #1,
get off at Jan Pieter Heijestraat, Anna van Den Vondelstraat 6, tel.
020/683-3013, fax 020/685-3750, www.hotelfilosoof.nl, reservations
@hotelfilosoof.nl).

$$ Hotel Alexander is a modern, newly renovated, 32-room
hotel on a quiet street. Some of the rooms overlook the garden
patio out back (Db-€120, includes breakfast, prices soft in winter,
elevator, tel. 020/589-4020, fax 020/589-4025, Vondelstratt 44-46,
www.hotelalexander.nl, info@hotelalexander.nl).

$$ Hotel Hestia, on a safe and sane street, is efficient and
family-run, with 18 clean, airy, and generally spacious rooms
(Sb-€80–90, very small Db-€98–115, standard Db-€125–145,
Tb-€155–173, Qb-€185–203, Quint/b-€215–233, elevator, Roemer
Visscherstraat 7, tel. 020/618-0801, fax 020/685-1382, www
.hotel-hestia.nl, info@hotel-hestia.nl).

$$ Hotel Parkzicht, an old-fashioned place with extremely steep stairs, rents 13 big, plain rooms on a street bordering Vondelpark (S-€39, Sb-€49, Db-€78–94, Tb-€110–120, Qb-€120–130, closed Nov–March, some noise from neighboring youth hostel, Roemer Visscherstraat 33, tel. 020/618-1954, fax 020/618-0897, www.parkzicht.nl, hotel@parkzicht.nl).

$$ Tulips B&B, with a bunch of cozy rooms—some on a canal—is run by a friendly Englishwoman, Karen, and her Dutch husband, Paul. Rooms are clean, white, and bright, with red carpeting, plants, and flowers (D-€60–80, Db-€105, suite-€140, family deals, includes milk-and-cereal breakfast, cash only, prefer 3-night stays on weekends, no shoes, south end of Vondelpark at Sloterkade 65, directions sent when you book, tel. 020/679-2753, fax 020/408-3028, www.bedandbreakfastamsterdam.net).

IN CENTRAL AMSTERDAM

Basic Hotels in the City Center

You won't get a warm welcome at either of the two following hotels. But if you're looking for a no-nonsense room that's convenient to plenty of tram lines, these hotels fit the bill.

$$ Hotel Résidence Le Coin offers 42 larger-than-average rooms complete with small kitchenettes. Located near the Mint Tower, this hotel is a two-minute walk to the Flower Market and a five-minute walk to Rembrandtplein. You won't get fancy extras here—just good, solid rooms in an all-business hotel (Sb-€112, small Db-€132, bigger Db-€147, family room-€220, extra bed-€35, breakfast-€10, by the University at Nieuwe Doelenstraat 5, tel. 020/524-6800, fax 020/524-6801, www.lecoin.nl, hotel@lecoin.nl).

$$ Ibis Amsterdam Hotel, located next door to the Central Station, is a modern, efficient, 187-room place. It offers a central location, comfort, and good value, without a hint of charm (Db-€100–160, breakfast-€14, highest prices Fri–Sat, check website for deals, book long in advance, air-con; facing the Central Station, go left towards the multistory bicycle garage to Stationsplein 49; tel. 020/638-9999, fax 020/620-0156, www.ibishotel.com, h1556@accor.com). When business is slow, they often rent rooms to same-day drop-ins for around €100.

Budget Hotels Between Dam Square and the Anne Frank House: Inexpensive, well-worn hotels line the convenient but noisy main drag, Raadhuisstraat. Expect a long, steep, and depressing stairway, with noisy rooms in the front and quieter rooms in the back. For locations, see the map on page 170.

$ Hotel Pax has 11 large, plain, but airy rooms with Ikea furniture—a lot like a European dorm room (S-€35–45, D-€65, Db-€80, T-€80, Tb-€95, Q-€100, no breakfast, prices drop

Hotels and Restaurants in Central Amsterdam

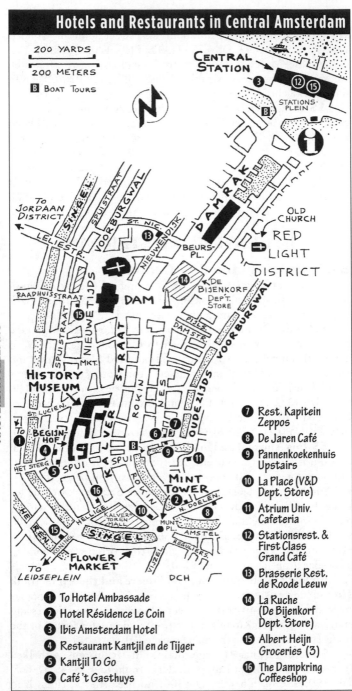

AMSTERDAM SLEEPING

200 YARDS

200 METERS

B BOAT TOURS

CENTRAL STATION

STATIONS-PLEIN

TO JORDAAN DISTRICT

OLD CHURCH

RED LIGHT DISTRICT

ST. NIC.

BEURS-PL.

De Bijenkorf Dept. Store

RAADHUISSTRAAT

DAM

DAMSTR.

HISTORY MUSEUM

ST. LUCIEN.

BEGIN-HOF

HET STEEG

SPUI

MINT TOWER

N. DOELEN.

KALVER-TOREN MALL

MUNT-PL.

AMSTEL

FLOWER MARKET

TO LEIDSEPLEIN

DCH

7 Rest. Kapitein Zeppos

8 De Jaren Café

9 Pannenkoekenhuis Upstairs

10 La Place (V&D Dept. Store)

11 Atrium Univ. Cafeteria

12 Stationsrest. & First Class Grand Café

13 Brasserie Rest. de Roode Leeuw

14 La Ruche (De Bijenkorf Dept. Store)

15 Albert Heijn Groceries (3)

16 The Dampkring Coffeeshop

1 To Hotel Ambassade

2 Hotel Résidence Le Coin

3 Ibis Amsterdam Hotel

4 Restaurant Kantjil en de Tijger

5 Kantjil To Go

6 Café 't Gasthuys

dramatically in winter, six rooms share two showers and two toilets, Raadhuisstraat 37, tel. 020/624-9735, run by go-getters Philip and Pieter).

$ Hotel Aspen, a few doors away and a good value for a budget hotel, has eight tidy, stark, and well-maintained rooms (S-€40, tiny D-€55–60, Db-€75–80, Tb-€95, Qb-€110, no breakfast, Wi-Fi, Raadhuisstraat 31, tel. 020/626-6714, fax 020/620-0866, www.hotelaspen.nl, info@hotelaspen.nl, run by Rudy and Esam).

HOSTELS

Amsterdam has a world of good, cheap hostels located throughout the city. Most are designed for the party crowd, but here are a few quieter options. They all offer dorm beds; Stayokay Vondelpark also has some basic doubles.

In the Jordaan: **$ The Shelter Jordan** is a scruffy, friendly, Christian-run, 100-bed place in a great neighborhood. While most of Amsterdam's hostels are pretty wild, this place is drug-free and alcohol-free, with boys on one floor and girls on another. These are Amsterdam's best budget beds, in 4- to 20-bed dorms (€24/ bed with sheets and breakfast, €3 extra Fri–Sat, maximum age 35, Internet access in lobby; near Anne Frank House at Bloemstraat 179; tel. 020/624-4717, www.shelter.nl, jordan@shelter.nl). The Shelter serves hot meals, runs a snack bar in its big, relaxing lounge, offers lockers, and leads nightly Bible studies.

In the Red Light District: **$ The Shelter City** is Shelter Jordan's sister—similar, but definitely not preaching to the choir. While its 180 beds are buried in the heart of the red lights, it feels very well-run and perfectly safe (€24/bed with sheets and breakfast in 4- to 20-bed dorms, maximum age 35, curfew, Barndesteeg 21, see map on page 91, tel. 020/625-3230, fax 020/623-2282, www.shelter.nl, city@shelter.nl).

In Vondelpark: **$ Stayokay Vondelpark (IYHF)**, with 500 beds in 130 rooms, is one of Amsterdam's top hostels (€23–30/bed in 4- to 20-bed dorms, D-€65–90, higher prices are for March–Oct, members save €2.50, family rooms, lots of school groups, €2 lockers, right on Vondelpark at Zandpad 5, tel. 020/589-8996, fax 020/589-8955, www.stayokay.com). Though Stayokay Vondelpark and Stayokay Stadsdoelen (listed next) are generally booked long in advance, occasionally a few beds open up each day at 11:00.

Near Waterlooplein: **$ Stayokay Stadsdoelen (IYHF)**, smaller and simpler than its Vondelpark sister (listed above), has only large dorms and no private bathrooms, but is free of large school groups (€23–30/bed with sheets and breakfast in 10-bed dorms, members save €2.50, lockers, Kloveniersburgwal 97, see map on page 61, tel. 020/624-6832, fax 020/639-1035, www.stayokay.com).

Farthest East: **$ Stayokay Zeeburg Hostel (IYHF)** is a new 500-bed hostel with all the modern services. While it's pretty far from the center, by tram or bike you're just 15 minutes from Damrak street (€20–30/bed in 6- to 14-bed dorms, Internet access and Wi-Fi, lockers, games, restaurant, bike rental, tram #14 to Timorplein 21, tel. 020/551-3190, www.stayokay.com, zeeburg @stayokay.com).

EATING

Traditional Dutch food is basic and hearty, with lots of bread, cheese, soup, and fish. Lunch and dinner are served at American times (roughly 12:00–14:00 and 18:00–21:00).

Dutch treats include cheese, pancakes *(pannenkoeken),* and "syrup waffles" *(stroopwafels).* Popular drinks are light, pilsner-type beer and gin *(jenever).*

Experiences you owe your tongue in Holland: Try a pickled herring at an outdoor herring stand, linger over coffee in a "brown café," sip an old *jenever* with a new friend, and consume an Indonesian feast—a *rijsttafel.*

Budget Tips: To dine cheaply yet memorably alongside the big spenders, grab a meal to go, then find a bench on a lively neighborhood square or along a canal. Sandwiches *(broodjes)* of delicious cheese on fresh bread are cheap at snack bars, delis, and *broodjes* restaurants. Ethnic restaurants serve cheap, splittable carryout meals. Ethnic fast-food stands abound, offering a variety of meats wrapped in pita bread. Easy to buy at grocery stores, yogurt in the Netherlands (and throughout northern Europe) is delicious and often drinkable right out of its plastic container.

Types of Eateries

Any place labeled "restaurant" will serve full, sit-down meals for lunch or dinner. But there are other places to fill the tank.

An *eetcafé* is a simple restaurant serving basic soups, salads, sandwiches, as well as traditional meat-and-potatoes meals in a generally comfortable but no-nonsense setting.

A *salon de thé* serves tea and coffee, but also croissants, pastries, and sandwiches for a light brunch, lunch, or afternoon snack.

Cafés are all-purpose establishments, serving light meals at mealtimes and coffee, drinks, and snacks the rest of the day and night. *Bruin* cafés ("brown cafés") are named for their nicotine-stained walls—until smoking was banned indoors in 2008, they were filled with tobacco smoke. These places are usually a little more bar-like, with dimmer lighting and wood paneling.

A *proeflokaal* is a bar (with snacks) for tasting wine, spirits, or beer. "Coffeeshop" is the code word for an establishment where marijuana is sold and consumed, though most offer drinks and munchies, too (for details, see Smoking chapter on page 190).

There's no shortage of stand-up, take-out places serving fast food, sandwiches, and all kinds of quick ethnic fare.

No matter what type of establishment you choose, expect it to be *gezellig*—a much-prized Dutch virtue, meaning an atmosphere of relaxed coziness.

Etiquette and Tipping

The Dutch are easygoing. Pay as you go or pay after? Usually it's your choice. Wait for table service or order at the bar? Whatever you do, you won't be scolded for your faux pas, as you might be in France or Italy. Dutch establishments are mellow. Still, here are some guidelines:

• Tipping is not necessary in restaurants (15 percent service is usually already included in the menu price), but a tip of about 5–10 percent is a nice reward for good service. In bars, rounding up to the next euro ("keep the change") is appropriate if you get table service, rather than order at the bar.

• When ordering drinks in a café or bar, you can just pay as you go (especially if the bar is crowded), or wait until the end to settle up, as many locals do. If you get table service, take the cue from your waiter.

• Cafés with outdoor tables generally do not charge more if you sit outside (unlike in France or Italy).

• Waiters constantly say, *"Alstublieft"* (AHL-stoo-bleeft). It's a catch-all polite word meaning, "please," "here's your order," "enjoy," and "you're welcome." You can respond with a thank you by saying, "Dank u wel" (dahnk oo vehl).

Typical Meals

Breakfast: Breakfasts are big by continental standards—bread, meat, cheese, and maybe an egg or omelet. Hotels generally put out a buffet spread, including juice and cereal.

Lunch: Simple sandwiches are called *broodjes* (most commonly made with cheese and/or ham). An open-face sandwich of ham and cheese topped with two fried eggs is an *uitsmijter* (OUTS-mi-ter). Soup is popular for lunch.

Snacks and Take-Out Food: Small stands sell french fries *(frites)* with mayonnaise; pickled herring; falafels (fried chickpea balls in pita bread); *shoarmas* (lamb tucked in pita bread); and *döner kebabs* (Turkish version of a *shoarma*). Delis have deep-fried croquettes *(kroketten).*

Dinner: It's the biggest meal of the day, consisting of meat or seafood with boiled potatoes, cooked vegetables, and a salad. Hearty stews are served in winter. These days, many people eat more vegetarian fare.

Sweets: Try *poffertjes* (small, sugared doughnuts without holes), *pannenkoeken* (pancakes with fruit and cream), *stroopwafels* (syrup waffles), and *appelgebak* (apple pie).

Local Specialties

Cheeses: Edam (covered with red wax) or Gouda (HHHOW-dah). Gouda can be young or old—*jong* is mellow, and *oude* is salty, crumbly, and strong, sometimes seasoned with cumin or cloves.

French Fries: Commonly served with mayonnaise (ketchup and curry sauce are often available) on a paper tray or in a newspaper cone. Flemish *(Vlaamse) frites* are made from whole potatoes, not pulp.

Haring **(herring):** Pickled herring, often served with onions or pickles, sometimes with sour cream, on a thick, soft, white bun.

Hutspot: Hearty meat stew with mashed potatoes, onions, and carrots, especially popular on winter days.

Kroketten **(croquettes):** Log-shaped rolls of meats and vegetables (kind of like corn dogs) breaded and deep-fried, such as *bitter-ballen* (meatballs), *frikandelen* (sausage), or *vlammetjes* (spring rolls).

Pannenkoeken: Either sweet dessert pancakes or crêpe-like, savory dinner pancakes.

Ethnic Foods

If you're not in the mood for meat and potatoes, sample some of Amsterdam's abundant ethnic offerings.

Indonesian *(Indisch):* The tastiest "Dutch" food is Indonesian, from the former colony. Find any Indisch restaurant and experience a *rijsttafel* (literally, "rice table"). With as many as 30 spicy dishes (ranging from small sides to entrée-sized plates) and a big bowl of rice (or noodles), a *rijsttafel* can be split and still fill two hungry tourists. Vegetarian versions are

Birgit Jons' Diary

9:00 Had coffee with breakfast of bread, cheese, ham, and a boiled egg.

11:00 Stopped at a *salon de thé* for an *uitsmijter* sandwich.

12:30 Cold out, so warmed up with *erwtensoep* at an *eetcafé*. Also had more bread, cheese, and ham, and a small salad.

15:00 Dirk bought me a *shoarma* with fries and mayonnaise. Topped it off at a stand selling—mmm!—*poffertjes*.

16:30 Work's done! Sat in the sun along a canal outside a *proeflokaal* and sipped...was it fruit brandy? Got courage to swallow pickled herring from kiosk—mistake!

17:30 Cappuccino and *appelgebak*.

19:00 Finally, dinner! I've been starving myself all day. First, fresh Zeeland oysters. Next, the main course: meat, potatoes, and white asparagus, all heaped on one plate. For dessert, *pannenkoeken* topped with strawberries and whipped cream, with coffee and a weird liqueur.

21:00 Party! We met at De Prins for a *pils* and an *oude jenever*.

23:00 Need grease—inhaled two *frikandellen* at late-night deli. Fortified for tomorrow—another busy day!

yours for the asking.

Nasi rames is a cheaper, smaller version of a *rijsttafel*. Another popular dish is *bami goreng*—stir-fried noodles served with meat, vegetables, and *rijsttafel* items. *Nasi goreng* is like *bami*, but comes with fried rice. *Saté* is skewered meat, and *gado-gado* consists of steamed vegetables and hard-boiled eggs with peanut sauce. Among the most common sauces are peanut, red chili *(sambal)*, and dark soy.

Middle Eastern: Try a *shoarma* (roasted lamb with garlic in pita bread, served with bowls of different sauces), falafel, gyros, or a *döner kebab*.

Surinamese *(Surinaamse)*: Surinamese cuisine is a mix of Caribbean and Indonesian influences, featuring *roti* (spiced chicken wrapped in a tortilla) and rice (white or fried) served with meats in sauces (curry and spices). Why Surinamese food in Amsterdam? In 1667, Holland traded New York City ("New

Amsterdam") to Britain in exchange for the small country of Suriname (which borders Guyana on the northeast coast of South America). For the next three centuries, Suriname (renamed Dutch Guyana) was a Dutch colony, which is why it has indigenous Indians, Creoles, and Indonesian immigrants who all speak Dutch. When Suriname gained independence in 1975, 100,000 Surinamese immigrated to Amsterdam, sparking a rash of Surinamese fast-food outlets.

Drinks

Beer: Order "a beer," and you'll get a *pils,* a light lager/pilsner-type beer in a 10-ounce glass with a thick head leveled off with a stick. (Typical brands are Heineken, Grolsch, Oranjeboom, and Amstel.) A common tap beer is Palm Speciale, an amber ale served in a stemmed, wide-mouth glass. Belgian beers are popular, always available in bottles and sometimes on tap (for more information, see page 367). *Witte* (white) beer is light-colored and summery, sometimes served with a lemon slice (it's like American Hefeweizen, but yeastier).

Jenever: Try this Dutch gin made from juniper berries. *Jong* (young) is sharper; *oude* (old) is mellow. Served chilled, *jenever* (yah-NAY-ver) is meant to be chugged with a *pils* chaser (this combination is called a *kopstoot*—head-butt). While cheese gets harder and sharper with age, *jenever* grows smooth and soft, so old *jenever* is best.

Liqueur: You'll find a variety of local fruit brandies and cognacs.

Wine: Dutch people drink a lot of fine wine, but it's almost all imported.

Coffee: The Dutch love their coffee, enjoying many of the same drinks (espresso, cappuccino) served in American or Italian coffee shops. Coffee usually comes with a small spice cookie. A *koffie verkeerd* (fer-KEERT, "coffee wrong") is an espresso with a lot of steamed milk.

Soft Drinks: You'll find the full array.

Orange Juice: Many cafés/bars have a juicer for making fresh-squeezed orange juice.

Water: The Dutch (unlike many Europeans) drink tap water with meals, but many prefer mineral water, still or sparkling (Spa brand is popular).

RESTAURANTS

Of Amsterdam's thousand-plus restaurants, no one knows which are best. I'd pick an area and wander. The rowdy food ghetto thrives around Leidseplein; wander along Leidsedwarsstraat, Restaurant Row. The area around Spui canal and that end of Spuistraat is also trendy and not as noisy. For fewer crowds and more charm, find something in the Jordaan district. Most hoteliers keep a reliable eating list for their neighborhood and know which places keep their travelers happy.

Here are some handy places to consider.

IN CENTRAL AMSTERDAM

For the locations of these eateries, see the "Hotels and Restaurants in Central Amsterdam" map on page 176.

On and near Spui

Restaurant Kantjil en de Tijger is a thriving place with a plain and noisy ambience, full of happy eaters who know a good value. The food is purely Indonesian; the waiters are happy to explain your many enticing options. Their three *rijsttafels* (traditional "rice tables" with about a dozen small courses) range from €20–30 per person. While they are designed for two people, three people can make a meal by getting a *rijsttafel* for two and ordering a soup or light dish for the third person. A good budget alternative to the full-blown *rijsttafel* is a *nasi rames*—10 small dishes on one big plate for €13 (daily 16:30–23:00, early-bird €9.50 dinner daily 16:30–18:45, reservations smart, mostly indoor with a little outdoor seating, Spuistraat 291, tel. 020/620-0994).

Kantjil to Go, run by Restaurant Kantjil, is a tiny take-out bar serving up inexpensive but delicious Indonesian fare (€5 for 300 grams, €6.50 for 600 grams, vegetarian specials, daily 12:00–21:00, storefront at Nieuwezijds Voorburgwal 342, around the corner from the sit-down restaurant listed above, tel. 020/620-3074). Split a large box (they'll happily give you an empty extra box for your dining pleasure), grab a bench on the charming Spui Square around the corner, and you've got perhaps the cheapest hot meal in town.

Near the Mint Tower

Café 't Gasthuys, one of Amsterdam's many brown cafés (so called for their smoke-stained walls), has a busy dumbwaiter cranking out light lunches, sandwiches, and reasonably priced dinners. It offers a long bar, a fine secluded back room, peaceful canalside seating, and sometimes slow service (€5–9 lunch plates, €10–14 dinner plates, daily 12:00–16:30 & 17:30–22:00; Grimburgwal 7—from the Rondvaart Kooij boat dock, head down Langebrugsteeg, and it's one block down on the left; tel. 020/624-8230).

Restaurant Kapitein Zeppos, named for an old-time TV star, serves International-Dutch food and salads amid dressy yet unpretentious 1940s ambience. They offer both a restaurant (upstairs, with waiters in nice suits) and a charming, spacious pub (downstairs, good Belgian beers on tap at the big woody bar). The light lunch specials—soups and sandwiches—cost €5–10. Dinners go for about €17 in the pub and for €20–30 in the classy restaurant (food served daily 11:00–15:30 & 17:30–22:30, just off Grimburgwal at Gebed Zonder End 5—a small pedestrian alleyway, tel. 020/624-2057).

De Jaren Café ("The Years Café") is a chic yet inviting place—clearly a favorite with locals. Upstairs is the minimalist restaurant with a top-notch salad bar and a canal-view deck (serving €14–18 dinners after 17:30, including fish, meat, and veggie dishes, and salad bar, or €11 for salad bar only). Downstairs is a modern Amsterdam café, great for light lunches (soups, salads, and sandwiches served all day and evening), or just coffee over a newspaper. On a sunny day, the café's canalside patio is a fine spot to nurse a drink; this is also a nice place to go just for a drink in the evening and enjoy the spacious Art Deco setting (daily 10:00–24:00, Nieuwe Doelenstraat 20–22, a long block up from Muntplein, tel. 020/625-5771).

Pannenkoekenhuis Upstairs is a tiny and characteristic perch up some extremely steep stairs, where Arno Jakobs cooks and serves delicious €7 pancakes to four tables throughout the afternoon (Fri 12:00–19:00, Sat 12:00–18:00, Sun 12:00–17:00, closed Mon–Thu, Grimburgwal 2, tel. 020/626-5603).

La Place, on the ground floor of the V&D department store, has an abundant, colorful array of fresh, appealing food served

cafeteria-style. A multi-story eatery that seats 300, it has a small outdoor terrace upstairs. Explore before you make your choice. This bustling spot has a lively market feel, with everything from made-on-the-spot beef stir-fry, to fresh juice, to veggie soups (€3 pizza and €4 sandwiches, Mon–Sat 10:00–20:00, Sun 12:00–20:00, at the end of Kalverstraat near Mint Tower, tel. 020/622-0171). For fast and healthy take-out food (sandwiches, yogurt, fruit cups, and more), try the bakery on the department store's ground floor. (They run another branch, which has the city's ultimate view terrace, on the top floor of the **Central Library**—Openbare Bibliotheek Amsterdam—near Central Station.)

Atrium University Cafeteria, a three-minute walk from Mint Tower, feeds travelers and students from Amsterdam University for great prices, but only on weekdays (€6 meals, Mon–Fri 11:00–15:00 & 17:00–19:30, closed Sat–Sun; from Spui, walk west down

Landebrug Steeg past canalside Café 't Gasthuys three blocks to Oudezijds Achterburgwal 237, go through arched doorway on the right; tel. 020/525-3999).

In Central Station

Stationsrestauratie is a surprisingly good, budget, self-service option inside Central Station on platform 2 (daily 8:00–20:00). This entire platform is lined with eateries, including the tall, venerable, 1920s-style **First Class Grand Café.** For picnics, there's a handy **Albert Heijn** supermarket at the end of the underpass beneath the tracks.

Between Central Station and Dam Square

Brasserie Restaurant de Roode Leeuw (*roode leeuw* means "red lion") offers a peaceful, calm respite from the crush of Damrak. During the day, the whole restaurant shares the same menu, but at night, it's split roughly in half, with finer service, cloth tablecloths, and higher prices in back, and a more casual setup (and better people-watching on Damrak street) up front. Either way, you'll get a menu filled with traditional Dutch food, good service, and the company of plenty of tourists. Call ahead to reserve a window seat (restaurant: €20 entrées, €35 three-course fixed-price meal with all the most Dutch choices; brasserie: €10–15 entrées; daily 12:00–22:00, Damrak 93–94, tel. 020/555-0666).

La Ruche, inside the De Bijenkorf department store on Dam Square, has a cafeteria-style lineup of inexpensive salads, soups, sandwiches, and pizzas. On the second floor, with views of busy Damrak, comfortable seating, and an upscale café vibe, this place feels miles above the chaotic streets below (€6–10 plates, daily generally 11:00–19:00, Dam 1, tel. 0900-0919—€0.20/min). De Bijenkorf also has a fancy bakery on the first floor.

Munching Cheap

Traditional fish stands sell €3 herring sandwiches and other salty treats, usually from easy-to-understand photo menus. **Stubbe's Haring,** where the Stubbe family has been selling herring for 100 years, is handy and well-estab-lished, a few blocks from Central Station (Tue–Fri 10:00–18:00, Sat 10:00–17:00, closed Sun–Mon, at the locks where Singel canal boat arrives at the train station, see map on page 170). Grab a sand-wich and have a picnic canalside.

Supermarkets: You'll see **Albert Heijn** grocery stores (daily 8:00–22:00) all over town.

Three helpful, central locations are: Dam Square (Nieuwezijds Voorburgwal 226), Mint Tower (Koningsplein 4), and Central Station (far end of passage under the tracks).

IN WEST AMSTERDAM

Near the Anne Frank House and in the Jordaan District

Nearly all of these places are within a few scenic blocks of the Anne Frank House, providing handy lunches and atmospheric dinners in Amsterdam's most characteristic neighborhood. For locations, see the map on page 170.

Restaurant de Luwte is romantic, located on a picturesque street overlooking a canal. It has lots of candles, a muted but fresh modern interior, spacious seating, a few cool outdoor canalside tables, and French Mediterranean cuisine (€19.50 entrées, €29.50 three-course fixed-price meal, big dinner salads for €17.50, daily 18:00–22:00, Leliegracht 26–28, tel. 020/625-8548, manager Marko Depender). Ask about their specials.

De Bolhoed has serious vegetarian and vegan food in a colorful setting that Buddha would dig, with a clientele that appears to dig Buddha (big splittable portions, €15 dinners, light lunches, daily 12:00–22:00, dinner starts at 17:00, Prinsengracht 60, tel. 020/626-1803).

Café Restaurant de Reiger must offer the best cooking of any *eetcafé* in the Jordaan. Famous for its fresh ingredients and delightful bistro ambience, it's part of the classic Jordaan scene. In addition to an English menu, ask for a translation of the €17.50–20 daily specials on the chalkboard. They're proud of their fresh fish and French-Dutch cuisine. The café, which is crowded late and on weekends, takes no reservations, but you're welcome to have a drink (€3 house wine and fun little bar munchies menu) at the bar while you wait (daily 18:00–24:00, veggie options, Nieuwe Leliestraat 34, tel. 020/624-7426).

Café 't Smalle is extremely charming, with three zones where you can enjoy a light lunch or a drink: canalside, inside around the bar, and up some steep stairs in a quaint little back room. The café is open daily until midnight, and simple meals (salads, soup, and fresh sandwiches) are served 11:00–17:30 (plenty of fine €2–3 Belgian beers on tap and interesting wines by the glass, at Egelantiersgracht 12 where it hits Prinsengracht, tel. 020/623-9617).

Restaurant Vliegende Schotel, which may have new ownership in 2010, is a folksy, unvarnished little Jordaan eatery with a cheap, fun menu featuring fish and vegetarian fare. Nothing trendy about this place—just locals who like healthful food and don't want to cook. The €8 *Vliegende Schotel* salad is a vegetarian extravaganza (€10–12 entrées, daily from 17:30, kitchen closes at 21:30, wine by the glass, order at the counter, Nieuwe Leliestraat 162, tel. 020/625-2041).

Top Thai, a block from Hotel Toren, offers top-quality meals for €20 (less for takeout) in their cozy, 10-table restaurant (daily 16:00–22:30, good veggie options, Herenstraat 22, tel. 020/623-4633).

Toscana Italian Restaurant is the Jordaan's favorite place for good, inexpensive Italian cuisine, including pizza, in a woody Dutch-beer-hall setting (€6–8 pizza and pastas, €15 main courses, daily 16:00–24:00, Haarlemmerstraat 130, tel. 020/622-0353).

Sara's Pancake House is a basic pancake diner where extremely hardworking Sara cranks out sweet and savory €8–10 flapjacks (open daily from early until late, breakfast served until noon, Raadhuisstraat 45, tel. 020/320-0662).

Bistro 't Stuivertje is a small, family-run neighborhood favorite tucked away in the Jordaan, serving French-Dutch cuisine in a cozy but unpretentious atmosphere (€15 main courses, dinner salads, Wed–Sun 17:30–22:00, closed Mon–Tue, Hazenstraat 58 near Elandsgracht, tel. 020/623-1349).

Ristorante Toscanini is an up-market Italian place that's always packed. It's so popular that the staff can be a bit arrogant, but the lively, spacious ambience and great Italian cuisine more than make up for that—if you can get a seat. Reservations are essentially required. Your best bet is to eat when they open at 18:00 (€14 first courses, €20 main courses, Mon–Sat 18:00–22:30, closed Sun, deep in the Jordaan at Lindengracht 75, tel. 020/623-2813).

Drinks Only: **Café 't Papeneiland** is a classic brown café with Delft tiles, an evocative old stove, and a stay-awhile perch overlooking a canal with welcoming benches. It's been the neighborhood hangout since the 17th century (drinks but no food, overlooking northwest end of Prinsengracht at #2, tel. 020/624-1989). It feels a little exclusive; patrons who come here to drink and chat aren't eager to see it overrun by tourists. The café's name means "Papists' Island," since this was once a refuge for Catholics; there used to be an escape tunnel here for priests on the run.

IN SOUTHWEST AMSTERDAM

Near Leidseplein

Stroll through the colorful cancan of eateries on Leidsedwarsstraat, Restaurant Row, just off Leidseplein, and choose your favorite. Nearby, the busy Leidsestraat offers plenty of starving-student options (between the Prinsengracht and the Herengracht) offering fast and fun food for around €5 a meal.

Beyond the Rijksmuseum

Restaurant Bazar offers one of the most memorable and fun budget eating experiences in town. Converted from a church, it has spacious seating and mod belly-dance music, and is filled with young locals enjoying good, cheap Middle Eastern and North African cuisine. Reservations are necessary if you plan to eat after 20:00 (fill up with the €8.50 daily plate, delicious €13 couscous, or €16 three-course meal of the day; daily 11:00–24:00, Albert Cuypstraat 182, tel. 020/675-0544, www.bazaramsterdam.nl). Restaurant Bazar marks the center of the thriving Albert Cuyp market, which is wrapped up by about 17:00, though the restaurant is open late.

In Vondelpark

Café Vertigo offers a fun selection of excellent soups, salads, and sandwiches. It's a surprisingly large complex of outdoor tables, an indoor pub, and an elegant, candlelit, back-room restaurant. The service can be slow, but if you grab an outdoor table, you can watch the world spin by (daily 10:00–24:00, beneath Film Museum, Vondelpark 3, tel. 020/612-3021).

IN SOUTHEAST AMSTERDAM

Near the Dutch Resistance Museum

For locations of the following eateries, see the map on page 61.

Restaurant Plancius, adjacent to the Dutch Resistance Museum, is a modern and handy spot for lunch. Its good indoor and outdoor seating make it popular with the museum staff and broadcasters from the nearby local TV studios (creative breakfasts, hearty fresh sandwiches, light €4–8 lunches and €16–19 dinners, daily 10:00–22:00, Sun until 21:00, Plantage Kerklaan 61a, tel. 020/330-9469).

Café Koosje, located halfway between the Dutch Resistance Museum and the Dutch Theater, is a corner lunchtime pub/bar ringed with outdoor seating. Inside, casual wooden tables and benches huddle under chandeliers, and the hip, young waitstaff serves beer and salads big enough for two (€5 sandwiches, €11 salads, Plantage Middenlaan 37, on the corner of Plantage Kerklaan, tel. 020/320-0817).

Taman Sari Restaurant is the local choice for Indonesian, serving hearty, quality €10 dinners and *rijsttafel* dinners for €16–23 (daily 17:00–22:00, Plantage Kerklaan 32, tel. 020/623-7130).

SMOKING

Tobacco

A third of Dutch people smoke tobacco. Holland has a long tradition as a smoking culture, being among the first to import the tobacco plant from the New World. (For a history of smoking, visit the Pipe Museum, listed on page 84.)

Tobacco shops, such as the House of Hajenius (see page 81), glorify the habit, yet the Dutch people are among the healthiest in the world. Tanned, trim, firm, 60-something Dutch people sip their beer, take a drag, and ask me why Americans murder themselves with Big Macs.

Still, their version of the Surgeon General has finally woken up to the drug's many potential health problems. Warning stickers bigger than America's are required on cigarette packs, and some of them are almost comically blunt, such as: "Smoking will make you impotent...and then you die." (The warnings have prompted gag stickers like, "Life can kill you.")

Since 2008, a Dutch law has outlawed smoking tobacco almost everywhere indoors: on trains, and in hotel rooms, restaurants, cafés, and bars.

Marijuana (a.k.a. Cannabis)

Amsterdam, Europe's counterculture mecca, thinks the concept of a "victimless crime" is a contradiction in terms. Drive under the influence of anything and you're toast. Heroin and cocaine are strictly illegal in the Netherlands, and the police stringently enforce laws prohibiting their sale and use. But, while hard drugs are definitely out, marijuana causes about as much excitement as a bottle of beer. When tourists call an ambulance after smoking too much pot, medics just say, "Drink something sweet and walk it off."

Throughout the Netherlands, you'll see "coffeeshops"—pubs

selling marijuana, with display cases showing various joints or baggies for sale. The minimum age for purchase is 18, and coffeeshops
can sell up to five grams of mari-
juana per person per day. Locals
buy marijuana by asking, "Can I
see the cannabis menu?" Because
it's illegal to advertise marijuana,
the buyer has to take the initia-
tive and request a menu. In some
places there's actually a button
you must push and hold down
to see an illuminated menu, the
contents of which look like the
inventory of a drug bust.

The big buzz on the coffeeshop scene is the new smoking ban.
The new laws pertain to tobacco smoke, not pot smoke. But the
Dutch, like the rest of Europe, mix their marijuana with tobacco. It
might seem strange to an American, but these days, if a coffeeshop
is busted, it's for tobacco. Coffeeshops with a few outdoor seats
have a huge advantage, as their customers can light up outside.
Shops without the outdoor option are in for an extra challenge, as
many local smokers would rather get their weed to-go than smoke
it without tobacco at their neighborhood coffeeshop. As a sub-
stitute for tobacco, shops have started mixing a kind of herb tea
into joints. Pre-rolled joints are now sold three ways: pure, with
the non-tobacco "hamburger helper" herb mix, or with tobacco. If
you like your joint tobacco-free anyway, pure marijuana joints are
much easier to buy now than a year ago.

Shops sell marijuana and hashish both in pre-rolled joints and
in little baggies. Some places sell individual joints (€2–5). Others
sell only small packs of three or four joints. Baggies of marijuana
usually cost €10–15. Some shops charge per gram. The better pot,
while costlier, is actually a better value, as it takes less to get high—
and it's a better high. Shops have loaner bongs and inhalers, and
they dispense cigarette papers like toothpicks. As long as you're a
paying customer (e.g., buy a cup of coffee), you can pop into any
coffeeshop and light up, even if you didn't buy your pot there.

Pot should never be bought on the street in Amsterdam, and
don't smoke marijuana openly while walking down the street.
Well-established coffeeshops are considered much safer, and
coffeeshop owners have an interest in keeping their trade safe and
healthy. They warn Americans—unused to the strength of the
local stuff—to try a lighter leaf. In fact, they are generally very
patient in explaining the varieties available.

Several forms of the cannabis plant are sold. Locals smoke
more hashish (the sap of the cannabis plant) than the leaf of the

plant (which they call "marijuana" or "grass"). While each shop has different brands, it's all derived from two types of marijuana plant: *Cannabis indica* and *Cannabis sativa*. *Indica* gets you a "stoned, heavy, mellow, couch-weed" high. *Sativa* is light, fun, "uplifting," and more psychedelic. *Sativa* makes you giggle.

Most of the pot you'll see is locally grown. Technological advances have made it easier to cultivate exotic yet local strains. Coffeeshops know it's much safer to deal with Dutch-grown plants than to import marijuana from a foreign land (international trafficking gives rise to a whole different level of legal complexity than just growing your own). Most shops get their inventory from the pot equivalent of local home-brewers or micro-brewers. Shops with better "boutique suppliers" get the reputation for having better quality weed (and regularly win the annual Cannabis Cup).

Each shop is allowed to keep an inventory of up to 500 grams (about a pound) in stock—the tax authorities don't want to see more than this on the books at the end of each accounting cycle, and a shop can lose its license if it exceeds this amount. However, the wholesale dimension of the business is the famous "gray area" in the law: A shop can sell a ton of pot with no legal problems, as long as it maintains that tiny stock of 500 grams and just refills it as needed. The mayor of Amsterdam, seeking to cut down on the high volume of small-time deliveries, has proposed doubling the allowable inventory level (to one kilo). The reason the inventory level is kept so low: Authorities want shops to stay small and not become bases for exportation. Providing pot to neighboring countries would bring more international pressure on the Netherlands to crack down on its coffeeshop culture.

The other legal trend is that licenses are not being renewed in some neighborhoods, as the city seeks to maintain a wide smattering of shops, avoiding too big a concentration in any one area. A national law which goes into effect in 2011 would close all coffeeshops near schools, including the landmark Bulldog Café on Liedseplein. But Amsterdam's mayor has vowed to look for a way to keep its central coffeeshops open. Stay tuned.

So what am I? Pro-marijuana? Let's put it this way: I agree with the Dutch people, who remind me that a society either has to allow alternative lifestyles...or build more prisons. As many as 800,000 Americans are arrested for marijuana use in one year alone. (Only the US and Russia lock up more than 1 percent of their citizens.)

The Dutch are not necessarily pro-marijuana, but they do believe that a prohibition on marijuana would cause more problems than it solves. Statistics support the Dutch belief that their system works. They have fewer hard drug problems than other countries. And they believe America's policy is based on fear, misinformation, and electoral politics, rather than rationality. The Dutch have found that their drug policy, with its 10-year track record, does not result in more pot smoking. Statistically, Americans smoke twice as much pot as the Dutch.

If you'd like to learn more about marijuana (and don't feel like Googling "Rick Steves marijuana"), drop by Amsterdam's Cannabis College or the Hash, Marijuana, and Hemp Museum. To see where cannabis growers buy their seeds, stop by the Sensi Seed Bank Store. These three places are located on Oudezijds Achterburgwal street (see pages 100–101). Back home, if you'd like to support an outfit dedicated to taking the crime out of pot, read up on the National Organization for the Reform of Marijuana Laws (www.norml.org).

Coffeeshops

Most of downtown Amsterdam's coffeeshops feel grungy and fore-boding to a typical middle-aged American traveler. The neighbor-hood places (and those in small towns around the countryside) are much more inviting to people without piercings, tattoos, and favorite techno artists. I've listed a few places with a more pub-like ambience for Americans wanting to go local, but within reason. For locations, see the maps in the Sleeping chapter.

Paradox is the most *gezellig* (cozy) coffeeshop I found—a mellow, graceful place. The managers, Ludo and Wiljan, and their

staff are patient with descriptions and happy to walk you through all your options. This is a rare coffee-shop that serves light meals. The juice is fresh, the music is easy, and the neighborhood is charming (single tobacco-free joints-€3, loaner bongs, games, daily 10:00–20:00, two blocks from Anne Frank House at Eerste Bloemdwarsstraat 2, tel. 020/623-5639, www.paradoxamsterdam.demon.nl).

The Grey Area coffeeshop—a hole-in-the-wall spot with three tiny tables—is a cool, welcoming, and smoky place appreci-ated among local aficionados as a perennial winner of Amsterdam's Cannabis Cup awards. Judging by the autographed photos on the wall, many famous Americans have dropped in (say hi to Willie Nelson). You're welcome to just nurse a bottomless cup of coffee (daily 12:00–20:00, they close relatively early out of consideration for their neighbors, between Dam Square and Anne Frank House at Oude Leliestraat 2, tel. 020/420-4301). The Grey Area is run by two friendly Americans, Adam and Jon. They are helpful and even have a vaporizer if you want to "smoke" without smoking.

Siberië Coffeeshop is a short walk from Central Station, but feels cozy, with a friendly canalside ambience. Clean, big, and bright, this place has the vibe of a not-too-far-out Starbucks (daily 11:00–23:00, Fri–Sat until 24:00, free Internet access, helpful staff, English menu, Brouwersgracht 11, tel. 020/623-5909, www.siberie.nl).

La Tertulia is a sweet little mother-and-daughter-run place with pastel decor and a cheery terrarium atmosphere (Tue–Sat 11:00–19:00, closed Sun–Mon, sandwiches, brownies, games, Prinsengracht 312, www.coffeeshopamsterdam.com).

The Bulldog is the high-profile, leading touristy chain of coffee-shops. These establishments are young but welcoming, with reliable selections. They're pretty comfortable for green tourists wanting to just hang out for a while. The flagship branch, in a former police station right on Leidseplein, is very handy, offering alcohol upstairs, pot downstairs, and fun outdoor seating where you can watch the world skateboard by. There's a chance it may close because it's considered too near a school, but it will likely stay open (daily 10:00–
1:00 in the morning, Fri–Sat until 2:00, Leidseplein 17, tel. 020/625-6278, www.bulldog.nl). They opened their first café (on the canal near the Old Church in the Red Light District) in 1975.

The Dampkring is a rough-and-ready constant party. It's a high-profile and busy place, filled with a young clientele and loud music, but the owners still take the time to explain what they offer. Scenes from the movie *Ocean's Twelve* were filmed here (daily 11:00–22:00, later on Fri–Sat, close to Spui at Handboogstraat 29, tel. 020/638-0705).

Smartshops

These business establishments (one is listed on page 83) sell "natural" drugs that are legal. Many are harmless nutritional supplements, but they also sell stimulants similar to Ecstasy and strange drug cocktails rolled into joints. It's all perfectly legal, but if you've never taken drugs recreationally, don't start here.

SHOPPING

Amsterdam brings out the browser even in those who were not born to shop. Ten general markets, open six days a week (generally 9:30–17:00, closed Sun), keep folks who brake for garage sales pulling U-turns. Markets include Waterlooplein (the flea market), the huge Albert Cuyp street market, and various flower markets (such as the Singel canal Flower Market near Mint Tower).

For information on shopping, pick up the TI's *Shopping in Amsterdam* brochure. To find out how to get a VAT (Value Added Tax) refund on your purchases, see page 11.

Most shops in the center are open 10:00–18:00 (Thu until 21:00); the businesslike Dutch know no siesta, but many shopkeepers take Sunday and Monday mornings off. Supermarkets are open Monday–Saturday 8:00–20:00.

Department Stores

When you need to buy something but don't know where to go, two chain stores—Hema and Vroom & Dreesmann (V&D)—are handy for everything from inexpensive clothes and notebooks to food and cosmetics. **Hema** is at Kalverstraat 212, in the Kalvertoren mall (Mon 11:00–18:30, Tue–Sat 9:30–18:30, Thu until 21:00, Sun 12:00–18:30). **Vroom & Dreesmann,** with its great La Place cafeteria, is at Kalverstraat 203 (Mon and Sun 11:00–19:00, Tue–Sat 10:00–20:00, Thu until 21:00; cafeteria on ground floor—see page 185).

The **De Bijenkorf** department store is old-time fancy and central on Dam Square, with a nice café on the second floor (see page 186). **Metz & Co.** is decent but getting dowdy, and its sixth-floor café has good views (located where Leidsestraat intersects Herengracht).

Amsterdam's Top Shopping Zones

Jordaan—The colorful, old, working-class district of the Jordaan and its main drag, Westerstraat, are a veritable wonderland of funky, artsy shops. On Mondays, you'll find the busy Noordermarkt market at the end of Westerstraat and spilling onto the neighboring street, Lindengracht.

Leidsestraat—This bustling shopping street has elegant and trendy shops, along with the Metz & Co. department store.

The Nine Little Streets—De Negen Straatjes is home to 190 diverse shops mixing festive, creative, nostalgic, practical, and artistic items. The cross streets make a tic-tac-toe with a couple of canals and bicycle-friendly canalside streets just west of Kalverstraat. (Look for the zone where Hartenstraat, Wolvenstraat, and Huidenstraat cross the Keizersgracht and Herengracht canals—see the color map at the beginning of this book.)

Kalverstraat–Heiligeweg–Spui—This is the busiest shopping corridor in town. Kalverstraat, a pedestrian street, is a human traffic jam of low-end shoppers. It feels soulless, but if you explore the fringes, there are some interesting places.

Spiegelkwartier—Located between the Rijksmuseum and the city center, this is *the* place for art and antiques. You'll find 70 dealers offering 17th-century furniture, old Delftware, Oriental art, clocks, jewelry, and Art Nouveau doodads. Wander down Spiegelgracht and Nieuwe Spiegelstraat.

Prinsheerlijk—Along Herenstraat and Prinsenstraat, you'll find top-end fashion, interior design, and gift shops. If you're looking for jewelry, accessories, trendy clothing, and fancy delicatessens, this may be an expensive but rewarding stroll.

Magna Plaza Shopping Center—Formerly the main post office, this grand 19th-century building has been transformed into a stylish mall with 40 boutiques. You'll find fashion, luxury goods, and gift shops galore. It's just behind the Royal Palace a block off Dam Square (see page 103).

P. C. Hooftstraat—The most expensive shopping street is between Museumplein and Vondelpark.

Albert Cuyp Market—Amsterdam's biggest open-air market, stretching for several blocks along Albert Cuypstraat, bustles daily (roughly 9:00–17:00) except Sunday. You'll find fish, exotic vegetables, bolts of fabric, pantyhose, bargain clothes, native Dutch and ethnic food stands (especially *stroopwafels* and Surinamese *rotis*), and great people-watching. It's located a 10-minute walk east of Museumplein and a block south of the Heineken Experience (tram #16 or #24).

Popular Souvenirs

Amsterdam has lots of one-of-a-kind specialty stores. Poke around and see what you can find. If you want to bring home edibles and drinkables, first check "Customs for American Shoppers" (page 12).

Wooden Shoes—Once crucial for navigating soggy Amsterdam, now something to clomp around in.

Delftware—Ceramic plates, vases, and tiles decorated with a fake Chinese blue-and-white design popularized in the 1600s. Only a few licensed places sell the real stuff (expensive) and antiques (very expensive). You can find fireplace tiles (cheap) at most gift shops.

Diamonds—Cut or uncut, expensive or really expensive. Diamond dealers offer free cutting and polishing demos at their shops. Gassan Diamonds, near Rembrandt's House, is best (page 62); Coster is on Potterstraat, behind the Rijksmuseum (page 49).

Beers—A yeasty, frothy souvenir.

Jenever—Dutch gin (made from juniper berries) sold in traditional stone bottles.

Marijuana Pipes—These need to be clean and unused, because even a little residue can get you busted at US Customs. Note that, these days, American laws are written in a way that—technically—even importing an unused pipe could get you arrested.

Chocolate—Belgian or Dutch Verkade or Droste cocoa in tins.

Flower Seeds and Bulbs—Look for ones that are packed with a seal that promises they are US Customs–friendly.

Posters and Art Postcards—Good selection at the Van Gogh Museum bookshop (also sells protective mailing tubes).

Old Maps—Capturing the Golden Age.

Old Books—Treasures found in musty bookstores.

NIGHTLIFE

Amsterdam hotels serve breakfast until 11:00 because so many people—visitors and locals—live for nighttime in Amsterdam.

On summer evenings, people flock to the main squares for drinks at outdoor tables. Leidseplein is the liveliest, surrounded by theaters, restaurants, and nightclubs. The slightly quieter Rembrandtplein (with adjoining Thorbeckeplein and nearby Reguliersdwarsstraat) is the center of gay clubs and nightlife. Spui features a full city block of bars. And Nieuwmarkt, on the east edge of the Red Light District, is a bit rough, but is probably the most local.

The Red Light District (particularly Oudezijds Achterburgwal) is less sleazy in the early evening, almost carnival-like, as the neon comes on and the streets fill with tour groups. But it starts to feel scuzzy after about 22:30 (✪ see Red Light District Walk, page 88).

Information

Pick up one of these free papers for listings of festivals and performances of theater, film, dance, cabaret, and live rock, pop, jazz, and classical music. *Amsterdam Weekly* is a free, local English-language paper that lists cutting-edge art, movies, and concerts (available in bookstores every Wed, see list on pages 36–37, also online at www .amsterdamweekly.nl). The irreverent *Boom!* has the lowdown on the youth and nightlife scene, and it's packed with practical tips and countercultural insights (includes €3 discount on the Boom Chicago R-rated comedy theater act described on the next page, available at TIs and many bars). *Uitkrant* is in Dutch, but it's just a calendar of events, and anyone can figure out the name of the event and its date, time, and location (available at TIs and many bars).

There's also *What's On in Amsterdam, Time Out Amsterdam,* the Thursday edition of many Dutch papers, and the *International Herald Tribune*'s special Netherlands inserts (all sold at newsstands).

Box Office: The Last Minute Ticket Shop at Stadsschouwburg Theater is the best one-stop-shopping box office for theater, classical music, and major rock shows. They also sell half-price, same-day tickets to certain shows (daily 12:00–19:30, Leidseplein 26, tel. 0900-0191—€0.40/min, www.lastminuteticketshop.nl).

Music

You'll find classical music at the **Concertgebouw** (free 12:30 lunch concerts on Wed Sept–mid-June, no concerts mid-June–Aug; arrive at 12:00 for best first-come, first-serve seating; at far south end of Museumplein, tel. 020/671-8345, www.concertgebouw.nl) and at the former Beurs (on Damrak). For opera and dance, try the opera house on Waterlooplein (tel. 020/551-8100). In the summer, Vondelpark hosts open-air concerts.

Two rock music (and hip-hop) clubs near Leidseplein are **Melkweg** (Lijnbaansgracht 234a, tel. 020/531-8181, www.melkweg.nl) and **Paradiso** (Weteringschans 6, tel. 020/626-4521, www.paradiso.nl; see page 86). They present big-name acts that you might recognize if you're younger than I am.

Jazz has a long tradition at the **Bimhuis** nightclub, east of the Red Light District (concerts Thu–Sat, Oude Schans 73–77, tel. 020/788-2150, www.bimhuis.nl).

The nearby town of Haarlem offers free pipe organ concerts on Tuesday evenings in summer at its 15th-century church, the **Grote Kerk** (at 20:15 mid-May–mid-Oct, see page 206).

Comedy

Boom Chicago, an R-rated comedy improv act, was started 15 years ago by a group of Americans on a graduation tour. They have been entertaining tourists and locals ever since. The two-hour, English-only show is a series of rude, clever, and high-powered improvisational skits offering a raucous look at Dutch culture and local tourism (€20, more on Sat, less for second Friday show; shows run Sun–Fri at 20:15, second show Fri at 23:30, Sat shows at 19:30 and 22:30, confirm times when you buy your ticket; ticket office open Mon–Thu 11:00–20:30, Fri–Sat 11:00–23:30, closed Sun; no Mon shows Jan–March; in 300-seat Leidseplein Theater, optional meal and drink service, enter through the skinny Boom Bar, Leidseplein 12, tel. 020/423-0101, www.boomchicago.nl). They do *Best of Boom* (a collection of their greatest hits over the years) as well as new shows for locals and return customers. When sales are slow, ticket-sellers on the street out front offer steeply discounted tickets, with a drink included (drop by that afternoon and see what's up).

Theater

Amsterdam is one of the world centers for experimental live theater (much of it in English). Many theaters cluster around the street called the Nes, which stretches south from Dam Square.

Movies

It's not unusual for movies at many cinemas to be sold out—consider buying tickets during the day. Catch modern movies in the 1920s setting of the classic **Tuschinski Theater** (between Muntplein and Rembrandtplein, described on page 51).

Museums

Several of Amsterdam's museums stay open late. The **Anne Frank House** is open daily until 22:00 in July and August, and until at least 19:00 the rest of the year. The **Rijksmuseum** and **Van Gogh Museum** are open on Fridays until 20:30 and 22:00, respectively (the Van Gogh sometimes has music and a wine bar in the lobby). The **Hermitage Amsterdam** stays open until 20:00 on Wednesday.

The **Hash, Marijuana, and Hemp Museum** is open daily until 22:00. And the **sex museums** always stay open late (Damrak Sex Museum until 23:00, Erotic Museum until 24:00).

Skating After Dark

While there hasn't been a good canal freeze since 1996, Amsterdammers still get their skating fix on wheels every Friday night in summer and early fall. Huge groups don inline skates and meet at the Film Museum in Vondelpark (around 20:15). Tourists can roll along; there's a skate-rental shop at the far end of the park (Vondel Tuin Rental, daily 11:00–24:00 in good weather; first hour–€5, then €2.50/hour; price includes helmet, wrist guards, and knee guards; at southeastern edge of park, tel. 020/664-5091, www.vondeltuin.nl).

HAARLEM

ORIENTATION AND SIGHTS

Cute and cozy, yet authentic and handy to the airport, Haarlem is a fine home base, giving you small-town warmth overnight, with easy access (20 min by train) to wild and crazy Amsterdam during the day.

Bustling Haarlem gave America's Harlem its name back when New York was New Amsterdam, a Dutch colony. For centuries, Haarlem has been a market town, buzzing with shoppers heading home with fresh bouquets, nowadays by bike.

Enjoy the market on Monday (clothing) or Saturday (general), when the town's atmospheric main square bustles like a Brueghel painting, with cheese, fish, flowers, and families. Make yourself at home; buy some flowers to brighten your hotel room.

OVERVIEW

(area code: 023)

Tourist Information

Haarlem's TI (VVV), in the town center, is friendlier, more help-ful, and less crowded than Amsterdam's, so ask your Amsterdam questions here (April–Sept Mon–Fri 9:00–17:30, Sat 10:00–16:00, closed Sun; Oct–March Mon–Fri 9:30–17:00, Sat 10:00–14:00, closed Sun; across from V&D department store at Verwulft 11, tel. 0900-616-1600—€0.50/min, www.vvvhaarlem.nl, info@vvv haarlem.nl).

The TI offers a good selection of maps and sightseeing and walking tour brochures, and sells discounted tickets (€1–2 off) for the Frans Hals Museum and the Teylers Museum.

The little yellow computer terminal on the curb outside the

train station prints out free maps anytime. (It's fun...just dial the street and hit "print." Drivers will also find these terminals stationed at roads coming into town.)

Arrival in Haarlem

By Train: Lockers are available at Haarlem's train station (€3.50/day, no coins—use a debit card or a "Chipknip" prepaid debit card, which you can purchase at a ticket window). Two parallel streets flank the train station (Kruisweg and Jansweg). Head up either street, and you'll reach the town square and church within 10 minutes. If you need help, ask a local person to point you toward the Grote Markt (Market Square).

By Car: Parking is expensive on the streets (€2.50/hr) and cheaper in several central garages (€2/hr). Three main garages let you park overnight for €2.50: at the train station, near the Teylers Museum (follow signs to the museum) and near the Frans Hals Museum (again, follow signs).

By Plane: For details on getting from Schiphol Airport into Haarlem, see page 306.

Helpful Hints

Blue Monday: Most sights are closed on Monday, except the church.

Money: The handy **GWK** currency exchange office at the train station offers fair rates (Mon–Fri 8:00–20:00, Sat 9:00–17:00, Sun 10:00–17:00).

Internet Access: Try **Hotel Amadeus** (overlooking Market Square, €1.20/15 min, 25 percent discount with this book), **High Times Coffeeshop** (free if you buy some pot), or **Suny Teletechniques** (€2/hr, daily 10:00–24:00, near train station at Lange Herenstraat 4, tel. 023/551-0037).

Post Office: It's at Gedempte Oude Gracht 2 (Mon–Fri 9:00–18:00, Sat 10:00–13:30, closed Sun, has ATM).

Laundry: **My Beautiful Launderette** is handy and fairly central (€6 self-service wash and dry, daily 8:30–20:30, €9 full service available Mon–Fri 9:00–17:00, near V&D department store at Boter Markt 20).

Bike Rental: You can rent bikes at the train station (€7.50/day, €50 deposit and passport number, Mon–Sat 6:00–24:00, Sun 7:30–24:00). They have only 50 bikes to rent and often run out by midmorning—especially when the weather's good.

Taxi: The drop charge of €7.50 gets you a little over a mile.

Local Guide: For a historical look at Haarlem, consider hiring **Walter Schelfhout** (€75/2 hrs, tel. 023/535-5715, mobile 06-1258-9299, schelfhout@dutch.nl).

Best View: At **La Place** (top-floor cafeteria of the V&D department store—see page 237), you get wraparound views of the city as you sip your €2 self-serve tea.

Best Ice Cream: Gelateria Bartoli (on the south side of the Grote Kerk) is the local favorite.

SELF-GUIDED WALK

Welcome to Haarlem's Market Square

Haarlem's market square (Grote Markt), where 10 streets converge, is a ▲▲ sight and the town's delightful centerpiece...as it has been

for 700 years. To enjoy a coffee or beer here, simmering in Dutch good living, is a quintessential European experience. In a recent study, the Dutch were found to be the most content people in Europe; in another study, the people of Haarlem were found to be the most content in the Netherlands. Observe. Sit and gaze at the church, appreciating essentially the same scene that Dutch artists captured centuries ago in oil paintings that now hang in museums.

Just a few years ago, trolleys ran through the square, and cars were parked everywhere. But today, it's a pedestrian zone, with market stalls filling the square on Mondays and Saturdays, and café tables dominating on other days.

This is a fun place to build a picnic with Haarlem finger foods—pickled herring (take-away stand on the square), local cheese (Gouda and Edam—tasty shop a block away on Barteljorisstraat), french fries with mayonnaise (recommended old-time fries place behind the church on Warmoesstraat), *stroopwafels* (waffles with built-in syrup), and *poffertjes* (little sugar doughnuts, cooked on the spot, great seating on the square).

• *Overseeing the square is the...*

L. J. Coster Statue: Forty years before Gutenberg invented movable type, this man carved the letter *A* out of wood, dropped it into some wet sand, and saw the imprint it left. He got the idea of making movable type out of wood (and later, he may have tried using lead). For Haarlemmers, that was good enough, and

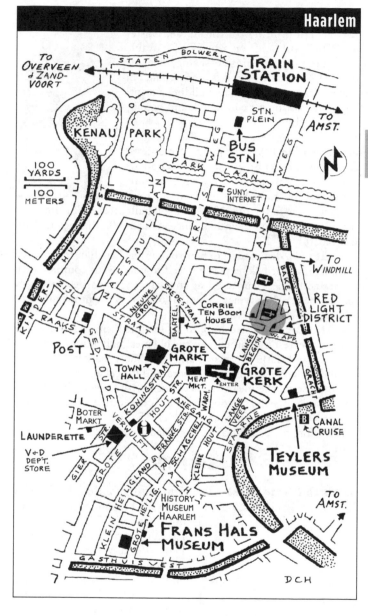

Haarlem

TO
OVERVEEN
& ZAND-
VOORT

STATEN BOLWERK

TRAIN
STATION

TO
Amst.

STN.
PLEIN

BUS
STN.

KENAU PARK

PARK LAAN

KRUIS JANS WEG

HUIS VEST

100
YARDS
100
METERS

SUNY
INTERNET

TO
WINDMILL

NIEUWE GROEN

BARTEL JORIS STRAAT

SMEDESTRAAT

Corrie
Ten Boom
House

RED
LIGHT
DISTRICT

KINDER ZIJL

RAAKS

GED. OUDE GRACHT

Post

TOWN
HALL

GROTE
MARKT

LANGE BEGIJN

KONINGSTRAAT

HOUT STR.

MEAT
MKT.

WARM.

ENTER

GROTE
KERK

GRACHT

BOTER
MARKT

VERWULFT

ANEGANG

FRANKE STR.

LANGE VEEK

SPAARNE

B CANAL
CRUISE

LAUNDERETTE

GIER STR.

GROTE HEILIGLAND

SCHAGCHEL STR.

KLEINE HOUT

TEYLERS
MUSEUM

V&D
DEPT.
STORE

HISTORY
MUSEUM
HAARLEM

KLEIN HEILIGLAND

GROTE HEILIG.

FRANS HALS
MUSEUM

GASTHUIS VEST

TO
Amst.

DCH

206 Rick Steves' Amsterdam, Bruges & Brussels

they credit their man, Coster, with inventing modern printing. In the statue, Coster (c. 1370–1440) holds up a block of movable type and points to himself, saying, "I made this." How much Coster did is uncertain, but Gutenberg trumped him by building a printing press, casting type in metal, and pounding out the Bible.

• *Coster is facing the...*

Town Hall: While most of medieval Europe was ruled by kings, dukes, and barons, Haarlem has been largely self-governing since 1425. The town hall—built from a royal hunting lodge in the mid-1200s, then rebuilt after a 1351 fire—has served as Haarlem's town hall since about 1400. The facade dates from 1630.

The town drunk used to hang out on the bench in front of the town hall, where he'd expose himself to newlyweds coming down the stairs. Rather than arresting the man, the townspeople simply moved the bench (a typically Dutch solution to the problem).

• *Next to the church is the...*

Meat Market (Vleeshal), 1603: The fine Flemish Renaissance building nearest the cathedral is the old meat hall, built by the rich butchers' and leatherworkers' guilds. The meat market was on the ground floor, the leather was upstairs, and the cellar was filled with ice to preserve the meat. It's decorated with carved bits of early advertising—sheep and cows for sale. Today, rather than meat, the hall shows off temporary art exhibits (€5, Tue–Sun 11:00–17:00, closed Mon, tel. 023/511-5775, www.dehallen.com).

SIGHTS

▲**Church (Grote Kerk)**—This 15th-century Gothic church (now Protestant) is worth a look, if only to see Holland's greatest pipe organ (from 1738, 100 feet high).

Its 5,000 pipes impressed both Handel and Mozart. Note how the organ, which fills the west end, seems to steal the show from the altar. Quirky highlights of the church include a replica of Foucault's pendulum, the "Dog-Whipper's Chapel," and a 400-year-old cannonball.

To enter, find the small *Entrée* sign behind the church at

Haarlem of the Golden Age

Parts of Haarlem still look like they did four centuries ago, when the city was a bustling commercial center rivaling Amsterdam. It's easy to imagine local merchants and their wives dressed in black with ruff collars, promenading Market Square.

Back then, the town was a port on the large Haarlemmer Lake, with the North Sea only about five miles away. As well as being the tulip capital of the country, Haarlem was a manufacturing center, producing wool, silk, lace, damask cloth, furniture, smoking pipes (along with cheap, locally grown tobacco), and mass quantities of beer. Haarlemmers were notorious consumers of beer—it was a popular breakfast drink, and the average person drank six pints a day.

In 1585, the city got an influx of wealthy merchants when Spanish troops invaded the culturally rich city of Antwerp, driving Protestants and Jews north. Even when hard-line, moralistic Calvinists dominated Haarlem's politics, the city remained culturally and religiously diverse.

In the 1700s, Haarlem's economy declined, along with that of the Netherlands. In the succeeding centuries, industry—printing, textiles, ship building—once again made the city an economic force.

Oude Groenmarkt 23 (€2, Mon–Sat 10:00–16:00, closed Sun to tourists, tel. 023/553-2040).

Consider attending (even part of) a **concert** to hear the Oz-like pipe organ (regular free concerts Tue at 20:15 mid-May–mid-Oct, additional concerts Thu at 15:00 late June–Aug, concerts nearly nightly at 20:15 during the organ competition in July, confirm schedule at TI or at www.bavo.nl; bring a sweater—the church isn't heated).

○ See Grote Kerk Tour, page 212.

▲▲**Frans Hals Museum**—Haarlem is the hometown of Frans Hals, the foremost Dutch portrait painter of the 17th-century Golden Age. This refreshing museum, once an almshouse for old men back in 1610, displays many of his greatest paintings, done in his nearly Impressionistic style. You'll see group portraits and take-me-back paintings of old-time Haarlem (€7.50, Tue–Sat 11:00–17:00, Sun 12:00–17:00, closed Mon, Groot Heiligland 62, tel. 023/511-5775, www.franshalsmuseum.nl).

○ See Frans Hals Museum Tour, page 221.

History Museum Haarlem—This small museum, across the street from the Frans Hals Museum, offers a glimpse of old Haarlem. Request the English version of the 10-minute video, low-key Haarlem's version of a sound-and-light show. Study the large-scale model of Haarlem in 1822 (when its fortifications were still intact), and wander the two rooms without English descriptions (overpriced at €4, Tue–Sat 12:00–17:00, Sun 13:00–17:00, closed Mon, Groot Heiligland 47, tel. 023/542-2427, www.historisch museumhaarlem.nl). The adjacent architecture center (free) may be of interest to architects.

▲**Corrie ten Boom House**—Haarlem was home to Corrie ten Boom, popularized by her inspirational book (and the movie that followed), *The Hiding Place*. Both tell about the Ten Boom family's experience protecting Jews from the Nazis. Corrie ten Boom gives the other half of the Anne Frank story—the point of view of those who risked their lives to hide Dutch Jews during the Nazi occupation (1940–1945).

The clock shop was the Ten Boom family business. The elderly father and his two daughters—Corrie and Betsy, both in their 50s—lived above the store and in the brick building attached in back (along Schoutensteeg alley). Corrie's bedroom was on the top floor at the back. This room was tiny to start with, but then the family built a second, secret room (less than a yard deep) at the very back—"the hiding place," where they could hide six Jews at a time. Devoutly religious, the family had a long tradition of tolerance, having hosted prayer meetings here in their home for both Jews and Christians for generations.

The Gestapo, tipped off that the family was harboring Jews, burst into the Ten Boom house. Finding a suspicious number of ration coupons, the Nazis arrested the family, but failed to find the six Jews (who later escaped) in the hiding place. Corrie's father and sister died while in prison, but Corrie survived the Ravensbruck concentration camp to tell her story in her memoir.

The Ten Boom House is open only for 60-minute English tours—check the sign on the door for the next start time. The gentle and loving tours come with a little evangelizing that some atheists may find objectionable (donation accepted; April–Oct Tue–Sat first tour at 10:00, last tour at 15:30; Nov–March Tue–Sat first tour at 11:00, last tour at 15:00; closed Sun–Mon; 50 yards north of Market Square at Barteljorisstraat 19; the clock-shop people get all wound up if you go inside—wait in the little side street at the door, where hourly tour times are posted; tel. 023/531-0823, www .corrietenboom.com).

▲**Teylers Museum**—Famous as the oldest museum in Holland, Teylers is a time-warp experience, filled with all sorts of fun curios for science buffs: fossils, minerals, primitive electronic gadgetry, and examples of 18th- and 19th-century technology. This place feels like a museum of a museum. They're serious about authenticity here: The presentation is perfectly preserved, right down to the original labels. Since there was no electricity in the olden days, you'll find little electric lighting...if it's dark outside, it's dark inside. The museum's benefactor, Pieter Teyler van der Hulst, was a very wealthy merchant who willed his estate, worth the equivalent of €80 million today, to a foundation whose mission was to "create and maintain a museum to stimulate art and science." The museum opened in 1784, six years after Teyler's death (his last euro was spent in 1983—now it's a national museum). Add your name to the guest book, which goes back to before Napoleon's visit here. The oval room—a temple of science and learning—is the core of the museum; the art gallery hangs paintings in the old style. While there are no English descriptions, an excellent (and, I'd say, essential) audioguide is included (€7, Tue–Sat 10:00–17:00, Sun 12:00–17:00, closed Mon, Spaarne 16, tel. 023/516-0960, www .teylersmuseum.nl). The museum's modern café has good prices and faces a delightful garden.

▲**De Adriaan Windmill**—Haarlem's old-time windmill, located just a 10-minute walk from the station and Teylers Museum, welcomes visitors with a short video, little museum, and fine town views (€2, Wed–Fri 13:00–16:00, Sat–Sun 10:00–16:00, closed Mon–Tue, Papentorenvest 1, tel. 023/545-0259, www.molen adriaan.nl—in Dutch only).

Canal Cruise—Making a scenic 50-minute loop through and around Haarlem with a live guide who speaks Dutch and sometimes English, these little trips are more relaxing than informative (€10; April–Oct Tue–Sun departures at the top of each hour from 12:00–16:00, closed Mon; across canal from Teylers Museum at Spaarne 11a, tel. 023/535-7723, www.woltheuscruises.nl).

▲**Red Light District**—Wander through a little Red Light District that's as precious as a Barbie doll—and legal since the 1980s (2 blocks northeast of Market Square, off Lange Begijnestraat, no senior or student discounts). Don't miss the mall on Begijnesteeg marked by the red neon sign reading *'t Steegje* ("free"). Just beyond that, the nearby 't Poortje ("office park") costs €6 to enter. Jog to the right to pop into the much more inviting "Red Lantern" (window-shopping welcome, at Korte Begijnestraat 27). As you wander through this area, remember that the people here don't condone prostitution any more than your own community back home probably does; they just find it practical not to criminalize it and drive it underground, but instead to regulate it and keep the practice as safe as possible.

The Haarlemmermeer

The land between Haarlem and Amsterdam—where trains speed through, cattle graze, and 747s touch down—was once a lake the size of Washington, D.C. called the Haarlemmermeer.

In the 1500s, a series of high tides and storms caused the IJ River to breach its banks, flooding this sub-sea-level area and turning a bunch of shallow lakes into a single one nearly 15 feet deep, covering 70 square miles. By the 1800s, floods were licking at the borders of Haarlem and Amsterdam, and the residents needed to act. First, they dug a ring canal to channel away water (and preserve the lake's shipping business). Then, using steam engines, they pumped the lake dry, turning marshy soil into fertile ground. The Amsterdam-Haarlem train line that soon crossed the former lakebed was the country's first.

Amsterdam to Haarlem Train Tour

Since you'll be commuting from Amsterdam to Haarlem, here's an out-the-window tour to keep you entertained while you travel. Departing from Amsterdam, grab a seat on the right (with your back to Amsterdam, top deck if possible). Everything is on the right unless I say it's on the left.

You're riding the oldest train line in Holland.

Leaving Amsterdam, you'll see the cranes and ships of its harbor—sizable, but nothing like Europe's biggest in nearby Rotterdam.

On your left, a few minutes out of Amsterdam, find the old **windmill.** In front of it, the little garden plots and cottages are escapes for big-city people who probably don't even have a balcony.

Coming into the **Sloterdijk Station** (where trains connect for Amsterdam airport), you'll see huge office buildings, such as Dutch Telecom KPN. These grew up after the station made commuting easy. On the horizon, sleek and modern windmills whirl.

Passing through a forest and by some houseboats, you enter a *polder*—an area of reclaimed land. This is part of an ecologically sound farm zone, run without chemicals. Cows, pigs, and chickens run free—they're not raised in cages. The train tracks are on a dike, which provides a solid foundation not susceptible to floods. This way, the transportation system functions right through any calamity. Looking out at the distant dike, remember you're in the most densely populated country in Europe.

On the right, just after the Ikea building, find a big beige-and-white building. This is the **mint,** where currency is printed (top security, no advertising). This has long been a family business—see the name: Johan Enschede.

As the train slows down, you're passing through the Netherlands' biggest train-car-maintenance facility, and entering Haarlem. Look left. The domed building is a **prison,** built in 1901 and still in use. The windmill burned down in 1932 and was rebuilt in 2002.

When you cross the Spaarne River, you'll see the great **church spire** towering over Haarlem, as it has since medieval times—back when a fortified wall circled the town. Notice the white version of the same spire capping the smaller church (between the prison and the big church)—this was the original sandstone steeple that stood atop the big church. However, structural problems forced its move to another church, and a new spire was built for the big church.

Exit the train into one of Holland's oldest stations, adorned with Art Nouveau decor from 1908. Welcome to Haarlem.

GROTE KERK TOUR

Haarlem's impressive Grote Kerk (Great Church), one of the best-known landmarks in the Netherlands, is visible from miles around, rising above the flat plain that surrounds it. From the Market Square, you see the church at a three-quarters angle, emphasizing both its length (240 feet) and its height (260 feet).

ORIENTATION

Cost: €2.

Hours: Mon–Sat 10:00–16:00, closed Sun to tourists, Sun service at 10:00 (May–Sept). There's a daily 15-minute prayer service at 12:45 and, in July–Aug, an evensong service on Sun at 19:00. Occasionally, the church is closed for a wedding or a funeral; if you see a closed sign when it's supposed to be open, return in a couple of hours.

Getting There: The church is on the main square, a 10-minute walk south of the train station.

Information: While rich in heritage, the church doesn't do much to share its history with non-Dutch-speaking visitors. It offers no tours and very little information in English. Tel. 023/553-2040, www.bavo.nl.

WC: A handy WC is inside near the café.

Music: Consider attending even just part of a concert to hear Holland's greatest pipe organ. Free concerts are generally offered throughout the summer (Tue at 20:15 mid-May–mid-Oct, additional concerts Thu at 15:00 late June–Aug; confirm schedule at TI or at website listed above). If you're coming for a concert, bring a sweater—the thick stone walls keep the church cool, even during summer.

Length of This Tour: Allow one hour.

OVERVIEW

After a fire destroyed the old church (1328), the Grote Kerk was built over a 150-year period (c. 1390–1540) in the late Gothic style of red and gray brick, topped with a slate-covered wood roof and a stacked tower bearing a golden crown and a rooster weathervane.

Builders raised money by cleverly hitting up both popes—back when there were two competing pontiffs, one in Avignon and one in Rome. The builders came home with two different "absolution bills," authorizing them to grant forgiveness to parishioners for donations. Apparently, Haarlem's sinners—not knowing for sure which pope was *the* pope—covered all their bases by giving twice for their forgiveness.

Originally Catholic, the church was named after St. Bavo, a local noble who frequented seventh-century Red Light Districts during his youth. After his conversion, he moved out of his castle and into a hollow tree, where he spent his days fasting and praying. In the late 1500s, the St. Bavo Church became Protestant (Dutch Reformed) along with much of the country. From then on, the anti-saint Protestants simply called it the Great Church.

THE TOUR BEGINS

• *You'll enter the church from the side opposite the square. As you walk around the building, check out a few details…*

Exterior

Notice the rough buttress anchors, which were never needed. Money ran out, and the planned stone ceiling (which would have

required these buttresses) was replaced by a lighter wooden one. Some windows are bricked up because the organ fills the wall.

The original stone tower crowned the church from 1522 until 1530, when the church began sinking under its weight. It was removed and replaced by the lighter, wood-covered-with-lead version you see today. (The frugal Dutch recycled the old tower, using it to cap the Bakenesser church, a short walk away.)

Because the tower was used as a lookout by Napoleon, it was classified as part of the town's defense. As a result, the tower (but not the rest of the church) became city property, and, since Haarlem's citizens own it, they must help pay to maintain it.

The base of the church is encrusted, barnacle-like, with

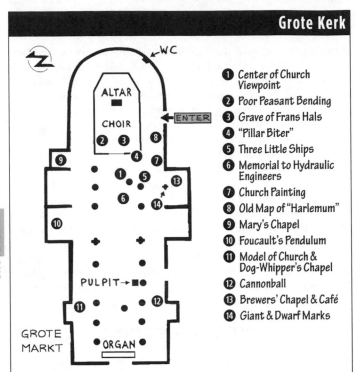

Grote Kerk

❶ Center of Church Viewpoint
❷ Poor Peasant Bending
❸ Grave of Frans Hals
❹ "Pillar Biter"
❺ Three Little Ships
❻ Memorial to Hydraulic Engineers
❼ Church Painting
❽ Old Map of "Harlemum"
❾ Mary's Chapel
❿ Foucault's Pendulum
⓫ Model of Church & Dog-Whipper's Chapel
⓬ Cannonball
⓭ Brewers' Chapel & Café
⓮ Giant & Dwarf Marks

GROTE KERK TOUR

shops—selling jewelry, souvenirs, haircuts, and artwork in the colonnaded former fish market—harkening back to medieval times, when religion and commerce were more intertwined. The little shops around the cathedral have long been church-owned, rented out to bring in a little cash.

During the day, a machine plays music on the bells of the Grote Kerk's carillon (live carillonneurs play occasionally). If you're in Haarlem at night, you'll hear the carillon chiming a simple "de dong dong, de dong dong" ("Don't worry, be hap-py") at 21:00. In days gone by, this used to warn citizens that the city gates would soon close for the night.

• *Enter the church at Oude Groenmarkt 23 (look for the small* Entrée *sign). Stand in the center of the church and take it all in.*

Interior

Simple white walls, a black floor, a brown ceiling, and a mahogany-colored organ make this spacious church feel vast, light, and airy. Considering it was built during a span of 150 years, its architecture is surprisingly homogenous. Originally, much of the interior was painted in bright patterns, similar to the carpet-like frescoes on

some columns near the center of the church. But in 1566, Protestant extremists stripped the church of its graven images and ornate Catholic trappings, leaving it relatively stark, with minimal decoration. They whitewashed everything. The frescoes you see today were restored when the whitewash was removed in the 1980s.

Look up to see the fan-vaulted cedar ceiling from 1530. Look down to see tombstones paving the floor. And look midway up the walls to catch squatting characters supporting the pilasters. The three-story organ fills the west wall.

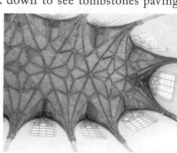

• *We'll circle the church, but first stand at the candle-lined, fence-like brass barrier and look into an enclosed area of wooden benches ("stalls") and the altar, known as the...*

Choir

After the church's foundation was laid, the choir was built first

and used for worship for more than a century while the rest of the building was completed.

Today, the brass-and-wood barrier keeps tourists from entering the most sacred area, just as peasants were kept out in medieval times. While the commoners had to stand during services, local big shots got to perch their heinies on the little ledges (called misericords, carved in 1512) of the **wooden stalls** that line the choir; the eighth stall along the left-hand side shows a poor peasant bending over to bear a rich guy's bum on his back. The stalls are also decorated with the coats of arms of noble families, whose second sons traditionally became priests.

The choir's floor holds a simple slab marked with a lantern—the **Grave of Frans Hals** (Graf van Frans Hals), Haarlem's own master artist of the Golden Age. When he was a child, Hals' family moved to Haarlem, and he lived and worked here all his life, worshipping in the Grote Kerk. A friend of mayors and preachers, he chronicled middle-class citizens and tavern life, producing hundreds of masterpieces...and 10 kids. (☉ See the Frans Hals Museum Tour, page 221.)

At both ends of the brass barrier, look for the endearing knee-level carvings of the "pillar biter." The message of these carvings, aimed at those who were "more Catholic than even the Pope," was this: Don't go overboard on devotion.

More than a thousand wealthy people are buried under the church's pavement stones. Only those with piles of money to give to the church could be buried in a way that gave them an advantage in the salvation derby. But even though the dead bodies were embalmed, they stunk. Imagine being a peasant sitting here, trying to think about God... and thinking only of the stench of well-fed bodies rotting below. Here is where the phrase "stinking rich" was born.

• *Looking down the nave (without actually walking there yet), on the left side is the...*

Pulpit

The pulpit, elaborately carved from oak in 1679, is topped with a tower-shaped roof. Brass handrails snake down the staircase, serpents fleeing the word of God. In this simply decorated Protestant church, the pulpit is perhaps the most ornate element, directing worshippers' eyes to the speaker. During the Reformation, Protestants changed the worship service. As teaching became more important than ritual, the pulpit was given a higher profile.

• *Suspended between columns, between the center of the church and the tourists' entrance, are...*

Three Little Ships

Sailing under the red-white-and-blue Dutch flag and the flag of a rearing lion, ships like these helped make Holland the world's number one sea-trading nation in the 1600s.

The biggest model ship of the three is a frigate. These fast, heavily armed, three-masted, fully rigged ships rode shotgun for merchant vessels, protecting them from pirates in their two-year journey to the Far East and back. This one has a flat-bottomed hull, necessary to ply Amsterdam's shallow harbor. It could fire a 21-gun salute from each side. Extra cannons on the poop deck and forecastle made it more powerful than the average frigate. The keel has an iron saw, a Dutch military specialty for slicing through the chains that commonly blocked harbors (see the chain between two towers near the bow).

• *Three yards away, just to the right, find the...*

Memorial to Hydraulic Engineers
The marble relief shows Neptune in his water chariot. In low-lying Holland of the 1800s, when flooding could mean life or death, hydraulic engineers were heroes.

Twenty yards beyond the memorial (near where you entered, just left of the café) is a painting done when the church was commissioned. This provided a model for the architects to follow.

• *From here, circle the church counterclockwise, starting back near the tourists' entrance. On the wall near the tourists' entrance hangs an...*

Old Map of "Harlemum"
The map shows the walled city in 1688, with ramparts and a moat. Surrounding panels showcase Haarlem's 750-year history. The

lower-left panel shows the 1572–1573 Siege of Haarlem (described below), as brave Haarlem women join their menfolk in battle—bombs exploding around them—to fight off invading Spanish troops.

The bottom-right panel shows knights kneeling before a king in the 12th century, while in the distance, ships sail right along the city walls.

Up until the 1840s, when it was drained and reclaimed, there was a large lake (the Haarlemmermeer) standing between Haarlem and Amsterdam (see page 210). The Grote Kerk, when viewed by distant travelers, seemed to float like a stately ship on the lake, as seen in the landscape along the bottom of the map.

• *Circle around the altar to the other side of the church, to...*

Mary's Chapel (Maria Kapel)

Inside the iron cage on the back wall is an old wood-and-iron chest that served as a safe for the church's cash and precious documents—such as those papers granting the power to sell forgiveness. See the board of keys for the many doors in this huge complex. Notice also the sarcophagi. Once filled with the "stinking rich," boxes like this were buried five deep below the church floor. Such high-density burying maximized the revenue generated by selling burial spots.

Foucault's Pendulum

In the north transept, a ball on a wire hangs from the ceiling (see the brass sphere in the far right corner). When set in motion (by a church tour guide, mostly on Saturdays), it swings across a dial on the floor, re-creating physicist Léon Foucault's pendulum experiment in Paris in 1851. If it's swinging, stand here patiently and watch the earth rotate on its axis.

As the pendulum swings steadily back and forth, the earth rotates counterclockwise underneath it, making the pendulum appear to rotate clockwise around the dial. The earth rotates once every 24 hours, of course, but at Haarlem's latitude of 52 degrees, it makes the pendulum (appear to) sweep 360 degrees every 30 hours, 27 minutes (to knock over the bowling pin). Stand here for five minutes, and you'll see the earth move one degree.

As the world turns, find several small relief statues (in a niche on the right-hand wall) with beheaded heads and defaced faces—victims of the 1566 Iconoclast rampage, when angry Protestant extremists vandalized Dutch Catholic churches (as this once was).

Model of Church

A hundred times smaller than the church itself, this model still took a thousand work-hours to build. On the wall, some of the building materials are displayed: matchsticks, washers, screens, glue, wire, and paper clips.

• *Ten yards farther on, the shallow niche is the...*

Dog-Whipper's Chapel

In a sculpted relief (top of column at left end of chapel, above eye level), an angry man whips an angry dog while striding over another angry dog's head. Back when churches served as rainy-day marketplaces, this man's responsibility was to keep Haarlem's dogs out of the church.

The Organ

Even silent, this organ impresses. Finished in 1738 by Amsterdam's Christian Muller, it features a mahogany-colored casing with tin pipes and gold trim, studded with statues of musicians and an eight-piece combo of angels. Lions on the top hold Haarlem's coat of arms—a sword, surrounded by stars, over a banner reading *Vicit Vim Virtus* ("Truth Overcomes Force"). There are larger pipe organs in the world, but this is one of the best.

With three keyboards, a forest of pedals, and 65 stops (the knobs on either side of the keyboards), this magnificent organ produces an awesome majesty of

sound. Picture 10-year-old Mozart at the controls of this 5,000-pipe sound machine. In 1766, he played Haarlem at the tail end of his triumphant, three-year, whirlwind tour of Europe. He'd just returned from London, where he met J. C. Bach, the youngest son of Johann Sebastian Bach (1685–1750), the grandfather of organ music. Mozart had recently written several pieces inspired by Bach, and he may have tried them out here.

"Hal-le-lu-jah!" That famous four-note riff may have echoed around the church when Handel played here in 1740, the year before his famous oratorio, *Messiah*, debuted. The 20th-century organist/humanitarian Albert Schweitzer also performed here.

The organist sits unseen amid the pipes, behind the section that juts out at the bottom. While the bellows generate pressurized air, the organist presses a key, which opens a valve, admitting forced air through a pipe and out its narrow opening, producing a tone. An eight-foot-long pipe plays middle C. A four-foot-long pipe plays C exactly one octave up. A 20-foot pipe rumbles the rafters. With 5,068 pipes ranging from more than 20 feet tall to just a few inches, this organ can cover eight octaves (a piano plays seven), and each key can play a variety of sounds. By pulling one of the stops (such as "flute" or "trumpet"), the organist can channel the air into certain sets of pipes tuned to play together to mimic other instruments. For maximum power, you "pull out all the stops."

A Cannonball in the Wall, and the Siege of Haarlem

Duck! On the wall (left of the chapel with the green metal gate, above eye level) sits a cannonball, placed here in 1573 to commemorate the city's finest hour—the Siege of Haarlem.

In the winter of 1572–1573, Holland was rebelling against its Spanish oppressors. Haarlem proclaimed its alliance with William of Orange (and thus, independence from Spain). In response, the angry Spanish governor—camped in Amsterdam—laid siege to

Haarlem. The winter was cold, food ran low, and the city was bombarded by Spanish cannons. Inside huddled 4,000 cold, hungry Calvinists. At one point, the city's women even joined the men on the barricades, brandishing kitchen knives.

But Spain had blockaded the Haarlem Lake (the Haarlem-mermeer), and on June 12, 1573, Haarlem had to surrender. The Spanish rounded up 1,500 ringleaders and executed them to send a message to the rest of the country. Still, Haarlem's brave seven-month stand against overwhelming odds became a kind of Dutch Alamo, inspiring their countrymen to fight on.

Following Haarlem's brave lead, other Dutch towns rebelled, including Amsterdam (see page 442). Though Holland and Spain would skirmish for another five decades, the battles soon moved southward, and Spanish troops would never again seriously penetrate the country's borders.

• *Finish in the chapel now housing the café...*

Brewers' Chapel (Brouwerskapel): Giant and Dwarf Marks

The long and short of the city's 750-year history are found on the chapel's central pillar. Black lines on the column mark the height of Haarlem's shortest citizen, thigh-high (33 inches) Simon Paap, who supposedly died in a dwarf-tossing incident, and—wow!—8-foot-8-inch-tall Daniel Cajanus. Who said, "When you've seen one Gothic church, you've seen 'em all"?

FRANS HALS MUSEUM TOUR

Frans Hals (c. 1582–1666) is Haarlem's most famous son. He was a bold humanist who painted everyday people in their warts-and-all glory, a forerunner of Impressionist brushwork, a master of composition, and an articulate visual spokesman for his generation—the generation of Holland's Golden Age.

Stand eye-to-eye with life-size, lifelike portraits of Haarlem's citizens—brewers, preachers, workers, bureaucrats, and housewives. Take a close look at the people who built the Golden Age, and then watched it start to fade.

ORIENTATION

Cost: €7.50 (often €10 when entry includes a special exhibit).

Hours: Tue–Sat 11:00–17:00, Sun 12:00–17:00, closed Mon.

Getting There: The museum is at Groot Heiligland 62, a delightful five-minute stroll from the main square.

Information: While Frans Hals' masterpieces never leave Room 14 (and nearby rooms), the other paintings can rotate—ask a guard if you can't locate them easily. The entire museum is thoughtfully described in English. Tel. 023/511-5775, www.franshalsmuseum.nl.

If you'll be visiting six or more museums in the Netherlands, consider buying the €39.95 Museumkaart pass here. It covers your entry to both the Frans Hals and Teylers museums in Haarlem, and lets you skip the ticket-buying line at bigger sights, such as the Van Gogh Museum in Amsterdam (for more on sightseeing passes, including the Museumkaart, see page 34).

Length of This Tour: Allow one hour.

Cuisine Art: The Frans Hals Lunchcafé serves sandwiches and other simple food (daily 12:00–16:30).

Overview

Frans Hals' paintings are just one part of the collection. The museum fancies itself as *the* museum of the Golden Age, offering you the rare opportunity of enjoying 17th-century art in a 17th-century building. Well-described exhibits unfold as the rectangular museum wraps around a peaceful central courtyard. The building's layout makes sense when you realize it was built as subsidized housing for poor old men (in 1610).

Circle counterclockwise, through the art of Hals' predecessors and colleagues, to the back. The lush still lifes give a sense of how good life is and how important it is to embrace it before it all rots and falls away. Your visit begins with "Haarlem in the 17th Century," showing Dutch slice-of-life painting alongside exhibits on the things that concerned everyday Golden Agers: tulips, trading, linen-weaving, militias, "women power," and beer.

To see the Frans Hals paintings described in this chapter, start in Room 14, with four large Civic Guard portraits, each a masterpiece. Then see his portraits and smaller works nearby (Rooms 16–19).

THE TOUR BEGINS

• *Make your way to large Room 14, where you're well-guarded by canvases full of companies of men in uniform. We'll start with the men in the bright red sashes.*

Banquet of the Officers of the St. George Civic Guard (1616)

In 1616, tiny Holland was the richest country on earth, and these Haarlem men are enjoying the fruits of their labor. The bright red sashes, the jaunty poses, the smiles, the rich food, the sweeping tilt of the flags...the exuberant spirit of the Golden Age. These weekend warriors have finished their ceremonial parade through town and hung their weapons on the wall, and now they sit down for a relaxed, after-the-show party.

The man in the middle (next to the flag-bearer, facing us) is about to carve the chicken, when the meal is interrupted. It's us, arriving late through the back door, and heads turn to greet us.

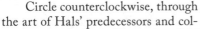

Frans Hals Museum—Room 14

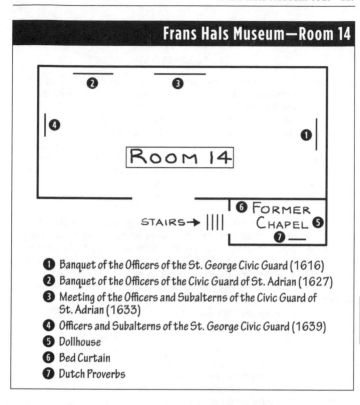

❶ Banquet of the Officers of the St. George Civic Guard (1616)
❷ Banquet of the Officers of the Civic Guard of St. Adrian (1627)
❸ Meeting of the Officers and Subalterns of the Civic Guard of St. Adrian (1633)
❹ Officers and Subalterns of the St. George Civic Guard (1639)
❺ Dollhouse
❻ Bed Curtain
❼ Dutch Proverbs

Rosy-cheeked Nicolaes Woutersz van der Meer (see his portrait, page 227), hand on hip, turns around with a friendly look, while the man to the right, the colonel in charge, waves us in. Frans Hals knew these men well as friends and colleagues, since he himself was a lifelong member of this Civic Guard company.

This band of brothers is united by common gestures—two men have hands on hips, three turn their palms up, two plant their hands downward, three clutch wine glasses. But mostly, they're joined by the uniform sashes. The red sashes slant both left and right, perfectly forming opposing diagonals.

With this painting, Frans Hals broke the mold of stuffy group portraits. He relegates the traditional symbolic weapons to the shelf (upper right) and breaks up the traditional chorus line of soldiers by placing the men naturally around a table. Van der Meer

Frans Hals
(c. 1582–1666)

At age 10, Frans Hals, the son of a weaver, moved with his family to Haarlem. He would spend the rest of his life there, rarely traveling even to nearby Amsterdam.

His early years are known to us only through his paintings of taverns and drunks, musicians and actors, done in a free and colorful style (like the Rijksmuseum's *Merry Drinker*, page 117). In 1610, he married and joined Haarlem's St. Luke's Guild of painters. In 1612, he was admitted to the prestigious St. George Civic Guard. In 1617, widowed Hals married again, producing (altogether) ten children, five of whom took up painting.

Hals' group portrait of the St. George Civic Guard (1616) put him on the map as Haarlem's premier portrait painter. For the next five decades, he abandoned the lighthearted slice-of-life scenes of his youth and dedicated himself to chronicling Haarlem's prosperous, middle-class world of businessmen and professionals—people he knew personally, as well as professionally.

Despite his success, Hals had trouble with money. In 1654, he had to sell his belongings to pay debts, and he fought poverty the rest of his life. Commissions became scarce, as the public now preferred more elegant, flattering portraits. His final works (1650–1666) are dark and somber, with increasingly rough and simple brushwork.

In 1664, the city granted him a pension for his years of service. When he died two years later, his work quickly passed out of fashion, dismissed as mere portraiture. In the 1800s, the Impressionists rediscovered him, and today he's recognized for his innovations, craftsmanship, and unique style.

FRANS HALS MUSEUM

sticks his elbow in our faces (another Hals trademark) to define a distinct foreground, while the flag-bearer stakes out the middle ground, and a window at the back opens up to a distant, airy background.

Then Hals sets the scene in motion. A guy on the left side leans over to tell a joke to his friend. The dashing young flag-bearer in the middle turns back to listen to the bald-headed man. An ensign (standing, right side) enters and doffs his cap to Captain Van der Meer. And then we barge in, interrupting the banquet, but welcomed as one of the boys.

Banquet of the Officers of the Civic Guard of St. Adrian (1627)

The men are bunched into two symmetrical groups, left and right, with a window in the back. The figures form a Y, with a tilted

Civic Guard Portraits

The fathers of the men pictured in this room fought, suffered imprisonment, and died in the great Siege of Haarlem (1572-1573), which helped turn the tide against Spanish oppression. But their sons were bankers, merchants, traders, and sailors, boldly conquering Europe on the new frontier of capitalism. Civic Guards became less of a militia and more a social club for upwardly mobile men. Their feasts—huge eating and drinking binges, punctuated by endless toasts, poems, skits, readings, dirty limericks, and ceremonial courses—could last for days on end.

Standard Civic Guard portraits (see page 78 of Amsterdam City Walk) always showed the soldiers in the same way—two neat rows of men, with everyone looking straight out, holding medieval weapons that tell us their ranks. It took master artists like Hals and Rembrandt to turn these boring visual documents into art.

flag marking the right diagonal (echoed by several tilted ruffs), and a slanting row of heads forming the left diagonal (echoed by several slanting sashes). The diagonals meet at the back of the table, marking the center of the composition, where the two groups of men exchange food, drink, and meaningful eye contact.

Meeting of the Officers and Subalterns of the Civic Guard of St. Adrian (1633)

Six years later, Hals painted many of these same men gathered around an outdoor table. The horizontal row of faces is punctuated by three men standing sideways, elbows out. Again, the men are united by sashes that slant in (generally) the same direction and by repeated gestures—hands on hips, hands on hearts, and so on.

Officers and Subalterns of the St. George Civic Guard (1639)

When 57-year-old Frans Hals painted this, his last Civic Guard portrait, he included himself among his St. George buddies. (Find

Frans in the upper left, second from left, under the faint gray number 19.)

As he got older, Hals refined and simplified his group-portrait style, using quieter colors, the classic two horizontal rows of soldiers, and the traditional symbolic weapons.

A decade after this was painted, Holland officially ended its war with Spain (Treaty of Munster, 1648), Civic Guards lost their military purpose, businessmen preferred portraits showing themselves as elegant gentlemen rather than crusty soldiers, and the tradition of Civic Guard group portraits quickly died out.

• *Backtrack and look for the* Poppenhuis *sign, pointing left. Head up five steps to the...*

Former Chapel

Take a look inside. You'll find a **fancy dollhouse** *(poppenhuis)*, the hobby of the lady of the house (her portrait is on the left). Handmade by the finest local craftsmen, this delicately crafted dollhouse offers a glimpse of wealthy 18th-century living.

The exquisite **bed curtain,** brought back from New England, decorated the bed of a wealthy Dutch family who lived in colonial America. It's embroidered with bulb flowers known during the 17th century—and well-described in English.

On the wall is ***Dutch Proverbs** (Vlaamsche Spreekwoorden)*, a fun painting that shows 72 charming Flemish scenes representing different folk sayings. (It's a copy of a 17th-century work by Pieter Brueghel the Younger.) Pick up the chart to identify these clever bits of everyday wisdom. True to form, this piece of Flemish art isn't preachy religious art or political propaganda; rather, it shares the simple and decent morals of these hardworking Dutch people.

• *Continue counterclockwise around the museum, pausing to enjoy the exquisite still lifes in Room 16. When you reach the hallway that is Room 17, look for the...*

Portrait of Jacobus Zaffius (1611)

Arr-r-r-r-rh! This fierce, intense, rough-hewn man is not a pirate, but a priest, the rogue leader of an outlawed religion in

Haarlem—Catholicism. In the 1600s, Haarlem was a Protestant town in the midst of a war against Catholic Spain, and local Catholics were guilty by association. But Zaffius refused to be silenced. He turns to glare and snarl at the Protestant town fathers. He was so personally imposing that the city tolerated his outspokenness.

The face jumps out from a background of neutral gray-brown-black. His features are alive—head turning, mouth twisting, face wrinkling up, beard bristling. Hals captures him in action, using a slow shutter speed. The rough brushstrokes of the fur coat and beard suggest the blur of motion of this agitated individual. This is Frans Hals' first known portrait, painted when he—a late starter in the art world—was nearly 30.

• *Make a left into Room 18 to see the...*

Portraits of Nicolaes Woutersz van der Meer and his wife, Cornelia Claesdr Vooght (1631)

Hals knew Nicolaes van der Meer, a fellow Civic Guard lodge member, personally. Van der Meer was a brewer, an important post in a city where average beer consumption was six pints a day per person (man, woman, and child). He was also the mayor, so

his pose is official and dignified, larger than life-size. But the face is pure Golden Age—red-cheeked and healthy, confident and intelligent, his even gaze tinged with wisdom. This mayor kept a steady hand on the tiller of Haarlem's ship of state.

The face is literally the focus of this otherwise messy painting. The ruffled collar is a tangle of simple, figure-eight swirls of white paint; the brocaded coat is a patchwork of white lines; and the lace cuffs are a few broad outlines. But out of the rough brushwork and somber background, Van der Meer's crystal-clear eyes meet ours. The finely etched crow's-feet around his eyes suggest that Hals had seen this imposing man break into a warm smile. Hey, I'd vote for him as my mayor.

The companion painting shows Van der Meer's companion, his wife, **Cornelia.** Husband-and-wife portraits were hung together—notice that they share the same background, and the two figures turn in toward each other. Still, both people are looking out at us,

Frans Hals' Style

- Hals' forte is portraits. Of his 240 paintings, 195 are individual or group portraits, mostly of Haarlem's citizens.
- His paintings are life-size and realistic, capturing everyday people, even downright ugly people, without airbrushing out their blemishes or character flaws.
- Hals uses rough, Impressionistic brushwork, where a few thick, simple strokes blend at a distance to create details. He worked quickly, often making the rough sketch the final, oil version.
- His stop-action technique captures the sitter in mid-motion. Aided by his rough brushwork, this creates a blur that suggests the person is still moving.
- Hals adds 3-D depth to otherwise horizontal, widescreen canvases. (Men with their elbows sticking out serve to define the foreground.)
- His canvases are unified by people wearing matching colors, using similar poses and gestures, and gathered in symmetrical groups.
- His paintings have a relaxed, light-hearted, even comical atmosphere. In group portraits, the subjects interact with one another. Individual portraits meet your eyes as if meeting an old friend.
- His works show nothing religious—no Madonnas, Crucifixions, angels, or Bible scenes. If anything, he imbues everyday objects with heavenly beauty and grants ordinary people the status of saints.

not clinging to each other, suggesting mature partners more than lovey-dovey newlyweds. Married couples in Golden Age Holland divvied up the work—men ran the business, women ran the home—and prided themselves on their mutual independence. (Even today in progressive Holland, fewer women join the workforce than in many other industrial nations.) Cornelia's body is as imposing as her husband's, with big, manly hands and a practical, slightly suspicious look. The intricate work in her ruff collar tells us that Hals certainly could sweat the details when it suited his purpose.

Regents of the St. Elisabeth Hospital of Haarlem (1641)

These aren't the Dutch Masters cigar boys, though it looks like Rembrandt's famous (and later) *De Staalmeesters* (see page 124 in the Rijksmuseum Tour). It's a board meeting, where five men in black hats and black suits with lace collars and cuffs—the Golden Age power suit—sit around a table in a brown room.

Pretty boring stuff, but Hals was hired to paint their portraits, and he does his best. Behind the suits, he captures five distinct men. The man on the far left is pondering the universe or raising a belch. The man in the middle (facing us) looks like the classic Golden Age poster boy, with moustache, goatee, ruddy cheeks, and long hair. Another is clean-shaven, while the guy on the far right adds a fashion twist with moustache wax. Hals links these five unique faces with one of his trademark techniques—similar poses and gestures. The burping man and the goateed man are a mirror image of the same pose—leaning on the table, hand on chest. Several have cupped hands, several have hands laid flat, or on their chests, or on the table. And the one guy keeps working on that burp.

• *Continue to Room 19. On the wall straight ahead are the...*

Regents of the Old Men's Almshouse (1664)

These men look tired. So was Holland. So was Hals. At 82, Hals, despite years of success, was poor and dependent on the charity of the city, which granted him a small pension.

He was hired to paint the board of directors of the Old Men's

Almshouse, located here in the building that now houses the Frans Hals Museum. Though Hals himself never lived in the almshouse, he fully understood what it was to be penniless and have to rely on money doled out by men like these.

The portrait is unflattering, drained of color. Somber men dressed in black peer out of a shadowy room. These men were trying to administer a dwindling budget to house and feed an aging population. Holland's Golden Age was losing its luster.

The style is nearly Impressionistic—collars, cuffs, and gloves rendered with a few messy brushstrokes of paint. Hands and faces are a patchwork of light and dark splotches. Despite the sketchiness, each face captures the man's essence.

Historians speculate that this unflattering portrait was Hals' revenge on tightwad benefactors, but the fact is that the regents were satisfied with their portrait. By the way, the man just to the right of center isn't drunk, but suffering from facial paralysis. To the end, Hals respected unvarnished reality.

• *Directly behind you, find the...*

Regentesses of the Old Men's Almshouse (1664)

These women ran the women's wing of the almshouse, located across the street. Except for a little rouge on the women's pale-as-death faces, this canvas is almost a study in gray and black, as Hals pared his palette down to the bare essentials. The faces are subtle variations on old age. Only the woman on the right resolutely returns our gaze.

The man who painted this was old, poor, out of fashion, in failing health, perhaps bitter, and dying. In contrast with the lively group scenes of Hals' youth, these individuals stand forever isolated. They don't look at each other, each lost in their own thoughts, perhaps contemplating their own mortality (or stifling belches). Their only link to one another is the tenuous, slanting line formed by their hands, leading to the servant who enters the room with a mysterious message.

Could that message be...death? Or just that this tour is over?

SLEEPING, EATING, and NIGHTLIFE

The helpful Haarlem TI can nearly always find you a €25 bed in a private home (but for a €6-per-person fee, plus a cut of your host's money; two-night minimum). Avoid this if you can; it's cheaper to reserve by calling direct. Nearly every Dutch person you'll encounter speaks English.

Haarlem is most crowded on Easter weekend (April 2–4 in 2010), in April (particularly the flower parade—on April 24 in 2010—and Queen's Day, on April 30), May, July, and August. Also see "Major Holidays and Weekends" on page 4.

The listed prices include breakfast (unless otherwise noted) and usually include the €2-per-person-per-day tourist tax. To avoid this town's louder-than-normal street noises, forgo views for a room in the back. Hotels and the TI have a useful parking brochure.

SLEEPING

In the Center
Hotels and B&Bs
$$$ Hotel Lion D'Or is a classy, 34-room business hotel with all the professional comforts and a handy location (Db-€150, Fri–Sat Db-€125, extra bed-€15, 8 percent discount to Rick Steves readers for 2-night stays when you book direct, air-con, elevator, Wi-Fi, across the street from train station at Kruisweg 34, tel. 023/532-1750, fax 023/532-9543, www.hotelliondor.nl, reservations@hotelliondor.nl, Dirk Pauw).

$$$ Stempels Hotel, modern yet elegant, is located in a recently renovated, 250-year-old building. With bare floors, comfy high-quality beds, and minimalist touches in its 17 rooms, what it lacks in warmth it makes up for in style and value. Double-paned windows help keep down the noise, since it's a block east of Market

Sleep Code

(€1 = about $1.40, country code: 31, area code: 023)
S = Single, D = Double/Twin, T = Triple, Q = Quad, b = bathroom, s = shower only. Credit cards are accepted unless otherwise noted.

To help you easily sort through these listings, I've divided the rooms into three categories, based on the price for a standard double room with bath:

$$$ Higher Priced—Most rooms €85 or more.
$$ Moderately Priced—Most rooms between €60–85.
$ Lower Priced—Most rooms €60 or less.

Square, with a bustling brasserie and bar downstairs (standard Sb-€80, Db-€95–108, breakfast-€10, in-room computers with free Internet access and Wi-Fi, Klokhuisplein 9, tel. 023/512-3910, www.stempelsinhaarlem.nl, info@stempelsinhaarlem.nl).

$$$ Hotel Amadeus, on Market Square, has 15 small, bright, and basic rooms, some with views of the square. This characteristic hotel, ideally located above an early 20th-century dinner café, is relatively quiet, especially if you take a room in the back. Its lush old lounge/breakfast room on the second floor overlooks the square, and Mike and Inez take good care of their guests (Sb-€60, Db-€85, Tb-€110, 5 percent Rick Steves discount with 2-night stay and cash, 10-min walk from train station, steep climb to lounge and then an elevator, fee for Internet access and Wi-Fi, Grote Markt 10, tel. 023/532-4530, fax 023/532-2328, www.amadeus-hotel.com, info@amadeus-hotel.com). The Hotel Amadeus' breakfast room overlooking the main square is a great place to watch the town greet a new day—one of my favorite Haarlem moments.

$$$ Ambassador City Centre Hotel, with 29 comfortable rooms in a big, plain hotel, is located just behind the Grote Kerk (Db-€100, breakfast buffet-€14, free Internet access and Wi-Fi, Oude Groenmarkt 20, tel. 023/512-5300, www.acc-hotel.nl, info @acc-hotel.nl). They rent studios with kitchenettes for 2–4 people (€120–150 depending on season and number of people). They also run Hotel Joops a block away (rooms are €10 cheaper; studios and apartments with kitchenettes for 2–4 people).

$$ Hotel Malts, which just opened in late 2008, is well-located and rents 12 bright, simple, and fresh rooms for a good price (small Db-€55, medium Db-€70, big Db-€85, breakfast-€7.50, free Wi-Fi, Zijlstraat 56, tel. 023/551-2385, www.maltshotel.nl, info @degraaf-schreurs.nl, Marco).

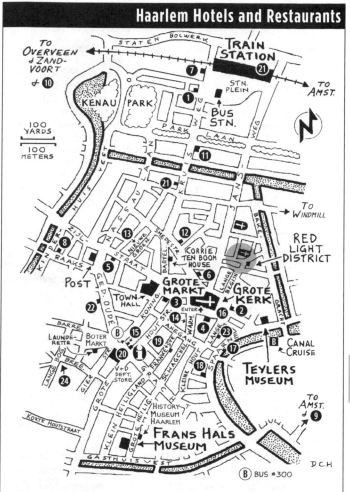

Haarlem Hotels and Restaurants

1. Hotel Lion D'Or
2. Stempels Hotel
3. Hotel Amadeus
4. Ambassador City Centre Hotel
5. Hotel Malts
6. Hotel Carillon
7. Indrapoera Hotel & Hostel
8. Die Raeckse Hotel
9. To Hotel Haarlem Zuid
10. To Stayokay Haarlem Hostel
11. Pannenkoekhuis de Smikkel
12. Vlam in de Pan & 't Theehuis Coffeeshop
13. Vincent's Eethuis
14. Jacobus Pieck Eetlokaal & Friethuis de Vlaminck
15. Pizzeria-Rist. Venezia
16. La Plume Restaurant
17. Spaarne 66 Restaurant Bar
18. Lambermon's Restaurant
19. De Lachende Javaan Rest.
20. La Place Cafeteria
21. Albert Heijn Supermarkets (2)
22. DekaMarkt Supermarket
23. High Times Coffeehouse
25. Vijfhoek (Five Corners)

Jan-Kees Doodle Dandy

Haarlem isn't the only Dutch town that sounds familiar to American ears. Given that it was Dutch settlers who founded New York (a.k.a. "Nieuw Amsterdam"), it's no surprise that plenty of places in and around New York have Dutch sources: Brooklyn was named after Breukelen, a town south of Amsterdam, and the land that once belonged to émigré farmer Jonas Bronk became (care to guess?)... the Bronx. Other familiar place names come from straightforward descriptions of what the Dutch found there: Coney Island was once "Coyne Eylandt" (rabbit island), Rhode Island was "Roode Eylandt" (red island), Flatbush was "Vlakke bos" (wooded plain), and Catskill was "Kaatskil" (cat creek). Even "Yankee"—which originally referred only to Dutch settlers—quite likely came from a common Dutch first name, Jan-Kees.

Rooms in Restaurants

These places are all run as sidelines by restaurants, and you'll know it by the style of service and rooms. Lobbies are in the restaurant, and there are no public spaces. Still, they are handy and—for Haarlem—inexpensive.

$$ Hotel Carillon overlooks the town square and comes with a little traffic and bell-tower chimes. It rents 20 spartan and run-down rooms at the top of st-e-e-e-p stairs. The front rooms come with more street noise and great town-square views (tiny loft S-€40, Db-€78–80, Tb-€99, Qb-€108, 5 percent discount for Rick Steves readers—claim when booking and show book on arrival, no elevator, free Wi-Fi, Grote Markt 27, tel. 023/531-0591, fax 023/531-4909, www.hotelcarillon.com, info@hotelcarillon.com, owners Kelly Kuo, Andres Haas, and June).

$$ Indrapoera Hotel and Hostel, a humid little place with too much carpeting, has eight cheap hotel rooms and five new hostel rooms just across the street from the train station. Their stark-yet-modern, six- to eight-bed dorms have lockers and share one big modern bathroom (hotel—Db-€75, hostel—€25–30/bed with sheets and breakfast, trains stop by midnight, Kruisweg 18, tel. 023/532-0393, yeh@yeh.speedxs.nl, Yeh family).

$$ Die Raeckse Hotel, family-run and friendly, is not as central as the others and has less character and more traffic noise—but its 21 rooms are decent and comfortable. Noisy rooms on the street are cheaper than the quiet ones in the back, but it's worth asking for a quiet room (Sb-€55, small Db-€70, big Db-€85, Tb-€90–110, Qb-€120–135, €5/night discount for 2-night stay, includes breakfast, these special Rick Steves prices only for direct bookings, fee for Internet access and Wi-Fi, Raaks Straat 1, tel. 023/532-6629, fax 023/531-7937, www.die-raeckse.nl, dieraeckse@zonnet.nl).

Near Haarlem

$$$ Hotel Haarlem Zuid, with 300 modern rooms, is sterile but a good value for drivers. It sits in an industrial zone a 20-minute walk from the center, on the road to the airport (Db-€84–98, breakfast-€12, elevator, free parking, laundry service, fitness center-€5, inexpensive hotel restaurant, Toekanweg 2, tel. 023/536-7500, fax 023/536-7980, www.hotelhaarlemzuid.nl, haarlemzuid @valk.com). Bus #300 (runs every 10 min) conveniently connects the hotel with the train station, Market Square, and the airport.

$ Stayokay Haarlem Hostel, completely renovated and with all the youth-hostel comforts, charges €25–30 for beds in four- and six-bed dorms. They also rent simple €60–80 doubles (€2.50 less for members, includes sheets and breakfast, save by booking on their website, laundry service, daily 8:00–24:00, Jan Gijzenpad 3, two miles from Haarlem station—take bus #2 from station, or a 10-min walk from Santpoort Zuid train station, tel. 023/537-3793, www.stayokay.com/haarlem, haarlem@stayokay.com).

EATING

North of Market Square

Pannenkoekhuis de Smikkel, a well-worn fixture in town, serves a big selection of pancakes for lunch or dinner (meat, cheese, etc.) and dessert. The €8–12 pancakes are large but pricey and only a good value if you split them. Two people can split one savory and one sweet selection to eat economically (Tue–Sun 12:00–21:00, closed Mon, 2 blocks in front of station, Kruisweg 57, tel. 023/532-0631).

At **Vlam in de Pan,** a dynamo named Femke serves vegetarian delights: soup, salad, veggie sushi, quiches, and other fresh foods. Sit family-style at the long tables, or get your food to take away (€6–10 plates, Tue–Fri 16:00–21:00, closed Sat–Mon, Smedestraat 13, tel. 023/551-1738).

Vincent's Eethuis, the cheapest restaurant in town, offers basic Dutch food and a friendly staff. This former St. Vincent's soup kitchen now feeds more gainfully employed locals than poor people in a homey dining hall. Just grab a plate and hit the buffet line (two €6 daily plates to choose from, price includes second helping, dessert and drinks extra, Mon–Fri from 17:30, last serving at 19:30, closed Sat–Sun, Nieuwe Groenmarkt 22).

Supermarkets: Albert Heijn has two convenient locations. One is in the train station (Mon–Fri 6:30–21:30, Sat 7:00–21:30, Sun 8:00–21:30, cash only) and the other is at Kruisstraat 10 (Mon–Sat 8:00–20:00, closed Sun, cash only). The **DekaMarkt** is a few blocks east of Market Square (Mon 10:00–20:00, Tue–Wed 8:30–20:00, Thu–Fri 8:30–21:00, Sat 8:30–20:00, closed Sun,

Marijuana in Haarlem

Haarlem is a laid-back place for observing the Dutch approach to recreational marijuana. The town is dotted with about a dozen coffeeshops, where pot is casually sold and smoked by relaxed, noncriminal types. These easygoing coffeeshops are more welcoming than they may feel—bartenders under-stand that Yankee travelers might be a bit out of their ele-ment and are happy to answer questions.

If you don't like the smell of pot, avoid places sporting wildly painted walls, plants in the windows, or Rastafarian yellow, red, and green colors. The following two shops are inviting and particularly friendly to American visitors:

The tiny **'t Theehuis,** which feels like a hippie teahouse, was Haarlem's first coffeeshop (c. 1984). Along with a global selection of pot, it has 50 different varieties of tea on the menu, and a friendly staff. Martijn, who offers weekly menus, is happy to roll you the €3 joint of your choice (daily 13:00–22:00, a block off Market Square at Smedestraat 25).

High Times, with a living room ambience and loaner bongs, offers smokers 12 varieties of joints in racks behind the bar (neatly pre-packed in trademarked "Joint Packs," €3-4.50, daily 8:00–23:00, Internet access, Lange Veerstraat 47). Across the street at Crackers Pub, you can see what too much alcohol does to people.

Gedempte Oude Gracht 54, between V&D department store and post office).

South of Market Square

Jacobus Pieck Eetlokaal is popular with locals for its fine-value "global cuisine," good salads, and peaceful garden courtyard. The Oriental Peak Salad is a perennial favorite, and the dish of the day (*dagschotel*, €12) always sells out (great €6 sandwiches at lunch, Tue–Sat 10:00–22:00, closed Sun–Mon, cash only, Warmoesstraat 18, behind church, tel. 023/532-6144).

Friethuis de Vlaminck is your best bet for a cone of old-fashioned, fresh Flemish-style fries (€2, daily 11:00–18:30, Warmoesstraat 3, behind church, tel. 023/532-1084). Winnie offers a dazzling array of sauces. With his help, you can be adventurous.

Pizzeria-Ristorante Venezia, run for 10 years by the same Italian family from Bari, is the place to go for pizza or pasta (€8–10 choices, daily 13:00–23:00, facing V&D department store at Verwulft 7, tel. 023/531-7753). You'll feel like you're in Rome at a good indoor table, or sit outdoors in a busy people-zone.

La Plume Restaurant steakhouse is noisy, with a happy, local, and carnivorous crowd (€15–20 meals, daily from 17:30, *satay* and ribs are favorites, Lange Veerstraat 1, tel. 023/531-3202). The relaxing outdoor seating faces the church and a lively pedestrian mall.

Lange Veerstraat Restaurant Row: If you don't know what you want to eat, stroll the delightful Lange Veerstraat behind the church and survey a fun range of restaurants (from cheap falafels to Cuban, and much more).

On the Spaarne River Canal: Haarlem seems to turn its back on its river with most of the eating energy a couple of blocks away. To enjoy a meal with a fine canal view, consider the **Spaarne 66 Restaurant Bar.** The Lemmers girls (a mom and her daughters) run this cozy eatery, with a woody, old-time interior and fine, outdoor canalside seating (light €7 lunches, €20 Mediterranean/Dutch dinner plates, Wed–Mon 11:00–24:00, closed Tue, Spaarne 66, tel. 023/551-3800).

Dressy Splurge: Romantic **Lambermon's** has tables gathered around a busy, modern open kitchen and an intriguing and popular-in-Haarlem formula. Chef Pascal Smit offers a kind of "cooking theater" that serves up an orderly succession of eight French/Dutch courses (€10/course, optional paired wines-€5/glass). Each successive course is served on the half-hour starting at 18:30. You only get what's served that day, and you can arrive when it suits you. Jump in at the cheese and/or dessert course, then finish when you like (closed Sun–Mon, Spaarne 96, tel. 023/542-7804).

De Lachende Javaan ("The Laughing Javanese") is a long-established Indonesian place serving a memorable *rijsttafel* (€20–24, Tue–Sun 17:00–22:00, closed Mon, Frankestraat 27, tel. 023/532-8792). The jury's still out on the new Indonesian place in town, **Wisma Hilda,** which is closer to the station and has a cheerier interior (Kruisweg 70, tel. 023/551-3197).

La Place dishes up fresh, healthy, budget food with Haarlem's best view. Sit on the top floor or roof garden of the V&D department store (Mon 11:00–18:00, Tue–Sat 9:30–18:00, Thu until 21:00, closed Sun except for first Sun of month 12:00–17:00, Grote Houtstraat 70, on corner of Gedempte Oude Gracht, tel. 023/515-8700).

NIGHTLIFE

Haarlem's evening scene is great. Consider four basic zones: Market Square in the shadow of the Grote Kerk; Lange Veerstraat; Boter Market Square; and Vijfhoek (Five Corners).

Market Square is lined with trendy bars (Café Studio is generally the hot spot for a drink here) that seem made for nursing a drink. Lange Veerstraat (behind the Grote Kerk) is colorful and bordered with lively spots. Boter Market Square is more convivial and local, as it's less central and away from the tourists. And Vijfhoek, named for the five lanes that converge here, is incredibly charming, although it has only one pub (with plenty of drinks, bar snacks, a relaxed local crowd, and fine indoor or outdoor seating). The area from this cutest corner in town to the New Church (Nieuwe Kerk, a couple of blocks away) is worth exploring. If you want a more high-powered scene, Amsterdam is just 20 minutes away by train.

DELFT and THE HAGUE

These adjoining cities, both conveniently situated just an hour southwest of Amsterdam, are as different as night and day. Sleepy Delft is the charming cultural capital, with soothing canals, an inviting square, royal tombs squirreled away under an exclamation-point church tower, and ties to Vermeer. The citified Eurocrat center of The Hague offers sightseers a few busy but rewarding hours of urban museum-hopping, including the chance to meet a famous girl with a pearl earring.

The two cities are linked by a simple tram or train ride (explained on page 248). Together, they form a handy yin and yang of enjoyable experiences to round out your Dutch travels.

Planning Your Time

It's easy to day-trip to Delft and The Hague from Amsterdam or Haarlem. But if you spend the night anywhere in the Netherlands outside the capital...make it Delft.

Whether side-tripping or home-basing, for a busy day of contrasts, visit both Delft and The Hague. In the morning, take in The Hague's sights (the Mauritshuis museum is tops). Then, continue to Delft to visit its churches, Vermeer Center, and Royal Dutch Delftware Manufactory (last tour departs at 16:00)...or to simply mellow out by a canal.

Delft

Peaceful as a Vermeer painting and as lovely as its porcelain, Delft has a special soul. Enjoy this typically Dutch, "I could live here"

town best by simply wandering around, watching people, munching local syrup waffles, or daydreaming on the canal bridges. If you're eager for some sightseeing, visit a pair of churches, learn more about favorite son Vermeer, or tour the famous porcelain factory.

Think of Delft as an alternative to Haarlem: a low-key, mid-sized city with fast and easy connections to a big metropolis (The Hague). And, laced with tranquil and picturesque canals, Delft might even win the cuteness contest.

ORIENTATION

(area code: 015)

Delft feels much smaller than its population of 95,000. (Because they're squeezed between the two giant cities of Rotterdam and The Hague, locals describe Delft as a "small town.") Almost everything of interest (except the porcelain factory) clusters within the former walls of the canal-lined Old Town, across the street from the train station. The vast Market Square (Markt), with the tall and skinny spire of the New Church, marks the center of the Old Town. A couple of blocks to the southeast is the lively, restaurant-lined Beestenmarkt ("Beast Market"). You could walk from one end of the Old Town to the other in about 15 minutes.

Tourist Information

This TI is a tourist's dream. Pick up the good free brochure on Delft, which includes an excellent map (April–Sept Sun–Mon 10:00–16:00, Tue–Fri 9:00–18:00, Sat 10:00–17:00; Oct–March Mon 11:00–16:00, Tue–Sat 10:00–16:00, Sun 11:00–15:00; free Internet access, 2-min walk north of Market Square to Hippolytusbuurt 4, tel. 015/215-4051, www.delft.nl).

Tours: The TI sells four different brochures (€2.50 each) describing self-guided walking tours. In the summer (mid-April–Sept), they offer a €10, two-hour walking tour of town that includes a canal-boat trip (Sun–Fri at 11:30, Sat at 12:30, also in Oct on weekends only).

Arrival in Delft

From the train station (ATM on left as you leave), it's about a five-minute walk to Market Square at the center of the Old Town: Exit straight ahead, walk across the canal, then continue straight into town, following signs for *Centrum*. Drivers take the Delft exit #9 off the A-13 expressway.

SIGHTS

In the Old Town

▲**Churches**—Delft has two churches that hold tombs of prominent local residents. They're both covered by the same €3.20 ticket and are open the same hours (April–Oct Mon–Sat 9:00–18:00; Nov–March Mon–Fri 11:00–16:00, Sat 10:00–17:00; closed to tourists Sun year-round, tel. 015/212-3025, www.nieuwekerk-delft.nl).

The giant, Gothic **New Church** (Nieuwe Kerk) boldly dominates the town from its prominent position overlooking Market Square. Inside are buried the beloved Dutch ruler William I ("The Silent") of Orange (1533-1584) and the Dutch royalty that succeeded him. It was William who rallied the Dutch to begin their revolt against the Spanish Habsburg rulers. William's ornate tomb—a canopied monument to his greatness—dominates the choir area. It features two representations of William: one of white marble, reclining peacefully; and a strong, armored king in bronze, sitting royally. At the corners of his monument are female statues representing Liberty, Justice, Religion, and Fortitude. The sweet dog at his feet symbolizes loyalty. Unfortunately, all these fine virtues could not save William from being gunned down by an assassin's bullet (just up the street, right here in Delft).

William I was the founder of the dynasty that still (in name) rules the Netherlands. His most famous descendant is one of the few not buried here. William III of Orange (1650–1702), as grandson of the English king, was called upon by the English Parliament to bring peace and order after the turmoil of England's Civil War. William III was crowned King of England and ruled alongside his wife Mary. The two gave their name to a

DELFT

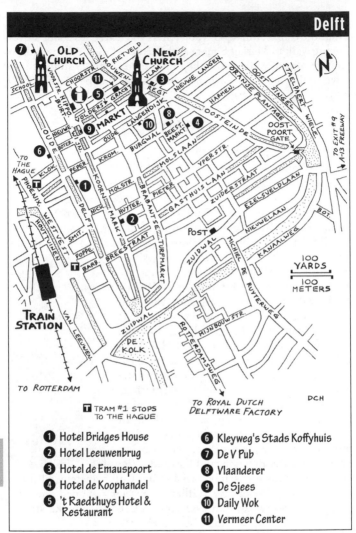

Delft

Map labels:

OLD CHURCH
NEW CHURCH
MARKT
SCHOOL
VOORT. BURT.
HIPPO.
CHOORSTR.
VROUWEN.
VR.RIETVELD
VLAM.
NIEUWE LANGEN
HARMEN.
ORANJE PLANTAGE
OOST SINGEL
STAELPAERT WIELE
VOLDERS GRACHT
REGT
OUDE
NIEUWE
BOTER
KOORN MARKT
PEPER
KLOK
PHOENIX
WESTVEST
HOUTTUINEN
SMIT
POPPE
BARB
VAN LEEUWEN.
NIEUWE DELFT
WICK.
HUYTER
BREESTRAAT
OOSTEINDE
OOSTPOORT GATE
LANGENDIJK
BEEST MARKT
BURGWAL
OUDE
KROM
MOLSLAAN
BRABANTSE TURFMARKT
PIETER
GASTHUISLAAN
VIPER STR.
ZUIDERSTRAAT
EZELSVELDLAAN
BOT
NIEUWELAAN
KANAALWEG
ZUIDWAL
POST
MICHIEL DE RUYTERWEG
ZUIDWAL
DE KOLK
ROTTERDAMSWEG
MIJNBOUWSTR.
DCH
TRAIN STATION
TO THE HAGUE
TO ROTTERDAM
TO EXIT #9 A-13 FREEWAY
TO ROYAL DUTCH DELFTWARE FACTORY

100 YARDS
100 METERS

T TRAM #1 STOPS TO THE HAGUE

1 Hotel Bridges House
2 Hotel Leeuwenbrug
3 Hotel de Emauspoort
4 Hotel de Koophandel
5 't Raedthuys Hotel & Restaurant

6 Kleyweg's Stads Koffyhuis
7 De V Pub
8 Vlaanderer
9 De Sjees
10 Daily Wok
11 Vermeer Center

DELFT

fledgling college in the American Colonies (and William III lies buried in London).

Most of William I's descendants of the House of Orange are also buried in this church. A few paces in front of William (near the transept), a large stone slab marks the entrance to the sprawling underground labyrinth that holds crates of Oranges. (The crypt is strictly off-limits for anyone unrelated.) Besides ruling Holland, the Orange family had owned the independent principality of Orange in the south of France since medieval times. The Royal Family's official color was—what else?—orange, which is

Johannes Vermeer
(1632–1675)

The great Golden Age painter Johannes Vermeer was born in Delft, grew up near Market Square, and set a number of his paintings here. His father, an art dealer, gave Johannes a passion for painting. Late in the artist's career, with Holland fighting draining wars against England, the demand for art and luxuries went sour in the Netherlands, forcing Vermeer to downsize—he sold his big home, packed up his wife and 14 children, and moved in with his mother-in-law. He died two years later.

Vermeer painted some 37 surviving works (though experts debate whether all of them were actually his). Although Vermeer painted landscapes and scenes from mythology and the Bible, he specialized in depicting the everyday actions of regular people. While his scenes are usually still and peaceful, he artfully conveys deep tension, and suggests a complicated story with subtle body language (the subject glances at something out of view) or the inclusion of a small item (a letter that seems pregnant with significance). Vermeer was also a master of light, capturing it with an artistry that would make the Impressionists jealous two centuries later.

After centuries of relative obscurity—we still know very little about him—Vermeer and his paintings are now much appreciated. Delft owns none of his works (you'll have to visit Amsterdam's Rijksmuseum, with four masterpieces—see page 113; or The Hague's Mauritshuis museum—see page 251). However, the town's new Vermeer Center pays tribute to the talent of this great artist.

DELFT

why today's Dutch wear orange to soccer matches and consider it their national color.

If you want to work off your *pannenkoeken*, you can climb the New Church's **tower** (€2.70, three levels and 376 steps, last entry one hour before church closes, may close in bad weather).

A few blocks away, listing over a canal as if it's about to tip in, is the **Old Church** (Oude Kerk). Although smaller and less impressive (inside and out) than the New Church, this church feels more lived-in. Light filters through stained-glass windows, falling on the tombs of two local boys done good: Johannes Vermeer and Anton van Leuwenhoek (who invented the microscope, then used it to discover bacteria). Vermeer usually wins the "most flowers" award...tulips, of course. Aside from these talented bones, the church is as dead as its residents.

▲**Vermeer Center (Vermeercentrum)**—While it doesn't have any Vermeer originals, this intelligent new exhibit does a fine job of tracing the career and unique creative mind of Delft's favorite resident. Everything is well-described in English. Begin in the basement, where a good movie orients you to Vermeer and his ties to Delft. Then, view copies of all 37 known Vermeer paintings, arranged chronologically. Upstairs, a mock-up of "Vermeer's studio" thoughtfully analyzes and explains some of Vermeer's techniques, using modern technology to emphasize his mastery of light and color (€6, daily 10:00–17:00, a block from Market Square—through the gap where Vermeer's house used to be—at Voldersgracht 21, tel. 015/213-8588, www.vermeerdelft.nl). The café is good for a drink or snack, and the shop is the perfect place to buy some sou-vermeers.

Markets—Multiple all-day markets are held on Thursdays (general on Market Square, flower market on Hippolytusbuurt Square) and on Saturdays (general on Brabantse Turfmarkt and Burgwal, flea market at Hippolytusbuurt Square, and sometimes an art market at Heilige Geestkerkhof).

Royal Dutch Delftware Manufactory (Koninklijke Porceleyne Fles)

The Delft Blue earthenware made at this factory is famous world-

wide, making this the biggest tourist attraction in town. The Dutch East India Company, partly headquartered in Delft, imported many exotic goods, including Chinese porcelain. The Chinese designs became trendy and were copied by many of the local potters. Three centuries later, their descendants are still going strong, and you can see them at work in this factory—

the only one left of an original 32 factories (€6.50; April–Oct daily 9:00–17:00; Nov–March Mon–Sat 9:00–17:00, closed Sun; Rotterdamsweg 196, tel. 015/251-2030, www.royaldelft.com).

While it's basically a small museum exhibit attached to a giant shop—and, for some, doesn't merit the trip—for those who enjoy porcelain, this is worthwhile, especially if you catch one of the English-language tours, included in the entry price (mid-March–mid-Oct on the hour daily 11:00–16:00).

If you miss the tour, good posted English information helps you explore the complex on your own. First you'll watch the five-minute video (ask for English as you enter), then follow the small tile arrows through the collection. Along with tableware, you'll also see gorgeous pictures made from tiles (including a giant replica of Rembrandt's *The Night Watch*), and outdoor architectural

Delft Blue Manufacturing Process

Delft Blue earthenware is made from a soupy mix of clay and water. To make plates, the glop is rotated on a spinning disk until it looks like a traditional Dutch pancake. This "pancake" is then placed in a plate mold, where a design is pressed into it.

To make vases, pitchers, cups, and figurines, the liquid clay is poured into hollow plaster molds. These porous molds work like a sponge, sucking the water out of the clay to leave a layer of dry clay along the mold walls. Once the interior walls have reached the correct thickness, all excess clay within is poured off and recycled.

After the clay object is removed from the mold, it's fired in the kiln for 24 hours. The pottery removed from the kiln is called "biscuit." Next, painters trace traditional decorations with sable-hair pencils onto the biscuit pottery; these are then painted with a black paint containing cobalt oxide. The biscuit immediately soaks up the paint—making it a very unforgiving medium for mistakes.

The objects are dipped into an opaque white glaze and then fired a second time. A chemical reaction transforms the black paint into the famous Delft Blue, and the white glaze melts into a translucent, glasslike outer layer.

elements (such as chimneys). After the museum, you'll walk through part of the factory, past racks upon racks of unfired pieces. Take some time to watch artisans at work—and feel free to stop and chat with them.

Getting There: It's about a 15-minute walk south of the Old Town. From the train station, catch bus #63, #121, or #129 and get off at TU Aula/Jaffalaan (a five-minute walk from the factory). You can also catch the "Delft Express" tourist train in front of the train station (€2, runs hourly, 20-min ride loops around the north end of the Old Town with commentary en route to the factory). Or, from the Market Square, you can hire a bike-taxi to take you there for about €3 one-way.

Near Delft: Rotterdam

The Hague isn't the only big Dutch city near Delft. About the same distance in the opposite direction is the Netherlands' (and Europe's) largest port, Rotterdam—which bounced back after being bombed flat in World War II. While it lacks the charm of Delft, and the great museums of The Hague, it might be worth a

Sleep Code

(**€1 = about $1.40, country code: 31, area code: 015**)
S = Single, **D** = Double/Twin, **T** = Triple, **Q** = Quad, **b** = bathroom,
s = shower only. Unless otherwise noted, credit cards are
accepted, breakfast is included, and hoteliers speak English.

To help you easily sort through these listings, I've divided
the rooms into three categories, based on the price for a
standard double room with bath:

$$$ Higher Priced—Most rooms €100 or more.
  $$ Moderately Priced—Most rooms between €70–100.
    $ Lower Priced—Most rooms €70 or less.

visit if you're curious to round out your Dutch urban experience.
See its towering Euromast, take a harbor tour, and stroll its great
pedestrian zone (**TI** tel. 0900-403-4065—costs €0.35/min, www
.vvv.rotterdam.nl).

SLEEPING

Delft's accommodations aren't cheap, but the ones listed here are
well-run and offer good value for the money.

$$$ Hotel Bridges House, with 10 rooms around the corner
from Market Square, is wood-beamed elegant and was once the
home of painter Jan Steen. Energetic Jan-Willem van der Blom
works hard to bring class and charm to this canalside splurge
(Sb-€128.50–163.50, Db-€152.50–197.50, higher prices are for very
roomy junior suites, extra bed-€20, includes breakfast, free Internet
access and Wi-Fi, air-con in junior suites only, Oude Delft 74, tel.
015/212-4036, fax 015/213-3600, www.bridges-house.com, info
@bridges-house.com).

$$$ Hotel Leeuwenbrug, a former warehouse and now a
business-class hotel, has 36 clean rooms, Old World atmosphere,
and a helpful staff (very small Sb-€55, standard Sb-€83–102, deluxe
Sb-€125, standard Db-€98–112, deluxe Db-€135, cheaper Fri–Sun
in Aug–Feb, elevator, free Internet access and Wi-Fi, Koornmarkt
16, tel. 015/214-7741, fax 015/215-9759, www.leeuwenbrug.nl,
sales@leeuwenbrug.nl, Mr. Wubben).

$$ Hotel de Emauspoort, picture-perfect and family-run,
is relaxed, friendly, and wrapped around the family's 87-year-old
bakery. It's ideally located one block from Market Square. The 23
rooms, decorated with pleasantly old-fashioned wooden furniture
and named for sea heroes and Delft artists (most you've never
heard of), overlook a canal or peek into the courtyard. Romantics

can stay in one of their two "Gypsy caravans"—"Pipo de Clown" or "Mammaloe" (Sb-€88, Db-€99, "Vermeer Room" Db-€150, Tb-€137.50, Qb-€175, includes breakfast, free Internet access and fee for Wi-Fi, behind church/Market Square at Vrouwenregt 9–11, tel. 015/219-0219, fax 015/214-8251, www.emauspoort.nl, emauspoort @emauspoort.nl).

$$ Hotel de Koophandel has 25 painting-over-the-bed rooms right on the charming, lively, tree-and-restaurant-lined Beestenmarkt square (Sb-€85, Db-€99, extra bed-€25, reception closed 23:00–7:00, Beestenmarkt 30, tel. 015/214-2302, fax 015/212-0674, www.hoteldekoophandel.nl, hotel@hotelde koophandel.nl).

$ 't Raedthuys is a hotel/restaurant right on Market Square, renting seven basic, lightly renovated rooms. Some rooms have tiny bathrooms shoehorned into a corner. The location couldn't be more central, but this is best suited for travelers on a tight budget (S-€52, Sb-€62, D-€59, Db-€69, Tb-€99, breakfast-€7, Markt 38–40, tel. 015/212-5115, fax 015/213-6069, www.raadhuisdelft.nl).

EATING

As Delft is a university town, well-priced and lively eateries abound. Most places have outdoor seating, sometimes on an inviting square or on a little barge floating in the canal out front.

Kleyweg's Stads Koffyhuis is a local institution that's won prizes for its sandwiches (see the trophies above the counter). This is a great spot for an affordable bite, either in the country-cozy interior or out on a canal barge (€5–7 sandwiches, €6–10 pancakes, big €11 salads, Mon–Fri 9:00–20:00—until 19:00 Oct–March, Sat 9:00–18:00, closed Sun, just down the canal from the Old Church at Oude Delft 133, tel. 015/212-4625).

De V is a lively pub with a local following loyal to its straightforward and well-priced food. Sit in the crowded area near the bar, or elbow your way up top to the glassed-in patio (€8 daily specials, €10–15 main dishes, daily 16:00–24:00, just past the TI and Old Church along the canal at Voorstraat 9, tel. 015/214-0916).

Around Beestenmarkt: Literally "Beast Market" for the livestock that was once sold here, this square is more local-feeling and appealing than the more prominent Market Square (described below). Do a spin around the square to scope out the food and seating (indoor or outdoor) you like best. I ate well at **Vlaanderer,** serving good, trendy, pricey, well-presented food. You can sit out on the square; in the dimly lit, old-fashioned dining room; or in the partly glassed-in patio out back (€19–22 main dishes, €35 fixed-price meals, daily 12:00–24:00, Beestenmarkt 16, tel. 015/213-3311).

Around Market Square (Markt): Delft's giant Market Square, under the looming tower of the New Church, is a scenic spot for a meal. Most of the places around here are interchangeable, but tucked behind the Town Hall (across the square from the church) are some good options that also have outdoor seating. **De Sjees** features an interior that's a nice mix of new and old, with an atmosphere that's mellow but still fun (€10 daily chalkboard special, €15–18 main dishes, daily 10:00–24:00, Markt 5, tel. 015/214-4647).

Asian: For a break from flapjacks, try **Daily Wok,** a mod Thai eatery serving up affordable but good food just a few steps off Market Square (€4–7 meals, Mon–Sat 12:30–21:00, Sun 15:00–21:00, Oude Langendijk 230, tel. 015/213-7222).

TRANSPORTATION CONNECTIONS

From Delft to The Hague

There are two options for connecting these two cities, both departing from Delft's train station.

Tram #1 leaves from in front of the Delft station and clatters through residential neighborhoods to The Hague. This connection is frequent, comes with nice urban scenery, and delivers you right to the center of The Hague's tourist zone, but it takes longer than the train (runs about every 5 min, costs 5 *strippenkaart* strips, take tram going in direction: Scheveningen Noorderstrand, get off after about 30 min at The Hague's Centrum stop for TI, parliament area, and most sights). You can continue on this tram directly to the Peace Palace (Vredespaleis stop, about 5 min beyond Centrum stop) or go all the way to the beach at Scheveningen (Kurhaus stop, about 15 min beyond Centrum stop).

Regular **trains** depart from Delft's station for The Hague (4/hr, 15 min, €2.30 one way, €3.60 round-trip). Get off at The Hague's Central Station (CS), not the Hollands Spoor station (HS). The train appears to be faster than the tram, but from The Hague's Central Station it's still a 15-minute walk or a 5-minute tram ride to reach the TI and tourist zone (for details, see "Arrival in The Hague," on next page).

By Train from Delft

From Delft, trains go to **Amsterdam** Central Station (4/hr, 60 min, some transfer in The Hague), **Haarlem** (2/hr direct, 40 min), and **Arnhem** (2/hr, 1.75 hrs, transfer in The Hague; more with transfers in Rotterdam and Utrecht).

The Hague (Den Haag)

While the Dutch constitution identifies Amsterdam as the official "capital," The Hague has been the Netherlands' seat of government since 1588. Or, as locals say, the money is made in Rotterdam, divided in The Hague, and spent in Amsterdam.

The Hague is the home of several fine museums—including the excellent Mauritshuis art gallery—and international organizations such as the International Court of Justice (at the Peace Palace, where nations try to settle their disputes without bloodshed; tourable and described on page 253) and the UN International Criminal Tribunal for the Former Yugoslavia (not tourable). Urban but still manageable—if not exactly charming—The Hague is ideal for a few engaging hours of sightseeing.

ORIENTATION

(area code: 070)
Though it has nearly a half-million residents (the Netherlands' third-largest city), The Hague feels manageable for a sightseer. On a quick visit, begin at the Centrum tram stop, between the TI and the parliament complex; most worthwhile museums are near here. I list no hotels for The Hague because Delft—so close it's practically a neighborhood of this city—is a much more appealing place to hang your hat.

Tourist Information
The TI is opposite the Parliament building on Hofweg 1, near the Centrum stop for tram #1. Pick up the free map; the better €2 map isn't worth it, but the €1 information guide—while heavy on glossy promotion—is worth having for a longer visit (Mon–Fri 10:00–18:00, Sat 10:00–17:00, Sun 12:00–17:00, toll tel. 0900-340-3505—costs €0.45/min, www.vvvdenhaag.nl).

Arrival in The Hague
The major sights in The Hague are well-signed—just look for the black-and-gold directional arrows.

By Train: The Hague has two train stations: Central Station ("Den Haag CS," or just "Centraal Station") and Hollands Spoor

("Den Haag HS," used by more international trains). Central Station is closer to the tourist area.

From Central Station, exit toward the sign for *Uitgang Centrum* (to the left with your back to the tracks, near the Burger King). Here you can catch tram #16 (direction: Wateringen) and take it two stops to the Centrum stop. Or, for a 15-minute walk, turn right and walk past the big bike-parking lot, then turn left, cross the tram tracks, and head up Bezuidenhoutseweg. After the road changes names a few times, it leads you to Hofweg; the TI is a block to the right, across the street.

If you arrive at the Hollands Spoor station, walk out front and hop on tram #1 (direction: Scheveningen Noorderstrand) to the Centrum stop.

By Tram: If coming on tram #1 from Delft, get off at the Centrum stop. The TI is about a block farther up along the tram tracks.

SIGHTS

In The Hague's City Center

All of these attractions are within a 10-minute walk of the TI (most are even closer).

Binnenhof Parliament Complex—The castle-like Binnenhof complex, overlooking a giant pond right in the center of The Hague, is the seat of Dutch political power. The prime minister's office is here, and it's also the meeting place of the two-house parliament, or Staten-Generaal. Most of the power resides in the directly elected Second Chamber

(a.k.a. House of Representatives), while the mostly figurehead First Chamber (a.k.a. Senate, but actually more like the UK's House of Lords) meets once weekly to harrumph their approval.

It's surprisingly easy to dip into the low-key parliament complex (just saunter through the brick gateway across the street from the TI). In the inner courtyard—surrounded by orange-and-white-striped awnings—you'll find a golden fountain depicting the Netherlands' current Queen Beatrix, a reminder that the respectful Dutch parliamentarians govern with her symbolic approval. Dominating the middle of the complex is the historic Knights' Hall (Ridderzaal), where the two houses meet jointly on special occasions. Tours of the complex are sometimes possible (ask at the office downstairs around the right side of the Knights' Hall, call 070/364-6144, or check www.binnenhofbezoek.nl).

▲▲Mauritshuis Royal Picture Gallery—The Hague's top art gallery features an easy-to-appreciate collection of Dutch Golden Age art, including top-notch

pieces by Vermeer (his famous *Girl with a Pearl Earring*), Rembrandt, Rubens, and many others. The beautifully restored 17th-century palace is an ideal setting for this exquisite art. While calling it a "mini-Rijksmuseum" might be a stretch, and the ticket price is steep, the Mauritshuis is well worth a visit.

Cost, Hours, Location: €9.50, covered by Museumkaart—see page 35, extra charge for special exhibitions, includes great English audioguide; April–Aug Mon–Sat 10:00–17:00, Sun 11:00–17:00; Sept–March Tue–Sat 10:00–17:00, Sun 11:00–17:00, closed Mon; café, no photography, mandatory bag check, next door to the Binnenhof parliament complex at Korte Vijverberg 8, tel. 070/302-3456, www.mauritshuis.nl. From the TI, it's on the far side of the parliament; cut straight through the Binnenhof courtyard (described on previous page) and look left when you pop out on the other side.

Ɔ Self-Guided Tour: The included audioguide is excellent, but this tour covers the basics. The collection, exhibited on two floors, is constantly moved around—pick up a floor plan as you enter to find the current location of these pieces.

Vermeer, *Girl with a Pearl Earring* (c. 1665): Sometimes called "the Dutch *Mona Lisa*" for its enigmatic qualities, this canvas became a sensation in recent years as the subject of a popular book and film. This is a "tronie" (TROH-nee)—the painter's goal is not to depict a particular person, but to capture a mood or character. In fact, we don't even know who this mysterious girl is. Wearing a blue turban and with a gigantic pearl dangling from her earlobe, she glances over her shoulder and catches the viewer's gaze...expectantly, maybe even seductively. Vermeer's straightforward scene subtly implies a much more complicated story than we'll ever know. The artist was also a master of color and at suggesting shape with light—looking closely, you'll see that the famous pearl is essentially formed by two simple brushstrokes. For more on Vermeer, see page 125.

Vermeer, *View of Delft* (c. 1660–1661): If this were a photograph, it'd be a bad one...you'd want to wait for the clouds to pass to snap another one with the entire scene bathed in light. But Vermeer, an expert at capturing light effects on canvas, uses the cloudy/sunny contrast to his advantage, illuminating the foreground and the distant, inner part of town instead of the more predictable middle ground. This makes your eye probe deeply into the canvas, subconsciously immersing you in Vermeer's world.

Rembrandt, *The Anatomy Lesson of Dr. Nicolaes Tulp* (1632): Notice Rembrandt's uniquely engaging version of a (typically dull) group portrait—inquisitive faces lean in, hanging on the doctor's every word. The cadaver resembles a notorious criminal of the day. For more on Rembrandt, see page 123.

Rembrandt, *Portrait of an Elderly Man* (1667): Painted when Rembrandt was 61, this portrait is typical of his style: The clothes are painted lightly, but the face is caked on. Look closely at his ruddy cheeks, built up by layer after layer of paint, carefully slathered on by the master.

Peter Paul Rubens, *Old Woman and a Boy with Candles* (c. 1616–1617): In this touching scene, the elderly woman passes her light to the boy—encouraging him to enjoy life in a way that she perhaps hasn't. Her serene smile suggests her hope that he won't have the same regrets she does.

Frans Hals, *Laughing Boy* (c. 1625): This loveable painting depicts an exuberant scamp grinning widely despite his decaying teeth and rat's-nest hair. Like *Girl with a Pearl Earring,* this is a "tronie," or character study, rather than a portrait of an important person. For more on Frans Hals, see page 224.

Jan Steen, *Girl Eating Oysters* (c. 1658–1660): This seemingly innocent scene—a still life combined with a portrait, on the smallest canvas Steen ever painted—is loaded with 17th-century sexual innuendo. Oysters were considered a powerful aphrodisiac, and behind the subject, peeking through the curtains, we can see a bed. Her impish grin seals the deal that she's got more than shellfish on her mind.

And Lots More: These paintings are just the beginning. Look around to find works by Jan Breughel the Elder (a painting of the Garden of Eden, done jointly with Rubens), Hans Holbein, Anthony van Dyck, Hans Memling, and many other famous painters. The gallery also hosts good temporary exhibits.

Prison Tower Museum (Gevangenpoort)—This torture museum, in a 13th-century gatehouse that once protected a castle on the site of today's parliament, shows the medieval mind at its worst. First you'll watch a 20-minute film (with English subtitles) about a famous prisoner, then you'll tour the sight with a required 40-minute tour (usually in Dutch, but you can buy a €1 English guidebook). You'll get the full story on crime and punishment here from 1420 to 1823

(€4 entry, covered by Museumkaart—see page 35, Tue–Fri 10:00–17:00, Sat–Sun 12:00–17:00, closed Mon, tours depart on the hour, last tour leaves at 16:00, across from parliament at Buitenhof 33, tel. 070/346-0861, www.gevangenpoort.nl).

Panorama Mesdag—For a look at the 19th century's attempt at virtual reality, stand in the center of this 360-degree painting of nearby Scheveningen in the 1880s, with a 3-D, sandy-beach fore-ground. As you experience this nostalgic attraction, ponder that this sort of "art immersion" experience was once mind-blowingly cutting-edge (€6, Mon–Sat 10:00–17:00, Sun 12:00–17:00, a few blocks east of the TI/parliament area at Zeestraat 65, tel. 070/364-4544, www.panorama-mesdag.com).

Escher in the Palace (Escher in Het Paleis)—Compared to The Hague's other museums, this place is just a trifle...but an entertaining one. (Think of it as "art museum lite.") Celebrating Dutch optical illusionist M. C. Escher (1898–1972), the exhibit displays replicas of many of his works and traces his artistic evolu-tion—from the Mediterranean landscapes of his beloved Italy, to shapes that melt into each other, to mind-bending experiments in angles and perspective. Hands-on displays let you step right into an Escher engraving (€7.50, Tue–Sun 11:00–17:00, closed Mon, Lange Voorhout 74, tel. 070/427-7730, www.escherinhetpaleis.nl).

Other Museums—Top options include the **Historical Museum of The Hague** (Haagshistorischmuseum), with pieces from the Rijksmuseum's collection on Dutch history (€4, Tue–Fri 10:00–17:00, Sat–Sun 12:00–17:00, closed Mon, across the pond from parliament at Korte Vijverberg 7, tel. 070/364-6940, www.haagshistorischmuseum.nl); and the **Gemeentemuseum,** display-ing modern and contemporary art, including a large collection by Dutchman Piet Mondrian (€8.50, covered by Museumkaart—see page 35, Tue–Sun 11:00–17:00, closed Mon, farther out at Stadhouderslaan 41, tram #17 or bus #24 from Central Station, tel. 070/338-1111, www.gemeentemuseum.nl). For details on these and other attractions, ask at the TI.

Outside The Hague's City Center

All of these sights lie north of the main tourist zone. While worth-while for the thorough sightseer, they're more difficult to reach than the sights listed above.

▲**Peace Palace (Vredespaleis)**—The palace houses the International Court of Justice and the Permanent Court of Arbitration. These two Peace Palace courts attempt to reach amicable settlements for international disagreements, such as border disputes. While the judicial process is interesting, the building itself is the big draw. A gift from American industrial-ist Andrew Carnegie, it's filled with opulent decorations donated

THE HAGUE

by grateful nations who found diplomatic peace here, from exquisite Japanese tapestries, to a Hungarian Zsolnay-tile fountain, to French inlay floors. On the required tour, you'll see the judicial chambers and the grandly decorated halls, and learn how modern nations attempt to resolve their disputes here instead of on the battlefield. Don't con-

fuse this place with the International Criminal Tribunal for the Former Yugoslavia, which is not open to the public.

Cost and Hours: €5; required guided tours Mon–Fri at 10:00, 11:00, 14:00, and 15:00, plus an additional tour at 16:00 May–Sept; closed Sat–Sun, when court is in session, or if there's an event at the palace; you must reserve in advance and bring your passport (required to enter), tel. 070/302-4137, www.vredespaleis.nl.

Getting There: Take tram #1 directly from Delft, or tram #10 or bus #24 from The Hague's Central Station, and get off at the Vredespaleis stop (right in front of the palace).

Scheveningen—This "Dutch Coney Island," with its broad sandy beach, is at its liveliest on sunny summer afternoons (but

is dead when the weather cools). Its biggest appeal is watching urbanites from The Hague and Delft enjoy a day at the seashore. Dominating the scene is the long double-decker pleasure pier, with shops down below, a boardwalk

up top, and a bungee-jumping pavilion at the far end. A café-lined promenade stretches along the sand. Take northbound tram #1 from Delft or from the street in front of The Hague's TI, or take tram #9 from The Hague's Central Station. Get out at Kurhaus (one stop before the end of the line) and follow signs for *Boulevard/Strand* and *Pier*.

By the way, if you can't pronounce this tongue-twisting name (roughly SKHHHEH-veh-ning-eh), you're not alone. In World War II, Dutch soldiers would quiz suspicious visitors on how to pronounce this name as a test to determine who was Dutch-born and ferret out potential German spies.

Madurodam—The mini-Holland amusement park, with min-iature city buildings that make you feel like Godzilla, is fun for kids (adults-€13.75, kids 3–11-€9.75, daily mid-March–June

9:00–20:00, July–Aug 9:00–23:00, Sept–mid-March 9:00–18:00, George Maduroplein 1, tram #9 or bus #22 from Central Station, tel. 070/416-2400, www.madurodam.nl).

TRANSPORTATION CONNECTIONS

Remember that The Hague has two train stations: the Central Station (CS) is handier for local sightseers, while the Hollands Spoor station (HS) is used mostly for international trains. Note that if you're taking tram #1 to Delft, take it in the direction of Delft Tanthof.

From The Hague's Central Station by Train to: Delft (4/hr, 15 min, see page 248), **Amsterdam** (6/hr, 50 min, may require transfer in Leiden), **Haarlem** (4/hr, 40 min, some transfer in Leiden), **Arnhem** (2–4/hr, 1.5 hrs, some transfer in Utrecht).

NEAR ARNHEM

Arnhem Open-Air Folk Museum
• Kröller-Müller Museum

While the city of Arnhem itself is nothing special, it's close to a pair of fun and worthwhile side-trips: the Arnhem Open-Air Folk Museum and the exceptional Kröller-Müller Museum.

Of all the Netherlands' open-air folk museums, Arnhem's feels the most authentic. Its classically Dutch buildings sprawl across rolling hills, with rich details around every corner. Nearby, the Kröller-Müller Museum displays a world-class collection of modern art (including roomfuls of Van Goghs). The art museum is located in the middle of Hoge Veluwe National Park—a delight to pedal through on free white bikes.

The open-air folk museum is just within Arnhem's city limits, but the Kröller-Müller Museum and national park are technically in the next town.

Planning Your Time

Arnhem, an hour and 15 minutes southeast of Amsterdam by train, is doable as a side-trip from Amsterdam. Unfortunately, the two main sights are far from each other, and far from Arnhem's Central Station—so you'll need to allow extra time to catch the bus to either one. But both are superb and worth the effort.

By Car: Drivers with short attention spans can visit both the open-air folk museum and Kröller-Müller Museum within a day... and might have time left to park the car and go for a pedal through the national park. Figure just over an hour's drive from Amsterdam to Arnhem, then about a 20-minute ride into the national park, then an hour back to Amsterdam.

By Public Transportation: It's possible to get to both the Arnhem Open-Air Folk Museum and the Kröller-Müller Museum in one very long but fulfilling day of sightseeing—but it's only worthwhile for the energetically ambitious. Because no

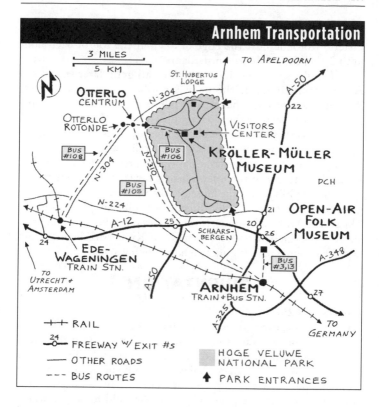

Arnhem Transportation

3 MILES
5 KM

TO APELDOORN

ST. HUBERTUS LODGE

OTTERLO CENTRUM

OTTERLO ROTONDE

N-304

A-50

22

VISITORS CENTER

KRÖLLER-MÜLLER MUSEUM

BUS #108

BUS #106

N-304

N-310

BUS #105

N-224

A-12

25

SCHAARS-BERGEN

21

20

26

OPEN-AIR FOLK MUSEUM

DCH

24

EDE-WAGENINGEN TRAIN STN.

TO UTRECHT & AMSTERDAM

A-50

BUS #3,13

A-348

ARNHEM TRAIN & BUS STN.

27

A-325

TO GERMANY

+++ RAIL

24
—○— FREEWAY W/ EXIT #S

—— OTHER ROADS

--- BUS ROUTES

HOGE VELUWE NATIONAL PARK

▲ PARK ENTRANCES

bus connects the open-air folk museum and the Kröller-Müller Museum, you'll have to return to Arnhem's bus station between sights—limiting the amount of time you'll have at each place. If you prefer to take your time (and these sights deserve it), it's more rewarding to choose just one, or to spend the night in the area (best in Otterlo, near the national park—see page 268).

To do everything in one day, I'd catch an early train from Amsterdam Central Station to Arnhem (4/hr, 1.25 hrs, some transfer in Utrecht, www.ns.nl), then go next door to the bus station and hop a bus for the Arnhem Open-Air Folk Museum (opens at 10:00). When finished at this museum, bus back to the Arnhem station and catch another bus to Otterlo, near Hogue Veluwe National Park. Once in Otterlo, you can take yet another bus directly to the Kröller-Müller Museum (in the middle of the national park), or walk 15 minutes to the entrance of the park and borrow a bike to ride there (for all the details on Otterlo, see page 268). In the national park, do the museum first (closes at 17:00 in summer), then the Visitors Center (closes at 18:00 in summer), then wind down your day by biking around the park. Plan on a long day and a late return to Amsterdam (bus or walk back into Otterlo, catch bus #108 to Ede-Wageningen—departs from Otterlo Rotonde near the edge of town at the top of each hour until 23:00, then train to Amsterdam).

If you're spending the night, you can get a later start from Amsterdam, linger at the open-air folk museum (lockers at Arnhem station), relax that evening in Otterlo, and do the national park at a leisurely pace the next morning.

For specifics on the complicated connections between these sights, and the towns they're near, see each listing.

By Bike: Pedal enthusiasts may want to rent some wheels once in Arnhem to get to the open-air folk museum; it's a strenuous 30-minute uphill ride to the museum, then a breezy, easy 15-minute glide back into town (ask for directions at bike shop, listed under "Arrival in Arnhem," below). If you're a serious biker—and in great shape—you can bike from Arnhem to the Kröller-Müller Museum and the national park (figure two hours each way).

ORIENTATION

(area code: 026)

Arnhem is a dreary urban city of about 140,000 people. Tourists view Arnhem as a transit hub useful only for reaching the open-air folk museum on its outskirts and the nearby Kröller-Müller Museum and national park. A few hotels line up across from the train station, but I'd rather sleep in charming little Otterlo, near the park entrance (see page 268). Arnhem's old town—nowhere near as charming as similar towns in the Netherlands (such as Haarlem, Delft, or Alkmaar)—is just across the busy ring road from the train and bus stations. There, restaurants with outdoor seating cluster around the square called Korenmarkt and, a few steps deeper into the old town, around Jaansplaats.

Tourist Information

Arnhem's TI is across the street from the bus station (Mon–Fri 9:30–17:30, Sat 9:30–17:00, closed Sun, Stationsplein 13, tel. 0900-112-2344—€0.45/min, www.vvvarnhem.nl). The TI sells a simple €0.50 city map and a detailed €6 regional map that includes the national park and the Kröller-Müller Museum.

Arrival in Arnhem

Arnhem's **train station** is surrounded by a sea of construction and urban blight, as they're in the midst of a multi-year project to build a super-modern station complex, which won't likely be finished before 2011. In any case, expect changes to the following information.

The station has **WCs** (€0.40) and **lockers** (€3.40/24 hrs; no coins—you must buy a €5 "Chipknip" prepaid debit card at the ticket office before loading and paying for your locker). You'll also find a Rijwiel **bike-rental shop** (€7.50/day for 3-speed bike—you'll need all 3 speeds—plus €50 refundable deposit, open daily very long hours; exit the station to the left and look for stairs up to bike shop (location subject to change).

The **bus station** is to the right as you exit the train station, along the busy street. Along the way is the convenient Connexxion bus-information office—ideal for confirming bus schedules or buying a *strippenkaart* (Mon–Fri 7:00–19:00, Sat 9:00–12:30 & 13:00–17:00, Sun 10:00–12:30 & 13:00–17:00; location subject to change). The station is actually a giant garage with lettered bus bays. Check the sign near the entry to the bus area to find the departure bay for your bus. For the Openluchtmuseum (Arnhem Open-Air Folk Museum), take bus #3 or #13; for Otterlo (near the Kröller-Müller Museum and national park), take bus #105.

Arnhem Open-Air Folk Museum (Openluchtmuseum)

Arnhem has the Netherlands' first, biggest, and best folk museum, rated ▲▲. You'll enjoy a huge park of windmills, old farmhouses and other buildings (relocated from throughout the Netherlands), traditional crafts in action, and a pleasant education-by-immersion in Dutch culture. It's great for families.

ORIENTATION

Cost and Hours: €13.60 during peak season, April–Oct daily 10:00–17:00; €12 during winter festival, Dec–mid-Jan daily 12:00–20:00, €4 in Nov and mid-Jan–March daily 11:00–16:30 when the buildings are closed but the grounds are open.

Getting There: To reach the open-air folk museum from the Arnhem bus station, take one of two **buses** (check the board for the departure bay): In July and Aug (and on some holidays), handy bus #13 zips you directly to the town's zoo, then to the museum entrance (3–4/hr, €1). At other times, take bus #3 (make sure it's marked *Alteveer*, as some #3 buses go elsewhere; about 2/hr, 20 min, €1 ticket or 3 *strippenkaart* strips). Bus #3 drops you a five-minute walk from the museum entrance: Cross the street, head down the tree-lined avenue to the roundabout, then turn right (following signs for *Openluchtmuseum*). From the Arnhem train station, you can also **walk** or ride a **bike** (gradually uphill most of the way, figure 30 min by foot or 20 min by bike). A **taxi** from the station costs about €16.

By **car** from Amsterdam, take A-2 south to Utrecht, then A-12 east to Arnhem. Just before Arnhem, take the Arnhem Nord exit (#26) and follow *Openluchtmuseum* signs to the museum (€4.50 parking, buy parking ticket when you buy entrance ticket). If driving from Haarlem, skirt Amsterdam to the south on A-9, take A-2 south to Utrecht, and then follow the previous instructions (via A-12).

Information: Tel. 026/357-6111, www.openluchtmuseum.nl.

Tours: On Sunday, there's usually a free one-hour English-language tour at 13:00 (confirm when you buy your ticket).

Getting Around: A free, old-fashioned tram does a lazy counterclockwise circle around the museum grounds, making six stops (well-marked on park maps).

SELF-GUIDED TOUR

You could spend the whole day exploring this open-air museum. But to hit a few highlights, follow this tour. Because the layout of the grounds can be confusing, pick up the good free map at the entry—I've used the numbers on that map to help you navigate this tour. Don't hesitate to dip into any buildings that intrigue you, even if they're not on this tour—most have brief English explanations outside, and some have English-speaking docents inside. (Ask them questions...that's their job.) Especially with kids, it would be a shame to do this place in a rush—there's so much to experience.

• *Start in the...*

Entrance Pavilion: Consider buying the in-depth English guidebook, and ask about special events and activities, especially for kids. Downstairs are exhibits on traditional Dutch costumes and replicas of various storefronts. You'll also find Arnhem's effort to keep up with the Disneys: the high-tech **"HollandRama"** multimedia experience (inside the big copper blob you saw out front; runs about hourly—schedule posted by stairs). You'll sit on a giant platform that rotates inside a spherical theater to gradually reveal various Dutch dioramas: windmills, a snowy countryside, house and store interiors, and so on. Although the narration is only in Dutch, the 20-minute presentation is an enjoyable rest.

• *To hit the park, exit straight out of the entrance pavilion and walk up the path. After a few buildings on the left, step inside the one-story...*

"Cheese-Cover" Farmhouse (#4.1, just before the pond): The cows lived on one side of this house from 1745, and the people on the other (notice the claustrophobic cupboard-beds). Along the cow stalls, see the patterns the farmwife would make with fresh sand and seashells each summer to show off family status.

• *Nearby, cross the...*

Yellow Drawbridge (#4.2): Dating from 1358, this takes you to perhaps the most scenic part of the park: a pond surrounded by

windmills and cabins (inspired by the Waterland area around Marken—see page 280). Pause on the bridge to look toward the sawmill. You might see kids playing with a small, rope-pulled ferryboat.

Continue across the drawbridge into the little **village.** Along the way are some tempting shops where you can pick up an edible souvenir, including a well-stocked general store, a bakery, and a fragrant candy store.

Village Square (#4.13): you can play here with toys from the 1800s. See if you can make the "flying Dutchman" fly, or try to ride an original "high-wheeled velocipede" without falling off. On the square is a restaurant specializing in *poffertjes* (mini-pancakes dusted with powdered sugar), with indoor and outdoor seating.

• *Behind the* poffertje *shop, cross the little bridge toward the windmills, pass the boat workshop, and enter the...*

Fisherman's Cottage (#4.11): The black-tarred exterior hides a bright and colorful interior. Notice the rope-controlled smoke hatch, rather than a chimney. Wooden cottages like these were nicknamed "smokehouses." In front of the cottage is the boatyard, where vessels could be pulled out of the water to scrape off the barnacles.

• *Backtrack through the village square, then continue on to the...*

Laundry (#5.1, on the right): Inside, an industrial-strength agitator furiously pounds stubborn stains to smithereens. (There was no "delicate cycle" back then.) On nice days, the clean sheets are spread out on the lawn to dry.

• *For an optional detour (best for train buffs), hook around through the little cottages across the street, then turn right to reach the...*

Train Depot (#6.1): Inside, you can actually walk underneath a train to check out its undercarriage. The adjacent **goods shed** (#6.8) holds a virtual-reality postal carriage.

• *Head back past the laundry, then go beyond the cafeteria to reach the small, yellow windmill. Here, turn left and walk up the path, watching for the low-profile brown building through the trees on your right, near the bridge.*

Paper Mill (#5.4): At this building, dating from around 1850, you'll learn that farmers often made paper in their spare time to help make ends meet. Inside, you might see a demonstration of linen rags being turned into pulp, and then into paper. Peek upstairs at the finished paper hanging to dry.

• *Leaving the mill, walk straight ahead on the brick path, passing various buildings on your right-hand side until you reach the...*

Herb Garden (#11.1): This tranquil, hedge-lined garden is worth exploring. The map at the entry explains the various parts of the garden, each growing herbs for different purposes: dyes, food, medicine, and so on. Listen for the squeals of lively children from the playground behind the garden.

• *Continue past the garden and cross the tram tracks to the...*

Freia Steam-Dairy Factory (at #7.1, with the big smoke-stack): Named after Freia, the Norse goddess of agriculture, this was the Netherlands' first, privately owned cheese and butter factory. Borrow the English explanations at the entry, sample some free cheese, and try to follow the huge belt of the steam engine as it whirls through the factory.

• *Leaving the factory, loop around to the right—past the little black-and-green windmill—then turn right again, down the path just before the brick-and-thatch forest hut. On the right, look for the...*

Peat Hut (#7.6): Humble little huts like these were used by day laborers and covered with the same turf that those laborers were paid so poorly to gather.

• *Continue to a big, thatched-roof...*

Farmhouse (#8.1): Step into the vast and rough 1700s interior, listen to recorded animal noises, and scope out the layout: grain stored up above, cows along the main room, and at the far end, a (no doubt smelly) residential zone for people.

• *Cross the tram tracks in front of the farmhouse to reach the tiny...*

Schoolhouse (#8.2): Aside from its brick construction (most were made of clay), this is typical of village schoolhouses from around 1730. Only boys from 6 to 12 years old attended school, with an emphasis on reading and writing, and summers off to help on the farm. Imagine the schoolhouse back then, fragrant with smoke from the peat fire. Notice the slates used to follow along with lessons (stored in the wooden "lockers" on the walls). An underperforming student would have to wear the donkey picture around his neck.

Just beyond the schoolhouse is the **Pancake House** (#9.1; good for a snack or meal—see "Eating," next page), with an adjacent playground.

• *Cross the tram tracks to peek into the...*

Church (#10.1): In the typical Dutch style, the church has an austere white interior, central pulpit, and wooden pews.

• *Then continue along the tracks through the village, past the **Brabant***

*Café (#12.3; see "Eating," below), to the modern, working **brewery** (#12.4, on the left), where you can duck inside for a free sample.*

Just beyond, on the left, look for the...

Four Laborers' Houses (#12.5): These houses offer a fascinating glimpse into the lifestyles of four generations of workers: from 1870, 1910, 1954, and 1970. See how home fashion and amenities progressed from the rustic 1870s to the garish 1970s.

• *Continuing through the village, the **hospital** on the left (#12.9), from 1955, really does smell like a hospital. Next, the long **collection center** (#13.8) shows off a mind-numbing array of Dutch bric-a-brac, with futuristic exhibits about recycling and conservation. Just beyond it is a formal hedge garden. Finally, cross the tram tracks and walk to the big, white...*

Platform Windmill (#15.6): Hike up the steep steps of the park's centerpiece for an aerial view over the museums.

• *Our tour is over. Head back to the entrance, or continue exploring to your heart's content.*

EATING

At the Arnhem Open-Air Folk Museum

The park has several good budget restaurants and covered picnic areas. The **café** in the entrance pavilion is inexpensive but has limited choices (€3.50 sandwiches)—it's more enjoyable to eat inside the park. The rustic **Pancake House** (Pannekoeken Huis, a.k.a. "Restaurant de Hanekamp") serves hearty and sweet, splittable Dutch flapjacks (€6–9 pancakes, soups, salads, and sandwiches). **Brabant Café,** in the "village" of Budel, resembles an old-fashioned farmhouse café. The **De Kasteelboerderij Café-Restaurant** at the Oud-Beijerland Manor is a giant place that can feed 300 visitors at once (traditional €8 *dagmenu,* or plate of the day; open daily July–Aug, otherwise Sun only).

TRANSPORTATION CONNECTIONS

From Arnhem by Train to: Amsterdam (2–4/hr, 1.25 hrs, some transfer in Utrecht), **The Hague** (2–4/hr, 1.5 hrs, some transfer in Utrecht; then another 15 min to **Delft**).

Kröller-Müller Museum

The Kröller-Müller Museum of top-notch modern art, rated ▲▲, is located within Hoge Veluwe National Park, the Netherlands' largest at 13,000 acres. While the south end of the park is just outside Arnhem, the museum is buried deep in the forest close to the opposite end of the park, near the town of Otterlo.

ORIENTATION

Cost, Hours, Information: €14 combo-ticket includes park entry, open Tue–Sun 10:00–17:00, sculpture garden until 16:30, closed Mon, Houtkampweg 6, tel. 031/859-1241, www.kmm.nl.

Getting There: Public-transportation connections to the Kröller-Müller Museum and Hoge Veluwe National Park are complicated, potentially involving several changes. (Even locals who work at the park don't bother trying to commute by bus.) Give yourself plenty of time, and try to confirm bus schedules when planning your day. These instructions get you to the northwest entrance of the park, near Otterlo, just over a mile from the Kröller-Müller Museum.

From Amsterdam: First, take the train to Ede-Wageningen (4/hr, 1 hr, some with a transfer in Utrecht). Exit the Ede-Wageningen station toward signs marked *Centrum* to find the bus stops, where you can catch bus #108 to Otterlo (bus marked *Apeldoorn*, runs hourly about :40 past the hour, or 2/hr on weekday mornings before 11:00, 15 min, costs 5 *strippenkaart* strips). Hop off the bus at Otterlo Rotonde (a roundabout on the edge of town). From here, walk five minutes into the town center, and then hang a left to the park entrance (about 20 minutes total), where you can buy your ticket and hop on a free white bike to ride to the Kröller-Müller Museum or the park's Visitors Center.

If you'd rather wait for a ride, bus #106 goes from Otterlo Rotonde to Otterlo Centrum, and then continues into the park (1–2/hr, bus marked *Hoenderloo*, check posted schedule to see how long you'll wait; see "Getting Around Hoge Veluwe National Park," next page).

If the schedules don't line up well, you can also get from Amsterdam to the park via Arnhem (see below).

From Arnhem Central Station: Remember, Arnhem is a 1.25-hour train ride from Amsterdam. From Arnhem Central Station, the Kröller-Müller Museum is 12 miles away. There's no direct bus to the museum, so you'll go via the town of Otterlo: Go next door to Arnhem's bus station (see "Arrival in Arnhem," page 258), take bus #105, and get off at Otterlo Centrum (1–2/hr, 20 min, 5 *strippenkaart* strips each way; when you get off, note return times). Once in Otterlo, you can take bus #106 or walk to the park (both options described under "Arrival in Otterlo," page 268). You can hire a taxi from Arnhem's station, but it's expensive (about €45).

Alternatively, if you have plenty of time and want to **bike,** take bus #2 from Arnhem toward Schaarsbergen, and enter the park through this southern entrance. From here, you can borrow a white bike for the long pedal to the Kröller-Müller Museum (figure about 10 miles each way). Renting a bike at the Arnhem train station also works, but adds another 30 minutes of uphill biking to reach the park (see "Planning Your Time—By Bike," page 258).

By Car: From Amsterdam, take A-1 southeast, then exit on N-310 to Otterlo. From Arnhem, take A-12 north, then pick up N-310 to Otterlo. Parking inside the park costs €6, or you can pay €2 to park at the entrance and bike or walk in.

Getting Around Hoge Veluwe National Park: Once at Hoge Veluwe, you have various options for connecting the attractions. My favorite plan: Bus from Otterlo directly to the Kröller-Müller Museum, pick up a free white bike to pedal to the Visitors Center, then bike back to the entrance (or, with more time, bike around the park).

By Bike: The park has 1,700 white bikes—an endearing remnant of Holland's hippie past—that you're free to use to make your explorations more fun. The one-speed bikes, with no hand brakes (just pedal brakes), are good enough to get around on, but not good enough to get stolen. Just pick one up (or drop one off) wherever you see a bike rack, including at park entrances or at any attraction. While riding through the vast green woods, make a point of getting off your bike to climb an inland sand dune.

By Bus: Bus #106 does a convenient circuit around the park, connecting Otterlo Rotonde (at the edge of town), Otterlo Centrum (in the town center), the entrance to the park (where you'll have to get off to buy the entry ticket), a stop 200 yards from the Kröller-Müller Museum, and at the Visitors Center. Unfortunately, its frequency isn't ideal (1–2/hr depending on time of day, stops running after the sights close—last departure from Visitors Center in summer at 17:46, costs 2 *strippenkaart* strips from Otterlo into the park). But it can be a handy way to connect the dots if you're tired or in a hurry.

SELF-GUIDED TOUR

This memorable museum shows off the collection of Helene Kröller-Müller (1869–1939), who was a wealthy fan of avant-garde art. The modern museum seamlessly blends artistic beauty and its own peaceful park setting. Stroll through the delightfully landscaped sculpture garden, and spend some time with virtually all the top artists of the late 19th and early 20th centuries.

A stern-looking statue of Monsieur Jacques (the museum's mascot) greets you on the entry path. Once inside, pick up the informative guidebooklet and drop your bag at the mandatory bag check. Computers near the entry let you tailor a self-guided tour to your interests. Each work is labeled (but not described) in English, and there is no audioguide.

There are two parts to the museum: the outside sculpture garden and the interior art collection.

The **sculpture garden** shows off more than a hundred sculptures, entertainingly displayed on 60

rolling acres of lawn. You can appreciate works by Auguste Rodin, Barbara Hepworth, Claes Oldenburg, Christo, and others—or just enjoy this excuse for a walk in a pretty park with something fun to look at. Look for Jean Dubuffet's beloved *Garden of Enamel*, a giant, psychedelic, black-and-white roller rink you can climb around on. Since the garden closes at 16:30, head here first if you're arriving later in the day.

Inside, the permanent **art collection** is like a Who's Who of modern art. The works are displayed chronologically and grouped by movement, in keeping with Helene Kröller-Müller's wishes to foster understanding and appreciation of new art styles. You'll go from the hazy landscapes of the Impressionists (Monet, Manet, Renoir), to the intricate compositions of the Pointillists (Seurat, Pissarro), to the bold innovations of the Post-Impressionists (Gauguin, Van Gogh), to the slinky scenes of Art Nouveau (Toulouse-Lautrec), to the shattered-glass canvases of the Cubists (Picasso, Braque, and Gris), and to the colorful grids of Dutchman Piet Mondrian.

The museum's highlight is its Vincent van Gogh collection, the second-largest in the world (after Amsterdam's Van Gogh Museum; Kröller-Müller usually displays about 50 of their 87 Vincent canvases). Look for some famous pieces, including various self-portraits,

some *Sunflowers*, and *Café de Nuit*, the famous scene of an al fresco café on a floodlit Arles square. Notice how thickly the paint is caked on to create the almost 3-D lamp, the work's focal point.

Eating at Kröller-Müller Museum: Consider the self-service restaurant Monsieur Jacques (€4 soups and sandwiches, €9 salads, Tue–Sun 10:00–16:30, closed Mon).

After visiting the museum, grab a free white bike for the three-quarter-mile pedal to the national park's Visitors Center, described below.

MORE SIGHTS

▲▲Hoge Veluwe National Park (Nationaal Park de Hoge Veluwe)

The Netherlands' biggest national park is a delight to explore. On a quick visit, a short pedal and a visit to the Kröller-Müller Museum are enough; with more time, also swing by the Visitors Center and bike to your heart's content. The hunting lodge (described on next page) makes a fun destination. If you head deeper into the park, you'll find a surprising diversity of terrain, from inland sand dunes to lakes to moorland. Get advice, maps, and brochures at the park entrances or at the Visitors Center.

Cost, Hours, Information: Entry to the park costs €7; a €14 combo-ticket includes the Kröller-Müller Museum. The park is open daily June–July 8:00–22:00, May and Aug 8:00–21:00, April 8:00–20:00, Sept 9:00–20:00, Oct 9:00–19:00, Nov–March 9:00–18:00, last entry one hour before closing (park tel. 055/378-8100, www.hogeveluwe.nl).

Visitors Center (Bezoekerscentrum)—This fine center is a good place to get your bearings in the park, with a helpful information desk, nature exhibit, WCs, playground, restaurant, and hub for free loaner bikes (daily April–Oct 9:30–18:00, Nov–March 9:30–17:00, park tel. 055/378-8100, www.hogeveluwe.nl). Browse the collection of brochures and maps, including the good €2.50 map of the park, and the €1 self-guided bike tour, with commentary on the main stops.

The **nature exhibit** features interactive, kid-oriented exhibits, well-explained in English. It's divided into two parts: An above-ground section focuses on the parks' various landscapes and the animals that live above ground; then you'll go through a tunnel to reach the second section, called the "Museonder," which shows life underground (animals, fossils, the water table), with conservation-themed displays. Ask for an English showing of the nature films when you enter (a favorite is the 20-minute movie about park deer).

Eating at the Visitors Center: The good **Restaurant de Koperen Kop** serves up surprisingly tasty, self-service cafeteria food, with indoor or outdoor seating (€8–12 plates, daily May–Sept 9:30–18:00, April and Oct 9:30–17:30, Nov–March 9:30–16:30).

St. Hubertus Lodge—This dramatic hunting lodge, at the north end of the park, is another popular excuse for a bike ride. Once the countryside residence of the modern art-collecting Kröller-Müller family, it's perched on the edge of a lake with a characteristic tower looming overhead. Designed to resemble the antlers of a stag, this structure evokes the story of St. Hubert, who supposedly discovered a crucifix miraculously dangling between a deer's antlers (sporadic tours, in Dutch only). The 45-minute walk around the adjacent lake is dotted with sculptures. Combining this lodge, the Kröller-Müller Museum, and the Visitors Center makes for a fun 6.5-mile biking loop.

Otterlo

The village of Otterlo is located just outside the Hoge Veluwe National Park entrance that's closest to the Kröller-Müller Museum. While not exciting, it's a fine place to spend the night near the park (see "Sleeping," below). Otterlo is a tiny town with tandem-bike tourists zipping through on their way to the park. The town also has cafés and a meager **TI** (100 yards south of the town center, open Sat 10:00–12:30 year-round, also May–Sept Mon–Fri 10:00–15:30, ATM in lobby, Arnhemseweg 14, tel. 0318/591-254, www.vvvotterlo.nl—in Dutch only).

Arrival in Otterlo: Note that there are two different bus stops in Otterlo. "Otterlo Rotonde" is at a roundabout on the busy road that skirts the edge of town; from here, it's about a five-minute walk into the town center. "Otterlo Centrum" is right in the middle of town (described below). Buses #105 (from Arnhem) and #106 (into the park itself) stop at both Rotonde and Centrum, while bus #108 (from Ede-Wageningen and trains to Amsterdam) stops only at the Rotonde stop.

From **Otterlo Centrum,** follow the directional signs: The TI is along the main road, and the park is down the major intersecting road. From here, it's about a 15-minute walk to the park entrance (or hop on bus #106).

SLEEPING

In Otterlo, near the National Park Entrance

Consider spending the night in Otterlo if you'd like to have a relaxing time at the museum, the park, and nearby Arnhem.

Both of these accommodations are on the road between Otterlo Centrum and the park entrance; Sterrenberg is closer to the park, while Kruller is closer to the town center.

$$ Boutique Hotel Sterrenberg, located 400 yards from the park entrance, is a Dutch designer's take on a traditional hunting lodge. With woodsy touches and modern flair in its 33 rooms, it's a pleasant splurge (Sb-€100–150, Db-€130–190, price depends on season and room size, great Sunday-night deals include dinner, non-smoking, elevator, free Internet access and fee for Wi-Fi, restaurant with terrace, swimming pool, sauna, 6 rentable bikes for guests—€7/day—or use free white bikes within nearby park gates, about a quarter-mile to park entrance and 1.5 miles to Kröller-Müller Museum, Houtkampweg 1, tel. 0318/591-228, fax 0138/591-693, www.sterrenberg.nl, info@sterrenberg.nl).

$ Hotel Kruller has 17 playfully decorated rooms over a busy restaurant (small Sb-€58, mid-size Sb-€73, small Db-€75, mid-size Db-€90, large Db-€105, cheaper for two or more nights, Dorpsstraat 19, tel. 0318/591-231, fax 0318/592-034, www.kruller .nl, info@kruller.nl).

Utrecht

The city of Utrecht lies smack-dab between Arnhem to the east, The Hague (and Delft and Rotterdam) to the west, and Amsterdam to the north. You might change trains here; if so, and if you have time to kill, consider poking around the central zone. The **National Museum from Musical Clock to Street Organ** (Nationaal Museum van Speelklok tot Pierement), which you can visit only with a free, guided hour-long tour, demonstrates musical clocks, calliopes, and street organs (€8, tours on the hour Tue–Sun 10:00–17:00, closed Mon, last tour at 16:00, 10-min walk from station, located on busy shopping street in city center at Steenweg 6, tel. 030/231-2789, www.museumspeelklok.nl).

DUTCH DAY TRIPS

The Historic Triangle • Waterland • Near Haarlem • Alkmaar and Zaanse Schans • Schokland and Flevoland

Any Dutch native will tell you: To really experience everyday life in the Netherlands, get out of Amsterdam. In a country as tiny as Holland, day-tripping is easy to do. Within a half-hour of leaving Central Station, you can be deep in the Dutch countryside—lush, green, and filled with tulips, red-brick houses, quaint canals, and black-and-white cows. It's a refreshing break from urban Amsterdam. Match your interest with the village's specialty: flower auctions, wooden-shoe folk museums, fresh cheese, Delft Blue porcelain, or modern art. Take some time to learn a few basic Dutch phrases for the sake of politeness (see page 471), but don't obsess—even outside of Amsterdam, just about everyone speaks English.

I describe three Dutch open-air museums in this book: Arnhem, Zuiderzee in Enkhuizen, and Zaanse Schans. Doing more than one is overkill for most visitors—read my descriptions and choose one. Arnhem's is the granddaddy of them all, but the farthest from Amsterdam. Enkhuizen's Zuiderzee can be conveniently combined with a fun steam-train ride (practically a museum experience in itself) on the "Historic Triangle" route. Zaanse Schans is the least appealing (and impossible to pronounce), but the closest to Amsterdam.

Transportation Tips

Train: If you're day-tripping, ask about "day return" tickets (same-day round-trip), which are cheaper than two one-way tickets. Before you board at Amsterdam's Central Station, check the yellow train-schedule boards or ask at the information counter to confirm the details of your trip (such as times, necessary transfers, delays, and the name of the station you'll be using—for example, to get to Zaanse Schans, you'll get off at the Koog-Zaandijk station). When riding a train to any big town, note that "CS" always stands for "Central Station"—usually the one you want (unless I note otherwise). You'll find train information online at www.ns.nl.

Driving: Although the roads are excellent, densely populated Holland can be a time-consuming place for drivers. Traffic congestion is epidemic, especially around rush hour near Amsterdam, Rotterdam, Utrecht, The Hague, and other big cities. Everything in this book is covered by the excellent, detailed ANWB Wegenkaart *Nederland midden* map (1:200,000, €6, sold at bookstores).

The Historic Triangle

The Historic Triangle (De Historische Driehoek) is a manageable and enjoyable one-day journey through the Dutch countryside.

You'll start in the small town of Hoorn (an easy train trip from Amsterdam or Haarlem), catch a toot-toot steam train to the town of Medemblik, then sail on a 1920s-era boat to Enkhuizen, home of an excellent open-air folk museum (see route on map on page 273). Particularly good for families—and a fantasyland for trainspotters—the Historic Triangle trip is a charming way to pass a day. Dutch grandmothers feed snacks to towheaded toddlers, gusts of steam billow gracefully behind the engine, and cows nod sleepily in the fields.

ORIENTATION

Cost: Allow about €50 per adult for the entire trip, including the open-air museum in Enkhuizen. Here's how the price breaks down per leg: Train from Amsterdam to Hoorn-€7.10; steam train to Medemblik-€10.70; boat to Enkhuizen-€8.90; museum entry-€12.50; train from Enkhuizen back to Amsterdam-€9.70 (Enkhuizen to Hoorn is €3.50). A railpass only covers the Amsterdam–Hoorn and Enkhuizen–Amsterdam sections (not the steam train or boat). If you're in a hurry, you can skip the steam train and boat and go directly by train from Amsterdam to Enkhuizen (€17.80 day return ticket).

A variety of **combo-tickets** are available to save you a couple of euros. If you're not doing the museum in Enkhuizen, get the €18.50 ticket covering just the steam train and boat (then buy your Amsterdam–Hoorn and Enkhuizen–Amsterdam train tickets

Dutch Day Trips at a Glance

If you only have a day or two to venture outside of Amsterdam or Haarlem, use this list to help you decide where to go.

▲▲▲**Keukenhof** This can't-miss garden show, in the town of Lisse, is open for only two months every spring (March 18–May 16 in 2010). See page 287.

▲▲**The Historic Triangle** This enjoyable all-day trip connects two towns and a fine open-air folk museum (in Enkhuizen) by old-fashioned steam train and boat. See page 271.

▲▲**Edam** In this quiet town, you can mellow out like a hunk of aging cheese. There are no real sights, but its tiny main square and peaceful canals may win you over. See page 281.

▲▲**Arnhem Open-Air Folk Museum** Holland's original, biggest, and best open-air folk museum, Arnhem sprinkles traditional buildings from around Holland across a delightful park, and populates them with chatty docents to give you a flavor of old-time lifestyles. See page 259.

▲▲**FloraHolland Aalsmeer Flower Auction** Close to the airport, this vast auction warehouse shows you the business side of the Netherlands' beautiful flower scene (open mornings only year-round). See page 287.

▲▲**Delft** This lovely hometown of the painter Vermeer and the Delftware factory is a delightful place to relax by a canal. For more activity, zip into The Hague. See page 240.

▲▲**The Hague** Next door to Delft (and ideal for side-tripping), this big-city seat of Dutch government offers good museums, including the excellent Mauritshuis art gallery. See page 249.

▲▲**Kröller-Müller Museum** This excellent modern art museum has dozens of Van Goghs and a sculpture garden. Near Arnhem, it's located within the vast Hoge Veluwe National Park, which has free loaner bikes you can ride to the museum. See page 264.

▲**Enkhuizen Zuiderzee Museum** With an emphasis on seaside lifestyles, this well-presented, open-air folk museum is the grand finale of a Historic Triangle day, or can be visited directly from Amsterdam. See page 277.

▲**Alkmaar** This likeable town is especially fun to visit, and worth ▲▲, during its Friday-morning cheese market (early April–early Sept only, 10:00–12:30). See page 289.

Dutch Day Trips

RAIL
BUS
BOAT
AIRPORT

N

NOT TO SCALE
AMST.-HAARLEM = 15 MILES / 25 KM

NORTH
SEA

DEN HELDER

HARLINGEN   LEEUWARDEN

MEDEM-
BLIK

HINDELOOPEN

IJSSEL-
MEER   URK

SCHOKLAND

ALKMAAR

ENKHUIZEN

HOORN

LELYSTAD

ZAANSE
SCHANS

VOLENDAM

FLEVO-
LAND

ZANDVOORT

EDAM

MARKEN

KOOG-
ZAANDIJK

HAARLEM

SLOT.

AMSTERDAM

LISSE
(KEUKENHOF)

LEIDEN

KRÖLLER-
MÜLLER
MUSEUM

SCHEV.

AALS-
MEER

THE
HAGUE

SCHIPHOL

OTTERLO

OPEN-AIR
MUSEUM

TRAM

DELFT

GOUDA

EDE-W.

HOEK

UTRECHT

ARNHEM

TO
HARWICH
(ENG.)

ROTTERDAM

TO
KÖLN +
RHINE

TO BRUSSELS
+ PARIS

DCH

▲**Schokland** A former island left high and dry when the surrounding sea was drained, this village is now a museum in the middle of reclaimed farmland. While the farthest from Amsterdam of these day trips, it's interesting. See page 297.

Marken Once an island, and now connected by a causeway to the mainland, this time-warp fishing village preserves traditional buildings and lifestyles. See page 285.

Volendam A transit hub for the Waterland region, this workaday town has a fine seafront promenade and a boat across to Marken. See page 284.

Zaanse Schans Open-Air Museum Packed with windmills (and greedy shops), this sight is just a quick 15-minute train ride (plus a 15-min walk) from central Amsterdam. See page 292.

Zandvoort This lively beach resort town, practically a suburb of Haarlem, is handy for a quick getaway. See page 288.

separately). If you're doing the whole thing, the €34 combo-ticket also covers museum entry and the train from Enkhuizen back to Hoorn (though not all the way back to Amsterdam)—saving you about €0.50. This combo-ticket combines perfectly with a €13.20 day return ticket between Amsterdam and Hoorn—making your total cost €47.20.

You can buy the combo-tickets only at the station in Hoorn; buy the regular train tickets at the station in Amsterdam.

Schedule: The Historic Triangle trip is offered from mid-March through November, with the timing and frequency determined by the season. Start times from Hoorn: mid-July–mid-Aug 2/day at 11:00 and 13:30 (may be more departures on certain days); mid-April–mid-July and mid-Aug–Sept Tue–Sun at 11:00 only (no trains Mon); mid-March–mid-April and Oct–Nov Sat–Sun only at 11:00 or 12:00 (no trains Mon–Fri). The trip doesn't run Dec–Feb. Because holidays or special events can tweak the schedule, it's smart to confirm train departure times (tel. 0229/214-862, www.museumstoomtram.nl, info@museumstoomtram.nl). Reservations are not necessary or even possible, except for big groups (if they run out of room, they just add more cars to the train).

Note that on summer days when there are two (or more) departures, you must take the 11:00 train if you want to arrive in Enkhuizen in time to see the open-air museum. If you start from Hoorn at 11:00 and visit the open-air museum in the afternoon, you'll likely get back to Amsterdam about 18:30 (museum closes at 17:00).

In summer, extra departures open up more options beyond the basic route I've described here. For example, you could hop off the steam train in Twisk, get on a shuttle bus (included in your combo-ticket) to Medemblik's steam engine museum, then continue on the bus directly to the boat. Or you could just do the boat and steam train both ways (skipping the open-air museum). For more on these options, ask at the station in Hoorn.

HISTORIC TRIANGLE TOUR

Train from Amsterdam to Hoorn

To do the basic trip, your best bet is to catch the 11:00 steam train in Hoorn. To make this connection, leave Amsterdam's Central Station on the 9:33 train (train from Amsterdam to Hoorn: 2/hr, 42 min). Once in Hoorn, this gives you about 45 minutes to buy your tickets and poke around the interesting old station before boarding the steam train. (Take the 9:03 train if you want more time to peruse the Hoorn station exhibits—open at 10:00; late-risers can leave Amsterdam at 10:03, which gives you a tight 15 minutes in Hoorn to make a beeline for the steam train.)

▲Hoorn Station

While pleasant, the town of Hoorn itself has little to offer (**TI** is a 2-min walk from the train station, open Mon 13:00–18:00, Tue–Fri 9:30–18:00, until 17:00 Sept–April, Sat 9:30–17:00, closed Sun, Veemarkt 4, tel. 072/511-4284, www.vvvhoorn.nl).

Coming from Amsterdam, you'll arrive at Hoorn's modern train station. Exit the train and find the modern pedestrian overpass (following *stoomtram* signs) that runs up and over the tracks, leading to the small, old-timey station. (Both old and new trains share the same train tracks, but on opposite sides.) Buy your combo-ticket here for the steam train, boat, and open-air museum. Then poke around to kill time while you wait for the steam train's departure.

The station has a genteel little waiting room where you can buy coffee or snacks (also available on the train). Outside, you can climb up the stairs to the cute signal house *(seinhuis),* where the conductor pulls a long line of levers to change tracks (see the complex diagram posted overhead). As he demonstrates pull-

ing the levers, watch the signals flip at the far end of the tracks to notify the trains.

Then head alongside those tracks and into the workshop *(werkplaats),* where a crew of devoted engineers keeps all those proud old steam trains in working order. You can actually climb the steep stepladders into some of the gorgeously reconstructed locomotives, and imagine pulling levers, turning valves, and shoveling coal to keep the "iron horse" moving.

Before long...all abooooard!

▲▲"Museum Steam Train" from Hoorn to Medemblik

From Hoorn, it's a relaxing 1.25-hour steam-train ride to Medemblik. The trains are the kind that ran through Holland from 1879 through 1966; the train you'll be riding has a chassis

from the 1920s, but the cars are furnished circa 1950s. It's a time-warp back to when train trips really had style, with wooden-bench seats, leather belts to keep windows secured in place, and nattily uniformed conductors.

After you choose a seat inside the train, you can get up and walk around. The best views (farthest from the soot, noise, and vibrations of the engine) are standing on the train balcony at the very back of the train. You'll feel like a whistle-stop presidential candidate as the train plods through the Dutch countryside.

The train makes two stops: ten minutes in Wognum-Nibbixwoud and about three minutes in Twisk. Both have doll-house-cute stations, recently renovated and decorated to evoke times past. Notice the little potbellied stoves between rooms and the old travel posters on the walls. At Wognum, peek into the old-fashioned outhouses. Stops are also a good chance to walk around and peek inside the locomotive, where you can see engineers constantly adjusting valves and levers, and opening the little door to shovel in more coal from the pile at their feet.

The costumed conductor occasionally walks through the cars, giving instructions in Dutch (if you're curious, ask him to repeat what he said in English when he passes). The train periodically stops so a conductor can hop out, scurry out in front of the engine, and flag traffic to a stop the old-fashioned way.

But don't fret the details...this is simply a serene, old-fashioned joyride. Enjoy the purely Dutch countryside. Count sheep. Moo at cows. Watch horses playfully run alongside the train. Look for ducks in the canals and pheasants in the fields. If you see little Dutch kids waving to the train from their backyards, wave back. The modern white windmills in the distance jolt you back into the 21st century, just in time to arrive at...

Medemblik

You'll have about an hour in this pleasant one-street town before boarding the boat (confirm the boat's exact departure time before leaving the train station). Exit the station and bear left, then right, to walk up the main drag—a pretty market street lined with cafés, bakeries, shops, and postcard stands. Because time is short here, you'll have to pick and choose: If you're hungry, you could grab a quick sandwich or a coffee and snack at an outdoor café, but you likely won't have time for a full meal. (Note that there's also basic food available on the upcoming boat ride.)

Or, if you feel like sightseeing, on the first block of the main street (on the right) is a cute, if overpriced, **bakery museum.** Displayed on two floors of an old bakery, the exhibit shows off baking bric-a-brac and covers everything from Christmas spice cookies and sugar sculptures to chocolate and marzipan. The live demonstrations are the highlight—depending on the day, you might see a baker making cookies, candies, or ice cream in an old-fashioned machine (€5, Tue–Sun 12:00–17:00, closed Mon, Nieuwstraat 8, tel. 0227/545-014, www.deoudebakkerij.nl).

Two other sights—a steam engine museum and a castle museum—are too far from the station to visit in the one hour between the steam train and boat. But if you have more time, the **TI**—at the end of the main street on the right—has information on both, as well as a €3 self-guided tour brochure for the town (July–Aug Mon–Sat 10:00–12:30 & 13:00–17:00, May–June and Sept Mon–Sat 11:00–16:00, April and Oct Mon–Sat 11:00–15:00, closed Sun and Nov–March, Kaasmarkt 1, tel. 0227/542-852).

Shortcut Back to Hoorn: If you want to skip the boat trip and open-air museum at Enkhuizen, and instead go directly back to Hoorn, you can ride back on the steam train, or catch the bus (bus #39, 2/hr on weekdays, 1/hr on weekends, 25 min, €2 ticket from driver is cheaper than 7 *strippenkaart* strips; slower milk-run bus #44 runs hourly weekdays only, 1 hour). Note that there's usually no direct overland connection from Medemblik to Enkhuizen (except the boat)—you'll have to take the bus to Hoorn, then the train or bus from there to Enkhuizen.

Boat from Medemblik to Enkhuizen

Catch the *MS Friesland* to Enkhuizen just over the dike from the

train station (you'll see the boat moored there as the train pulls in). It's a 90-minute putter along the coast to Enkhuizen. If you didn't eat in Medemblik, you can grab a bite in the boat's surprisingly comfortable dining room (€2–2.50 sandwiches and meatloaf-like "hamburgers"). If you've brought a picnic, grab a wicker chair and enjoy the peaceful, windswept deck. Kids can safely run around on the open spaces of the top deck, or play wooden board games in the lounge. In good weather, you'll pass small pleasure craft—little sailboats and windsurfers—close enough to shake hands.

▲Enkhuizen Zuiderzee Museum

The boat from Medemblik drops you right at the rear entrance of this wonderful open-air folk museum. It's a low-key, re-created village patterned after a salty old Dutch fishing town. The museum's original buildings were collected from around the Zuiderzee ("South Sea"), which was diked off in 1932 to become a lake called the IJsselmeer. With the ensuing transition from saltwater to freshwater, and the later reclamation and repurposing of land, the traditional culture on display at this museum became virtually extinct. You'll meet people who do a convincing job of role-playing no-nonsense 1905 villagers. You're welcome to take their picture, but they won't smile—no one said "Have a nice day" back then. On weekends, children enjoy trying out old-time games, playing at the dress-up chest (€1), and making sailing ships out of old wooden shoes (€2.50).

Cost and Hours: €12.50, April–Oct daily 10:00–17:00; also open Nov–March daily 10:00–17:00, but the buildings are closed, making it a pricey ticket to see just the indoor museum and deserted grounds; tel. 0228/351-111, www.zuiderzeemuseum.nl.

Getting There: If you don't want to do the whole Historic Triangle trip (described previously), it's also possible to take the train to the museum from Amsterdam (or Haarlem). Trains make the one-hour trip between Amsterdam and Enkhuizen every half-hour. From the Enkhuizen station, take the shuttle boat or walk 20 minutes to the museum (see "Back to Amsterdam" at the end of this tour).

◑ Self-Guided Tour: The Zuiderzee Museum is a delight to explore. This tour is a start, but don't be afraid to poke into houses (even if they seem to be populated) and backyards.

A museum attendant will greet you at the **dock** where the boats arrive (from Medemblik and the Historic Triangle trip—described above; or from the Enkhuizen train station—described under "Back to Amsterdam," page 280). Show your Historic Triangle ticket, or (if you don't have one) buy a museum ticket. From here, you can head to the right into a nature preserve, or go to the left to the museum buildings. Follow signs for *Informatiecentrum* into the row of brick houses, where you can pick up a map at the information center.

The museum is organized into units. Use the map to visit these in counterclockwise order. Throughout the open-air museum, notice that every building has a little plaque with a brief English description and a map showing the building's original location in the Zuiderzee region. The first section, the **fishing village**, includes many residential homes that are fun to explore. On some days (likely Tue and Thu), dressed-up locals populate the ramshackle village street from Urk—once a remote island across the Zuiderzee, now a strange little lump on a vast, flat *polder*.

Head to the *polder* area, near the windmill. In addition to being a pretty symbol for the Netherlands, windmills like the one

here harness the power of the wind to turn Archimedes' screws, which, by rotating in a tube, pump water up over a dike and into the sea—continuing to drain reclaimed *polder* land. Nearby are big vats used to cure fishing nets and a smokehouse where you can pick up a tasty snack: smoked herring (€1.50) or eel (€4).

Next, circle around to the **urban canal** zone (near the pavilion), lined with shops—such as a bakery, gift shop, and cheese shop where 15,000 clumps of Gouda could be aged. Don't miss the pharmacy (marked *Apotheke "De Groote Gaper,"* under the queen with her mouth hanging open). Past the counter where the pharmacist weighs out little bottles of camphor, you'll find a room full of open-mouthed giant heads. Traditionally, Dutch pharmacies were marked by a head with a gaping mouth (opening wide to say "aaaah" for the doctor, or for taking a pill). Many of these original heads are dark-skinned—since medicine, like people from the east or south of Europe, was considered mysterious and magical.

A nearby theater shows a dramatic film that includes some grainy black-and-white footage of traditional Zuiderzee life (with English subtitles). As you curl around along the little canal, you'll find other trades represented, such as a barber and a cooper (barrel-maker).

Afterwards, head into the **church district,** surrounding a reconstructed church dating from the 15th century. Because local builders were more familiar with boats than buildings, standing inside this church feels like being under an overturned boat (a common feeling in many Dutch village churches). Around the church are more shops, including the blacksmith. Don't miss the schoolhouse, with two period classrooms: one from 1905 and another from 1930. Just across the canal from the church area is a big self-service restaurant, with indoor and outdoor seating (€3 sandwiches, €5–10 meals).

Finally, walk toward the cute, enclosed **harbor,** filled with Zuiderzee watercraft from ages past (just beyond it is a modern harbor, filled with pleasure boats). The little cluster of houses just beyond the harbor (where you can pay €1 to see a rope-making demonstration) is based on the island village of Marken (see page 285).

As you leave the park through the main entrance, you can pay a visit to the **indoor museum** (same ticket and hours): Exit to the left and walk two blocks, watching for the museum on your right. This space shows off temporary exhibits (only some of which relate to the Zuiderzee), as well as an impressive hall filled with nine old Zuiderzee boats. Notice that many of them have big, flat fins on the sides. Because the Zuiderzee could be very shallow, these boats didn't have a keel; the fins could be extended down into the water to provide more stability.

Back to Amsterdam

From the indoor museum, it's a scenic 15-minute walk, mostly along the water, through the bricks-and-canals town to the Enkhuizen train station: Exit the indoor museum to the right, follow the wall, and cross three bridges (watching for *Station* directional signs). Or you can catch a shuttle boat between the museum and the station (free with museum ticket, 4/hr, 10-min trip, last trips from museum at 17:15 and 17:30).

Waterland

The aptly named region of Waterland (VAH-ter-land), just north of Amsterdam on the west shore of the IJsselmeer, is laced with canals and sprinkled with picturesque red-brick villages. Three in particular—the homey cheesemaking village of Edam, the workaday waterfront town of Volendam, and the trapped-in-a-time-warp hamlet of Marken—offer an enticing peek at rural Holland. If choosing just one Waterland town, make it Edam—and consider spending the night. Because of its charm and its proximity to Amsterdam, this region is popular, especially on summer weekends. But if you'd like to get a taste of traditional Dutch living, it's worth joining the crowds.

Planning Your Time: The Waterland Loop

The most efficient way to see this area is as a one-day loop trip by public transportation from Amsterdam (or Haarlem). Begin with a bus from Amsterdam to Edam. Then, after enjoying Edam, continue by bus to Volendam for a stroll and to catch the boat across to Marken. Poke around salty Marken before taking the bus back to Amsterdam. The entire loop is covered by the €6 "Waterland Ticket" from the Arriva bus company (or €10 for a "Family Day Pass" covering up to five people). You can also do the loop in reverse: Marken, then Volendam, then Edam.

The Volendam–Marken boat doesn't take cars, so drivers must

leave their cars in Volendam while they take the round-trip boat ride to Marken.

Edam

This adorable cheesemaking village is sweet but palatable, and just 30 minutes by bus from Amsterdam. It's mostly the terrain of day-trippers, who can mob the place on summer weekends. For

the ultimate in cuteness and peace, make your home in tiny Edam.

While Edam is known today for cheese, it was once an industrious ship-yard and port. But having a canal to the sea caused such severe flooding in town—cracking walls and spilling into homes—that one frustrated resident even built a floating cellar (now in the Edams Museum, next page). To stop the flooding, the harbor was closed off with locked gates (you'll see the gates at Dam Square next to the TI). Eventually the harbor silted up, forcing the decline of the shipbuilding trade.

Edam's Wednesday market is held year-round, but it's best in July and early August, when the focus is on cheese. You, along with piles of other tourists, can meet the cheese traders and local farmers.

ORIENTATION

(area code: 0299)

Edam is a very small town—you can see it all in a lazy 10-minute stroll. Dam Square, with the City Hall and TI, is right along the big canal called Spui; the town's lone museum is just over the big bridge.

Tourist Information

The TI, often staffed by volunteers, is in City Hall on Dam Square. Pick up the €0.50 *Edam Holland* brochure and consider the €2.50 *A Stroll Through Edam* brochure outlining a self-guided walking tour (July–Aug Mon–Sat 10:00–17:00, Sun 12:30–16:30; early March–June and Sept–Oct Mon–Sat 10:00–17:00, closed Sun; Nov–early March Mon–Sat 10:00–15:00, closed Sun; WC and ATM just outside, tel. 0299/315-125, www.vvv-edam.nl).

Internet Access: Edam has a two-computer Internet café close to Dam Square, called **Cor Graphics** (Tue–Fri 9:30–17:30, Sat 9:30–16:00, closed Sun–Mon, along the canal just behind City

Hall at Voorhaven 141, tel. 0299/315-587, www.cor-graphics.com).

Arrival in Edam

To get from the bus "station"—really just a parking lot for buses—to Dam Square and the TI, take a five-minute walk toward the gray-and-gold bell tower just east of the main square. Head for the big canal, then turn right and walk alongside it for a while. Cross the first bridge you come to, and head straight up the street. Hook right around the church, and you'll wind up across the canal from Dam Square.

SIGHTS

Introductory Walk—To get the lay of the land, take this stroll through the heart of Edam. From Dam Square, walk over the bridge to the Edams Museum (see below). Exiting the museum, turn right and walk one block along the Spui canal, then turn right down Prinsenstraat. This leads to the traditional cheese-market square (Niewhuizenplein), with the big Matthijs Tinxgracht canal just beyond. Peek into the old "cheese weigh house," then continue down the street to see the town's main church, or Grote Kerk. Take a look at the cows chewing their cud in the field across the canal, and you've pretty much seen all there is in Edam.

Edams Museum/Historical Collection—This small, quirky museum—and a nearby 400-year-old historical home with a floating cellar (covered by the same ticket)—offer a fun peek into Edam's past. At the museum, learn about Edam's trading history upstairs, and about Fris Pottery on the top floor (€3, late March–Oct Tue–Sat 10:00–16:30, Sun 13:00–16:30, closed Mon and Nov–late March, historical house at Dam Square 8, museum in city hall with TI, tel. 0299/372-644, www.edams museum.nl).

SLEEPING

There are only two hotels in town, but they're both distinctive, classy, and expensive (when there's a range, the price depends on room size and amenities). The TI has a list of cheaper rooms in private homes.

$$ Damhotel, centrally located on a canal across the street from the TI, has 11 newly renovated rooms with over-the-top plush decor—each one a bit different (Db-€125–165, Tb-€160, Qb-€185, air-con, free Wi-Fi, Keizersgracht 1, tel. 0299/371-766, fax 0299/374-031, www.damhotel.nl, info@damhotel.nl).

$ Hotel de Fortuna is an eccentric, canalside place with flowers and sounds of ducks and other birds. It offers steep stairs and

Sleep Code

(€1 = about $1.40, country code: 31, area code: 0299)
S = Single, **D** = Double/Twin, **T** = Triple, **Q** = Quad, **b** = bathroom,
s = shower only. Unless otherwise noted, credit cards are
accepted, breakfast is included, and hoteliers speak English.

To help you easily sort through these listings, I've divided
the rooms into two categories, based on the price for a
standard double room with bath:

$$ **Higher Priced**—Most rooms €125 or more.
$ **Lower Priced**—Most rooms less than €125.

23 low-ceilinged rooms in
a complex of five ancient
buildings in the old center of
Edam. It's been run by the
Dekker family for more than
30 years (Sb-€67.50–97.50,
Db-€95–127.50, free Wi-Fi,
Spuistraat 3, tel. 0299/371-
671, fax 0299/371-469, www
.fortuna-edam.nl, fortuna@fortuna-edam.nl).

EATING

Edam's lanes are lined with tourist-friendly restaurants (all of these
are within a block of Dam Square). Considering how close it is to
Amsterdam, I'd come here for a romantic dinner in the country-
side, then head back to my lodgings in the big city.

Hotel de Fortuna and **Damhotel,** both listed on previous
page, each have a fine restaurant with classy, high-priced food
(reservations smart on weekends). Hotel de Fortuna has more rus-
tic charm, with a romantic dining room and seating in a gorgeous
garden alongside a picturesque canal (€20–25 main dishes, three-
course "Fortuna *menu*" for €32.50, pricier fixed-price meals also
available, daily 12:00–15:00 & 18:00–21:30). Damhotel's outdoor
seating is right on Dam Square, in the shadow of the Town Hall,
and their interior feels dressy (€20–30 main dishes, €35–45 fixed-
price meals, daily 8:00–24:00).

De Prinsen Bar and Eetcafé is a good bet for a light lunch
or a midday snack. Their €7 *Portie gemengde Hollandse Kaas* is a
sampler of bread, olives, and regional cheeses. It's a good nibbler
plate for two and goes well with a little Belgian *beerje* (€3.50 soups,
€3.50–4.50 salads, €6–10 pub grub meals, daily 12:00–24:00, food

served all the time June–Aug but only Sat–Sun 12:00–16:00 in off-season, Prinsenstraat 8, tel. 0299/372-911).

Picnickers can stock up at the **Topper Supermarket/Delicatessen** (Mon–Fri 9:00–18:00, Sat 8:30–16:00, Sun 10:00–17:00, next door to cheese shop overlooking Spui canal across from Dam Square, tel. 0299/373-069).

TRANSPORTATION CONNECTIONS

Edam and **Amsterdam** are connected by frequent buses. From Amsterdam, bus #112 is the most direct option (2/hr Mon–Sat, 30-min trip, no buses after 19:00). You can also take bus #116 (2/hr Mon–Sat, similar duration, no buses after 19:00), bus #110 (2/hr Mon–Sat, slower and with more stops, no buses after 19:00), or bus #118 (2/hr daily, much slower and lots of stops but runs Sun and until 24:00). The trip between Amsterdam and Edam costs 7 *strippenkaart* strips. To find the Edam-bound bus stop from Amsterdam's Central Station, exit the station to the left and go beyond all the tram stops.

By Bus to Volendam on the "Waterland Loop": Buses #110, #116, and #118 zip you from Edam to Volendam in just a few minutes. Hop off at the Zeestraat stop (bus #110 or #118) or the Julianaweg/Centrum stop (bus #116)—ask the driver if you're unsure (6/hr Mon–Sat, 2/hr Sun, costs 2 *strippenkaart* strips). Other buses also go to Volendam, but not to these handy town-center stops.

Volendam

Less cute and more functional than the other two Waterland towns, Volendam enjoys some workaday charm of its own—including a lively dike-top walkway stretching along a shimmering bay, and an appealing town museum.

Arrival in Volendam: If arriving by bus from Edam, get off at the Zeestraat or Julianaweg/Centrum stop. The town's museum and TI are within a block of these bus stops. To reach the boat to Marken, walk straight from the bus stop toward the water, then turn left and walk along the dike.

Sights: The town's lone sight is the **Volendams Museum.** This hokey but endearing little collection, in the modern part of town, oozes Volendam local pride. You'll wander through displays of traditional local costumes, replica house and shop interiors, scenes from village life, and nostalgic old grainy black-and-white movies that are worth watching even if you don't speak Dutch. The highlight is the Cigarband House, where a local artist glued 11 million cigarbands to big boards to create giant images—from Dutch windmills to Venice to the Statue of Liberty (€2, borrow English descriptions at entry, mid-March–mid-Oct daily 10:00–17:00, closed off-season, Zeestraat 41, tel. 0299/369-258, www.volendams

museum.nl). The town's **TI** is in the same building (closed Sun, tel. 0299/363-747, www.vvv-volendam.nl).

Along the waterfront, Volendam's inviting **promenade,** with a lively boardwalk appeal, is lined with souvenir shops, indoor/outdoor eateries, and Dutch clichés—a good place to kill time waiting for your boat. The **Hotel Spaander**'s walls are decorated with paintings by starving artists who slept or ate there. Don't miss the maze of sleepy residential courtyards below sea level just behind the promenade, with an adorable dollhouse charm and fewer crowds.

"Marken Express": This boat connects Volendam with Marken (€4.50 one-way, €7 round-trip, bike-€1 extra each way, March–Oct daily from about 11:00–17:30, departs every 20 min July–Aug, every 30–45 min March–June and Sept–Oct, by appointment only Nov–Feb, 30-min crossing, tel. 0299/363-331, www.marken-express.nl).

Marken

Famous as one of the Netherlands' most traditional fishing communities, Marken is a time-passed hamlet in a bottle...once virtually abandoned, now revived but kept alive solely as a tourist attraction. This island town once had a harbor for whaling and herring fishing. But when the Zuiderzee began to silt up in the late

17th century, it became more and more difficult to eke out a living here, and many people from Marken fled to easier conditions on the mainland. Once the Zuiderzee was diked off in 1932 to become a giant freshwater lake (the IJsselmeer), it forced saltwater fishermen to

adapt or to find a new calling (which most did). Marken became a virtual ghost town. But in 1957, a long causeway was constructed from the mainland to the hamlet, which allowed easy access for visitors—who today come in droves to walk its tiny lanes.

Arrival in Marken: From the boat dock at the little harbor, follow signs to the museum in the town center. Marken has no TI; the nearest is in Volendam.

Sights: The village of Marken has two districts: Havenbuurt, near the harbor, and Kerkbuurt, near the church. Arriving by boat, you'll first wander through the colorful Havenbuurt, then head for the charming Kerkbuurt to get a taste of Marken's old-time charm. As you walk, notice the unique local architecture, adapted to survive the challenging local conditions: Because the tides could be so temperamental, houses here tend to cluster on little hills called *werven*, or are built on pilings to keep them high and dry. Traditional Marken homes, while dull and black-tarred outside, are painted a cheerful yellow and blue inside.

The town's main attraction is the modest **Marken Museum,** celebrating the 16th-century costumes (still worn for special events) and traditional lifestyles of the people of Marken. As you enter, ask for an English showing of the good, eight-minute movie (€2.50, April–Oct Mon–Sat 10:00–16:30, Sun 12:00–16:00, closed Nov–March, tel. 0299/601-904).

Just outside town, on the way to the parking lot and bus stop, you'll pass Marken's raised **cemetery,** where graves are marked with numbers rather than names. With more time, you can walk (about 40 min) out to the **lighthouse,** dubbed Paard van Marken ("Horse of Marken"), picturesquely situated at the far end of the island, at the tip of a sandy spit.

Transportation Connections: Bus #111 connects Marken with Amsterdam (2/hr, 40 min, 6 *strippenkaart* strips). In Marken, catch the bus along the main road that skirts the town, just past the big parking lot.

Near Haarlem

These side-trips are near the good home-base town of Haarlem. Among all the day trips, these three require the least brainpower: two flower experiences (a garden show and a flower auction) and a beach retreat.

▲▲▲Keukenhof

This is the greatest bulb-flower garden on earth, open for only two months in spring. Each spring, seven million flowers, enjoying the sandy soil of the Dutch dunes and *polderland,* conspire to make even a total garden-hater enjoy them. This 80-acre park is packed with tour groups daily; for the least crowds and the best light, go late in the day.

Cost and Hours: €13.50, open March 18–May 16 in 2010, daily 8:00–19:30, last entry at 18:00, at the northern tip of the town of Lisse, tel. 0252/465-555, www.keukenhof.nl.

Getting There: Take the train to Leiden, then catch bus #54 (Keukenhof Express) straight to the garden (allow 1.25 hrs total from Amsterdam, 45 min total from Haarlem). Bus #58 connects Schiphol Airport directly to Keukenhof (20 min). Drivers will find Lisse well-marked from the A-6 expressway south of Amsterdam.

▲▲FloraHolland Aalsmeer Flower Auction (Bloemenveiling)

Get a bird's-eye view of the huge Dutch flower industry in this cavernous building where the world's flower prices are set. You'll wan-

der on elevated walkways (through what's claimed to be the biggest commercial building on earth) over literally trainloads of freshly cut flowers. About half of all the flowers exported from Holland are auctioned off here, in four huge auditoriums. The flowers are shipped here overnight (for maximum freshness), auctioned at the crack of dawn, and distributed as quickly as possible. For the best floral variety and auction action, the earlier, the better (things wilt after 9:30 and on Thu, and the auction closes down by 11:00).

Standing above all those blooms, take a deep, fragrant breath, and hold it in. As you wander, keep an eye out for tulip-shaped "listening posts," and press the English button for on-the-spot information. Peering into the auction halls, you'll see that clocks are projected on two big screens. This is a "Dutch auction," meaning that the price starts high and then ticks down, until buyers push the button at the price they're willing to pay. Think about the high stakes and the need for decisiveness...there's no time to think things over as the auctioneer calls, "Going once, going twice..."

Most of the flowers are purchased by wholesalers and exporters. You'll see the busy beehive of the distribution process, as workers scurry to load carts of flowers onto little tractors to zip to awaiting buyers. Up along the ceiling, look for the suspended orange trams. This "Aalsmeer Shuttle" zips loads of flowers over the workers' heads to the distribution center across the street, far more quickly and efficiently than trucks.

You'll wind up at the even more elaborate Rose Market, where 450 buyers keep their eyes peeled on three different auction clocks as they jostle to buy the auction's most popular item. As you circle back to the entrance, you'll see the company's testing lab, where they actually create and test new varieties of flowers.

Cost and Hours: €5, Mon–Fri 7:00–11:00, closed Sat–Sun, gift shop, cafeteria, tel. 0297/392-185, www.floraholland.com.

Getting There: By bus, you can reach the flower auction from Amsterdam (Connexxion bus #172 from Central Station, 4/hr, 50 min) or from Haarlem (take bus #198 or #140 to the town of Aalsmeer, where you can transfer to bus #172, 2/hr, 60 min). Aalsmeer, which is close to the airport, makes a handy last fling for **drivers** before dropping off your car at the airport and catching a late-morning weekday flight out (but there's usually no bus connection from the auction to the airport). From the A-6 expressway south of Amsterdam, drivers take the Aalsmeer exit (#3) and follow signs for *Aalsmeer*, then *Bloemenveiling*. Once you reach the complex, carefully follow the *P Tourist* signs to park on top of the garage, then take the elevator downstairs and follow *Tourist* signs to the visitors center.

Zandvoort

For a quick and easy look at the windy coastline in a shell-lover's Shangri-la, visit the beach burg of Zandvoort. This pretty, manicured resort has plenty of cafés, ice-cream parlors, *Vlaamse frites* stands, restaurants, and boutiques.

Just beyond the town is the vast and sandy beach, lined with cafés and rentable chairs. Above it all is a pedestrian promenade and a line of high-rise hotels. South of the main beach, sunbathers work on all-over tans. Come to Zandvoort if the weather's hot and you want a

taste of the sea and sun, if you want to see how Dutch and German holiday-makers have fun, or if you just want an excuse for a long bike ride from Haarlem (helpful **TI** open Mon–Fri 9:00–12:30 & 13:30–16:30, Sat 10:00–16:00—until 14:00 Oct–March, closed Sun, on Bakkerstraat, tel. 023/571-7947, www.vvvzandvoort.nl).

Getting There: It's easy to reach by **train** (2/hr, 12 min from Haarlem, 30 min from Amsterdam). For a breezy 45-minute **bike** ride west of Haarlem, follow road signs for *Bloemendaal,* then *Zandvoort.*

Alkmaar and Zaanse Schans

Two handy day trips line up north of Amsterdam: Alkmaar is a famous cheesemaking town with a charming square and a bustling cheese market. Zaanse Schans, while perhaps the tackiest of Holland's open-air museums, is also its most convenient—offering a taste of traditional life a stone's throw from the capital. Consider combining the two destinations for a full day of sightseeing (best on summer Fridays, when Alkmaar's festive cheese market enlivens the town).

Alkmaar

Alkmaar is Holland's cheese capital (and, perhaps, the unofficial capital of high cholesterol). In addition to being an all-around delightful city, Alkmaar has a rich history and a zesty cheese-loving spirit. While it's enjoyable to visit any time, don't miss this town during its bustling Friday-morning cheese market in the summer.

ORIENTATION

(area code: 072)

Once a stoutly walled city, Alkmaar (pop. 95,000) now has a fine and tidy Old Town laced by canals. The main square, Waagplein, is named for Alkmaar's cheese-weighing. The mighty Weigh House, containing the TI and Cheese Museum, is at one end of the square, and the Beer Museum is at the other. (Think of it as "Holland's Wisconsin.") From this area, the main pedestrian drag, Langestraat, leads to the Grote Kerk and Stedelijk Museum.

Tourist Information

Alkmaar's TI, in the old Weigh House, sells a €2 town walking tour brochure (April–Sept Mon–Thu 10:00–17:30, Fri 9:00–17:30, Sat 9:30–17:00, closed Sun; Oct–March Mon–Fri 10:00–17:30, Sat 9:30–17:00, closed Sun; Waagplein 2, tel. 072/511-4284, www.vvvalkmaar.nl).

Arrival in Alkmaar

From the train station, it's a 15-minute walk to the town center. The route is well-marked (just follow signs for *Centrum*): Exit the station to the right, then turn left (onto Scharlo) when the street dead-ends. Soon you'll cross a canal and see the big church (Grote Kerk), with the Stedelijk Museum nearby. From the church, walk straight up the main pedestrian street (Langestraat). When you reach the next canal, turn left and walk one more block to the main square and TI.

SIGHTS

▲▲Cheese Market (Kaasmarkt)—Tellingly, Alkmaar's biggest building isn't the church or the town hall, but the richly decorated **Weigh House** (Waaggebouw), used since the 16th century for weighing cheese. (It was converted from an old chapel.) The right to weigh, sell, and tax cheese is what put Alkmaar on the map in the Middle Ages, and it's still what the town is celebrated for today.

Think about the udder importance of cheese to this culture—wheying the fact that it has long kept the Dutch economy moo-ving. If you travel through the Dutch countryside, you'll pass endless fields filled with cows, which are more reliable than crops in this marshy landscape. Because cheese offers similar nutritional value to milk, but lasts much longer without refrigeration, it was a staple on long sea voyages—and Holland was the first country to export it. Today the Netherlands remains the world's biggest cheese exporter.

There's no better time to sample a sliver of this proud wedge of Dutch culture than during Alkmaar's **cheese market,** which takes place on Fridays in the summer (early April–early Sept, 10:00–12:30). Early in the morning, cheesemakers line up their giant orange wheels in neat rows on the square. Prospective buyers (mostly wholesalers) examine and sample the cheeses and make their selections. Then the cheese is sold off with much fanfare, as

an emcee narrates the action (in Dutch and English). To close the deal, costumed cheese carriers run the giant wheels back and forth to the Weigh House just as they have for centuries: They load a wheel onto a "cheese-barrow"—kind of a wooden stretcher—then sling each end over their shoulders on ropes and run it to and fro. The cheese carriers' guild has four "fraternities" of seven carriers each: red, yellow, blue, and green (with color-coded hats, cheese-barrows, and scales). Each fraternity is headed by a "cheese father," who enforces the strict rules and levies fines on carriers who show up late or drink beer before carrying cheese (which is strictly forbidden).

On cheese market days, the town erupts in a carnival atmosphere, becoming one big street fair with festive entertainers and vendors selling souvenirs, snacks...and, of course, cheese. It can get crowded—especially midmorning—but the Cheese Museum (below) is surprisingly uncrowded, and its windows allow great unobstructed views of the action below.

▲**Cheese Museum (Het Hollands Kaas Museum)**—This is probably the Netherlands' best cheese museum...and in this country, that's saying something. With displays on two floors above the TI in the Weigh House, the museum explains both traditional and modern methods of cheesemaking. You'll learn that as the economy evolved, cheesemaking went from being the work of farmers' wives to factory workers. You'll find old equipment (much of it still used for today's cheese market), such as big scales, wagons, cheese-barrows, and (upstairs) old presses for squeezing the last bit of whey out of the cheese molds. Ask for an English showing of the 15-minute movie that traces the history and traditions of Alkmaar cheesemaking. (You'll find out what a "cheesehead" really is, and the technical difference between Gouda and Edam cheeses.) Other, smaller screens around the museum show informative movies—press the flag for English subtitles (€3, April–Oct Mon–Sat 10:00–16:00, Fri from 9:00 during cheese market, closed Sun and Nov–March, enter TI at Waagplein 2 and walk up the stairs to the museum, tel. 072/511-4284, www.cheesemuseum.com).

Beer Museum (Nationaal Biermuseum De Boom)—This hokey old museum, in a former brewery, shows off an endearing collection about beer production across the centuries—from the days of barrels to the earliest bottling plants. The 1700s-era replica bar has sand on the floor, from a time when men were men and didn't have to aim into a spittoon. While interesting, the museum's explanations are scant (pick up the English descriptions as you enter). If you're not a beer-lover or a backyard brewer, I'd skip it (€3.50, Mon–Sat 13:00–16:00, Fri from 10:00 during cheese market, closed Sun, across Waagplein from the Weigh House at Houttil 1, tel. 072/511-3801, www.biermuseum.nl).

Grote Kerk—Alkmaar's "Great Church" is similar to others in Holland (such as Haarlem's and Delft's). Visit if you want to see a typically austere Dutch interior (€2.50, June–Aug Tue–Sun 10:00–17:00, closed Mon; Sept–May open only for cheese-market Fridays, concerts, and special events). The church also hosts frequent concerts (for schedules, call tel. 072/514-0707 or see www.grotekerk-alkmaar.nl).

Stedelijk Museum Alkmaar—The Stedelijk, which also has a big branch in Amsterdam, recently opened this facility in little Alkmaar. The museum has two parts: a permanent collection about the history of Alkmaar and a space for temporary exhibits. The 15-minute movie in the town history section is excellent, enlivened by props and sound effects (ask to see it in English). But the rest of the history exhibit—with stiff group portraits, other paintings, and artifacts from the town's illustrious past—is only in Dutch and difficult for non-locals to appreciate. Visit here only if the temporary exhibit intrigues you (€4.50, Tue–Fri 10:00–17:00, Sat–Sun 13:00–17:00, closed Mon, Canadaplein 1, tel. 072/548-9789, www.stedelijkmuseumalkmaar.nl).

TRANSPORTATION CONNECTIONS

Alkmaar is connected by frequent fast trains to **Amsterdam** (4/hr, 35–45 min). However, these trains do not stop at the Zaanse Schans museum (see below). To visit the **Zaanse Schans** museum on your way back to Amsterdam, take a train from Alkmaar to Uitgeest, where you can transfer to a slower regional train (typically just across the platform) to Koog-Zaandijk (sometimes abbreviated as "Koog Z."). On busy days, the info desk in the tunnel of the Alkmaar train station hands out schedules for this connection.

Zaanse Schans
Open-Air Museum

This re-created 17th-century town puts Dutch culture—from cheesemaking to wooden-shoe carving—on a lazy Susan. Located on the Zaan River in the town of Zaandijk, the museum is devoted to the traditional lifestyles along the Zaan—once lined with hundreds of windmills, used for every imaginable purpose, and today heavily industrialized (including a giant corporate chocolate

factory you'll pass on the way). In the 1960s, houses from around the region were transplanted here to preserve traditional culture. Most of the exhibits are run by quirky locals who've found their niche in life, and do it with gusto.

Less a coherent "museum" (like Arnhem or Zuiderzee), and more a hodgepodge of loosely related attractions in a pretty park with old houses, Zaanse Schans feels less organized than the others. And, since each attraction charges a separate entry fee (and those that are free are either selling or promoting something), it also feels more crassly commercial...you'll be nickel-and-dimed for your cultural education. But it's undeniably handy, just 15 minutes by train (plus a 15-minute walk) from downtown Amsterdam. Two of the attractions here—the Dutch Clock Museum and the tour-able, working windmills—are unique and genuinely interesting. Because it's the easiest one-stop look at the Netherlands' traditional culture, Zaanse Schans can be flooded at midday by busloads of tour groups—to avoid the hordes, come early or late.

Getting There: From Amsterdam, catch a slow **train** going towards Uitgeest (4/hr, €2.90 one-way, €4.70 day return), ride for about 15 minutes, then hop out at Koog-Zaandijk (or "Koog Z."). From Alkmaar, reaching Koog-Zaandijk requires a change in Uitgeest (see "Transportation Connections" for Alkmaar, on previous page).

Once at the Koog-Zaandijk station, it's about a 15-minute walk to the museum (well-marked, just follow the signs...and the other tourists). Go through the underpass and exit straight ahead, watching on your left for a TI machine where you can pull the crank to get a map. Then continue straight until the road forks. From here, follow *Zaanse Schans* signs. If the new road bridge is finished, you'll turn left, then right across the river. If the bridge isn't finished yet, you'll turn right, walk a few more steps, then catch a free little shuttle boat across the river (every 10 min). Either way, you'll end up at the "back entrance" to the park, near the Clock Museum (signs to *Ned. Uurwerkmuseum*).

If **driving** from Amsterdam, take A-8 (direction: Zaanstad/ Purmerend), turn off at *Purmerend A-7*, then follow signs to *Zaanse Schans* (parking—€6.50).

Cost: Entry is free, but it costs a euro or two to visit each historical presentation, and these costs can quickly add up. If you want to do everything, it's simplest to spring for the €13 Zaanse Schans Pass, which gets you into four museums (main Zaans Museum, Noorderhuis, Dutch Clock Museum, and Bakery Museum), plus your choice of one windmill; and 10 percent discounts at a few minor attractions (can buy pass only at either end of park—Zaanse Museum or Dutch Clock Museum).

Hours: The grounds are open all the time (since people actually live here). In the summer (April–Sept), most of the building interiors are open daily 9:00–17:00 (though many are closed Mon, and individual opening and closing times can vary by up to an hour, as noted below in each listing). After about 16:30, things get really quiet. In the winter (Oct–March), only some of the buildings are open (roughly 9:00–17:00 on Sat–Sun, shorter hours or closed entirely Mon–Fri; specific month-to-month hours listed at www.zaanseschans-museum.nl).

Information: The Visitors Center, located in the Zaanse Museum building, has a good, free map of the grounds. Ask if any events are scheduled for that day (daily 9:00–17:00, lockers, free WCs in museum, otherwise €0.50 in park, tel. 075/616-8218).

SIGHTS

I've arranged these sights in order from the train station. Drivers should park at the Zaanse Museum and then visit these in reverse order, or walk five minutes to the Dutch Clock Museum and begin there.

▲**Dutch Clock Museum (Museum van het Nederlandse Uurwerk)**—More interesting than it sounds, this collection is brought to life by its curator, clock enthusiast Pier van Leeuwen. If he's not too busy, Pier can show you around and will lovingly describe his favorite pieces. Or pick up the free brochure and explore seven centuries' worth of timepieces on your own. Upstairs is a big, bulky, crank-wound turret clock from around 1520. Back then, the length of an "hour" wasn't fixed—there were simply 12 of them between sunrise and sunset, so the clock's weights could be adjusted to modify the length of an hour at different times of year. Also up here are the museum's prized possessions: two of the world's four surviving, original 17th-century pendulum clocks, which allowed for more precision in timekeeping. Downstairs, appreciate the fine craftsmanship of the Zaans clocks (one clock is wound by being pushed up on a rack, rather than pulling a chain) and Amsterdam clocks (€4; April–Oct Tue–Sun 10:00–17:00, closed Mon; Nov–March Sat–Sun 12:00–16:30, closed Mon–Fri; tel. 075/617-9769, www.mnuurwerk.nl).

• *Next door is the...*

Albert Heijn Grocery "Museum" (Museumwinkel)—Little more than a thinly veiled advertisement for the Dutch supermarket chain, this replica grocery store from the 1880s re-creates the first shop run by Albert Heijn. The scant exhibits lead to a room promoting Heijn coffee (free, get English description sheet;

Easter–Oct Tue–Sun 10:30–13:00 & 13:30–16:00, closed Mon; Nov–Easter Sat–Sun 12:00–16:00, closed Mon–Fri).

• A few doors up the street is...

Het Noorderhuis Museum—Walk through this old merchant's house from 1670, with two diorama scenes showing local lifestyles around 1800 and 1900 (€1.50, Tue–Sat 10:00–17:00, Sun 12:00–17:00, closed Mon).

• Just beyond the De Hoop op d'Swarte Walvis restaurant (see "Eating," page 297) is the dock for the...

Boat Cruise (Rederij de Schans Rondvaarten)—This 45-minute boat tour floats visitors through the park and adjacent town (€6, departs on the hour Tue–Sun 11:00–16:00, closed Mon except July–Aug, closed Oct–March, tel. 065/329-4467, www .rederijdeschans.nl).

• From here, enjoy a fine view of the windmills. But before you go on to visit them, poke into the little village area across from the boat landing. First you'll pass an adorable curiosity shop that's a pack-rat's heaven. Then you'll encounter the...

Bakery Museum (Bakkerijmuseum)—This fragrant and very modest "museum" displays old bakery equipment (including cookie molds) and sells what it bakes. Borrow the English descriptions to navigate the slapdash exhibit (€1 to enter museum, various treats available—most around €2.50, Tue–Sun 10:00–17:00, closed Mon).

• Now head for the...

▲Windmills (Molens)—The very industrious Zaan region is

typified by these hardworking windmills, which you'll see everywhere. Mills are built with sturdy oak timber frames to withstand the constant tension of movement. To catch the desired amount of wind, millers—like expert sailors—know just how much to unfurl the sails. When the direction of the wind shifts, the miller turns the cap of the building, which weighs several tons, to face the breeze.

You can tour several of Zaanse Schans' old-fashioned windmills, each one used for a different purpose (€2.50 per mill, hours vary, www.zaansemolen .nl). **De Gekroonde Poelenburg** is a sawmill, where stout logs are turned into building lumber (open sporadically). **De Kat** ("The Cat") grinds dyes. Watch its gigantic millstones rolling over the colored dust again and again, as wooden chutes keep it on its path. Climb the steep steps (practically a ladder) for a closer look at the wooden gears, and the fine views out over the museum grounds (March–Oct Tue–Sun 9:00–17:00, closed Mon). **De Zoeker** ("The Seeker") crushes oil from seeds and nuts, a drop at a time—up to an incredible 100 quarts per day (March–Oct daily 9:30–16:30). Other mills may also be open for your visit. If deciding which mill to visit, choose one that's spinning—you'll see more action inside. While these structures appear graceful, and even whimsical from the outside, on a windy day you can really experience the awesome power of the mills by getting up close to their grinding gears.

• *After exploring the windmills, cross the little canal to the big...*

De Catharina Hoeve Cheese Farm (Kaasmakerij)—Essentially a giant cheese shop, this is worthwhile only if you catch one of their presentations. A movie shows how cheese is made, and periodically a costumed Dutch maiden explains the process in person (about five quarts of milk are used to make about a pound of cheese) and dispenses samples...followed by a confident sales pitch (free entry, daily 8:00–18:00).

• *Walk past the mini-windmill to a shopping zone, which includes the...*

Wooden Shoe Workshop (Klompenmakerij)—More engaging than the park's other free attractions, this shoe store features a well-presented display of clogs from different regions of the Netherlands. You'll see how clogs were adapted for various purposes, including wooden clogs with boot-like leather to the knee, frilly decorative clogs for weddings, and spiky clogs for ice fishing. Watch the videos, and try to catch the live demonstration that sends wood chips flying as a machine carves a shoe. Your visit ends—where else?—in the vast clog shop (free entry, daily 8:00–18:00).

• *Nearby is the huge De Kraai restaurant (see "Eating," opposite page), and just across the big parking lot is the final attraction, the...*

▲Zaanse Museum—This museum, whose modern structure evokes both the hull of a ship and the curved body of a whale, is the focal point of the complex. In addition to housing the Visitors Center, it has a fresh, modern multimedia presentation that explains Holland's industrial past and present with the help of a fine included audioguide. The exhibit, with some English descriptions, is thematically divided into four parts: life, work, wind, and water (€4.50, Tue–Sat 10:00–17:00, Sun 12:00–17:00, closed Mon, tel. 075/616-2862). In 2009, a new exhibit dedicated to the Verkade candy company (a local favorite) opened adjacent to the museum.

EATING

Pannenkoeken Restaurant de Kraai, located in the open-air museum, is a self-service eatery offering traditional sweet and savory pancakes that come with all the fillings you might select for an omelet—cheese, ham, mushrooms, and so on (€8–10 pancakes, daily until 18:00, closed Jan, with indoor and outdoor seating). **De Hoop op d'Swarte Walvis** ("The Hope of the Black Whale") is the park's splurge, with a white-tablecloth interior, outdoor seating, and an ambitiously priced menu (€6–7 sandwiches, €35–45 main dishes at dinner, Tue–Sun from 11:00 for lunch and from 17:00 for dinner, closed Mon, tel. 075/616-5629).

Schokland and Flevoland

The Dutch have always had a love/hate relationship with the tempestuous Zuiderzee ("South Sea"). While it provided the Dutch

with a convenient source of fish and trade—and an outlet to the Atlantic—the unpredictable bay also made life challenging. Over the centuries, entire towns were gradually eroded off the map.

But in 1918, the Dutch fought back and began to ingeniously tame the sea and "reclaim" their land with the Zuiderzee Works: First they built a sturdy dike (the Afsluitdijk) across the mouth of the sea to turn a dangerous, raging ocean into a mild puddle (the IJsselmeer); then they began to partition pieces of the sea floor, dike them off, and drain the water. The salty new seabed soil was treated organically and eventually became fertile farmland.

Today, about a fifth of the Netherlands is reclaimed land—much of it a short drive northeast of Amsterdam. In Flevoland, the Netherlands' newest state, some of the residents are older than the land they live on, which was reclaimed in the 1960s. The roads, commercial centers, and neighborhoods—made affordable to the masses—are all carefully planned and tidy as can be. This area offers a fascinating joyride for engineers or anyone else who wants to appreciate the way the Dutch have confidently grabbed the reins from Mother Nature.

The most interesting place to understand what the Dutch have achieved (and what the sea did to deserve it) is the museum at Schokland. Once a long and skinny island with a few scant villages, Schokland was gradually enveloped by the sea, until the king condemned and evacuated it in 1859. But after the sea around it was tamed and drained, Schokland was turned into a museum of Dutch traditions...and engineering prowess. Today Schokland is a long way to go for a little museum, and won't fascinate everyone. But those intrigued by this chapter of Dutch history will find it worth the journey.

Cost and Hours: €3.50; July–Aug daily 11:00–17:00; April–June and Sept–Oct Tue–Sun 11:00–17:00, closed Mon; Nov–March Fri–Sun 11:00–17:00, closed Mon–Thu; Middelbuurt 3, tel. 0527/251-396, www.schokland.nl.

Getting There: It's about an hour's **drive** north of Amsterdam (assuming there's no traffic), but the trip offers an insightful glimpse at Dutch land reclamation. From Amsterdam's ring freeway, follow signs for *Almere*—first southeast on A-1, then northeast on A-6. You'll drive the length of the very flat reclaimed island of Flevoland (past the towns of Almere and Lelystad), and pass a striking line of power-generating windmills spinning like gigantic pinwheels as you cross out of Flevoland and into Noordoostpolder—the reclaimed "Northeast Polder" that includes Schokland. Take the Urk exit (#13), turn right, and follow blue signs for *Schokland*. By **public transportation,** it's possible but not worth the effort (train from Amsterdam to Lelystad, bus to Emmeloord, then bus to Ens, then a 2-mile walk to Schokland).

◑ Self-Guided Tour: After buying your ticket, you'll watch a 15-minute **film** (press button to start in English) about the history of the town, its loss to the sea, and its reclamation.

Then tour the exposition called **Schokland: An Island in Time,** which explains how Schokland was reclaimed as part of the Northeast Polder beginning in 1936. After being enclosed by a sturdy dike, a year-long project drained this area of water in 1942 (while the Netherlands was occupied by the Nazis). Various Allied bombers were shot down and crashed into what would become the Northeast Polder (including one whose mangled propeller is displayed just outside the museum), joining the dozens of shipwrecks that already littered the seafloor.

A model shows the full territory of the Northeast Polder, which is carefully planned in concentric circles around the central town of Emmeloord (with Schokland and another former island, Urk, creating a pair of oddball bulges in the otherwise tidy pattern).

The exhibit explains that this isn't the first time this area has been dry land. From prehistoric times through the Middle Ages, much of what is today the Northeast Polder was farmed (many old tools have been discovered). In 1100, medieval engineers even attempted a primitive (and ultimately unsuccessful) effort to reclaim the land. Other remains from former residents include bones from mammoths and other prehistoric mammals, and a primitive 2,450-year-old canoe.

Then you'll head into the **Schokkerhuisje** to learn about the people who lived here (called *Schokkers*) until they were evacuated in 1859. Up to 650 people at a time lived on Schokland, residing in settlements on hills called *terpen* while they farmed the often-flooded land below. Like the rest of the Netherlands, this little island was divided in half by religion: part Catholic, part Protestant. This museum holds artifacts from the former town of Middelbuurt. You'll see traditional *Schokker* costumes (abandoned when they left the island) and a map of the entire island.

Back outside, go into the former **town church,** with a ceiling like the hull of a ship, a pulpit like a crow's nest, and a model ship hanging from the ceiling—appropriate for the seafaring residents of a once practically submerged island.

Finally, follow the path (below the church) to walk around the base of the former island—now surrounded by **farm fields.** When farmers first tilled their newly reclaimed soil a half-century ago, they uncovered more than just muck and mollusks. You'll see a pair of rusty anchors and a giant buoy that used to bob in the harbor—now lying on its side and still tethered to the ground. Examine the stone dike and black wooden seawall built by residents in a futile attempt to stay above water. The post with the blue strip helped residents keep an eye on the ever-rising water level.

If you're intrigued by all of this, you can walk a six-mile path (with posted information) that covers the entire length of the former island (get a map from the museum). Or, for a quick look, drive to the forlorn old **lighthouse,** improbably perched overlooking a vast field of grazing cows—without a  coastline in sight. In fact, the lighthouse marks the far tip of what was Schokland Island—and, because it was situated along a major trade route, this lighthouse was once extremely important. Today, this white elephant is an evocative symbol of Holland's complex relationship with the sea. To get there by car, leave the museum parking lot and turn left onto the main road, then take the first right (marked *Oude Haven Schokland*) and follow the road through the woods for about three minutes. When you reach the next big road, turn right, then look for the lighthouse on the left (with parking nearby).

TRANSPORTATION CONNECTIONS

The Netherlands

The Netherlands is so small, level, and well-covered by trains and buses that transportation is a snap. Major cities are connected by speedy trains that come and go every 15 minutes. Buses take you where trains don't go, and bicycles take you where buses don't go. Bus stations and bike-rental shops cluster around train stations.

Amsterdam

Trains

The easiest way to reach nearly any Dutch destination is by train. Connections are fast and frequent, and you'll rarely wait more than a few minutes. Intercity (IC) trains are speediest, connecting big cities; *sneltreins* connect smaller towns; *stoptreins* are pokey milk-run trains that stop at every station; and the misnamed "Sprinter" trains are actually slow *stoptreins*. Throughout the Netherlands, smoking is prohibited in trains and train stations.

Train Schedules: To get train schedules in advance, use the German Rail (Deutsche Bahn) website, which has comprehensive schedules for virtually anywhere in Europe (http://bahn.hafas .de/bin/query.exe/en). Or try the Dutch Rail site (www.ns.nl for domestic trains, www.nsinternationaal.nl for trains to Belgium and beyond). For phone information, dial 0900-9292 for local trains or 0900-9296 for international trains (€0.50/min, daily 7:00–24:00, wait through recording and hold...hold...hold...). The numbers listed in this chapter are frustrating phone trees in Dutch and—if you wait—maybe in English.

To find schedules at the station, check the yellow schedule posters, or look for TV screens listing upcoming departures. If

Train Lines in the Low Countries

✈ AIRPORT

50 MILES

100 KM

See Day Trips Detail Map

NORTH SEA

NETHERLANDS

HAARLEM

THE HAGUE

DELFT

ROTTERDAM

AMSTERDAM

GRONINGEN

LEEUW.

MEPPEL

DEVENTER   HENGELO

UTRECHT

GOUDA   ARNHEM

RHINE   GERMANY

Roos.

EINDHOVEN

BRUGES

OSTENDE

FLANDERS

EUROSTAR

TO LONDON

LILLE

GHENT

BELGIUM

ANTWERP

BRUSSELS

MAAS-TRICHT

KÖLN

AACHEN

RHINE

MONS   NAMUR

WALLONIE

LIEGE

KOBLENZ

BASTOGNE

LUX.

N

TO PARIS

FRANCE

DCH

TRIER

LUXEMBOURG CITY

you can't find your train, or are unclear on departure details, visit a yellow information booth or enlist the help of any official-looking employee (most wear portable computers with timetables).

Buying Train Tickets: You have two options for buying tickets in the Netherlands—at a ticket window (€0.50 extra, worth it if the lines are short), or at an automated machine. While the machines levy no additional fees, they can be a trial to use. Most machines have instructions in English (press the British flag). Before committing to quality time with a machine, check the upper-right corner of the screen to see what forms of payment are accepted: euro coins, euro bills, credit cards, and so on (items with an "X" through them are not accepted). If the machine accepts your credit card, you'll be required to enter a PIN. Note that same-day round-trip tickets ("day return") are discounted—handy for day trips.

Amsterdam Central Station (and Alternatives): Amsterdam's Central Train Station is being renovated—a messy construction project that's expected to last through 2012 (see "Arrival in Amsterdam" on page 35 for more details on the station). The station's train-information center can require a long wait. Save lots of time by getting train tickets and information in a small-town station (such as Haarlem), at the airport upon arrival (wonderful service), or from a travel agency. You can buy tickets ahead of time for the next day. If you plan to use a Eurailpass and Amsterdam is your first stop, validate it at Schiphol Airport when you arrive (best choice), or at Amsterdam's international train office at platform #2 (take a number and expect a wait).

From Amsterdam Central Station by Train to Domestic Destinations: Schiphol Airport (4–6/hr, 20 min, €3.80, have coins handy to buy from a machine to avoid lines), **Haarlem** (6/hr, 20 min, €3.80 one-way, €6.40 same-day round-trip), **Zandvoort** (2/hr direct, 30 min), **The Hague/Den Haag** (6/hr, 50 min, may require switch in Leiden to reach The Hague's Central Station), **Delft** (4–5/hr, 60 min, some transfer in Leiden or The Hague), **Rotterdam** (7/hr, 60–70 min, some transfer in Leiden), **Utrecht** (4/hr, 30 min), **Hoorn** and the start of the Historic Triangle (2/hr, 42 min), **Enkhuizen** and its Zuiderzee Open-Air Museum (2/hr, 1 hr), **Alkmaar** (4/hr, 35–45 min), **Koog-Zaandijk** near Zaanse Schans Open-Air Museum (train direction: Uitgeest, 4/hr, 15 min), **Arnhem** (4/hr, 1.25 hrs, some transfer in Utrecht), **Ede-Wageningen** near Hoge Veluwe National Park (4/hr, 1 hr, some transfer in Utrecht; once in Ede-Wageningen, wait to take a 15-min bus to Otterlo near park entrance). For Waterland destinations including **Edam, Volendam,** and **Marken,** or for the **Aalsmeer Flower Auction,** take the bus (see next page).

By Train to International Destinations: Bruges/Brugge (hourly, 3.5–4 hrs, transfer at Antwerp Central or Brussels Midi; transfer can be timed closely—be alert and check with conductor), **Brussels** (hourly, 2.75 hrs, €35), **Ostende** (hourly, 4 hrs, change in Antwerp), **London** (hourly, 5.5 hrs, with transfer to Eurostar Chunnel train in Brussels; Eurostar discounted with railpass, www.eurostar.com), **Copenhagen** (9/day, 11–18 hrs, most require multiple transfers), **Frankfurt** (every 2 hours, 4 hrs direct, more with transfer in Köln or Duisburg), **Munich** (hourly, 7–8 hrs, transfer in Frankfurt or Düsseldorf, night train possible), **Bonn** (10/day, 3 hrs, some direct but most transfer in Köln), **Bern** (5/day, 9 hrs, 1 direct but most transfer in Mannheim), **Paris** (nearly hourly, 4–5 hrs, requires fast Thalys train from Brussels with €14.50 second-class reservation, www.thalys.com; save money by taking a bus—described next).

Buses

While you'll mostly use trains in the Netherlands, a few destinations are reachable only by bus. The national bus system, both within and between cities, runs on a uniform system of strip tickets *(strippenkaart)*; each time you board, the driver or conductor stamps your *strippenkaart,* deducting the fare of a ride. (Single-ride tickets are sometimes available, but usually cost more than using strips.) Buy *strippenkaart* at tobacco shops, newsstands, and machines at train stations, or—for an extra charge—from the driver. If you're caught riding without a strip ticket, you have to take off your clothes. For all the details on this seemingly complex but elegantly simple system, see "Strip Tickets" on page 38.

Confusingly, there's no unified national bus company—various destinations are served by different companies. The biggest companies serving towns near Amsterdam include Arriva (www.arriva.nl) and Connexxion (www.connexxion.nl).

From Amsterdam by Bus to: Edam and **Volendam** (Arriva buses #112, #116, #110, or #118; 30–45 min depending on bus—see page 284 for details), **Marken** (Arriva bus #111, 2/hr, 40 min), **Aalsmeer Flower Auction** (Connexxion bus #172, 4/hr, 50 min). Buses depart from just southeast of Amsterdam's Central Station (exit station to the left and cross the street). Once in the countryside, buses can also be helpful for connecting the dots (see the "Transportation Connections" for each destination).

To Paris by Bus: If you don't have a railpass, the cheapest way to get to Paris is by bus (Eurolines buses make the 8-hour trip every 2 hours, €35 one-way, €60 round-trip; check online for deals, bus station in Amsterdam at Julianaplein 5, Amstel Station, five stops by metro from Central Station, tel. 020/560-8788, www.eurolines.com).

Amsterdam's Schiphol Airport

Schiphol (SKIP-pol) Airport, is located about 10 miles southwest of Amsterdam's city center. Like most of Holland, it is user-friendly and below sea level. With an appealing array of shops, eateries, and other time-killing opportunities, Schiphol is a fine place to arrive, depart, or change planes. A truly international airport, Schiphol has done away with Dutch—signs are in English only.

Information: Schiphol flight information (tel. 0900-0141; from other countries dial +31-20-794-0800) can give you flight times and your airline's Amsterdam phone number for reconfirmation before going home (or visit www.schiphol.nl). To reach the airlines directly, call: KLM and Northwest—tel. 020/474-7747; Martinair—tel. 020/601-1767; SAS—tel. 0900-7466-3727 (toll call); British Airways—tel. 020/346-9559; and easyJet—tel. 0900-265-8022 (toll call).

Orientation: Schiphol has four terminals: Terminal 1 is for flights to most European countries (not including the UK); Terminals 2 and 3 are for flights to the UK, US, and other non-European countries; and the new, smaller Terminal 4 (attached to Terminal 3) is for low-cost carriers. Once inside the airport, the terminal waiting areas are called "Lounges" (e.g., "Lounge 1"), and are subdivided into lettered concourses (e.g., "D Gates"). An inviting shopping and eating zone called "Holland Boulevard" runs between Lounges 2 and 3.

Arrival at Schiphol: Conveniently, baggage claim areas for all terminals empty into the same arrival zone, called Schiphol Plaza—with ATMs, shops, eateries, a busy **TI** (near Terminal 2), a train station, and bus stops for getting into the city. You can validate your Eurailpass and hit the rails immediately, or, to stretch your railpass, buy an inexpensive ticket into Amsterdam today and start the pass later.

Airport Services: The ABN/AMRO **banks** offer fair exchange rates (in both arrivals and lounge areas). The GWK **public-transit office** is located in Schiphol Plaza and sells SIM cards for mobile phones. Surf the **Internet** and make phone calls at the Communication Centres (one on the top level of Lounge 2, another on the ground floor of Lounge 1; both are behind customs and not available once you've left the security checkpoint). Convenient luggage **lockers** are at various points around the airport—allowing you to leave your bag here on a lengthy layover (both short-term and long-term lockers; biggest bank of lockers near the train station at Schiphol Plaza).

Airport Train Ticket Counter: For a train ticket or train information, take advantage of the fantastic "Train Tickets and Services" counter (Schiphol Plaza ground level, just past Burger King). They have an easy info desk, almost no lines (much quicker than the ticket desk at the Amsterdam train station downtown), and issue international tickets for €3.50 and domestic tickets for €0.50.

Time-Killing Tips: If you have extra time to kill at Schiphol, check out the **Rijksmuseum Amsterdam Schiphol,** a little art gallery on Holland Boulevard. The Rijksmuseum loans a dozen or so of its minor masterpieces from the Golden Age to this unique airport museum, including actual Dutch Masters by Rembrandt, Vermeer, and others (free, daily 7:00–20:00, between Terminals 2 and 3). The museum is between the passport and security checks at Terminal 2, so it's technically not in the "secure" part of the airport. You can visit easily from Terminals 2 or 3, but if you visit from Terminal 1, you'll have to go back through security to reach your flight (allow plenty of time).

To escape the airport crowds, follow signs for the *Panorama*

Terrace to the third floor of Terminal 2, where you'll find a quieter, full-of-locals cafeteria, a kids' play area, and a view terrace where you can watch planes come and go while you nurse a coffee. If you plan to visit the terrace on arrival, stop there before you pass through customs.

From Schiphol Airport to Amsterdam: There's a direct **train** to Amsterdam's Central Station (4–6/hr, 20 min, €3.80, no strip tickets). The Connexxion **shuttle bus** takes you to your hotel neighborhood; since there are three different routes, ask the attendant which one works best for your hotel (2/hr, 20 min, €14 one-way, €22 round-trip, one route stops at Westerkerk near Anne Frank House and many recommended hotels, bus to other hotels may cost a couple euros more, departs from lane A7 in front of airport, tel. 020/653-4975, www.airporthotelshuttle.nl). Allow about €40 for a **taxi** to downtown Amsterdam. Bus #197 is handiest for those staying in the Leidseplein district (departs from lane B9 in front of airport, buy ticket from driver or use strip tickets).

From Schiphol Airport to Haarlem: The big red #300 **bus** is direct, stopping at Haarlem's train station and near the Market Square (4/hr, 40 min, €5.80—buy ticket from driver, or use 7 strips of a *strippenkaart*, departs from lane B2 in front of airport). The **train** is slightly cheaper and just as quick, but you'll have to transfer at the Amsterdam-Sloterdijk station (6/hr, 30–40 min, €5.30). Figure about €45 to Haarlem by **taxi**.

From Schiphol Airport by Train to: The Hague/Den Haag (2/hr, 30 min), **Delft** (4/hr, 45 min, transfer in The Hague or Leiden), **Rotterdam** (3/hr, 45 min). International trains to Belgium run every hour: **Brussels** (2.5 hrs), **Bruges/Brugge** (3.5 hrs, change in Antwerp or Brussels).

Haarlem

From Haarlem by Train to: Amsterdam (6/hr, 20 min, €3.80 one-way, €6.40 same-day round-trip), **The Hague/Den Haag** (4/hr, 40 min), **Delft** (2/hr, 40 min), **Rotterdam** (2/hr, 50 min, may require change in Leiden), **Hoorn** (2/hr, 1 hr), **Alkmaar** (2/hr, 45 min), **Brussels** (hourly, 2.75 hrs, transfer in Rotterdam), **Bruges/Brugge** (1–2/hr, 3.5 hrs, requires transfer).

To Schiphol Airport: Your options are the **bus** (4/hr, 40 min, €5.80—buy ticket from driver, or use 7 strips of a *strippenkaart*, bus #300, departs from Haarlem's train station in "Zuidtangent" lane), **train** (6/hr, 30–40 min, transfer at Amsterdam-Sloterdijk station, €5.30 one-way), or **taxi** (about €45).

BELGIUM

BELGIUM

Belgium falls through the cracks. It's nestled between Germany, France, and Britain, and it's famous for waffles, sprouts, endives, and a statue of a little boy peeing—no wonder many travelers don't even consider a stop here. But many who do visit remark that Belgium is one of Europe's best-kept secrets. There are tourists—but not as many as the country's charms merit.

Belgium is split between Wallonia in the south, where they speak French, and Flanders in the north, where they speak Flemish, a dialect of Dutch. French-speakers have often dominated the government, even though about 60 percent of the population speaks Flemish. Talk to locals to learn how deep the cultural rift is. The longstanding Flemish-Dutch rivalry has become especially intense in the last couple of years. Belgium's capital, Brussels, while mostly French-speaking, is officially bilingual. The country also has a small minority of German-speaking people. Because of Brussels' international importance as the capital of the European Union, more than 25 percent of its residents are foreigners.

It's here in Belgium that Europe comes together: where Romance languages meet Germanic languages, Catholics meet Protestants, and the Benelux union was established 40 years ago, planting the seed that today is sprouting into the unification of Europe. Belgium flies the flag of Europe more vigorously than any other place on the Continent.

Bruges and Brussels are the best two first bites of Belgium. Bruges is a wonderfully preserved medieval gem that expertly nurtures its tourist industry, bringing the town a prosperity it hasn't enjoyed for 500 years, when—as one of the largest cities in the world—it helped lead northern Europe out of the Middle Ages. Brussels is simply one of Europe's great cities.

Belgians brag that they eat as much as the Germans and as

Belgium Almanac

Official Name: Royaume de Belgique/Koninkrijk België, or simply Belgique in French and België in Flemish.

Population: Of its 10.5 million people, 58 percent are Flemish, 31 percent are Walloon, and 11 percent are "mixed or other." About three-quarters are Catholic, and the rest are Protestant or other.

Latitude and Longitude: 50°N and 4°E. The latitude is similar to Alberta, Canada.

Area: With only 12,000 square miles, it's one of the smallest countries in Europe.

Geography: Belgium's flat coastal plains in the northwest and central rolling hills make it easy to invade (just ask Napoleon or Hitler). There are some rugged mountains in the southeast Ardennes Forest. The climate is temperate.

Biggest Cities: The capital city of Brussels has about 1.8 million people, followed by Antwerp's 950,000.

Economy: With few natural resources, Belgium imports most of its raw materials and exports a large volume of manufactured goods, making its economy unusually dependent on world markets. It can be a sweet business—Belgium is the world's number one exporter of chocolate. It's prosperous, with a GDP per capita of $35,350. As the "crossroads" of Europe, Brussels is the headquarters of both the EU and NATO.

Government: A parliamentary democracy, Belgium's official head of state is King Albert II. Regional tensions dominate politics: Flemish-speaking, entrepreneurial Flanders wants more autonomy, while the French-speaking "rust belt" of Wallonia is reluctant to give it. The division has made it increasingly difficult for the Belgian Parliament to form a stable coalition government. One prime minister recently said that Belgians are united only by the king, a love of beer, and the national soccer team. Voting is compulsory. More than 90 percent of registered voters participated in the last general election (compared to approximately 62 percent in the US).

Flag: Belgium's flag is composed of three vertical bands of black, yellow, and red.

The Average Belgian: The average Belgian is 42 years old—five years older than the average American—and will live to be 79. He or she is also likely to be divorced—Belgium has the highest divorce rate in Europe, with 60 for every 100 marriages. Beer is the national beverage—on average Belgians drink 26 gallons a year, just behind the Austrians and just ahead of the Brits.

BELGIUM

Belgium

well as the French. They are among the world's leading beer consumers and carnivores. In Belgium, never bring chrysanthemums to a wedding—they symbolize death. And tweaking little kids on the ear is considered rude.

Ten and a half million Belgians are packed into a country only a little bigger than Maryland. With nearly 900 people per square mile, it's the second most densely populated country in Europe (after the Netherlands). This population concentration, coupled with a dense and well-lit rail and road system, causes Belgium to shine at night when viewed from space, a phenomenon NASA astronauts call the "Belgian Window."

BRUGES
Brugge

ORIENTATION

With Renoir canals, pointy gilded architecture, vivid time-tunnel art, and stay-a-while cafés, Bruges is a heavyweight sightseeing destination, as well as a joy. Where else can you ride a bike along a canal, munch mussels and wash them down with the world's best beer, savor heavenly chocolate, and see Flemish Primitives and a Michelangelo, all within 300 yards of a bell tower that jingles every 15 minutes? And do it all without worrying about a language barrier?

The town is Brugge (BROO-ghah) in Flemish, and Bruges (broozh) in French and English. Its name comes from the Viking word for wharf. Right from the start, Bruges was a trading center. In the 11th century, the city grew wealthy on the cloth trade.

By the 14th century, Bruges' population was 35,000, as large as London's. As the middleman in the sea trade between northern and southern Europe, it was one of the biggest cities in the world and an economic powerhouse. In addition, Bruges had become the most important cloth market in northern Europe.

In the 15th century, while England and France were slugging it out in the Hundred Years' War, Bruges was the favored residence of the powerful Dukes of Burgundy—and at peace. Commerce and the arts boomed. The artists Jan van Eyck and Hans Memling had studios here.

But by the 16th century, the harbor had silted up and the economy had collapsed. The Burgundian court left, Belgium became a minor Habsburg possession, and Bruges' Golden Age abruptly ended. For generations, Bruges was known as a mysterious and dead city. In the 19th century, a new port, Zeebrugge, brought renewed vitality to the area. And in the 20th century, tourists discovered the town.

Today, Bruges prospers because of tourism: It's a uniquely

well-preserved Gothic city and a handy gateway to Europe. It's no secret, but even with the crowds, it's the kind of place where you don't mind being a tourist.

Bruges' ultimate sight is the town itself, and the best way to enjoy it is to get lost on the back streets, away from the lace shops and ice-cream stands.

Planning Your Time

Bruges needs at least two nights and a full, well-organized day. Even non-shoppers enjoy browsing here, and the Belgian love of life makes a hectic itinerary seem a little senseless. With one day—other than a Monday, when the three museums are closed—the speedy visitor could do the Bruges blitz described below (also included in the Bruges City Walk on page 329):

9:30	Climb the bell tower on Market Square.
10:00	Tour the sights on Burg Square.
11:30	Tour the Groeninge Museum.
13:00	Eat lunch and buy chocolates.
14:00	Take a short canal cruise.
14:30	Visit the Church of Our Lady and see Michelangelo's *Madonna and Child*.
15:00	Tour the Memling Museum.
16:00	Catch the De Halve Maan Brewery tour (note that their last tour runs at 15:00 in winter on weekdays).
17:00	Calm down in the Begijnhof courtyard.
18:00	Ride a bike around the quiet back streets of town or take a horse-and-buggy tour.
20:00	Lose the tourists and find dinner.

If this schedule seems insane, skip the bell tower and the brewery—or stay another day.

OVERVIEW

The tourist's Bruges—and you'll be sharing it—is less than one square mile, contained within a canal (the former moat). Nearly everything of interest and importance is within a convenient cobbled swath between the train station and Market Square (a 20-min walk). Many of my quiet, charming, recommended accommodations lie just beyond Market Square.

Tourist Information

The main tourist office, called **In&Uit** ("In and Out"), is in the big, red concert hall on the square called 't Zand (daily 10:00–18:00, take a number from the touch-screen machines and wait, 't Zand 34, tel. 050-448-686, www.brugge.be). The other TI is at the train

---

Museum Tips

Admission prices are steep, but they include great audio-guides—so plan on spending some time and really getting into it. For information on all the museums, call 050-448-711 or visit www.brugge.be.

Combo-Tickets: The TIs and participating museums sell a museum combo-ticket (any five museums for €15, valid for three days). Since the Groeninge and Memling museums cost €8 each, art lovers will save money with this pass. Another combo-ticket offers any three museums and a one-day bike rental for €15 (get bike from Koffieboontje, listed under "Helpful Hints"; sold at bike shop or TI, open-ended validity period).

Blue Monday: In Bruges, nearly all museums are open Tuesday through Sunday year-round from 9:30 to 17:00 and are closed on Monday. If you're in Bruges on a Monday, the following attractions are still open: bell-tower climb on Market Square, Begijnhof, De Halve Maan Brewery Tour, Basilica of the Holy Blood, City Hall's Gothic Room, and chocolate shops and museum. You can also join a boat, bus, or walking tour, or rent a bike and pedal into the countryside.

---

station (Mon–Fri 10:00–17:00, Sat–Sun 10:00–14:00).

The TIs sell a great €1 *Bruges Visitors' Guide* with a map and listings of all the sights and services. You can also pick up a monthly English-language program called *events@brugge*. The TIs have information on train schedules and on the many tours available (see "Tours," page 316). Many hotels give out free maps with more detail than the map the TIs sell.

Arrival in Bruges

By Train: Coming in by train, you'll see the bell tower that marks the main square (Market Square, the center of town). Upon arrival, stop by the train station TI to pick up the €1 *Bruges Visitors' Guide* (with map). The station lacks ATMs, but has lockers (€3–4, daily 6:00–24:00).

The best way to get to the town center is by **bus.** Buses #1, #3, #4, #6, #11, #13, #14, and #16 (all marked *Centrum)* go directly to Market Square. Simply hop on, pay €1.60 (€1.20 if you buy in advance at train station), and in four minutes, you're there. Buses #4 and #14 continue to the northeast part of town (to the windmills and recommended accommodations on Carmersstraat). The **taxi** fare from the train station to most hotels is about €8.

It's a 20-minute **walk** from the station to the center—no fun with your luggage. If you want to walk to Market Square, cross the busy street and canal in front of the station, head up Oostmeers, and turn right on Zwidzandstraat. You can rent a **bike** at the station for the duration of your stay, but other bike rental shops are closer to the center (see "Helpful Hints," below).

By Car: Park in front of the train station in the handy two-story garage for just €2.50 for 24 hours. The parking fee includes a round-trip bus ticket into town and back for everyone in your car. There are pricier underground parking garages at the square called 't Zand and around town (€10/day, all of them well-marked). Paid parking on the street in Bruges is limited to four hours. Driving in town is very complicated because of the one-way system. The best plan for drivers: Park at the train station, visit the TI, and rent a bike or catch a bus into town.

Helpful Hints

Market Days: Bruges hosts markets on Wednesday morning (Market Square) and Saturday morning ('t Zand). On Saturday, Sunday, and public holidays, a flea market hops along Dijver in front of the Groeninge Museum. The Fish Market sells souvenirs and seafood Tuesday through Saturday mornings until 13:00.

Shopping: Shops are generally open from 10:00 to 18:00. Grocery stores are usually closed on Sunday. The main shopping street, Steenstraat, stretches from Market Square to 't Zand Square. The **Hema** department store is at Steenstraat 73 (Mon–Sat 9:00–18:00, closed Sun).

Internet Access: Punjeb Internet Shop, just a block off Market Square, is a good place to get online (€1.50/30 min, daily 10:00–22:00, 4 Philipstockstraat).

Post Office: It's on Market Square near the bell tower (Mon–Fri 9:00–18:00, Sat 9:30–12:30, closed Sun, tel. 050-331-411).

Laundry: Bruges has three self-service launderettes, each a five-minute walk from the center; ask your hotelier for the nearest one.

Bike Rental: Koffieboontje Bike Rental, just under the bell tower on Market Square, is the handiest place to rent bikes (€4/1 hr, €8/4 hrs, €12/24-hr day; special discount with this book: 24-hr rental for price of 4-hr rental; free city maps and child seats, daily 9:00–22:00, Hallestraat 4, tel. 050-338-027, www.hotel -koffieboontje.be). The €15 bike-plus-any-three-museums combo-ticket works only with this outfit (and can save enough to pay for lunch).

Fietsen Popelier Bike Rental is also good (€3.50/hr, €7/4 hrs, €10/day, 24-hour day is OK if your hotel has a safe place to store bike, daily 10:00–19:00, Mariastraat 26, tel. 050-343-262). Other rental places include the less-central **De Ketting** (cheap at €5/day, daily 9:00–18:30, Gentpoortstraat 23,

tel. 050-344-196, www.de
ketting.be) and the **train
station** (ticket window
labeled *verhuring fietsen*,
€9.50/day, €6.50/half-day
after 14:00, €13 deposit, daily
7:00–19:30, blue lockers here
for day-trippers leaving bags).

Best Town View: The bell tower
overlooking Market Square rewards those who climb it with
the ultimate town view.

Getting Around Bruges

Most of the city is easily walkable, but you may want to take the
bus or taxi between the train station and the city center at Market
Square (especially if you have heavy luggage).

By Bus: A bus ticket is good for an hour (€1.20 if you buy
in advance at train station, or €1.60 on the bus). While there are
various day passes, there's really no need to buy one for your visit.
Nearly all city buses go directly from the train station to Market
Square and fan out from there; they then return to Market Square
and go back to the train station. Note that buses returning to the
train station from Market Square also leave from the library bus
stop, a block off the square on nearby Kuiperstraat (every 5 min).
Your key: Use buses that say either *Station* or *Centrum*.

By Taxi: You'll find taxi stands at the station and on Market
Square (€8/first 2 km; to get a cab in the center, call 050-334-444).

TOURS

Bruges

Bruges by Boat—The most relaxing and scenic (though not informative) way to see this city of canals is by boat, with the captain

narrating. The city carefully controls
this standard tourist activity, so the
many companies all offer essentially
the same thing: a 30-minute route
(4/hr, daily 10:00–17:00), a price of
€6.50, and narration in three or four
languages. Qualitative differences
are because of individual guides...
not companies. Always let them
know you speak English to ensure
you'll understand the spiel. Two
companies give a €1 discount with
this book: Boten Stael (just over the

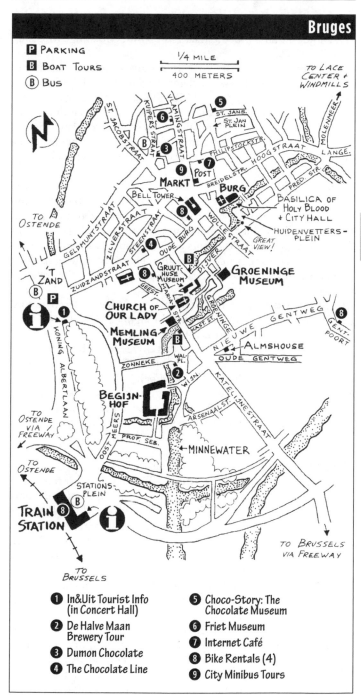

Bruges

P Parking
B Boat Tours
Ⓑ Bus

¼ MILE
400 METERS

TO LACE
CENTER &
WINDMILLS

N

TO
OSTENDE

'T
ZAND

TO
OSTENDE
VIA
FREEWAY

TO
OSTENDE

ST. JACOBSTRAAT

KUIPERS STRAAT

VLAMINGSTRAAT

ST. JANS

St. Jan
Plein

PHILIPSTOCKSTR.

HOOG STRAAT

PRED. STR.

MOLENMEER

LANGE.

❺
❻
❸
❾ ❼
Post
MARKT
Bell Tower
❽

BURG
BREIDELSTR.

**BASILICA OF
HOLY BLOOD
& CITY HALL**

HUIDENVETTERS-
PLEIN

GREAT
VIEW!

WOLLE STRAAT

GELDMUNTSTRAAT

ZILVERSTRAAT

STEENSTRAAT

❹ OUDE
BURG

**GROENINGE
MUSEUM**

ZUIDZANDSTRAAT

GEEST.

❽
**GRUUT-
HUSE
MUSEUM**

DIJVER

MARIA STR.

KAST. ST.

GROENINGE

NIEUWE

GENTWEG

❽

GENT-
POORT

**CHURCH OF
OUR LADY**

**MEMLING
MUSEUM**

KONING ALBERTLAAN

ZONNEKE

WAL-
PL.

❷

W. STR.

ALMSHOUSE

OUDE GENTWEG

❶ ❷

**BEGIJN-
HOF**

OOST MEERS

PROF. SEB.

ARSENAALSTRAAT

KATELIJNESTRAAT

← **MINNEWATER**

TO BRUSSELS
VIA FREEWAY

STATIONS-
PLEIN

Ⓑ
❽

**TRAIN
STATION**

TO
BRUSSELS

BRUGES ORIENTATION

❶ In&Uit Tourist Info
(in Concert Hall)

❷ De Halve Maan
Brewery Tour

❸ Dumon Chocolate

❹ The Chocolate Line

❺ Choco-Story: The
Chocolate Museum

❻ Friet Museum

❼ Internet Café

❽ Bike Rentals (4)

❾ City Minibus Tours

canal from Memling Museum at Katelijnestraat 4, tel. 050-332-771) and Gruuthuse (Nieuwstraat 11, opposite Groeninge Museum, tel. 050-333-393).

City Minibus Tour—City Tour Bruges gives a rolling overview of the town in an 18-seat, two-skylight minibus with dial-a-language headsets and video support (€11.50, 50 min, pay driver). The tour leaves hourly from Market Square (10:00–20:00 in summer, until 18:00 in spring, until 17:00 in fall, less in winter, tel. 050-355-024, www.citytour.be). The narration, while clear, is slow-moving and a bit boring. But the tour is a lazy way to cruise past virtually every sight in Bruges.

Walking Tour—Local guides walk small groups through the core of town (€7, 2 hours, daily July–Aug, June and Sept Sat–Sun only, no tours Oct–May, depart from TI on 't Zand Square at 14:30—just drop in a few minutes early and buy tickets at the TI desk). Though earnest, the tours are heavy on history and given in two languages, so they may be less than peppy. Still, to propel you beyond the pretty gables and canal swans of Bruges, they're good medicine.

Private Guide—A private two-hour guided tour costs €60 (reserve at least one week in advance through TI, tel. 050-448-686). Or contact Christian and Danielle Scharle, who give two-hour walks for €60 and three-hour guided drives for €110 (Christian's mobile 0475-659-507, Danielle's mobile 0476-493-203, www.tourmanagementbelgium.be, tmb@skynet.be).

Horse-and-Buggy Tour—The buggies around town can take you on a clip-clop tour (€30, 35 min; price is per carriage, not per person). When divided among four or five people, this can be a good value.

Near Bruges

Quasimodo Countryside Tours—This company offers those with extra time two entertaining, all-day, English-only bus tours through the rarely visited Flemish countryside. The "Flanders Fields" tour concentrates on WWI battlefields, trenches, memorials, and poppy-splattered fields (April–Oct Tue–Sun; Nov–March Sun, Tue, and Thu only; departs at 9:15, 8 hours, visit to In Flanders Fields Museum not included). The other tour, "Triple Treat," focuses on Flanders' medieval past and rich culture, with tastes of chocolate, waffles, and beer (departs Mon, Wed, and Fri at 9:15, 8 hours). Be ready for lots of walking.

Tours cost €55, or €45 if you're under 26 (includes a picnic lunch, 9- or 30-seat bus depending on demand, non-smoking, reservations required—call tel. 050-370-470 or toll-free tel. 0800-97525, www.quasimodo.be). After making a few big-hotel pickups, the buses leave town from the Park Hotel on 't Zand Square.

Daytours—Tour guide Nathan loves leading small groups on fascinating "Flanders Fields Battlefield" day trips. This tour is like Quasimodo's (listed above), but more expensive. The differences: eight travelers on a minibus rather than a big busload; pickup from any hotel or B&B (because the small bus is allowed in the town center); restaurant lunch included rather than a picnic; and a little more serious lecturing and a stricter focus on World War I. For instance, you actually visit the In Flanders Fields Museum in Ieper—Ypres in French (€65, €3 discount when booked direct using this book, departs Tue–Sun at 9:00, 8.5 hours, call 050-346-060 or toll-free 0800-99133 to reserve, www.visitbruges.org).

Bruges by Bike—**QuasiMundo Bike Tours** leads daily five-mile bike tours around the city (English only, departs at 10:00, 2.5 hours). Their other tour, "Border by Bike," goes through the

nearby countryside to Damme (March–Oct, departs at 13:00, 15 miles, 4 hours). Either tour costs €22, but you'll get €3 off with this book (tel. 050-330-775, www.quasimundo.com). Both tours include bike rental, a light raincoat (if necessary), water, and a drink in a local café. Meet on Burg Square. If you already have a bike, you're welcome to join either tour for €14. Jos, who leads most departures, is a high-energy and entertaining guide.

Charming Mieke of **Pink Bear Bike Tours** leads small groups on an easy and delightful 3.5-hour guided pedal along a canal to the historic town of Damme and back, finishing with a brief tour of Bruges. English tours go daily through peak season and nearly daily the rest of the year (€20, €2 discount with this book, €14 if you already have a bike, meet at 10:25 under bell tower on Market Square, tel. 050-616-686, mobile 0476-744-525, www.pinkbear.freeservers.com).

For a do-it-yourself bike tour, see page 326. For bike rental shops in Bruges, see page 315.

SIGHTS

These sights are listed in walking order, from Market Square, to Burg Square, to the cluster of museums around the Church of Our Lady, to the Begijnhof (10-min walk from beginning to end, without stops). For a self-guided walk and more information on each major sight, ✪ see the Bruges City Walk, page 329.

▲**Market Square (Markt)**—Ringed by a bank, the post office, lots of restaurant terraces, great old gabled buildings, and the iconic bell tower, this is the modern heart of the city (most city buses run from near here to the train station—it's a block down Kuiperstraat at the library bus stop). Under the bell tower are two great Belgian-style french-fry stands, a quadrilingual Braille description of the old town, and a metal model of the tower. In Bruges' heyday as a trading center, a canal came right up to this square. Geldmuntstraat, just off the square, is a delightful street with many fun and practical shops and eateries.

▲▲**Bell Tower (Belfort)**—Most of this bell tower has presided over Market Square since 1300, serenading passersby with carillon music. The octagonal lantern was added in 1486, making it 290 feet high—that's 366 steps. The view is worth the climb and the €5 (daily 9:30–17:00, last entry 45 min before closing, €0.40 WC in courtyard).

▲▲**Burg Square**—This opulent square is Bruges' civic center, historically the birthplace of Bruges and the site of the ninth-century castle of the first count of Flanders. Today, it's an atmospheric place to take in an outdoor concert while surrounded by six centuries of architecture.

▲**Basilica of the Holy Blood**—Originally the Chapel of Saint Basil, this church is famous for its relic of the blood of Christ, which, according to tradition, was brought to Bruges in 1150 after the Second Crusade. The lower chapel is dark and solid—a fine example of Romanesque style. The upper chapel (separate entrance, climb the stairs) is decorated Gothic. An interesting treasury museum is next to the upper chapel (treasury entry-€1.50; April–Sept Thu–Tue 9:30–12:00 & 14:00–18:00, Wed 9:30–11:45 only; Oct–March Thu–Tue 10:00–12:00 & 14:00–16:00, Wed 10:00–11:45 only; Burg Square, tel. 050-336-792, www.holyblood.com).

▲**City Hall**—This complex houses several interesting sights. Your €2.50 ticket includes an audioguide; access to a room full of old town maps and paintings; the grand, beautifully restored **Gothic Room** from 1400, starring a painted and carved wooden ceiling adorned with hanging arches (daily 9:30–17:00, Burg 12); and the less impressive **Renaissance Hall** (Brugse Vrije), basically just one ornate room with a Renaissance chimney (daily 9:30–17:00, separate entrance—in corner of square at Burg 11a).

▲▲▲**Groeninge Museum**—This museum houses a world-class collection of mostly Flemish art, from Memling to Magritte. While there's plenty of worthwhile modern art, the highlights are the vivid and pristine Flemish Primitives. ("Primitive" here means "before the Renaissance.") Flemish art is shaped by its love of detail, its merchant patrons' egos, and the power of the Church. Lose yourself in the halls of Groeninge: Gaze across 15th-century canals, into the eyes of reassuring Marys, and through town squares littered with leotards, lace, and lopped-off heads (€8, includes audioguide, Tue–Sun 9:30–17:00, closed Mon, mid-Aug–Oct 2010, Dijver 12, tel. 050-448-743).

○ See Groeninge Museum Tour, page 344.

Gruuthuse Museum—Once a wealthy brewer's home, this 15th-century mansion is a sprawling smattering of everything from medieval bedpans to a guillotine. A fine museum, it's now in disarray—some rooms are closed until 2011 due to an extensive reorganization and renovation (€6, includes entry to apse in Church of Our Lady, Tue–Sun 9:30–17:00, closed Mon, Dijver 17, Bruges museums tel. 050-448-711, www.brugge.be).

▲▲**Church of Our Lady**—The church stands as a memorial to the power and wealth of Bruges in its heyday. A delicate *Madonna and Child* by Michelangelo is near the apse (to the right if you're facing the altar). It's said to be the only Michelangelo statue to leave Italy in his lifetime (thanks to the wealth generated by Bruges' cloth trade). If you like tombs and church art, pay to wander through the apse (Michelangelo viewing is free, art-filled apse-€2.50, covered by €6 Gruuthuse admission or museum combo-ticket—see previous entry; church open Mon–Fri 9:30–17:00, Sat 9:30–16:45, Sun 13:30–17:00; museum and apse closed Mon; Mariastraat, www.brugge.be).

▲▲**Memling Museum/St. John's Hospital (Sint Janshospitaal)**—The former monastery/hospital complex has a fine

Bruges at a Glance

▲▲▲**Groeninge Museum** Top-notch collection of mainly Flemish art. **Hours:** Tue–Sun 9:30–17:00, closed Mon. See page 321.

▲▲**Bell Tower** Overlooking Market Square, with 366 steps to a worthwhile view and a carillon close-up. **Hours:** Daily 9:30–17:00. See page 332.

▲▲**Burg Square** Historic square with sights and impressive architecture. **Hours:** Always open. See page 333.

▲▲**Memling Museum/St. John's Hospital** Art by the greatest of the Flemish Primitives. **Hours:** Tue–Sun 9:30–17:00, closed Mon. See page 321.

▲▲**Church of Our Lady** Tombs and church art, including Michelangelo's *Madonna and Child*. **Hours:** Church open Mon–Fri 9:30–17:00, Sat 9:30–16:45, Sun 13:30–17:00 only; museum and apse closed Mon. See page 321.

▲▲**Begijnhof** Benedictine nuns' peaceful courtyard and Beguine's House museum. **Hours:** Courtyard always open, museum open daily 10:00–17:00, shorter hours off-season. See below.

▲▲**De Halve Maan Brewery Tour** Fun tour that includes beer. **Hours:** April–Oct daily on the hour 11:00–16:00, Sat until 17:00; Nov–March Mon–Fri at 11:00 and 15:00 only, Sat–Sun on the hour 11:00–16:00. See page 324.

▲▲**Biking** Exploring the countryside and pedaling to nearby Damme. **Hours:** Rental shops generally open daily 9:00–19:00. See page 326.

museum in what was once the monks' church. It contains six much-loved paintings by the greatest of the Flemish Primitives, Hans Memling. His *Mystical Wedding of St. Catherine* triptych is a highlight, as is the miniature, gilded-oak shrine to St. Ursula (€8, includes fine audioguide, Tue–Sun 9:30–17:00, closed Mon, across the street from the Church of Our Lady, Mariastraat 38, Bruges museums tel. 050-448-711, www.brugge.be).

✪ See Memling Museum Tour, page 353.

▲▲**Begijnhof**—Inhabited by Benedictine nuns, the Begijnhof courtyard (free and always open) almost makes you want to don a habit and fold your hands as you walk under its wispy trees and whisper past its frugal little homes. For a good slice of Begijnhof

▲**Market Square** Main square that is the modern heart of the city, with carillon bell tower (described on opposite page). **Hours:** Always open. See page 330.

▲**Basilica of the Holy Blood** Romanesque and Gothic church housing a relic of the blood of Christ. **Hours:** April–Sept Thu–Tue 9:30–12:00 & 14:00–18:00, Wed 9:30–11:45 only; Oct–March Thu–Tue 10:00–12:00 & 14:00–16:00, Wed 10:00–11:45 only. See page 333.

▲**City Hall** Beautifully restored Gothic Room from 1400, plus the Renaissance Hall. **Hours:** Daily 9:30–17:00. See page 321.

▲**Chocolate Shops** Bruges' specialty, sold at Dumon, The Chocolate Line, and on and on. **Hours:** Shops generally open 10:00–18:00. See page 324.

Gruuthuse Museum 15th-century mansion displaying an eclectic collection that includes furniture, tapestries, and lots more. **Hours:** Tue–Sun 9:30–17:00, closed Mon, some rooms closed until 2011. See page 321.

Choco-Story: The Chocolate Museum The whole delicious story of Belgium's favorite treat. **Hours:** Daily 10:00–17:00. See page 325.

In Flanders Fields Museum Moving WWI museum in Ypres, southwest of Bruges, easy to reach on a bus tour from Bruges. **Hours:** April–mid-Nov daily 10:00–18:00; mid-Nov–March Tue–Sun 10:00–17:00, closed Mon and for three weeks in Jan. See page 328.

life, walk through the simple museum, the Beguine's House museum (€2, daily 10:00–17:00, shorter hours off-season, English explanations, museum is left of entry gate).

Minnewater—Just south of the Begijnhof is Minnewater, an idyllic world of flower boxes, canals, and swans.

Almshouses—Walking from the Begijnhof back to the town center, you might detour along Nieuwe Gentweg to visit one of about 20 almshouses in the city. At #8, go through the door marked *Godshuis de Meulenaere 1613* into the peaceful courtyard (free). This was a medieval form of housing for the poor. The rich would pay for someone's tiny room here in return for lots of prayers.

Bruges Experiences: Beer, Chocolate, Windmills, and Biking

▲▲**De Halve Maan Brewery Tour**—Belgians are Europe's beer connoisseurs. This fun, handy tour is a great way to pay your

respects. The "Brugse Zot" is the only beer still brewed in Bruges, and the happy gang at this working-family brewery gives entertaining and informative, 45-minute tours in two languages. Avoid crowds by visiting at 11:00 or 15:00 (€5.50 includes a beer, lots of very steep steps, great rooftop panorama; tours run April–Oct daily on the hour 11:00–16:00, Sat until 17:00; Nov–March Mon–Fri 11:00 and 15:00 only, Sat–Sun on the hour 11:00–16:00; take a right down skinny Stoofstraat to #26 on Walplein, tel. 050-444-223, www .halvemaan.be).

During your tour, you'll learn that "the components of the beer are vitally necessary and contribute to a well-balanced life pattern. Nerves, muscles, visual sentience, and healthy skin are stimulated by these in a positive manner. For longevity and life-long equilibrium, drink Brugse Zot in moderation!"

Their bistro, where you'll be given your included beer, serves quick, hearty lunch plates. You can eat indoors with the smell of hops, or outdoors with the smell of hops. This is a good place to wait for your tour or to linger afterward. For more on beer, see page 367.

▲**Chocolate Shops**—Bruggians are connoisseurs of fine chocolate. You'll be tempted by chocolate-filled display windows all over town. While Godiva is the best big-factory/high-price/high-quality brand, there are plenty of smaller, family-run places in Bruges that offer exquisite handmade chocolates. Both of the following chocolatiers are proud of their creative varieties, generous with their samples, and welcome you to assemble a 100-gram assortment of five or six chocolates.

Dumon: Perhaps Bruges' smoothest and creamiest chocolates are at Dumon (€2.10/100 grams). Madame Dumon and her children (Stefaan, Natale, and Christophe) make their top-notch chocolate daily and sell it fresh just off Market Square (Thu–Tue 10:00–18:00, closed Wed, old chocolate molds on display in basement, Eiermarkt 6, tel. 050-346-282). The Dumons don't provide English labels because they believe it's best to describe their chocolates in person—and they do it with an evangelical fervor. Try a small mix-and-match box to sample a few out-of-this-world flavors, and come back for more of your favorites.

The Chocolate Line: Locals and tourists alike flock to The Chocolate Line (pricey at €4.40/100 grams) to taste the *gastronomique* varieties concocted by Dominique Person—the mad scientist of chocolate. His unique creations include Havana cigar (marinated in rum, cognac, and Cuban tobacco leaves—so therefore technically illegal in the US), lemongrass, lavender, ginger (shaped like a Buddha), saffron curry, spicy chili, and Moroccan mint. New combinations from Dominique's imagination are a Pop Rocks/cola chocolate, as well as "wine vinegar" chocolate (surprisingly good). The kitchen—busy whipping up 80 varieties—is on display in the back. Enjoy the window display, renewed monthly (daily 9:30–18:00, between Church of Our Lady and Market Square at Simon Stevinplein 19, tel. 050-341-090).

Choco-Story: The Chocolate Museum—This museum is rated ▲ for chocoholics. The Chocolate Fairy leads you through 2,600

years of chocolate history—explaining why, in the ancient Mexican world of the Mayas and the Aztecs, chocolate was considered the drink of the gods, and cocoa beans were used as a means of payment. With lots of artifacts well-described in English, the museum fills you in on the production of truffles, bonbons, hollow figures, and solid bars of chocolate. Then you'll view a delicious little video (8 min long, repeating continuously, alternating Flemish, French, and then English; peek into the theater to check the schedule. If you have time before the next English showing, visit the exhibits in the top room). Your finale is in the "demonstration room," where—after a 10-minute cooking demo—you get a taste (€6, €10 combo-ticket includes nearby Friet Museum, daily 10:00–17:00; where Wijnzakstraat meets Sint Jansstraat at Sint Jansplein, 3-min walk from Market Square; tel. 050-612-237, www.choco-story.be).

Friet Museum—It's the only place in the world that enthusiastically tells the story of french fries, which, of course, aren't even French—they're Belgian. As there are no real artifacts, you could just Google it and save the €6 entry fee (€10 combo-ticket includes Chocolate Museum, daily 10:00–17:00, Vlamingstraat 33, tel. 050-340-150, www.frietmuseum.be).

BRUGES SIGHTS

Windmills and Lace by the Moat—A 15-minute walk from the center to the northeast end of town brings you to four windmills strung along a pleasant grassy setting on the "big moat" canal. The St. Janshuysmolen **windmill** is open to visitors (€2, May–Aug daily 9:30–12:30 & 13:30–17:00, closed Sept–April, at the end of Carmersstraat, between Kruispoort and Dampoort, on Bruges side of the moat).

The **Folklore Museum,** in the same neighborhood, is cute but forgettable (€2, Tue–Sun 9:30–12:30 & 13:30–17:00, closed Mon, Balstraat 43, tel. 050-448-764). To find it, ask for the Jerusalem Church. On the same street is a lace shop with a good reputation—'t **Apostelientje** (Mon–Fri 9:30–18:00, Sat 10:00–17:00, Sun 10:00–13:00, Balstraat 11, tel. 050-337-860).

▲▲**Biking**—The Flemish word for bike is *fiets* (pronounced "feets"). While Bruges' sights are close enough for easy walking, the town is a treat for bikers, and a bike quickly gets you into dreamy back lanes without a hint of tourism. Take a peaceful evening ride through the town's nooks and crannies and around the outer canal. Consider keeping a bike for the duration of your stay—it's the way the locals get around in Bruges. Along the canal that circles the town, there is now a park with a delightful bike lane. Rental shops have maps and ideas (see "Bike Rental" on page 315 for more info).

○ Self-Guided Bike Ride to Damme: For the best short bike trip out of Bruges, rent a bike and pedal four miles to the nearby town of Damme. You'll enjoy a whiff of the countryside and see a working windmill while riding along a canal to this interesting city. Allow about two hours for the leisurely round-trip bike ride and a brief stop in Damme. The Belgium/Netherlands border is a 40-minute pedal (along the same canal) beyond Damme.

• *Head east from Bruges' Market Square through Burg Square and out to the canal. (You could stop to see the Jerusalem Church and a lace shop on the way—described above.) At the canal, circle to the left, passing several windmills (one is open for viewing, described above). At the last windmill, named Dampoort, head away from Bruges on the left (north) side of the Damme Canal, via Noorweegse Kaai/Damse Vaart-West.*

The Damme Canal: From Dampoort, you'll pedal straight and level along the canal directly to Damme. There's no opportunity to cross the canal until you reach the town. The farmland to your left is a *polder*—a salt marsh that flooded each spring, until it was reclaimed by industrious local farmers. The Damme Canal, also called the Napoleon Canal, was built in 1811 by Napoleon (actually by his Spanish prisoners) in a failed attempt to reinvigorate the city as a port. Today locals fish this canal for eels and wait for the next winter freeze. Old-timers have fond memories of skating to Holland on this canal—but it hasn't had a hard freeze for over a decade.

Windmill: Just before arriving in Damme, you'll come upon a working windmill that dates from 1867. More clever than the windmills in Bruges, this one is designed so just the wood cap turns to face the wind—rather than the entire building. If it's open, climb up through the creaking, spinning, wind-powered gears to the top floor (free, Sat–Sun 9:30–18:00).

In its day (13th–15th centuries), Bruges was one of the top five European ports and little Damme was important as well. Today all you see is land—the once-bustling former harbors silted up, causing the sea to retreat. Pause atop the bridge just beyond the windmill. From here you can see how, at Napoleon's instructions, the canal was designed to mimic a grand Parisian boulevard, leading to the towering Church of Our Lady back in Bruges.

• From here the canal continues straight to Holland. (If tempted...you're a third of the way to the border.) Cross the bridge and follow Kerkstraat, which cuts through the center of town, to Damme's main square and City Hall.

Damme: Once a thriving medieval port, and then a moated garrison town, today Damme is a tourist center—a tiny version of Bruges. It has a smaller-but-similar City Hall, a St. John's Hospital, and a big brick Church of Our Lady. You can tell by its 15th-century City Hall that, 500 years ago, Damme was rolling in herring money. Rather than being built with Belgian bricks (like other buildings around here), the City Hall was made of French limestone. Originally the ground floor was a market and fish warehouse, with government offices upstairs.

• Continue on Kerkstraat as it leads two blocks farther to the Church of Our Lady. Along the way, you could side-trip to the left, down Pottenbakkersstraat, which takes you to a quaint little square called Haringmarkt (named for the Herring Market that made Damme rich in the 15th century). The trees you see from here mark the lines of the town's long-gone, 17th-century ramparts. Returning to Kerkstraat, continue on to the big church.

The Church of Our Lady: This church, which rose and fell with the fortunes of Damme, dates from the 13th century. Inside

328 Rick Steves' Amsterdam, Bruges & Brussels

are two Virgin Marys: To the right of the altar, a 1630 wooden statue of Mary, and to the left, Our Lady of the Fishermen (c. 1650, in a glass case). Over the nave stands Belgium's oldest wooden statue, St. Andrew, with his X-shaped cross.

Outside, under the 13th-century church tower, is a three-faced, modern fiberglass sculpture by the Belgian artist Charles Delporte. Called *View of Light*, it evokes three lights: morning (grace), mid-day (kindness), and evening (gentleness). If you like his work, there's more at his nearby gallery.

• *To return to Bruges, continue past the church on Kerkstraat. Just before crossing the next bridge, follow a dirt lane to the right that leads scenically back to the Damme Canal (and Damse Vaart-Zuid). Take this road back to Bruges.*

Near Bruges

In Flanders Fields Museum—This World War I museum, about 40 miles southwest of Bruges, provides a moving look at the battles fought near Ieper (Ypres in French), where British losses totaled 60,000 dead and wounded in five weeks. Use its interactive computer displays to trace the wartime lives of individual soldiers and citizens. Powerful videos and ear-shattering audio complete the story (€8; April–mid-Nov daily 10:00–18:00; mid-Nov–March Tue–Sun 10:00–17:00, closed Mon and for three weeks in Jan; last entry one hour before closing, Grote Markt 34, Ieper, tel. 057-239-220, www.inflandersfields.be). From Bruges, catch a train to Ieper via Kortrijk (2 hrs), or take a tour (see "Tours," page 316). Drivers take E-403 to Kortrijk, then A-19 to Ieper, following signs to *Bellewaerde*.

BRUGES CITY WALK

This walk, which takes you from Market Square to the Burg to the cluster of museums around the Church of Our Lady (the Groeninge, Gruuthuse, and Memling), shows you the best of Bruges in a day.

ORIENTATION

Length of This Walk: Allow two hours for the walk, plus time for Bruges' two big museums (Groeninge and Memling—see tours on page 344 and page 353).

Bell Tower (Belfort): €5, daily 9:30–17:00, last entry 45 min before closing, on Market Square.

Basilica of the Holy Blood: Treasury entry-€1.50; April–Sept Thu–Tue 9:30–12:00 & 14:00–18:00, Wed 9:30–11:45 only; Oct–March Thu–Tue 10:00–12:00 & 14:00–16:00, Wed 10:00–11:45 only; Burg Square, tel. 050-336-792, www.holy blood.com.

City Hall's Gothic Room: €2.50, includes audioguide and entry to Renaissance Hall, daily 9:30–17:00, Burg 12.

Renaissance Hall (Brugse Vrije): €2.50, includes audioguide and admission to City Hall's Gothic Room, daily 9:30–17:00, entrance in corner of square at Burg 11a.

Groeninge Museum: €8, includes audioguide, Tue–Sun 9:30–17:00, closed Mon, Dijver 12, tel. 050-448-743.

Gruuthuse Museum: €6, includes entry to apse of Church of Our Lady, Tue–Sun 9:30–17:00, closed Mon, some rooms closed until 2011, Dijver 17, Bruges museums tel. 050-448-711.

Church of Our Lady: Free peek at Michelangelo sculpture, €2.50 for art-filled apse, covered by €6 Gruuthuse admission or museum combo-ticket—see page 321; church open Mon–Fri

9:30–17:00, Sat 9:30–16:45, Sun 13:30–17:00 only; museum and apse closed Mon, Mariastraat.

Memling Museum: €8, includes fine audioguide, Tue–Sun 9:30–17:00, closed Mon, Mariastraat 38.

De Halve Maan Brewery Tour: €5 tour includes a beer; April–Oct daily on the hour 11:00–16:00, Sat until 17:00; 11:00 and 15:00 are best to avoid groups; Nov–March Mon–Fri at 11:00 and 15:00 only, Sat–Sun on the hour 11:00–16:00; take a right down narrow Stoofstraat to #26 on Walplein, tel. 050-444-223, www.halvemaan.be.

Begijnhof: Courtyard free and always open; Beguine's House museum costs €2, open daily 10:00–17:00, shorter hours off-season.

THE WALK BEGINS

Market Square (Markt)

Ringed by the post office, lots of restaurant terraces, great old gabled buildings, and the bell tower, this is the modern heart of the city. And, in Bruges' heyday as a trading city, this was also the center. The "typical" old buildings here were rebuilt in the 19th century in an exaggerated Neo-Gothic style (Bruges is often called "more Gothic than Gothic"). This pre–Martin Luther style was a political statement for this Catholic town.

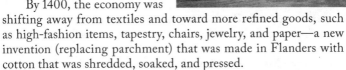

Formerly, a canal came right up to this square. Imagine boats moored where the post office stands today. In the 1300s, farmers shipped their cotton, wool, flax, and hemp to the port at Bruges. Before loading it onto outgoing boats, the industrious locals would spin, weave, and dye it into a finished product.

By 1400, the economy was shifting away from textiles and toward more refined goods, such as high-fashion items, tapestry, chairs, jewelry, and paper—a new invention (replacing parchment) that was made in Flanders with cotton that was shredded, soaked, and pressed.

The square is adorned with **flags,** including the red-white-and-blue lion flag of Bruges, the black-yellow-and-red flag of Belgium, and the blue-with-circle-of-yellow-stars flag of the European Union.

The **statue** depicts two friends, Jan Breidel and Pieter de Coninc, clutching sword and shield and looking towards France as they led a popular uprising against the French king in 1302.

1 Market Square
2 Bell Tower
3 Burg Square
4 Basilica of the Holy Blood
5 City Hall
6 Renaissance Hall
7 Crowne Plaza Hotel
8 Blinde Ezelstraat
9 Fish Market
10 Huidevettersplein
11 Postcard Canal View
12 Groeninge Museum
13 Gruuthuse Museum
14 Church of Our Lady
15 Memling Museum
16 De Halve Maan Brewery
17 Begijnhof
18 Minnewater

The rebels identified potential French spies by demanding they repeat two words—*schild en vriend* (shield and friend)—that only Flemish locals (or foreigners with phlegm) could pronounce. They won Flanders its freedom. Cleverly using hooks to pull knights from their horses, they scored the medieval world's first victory of foot soldiers over cavalry, and of common people over nobility. The French knights, thinking that fighting these Flemish peasants would be a cakewalk, had worn their dress uniforms. The peasants had a field day afterward scavenging all the golden spurs from the fallen soldiers after the Battle of the Golden Spurs (1302).

Geldmuntstraat, a block west of the square, has fun shops and eateries. Steenstraat is the main shopping street and is packed with people. Want a coffee? Stop by the Café-Brasserie Craenenburg on Market Square. Originally the house where Maximilian of Austria was imprisoned in 1488, it's been a café since 1905 (daily 7:30–24:00, Markt 16).

Bell Tower (Belfort)

Most of this bell tower has stood over Market Square since 1300. The octagonal lantern was added in 1486, making it 290 feet high.

The tower combines medieval crenellations, pointed Gothic arches, round Roman arches, flamboyant spires, and even a few small flying buttresses (two-thirds of the way up).

Try some Belgian-style fries from either stand at the bottom of the tower. Look for the small metal model of the tower and the Braille description of the old town. Enter the courtyard. At the base of the bell tower, find the posted schedule of free carillon concerts (normally June–Sept Mon, Wed, and Sat at 21:00; Oct–May Wed and Sun at 14:15, sit on benches in courtyard—a great experience). There's also a WC in the courtyard (€0.40).

Climb the tower (€5, 366 steps). Just before you reach the top, peek into the carillon room. The 47 bells can be played mechanically with the giant barrel and movable tabs (as they are on each quarter hour), or with a manual keyboard (as they are during concerts). The carillonneur uses his fists and feet, rather than fingers. Be there on the

quarter hour, when things ring. It's *bellissimo* at the top of the hour.

Atop the tower, survey Bruges. On the horizon, you can see the towns along the North Sea coast.

• *Leaving the bell tower, turn right (east) onto Breidelstraat, and thread yourself through the lace and waffles to Burg Square.*

Burg Square

This opulent square is Bruges' historical birthplace, political center, and religious heart. Today it's the scene of outdoor concerts and local festivals.

Pan the square to see six centuries of architecture. Starting with the view of the bell tower above the gables, sweep counter-

clockwise 360 degrees. You'll go from Romanesque (the interior of the fancy, gray-brick **Basilica of the Holy Blood** in the corner), to the pointed Gothic arches and prickly steeples of the white sandstone **City Hall,** to the well-proportioned Renaissance windows of the **Old Recorder's House** (next door, under the gilded statues), to the elaborate 17th-century Baroque of the **Provost's House** (past the park behind you). The **park** at the back of the square is the site of a cathedral that was demolished during the French Revolutionary period. Today, the foundation is open to the public in the **Crowne Plaza Hotel** basement (described on page 338). The modern, Japanese-designed **fountain** plays with motifs of lace and water, but locals simply call it "the car wash."

• *Complete your spin and walk to the small, fancy, gray-and-gold building in the corner of Burg Square.*

Basilica of the Holy Blood

The gleaming gold knights and ladies on the church's gray facade remind us that this double-decker church was built (c. 1150) by a brave Crusader to house the drops of Christ's blood he'd brought back from Jerusalem.

Lower Chapel: Enter the lower chapel through the door labeled *Basiliek.* Inside, the stark and dim decor reeks of the medieval piety that drove crusading Christian Europeans to persecute Muslims. With heavy columns and round arches, the style is pure Romanesque. The annex along

The Legend of the Holy Blood

Several drops of Christ's blood, washed from his lifeless body by Joseph of Arimathea, were preserved in a rock-crystal vial in Jerusalem. In 1150, the patriarch of Jerusalem gave the blood to a Flemish soldier, Derrick of Alsace, as thanks for rescuing his city from the Muslims during the Second Crusade. Derrick (also called Dedric or Thierry) returned home and donated it to the city. The old, dried blood suddenly turned to liquid, a miracle repeated every Friday for the next two centuries, and verified by thousands of pilgrims from around Europe who flocked here to adore it. The blood dried up for good in 1325.

Every year on Ascension Day (May 13 in 2010), Bruges' bankers, housewives, and waffle vendors put on old-time costumes for the parading of the vial through the city. Crusader knights re-enact the bringing of the relic, Joseph of Arimathea washes Christ's body, and ladies in medieval costume with hair tied up in horn-like hairnets come out to wave flags, while many Bruges citizens just take the day off.

the right aisle displays somber statues of Christ being tortured and entombed, plus a 12th-century relief panel over a doorway showing St. Basil (a fourth-century scholarly monk) being baptized by a double-jointed priest, and a man-size dove of the Holy Spirit.

• *Go back outside and up the staircase to reach the...*

Upper Chapel: After being gutted by Napoleon's secular-humanist crusaders in 1797, the upper chapel's original Romanesque decor was redone in a Neo-Gothic style. The nave is colorful, with a curved wooden ceiling, painted walls, and stained-glass windows of the dukes who ruled Flanders, along with their duchesses.

The painting at the main altar tells how the Holy Blood got here. Derrick of Alsace, having helped defend Jerusalem *(Hierosolyma)* and Bethlehem *(Bethlema)* from Muslim incursions in the Second Crusade, kneels (left) before the grateful Christian patriarch of Jerusalem, who rewards him with the relic. Derrick returns home (right) and kneels before Bruges' bishop to give him the vial of blood.

The relic itself—some red stuff preserved inside a clear, six-inch tube of rock crystal—is kept in the adjoining room (through the three arches). It's in the tall, silver tabernacle on the altar. (Each

Friday—and increasingly on other days, too—the tabernacle's doors will be open, so you can actually see the vial of blood.) On holy days, the relic is shifted across the room and displayed on the throne under the canopy.

Treasury (next to Upper Chapel): For €1.50, you can see the impressive gold-and-silver, gem-studded, hexagonal reliquary

(c. 1600, left wall) that the vial of blood is paraded around in on feast days. The vial is placed in the "casket" at the bottom of the four-foot-tall structure. On the wall, flanking the shrine, are paintings of kneeling residents who, for centuries, have tended the shrine and organized the pageantry as part of the 31-member Brotherhood of the Holy Blood. Elsewhere in the room are the Brothers' ceremonial necklaces, clothes, chalices, and so on.

In the display case by the entrance, find the lead box that protected the vial of blood from Protestant extremists (1578) and French Revolutionaries (1797) bent on destroying what, to them, was a glaring symbol of Catholic mumbo-jumbo. The broken rock-crystal tube with gold caps on either end is a replica of the vial, giving an idea of what the actual relic looks like. Opposite the reliquary are the original cartoons (from 1541) that provided the designs for the basilica's stained glass.

City Hall (Stadhuis)

Built in about 1400, when Bruges was a thriving bastion of capitalism with a population of 35,000, this building served as a model for town halls elsewhere, including Brussels. The white sand-

stone facade is studded with statues of knights, nobles, and saints with prickly Gothic steeples over their heads. A colorful double band of cities' coats of arms includes those of Bruges (Brugghe) and Dunkirk (Dunquerke). Back then, Bruges' jurisdiction included many towns in present-day France. The building is still the City Hall, and it's not unusual to see couples arriving here to get married.

Entrance Hall: The ground-level lobby (free, closed Mon) leads to a picture gallery with scenes from Belgium's history, from the Spanish king to the arrival of Napoleon, shown meeting the mayor here at the City Hall in 1803.

• *You can pay to climb the stairs for a look at the...*

Gothic Room: Some of modern democracy's roots lie in this ornate room, where, for centuries, the city council met to discuss the town's affairs (€2.50 entry includes audioguide—which explains both the upstairs and the ground floor—and entrance to the adjacent Renaissance Hall). In 1464, one of Europe's first parliaments, the Estates General of the Low Countries, convened here. The fireplace at the far end bears a proclamation from 1305, which says, "All the artisans, laborers...and citizens of Bruges are free—all of them" (provided they pay their taxes).

The elaborately carved and painted wooden ceiling (a Neo-Gothic reconstruction from the 19th century) features tracery in gold, red, and black. Five dangling arches ("pendentives") hang down the center, now adorned with modern floodlights. Notice the New Testament themes carved into the circular medallions that decorate the points where the arches meet.

The **wall murals** are late-19th-century Romantic paintings depicting episodes in the city's history. Start with the biggest painting along the left wall, and work clockwise, following the numbers found on the walls:

1. Hip, hip, hooray! Everyone cheers, flags wave, trumpets blare, and dogs bark, as Bruges' knights, dressed in gold with black Flemish lions, return triumphant after driving out French oppressors and winning Flanders' independence. The Battle of the Golden Spurs (1302) is remembered every July 11.

2. Bruges' high-water mark came perhaps at this elaborate ceremony, when Philip the Good of Burgundy (seated, in black) assembled his court here in Bruges and solemnly founded the knightly Order of the Golden Fleece (1429).

3. The Crusader knight, Derrick of Alsace, returns from the Holy Land and kneels at the entrance of St. Basil's Chapel to present the relic of Christ's Holy Blood (c. 1150).

4. A nun carries a basket of bread in this scene from St. John's Hospital.

5. A town leader stands at the podium and hands a sealed document to a German businessman, renewing the Hanseatic League's business license. Membership in this club of trading cities was a key to Bruges' prosperity.

6. As peasants cheer, a messenger of the local duke proclaims the town's right to self-government (1190).

7. The mayor visits a Bruges painting studio to shake the

hand of Jan van Eyck, the great Flemish Primitive painter (1433). Jan's wife, Margareta, is there, too. In the 1400s, Bruges rivaled Florence and Venice as Europe's cultural capital. See the town in the distance, out Van Eyck's window.

8. Skip it.

9. City fathers grab a ceremonial trowel from a pillow to lay the fancy cornerstone of the City Hall (1376). Bruges' familiar towers stand in the background.

10. Skip it.

11. It's a typical market day at the Halls (the courtyard behind the bell tower). Arabs mingle with Germans in fur-lined coats and beards in a market where they sell everything from armor to lemons.

12. A bishop blesses a new canal (1404) as ships sail right by the city. This was Bruges in its heyday, before the silting of the harbor. At the far right, the two bearded men with moustaches are the brothers who painted these murals.

In the adjoining room, old paintings and maps show how little the city has changed through the centuries. A map (on the right

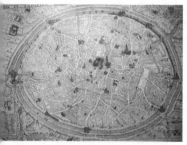

wall) shows in exquisite detail the city as it looked in 1562. (The map is oriented with south on top.) Find the bell tower, the Church of Our Lady, and Burg Square, which back then was bounded on the north by a cathedral. Notice the canal (on the west) leading from the North Sea right to Market Square. A moat encircled the city with its gates, unfinished wall, and 28 windmills (four of which survive today). The mills pumped water to the town's fountains, made paper, ground grain, and functioned as the motor of the Middle Ages. Most locals own a copy of this map that shows how their neighborhood looked 400 years ago.

• *Back on the square, leaving the City Hall, turn right and go to the corner.*

Renaissance Hall (Brugse Vrije)

This elaborately decorated room has a grand Renaissance chimney carved from oak by Bruges' Renaissance man, Lancelot Blondeel, in 1531. If you're into heraldry, the symbolism makes this room worth a five-minute stop. If you're not, you'll wonder where the rest of the museum is.

The centerpiece of the incredible carving is the Holy Roman Emperor Charles V. The hometown duke, on the far left, is related to Charles V. By making the connection to the Holy Roman Emperor clear, this carved family tree of Bruges' nobility helped substantiate their power. Notice the closely guarded family jewels. And check out the expressive little cherubs.

Crowne Plaza Hotel

One of the city's newest buildings (1992) sits atop the ruins of the town's oldest structures. In about A.D. 900, when Viking ships regularly docked here to rape and pillage, Baldwin Iron Arm built a fort *(castrum)* to protect his Flemish people. In 950, the fort was converted into St. Donatian's Church, which became one of the city's largest.

Ask politely at the hotel's reception desk to see the archaeological site—ruins of the fort and the church—in the basement. If there's no conference in progress, they'll let you walk down the stairs and have a peek.

In the basement of the modern hotel are conference rooms lined with old stone walls and display cases of objects found in the ruins of earlier structures. On the immediate left hangs a photo of a document announcing the *Vente de Materiaux* (sale of material). When Napoleon destroyed the church in the early 1800s, its bricks were auctioned off. A local builder bought them at auction, and now the pieces of the old cathedral are embedded in other buildings throughout Bruges.

See oak pilings, carved to a point, once driven into this former peat bog to support the fort and shore up its moat. Paintings show the immensity of the church that replaced it. The curved stone walls you walk among are from the foundations of the ambulatory around the church altar.

Excavators found a town water hole—a bonanza for archaeologists—turning up the refuse of a thousand years of habitation: pottery, animal skulls, rosary beads, dice, coins, keys, thimbles, pipes, spoons, and Delftware.

Don't miss the 14th-century painted sarcophagi—painted quickly for burial, with the crucifixion on the west end and the Virgin and Child on the east.

• *Back on Burg Square, walk south under the Goldfinger family (through the small archway) down the alleyway called...*

Blinde Ezelstraat

Midway down on the left side (knee level), see an original iron hinge from the city's south gate, back when the city was ringed by a moat and closed nightly at 22:00. On the right wall, at eye level, a black patch shows just how grimy the city had become before a 1960s cleaning. Despite the cleaning and a few fanciful reconstructions, the city looks today much as it did in centuries past.

The name "Blinde Ezelstraat" means "Blind Donkey Street." In medieval times, the donkeys, carrying fish from the North Sea on their backs, were stopped here so that their owners could put blinders on them. Otherwise, the donkeys wouldn't cross the water between the old city and the fish market.

• *Cross the bridge over what was the 13th-century city moat. On your left are the arcades of the...*

Fish Market (Vismarkt)

The North Sea is just 12 miles away, and the fresh catch is sold here (Tue–Sat 6:00–13:00). Once a thriving market, today it's mostly souvenirs...and the big catch is the tourists.

• *Take an immediate right (west), entering a courtyard called...*

Huidevettersplein

This tiny, picturesque, restaurant-filled square was originally the headquarters of the town's skinners and tanners. On the facade of the Hotel Duc de Bourgogne, four old relief panels show scenes from the leather trade—once a leading Bruges industry. First, they tan the hide in a bath of acid; then, with tongs, they pull it out to dry; then they beat it to make it soft; and finally, they scrape and clean it to make it ready for sale.

• *Continue a few steps to Rozenhoedkaai street, where you can look back to your right and get a great...*

Postcard Canal View

The bell tower reflected in a quiet canal lined with old houses—this view is the essence of Bruges. Seeing buildings rising straight

from the water makes you understand why this was the Venice of the North. Can you see the bell tower's tilt? It leans about four feet. The tilt has been carefully monitored since 1740, but no change has been detected.

To your left (west) down the Dijver canal (past a flea market on weekends) looms the huge spire of the Church of Our Lady, the tallest brick spire in the Low Countries. Between you and the church are the Europa College (a postgraduate institution for training future "Eurocrats" about the laws, economics, and politics of the European Union) and two fine museums.

• *Continue walking with the canal and bell tower on your right. About 100 yards ahead, on the left, is the copper-colored sign that points the way to the...*

Groeninge Museum

This sumptuous collection of paintings takes you from 1400 to 1945. The highlights are its Flemish Primitives, with all their glorious detail.

❍ See Groeninge Museum Tour on page 344.

• *Leaving the Groeninge, take your first left, into a courtyard. You'll see the prickly church steeple ahead. Head up and over the picture-perfect 19th-century pedestrian bridge.*

From the bridge, look up at the corner of the Gruuthuse mansion, where there's a teeny-tiny window, a toll-keeper's lookout. The bridge gives you a close-up look at Our Lady's big buttresses and round apse. Go slightly right, between the two huge buildings. On the right is a large stone courtyard, where you'll find the entrance to the...

Gruuthuse Museum

This 15th-century mansion of a wealthy Bruges merchant displays period furniture, tapestries, coins, and musical instruments. Extensive renovation will have this museum in a disappointing state of disarray until 2011. Use the leaflets in each room to browse through a collection of secular objects that are both functional and beautiful. Here are some highlights:

On the left, in the first room (or **Great Hall**), the big fireplace, oak table, and tapestries attest to the wealth of Louis Gruuthuse, who got rich providing a special herb used to spice up beer.

Tapestries like the ones you see here were a famous Flemish export product, made in local factories out of raw wool imported from England and silk brought from the Orient (via Italy). Both beautiful and useful (as insulation), they adorned many homes and palaces throughout Europe.

The Gruuthuse mansion abuts the Church of Our Lady and has a convenient little **chapel** (upstairs via the far corner of Room 16) with a window overlooking the interior of the huge church. In their private box seats above the choir, the family could attend services without leaving home. From the balcony, you can look down on two reclining gold statues in the church, marking the tombs of Charles the Bold and his daughter, Mary of Burgundy (the grandmother of powerful Charles V).

Leaving the museum, contemplate the mountain of bricks

that towers 400 feet above, as it has for 600 years. You're heading for that church.

• *Walk left out of the courtyard, doubling back the way you came, toward the pedestrian bridge. But this time, go right after the archway, circling clockwise around the outside of the church. Ahead on the right is the entrance to the...*

Church of Our Lady

This church stands as a memorial to the power and wealth of Bruges in its heyday.

A delicate *Madonna and Child* **by Michelangelo** (1504) is near the apse (to the right as you enter), somewhat overwhelmed by the ornate Baroque niche it sits in. It's said to be the only Michelangelo statue to leave Italy in his lifetime, bought in Tuscany by a wealthy Bruges businessman, who's buried beneath it.

As Michelangelo chipped away at the masterpiece of his youth, *David*, he took breaks by carving this one in 1504. Mary,

slightly smaller than life-size, sits, while young Jesus stands in front of her. Their expressions are mirror images—serene, but a bit melancholy, with downcast eyes, as though pondering the young child's dangerous future. Though they're lost in thought, their hands instinctively link, tenderly. The white Carrara marble is highly polished, something Michelangelo only did when he was certain he'd gotten it right.

If you like tombs and church art, pay €2.50 to wander through the apse (also covered by €6 Gruuthuse admission and museum combo-ticket). The highlight is the reclining statues marking the tombs of the last local rulers of Bruges, Mary of Burgundy, and her father, Charles the Bold. The dog and lion at their feet are symbols of fidelity and courage.

In 1482, when 25-year-old Mary of Burgundy tumbled from a horse and died, she left behind a toddler son and a husband who was heir to the Holy Roman Empire. Beside her lies her father, Charles the Bold, who also died prematurely, in war. Their twin deaths meant Bruges belonged to Austria, and would soon be swallowed up by the empire and ruled from afar by Habsburgs—who didn't understand or care about its problems. Trade routes shifted, and goods soon flowed through Antwerp, then Amsterdam, as Bruges' North Sea port silted up. After these developments, Bruges began four centuries of economic decline. The city was eventually mothballed. It was later discovered by modern-day tourists to be remarkably well-pickled—which explains its current affluence.

The balcony to the left of the main altar is part of the Gruuthuse mansion next door, providing the noble family with prime seats for Mass.

Excavations in 1979 turned up fascinating grave paintings on the tombs below and near the altar. Dating from the 13th century, these show Mary represented as Queen of Heaven (on a throne, carrying a crown and scepter) and Mother of God (with the baby Jesus on her lap). Since Mary is in charge of advocating with Jesus for your salvation, she's a good person to have painted on the wall of your tomb. Tombs also show lots of angels—generally patron saints of the dead person—swinging thuribles (incense burners).

• *Just across Mariastraat from the church entrance is the entry to the St. John's Hospital's Visitors Center (with a good Internet café and a €0.30 public WC). The entrance to the Memling Museum, which fills that hospital's church, is 20 yards south (to the left) on Mariastraat.*

Memling Museum

This medieval hospital contains some much-loved paintings by the greatest of the Flemish Primitives, Hans Memling. His *Mystical Wedding of St. Catherine* triptych deserves a close look. Catherine and her "mystical groom," the baby Jesus, are flanked by a headless John the Baptist and a pensive John the Evangelist. The chairs are there so you can study it. If you know the Book of Revelation, you'll understand St. John's wild and intricate vision. The St. Ursula Shrine, an ornate little mini-church in the same room, is filled with impressive detail.

  ❍ See Memling Museum Tour on page 353.

• *Continue south (with the museum behind you, turn right) about 150 yards on Mariastraat. Turn right on Walstraat (a small black-and-white sign points the way to Minnewater and the Begijnhof). It leads into the pleasant square called Walplein, where you'll find the...*

De Halve Maan Brewery Tour

If you like beer, take a tour here (Walplein 26). See page 324.
• *Leaving the brewery, head right, make your first right, and you'll see a pedestrian bridge on the right. From here, the lacy cuteness of Bruges crescendos as you approach the Begijnhof.*

Begijnhof

Begijnhofs (pronounced gutturally: buh-HHHINE-hof) were built to house women of the lay order, called Beguines, who spent their lives in piety and service without having to take the same vows a nun would. For military and other reasons, there were more women than men in the medieval Low Countries. The order of Beguines offered women (often single or widowed) a dignified place to live and work. When the order died out, many *begijnhofs* were taken over by towns for subsidized housing. Today, single religious women live in the small homes. Benedictine nuns live in a building

nearby. Tour the simple museum to get a sense of Beguine life.

In the church, the rope that dangles from the ceiling is yanked by a nun to announce a sung vespers service.

• *Exiting opposite the way you entered, you'll hook left and see a lake.*

Minnewater

Just south of the Begijnhof is Minnewater ("Water of Love"), a peaceful, lake-filled park with canals and swans. This was once far from quaint—a busy harbor where small boats shuttled cargo from the big, ocean-going ships into town. From this point, the cargo was transferred again to flat-bottomed boats that went through the town's canals to their respective warehouses and to Market Square.

When locals see these swans, they recall the 15th-century mayor—famous for his long neck—who collaborated with the Austrians. The townsfolk beheaded him as a traitor. The Austrians warned them that similarly long-necked swans would inhabit the place to forever remind them of this murder. And they do.

• *You're a five-minute walk from the train station, where you can catch a bus to Market Square, or a 15-minute walk from Market Square—take your pick.*

GROENINGE MUSEUM TOUR

In the 1400s, Bruges was northern Europe's richest, most cosmopolitan, and most cultured city. New ideas, fads, and painting techniques were imported and exported with each shipload. Beautiful paintings were soon an affordable luxury, like fancy clothes or furniture. Internationally known artists set up studios in Bruges, producing portraits and altarpieces for wealthy merchants from all over Europe.

The Groeninge Museum has one of the world's best collections of the art produced in the city and surrounding area. This early Flemish art is less appreciated and understood today than the Italian Renaissance art produced a century later. But by selecting 11 masterpieces, we'll get an introduction to this subtle, technically advanced, and beautiful style. Hey, if you can master the museum's name (HHHROON-ih-guh), you can certainly handle the art.

ORIENTATION

Cost: €8, includes audioguide.

Hours and Information: Tue–Sun 9:30–17:00, closed Mon. Tel. 050-448-743

Closure and Special Exhibit: The museum is closed from mid-August 2010 until October 29, 2010, when it reopens with an exhibit called "Van Eyck to Dürer." While the special exhibit is on, the permanent collection won't be on display.

Getting There: The museum is at Dijver 12, near the Gruuthuse Museum and Church of Our Lady. One big copper sign and several small *museum* signs mark the nearby area, leading you

to the Groeninge's modern, glass front door.
Length of This Tour: Allow one hour.

Overview

The included audioguide allows you to wander as you like. Use this chapter as background to the huge collection's highlights, then browse, punching in the numbers of the paintings you'd like to learn more about.

THE TOUR BEGINS

• *In Room 1, look for...*

Gerard David (c. 1455–1523)—*Judgment of Cambyses* (1498)

That's gotta hurt.

A man is stretched across a table and skinned alive in a very businesslike manner. The crowd hardly notices, and a dog just

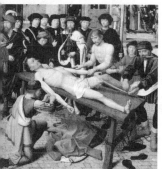

scratches himself. According to legend, the man was a judge arrested for corruption (left panel) and flayed (right panel), then his skin was draped (right panel background) over the new judge's throne.

Gerard David, Memling's successor as the city's leading artist, painted this for the City Hall. City councilors could ponder what might happen to them if they abused their offices.

By David's time, Bruges was in serious decline, with a failing economy and struggles against the powerful Austrian Habsburg family. The Primitive style was also fading. Italian art was popular, so David tries to spice up his retro-Primitive work with pseudo-Renaissance knickknacks—*putti* (baby angels, over the judgment throne), Roman-style medallions, and garlands. But he couldn't quite master the Italian specialty of 3-D perspective. We view the flayed man at an angle from slightly above, but the table he lies on is shown more from the side.

• *Head to Room 2 for...*

Jan van Eyck (c. 1390–1441)—*Virgin and Child with Canon Joris van der Paele* (1436)

Jan van Eyck was the world's first and greatest oil painter, and this is his masterpiece—three debatable but defensible assertions.

Mary, in a magnificent red gown, sits playing with her little baby, Jesus. Jesus glances up as St. George, the dragon-slaying

GROENINGE MUSEUM

knight, enters the room, tips his cap, and says, "I'd like to introduce my namesake, George (Joris)." Mary glances down at the kneeling Joris, a church official dressed in white. Joris takes off his glasses and looks up from his prayer book to see a bishop in blue, St. Donatian, patron of the church he hopes to be buried in.

Canon Joris, who hired Van Eyck, is not a pretty sight. He's old and wrinkled, with a double chin, weird earlobes, and bloodshot eyes. But the portrait isn't unflattering, it just shows unvarnished reality with crystal clarity.

Van Eyck brings Mary and the saints down from heaven and into a typical (rich) Bruges home. He strips off their haloes, banishes all angels, and pulls the plug on heavenly radiance. If this is a religious painting, then where's God?

God's in the details. From the bishop's damask robe and Mary's wispy hair to the folds in Jesus' baby fat and the oriental carpet to "Adonai" (Lord) written on St. George's breastplate, the painting is as complex and beautiful as God's creation. The color scheme—red Mary, white canon, and blue-and-gold saints—are Bruges' city colors, from its coat of arms.

Mary, crowned with a jeweled "halo" and surrounded by beautiful things, makes an appearance in 1400s Bruges, where she can be adored in all her human beauty by Canon Joris...and by us, reflected in the mirror-like shield on St. George's back.

Jan van Eyck—*Portrait of Margareta van Eyck* (1439)

At 35, shortly after moving to Bruges, Jan van Eyck married 20-year-old Margareta. They had two kids, and after Jan died,

Margareta took charge of his studio of assistants and kept it running until her death. This portrait (age 33), when paired with a matching self-portrait of Jan, was one of Europe's first husband-and-wife companion sets.

She sits half-turned, looking out of the frame. (Jan might have seen this "where-have-you-been?" expression in the window late one night.) She's dressed in a red, fur-lined coat, and we catch a glimpse of her wedding ring. Her hair is invisible— very fashionable at the time—pulled back

Flemish Primitives

Despite the "Primitive" label, the Low Countries of the 1400s (along with Venice and Florence) produced the most refined art in Europe. Here are some common features of Flemish Primitive art:

- **Primitive 3-D Perspective:** Expect unnaturally cramped-looking rooms, oddly slanted tables, and flat, cardboard-cutout people with stiff posture. Yes, these works are more primitive (hence the label) than those with the later Italian Renaissance perspective.
- **Realism:** Everyday bankers and clothmakers in their Sunday best are painted with clinical, warts-and-all precision. Even saints and heavenly visions are brought down to earth.
- **Details:** Like meticulous Bruges craftsmen, painters used fine-point brushes to capture almost microscopic details—flower petals, wrinkled foreheads, intricately patterned clothes, the sparkle in a ruby. The closer you get to a painting, the better it looks.
- **Oil Painted on Wood:** They were the pioneers of new-fangled oil-based paint (while Italy still used egg-yolk tempera), working on wood, before canvas became popular.
- **Portraits and Altarpieces:** Wealthy merchants and clergymen paid to have themselves painted either alone or mingling with saints.
- **Symbolism:** In earlier times, everyone understood that a dog symbolized fidelity, a lily meant chastity, and a rose was love.
- **Materialism:** Rich Flanders celebrated the beauty of luxury goods—the latest Italian dresses, jewels, carpets, oak tables—and the ordinary beauty that radiates from flesh-and-blood people.

tightly, bunched into horn-like hairnets, and draped with a headdress. Stray hairs along the perimeter were plucked to achieve the high forehead look.

This simple portrait is revolutionary—one of history's first individual portraits that wasn't of a saint, king, duke, or pope, and wasn't part of a religious work. It signals the advent of humanism, celebrating the glory of ordinary people. Van Eyck proudly signed the work on the original frame, with his motto saying he painted it *"als ik kan" (ALC IXH KAN)*..."as good as I can."

Rogier van der Weyden (c. 1399–1464)—*St. Luke Drawing the Virgin's Portrait* (c. 1435)

Rogier van der Weyden, the other giant among the Flemish

Primitives, adds the human touch to Van Eyck's rather detached precision.

As Mary prepares to nurse, baby Jesus can't contain his glee, wiggling his fingers and toes, anticipating lunch. Mary, dressed in everyday clothes, doesn't try to hide her love as she tilts her head down with a proud smile. Meanwhile, St. Luke (the patron saint of painters, who was said to have experienced this vision) looks on intently with a sketch pad in his hand, trying to catch the scene. These small gestures, movements, and facial expressions add an element of human emotion that later artists would amplify.

The painting is neatly divided by a spacious view out the window, showing a river stretching off to a spacious horizon. Van der Weyden experimented with 3-D effects like this one (though ultimately it's just window-dressing).

Rogier van der Weyden—*Duke Philip the Good* (c. 1450)

Tall, lean, and elegant, this charismatic duke transformed Bruges from a commercial powerhouse to a cultural one. In 1425, Philip moved his court to Bruges, making it the de facto capital of a Burgundian empire stretching from Amsterdam to Switzerland.

Philip wears a big hat to hide his hair, a fashion trend he himself began. He's also wearing the gold-chain necklace of the Order of the Golden Fleece, a distinguished knightly honor he gave himself. He inaugurated the Golden Fleece in a lavish ceremony at the Bruges City Hall, complete with parades, jousting, and festive pies that contained live people hiding inside to surprise his guests.

As a lover of painting, hunting, fine clothes, and many mistresses, Philip was a role model for Italian princes, such as Lorenzo the Magnificent—the *uomo universale,* or Renaissance Man.

Hugo van der Goes (c. 1430–c. 1482)—*Death of the Virgin* (c. 1470)

The long deathwatch is over—their beloved Mary has passed on, and the disciples are bleary-eyed and dazed with grief, as though hit with a spiritual two-by-four. Each etched face is a study in sad-

Oil Paint

Take vegetable oil pressed from linseeds (flax), blend in dry powdered pigments, whip to a paste the consistency of room-temperature butter, then brush onto a panel of white-washed oak—you're painting in oils. First popularized in the early 1400s, oil eventually overshadowed egg-yolk-based tempera. Though tempera was great for making fine lines shaded with simple blocks of color, oil could blend colors together seamlessly.

Watch a master create a single dog's hair: He paints a dark stroke of brown, then lets it dry. Then comes a second layer painted over it, of translucent orange. The brown shows through, blending with the orange to match the color of a collie. Finally, he applies a third, transparent layer (a "glaze"), giving the collie her healthy sheen.

Many great artists were not necessarily great painters (e.g., Michelangelo). Van Eyck, Rembrandt, Hals, Velázquez, and Rubens were master painters, meticulously building objects with successive layers of paint...but they're not everyone's favorite artists.

ness, as they all have their own way of coping—lighting a candle, fidgeting, praying, or just staring off into space. Blues and reds dominate, and there's little eye-catching ornamentation, which lets the lined faces and expressive hand gestures do the talking.

Hugo van der Goes painted this, his last major work, the

same year he attempted suicide. Hugo had built a successful career in Ghent, then abruptly dropped out to join a monastery. His paintings became increasingly emotionally charged, and his personality more troubled.

Above the bed floats a heavenly vision, as Jesus and the angels prepare to receive Mary's soul. Their smooth skin and serene expressions contrast with the gritty, wrinkled death pallor of those on earth. Caught up in their own grief, the disciples can't see the silver lining.

• *Head to Room 3 for the surreal scene that's...*

GROENINGE MUSEUM

Attributed to Hieronymus Bosch (c. 1450–1516)— *Last Judgment* (late 15th century)

It's the end of the world, and Christ descends in a bubble to pass judgment on puny humans. Little naked people dance and cavort in a theme park of medieval symbolism, desperately trying to squeeze

in their last bit of fun. Meanwhile, some wicked souls are being punished, victims either of their own stupidity or of genetically engineered demons. The good are sent to the left panel to frolic in the innocence of paradise, while the rest are damned to hell (right panel) to be tortured under a burning sky. Bosch paints the scenes with a high horizon line, making it seem that the chaos extends forever.

The bizarre work of Bosch (who, by the way, was not from Bruges) is open to many interpretations, but some see it as a warning for the turbulent times. He painted during the dawn of a new age. Secular ideas and materialism were encroaching, and the pious and serene medieval world was shattering into chaos.

• *At the entrance to Room 4 is...*

Jan Provoost (c. 1465–1529)—*Death and the Miser*

A Bruges businessman in his office strikes a deal with Death. The grinning skeleton lays coins on the table, and in return, the man—looking unhealthy and with fear in his eyes—reaches across the

divide in the panels to give Death a promissory note, then marks the transaction in his ledger book. He's trading away a few years of his life for a little more money. The worried man on the right (the artist's self-portrait) says, "Don't do it."

Jan Provoost (also known as Provost) worked for businessmen like this. He knew their offices, full of moneybags, paperwork, and books. Bruges' materialistic capitalism was at odds with Christian poverty, and society was divided over whether to praise or condemn it. Ironically, this painting's flip side is a religious work bought and paid for by...rich merchants.

Petrus Christus (c. 1420–c. 1475)—*Annunciation and Nativity* (1452)

Italian art was soon all the rage. Ships from Genoa and Venice would unload Renaissance paintings, wowing the Northerners

---

No Joke

An enthusiastic American teenager approaches the ticket seller at the Groeninge Museum:

"This is the Torture Museum, right?!"

"No," the ticket man replies, "it's art."

"Oh..." mumbles the kid, "art...."

And he walks away, not realizing that, for him, the Groeninge Museum would be torture.

---

with their window-on-the-world, 3-D realism. Petrus Christus, one of Jan van Eyck's students, studied the Italian style and set out to conquer space.

The focus of his *Annunciation* panel is not the winged angel

announcing Jesus' coming birth, nor is it the swooning, astonished Mary—it's the empty space between them. Your eye focuses back across the floor tiles and through the open doorway to gabled houses on a quiet canal in the far distance.

In the *Nativity* panel, the three angels hovering overhead really should be bigger, and the porch over the group looks a little rickety. Compared to the work of Florence's Renaissance painters, this is quite...primitive.

• *Fast-forward a few centuries (through Rooms 5–8), past paintings by no-name artists from Bruges' years of decline, to a couple of Belgium's 20th-century masters in Room 9...*

GROENINGE MUSEUM

Paul Delvaux (1897-1994)—*Serenity* (1970)

Perhaps there's some vague connection between Van Eyck's medieval symbols and the Surrealist images of Paul Delvaux. Regardless, Delvaux gained fame for his nudes sleepwalking through moonlit, video-game landscapes.

René Magritte (1898-1967)—*The Assault* (c. 1932)

Magritte had his own private reserve of symbolic images. The cloudy sky, female torso, windows, and horsebell (the ball with the slit) appear in other works as well. They're arranged here side by side as if they should mean something, but they—as well as the title—only serve to short-circuit your thoughts when you try to make sense of them. Magritte paints real objects with photographic clarity, then jumbles them together in new and provocative ways.

Scenes of Bruges

Remember that Jan van Eyck, Petrus Christus, Hans Memling, Gerard David, Jan Provoost, and possibly Rogier van der Weyden (for a few years) all lived and worked in Bruges.

In addition, many other artists included scenes of the picturesque city in their art, proving that it looks today much as it did way back when. Enjoy the many painted scenes of old Bruges as a slice-of-life peek into the city and its people back in its glory days.

MEMLING MUSEUM TOUR

Located in the former hospital wards and church of St. John's Hospital, the Memling Museum (Memling in Sint-Jan Hospitaalmuseum) offers a glimpse into medieval medicine, displaying surgical instruments, documents, and visual aids as you work your way to the museum's climax: several of Hans Memling's glowing masterpieces.

ORIENTATION

Cost: €8, includes fine audioguide and free loaner folding chairs (if you'd like to sit and study the paintings).

Hours: Tue–Sun 9:30–17:00, closed Mon.

Getting There: The museum is at Mariastraat 38, across the street from the Church of Our Lady.

Information: Bruges museums tel. 050-448-711.

Length of This Tour: Allow one hour.

Overview

Hans Memling's art was the culmination of Bruges' Flemish Primitive style. His serene, soft-focus, motionless scenes capture a medieval piety that was quickly fading. The popular style made Memling (c. 1430–1494) one of Bruges' wealthiest citizens, and his work was gobbled up by visiting Italian merchants, who took it home with them, cross-pollinating European art.

The displays on medieval medicine are all on one floor of the former church, with the Memlings in a chapel at the far end.

THE TOUR BEGINS

The Church as a Hospital

Some 500 years ago, the nave of this former church was lined with beds filled with the sick and dying. Nuns served as nurses. At the far end was the high altar, which once displayed Memling's *St. John Altarpiece* (which we'll see). Bedridden patients could gaze on this peaceful, colorful vision and gain a moment's comfort from their agonies.

As the museum displays make clear, medicine of the day was well-intentioned but very crude. In many ways, this was less a hos-

pital than a hospice, helping the down-and-out make the transition from this world to the next. Religious art (displayed further along in the museum) was therapeutic, addressing the patients' mental and spiritual health. The numerous Crucifixions reminded the sufferers that

Christ could feel their pain, having lived it himself.

• *Continue through the displays of religious art—past paintings that make you thankful for modern medicine. Head through the wooden archway to the black-and-white tiled room where Memling's paintings are displayed. A large triptych (three-paneled altarpiece) dominates the space.*

St. John Altarpiece (a.k.a. *The Mystical Marriage of St. Catherine,* 1474)

Sick and dying patients lay in their beds in the hospital and looked at this colorful, three-part work, which sat atop the hospital/church's high altar. The piece was dedicated to the hospital's patron saints, John the Baptist and John the Evangelist (see the inscription along the bottom frame), but Memling broadened the focus to take in a vision of heaven and the end of the world.

Central Panel: Mary, with baby Jesus on her lap, sits in a canopied chair, crowned by hovering blue angels. It's an imaginary gathering of conversing saints *(sacra conversazione),* though nobody in this meditative group is saying a word or even exchanging meaningful eye contact.

Some Memling Trademarks

- Serene symmetry, with little motion or emotion
- Serious faces that are realistic but timeless, with blemishes airbrushed out
- Eye-catching details like precious carpets, mirrors, and brocaded clothes
- Glowing colors, even lighting, no shadows
- Cityscape backgrounds

Mary is flanked by the two Johns—John the Baptist to the left, and John the Evangelist (in red) to the right. Everyone else

sits symmetrically around Mary. An organist angel to the left is matched by a book-holding acolyte to the right. St. Catherine (left, in white, red, and gold) balances St. Barbara, in green, who's absorbed in her book. Behind them, classical columns are also perfectly balanced left and right.

At the center of it all, baby Jesus tips the balance by leaning over to place a ring on Catherine's finger, sealing the "mystical marriage" between them.

St. Catherine of Alexandria, born rich, smart, and pagan to Roman parents, joined the outlawed Christian faith. She spoke out against pagan Rome, attracting the attention of the emperor, Maxentius, who sent 50 philosophers to talk some sense into her—but she countered every argument, even converting the emperor's own wife. Maxentius killed his wife, then asked Catherine to marry him. She refused, determined to remain true to the man she'd already "married" in a mystical vision—Christ.

Frustrated, Maxentius ordered Catherine to be stretched across a large, spiked wheel (the rather quaint-looking object at her feet), but the wheel flew apart, sparing her and killing many of her torturers. So they just cut her head off, which is why she has a sword, along with her "Catherine Wheel."

Looking through the columns, we see scenes of Bruges. Just to the right of the chair's canopy, the wooden contraption is a crane, used to hoist barrels from barges on Kraanplein.

Left Panel—The Beheading of John the Baptist: Even this gruesome scene, with blood still spurting from John's severed neck, becomes serene under Memling's gentle brush. Everyone is solemn, graceful, and emotionless—including both parts of the decapitated John. Memling depicts Salomé (in green) receiving the

head on her silver platter with a humble servant's downcast eyes, as if accepting her role in God's wonderful, if sometimes painful, plan.

In the background, left, we can look into Herod's palace, where he sits at a banquet table with his wife while Salomé dances modestly in front of him. Herod's lust is only hinted at with the naked statues—a man between two women—that adorn the palace exterior.

Right Panel—John the Evangelist's Vision of the Apocalypse: John sits on a high, rocky bluff on the island of Patmos and sees the end of the world as we know it...and he feels fine.

Overhead, in a rainbow bubble, God appears on his throne, resting his hand on a sealed book. A lamb steps up to open the seals, unleashing the awful events at the end of time. Standing at the bottom of the rainbow, an angel in green gestures to John and says, "Write this down." John starts to dip his quill into the inkwell (his other hand holds the quill-sharpener), but he pauses, absolutely transfixed, experiencing the Apocalypse now.

He sees wars, fires, and plagues on the horizon, the Virgin in the sky rebuking a red dragon, and many other wonders. Fervent fundamentalists should bring their Bibles along, because there are many specific references brought to life in a literal way.

In the center ride the dreaded Four Horsemen, wreaking havoc on the cosmos (galloping over either islands or clouds). Horseman number four is a skeleton, followed by a human-eating monster head. Helpless mortals on the right seek shelter in the rocks, but find none.

Memling has been criticized for building a career by copying the formulas of his predecessors, but this panel is a complete original. Its theme had never been so fully expressed, and the bright, contrasting colors and vivid imagery are almost modern. In the *St. John Altarpiece*, Memling shows us the full range of his palette, from medieval grace to Renaissance symmetry, from the real to the surreal.

• *In a glass case, find the...*

MEMLING MUSEUM TOUR

St. Ursula Shrine (c. 1489)

On October 21, 1489, the mortal remains of St. Ursula were brought here to the church and placed in this gilded oak shrine, built spe-

cially for the occasion and decorated with paintings by Memling. Ursula, yet another Christian martyred by the ancient Romans, became a sensation in the Middle Ages when builders in Germany's Köln (Cologne) unearthed a huge pile of bones believed to belong to her and her 11,000 slaughtered cohorts.

The shrine, carved of wood and covered with gold, looks like a miniature Gothic church (similar to the hospital church). Memling was asked to fill in the "church's" stained-glass windows with six arch-shaped paintings telling Ursula's well-known legend.

• *Stand in the middle of the room, facing the shrine. "Read" the shrine's story from left to right, circling counterclockwise, but begin with the...*

Left Panel: Ursula—in white and blue—arrives by boat at the city of Köln and enters through the city gate. She's on a pilgrimage to Rome, accompanied by 11,000 (female) virgins. That night (look in the two windows of the house in the background, right), an angel appears and tells her this trip will mean her death, but she is undaunted.

Center Panel: Continuing up the Rhine, they arrive in Basel. (Memling knew the Rhine, having grown up near it.) Memling condenses the 11,000 virgins to a more manageable 11, making each one pure enough for a thousand. From Basel, they set out on foot (in the background, right) over the snowy Alps.

Right Panel: They arrive in Rome—formally portrayed by a round Renaissance tower decorated with *putti* (little angels)— where Ursula falls to her knees before the pope at the church steps. Kneeling behind Ursula is her fiancé, Etherus, the pagan prince of England. She has agreed to marry him only if he becomes a Christian and refrains from the marriage bed long enough for her to make this three-year pilgrimage as a virgin (making, I guess, number 11,001). Inside the church on the right side, he is baptized a Christian.

Opposite Side—Left Panel: They head back home. Here, they're leaving Basel, boarding ships to go north on the Rhine. The pope was so inspired by these virgins that he joined them. These "crowd" scenes are hardly realistic—more like a collage of individual poses and faces. And Memling tells the story with extremely minimal acting. Perhaps his inspiration was the pomp and ceremony of Bruges parades, which were introduced by the

Burgundian dukes. He would have seen *tableaux vivants,* where Brugeois would pose in costume like human statues to enact an event from the Bible or from city history. (American "living Christmas crèches" carry on this dying art form.)

Middle Panel: Back in Köln, a surprise awaits them—the city has been taken over by vicious Huns. They grab Etherus and stab him. He dies in Ursula's arms.

Right Panel: The Hun king (in red with turban and beard) woos Ursula, placing his hand over his heart, but she says, "No

way." So a Hun soldier draws his arrow and prepares to shoot her dead. Even here, at the climax of the story, there are no histrionics. Even the dog just sits down, crosses his paws, and watches. The whole shrine cycle is as posed, motionless, and colorful as the *tableaux vivants* that may have inaugurated the shrine here in this church in 1489.

In the background behind Ursula, a Bruges couple looks on sympathetically. This may be Memling himself (in red coat with fur lining) and his wife, Anna, who bore his three children. Behind them, Memling renders an accurate city skyline of Köln, including a side view of the Köln Cathedral (missing its still-unfinished tall spires).

• *In the small adjoining room, find several more Memlings.*

Portrait of a Young Woman (1480)

Memling's bread-and-butter was portraits done for families of wealthy merchants (especially visiting Italians and Portuguese). This portrait takes us right back to that time.

The young woman looks out of the frame as if she were look-

ing out a window. Her hands rest on the "sill," with the fingertips sticking over. The frame is original, but the banner and Van Eyck–like lettering are not.

Her clothes look somewhat simple, but they were high-class in their day. A dark damask dress is brightened by a red sash and a detachable white collar. She's pulled her hair into a tight bun at the back, pinned there with a fez-like cap and draped with a transparent veil. She's shaved her hairline and plucked her brows to get that clean, high-forehead look. Her ensemble is animated by a well-placed necklace of small stones.

Memling accentuates her fashionably pale complexion and gives her a pensive, sober expression, portraying her like a medieval saint. Still, she keeps her personality, with distinct features like the broad nose, neck tendons, and realistic hands. She peers out from her subtly painted veil, which sweeps down over the side of her face. What's she thinking?

Diptych of Martin van Nieuwenhove (1489)

Three-dimensional effects—borrowed from the Italian Renaissance style—enliven this traditional two-panel altarpiece. Both Mary-and-Child and the 23-year-old Martin, though in different panels, inhabit the same room within the painting.

Stand right in front of Mary, facing her directly. If you line up

the paintings' horizons (seen in the distance, out the room's windows), you'll see that both panels depict the same room— a room with two windows at the back and two along the right wall.

Want proof? In the convex mirror on the back wall (just to the left of Mary), the scene is reflected back at us, showing Mary and Martin from behind, silhouetted in the two "windows" of the picture frames. Apparently, Mary makes house calls, appearing right in the living room of the young donor Martin, the wealthy, unique-looking heir to his father's business.

SLEEPING

Bruges is a great place to sleep, with Gothic spires out your window, no traffic noise, and the cheerily out-of-tune carillon heralding each new day at 8:00 sharp. (Thankfully, the bell tower is silent from 22:00 to 8:00.) Most Bruges accommodations are located between the train station and the old center, with the most distant (and best) being a few blocks to the north and east of Market Square.

B&Bs offer the best value (listed after "Hotels," on page 364). All are on quiet streets and (with a few exceptions) keep the same prices throughout the year.

Bruges is most crowded Friday and Saturday evenings from Easter through October, with July and August weekends being the worst. Many hotels charge a bit more on Friday and Saturday, and won't let you stay just one night if it's a Saturday.

Hotels

$$$ Hotel Heritage offers 24 rooms, with chandeliers that seem hung especially for you, in a solid and completely modernized old building with luxurious public spaces. Tastefully decorated and offering all the amenities, it's one of those places that does everything just right yet still feels warm and inviting—if you can afford it (Db-€192, superior Db-€238, deluxe Db-€286, includes breakfast, skipping their fine breakfast saves €17 per person, non-smoking, air-con, elevator, Internet access, sauna, tanning bed, fitness room, bike rental, Niklaas Desparsstraat 11, a block north of Market Square, tel. 050-444-444, fax 050-444-440, www .hotel-heritage.com, info@hotel-heritage.com). It's run by cheery and hardworking Johan and Isabelle Creytens.

$$$ Hotel Egmond is a creaky mansion located in the middle of the quietly idyllic Minnewater. Its eight 18th-century

Sleep Code

(€1 = about $1.40, country code: 32)
S = Single, **D** = Double/Twin, **T** = Triple, **Q** = Quad, **b** = bathroom,
s = shower only. Everyone speaks English. Unless otherwise
noted, credit cards are accepted.

To help you easily sort through these listings, I've divided
the rooms into three categories, based on the price for a
standard double room with bath:

$$$ Higher Priced—Most rooms €125 or more.
$$ Moderately Priced—Most rooms between €80–125.
$ Lower Priced—Most rooms €80 or less.

rooms are plain, with small modern baths shoehorned in, and the
guests-only garden is just waiting for a tea party. This hotel is ideal
for romantics who want a countryside setting—where you sleep
surrounded by a park, not a city (Sb-€97, small twin Db-€103,
larger Db-€125, Tb-€155, about €20 more Fri–Sat, parking-€10,
Minnewater 15, tel. 050-341-445, fax 050-342-940, www.egmond
.be, info@egmond.be).

$$ Hotel Adornes is small and classy—a great value situated
in the most charming part of town. This 17th-century canalside
house has 20 rooms with full modern bathrooms, free parking
(reserve in advance), free loaner bikes, and a cellar lounge with
games and videos (small Db-€120, larger Db-€140–150, Tb-€165,
Qb-€175, includes breakfast, elevator, near Carmersstraat at St.
Annarei 26, tel. 050-341-336, fax 050-342-085, www.adornes.be,
info@adornes.be). Nathalie runs the family business.

$$ Hotel Patritius, family-run and centrally located, is a
grand, circa-1830, Neoclassical mansion with hardwood oak floors
in its 16 stately rooms. It features a plush lounge, a chandeliered
breakfast room, and a courtyard garden. This is the best value in its
price range (Db-€100–122 depending on size, €10 more Fri–Sat;
Tb-€140, Qb-€165, €25 for extra bed, includes breakfast, coin-
op laundry, parking-€7, garage parking-€12, Riddersstraat 11,
tel. 050-338-454, fax 050-339-634, www.hotelpatritius.be, info
@hotelpatritius.be, Garrett and Elvi Spaey).

$$ Hotel Botaniek, quietly located a block from Astrid Park,
is a fine, pint-sized hotel with a comfy lounge, renting nine rooms
(Db-€92 weekday special for Rick Steves' readers, €98 Fri–Sat;
Tb-€120, Qb-€140, less for longer and off-season stays, free
museum-discount card, elevator, Waalsestraat 23, tel. 050-341-424,
fax 050-345-939, www.botaniek.be, info@botaniek.be, Yasmine).

$$ Hotel ter Reien is big and basic, with 26 rooms overlooking a canal in the town center (Db-€90–100, Tb-€110–130,

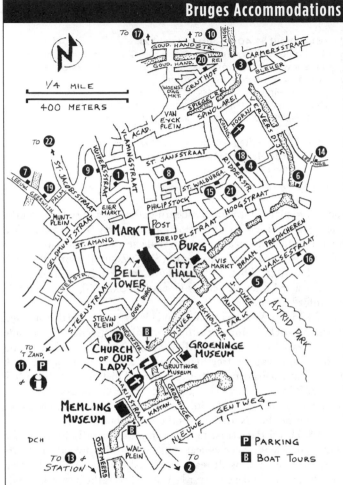

Bruges Accommodations

1. Hotels Heritage & Nicolas
2. To Hotel Egmond
3. Hotel Adornes
4. Hotel Patritius
5. Hotel Botaniek
6. Hotel ter Reien
7. Walwyck Cool Down Hotel
8. Hotel Cordoeanier
9. Hotel Cavalier
10. To Hotel de Pauw
11. To Hotel Imperial & Passage Hostel
12. Hotel Notre Dame
13. To Hotel 't Keizershof
14. Absoluut Verhulst B&B
15. B&B Setola
16. Dieltiens B&B
17. To Debruyne B&B
18. Gheeraert-Vandevelde B&B
19. 't Geerwijn B&B
20. Royal Stewart B&B
21. Charlie Rockets Hostel
22. To Snuffel Backpacker Hostel

Qb-€135–150, €10 off for viewless rooms, extra bed-€20, 10 percent Rick Steves discount if you ask when you reserve and show this book at check-in, includes breakfast, Internet access and Wi-Fi, Langestraat 1, tel. 050-349-100, fax 050-340-048, www.hotel terreien.be, info@hotelterreien.be, owners Diederik and Stephanie Pille-Maes).

$$ Walwyck Cool Down Hotel—a bit of modern comfort, chic design, and English verbiage in a medieval shell—is a new, nicely located hotel with 18 spacious rooms (Db-€90, includes breakfast, Wi-Fi, Leeuwstraat 8, tel. 050-616-360, www.walwyck .com, rooms@walwyck.com).

$ Hotel Cordoeanier, a charming family-run hotel, rents 22 bright, simple, well-worn rooms on a quiet street two blocks off Market Square. It's the best cheap hotel in town (Sb-€65–75, Db-€70–85, twin Db-€80–95, Tb-€90–105, Qb-€110, Quint/b-€130, these cash-only prices valid with this book, Cordoeanierstraat 16–18, tel. 050-339-051, fax 050-346-111, www .cordoeanier.be, info@cordoeanier.be, run by Kris, Veerle, and family).

$ Hotel Cavalier, with more stairs than character, rents eight decent rooms and serves a hearty buffet breakfast in a once-royal setting (Sb-€55, Db-€65, Tb-€78, Qb-€90, two lofty "backpackers' doubles" on fourth floor-€42 or €47, includes breakfast, Kuipers-straat 25, tel. 050-330-207, fax 050-347-199, www.hotelcavalier.be, info@hotelcavalier.be, run by friendly Viviane De Clerck).

$ Hotel de Pauw is tall, skinny, and family-run, with eight straightforward rooms on a quiet street next to a church (Sb-€65, Db-€70–80, free and easy street parking, Sint Gilliskerkhof 8, tel. 050-337-118, fax 050-345-140, www.hoteldepauw.be, info @hoteldepauw.be, Philippe and Hilde).

$ Hotel Nicolas feels like an old-time boarding house that missed Bruges' affluence bandwagon. Its 14 big, plain rooms are a good value, and the location is ideal—on a quiet street a block off Market Square (Sb-€50, Db-€60–62, Tb-€73, includes breakfast, Niklaas Desparsstraat 9, tel. 050-335-502, fax 050-343-544, www .hotelnicolas.be, hotel.nicolas@telenet.be, Yi-Ling and Thomas).

$ Hotel Imperial is an old-school hotel with seven old-school rooms. It's simple and well-run in a charming building on a handy, quiet street. The fact that Paul Bernolet and Hilde don't use email fits its character (Db-€65–80, includes breakfast, Dweersstraat 24, tel. 050-339-014, fax 050-344-306).

$ Hotel Notre Dame is a humble and blocky little budget option, renting 12 decent rooms in the busy thick of things (Db-€70–75, includes breakfast, Mariastraat 3, tel. 050-333-193, fax 050-337-608, www.hotelnotredame.be, info@hotelnotredame.be).

Near the Train Station: **$ Hotel 't Keizershof** is a dollhouse of a hotel that lives by its motto, "Spend a night...not a fortune." It's simple and tidy, with seven small, cheery, old-time rooms split between two floors, with a shower and toilet on each (S-€25, D-€44, T-€66, Q-€80, includes breakfast, cash only, free and easy parking, laundry service-€7.50, Oostmeers 126, a block in front of station, tel. 050-338-728, www.hotelkeizershof.be, info @hotelkeizershof.be). The hotel is run by Stefaan and Hilde, with decor by their children, Lorie and Fien.

Bed-and-Breakfasts

These B&Bs, run by people who enjoy their work, offer a better value than hotels. Most families rent out their entire top floor—generally three rooms and a small sitting area. And most are mod and stylish, they're just in medieval shells. Each is central, with lots of stairs and €70 doubles you'd pay €100 for in a hotel. Most places charge €10 extra for one-night stays. It's possible to find parking on the street in the evening (pay 9:00–19:00, 2-hour maximum for metered parking during the day, free overnight).

$$ Absoluut Verhulst is a great, modern-feeling B&B in a 400-year-old house, run by friendly Frieda and Benno (Db-€90, huge and lofty suite-€120 for two, €140 for three, and €160 for four, €10 more for one-night stays, cash only, non-smoking, Wi-Fi, five-minute walk east of Market Square at Verbrand Nieuwland 1, tel. 050-334-515, www.b-bverhulst.com, b-b.verhulst@pandora.be).

$ B&B Setola, run by Lut and Bruno Setola, offers three modern expansive rooms and a spacious breakfast/living room on the top floor of their house. The family room has a fun loft (Sb-€60, Db-€70, €20 per extra person, €10 more for one-night stays, Wi-Fi, 5-min walk from Market Square, Sint Walburgastraat 12, tel. 050-334-977, fax 050-332-551, www.bedandbreakfast-bruges .com, setola@bedandbreakfast-bruges.com).

$ Koen and Annemie Dieltiens are a friendly couple who enjoy getting to know their guests while sharing a wealth of information on Bruges. You'll eat a hearty breakfast around a big table in their comfortable house (Sb-€60, Db-€70, Tb-€90, €10 more for one-night stays, cash only, Wi-Fi, Waalse Straat 40, three blocks southeast of Burg Square, tel. 050-334-294, www.bedand breakfastbruges.be, dieltiens@bedandbreakfastbruges.be).

$ Debruyne B&B, run by Marie-Rose and her architect husband, Ronny, offers three rooms with artsy, original decor (check out the elephant-size white doors—Ronny's design) and genuine warmth. If Gothic is getting old, this is refreshingly modern (Sb-€55, Db-€60, Tb-€90, €10 more for one-night stays, cash only, Internet access, seven-minute walk north of Market Square, two blocks from the little church at Lange Raamstraat 18, tel. 050-347-

606, www.bedandbreakfastbruges.com, mietjedebruyne@yahoo .co.uk).

$ Paul and Roos Gheeraert-Vandevelde live in a Neoclassical mansion and rent three huge, bright, comfy rooms (Sb-€60, Db-€70, Tb-€90, two-night minimum stay required, cash only, strictly non-smoking, fridges in rooms, Internet access and Wi-Fi, Riddersstraat 9, 5-min walk east of Market Square, tel. 050-335-627, fax 050-345-201, www.bb-bruges.be, bb-bruges@skynet.be).

$ 't Geerwijn B&B, run by Chris de Loof, offers homey rooms in the old center. Check out the fun, lofty A-frame room upstairs (Ds/Db-€65, Tb-€75, pleasant breakfast room and a royal lounge, cash only, non-smoking, Geerwijnstraat 14, tel. 050-340-544, fax 050-343-721, www.geerwijn.be, chris.deloof@scarlet.be). Chris also rents an apartment that sleeps five (€100).

$ Royal Stewart B&B, run by Scottish Maggie and her husband, Gilbert, has three thoughtfully decorated rooms in a quiet, almost cloistered 17th-century house that was inhabited by nuns until 1953 (S-€45, D/Db-€62, Tb-€82, cash only, pleasant breakfast room, Genthof 25–27, 5-min walk from Market Square, tel. 050-337-918, fax 050-337-918, www.royalstewart.be, r.stewart @pandora.be).

Hostels

Bruges has several good hostels offering beds for around €15 in two- to eight-bed rooms. Breakfast is about €3 extra. The American-style **$ Charlie Rockets** hostel (and bar) is the liveliest and most central. The ground floor feels like a 19th-century sports bar, with a foosball-and-movie-posters party ambience. Upstairs is an industrial-strength pile of hostel dorms (90 beds, €16 per bed with sheets, 4–6 beds per room, D-€50, lockers, Hoogstraat 19, tel. 050-330-660, www.charlierockets.com). Other small, loose, and central places are **$ Snuffel Backpacker Hostel** (56 beds, €14–18 per bed includes sheets and breakfast, 4–14 beds per room, open 24/7, Ezelstraat 47, tel. 050-333-133, www.snuffel.be) and the minimal and funky **$ Passage** (€14, 4–7 beds per room, D-€50, Db-€65, prices include sheets, Dweerstraat 26, tel. 050-340-232, www.passagebruges.com, info@passagebruges.com).

EATING AND NIGHTLIFE

Belgium is where France meets northern Europe, and you'll find a good mix of both Flemish and French influences in Bruges and Brussels. As you're enjoying Belgian cuisine, it's interesting to note that the Flemish were ruled by the French and absorbed some of the fancy cuisine and etiquette of their overlords. The Dutch, on the other hand, were ruled by the Spanish for 80 years and picked up nothing.

Popular Throughout Belgium

Moules: Mussels are served everywhere, either cooked plain *(nature)*, with white wine *(vin blanc)*, with shallots or onions *(marinière)*, or in a tomato sauce *(provençale)*. You get a big-enough-for-two bucket and a pile of fries. Go local by using one empty shell to tweeze out the rest of the *moules*. When the mollusks are in season, from about mid-July through April, you'll get the big Dutch mussels. Locals take a break in May and June, when only the puny Danish kind are available.

Frites: Belgian-style fries (*Vlaamse frites,* or Flemish fries) taste so good because they're deep-fried twice—once to cook, and once to brown. The natives eat them with mayonnaise, not ketchup.

Flemish Specialties

These specialties are traditional to Bruges, but also available in Brussels.

Carbonnade: Rich beef stew flavored with onions and beer.

Chou rouge à la flamande: Red cabbage with onions and prunes.

Flamiche: Cheese pie with onions.

Flemish asparagus: White asparagus (fresh in springtime) in cream sauce.

Lapin à la flamande: Marinated rabbit braised in onions and prunes.
Soupe à la bière: Beer soup.
Stoemp: Mashed potatoes and vegetables.
Waterzooi: Creamy meat stew (chicken, eel, or fish).
...à la flamande: Anything cooked in the local Flemish style.

Brussels Specialties

These specialties are "native" to Brussels (which tends toward French cuisine), but you'll find them in Bruges, too.
Anguilles au vert: Eel in green herb sauce.
Caricoles: Sea snails. Very local, seasonal, and hard to find, these are usually sold hot by street vendors.
Cheeses: Remoudou and Djotte de Nivelles are made locally.
Choux de Bruxelles: Brussels sprouts (in cream sauce).
Crevettes: Shrimp, often served as croquettes (minced and stuffed in breaded, deep-fried rolls).
Croque monsieur: Grilled ham-and-cheese sandwich.
Endive: Typical Belgian vegetable (also called *chicoree* or *chicon*) served as a side dish.
Filet américain: Beware—for some reason, steak tartare (raw) is called "American."
Tartine de fromage blanc: Open-face cream-cheese sandwich, often enjoyed with a cherry Kriek beer.
...à la brabançonne: Anything cooked in the local Brabant (Brussels) style, such as *faisant* (pheasant) *à la brabançonne.*

Desserts and Snacks

Cramique: Currant roll.
Craquelin: Currant roll with sugar sprinkles.
Dame blanche: Hot-fudge sundae.
Gaufres: Waffles, sold hot in small shops.
Pistolets: Round croissants.
Pralines: Filled Belgian chocolates.
Spekuloos: Spicy gingerbread biscuits served with coffee.

Belgian Beers

Belgium has about 120 different varieties of beer and 580 different brands, more than any other country...and the locals take their beers as seriously as the French do their wines. Even small café menus include six to eight varieties. Connoisseurs and novices alike can be confused by the many choices, and casual drinkers probably won't like every kind offered, since some varieties don't even taste like beer. Belgian beer is generally yeastier and higher in alcohol than beers in other countries.

In Belgium, certain beers are paired with certain dishes. To bring out their flavor, different beers are served at cold, cool, or room temperature, and each has its own distinctive glass. Whether wide-mouthed, tall, or fluted, with or without a stem, the glass is meant to highlight the beer's qualities. A memorable Belgian beer experience is drinking a Kwak beer in its traditional tall glass. The glass, which widens at the base, stands in a wooden holder, and you pick the whole apparatus up—frame and glass—and drink. As you near the end, the beer in the wide bottom comes out at you quickly, with a "Kwak! Kwak! Kwak!" Critics say this gimmick distracts from the fact that Kwak beer is mediocre at best.

To get a draft beer in Bruges, where Flemish is the dominant language, ask for *een pintje* (ayn pinch-ya; a pint), and in Brussels, where French prevails, request *une bière* (oon bee-yair). Don't insist on beer from the tap. The only way to offer so many excellent beers fresh is to serve them bottled, and the best varieties are generally available only by the bottle. "Cheers" is *proost* or *gezondheid* in Flemish, and *santé* (sahn-tay) in French. The colorful cardboard coasters make nice, free souvenirs.

Here's a breakdown of types of beer, with some common brand names you'll find either on tap or in bottles. (Some beers require a second fermentation in the bottle, so they're only available in bottles.) This list is just a start, and you'll find many beers that don't fall into these neat categories. For encyclopedic information on Belgian beers, visit www.belgianstyle.com.

Ales (Blonde/Red/Amber/Brown): Ales are easily recognized by their color. Try a blonde or golden ale (Leffe Blonde, Duvel), a rare and bitter sour red (Rodenbach), an amber (Palm, De Koninck), or a brown (Leffe Bruin). The last surviving Bruges beer is the prize-winning Brugse Zot (Bruges Fool), a golden ale.

Lagers: These are the light, sparkling, Budweiser-type beers. Popular brands include Jupiler, Stella Artois, and Maes.

Lambics: Perhaps the most unusual and least beer-like, *lambics* are stored for years in wooden casks, fermenting from wild yeasts that occur naturally in the air. Tasting more like a dry and bitter farmhouse cider, pure *lambic* is often blended with fruits to counter the sour flavor. Some brand names include Cantillon, Lindemans, and Mort-Subite ("Sudden Death").

Fruit *lambics* include those made with cherries *(kriek)*, raspberries *(frambozen)*, peaches *(pêche)*, or black currants *(cassis)*. The result for each is a tart but sweet beer, similar to a dry pink champagne. People who don't usually enjoy beer tend to like these fruit-flavored varieties.

White *(Witte):* Based on wheat instead of hops, these are milky-yellow summertime beers. White beer, similar to a Hefeweizen in the United States, is often flavored with spices such as orange peel or coriander.

Trappist Beers: For centuries, between their vespers and matins, Trappist monks have been brewing heavily fermented, malty beers. Three typical Trappist beers (from the Westmalle monastery) are Trippel, with a blonde color, served cold with a frothy head; Dubbel, which is dark, sweet, and served cool; and Single, made especially by the monks for the monks, and considered a fair trade for a life of celibacy. Other Trappist monasteries include Rochefort, Chimay, and Orval. Try the Trappist Blauwe Chimay—extremely smooth, milkshake-like, and complex.

Strong Beers: The potent brands include Duvel (meaning "devil," because of its high octane, camouflaged by a pale color), Verboten Vrucht ("forbidden fruit," with Adam and Eve on the label), and the not-for-the-fainthearted brands of Judas, Satan, and Lucifer. Gouden Carolus is good and Delerium Tremens speaks for itself.

Mass-Produced Beers: Connoisseurs say you should avoid the mass-produced labels (Leffe, Stella, and Hoegaarden—all owned by InBev, which just bought Budweiser in America) when you can enjoy a Belgian microbrew (like Chimay) instead.

RESTAURANTS

Bruges' specialties include mussels cooked a variety of ways (one order can feed two), fish dishes, grilled meats, and french fries. Don't eat before 19:30 unless you like eating alone (or with other tourists).

Tax and service are always included in your bill (though a 5–10 percent tip is appreciated). You can't get free tap water; Belgian restaurateurs are emphatic about that. While tap water comes with a smile in Holland, France, and Germany, it's not the case in Belgium, where you'll either pay for water, enjoy the beer, or go thirsty.

You'll find plenty of affordable, touristy restaurants on floodlit squares and along dreamy canals. Bruges feeds 3.5 million tourists a year, and most are seduced by a high-profile location. These can be fine experiences for the magical setting and views, but the quality of food and service will likely be low. I wouldn't blame you for eating at one of these places, but I won't recommend any. I prefer the candle-cool bistros that flicker on back streets. Here are my favorites:

Rock Fort is a chic, eight-table spot with a modern, fresh coziness and a high-powered respect for good food. Two young chefs, Peter Laloo and Hermes Vanliefde, give their French

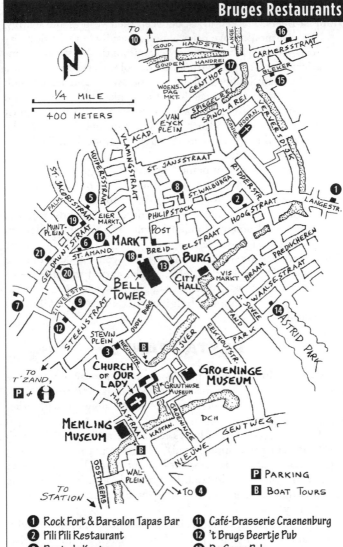

Bruges Restaurants

1. Rock Fort & Barsalon Tapas Bar
2. Pili Pili Restaurant
3. Rest. de Koetse
4. To Bistro de Bekoring
5. Bistro in den Wittenkop
6. Bistro den Amand & Medard Brasserie
7. The Flemish Pot
8. Lotus Vegetarian Restaurant
9. The Hobbit
10. To Tom's Diner

11. Café-Brasserie Craenenburg
12. 't Brugs Beertje Pub
13. De Garre Pub
14. L'Estaminet Restaurant
15. Herberg Vlissinghe Pub
16. Pub 't Gezelleke
17. Café Terrastje
18. Frituur Stands
19. Pickles Frituur
20. Laurenzino Waffles
21. Gelateria Da Vinci & Grocery

P Parking
B Boat Tours

cuisine a creative and gourmet twist. Reservations are required for dinner but not lunch. This place is a winner (€13 Mon–Fri lunch special with coffee, beautifully presented €19–24 dinner plates, fancy €49 fixed-price meal includes dessert, open Mon–Fri 12:00–14:30 & 18:30–23:00, closed Sat–Sun, great pastas and salads, Langestraat 15, tel. 050-334-113). They also run the Barsalon restaurant next door.

Barsalon Tapas Bar, more than a tapas bar, is the brainchild of Peter Laloo from Rock Fort (listed above), allowing him to spread his creative cooking energy. This long, skinny slice of L.A. thrives late into the evening with Bruges' beautiful people. Choose between the long bar, comfy stools, and bigger tables in back. Come early for fewer crowds. The playful menu comes with €6–10 "tapas" dishes taking you from Spain to Japan (three fill two hungry travelers) and more elaborate €14 plates. And don't overlook their daily "suggestions" board with some special wines by the glass and a "teaser" sampler plate of desserts. The €35 five-tapas special is a whole meal. Barsalon shares the same kitchen, hours, and dressy local clientele as the adjacent Rock Fort.

Pili Pili is a mod and inviting pasta eatery, where Gianna Santy handles the customers while husband Allan Hilverson prepares and serves pastas and great salads at good prices. It's clean, low-key, and brimming with quality food and snappy service (€10 lunch plate with wine, €8–10 pasta, Thu–Tue 12:00–14:30 & 18:00–22:30, closed Wed, Hoogstraat 17, tel. 050-491-149).

Restaurant de Koetse is a good bet for central, affordable, quality, local-style food. The feeling is traditional, a bit formal, and dressy yet accessible. The cuisine is Belgian and French, with an emphasis on grilled meat, seafood, and mussels (€28–37 three-course meals, €20–25 plates include vegetables and a salad, Fri–Wed 12:00–14:30 & 18:00–22:00, closed Thu, non-smoking section, Oude Burg 31, tel. 050-337-680, Piet).

Bistro de Bekoring, cute, candlelit, and Gothic, fills two almshouses and a delightful terrace with people thankful for good food. Rotund and friendly Chef Roland and his wife, Gerda, love to tempt the hungry—as the name of their bistro implies. They serve traditional Flemish food (especially eel and beer-soaked stew) from a small menu to people who like holding hands as they dine. Reservations are smart (€12 weekday lunch, €35 fixed-price dinners, €42 with wine, Wed–Sat 12:00–13:30 and from 18:30, closed Sun evening and Mon–Tue; out past the Begijnhof at Arsenaalstraat 53, tel. 050-344-157).

Bistro in den Wittenkop, very Flemish, is a stylishly cluttered, laid-back, old-time place specializing in the local favorites. While Lieve cooks, her husband Daniel serves in a cool-and-jazzy, candlelit ambience (€35 three-course meal, €20–25 plates, Tue–Sat

12:00–14:00 & 18:00–21:30, closed Sun–Mon, reserve ahead, terrace in back in summer, Sint Jakobsstraat 14, tel. 050-332-059).

Bistro den Amand, with a plain interior and a few outdoor tables, exudes unpretentious quality the moment you step in. In this mussels-free zone, Chef Arnout is enthusiastic about vegetables as his busy wok and fun salads prove. It's on a busy pedestrian lane a half-block off the Market Square (€30 three-course meal, €20 plates; Mon–Tue and Thu–Sat 12:00–14:00 & 18:00–21:00, closed Wed and Sun; Sint-Amandstraat 4, tel. 050-340-122, An Vissers and Arnout Beyaert). Reservations are smart for dinner.

The Flemish Pot (a.k.a. The Little Pancake House) is a hard-working eatery serving up traditional peasant-style meals. They crank out pancakes (savory and sweet) and homemade *wafels* for lunch. Then, at 18:00, enthusiastic chefs Mario and Rik stow their waffle irons and pull out a traditional menu of vintage Flemish specialties served in little iron pots and skillets. Seating is tight and cluttered. You'll enjoy huge portions, refills from the hovering "fries maiden," and a good selection of local beers (€26–30 three-course meals, €16–24 plates, Wed–Sun 12:00–22:00, closed Mon–Tue, reservations smart, family-friendly, just off Geldmuntstraat at Helmstraat 3, tel. 050-340-086).

Lotus Vegetarian Restaurant serves serious lunch plates (€10 *plat du jour* offered daily), salads, and homemade chocolate cake in a bustling and upscale setting without a trace of tie-dye. To keep carnivorous spouses happy, they also serve several very good, politically correct (a.k.a. organic) meat dishes (Mon–Sat from 11:45, last orders at 14:00, closed Sun, cash only, just off north of Burg Square at Wapenmakersstraat 5, tel. 050-331-078).

The Hobbit, featuring an entertaining menu, is always busy with happy eaters. For a swinging deal, try the all-you-can-eat spareribs with bread and salad for €16.50. It's nothing fancy, just good, basic food in a fun, traditional grill house (daily 18:00–24:00, family-friendly, Kemelstraat 8–10, reservations smart, tel. 050-335-520).

Tom's Diner is a trendy, stark little "bistro eetcafé" in a quiet, cobbled residential area a 10-minute walk from the center. Young chef Tom gives traditional dishes a delightful modern twist. If you want to flee the tourists and experience a popular neighborhood joint, this is it—the locals love it (€17 plates, Thu–Tue 18:00–24:00, closed Wed, north of Market Square near Sint-Gilliskerk at West-Gistelhof 23, tel. 050-333-382).

Market Square Restaurants: Most tourists seem to be eating on Market Square with the bell tower high overhead and horse carriages clip-clopping by. The square is ringed by tourist traps with aggressive waiters expert at getting you to consume more than you intended. Still, if you order smartly, you can have a memorable meal or drink here on one of the finest squares in Europe at a reasonable price. Consider **Café-Brasserie Craenenburg,** with a straightforward menu, where you can get pasta and beer for €14 and spend all the time you want ogling the magic of Bruges (daily 7:30–24:00, Markt 16, tel. 050-333-402).

Cheap Eats: **Medard Brasserie,** just a block off Market Square, serves the cheapest hot meal in town—hearty meat spaghetti (big plate-€3, huge plate-€5.50, sit inside or out, daily 11:00–20:30, Sint Amandstraat 18, tel. 050-348-684).

Bars Offering Light Meals, Beer, and Ambience

My best budget-eating tip for Bruges: Stop into one of the city's atmospheric bars for a simple meal and a couple of world-class beers with great Bruges ambience. For information on beer, see page 367. The last three pubs listed are in the wonderfully cozy *(gezellig)* quarter, northeast of Market Square.

The **'t Brugs Beertje** is young, convivial, and smoky. While any pub or restaurant carries the basic beers, you'll find a selection here of more than 300 types, including brews to suit any season. They serve light meals, including pâté, spaghetti, toasted sandwiches, and a traditional cheese plate. You're welcome to sit at the bar and talk with the staff (five cheeses, bread, and salad for €11; Thu–Tue 16:00–24:00, closed Wed, Kemelstraat 5, tel. 050-339-616, run by fun-loving manager Daisy).

De Garre is another good place to gain an appreciation of the Belgian beer culture. Rather than a noisy pub scene, it has a dressy, sit-down-and-focus-on-your-friend-and-the-fine-beer vibe. It's mature and cozy with tables, light meals (cold cuts, pâtés, and toasted sandwiches), and a selection of 150 beers (daily 12:00–24:00, additional seating up tiny staircase, off Breidelstraat between Burg and Markt, on tiny Garre alley, tel. 050-341-029).

L'Estaminet is a youthful, jazz-filled eatery, similar to one of Amsterdam's brown cafés. Don't be intimidated by its lack of tourists. Local students flock here for the Tolkien-chic ambience, hearty €9 spaghetti, and big dinner salads. Since this is Belgium, it serves more beer than wine. For outdoor dining under an all-weather canopy, enjoy the relaxed patio facing peaceful Astrid Park (Tue–Wed and Fri–Sun 11:30–24:00, Thu 16:00–24:00, closed Mon, Park 5, tel. 050-330-916).

Herberg Vlissinghe is the oldest pub in town (1515). Bruno keeps things simple and laid-back, serving simple plates (lasagna, grilled cheese sandwiches, and famous €8 angel-hair spaghetti) and great beer in the best old-time tavern atmosphere in town. This must have been the Dutch Masters' rec room. The garden outside comes with a *boules* court—free for guests to watch or play (Wed–Sat 11:00–24:00, Sun 11:00–19:00, closed Mon–Tue, Blekersstraat 2, tel. 050-343-737).

Pub 't Gezelleke lacks the mystique of the Vlissinghe, but it's a true neighborhood pub offering small, forgettable plates and a fine chance to drink with locals. Its name is an appropriate play on the word for cozy and the name of a great local poet (Mon–Fri 11:00–24:00, closed Sat–Sun, Carmersstraat 15, tel. 050-338-381, Peter and Gried).

Café Terrastje is a cozy pub serving light meals. Experience the grown-up ambience inside, or relax on the front terrace overlooking the canal and heart of the *gezellig* district (food served 12:00–21:00, open until 23:30, closed Thu, corner of Genthof and Langerei, tel. 050-330-919, Ian and Patricia).

Fries, Fast Food, and Picnics

Local french fries *(frites)* are a treat. Proud and traditional *frituurs* serve tubs of fries and various local-style shish kebabs. Belgians dip their *frites* in mayonnaise, but ketchup is there for the Yankees (along with spicier sauces). For a quick, cheap, hot, and scenic snack, hit a *frituur* and sit on the steps or benches overlooking Market Square (convenience benches are about 50 yards past the post office).

Market Square Frituur: Twin, take-away french fry carts are on Market Square at the base of the bell tower (daily 10:00–24:00). Skip the ketchup and have a sauce adventure. I find the cart on the left more user-friendly.

Pickles Frituur, a block off Market Square, is handy for sit-down fries. Its forte is greasy, fast, deep-fried Flemish fast food. The "menu 2" comes with three traditional gut bombs: shrimp, chicken, and "spicy gypsy" sausage (daily 11:30–24:00, at the corner of Geldmuntstraat and Sint Jakobstraat, tel. 050-337-957).

Delhaize-Proxy Supermarket is ideal for picnics. Its push-button produce pricer lets you buy as few as one mushroom (Mon–Sat 9:00–19:00, closed Sun, 3 blocks off Market Square on Geldmuntstraat). For midnight snacks, you'll find Indian-run corner grocery stores scattered around town.

Belgian Waffles and Ice Cream

While Americans think of "Belgian" waffles for breakfast, the Belgians (who don't eat waffles or pancakes for breakfast) think of *wafels* as Liège-style (dense, sweet, heated up, and eaten plain) and Brussels-style (lighter, often with powdered sugar or whipped cream and strawberries, served in teahouses only in the afternoons 14:00–18:00).

You'll see waffles sold at restaurants and take-away stands. **Laurenzino** is a favorite with Bruges' teens when they get the waffle munchies. Their classic waffle with chocolate costs €2.50 (daily 10:00–23:00, across from Gelateria Da Vinci at Noordzandstraat 1, tel. 050-345-854).

Gelateria Da Vinci, the local favorite for homemade ice cream, has creative flavors and a lively atmosphere. As you approach, you'll see a line of happy lickers. Before ordering, ask to sample the Ferrero Rocher (chocolate, nuts, and crunchy cookie) and plain yogurt (daily 10:00–24:00, Geldmuntstraat 34, run by Sylvia from Austria).

NIGHTLIFE

Herberg Vlissinghe and **De Garre,** listed on page 373, are great places to just nurse a beer and enjoy new friends.

Charlie Rockets is an American-style bar—lively and central—with foosball games, darts, and five pool tables (€9/hr) in the inviting back room. It also runs a youth hostel upstairs and therefore is filled with a young, international crowd (a block off Market Square at Hoogstraat 19). It's open nightly until 3:00 in the morning with non-stop rock 'n' roll.

Nighttime Bike Ride: Great as these pubs are, my favorite way to spend a late-summer evening in Bruges is in the twilight on a rental bike, savoring the cobbled wonders of its back streets, far from the touristic commotion.

Evening Carillon Concerts: The tiny courtyard behind the bell tower has a few benches where people can enjoy the free carillon concerts (generally Mon, Wed, and Sat at 21:00 in the summer; schedule posted on the wall).

BRUSSELS
Bruxelles

ORIENTATION

Six hundred years ago, Brussels was just a nice place to stop and buy a waffle on the way to Bruges. With no strategic importance, it was allowed to grow as a free trading town. Today, it's a city of 1.8 million, the capital of Belgium, the headquarters of NATO, and the center of the European Union.

The Bruxelloise are cultured and genteel—even a bit snobby. As the unofficial capital of Europe, the city is multicultural, hosting politicians and businessmen from around the globe and featuring a world of ethnic restaurants.

Brussels enjoyed a Golden Age of peace and prosperity (1400–1550) while England and France were duking it out in the Hundred Years' War. It was then that many of the fine structures that distinguish the city today were built. In the 1800s, Brussels had another growth spurt, fueled by industrialization, wealth taken from the Belgian Congo, and the exhilaration of the country's recent independence (1830).

Brussels speaks French. Bone up on *bonjour* and *s'il vous plaît* (see the French Survival Phrases in the appendix). Though the city (and country) is officially bilingual and filled with foreign visitors, 80 percent of the locals speak French first and English second, if at all. Language aside, the whole feel of the town is urban French, not rural Flemish.

Because Brussels sits smack-dab between Belgium's two linguistic groups (60 percent of Belgians speak Flemish, 40 percent speak French), most of Brussels' street signs and maps are in both languages. In this chapter, French names are generally used.

Tourists zipping between Amsterdam and Paris by train usually miss Brussels, but its rich, chocolaty mix of food and culture pleasantly surprises those who stop.

Brussels in Three Hours

Brussels makes a great stopover between trains. First check your bag at the Central Station and confirm your departure time and station (factoring in any necessary transit time to a different departure station) before heading into town. Then do this Brussels blitz:

Head directly for the Grand Place and take my Grand Place Walk (described on page 397). To streamline, skip the *Manneken-Pis* until later, and end the walk at the Bourse, where you'll catch bus #95 to Place Royale. Enjoy a handful of masterpieces at the Royal Museums of Fine Arts, then do the Upper Town Walk (page 409), which ends back at the *Manneken-Pis* and the Grand Place. Buy a box of chocolates and a bottle of Belgian beer, and pop the top as your train pulls out of the station. Ahhh!

Planning Your Time

Brussels is low on great sights and high on ambience. On a quick trip, a day and a night are enough for a good first taste. It could even be done as a day trip by train from Bruges (2/hr, 1 hr) or a stopover on the Amsterdam–Paris or Amsterdam–Bruges ride (hourly trains); for specifics, see the "Brussels in Three Hours" sidebar. The main reason to stop—the Grand Place—takes only a few minutes to see. With very limited time, skip the indoor sights and enjoy a coffee or a beer on the square.

Art lovers and novices alike can spend a couple of enjoyable hours at the Royal Museums of Fine Arts of Belgium (twin museums—ancient and modern—covered by the same ticket, and a new Magritte Museum), would-be Walloons can bone up on their Belgian history at the BELvue Museum, and even the tone-deaf can appreciate the Musical Instruments Museum. To see the impressive auto and military museums (side by side), plan on a three-hour excursion from the town center.

OVERVIEW

Central Brussels is surrounded by a ring of roads (which replaced the old city wall) called the Pentagon. (Romantics think it looks more like a heart.) All hotels and nearly all the sights I mention are within this ring. The epicenter holds the main square (the Grand Place), the TI, and Central Station (all within three blocks of each other).

What isn't so apparent from maps is that Brussels is a city divided by altitude. A ridgeline that runs north–south splits the town into the Upper Town (east half, elevation 200 feet) and Lower

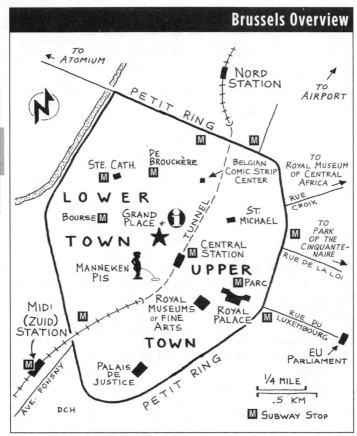

Brussels Overview

Town (west, at sea level), with the Central Station in between. The Upper Town, traditionally the home of nobility and the rich, has big marble palaces, broad boulevards, and the major museums. The Lower Town, with the Grand Place (Grote Markt in Flemish), narrow streets, old buildings, modern shops, colorful eateries, and the famous peeing-boy statue, has more character.

Outside the Pentagon-shaped center, sprawling suburbs and vast green zones contain some tourist attractions, including the European Parliament and the Park of the Cinquantenaire, along with Autoworld, the Royal Museum of the Army and Military History, and the Atomium.

Tourist Information

The TI at Rue du Marché-aux-Herbes 63 covers Brussels and Flanders, with a fine room-recommendation service (Mon–Sat 9:00–18:00, until 19:00 July–Aug, until 17:00 in winter; Sun 10:00–

17:00 year-round; three blocks downhill from Central Station, tel. 02-504-0390, www.brusselsinternational.be and www.visit flanders.com, fun Europe store nearby). There's another TI in the Town Hall on the Grand Place (summer daily 9:00–18:00, winter daily 10:00–14:00 except closed Sun Jan–Easter, tel. 02-513-8940).

The TIs have countless fliers. Day-trippers should pick up a free city map and a public transit map. The €4 *Brussels Guide & Map* booklet is worthwhile if you want a series of neighborhood walks (the Grand Place, plus three others farther afield), a map of greater Brussels, and a more complete explanation of the city's many museums. For current listings of concerts and other entertainment options, pick up the €3.50 *Bulletin* magazine, which has the monthly "What's On" inside. The **Brussels Card,** sold at the TIs, provides unlimited public transportation and free entrance to nearly all the major museums; it's worthwhile only if you plan to sightsee like mad (€20/24 hours, €28/48 hours, €33/72 hours, also sold at museums, public transportation offices, and some hotels, www.brusselsinternational.be).

Arrival in Brussels

By Train: Brussels can't decide which of its three stations (Central, Nord, and Midi) is the main one. Most international trains use the Nord and Midi stations. The Eurostar leaves from the Midi Station (also called Zuid, or South), getting you to London in less than three hours. The area around the Midi Station is a rough-and-tumble immigrant neighborhood (marked by its towering Ferris wheel); the area around the Nord Station is a seedy red light district. The Central Station, nearest to the sights and my recommended hotels, has handy services: a small grocery store, fast food, waiting rooms, and luggage storage (€4/bag—look for the *consigne* sign near track 1; or store two bags in a locker around the corner for half the price). Normally, only Belgian and Amsterdam trains stop at Central. Don't assume your train stops at more than one station; ask your conductor.

If you arrive at Nord or Midi, take a connecting train to the Central Station. Trains zip under the city, connecting all three stations every two minutes or so. It's an easy three-minute chore to connect from Nord or Midi to Central. The €1.50 ticket between the stations is covered by any train ticket into or out of Brussels (or use your railpass). Scan the departures board for trains leaving in the next few minutes and note which ones stop at Central. As you wait on the platform for your train, watch the track notice board that tells which train is approaching. They zip in and out constantly—so a train with an open door on your train's track—three minutes before your departure time—may well be the wrong train. Anxious travelers, who think their train has arrived early, often board the wrong train on the right track.

To get to the Grand Place from Central Station, exit the station from the top floor (to the left of the ticket windows), and you'll see Le Meridien Hôtel across the street. Pass through the arch of Le Meridien Hôtel, turn right, and walk downhill one block to a small square with a fountain. For the Grand Place, turn left at the far end of the square. Or, to head directly to the TI, exit the small square at the far end and continue straight for one block to Rue du Marché-aux-Herbes 63. Note that the hop-on, hop-off bus companies depart from just in front of the Central Station (you'll meet ticket hustlers as you leave). You could hop on one of these buses upon arrival to orient yourself from the top deck (see "Tours," page 384).

By Plane: See the Transportation Connections chapter, page 437.

Helpful Hints

Theft Alert: While I euphemistically describe Brussels as "earthy," it's also undeniably seedier than many European cities. Expect more grime on buildings, street people, and Gypsy ladies cradling their babies with a fake arm (while their hidden, real arm rifles your pockets). Muggings do occur. Some locals warn that it's not safe to be out late, especially after the Métro shuts down at midnight; troublemakers prey on people who missed that last ride. As in any other big city, use common sense and consider taking a taxi back to your hotel late at night.

Sightseeing Schedules: Brussels' most important museums are closed on Monday. But, of course, the city's single best sight—the Grand Place—is always open. You can also enjoy a bus tour any day of the week, or visit the more far-flung sights (which *are* open on Monday), such as the Atomium and the European Parliament. Most important, this is a city to browse and wander.

Department Store: Hema is at Nieuwstraat 13 (Mon–Sat 9:30–18:30, closed Sun, tel. 02-227-5210).

Laundry: There's a coin-op launderette at Rue du Midi 65 (daily 7:00–21:00, change machine).

Travel Agency and Discount Flights: The **Connections Agency** has a line on air and rail connections, including the Eurostar to London and the Thalys to Paris and Amsterdam (€10/person booking fee, Mon–Fri 9:30–18:30, opens Wed at 10:30, Sat 10:00–17:00, closed Sun, free coffee and WC, Rue du Midi 19–21, tel. 02-550-0130, www.connections.be).

Getting Around Brussels

Most of central Brussels' sights are walkable. But public transport is handy for connecting the train stations, climbing to the Upper Town (bus #95 from the Bourse), or visiting sights outside the central core. To reach these outlying sights, such as the European Parliament, take the Métro or jump on a hop-on, hop-off tour bus from Central Station (described under "Tours," next page; check tour bus route map to make sure it covers the sights you want to see). On summer weekends, a charming old-time trolley goes out to the Royal Museum of Central Africa (see page 396).

By Métro, Bus, Tram, and Train: A single €1.50 ticket is good for one hour on all public transportation—Métro, buses, trams, and even trains shuttling between Brussels' three train stations (notice the time when you first stamp it, stamp it again if you transfer lines, buy single tickets on buses or at Métro stations). Deals are available at the TI at Rue de Marché-aux-Herbes 63 and at Métro stations: an all-day pass for €4.20 (cheaper than three single tickets; on Sat–Sun and holidays, this pass covers two people); or a 10-ride card for €11. The free *Métro Tram Bus Plan* is excellent; pick it up at either TI or any Métro station. In 2009, the Mobib swipe-card system was introduced (similar to London's Oyster card), allowing you to use a "refillable" plastic card to pay for public transit (transit info: tel. 02-515-2000, www.mivb.be).

Brussels' Métro has three lines that run mostly east–west: 1A (Roi Baudouin-Debroux), 1B (Erasmus-Stokkel), and the circular 2 (Simonis-Clemenceau). A series of tram lines run north–south through the city center, connecting the Métro lines and the Nord, Central, and Midi train stations. Whether you're on a Métro train, bus, or tram, validate your ticket when you enter, feeding it into the breadbox-size orange machines.

Near the Grand Place are two transportation hubs: Central Station and the Bourse. Those staying in hotels northwest of the Grand Place have good access to the Métro system at the De Brouckère and Ste. Catherine stops.

By Taxi: Drivers in big-city Brussels are happy to take you for a ride; find out the approximate cost to your destination before you head out. Cabbies charge a €2.40 drop fee, as well as €1.35 per additional kilometer. After 22:00, you'll be hit with a €2 surcharge. You'll pay about €10 to ride from the center to the European Parliament. Convenient taxi stands are at the Bourse (near Grand Place) and at Place du Grand Sablon (in the Upper Town). To call a cab, try Taxi Bleu (tel. 02-268-0000).

TOURS

Hop-On, Hop-Off Bus Tours—Two different companies offer nearly identical "discovery" city tours. The 90-minute loop and recorded narration give you a once-over-lightly of the city from the top deck (open on sunny days) of a double-decker bus. While you can hop on and off for 24 hours with one ticket, schedules are sparse (about 2/hr, times listed on each flier; both companies run roughly April–Oct daily 10:00–16:00, Sat until 17:00; Nov–March daily 10:00–15:00, Sat until 16:00). Except for the trip out to the European Parliament and Cinquantenaire Park (which hosts the military and auto museums), I'd just stay on to enjoy the views and the minimal commentary. The fiercely competitive companies often both have hustlers at the Central Station trying to get you on board (offering "student" discounts to customers of all ages). The handiest starting points are the Central Station and the Bourse. The companies are **City Tours** (€18, tel. 02-513-7744, www.brussels-city-tours.com) and **Golden Tours** (€18, mobile 0486-053-981, www.goldentours.be).

Bus Tours—City Tours also offers a typical three-hour, guided (in up to five languages) bus tour, providing an easy way to get the grand perspective on Brussels. You start with a walk around the Grand Place, then jump on a tour bus (€27, year-round daily at 10:00 and 14:00, April–Oct extra tours Sat–Sun at 11:00; depart from their office a block off Grand Place at Rue du Marche aux Herbes 82; you can buy tickets there, at TI, or in your hotel; tel. 02-513-7744, www.brussels-city-tours.com). You'll get off the bus briefly at the Atomium for a quick photo stop.

Private Guide—Claude Janssens is good (€106/half-day, €200/day, mobile 0485-025-423, www.dobeltour.be, claude.janssens@pandora.be).

SIGHTS

On and near Grand Place

Brussels' Grand Place area sights, listed briefly below, are described in more detail in the ❂ Grand Place Walk on page 397.

▲▲▲**Grand Place**—Brussels' main square, aptly called Grand Place (grahn plahs, "Grote Markt" in Flemish), is the heart of the old town and Brussels' greatest sight. Any time of day, it's worth swinging by to see what's going on. Concerts, flower markets, sound-and-light shows, endless people-watching—it entertains (as do the streets around it). The museums on the square are well-advertised, but dull.

Town Hall (Hôtel de Ville), with the tallest spire, is the square's centerpiece, but its interior is no big deal. Admission is only possible with a 40-minute English tour, which also covers city history and the building's tapestries and architecture (€3, Tue–Wed at 15:15, Sun at 10:45 and 12:15, no Sun tours Oct–March). Only 25 people are allowed per tour; assure a spot by buying tickets from the guide exactly 40 minutes before the tour starts (in the court-yard behind the spire).

The **City Museum** (Musée de la Ville de Bruxelles) is opposite Town Hall in an 1875 Neo-Gothic building called the *Maison du Roi,* or "King's House" (but no king ever lived here). The top floor displays a chronological history of the city and an enjoyable room full of costumes dampened by the *Manneken-Pis* statue (see page 390). An engrossing video of tourist reactions to the statue plays constantly. The middle floor features maps and models of 13th- and 17th-century Brussels, and the bottom floor has tapestries and paintings (€3, Tue–Sun 10:00–17:00, closed Mon, Grand Place, tel. 02-279-4350). For local history, the best choice is not this museum—but the BELvue Museum (see page 391).

BRUSSELS SIGHTS

Brussels

TO NORD STATION

TO Ⓜ Rogier

N

R. DU GRAND

HOSPICE

R. DE LA BLANCH.

QUAI AUX BRIQUES

QUAI BOIS

R. DE FLANDRE

BRÛL

Ⓜ

PL. BEG.

Ste. Cath.

BLVD. ADOLPHE MAX

RUE NEUVE

BELGIAN COMIC BOOK CENTER

R. DE MARAIS

SABLES

FISH MKT.

De Brouckère

PLACE DE LA MONNAIE

PL. MART.

COMÉDIENS

BLVD. BERLAYMONT

RUE DANSAERT

PL. S. CATH.

Ⓜ Ste. Cath.

Ⓜ

FRIPIERS

FRIPIERS

R. MONTAUX

PRAET.

STE. CATH.

MARCHÉ

A. ORTS

ANSPACH

POULETS

R.

BOUCHERS

THEATRE ROYALE

GALERIES ST. HUBERT

V.

Bourse Ⓜ

Bourse Ⓑ

GRAND PLACE

MID.

ⓘ

MONT.

L'IMPERATRICE

OXUM

MERC.

ST. MICHAEL'S

COLONIES

TO Parc Ⓜ

Town Hall

ⓘ

Ⓜ Gare Central

CENTRAL STATION

R. ROYALE

DE

L'ETUVE

MANNEKEN-PIS

R. CHÊNE

ST. JEAN

LOMBARD

BLVD.

MAD

LOWER TOWN

Anneessens Ⓜ

R. POINÇON

ALEXIENS

Tour d'Angle

L'EMPEREUR

J. LEB.

MUSICAL INSTRUMENTS MUSEUM

BELVUE MUSEUM

PLACE DES PALAIS

BLVD.

ROLLE

ROYAL MUSEUMS OF FINE ARTS

PL. ROYALE

ROYAL PALACE

TO MIDI (ZUID) STATION

R. BLAES

R. HAUTE

BODEN

R. SABLONS

UPPER TOWN

MAGRITTE MUSEUM

R. RÉGENCE

NOTRE-DAME DU SABLON

TO PALACE OF JUSTICE

|||| STAIRS

Ⓜ SUBWAY STOP

Ⓑ TOUR BUS DEPARTURE POINTS (2)

→ 5 MIN. WALK - CENTRAL STATION TO GRAND PLACE

DCH

200 YARDS

200 METERS

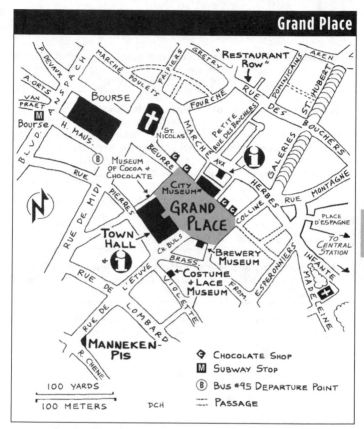

Grand Place

The **Brewery Museum** has one room of old brewing para-
phernalia and one room of new, plus a beer video in English. It's
pretty lame...but a good excuse for a beer (€5 includes an unnamed
local beer, daily 10:00–17:00, except Dec–March Sat–Sun opens at
12:00; Grand Place 10, tel. 02-511-4987).

The **Museum of Cocoa and Chocolate,** to the right of Town
Hall, is a delightful concept. But it's overpriced at €5 for a meager
set of displays, a second-rate video, a look at a "chocolate master" at
work, and a choco-sample (daily 10:00–16:30, until 17:00 July–Aug,
Rue de la Tête d'Or 9, www.mucc.be).

▲**Chocolate Shops on Grand Place**—For many, the best thing
about Grand Place is the chocolate sold at the four venerable
chocolate shops: Godiva, Neuhaus, Galler, and Leonidas (shops
generally open Mon–Sat 9:00–22:00, Sun 10:00–22:00). Each
has inviting displays and sells mixes of 100 grams (your choice of
6–8 pieces) or individual pieces for about €1.60. It takes a lot of

Brussels at a Glance

▲▲▲**Grand Place** Main square and spirited heart of the old town, surrounded by mediocre museums and delectable chocolate shops. **Hours:** Always open. See page 385.

▲▲▲**Royal Museums of Fine Arts of Belgium** Three museums in one, displaying ancient art (14th–18th centuries), modern art (19th–20th centuries), and works by Surrealist painter René Magritte. **Hours:** Ancient Art and Modern Art museums—Tue-Sun 10:00–17:00, closed Mon; Magritte Museum—Tue-Sun 10:00–17:00, Wed until 20:00, closed Mon. See page 390.

▲▲**BELvue Museum** Interesting Belgian history museum with a focus on the popular royal family. **Hours:** June–Sept Tue-Sun 10:00–18:00, Oct–May Tue-Sun 10:00–17:00, closed Mon year-round. See page 391.

▲▲**Royal Army and Military History Museum** Vast collection of weaponry and uniforms. **Hours:** Tue-Sun 9:00–16:45, closed Mon. See page 395.

▲**Chocolate on Grand Place** Choco-crawl through Godiva, Neuhaus, Galler, and Leonidas. **Hours:** Generally daily 9:00–22:00. See page 387.

▲**Musical Instruments Museum** More than 1,500 instruments, complete with audio. **Hours:** Tue-Fri 9:30–17:00, Sat-Sun 10:00–17:00, closed Mon. See page 391.

▲**St. Michael's Cathedral** White-stone Gothic church where Belgian royals are married and buried. **Hours:** Mon–Fri 7:00–18:00, Sat-Sun 8:30–18:00, until 19:00 in summer. See page 392.

▲**Belgian Comic Strip Center** Hometown heroes the Smurfs, Tintin, and Lucky Luke, plus many more. **Hours:** Tue-Sun 10:00–18:00, closed Mon. See page 392.

▲**European Parliament** Soaring home of Europe's governing body. **Hours:** Audioguide tours Mon–Thu at 10:00 and 15:00, also at 16:30 July-Aug; Fri at 10:00 only. See page 393.

Park of the Cinquantenaire Belgium's sprawling tribute to independence, near the European Parliament. **Hours:** Always open. See page 394.

▲**Autoworld** Hundreds of historic vehicles, including Mr. Benz's 1886 motorized tricycle. **Hours:** Daily April–Sept 10:00–18:00, Oct–March 10:00–17:00. See page 395.

▲**Royal Museum of Art and History** Filled with fine art, it's appropriately nicknamed "the local Louvre." **Hours:** Tue–Fri 9:30–17:00, Sat–Sun 10:00–17:00, closed Mon. See page 394.

▲**Royal Museum of Central Africa** Excellent but far-flung exhibit about the former Belgian Congo, featuring ethnology, artifacts, and wildlife. **Hours:** Tue–Fri 10:00–17:00, Sat–Sun 10:00–18:00, closed Mon. See page 396.

City Museum Costumes worn by the *Manneken-Pis* statue and models of Brussels' history. **Hours:** Tue–Sun 10:00–17:00, closed Mon. See page 385.

Costume and Lace Museum World-famous Brussels lace, as well as outfits, embroideries, and accessories from the 17th–20th centuries. **Hours:** Mon–Tue and Thu–Fri 10:00–12:30 & 13:30–17:00, Sat–Sun 14:00–17:00, closed Wed. See page 390.

Royal Belgian Institute of Natural Sciences Europe's largest dinosaur gallery. **Hours:** Tue–Fri 9:30–16:45, Sat–Sun 10:00–18:00, closed Mon. See page 396.

Atomium Fun space-age videos and displays, and an elevator ride to the panorama deck. **Hours:** Daily 10:00–19:00, later in summer. See page 396.

Mini-Europe Models of 350 famous European landmarks. **Hours:** Easter–Sept daily 9:30–18:00, July–Aug until 20:00; Oct–Dec 10:00–18:00; closed Jan-Easter. See page 396.

sampling to judge. See the "choco-crawl" described in the Grand Place Walk (page 401).

Manneken-Pis—Brussels is a great city with a cheesy mascot (apparently symbolizing the city's irreverence and love of the good life)—a statue of a little boy urinating. Read up on his story at any postcard stand. It's three short blocks off Grand Place, but, for exact directions, take my Grand Place Walk (page 397), look for small, white *Manneken-Pis* signs, or just ask a local, *"Où est le Manneken-Pis?"* The little squirt may be wearing some clever outfit, as costumes are sent to Brussels from around the world. Cases full of these are on display in the City Museum (described on page 385).

Costume and Lace Museum—This is worthwhile only to those who have devoted their lives to the making of lace (€3, Mon–Tue and Thu–Fri 10:00–12:30 & 13:30–17:00, Sat–Sun 14:00–17:00, closed Wed, Rue de la Violette 12, a block off Grand Place, tel. 02-213-4450).

Upper Town

Brussels' grandiose Upper Town, with its huge palace, is described in the ○ Upper Town Walk on page 409. Along that walk, you'll pass the following sights.

▲▲▲**Royal Museums of Fine Arts of Belgium (Musées Royaux des Beaux-Arts de Belgique)**—This sprawling complex is worth visiting for the three museums that hold its permanent collection.

The **Museum of Ancient Art** and the **Museum of Modern Art** are covered by the same €5 ticket (enter through the main foyer for both). The Museum of Ancient Art—featuring Flemish and Belgian art of the 14th–18th centuries—is packed with a dazzling collection of masterpieces by Van der Weyden, Brueghel, Bosch, and Rubens. The Museum of Modern Art gives an easy-to-enjoy walk through the art of the 19th and 20th centuries, from Neoclassical to Surrealism. Highlights here include works by Seurat, Gauguin, and David (Tue–Sun 10:00–17:00, closed Mon, last entry at 16:30, audioguide-€2.50, tour booklet-€2.50, pricey cafeteria with salad bar, Rue de la Régence 3, recorded info tel. 02-508-3211, www.fine-arts-museum.be).

The new **Magritte Museum,** honoring the Surrealist painter René Magritte, opened in the same museum complex in 2009 and contains over 150 works housed on three floors of a Neoclassical building (separate €8 ticket, Tue–Sun 10:00–17:00, Wed until 20:00, closed Mon). The Magritte Museum is the best art news in Brussels. Magritte's works are best described in his own words: *"My paintings are visible images which conceal nothing; they evoke mystery and, indeed, when one sees one of my pictures, one asks oneself* *this simple question, 'What does that mean'? It does not mean anything, because mystery means nothing either, it is unknowable."*

○ See Royal Museums of Fine Arts of Belgium Tour on page 418.

▲**Musical Instruments Museum (Musée des Instruments de Musique)**—One of Europe's best music museums (nicknamed "MIM") is housed in one of Brussels' most impressive Art

Nouveau buildings, the newly renovated Old English department store. Inside, you'll be given a pair of headphones and set free to wander several levels: folk instruments from around the world on the ground floor, a history of Western musical instruments on the first, and an entire floor devoted to strings and pianos on the second. Part of the **Royal Museum of Art and History** (described later in this chapter), this museum has more than 1,500 instruments—from Egyptian harps, to medieval lutes, to groundbreaking harpsichords, to the Brussels-built saxophone. As you approach an instrument, you hear it playing on your headphones (which actually work...most of the time). The museum is skimpy on English information—except for a laminated sheet in each section that simply identifies instruments—but the music you'll hear is an international language (€5, Tue–Fri 9:30–17:00, Sat–Sun 10:00–17:00, closed Mon, last entry 45 min before closing, Rue Montagne de la Cour 2, just downhill and toward Grand Place from the Royal Museums of Fine Arts, tel. 02-545-0130, www.mim.fgov.be). The sixth floor has a restaurant, a terrace, and a great view of Brussels (€10–15 *plats du jour*, same hours as museum, pick up free access pass at museum entrance).

▲▲**BELvue Museum**—This brilliant museum, which fills two palatial floors, offers far and away the best look in town at Belgian history. The exhibit, with lots of real historical artifacts, illustrates the short sweep of this nation's story, from its 1830 inception to today: kings, its bloody reign in the Congo, Art Nouveau, and world wars. The rooms proceed in chronological order, and outside in the hallway, displays on the monarchy provide a chance to get to know the generally much-loved royal family with intimate family photos. To make the most of your visit, follow along with the wonderful and

extensive flier translating all of the descriptions (€3, €5 combo-ticket includes Coudenberg Palace; June–Sept Tue–Sun 10:00–18:00, Oct–May Tue–Sun 10:00–17:00, closed Mon year-round, to the right of the palace at place des Palais 7, tel. 07-022-0492, www.belvue.be). Lunch is served in the lobby of this former princess' palace (€10–15 plates, same hours as museum).

Coudenberg Palace—The BELvue Museum stands atop the barren archaeological remains of a 12th-century Brussels palace. While well-lit and well-described, the ruins still aren't much to see. The best thing is the free orientation video you see before descending (€4, €5 combo-ticket includes BELvue Museum, same hours as BELvue).

North of Central Station

▲**St. Michael's Cathedral**—Belgium is largely Catholic, and St. Michael's Cathedral has been the center of Belgium's religious

life for nearly 1,000 years. While the Netherlands went in a Protestant direction in the 1500s, Belgium remains 80 percent Catholic (although only about 20 percent go to Mass). One of Europe's classic Gothic churches, built between roughly 1200 and 1500, Brussels' cathedral is made from white stone and topped by twin towers (Mon–Fri 7:00–18:00, Sat–Sun 8:30–18:00, until 19:00 in summer).

The church is where royal weddings and funerals take place. Photographs (to the right of the entrance) show the funeral of the popular King Baudouin, who died in 1993. He was succeeded by his younger brother, Albert II (whose face is on Belgium's euro coins). Albert will be succeeded by his son, Prince Philippe. Traditionally, the ruler was always a man, but in 1992 the constitution was changed, making it clear that the oldest child—boy or girl—would take the throne. In 1999, Prince Philippe and his bride, Mathilde—after a civil ceremony at the Town Hall—paraded up here for a two-hour Catholic ceremony with all the trimmings. They had a baby girl in 2001, and she is in line to become Belgium's Queen Elisabeth.

Before leaving, enjoy the great view from the outside porch of the Town Hall spire with its gold statue of St. Michael.

▲**Belgian Comic Strip Center (Centre Belge de la Bande Dessinée)**—Belgium has produced some of the world's most popular comic characters, including the Smurfs, Tintin, and Lucky Luke. You'll find these, and many less famous local comics, at the Comic Strip Center.

Just pop into the lobby to see the museum's groundbreaking Art Nouveau building (a former department store designed in

1903 by Belgian architect Victor Horta), browse through comics in the bookshop, and snap a photo with a three-foot-tall Smurf...and that's enough for many people. Kids especially might find the museum, like, totally boring. But those who appreciate art in general will enjoy this sometimes humorous, sometimes probing, often beautiful medium. The displays are in French and Flemish, but they loan out a helpful, if hard-to-follow, English guidebook.

You'll see how comics are made, watch early animated films (such as *Gertie the Dinosaur*, c. 1909), and see a sprawling exhibit on Tintin (the intrepid boy reporter with the button eyes and wavy shock of hair, launched in 1929 by Hergé and much loved by older Europeans). The top floor is dedicated to "serious" comics, where more adult themes and high-quality drawing aspire to turn kids' stuff into that "Ninth Art." These works can be grimly realistic, openly erotic or graphic, or darker in tone, featuring flawed anti-heroes (€7.50, Tue–Sun 10:00–18:00, closed Mon, 10-minute walk from Grand Place to Rue des Sables 20, tel. 02-219-1980, www.comicscenter.net).

▲**European Parliament**—Europe's governing body welcomes visitors with an information center and audioguide tours. This

towering complex of glass skyscrapers is a cacophony of black-suited politicians speaking 20 different Euro-languages. It's exciting just to be here—a mouse in the corner of a place that aspires to chart the future of Europe "with respect for all political thinking...con-solidating democracy in the spirit of peace and solidarity." The 785 parliament members, representing 28 countries and 457 million citizens, shape Europe with a €120 billion budget (from import duties, sales taxes, and a cut of each member country's GDP).

The **Info Point** is a welcoming place with 28 flags, enter-taining racks of freebies, and videos promoting the concept and beauties of the European Union (including bins of tiny *My Funda-mental Rights in the EU* booklets). Ask for the *Troubled Waters* comic book, which explains how the parliament works (free,

Mon–Fri 9:00–17:15, closed Sat–Sun, www.europarl.europa.eu). An adjacent, bigger-and-even-better center may open soon.

Audioguide tours, the only way to get inside the European Parliament, leave from the Info Point office (free, Mon–Thu at 10:00 and 15:00, also at 16:30 July–Aug; Fri only at 10:00; confirm tour time by calling 02-284-2111, arrive 30 min early, no visitors under 14 years old).

At the appointed time, enter the main hall through the double doors and meet your escort, who equips you with an audioguide and takes you to a balcony overlooking the huge "hemi-cycle" where the members of the European Parliament sit. Here you'll listen to a political-science lesson about the all-Europe system of governance. You'll learn how early visionary utopians (like Churchill, who in 1946 called for a "United States of Europe" to avoid future wars) led the way as Europe gradually evolved into the European Union (1992).

Getting There: The European Parliament is next to Place du Luxembourg. From the Bourse in downtown Brussels, take bus #95; from the museums at the Park of the Cinquantenaire or the Royal Palace, take bus #27. From Place du Luxembourg, go behind the old train station and look for the *Info Point* sign.

Park of the Cinquantenaire (Parc du Cinquantenaire)—The 19th-century Belgian king Leopold wanted Brussels to rival Paris. In 1880, he celebrated the 50th anniversary (cinquantenaire) of Belgian independence by building a huge monumental arch flanked by massive exhibition halls, which today house the Royal Museum of Art and History, Autoworld, and the military museum (see next listings). The Métro stop is 200  yards from the museums (follow signs to museum and walk to the statue crowning the big arch).

Connecting to Other Sights: If seeing both the Park of the Cinquantenaire and the European Parliament, take advantage of the wonderful public transportation connections that make this easy. The Métro zips you from the center out to the park in minutes (Métro stop: Merode). From the park (Métro stop: Gaulois), bus #27 runs four times an hour to the Luxembourg stop (for the European Parliament) and on to the Royal stop (for the Royal Palace and great nearby museums). It's cheap and easy, plus you'll feel quite clever doing it.

▲Royal Museum of Art and History—This is the "Belgian Louvre," with an impressive collection split between two wings:

European items in one wing, and antiquities and items from beyond Europe in the other. In the Europe wing, the basement takes you from pre-history, to Roman artifacts, to medieval Belgian. The ground floor is a chronological walk from Gothic to Renaissance to Baroque. Wandering the almost empty halls, you'll see fine tapestries, exquisite altarpieces, an impressive Islamic collection, Art Nouveau, and a "museum of the heart" donated by a local heart doctor. Unfortunately, the museum entrance is hidden behind Autoworld (€4, free and necessary audioguide, Tue–Fri 9:30–17:00, Sat–Sun 10:00 17:00, closed Mon; Jubelpark 10, Parc du Cinquantenaire, bus #27 goes to the Gaulois Métro stop a block away; tel. 02-741-7211).

▲**Autoworld**—Starting with Mr. Benz's motorized tricycle of

1886, you'll stroll through a giant hall filled with 400 historic cars. Car buffs can ogle circa-1905 models from Peugeot, Renault, Oldsmobile, Cadillac, and Rolls-Royce. It's well-described in English (€6, daily April–Sept 10:00–18:00, Oct–March 10:00–17:00, in Palais Mondial, Parc du Cinquantenaire 11, Métro: Merode, tel. 02-736-4165, www.auto world.be).

▲▲**Royal Army and Military History Museum (Musée Royal de l'Armée et d'Histoire Militaire)**—Wander through an enormous collection of 19th-century weaponry and uniforms,

and a giant hall dedicated to warplanes of the 20th century. There's a good display about the Belgian struggle for independence in the early 1800s and the best collection of WWI weaponry anywhere. Don't miss the primitive WWI tanks—able to break through the stalemated "Western Front," but

so clumsy that they couldn't do anything once in enemy territory. This place is filled with real, tangible history...but precious little English. Use the map and pay €3 for the essential audioguide to get the most out of your visit (free, Tue–Sun 9:00–16:45, closed Mon, Parc du Cinquantenaire 3, tel. 02-737-7811, www.klm-mra .be). While sections of the museum close from 12:00 to 13:00, most of it stays open.

Other Museums and Sights Away from the Center

Royal Belgian Institute of Natural Sciences (Institut Royal des Sciences Naturelles de Belgique)—Dinosaur enthusiasts come to this museum for the world's largest collection of iguanodon skeletons (€7, Tue–Fri 9:30–16:45, Sat–Sun 10:00–18:00, closed Mon, last entry 30 min before closing, Rue Vautier 29, bus #34 from the Bourse, tel. 02-627-4238, www.naturalsciences.be).

▲**Royal Museum of Central Africa (Musée Royal de l'Afrique Centrale)**—Remember the Belgian Congo? Just east of the city center, this fine museum covers the Congo and much more of Africa, including ethnography, sculpture, jewelry, colonial history, flora, and fauna. You'll learn about both the history of Belgian adventure in the Congo (when it was the king's private plantation) and the region's natural wonders. Unfortunately, there's barely a word of English (€4, Tue–Fri 10:00–17:00, Sat–Sun 10:00–18:00, closed Mon, Leuvensesteenweg 13, tel. 02-769-5211, www.africamuseum.be). The museum, housed in an immense palace, is surrounded by a vast and well-kept park. A trip out here puts you in a lush, wooded oasis a world away from the big, noisy city. To get here, take Métro #1B to Montgomery (direction: Stockel), and then catch tram #44 to its final stop, Tervuren. From there, walk 200 yards through the park to the palace.

Atomium—This giant, silvery iron molecule, with escalators connecting the various "atoms" and a view from the top sphere, was the über-optimistic symbol of the 1958 Universal Exhibition. Recently reopened after an extensive renovation, the Atomium now celebrates its kitschy past with fun space-age videos and displays. Your ticket includes an elevator ride to the panorama deck, as well as endless escalators and stairs. If you're scared of heights or tight spaces, tell your friends you'll wave to them... from the ground (€9, daily 10:00–19:00, later in summer, last entry one hour before closing,  on outskirts of town, Métro: Heysel and walk 5 min, tel. 02-475-4777, www.atomium.be).

Mini-Europe—This kid-pleasing sight, sharing a park with the Atomium, has 1:25-scale models of 350 famous European landmarks, such as Big Ben, the Eiffel Tower, and Venice. The new "Spirit of Europe" section is an interactive educational exhibit about the European Union (€13, Easter–Sept daily 9:30–18:00, July–Aug until 20:00, Oct–Dec 10:00–18:00, last entry one hour before closing, closed Jan–Easter, Métro: Heysel and walk 5 min, following signs to *Brupark*, tel. 02-474-1313, www.minieurope.com).

GRAND PLACE WALK

This walk takes in Brussels' delightful old center. After exploring the Grand Place itself, we'll loop a couple blocks north, see the Bourse, and then end south of the Grand Place at the *Manneken-Pis*.

ORIENTATION

Length of This Walk: Allow two hours.

Brewery Museum: €5, daily 10:00–17:00, except Dec–March opens on Sat–Sun at 12:00, Grand Place 10, tel. 02-511-4987.

City Museum: €3, Tue–Sun 10:00–17:00, closed Mon, Grand Place, tel. 02-279-4350.

Chocolate Shops: Generally open Mon–Sat 9:00–22:00, Sun 10:00–22:00, along the north side of the Grand Place.

Church of St. Nicolas: Rue de Tabora 6, tel. 02-513-8022.

THE WALK BEGINS

The Grand Place

This colorful cobblestone square is the heart—historically and geographically—of heart-shaped Brussels. As the town's market square for 1,000 years, this was where farmers and merchants sold their wares in open-air stalls, enticing travelers from the main east–west highway across Belgium, which ran a block north of the square. Today, shops and cafés sell chocolates, *gaufres* (waffles), beer, mussels, fries, lace, and flowers.

Brussels was born about 1,000 years ago around a long-gone castle put up by Germans to fight off the French (long before either of those countries actually existed). The villagers supplied the needs of the soldiers, and a city grew up on the banks of the Senne

The Grand Place: Center of Brussels

Face the Town Hall, with your back to the King's House. You're facing roughly southwest. The TI is one block behind you, and "restaurant row" is another block beyond that. To your right, a block away, catch a glimpse of the Bourse building (with buses, taxis, cafés). The Upper Town is to your left, rising up the hill beyond the Central Station. Over your left shoulder a few blocks away is St. Michael's Cathedral. And most important? The *Manneken-Pis* is three blocks ahead, down the street that runs along the left side of the Town Hall.

(not Seine) River, which today is completely bricked over. The river crossed the main road from Köln to Bruges.

Pan the square to get oriented. The **Town Hall** (Hôtel de

Ville) dominates the square with its 300-foot-tall tower, topped by a golden statue of St. Michael slaying a devil (skippable interior; see page 385 for tour times if you're interested). This was where the city council met to rule this free trading town. Brussels proudly maintained its self-governing independence while dukes, kings, and clergymen ruled much of Europe. These days, the Town Hall hosts weddings—Crown Prince Philippe got married here in 1999. (The Belgian government demands that all marriages first be performed in simple civil ceremonies.)

Opposite the Town Hall is the impressive, gray **King's House** (Maison du Roi), used by the Habsburg kings not as a house, but as an administrative center. Rebuilt in the 1890s, it's a stately and prickly Neo-Gothic building. Inside is the mildly interesting City Museum (described on page 400).

The fancy smaller buildings giving the square its uniquely grand medieval character are former **guild halls** (now mostly shops and restaurants), their impressive gabled roofs topped with statues. Once the home offices for the town's different professions (bakers, brewers, tanners, and *Manneken-Pis*-corkscrew-makers), they all date from shortly after

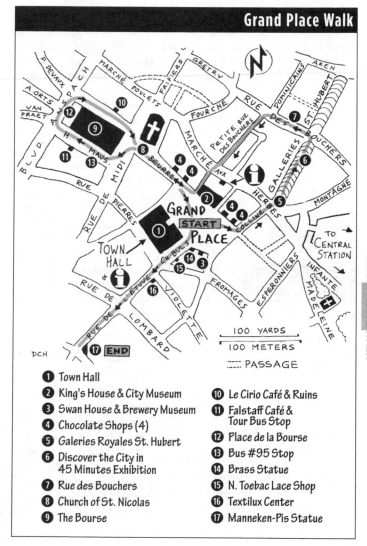

Grand Place Walk

1 Town Hall
2 King's House & City Museum
3 Swan House & Brewery Museum
4 Chocolate Shops (4)
5 Galeries Royales St. Hubert
6 Discover the City in 45 Minutes Exhibition
7 Rue des Bouchers
8 Church of St. Nicolas
9 The Bourse

10 Le Cirio Café & Ruins
11 Falstaff Café & Tour Bus Stop
12 Place de la Bourse
13 Bus #95 Stop
14 Brass Statue
15 N. Toebac Lace Shop
16 Textilux Center
17 Manneken-Pis Statue

1695—the year French king Louis XIV's troops surrounded the city, sighted their cannons on the Town Hall spire, and managed to level everything around it (4,000 wooden buildings) without ever hitting the spire itself. As a matter of pride, these Brussels businessmen rebuilt their offices better than ever, completing everything within seven years. They're in stone, taller, and with ornamented gables and classical statues.

The **Swan House** (#9, just to the left of the Town Hall) once housed a bar where Karl Marx and Friedrich Engels met in February of 1848 to write their *Communist Manifesto*. Later that year, when the treatise sparked socialist revolution around Europe, Brussels exiled them. Today, the once-proletarian bar is one of the city's most expensive restaurants. Next door (#10) was and still is the brewers' guild, now housing the **Brewery Museum** (see page 387).

The **statues** on the rooftops each come with their own uninteresting legend, but the Bruxelloise have an earthier explanation:

"What's that smell?" say the statues on the roof of the Swan House. "Someone farted." "Yeah," says the golden man riding a horse atop the Brewery Museum next door, "it was that guy over there," and he points north across the square to another statue. "It wasn't me," says that statue, "it was him—way over there." Follow his gaze to the southwest corner of the square, where a statue of St. Nicolas...hangs his head in shame.

• *In the King's House (across from the Town Hall) is the only museum of any importance on the square...*

City Museum

The museum's top floor has a roomful of goofy costumes the *Manneken* statue has pissed through, the middle floor features maps and models of old Brussels, and

the bottom floor has a few old paintings, fine carved altarpieces, and tapestries. On the ground floor, you'll see the original statues that once adorned the Town Hall. The local limestone is no match for the corrosive acidic air, so they were brought inside for protection. Most visitors aim straight for the *Manneken-Pis* outfits. Once up there, sit down and enjoy the video showing visitors' reactions to the ridiculous little statue.

But be sure to find the model of the city in the 13th century, on the second floor. (To follow the directions in this description, uphill is east.) The largest structure is St. Michael's Cathedral (northeast). The Upper Town hasn't a hint of its monumental future. The Grand Place's embryonic beginning is roughly in the center of town, amid a cluster of houses.

The city was a port town—see the crane unloading barges—since it was at this point that the shallow Senne became navigable. Grain from the area was processed in the watermills, then shipped downstream to the North Sea.

By the 1200s, Brussels—though tiny by today's standards—was an important commercial center, and St. Michael's was the region's religious hub. Still, most of the area inside the 2.5-mile-long city wall was farmland, dotted with a few churches, towers, markets, and convents (such as the Carmelite convent hugging the south wall).

The model in the far end of the room shows the city a couple centuries later—much bigger, but still within the same wall. By this time, the Upper and Lower Towns are clearly defined. In the Upper Town, the huge palace of the dukes of Burgundy marks the site of today's Royal Palace (described on page 410).

Taste Treats on the Grand Place

Cafés: Mussels in Brussels, Belgian-style french fries, yeasty local beers, waffles...if all you do is plop down at a café on the square, try some of these specialties, and watch the world go by—hey, that's a great afternoon in Brussels.

The outdoor cafés are casual and come with fair prices (a good Belgian beer costs €3.50—with no cover or service charge). Have a seat, and a waiter will serve you. The half-dozen or so cafés are all roughly equal in price and quality for simple drinks and foods—check the posted menus.

Choco-Crawl: The best chocolate shops all lie along the north (uphill) side of the square, starting with Godiva at the high end (that is, higher in both altitude and price). The cost goes down slightly as you descend to the other shops. Each shop has a mouth-watering display case of 20 or so chocolates and sells mixes of 100 grams—your choice of 6–8 pieces—for about €5, or individual pieces for about €1.60. Pralines are filled chocolates—uniquely Belgian (and totally different from the French praline). The shops are generally open daily from 9:00 to 22:00 (opening at 10:00 Sun).

Godiva, with the top reputation internationally, is synonymous with fine Belgian chocolate. Now owned by an American, Godiva still has its management and the original factory (built in 1926) in Belgium. This store, at Grand Place 22, was Godiva's first (est. 1937). The almond and honey goes way beyond almond roca.

Neuhaus, a few doors down at #27, has been encouraging local chocoholics since 1857. Look through the glass floor at the old-time choco-kitchen in the basement, and check out the historic photos on the walls. The enticing varieties are described in English, and Neuhaus publishes a fine little pamphlet (free, on the counter) explaining the products. The "caprice" (toffee with vanilla crème) tastes like Easter. Neuhaus claims to be the inventor of the filled chocolate.

History of Chocolate

In 1519, Montezuma served Cortés a cup of hot cocoa (*xocoatl*) made from cocoa beans, which were native to the New World.

It ignited a food fad in Europe—by 1700, elegant "chocolate houses" in Europe's capitals served hot chocolate (with milk and sugar added) to wealthy aristocrats. By the 1850s, the process of making chocolate candies for eating was developed, and Brussels, with a long tradition of quality handmade luxuries, was at the forefront.

Cocoa beans are husked, fermented, and roasted, then ground into chocolate paste. (Chocolate straight from the bean is very bitter.) The vegetable fat is pressed out to make cocoa butter. Cocoa butter and chocolate paste are mixed together and sweetened with sugar to make chocolates. In 1876, a Swiss man named Henry Nestlé added concentrated milk, creating milk chocolate—a lighter, sweeter variation, with less pure chocolate.

Galler, just off the square at Rue au Beurre 44, is homier and less famous because it doesn't export. Still family-run (and the royal favorite), it proudly serves less sugary chocolate—dark. The new top-end choice, 85 percent pure chocolate, is called simply "Black 85"—and worth a sample if you like chocolate without the sweetness. Galler's products are well-described in English.

At **Leonidas,** four doors down at Rue au Beurre 34, most locals sacrifice 10 percent in quality to double their take by getting their fix here (machine-made, only €1.60/100 grams). White chocolate is the specialty.

• *Exit the Grand Place next to Godiva (from the northeast, or uphill, corner of the square), and go north one block on Rue de la Colline (passing a popular Tintin shop at #13 and a Europe shop across the street) to Rue du Marché-aux-Herbes, which was once the main east–west highway through Belgium. Looking to the right, notice that it's all uphill from here to the Upper Town, another four blocks (and 200-foot elevation gain) beyond. Straight ahead, you enter the arcaded shopping mall called...*

Galeries Royales St. Hubert

Europe's oldest still-operating shopping mall, built in 1847, served as the glass-covered model that inspired many other malls. It celebrated the town's new modern attitude (having recently gained its independence from the Netherlands). Built in an age of expan-

sion and industrialization, the mall demonstrated efficient modern living, with elegant apartments upstairs above fine shops, theaters, and cafés. Originally, you had to pay to get in to see its fancy shops—that elite sensibility survives today.

Looking down the arcade, you'll notice that it bends halfway down, designed to lure shoppers further. Its iron-and-glass look is still popular today, but the decorative columns, cameos, and pastel colors evoke a more elegant time. It's Neo-Renaissance, like a pastel Florentine palace.

There's no Gap (yet), no Foot Locker, no Karmelkorn. Instead, you'll find hat, cane, and, umbrella stores that sell...hats, canes, and umbrellas—that's it, all made on the premises. At **Philippe**, have shoes made especially for the curves of your feet by a family that's done it for generations. Since 1857, **Neuhaus** has sold chocolates from here at its flagship store, where many locals buy their pralines. Across from Neuhaus, the **Taverne du Passage** restaurant serves the same local specialties that singer Jacques Brel used to come here for: *croquettes de crevettes* (shrimp croquettes), *tête de veau* (calf's head), *anguilles au vert* (eels with herb sauce), and *fondue au fromage* (cheese fondue; €10–20 meals, daily 12:00–24:00).

The **Brussels Discover the City in 45 Minutes Exhibition** (see the sign midway down the gallery) is the strangest thing: You enter through the back of a chocolate shop and descend into a huge underground exhibit that cleverly and artistically gives you the sweep of the city with fine English descriptions (€6, daily 10:00–17:00, tel. 02-512-5745).

• *Midway down the mall, where the two sections bend, turn left and exit the mall onto...*

Rue des Bouchers

Yikes! During meal times, this street is absolutely crawling with tourists browsing through wall-to-wall, midlevel-quality restaurants. Brussels is known worldwide for its food, serving all kinds of cuisine, but specializing in seafood (particularly mussels). You'll have plenty to choose from along this table-clogged "restaurant row." To get an idea of prices, compare their posted *menùs*—the fixed-price, several-course meal offered by most restaurants.

Many diners here are day-trippers. Colin from London, Marie from Paris, Martje from Holland, and Dietrich from Bonn could easily all "do lunch" together in Brussels—just three hours away.

The first intersection, with Petite Rue des Bouchers, is the heart of the restaurant quarter (and home to the recommended Chez Leon—see page 432), which sprawls for several blocks around. The street names tell what sorts of shops used to stand here—butchers *(bouchers)*, herbs, chickens, and cheese.

• *At this intersection, turn left onto Petite Rue des Bouchers and walk straight back to the Grand Place. (You'll see the City Hall tower ahead.) At the Grand Place, turn right (west) on Rue du Beurre. Comparison-shop a little more at the Galler and Leonidas chocolate stores and pass by the "Is it raining?" fountain. A block along, at the intersection with Rue du Midi, is the...*

Church of St. Nicolas

Since the 12th century, there's been a church here. Inside, see rough stones in some of the arches from the early church. Outside, notice the barnacle-like shops, such as De Witte Jewelers, built right into the church. The church was rebuilt 300 years ago with money provided by the town's jewelers. As thanks, they were given these shops with apartments upstairs. Close to God, this was prime real estate. And jewelers are still here.

• *Just west of the church, the big Neoclassical building you run into is the back entrance of...*

The Bourse (Stock Exchange) and Art Nouveau Cafés

The stock exchange was built in the 1870s in a Neo-everything style. Several **historic cafés** huddle around the Bourse. To the right is the woody, atmospheric Le Cirio with its delightful circa-1900 interior, and to the left is the Falstaff Café. Some Brussels cafés, like the Falstaff, are still decorated in the early-20th-century style called Art Nouveau. Ironwork columns twist and bend like flower stems, and lots of Tiffany-style stained glass and mirrors make them light and spacious. Slender, elegant, willowy Gibson Girls decorate the wallpaper, while waiters in bowties glide by.

The **ruins** under glass on the right side of the Bourse are from a 13th-century convent.

• *Circle around to the front of the Bourse, toward the busy Boulevard Anspach. Note that the street in front of the Falstaff Café is a convenient place to catch a hop-on, hop-off bus tour (see page 384).*

Place de la Bourse and Boulevard Anspach

Brussels is the political nerve center of Europe (only Washington, D.C., has more lobbyists), and the city sees several hundred demonstrations a year. When the local team wins a soccer match or some political group wants to make a statement, this is where people flock to wave flags and honk horns.

It's also where the old town meets the new. To the right along Boulevard Anspach are two shopping malls and several first-run movie theaters. Rue Neuve, which parallels Anspach, is a pedestrian-only shopping street.

Boulevard Anspach covers the still-flowing Senne River (which was open until 1850). Remember that Brussels was once a port, with North Sea boats coming as far as this point to unload their goods. But with frequent cholera epidemics killing thousands of its citizens, the city decided to cover up its stinky river.

• *For efficient sightseeing, consider catching bus #95 from alongside the Bourse (on Rue Henri Maus, just east of Falstaff Café) to the Place Royale, where you can follow my Upper Town Walk (see page 409), also ending at the* Manneken-Pis. *But if you'd rather stay in the Lower Town, return to the Grand Place.*

From the Grand Place to the *Manneken-Pis*

• *Leave the square kitty-corner, heading south down the street running along the left side of the Town Hall, Rue Charles Buls (which soon changes its name to Stoofstraat).*

Just five yards off the square, under the arch, is a well-polished, well-loved brass statue.

You'll see tourists and locals rubbing a **brass statue** of a reclining man. This was Mayor Evrard 't Serclaes, who in 1356 bravely refused to surrender the keys of the city to invaders, and so was tortured and killed. Touch him, and his misfortune becomes your good luck. Judging by the reverence with which locals go through this ritual, there must be something to it.

The **N. Toebac Lace Shop** is a welcoming place with fine

lace, a knowledgeable staff, and an interesting three-minute video. Brussels is perhaps the best-known city for traditional lacemaking, and this shop still sells handmade pieces in the old style: lace clothing, doilies, tablecloths, and ornamental pieces (daily 9:30–19:30, Rue Charles Buls 10). The shop gives travelers with this book a 15 percent discount. If you spend more than €125, you get a further 13 percent tax rebate. For more

Lace

In the 1500s, rich men and women decided that lace collars, sleeves, headdresses, and veils were fashionable. For the next 200 years, the fashion raged (peaking in about 1700). All this lace had to be made by hand, and many women earned extra income from the demand. The French Revolution of 1789 suddenly made lace for men undemocratic and unmanly. Then, in about 1800, machines replaced human hands, and except for ornamental pieces, the fashion died out.

These days, handmade lace is usually also homemade—not produced in factories, but at home by dedicated, sharp-eyed hobbyists who love their work. Unlike knitting, it requires total concentration as they follow intricate patterns. Women create their own patterns or trace tried-and-true designs. A piece of lace takes days, not hours, to make—which is why a handmade tablecloth can easily sell for €250.

There are two basic kinds of lace: bobbin lace (which originated in Bruges) and needle lace. To make bobbin lace, women juggle many different strands tied to bobbins, "weaving" a design by overlapping the threads. Because of the difficulties, the resulting pattern is usually rather rough and simple compared with other techniques.

Needle lace is more like sewing—stitching pre-made bits onto a pattern. For example, the "Renaissance" design is made by sewing a pre-made ribbon onto a pattern in a fancy design. This would then be attached as a fringe to a piece of linen—to make a fancy tablecloth, for instance.

In the "Princess" design, pre-made pieces are stitched onto a cotton net, making anything from a small doily to a full wedding veil.

"Rose point"—no longer practiced—used authentic bits of handmade antique lace as an ornament in a frame or filling a pendant. Antique pieces can be very expensive.

on lace, the Costume and Lace Museum is a block away and just around the corner (see page 390).

A block farther down the street, passing the always popular Waffle Factory (€4, freshly made, take-away, lots of fun toppings) step into the **Textilux Center** (Rue Lombard 41) for a good look at Belgian tapestries—both traditional wall-hangings and modern goods, such as tapestry purses and luggage in traditional designs.

• *Follow the crowds, noticing the excitement build, as in another block you reach the...*

> ## Tapestries
>
> In 1500, tapestry workshops in Brussels were famous, cranking out high-quality tapestries for the walls of Europe's palaces. They were functional (as insulation and propaganda for a church, king, or nobleman) and beautiful—an intricate design formed by colored thread. Even great painters (such as Rubens and Raphael) designed tapestries, which rivaled Renaissance canvases.
>
> First, neutral-colored threads (made from imported English wool) are stretched vertically over a loom. The design of the tapestry is created with the horizontal weave, from the colored threads that (mostly) overlay the vertical threads. Tapestry-making is much more difficult than basic weaving because each horizontal thread is only as long as the detail it's meant to create, so a single horizontal row can be made up of many individual pieces of thread. The weavers follow a pattern designed by an artist, called a "cartoon."
>
> Flanders and Paris (the Gobelins workshop) were the two centers of tapestry-making until the art died out, along with Europe's noble class.

Manneken-Pis

Even with low expectations, this bronze statue is smaller than

you'd think—the little squirt's under two feet tall, practically the size of a newborn. Still, the little peeing boy is an appropriately low-key symbol for the unpretentious Bruxelloise. The statue was made in 1619 to provide drinking water for the neighborhood. Sometimes, *Manneken-Pis* is dressed in one of the 700 different costumes that visiting VIPs have brought for him (including an Elvis Pissley outfit).

There are several different legends about *Manneken*—take

your pick. He was a naughty boy who peed inside a witch's house, so she froze him. A rich man lost his son and declared, "Find my son, and we'll make a statue of him doing what he did when found." Or—the locals' favorite version—the little tyke loved his beer, which came in handy when a fire threatened the wooden city: He bravely put it out. Want

the truth? The city commissioned it to show the joie de vivre of living in Brussels—where happy people eat, drink...and drink... and then pee.

The scene is made interesting by the crowds that gather. Hang out for a while and watch the commotion this little guy makes as tour groups come and go. When I was there, a Russian man marveled at the statue, shook his head, and said, "He never stop!"

UPPER TOWN WALK

The Upper Town has always had a more aristocratic feel than the medieval, commercial streets of the Lower Town. With broad boulevards, big marble buildings, palaces, museums, and so many things called "royal," it also seems much newer and a bit more sterile. But in fact, the Upper Town has a history that stretches back to Brussels' beginnings.

Use this 10-stop walk to get acquainted with this less-touristed part of town, sample some world-class museums, see the palace, explore art galleries, and stand on a viewpoint to get the lay of the land.

The tour starts half a block from the one essential art sight in town, the Royal Museums of Fine Arts of Belgium, which include museums of ancient and modern art, and—new in 2009—the Magritte Museum. Consider a visit while you're here (see tour on page 418). The Musical Instruments Museum is also in the neighborhood (also closed Mon, see page 391).

ORIENTATION

Length of This Walk: Allow 90 minutes.

Getting There: The walk begins at Place Royale in the Upper Town. You have several ways to get there:

    1. From the Grand Place, it's a 15-minute uphill walk (follow your map).

    2. From the Bourse, in front of the Falstaff Café, bus #95 leaves every few minutes for Place Royale (bus signs call it *Royale;* buy ticket from driver, validate it in machine).

    3. Catch a taxi (figure on €6 from the Bourse).

    4. Hop off here during a hop-on, hop-off bus tour (see page 384).

Route Overview: From Place Royale, walk south along the ridge, popping into a stained-glass-filled Gothic church, and on to the best view of the city from the towering Palace of Justice. Then backtrack a bit and descend through the well-worn tapestries of the Sablon Quarter's antiques, art, and cafés, and down to the *Manneken-Pis* at the foot of the hill.

THE WALK BEGINS

❶ Place Royale

At the crest of the hill sits Place Royale, encircled by cars and trams and enclosed by white, Neoclassical buildings forming a mirror image around a cobblestone square. A big, green statue of a horseman stands in the center.

The statue—a Belgium-born Crusader, Godfrey de Bouillon (who led the First Crusade, in 1096)—rides forward carrying a flag, gazing down on the Town Hall spire. If Godfrey turned and looked left down Rue de la Régence, he'd see the domed Palace of Justice at the end of the boulevard. Over his right shoulder, just outside the square, is the Royal Palace, the king's residence.

In the 1800s, as Belgium exerted itself to industrialize and modernize, this area was rebuilt as a sign that Brussels had arrived as a world capital. Broad vistas down wide boulevards ending in gleaming white, Greek-columned monuments—the look was all the rage, seen in Paris, London, Washington, D.C....and here.

The cupola of the Church of St. Jacques sur Coudenberg—the central portion of the square's ring of buildings—makes the church look more like a bank building. But St. Jacques' church goes back much further than this building (from 1787); it originated in the 13th century near a 12th-century castle. Nobles chose to build their mansions in the neighborhood, and later, so did the king.

The Musical Instruments Museum (see page 391) is 30 yards downhill from the square, housed in an early-20th-century, iron-and-glass former department store. Its Art Nouveau facade was a deliberate attempt to get beyond the retro-looking Greek columns and domes of the Place Royale. Even if you don't visit the museum, you can ride the elevator up to the museum café for a superb Lower Town view.

• *Brussels' world-class Royal Museums of Fine Arts of Belgium are 30 yards south of Place Royale on Rue de la Régence. But before heading*

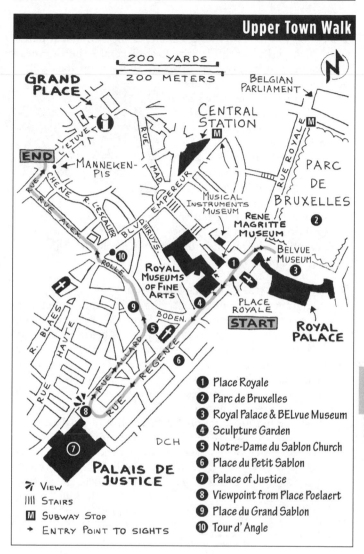

Upper Town Walk

200 YARDS
200 METERS

GRAND PLACE

BELGIAN PARLIAMENT

CENTRAL STATION Ⓜ

PARC DE BRUXELLES ➋

L'ETUVE ℹ

END

MANNEKEN-PIS

RUE MAD

RUE ROYALE Ⓜ

MUSICAL INSTRUMENTS MUSEUM

RENE MAGRITTE MUSEUM

BELVUE MUSEUM ➌

RUE CHENE

R. L'ESCALIER

RUE ALEX.

BLVD L'RUYS.

ROLLE

⑩

ROYAL MUSEUMS OF FINE ARTS

➊

PLACE ROYALE

START

ROYAL PALACE

➒

BODEN.

⑤

RUE BLAES

RUE HAUTE

⑥

④

RUE ALLARD

RUE REGENCE

⑧

⑦

PALAIS DE JUSTICE

DCH

➊ Place Royale
➋ Parc de Bruxelles
➌ Royal Palace & BELvue Museum
④ Sculpture Garden
⑤ Notre-Dame du Sablon Church
⑥ Place du Petit Sablon
⑦ Palace of Justice
⑧ Viewpoint from Place Poelaert
➒ Place du Grand Sablon
⑩ Tour d'Angle

🔭 VIEW
⫴⫴⫴ STAIRS
Ⓜ SUBWAY STOP
➔ ENTRY POINT TO SIGHTS

UPPER TOWN WALK

south, exit Place Royale on the north side (to the left as you face Godfrey), which opens up to a large, tree-lined park.

➋ Parc de Bruxelles

Copying Versailles, the Habsburg empress Maria Theresa of Austria (Marie-Antoinette's mom) had this symmetrical park laid out in 1776, when she ruled (but never visited) the city. This is just one of many large parks in Brussels, which expanded with an awareness of the importance of city planning.

At the far (north) end of the park (directly opposite the Royal Palace, no need to actually walk there) is the Parliament building. Which parliament? The city hosts several—the European Parliament, the Belgian Parliament, and several local, city-council-type parliaments. This is the Belgian Parliament, often seen on nightly newscasts as a backdrop for the country's politicians.

In 1830, Belgian patriots rose up and converged on the park, where they attacked the troops of the Dutch king. This was the first blow in a short, almost blood-less revolution that drove out the foreign-born king and gave the Belgians independence...and a different foreign-born king.

• *The long building facing the park is the...*

❸ Royal Palace (Palais Royale)

After Belgium struck out twice trying to convince someone to be their new king, Leopold I (r. 1831–1865), a nobleman from Germany, agreed. Leopold was a steadying influence as the country modernized. His son rebuilt this palace—near the site of earlier palaces, dating back to the 10th century—by linking a row of townhouse mansions with a unifying facade (around 1870).

Leopold's great-great-great-grandnephew, King Albert II, today uses the palace as an office. (His head is on Belgium's euro coins.) Albert and his wife, Queen Paola, live in a palace north

of here (near the Atomium) and on the French Riviera. If the Belgian flag (black-yellow-red) is flying from the palace, the king is somewhere in Belgium.

Albert II (born 1932) is a figurehead king, as in so many European democracies, but he serves an important function as a common bond between bickering Flemish and Walloons. His son, Prince Philippe, is slated to succeed him, though Philippe—awkward and standoffish—is not as popular as his wife, Mathilde, also a Belgian native. Their little girl, Elisabeth, born in 2001, will become the first Belgian queen.

The bulk of the palace is off-limits to tourists except for six weeks in summer (palace generally open from the last week of July until the first week of Sept, gardens open April–May), but you can see an impressive exhibit on Belgian history and the royal family in the adjacent BELvue Museum (see page 418).

• *Return to Place Royale, then continue south along Rue de la Régence, noticing the entrance to the Royal Museums of Fine Arts of Belgium (see tour on page 418). Just past the museums, on the right, you'll see a...*

❹ Sculpture Garden (Jardin de Sculpture)

This pleasant public garden—starring a statue by Rodin's contemporary, Aristide Maillol—looks like a great way to descend into the Sablon Quarter, but the gates at the bottom are often locked.

• *A hundred yards farther along, you reach the top of the Sablon neighborhood, dominated by the...*

❺ Notre-Dame du Sablon Church

The round, rose, stained-glass windows in the clerestory of this 14th-century Flamboyant Gothic church are nice by day, but are

thrilling at night, when the church is lit from inside. It glows like a lantern, enjoyed by locals at the cafés in the surrounding square.

Step inside. The glorious apse behind the altar—bathed in stained-glass light—is what Gothic is all about. Next to the altar, see a small wooden **statue of Mary** dressed in white with a lace veil. This is a copy,

made after iconoclastic Protestant vandals destroyed the original. The original statue was thought to have had miraculous powers that saved the town from plagues. In 1348, when the statue was in Antwerp, it spoke to a godly woman named Beatrix, prompting her to board a boat (see the small **wooden boat,** high above the entry door) and steal the statue away from Antwerp. When they tried to stop her, the Mary statue froze the Antwerp citizens in their tracks.

Beatrix and the statue arrived here, the Bruxelloise welcomed her with a joyous parade, and this large church was erected in her honor. Every summer, in Brussels' famous Ommegang, locals in tights and flamboyant costumes re-create the joyous arrival. With colorful banners and large puppets, they carry Mary from here through the city streets to the climax on the Grand Place.

• *On the other side of Rue de la Régence from the church is a leafy, fenced-off garden called the...*

❻ Place du Petit Sablon

This is a pleasant refuge from the busy street, part of why this neighborhood is considered so livable. The 48 small statues atop the wrought-iron fence represent the guilds—weavers, brewers, and butchers— of medieval Brussels. Inside the garden, 10 large statues represent hometown thinkers of the 16th century—a time of great intellectual accomplishments in Brussels. Gerardus Mercator (1512–1594), the Belgian mapmaker who devised a way

to show the spherical Earth on a flat surface, holds a globe.

• *We'll visit the Sablon neighborhood below the church later, but before losing elevation, let's continue along Rue de la Régence, passing the Music Academy and Brussels' main synagogue (its sidewalk fortified with concrete posts to keep car bombs at a distance), before reaching the long-scaffolded...*

❼ Palace of Justice (Palais de Justice)

This domed mountain of marble sits on the edge of the Upper Town ridge, dominating the Brussels skyline. Built in wedding-cake layers of Greek columns, it's topped with a dome taller than St. Peter's in Rome, rising 340 feet. Covering more than six acres, it's the size of a baseball stadium.

The palace was built in the time of King Leopold II (son of Leo I, r. 1865–1909) and epitomizes the brassy, look-at-me grandeur of his reign. Leopold became obscenely wealthy by turning Africa's Congo region—80 times the size of Belgium—into his personal colony. Whip-wielding Belgian masters forced African slaves to tend lucrative rubber plantations, exploiting the new craze for bicycle tires. Leopold spent much of this wealth expanding and beautifying the city of Brussels.

The building (which stands on the historic site of the town gallows) serves as a Hall of Justice, where major court cases are tried. If you pop into the lobby, you may see lawyers in black robes buzzing about.

• *On this square you'll notice a rack of city bikes. Like Paris, Brussels has a Cyclecity program that lets locals use bikes scattered all over town (note the map here) for a token €1 per hour. One of the best views of Brussels is immediately to the right of the Palace of Justice.*

❽ Viewpoint from Place Poelaert

You're standing 200 feet above the former Senne River Valley. Gazing west over the Lower Town, pan the valley from right (north) to left:

Near you is the stubby **clock tower** of the Minimen Church (which hosts lunchtime concerts in the summer). To the left of that, in the distance, past a tall square skyscraper, comes the lacy white Town Hall **spire** (marking the Grand Place).

In the far distance, six miles away, you can see one of the city's landmarks, the **Atomium.** (No doubt, someone atop it is looking back at you.) The Atomium's nine steel balls (all shiny after a 50th-anniversary restoration in 2008) form the shape of an iron molecule that is the size of the Palace of Justice behind you. Built for a 1958 World's Fair, it's now a middle-aged symbol of the dawn of the Atomic Era.

Next (closer to you) comes the **black-steepled roof** of the Notre-Dame de la Chapelle church, the city's oldest (from 1134,

with a spire that starts Gothic and ends Baroque). On the distant horizon, see **five boxy skyscrapers,** part of the residential sprawl of this city of 1.8 million, which now covers 62 square miles. Breaking the horizon is a **green dome**—it belongs to the Basilica of Koekelberg (fourth biggest in the world). And finally (panning quickly to the left), you see a **black glass skyscraper** marking the Midi (or South) train station, where you can catch the Eurostar to London.

At your feet lies the **Marolles neighborhood.** Once a funky, poor place where locals developed their own quirky dialogue, it remains somewhat seedy—and famous for its sprawling flea market (daily 7:00–14:00, best on weekends). Two of the streets just below you—Rue Haute and Rue Blaes—are lined with secondhand shops. An **elevator** connects Place Poelaert with the Marolles neighborhood (free, daily 6:00–23:00). People who brake for garage sales may want to cut out of this walk early and head to the Marolles from here.

Gazing off into the distance to the far left (south), you can't quite see the suburb of **Waterloo,** 10 miles away. But try to imagine it, because it was there that the tide of European history turned. On the morning of June 18, 1815, Napoleon waited two hours for the ground to dry before sending his troops into battle. That delay may have cost him the battle. His 72,000 soldiers could have defeated Wellington's 68,000, but the two-hour delay was just enough time for Wellington's reinforcements to arrive—45,000 Prussian troops. Napoleon had to surrender, his rule of Europe ended, and Belgium was placed under a Dutch king—until the Belgians won their independence in the 1830 revolution.

Behind you, in Place Poelaert, are two memorials to the two World Wars, both of which passed through Belgium with deadly force.

• *Backtrack east, descending to Place du Grand Sablon by walking down Rue Ernest Allard.*

❾ Place du Grand Sablon

The Sablon neighborhood features cafés and restaurants, antiques

stores, and art galleries. Chocolatier Wittamer (on the far side of the square, at #6) often has elaborate window displays. Every weekend, there's an antiques market on the square. On warm summer evenings, the square sparks magic, as sophisticated locals sip apéritifs at the café tables, admiring the glowing stained glass of the church.

• *Sloping Place du Grand Sablon funnels downhill into the pedestrian-only street called Rue de Rollebeek, which leads past fun shops to the busy Boulevard de l'Empereur. To the right on the boulevard, just past the bowling alley, is the...*

❿ Tour d'Angle

The "Corner Tower" is a rare surviving section of Brussels' 13th-century city wall, and was one of seven gates along the 2.5-mile-long wall that enclosed Brussels, one of Europe's great cities.

• *The Central Train station is two blocks directly ahead. Or continue downhill several blocks, and when you hit level ground, turn right on Rue L'Etuve, which leads directly back to the Grand Place. A block along, you'll run into our old friend* Manneken-Pis, *eternally relieving himself (if you're urine-ing to learn more about this leaky little tyke, see page 407).*

ROYAL MUSEUMS OF FINE ARTS OF BELGIUM TOUR

Musées Royaux des Beaux-Arts de Belgique

Two large buildings, each housing an art museum (ancient and modern), contain a vast collection covering the entire history of Western painting. The collection, while enjoyable, can be overwhelming, so this chapter gives a tour of a "Top 10" list highlighting the Ancient Art and Modern Art museums' strengths: Flemish and Belgian artists. In June of 2009, the complex added the new Magritte Museum, celebrating the work of the popular Belgian Surrealist with over 150 statues, paintings, and drawings.

ORIENTATION

Cost: €5 for Ancient Art and Modern Art museums; €8 for Magritte Museum.

Hours: Ancient Art and Modern Art museums—Tue–Sun 10:00–17:00, closed Mon, last entry at 16:30; Magritte Museum Tue–Sun 10:00–17:00, Wed until 20:00, closed Mon.

Getting There: The museums are at Rue de la Régence 3 in the Upper Town, just a five-minute walk uphill from Central Station (or take bus #20, #38, #71, or #95; or tram #92 or #94). You'll also encounter the museums if you take my Upper Town Walk on page 409.

Information: Consider the excellent €2.50 audioguide or the €2.50 tour booklet (*Twenty Masterpieces of the Art of Painting: A Brief Guided Tour*, sold in the museum shop). You can also choose among four self-guided tours, each marked with a different color: blue for the 15th and 16th centuries, brown for the 17th and 18th, and green for the 20th. Tel. 02-508-3211, www.fine-arts-museum.be.

Length of This Tour: Allow one hour.

Cuisine Art: The Greshem, a restaurant and tea room, is nearby at Place Royale (daily 11:00–18:00). See page 433 for other nearby lunchtime options. The museums also have a crummy café and a fancy brasserie on-site.

Overview

There are technically three museums here: the Ancient Art (pre-1800) and Modern Art (post-1800) museums are connected via a labyrinthine series of passageways. The museum complex sprawls over several wings and a dozen floors, and to see it all is a logistical nightmare. Your first stop should be the information desk, which has the latest on renovations, room closings, and the new Magritte Museum (located nearby in a separate building). Armed with the museum's free map (supplemented with the audioguide), make your way through the maze to find these 10 highlights.

THE TOUR BEGINS

• *Start with the Flemish masters, one floor up in the Ancient Art Museum, and follow the blue tour signs. In Room 11, you'll find...*

ANCIENT ART

Rogier van der Weyden (c. 1399–1464)—*Portrait of Anthony of Burgundy (Portrait d' Antoine de Bourgogne)*

Anthony was known in his day as the Great Bastard, the bravest and most distinguished of the many bastards fathered by prolific Duke Philip the Good (a Renaissance prince whose sense of style impressed Florence's young Lorenzo the Magnificent, patron of the arts).

Anthony, a member of the Archers Guild, fingers the arrow like a bow-string. From his gold necklace dangles a Golden Fleece, one of Europe's more prestigious knightly honors. Wearing a black cloak, a bowl-cut hairdo, and a dark-red cap, with his pale face and hand emerging from a dark background, the man who'd been called a bastard all his life gazes to the distance, his clear, sad eyes lit with a speckle of white paint.

Van der Weyden, Brussels' official portrait painter, faithfully rendered life-size, lifelike portraits of wealthy traders, bankers, and craftsmen. Here he captures the wrinkles in Anthony's neck, and the faint shadow his chin casts on his Adam's apple. Van der Weyden had also painted Philip the Good (in Bruges' Groeninge

Museum—see page 344), and young Anthony's long, elegant face and full lips are a mirror image—pretty convincing DNA evidence in a paternity suit.

Capitalist Flanders in the 1400s was one of the richest, most cultured, and progressive areas in Europe, rivaling Florence and Venice.
• *In Room 14, find...*

Hans Memling (c. 1430-1494)—*Martyrdom of St. Sebastian (Volets d'un Triptyque)*

Serene Sebastian is filled with arrows by a serene firing squad in a serene landscape. Sebastian, a Roman captain who'd converted to Christianity, was ordered to be shot to death. (He miraculously survived, so they clubbed him to death.)

Ready, freeze! Like a *tableaux vivant* (popular with Philip the Good's crowd), the well-dressed archers and saint freeze this moment in the martyrdom so the crowd can applaud the colorful costumes and painted cityscape backdrop.

Hans Memling, along with his former employer, Rogier van der Weyden, are called Flemish Primitives. Why "Primitive"? For the lack of 3-D realism so admired in Italy at the time (for more on Flemish Primitives, see sidebar on page 347). Sebastian's arm is tied to a branch that's not arching overhead, as it should be, but instead is behind him. An archer aims slightly behind, not at, Sebastian. The other archer strings his bow in a stilted pose. But Memling is clearly a master of detail, and the faces, beautiful textiles, and hazy landscape combine to create a meditative mood appropriate to the church altar in Bruges where this painting was once placed.
• *In Room 31, look for...*

Pieter Brueghel I, the Elder (c. 1527-1569)—*The Census at Bethlehem*

Perched at treetop level, you have a bird's-eye view over a snow-covered village near Brussels. The canals are frozen over, but life goes on, with everyone doing something. Kids throw snowballs and sled across the ice. A crowd gathers at the inn (lower left), where a woman holds a pan to catch blood while a man slaughters a pig. Most everyone has his or her back to us or head covered, so the figures speak through poses and motions.

Into the scene rides a woman on a donkey led by a man—it's Mary and husband Joseph hoping to find a room at the inn (or at

least a manger), because Mary's going into labor.

The year is 1566—the same year that Protestant extremists throughout the Low Countries vandalized Catholic churches, tearing down "idolatrous" statues and paintings of the Virgin Mary. Brueghel (more discreetly) brings Mary down to earth from her Triumphant Coronation in heaven, and places Jesus' birth in the humble here and now. The busy villagers put their heads down and work, oblivious to the future Mother of God and the wonder about to take place.

Brueghel the Elder was famous for his landscapes filled with crowds of peasants in motion. His religious paintings place the miraculous in everyday settings.

In this room, you'll see Brueghel's works, as well as those of his less-famous sons. Pieter Brueghel II, the younger Pieter, copied dad's style (and even some paintings, like the *Census at Bethlehem*). Another son, Jan, was known as the "Velvet Brueghel" for his glossy still lifes of flower arrangements.

• *Leave the blue tour and walk through to Room 34 and beyond, to the main hallway in this wing, in order to follow the brown tour signs. You'll find lots of Rubens in Rooms 52 and 53, including the wall-sized...*

Peter Paul Rubens (1577-1640)—*The Ascent to Calvary* (*La Montée au Calvaire*)

Life-size figures scale this 18-foot-tall canvas on the way to Christ's Crucifixion. The scene ripples with motion, from the windblown clothes to steroid-enhanced muscles to billowing flags and a troubled sky. Christ stumbles, and might get trampled by the surging crowd. Veronica kneels to gently wipe his bloody head.

This 200-square-foot canvas was manufactured by Rubens at his studio in Antwerp. Hiring top-notch assistants, Rubens could crank out large altarpieces for the area's Catholic churches. First, Rubens himself did a small-scale sketch in oil (like many of the studies in Room 52). He would then make other sketches, highlighting individual details. His assistants would reproduce them on the large canvas, and Rubens would then add the final touches.

This work is from late in Rubens' long and very successful career. He got a second wind in his 50s, when he married 16-year-old Hélène Fourment. She was the model for Veronica, who consoles the faltering Christ in this painting.

• *To get to the Modern Art wing, return to the ground floor and the large main entrance hall of the Ancient Museum. From there, a passageway leads to the Modern Art Museum. Once in the Modern Art wing (entering on Level −3), take the elevator—which is so slow, they actually provide chairs inside the elevator itself—down to the lowest level (−8), filled with paintings from the 19th and 20th centuries. Work your way back up, keeping an eye out for the paintings described below. Enlist the help of nearby guards if you can't find any of these pieces.*

MODERN ART

• *Watch Impressionism turn to Post-Impressionism in this wing, which features both. Paul Gauguin and Georges Seurat emerged from Paris' Impressionist community to forge their own styles. Begin by visiting with...*

Georges Seurat (1859–1891)—*The Seine at Grand-Jatte* (*La Seine à la Grande-Jatte, 1888*)

Seurat paints a Sunday-in-the-park view from his favorite island in the Seine. Taking Impressionism to its extreme, he builds the scene out of small points of primary colors that blend at a distance to form objects. The bright colors capture the dazzling, sunlit atmosphere of this hazy day.

Paul Gauguin (1848–1903)—*Breton Calvary* (*Calvaire Breton, 1889*; a.k.a. *The Green Christ/Le Christ Vert*)

Paul Gauguin returned to the bold, black, coloring-book outlines of more Primitive (pre-3-D) art. The Christian statue and countryside look less like Brittany and more like primitive Tahiti, where Gauguin would soon settle.

James Ensor (1860–1949)—*Shocked Masks (1883)*

At 22, James Ensor, an acclaimed child prodigy, proudly presented his lively Impressionist-style works to the Brussels Salon for exhibition. They were flatly rejected.

The artist withdrew from public view and, in seclusion, painted *Shocked Masks,* a dark and murky scene set in a small room of an ordinary couple wearing grotesque masks. Once again, everyone disliked this disturbing canvas and heaped more criticism on him. For the next six decades, Ensor painted

the world as he saw it—full of bizarre, carnival-masked, stupid-looking crowds of cruel strangers who mock the viewer.

Jacques-Louis David (1748–1825)—*The Death of Marat* (1793)

In a scene ripped from the day's headlines, Marat—a well-known crusading French journalist—has been stabbed to death in his

bathtub by Charlotte Corday, a conservative fanatic. Marat's life drains out of him, turning the bathwater red. With his last strength, he pens a final, patriotic, *"Vive la Révolution"* message to his fellow patriots. Corday, a young noblewoman angered by Marat's campaign to behead the French king, was arrested and guillotined three days later.

Jacques-Louis David, one of Marat's fellow revolutionaries, set to work painting a tribute to his fallen comrade. (He signed the painting: *"À Marat"*—"To Marat.")

David makes it a secular *pietà,* with the brave writer as a martyred Christ in a classic dangling-arm pose. Still, the deathly pallor and harsh lighting pull no punches, creating in-your-face realism.

David, the official art director of the French Revolution, supervised propaganda and the costumes worn for patriotic parades. A year later (1794), his extreme brand of revolution (which included guillotining thousands of supposed enemies) was squelched by moderates, and David was jailed. He emerged again as Napoleon's court painter. When Napoleon was exiled in 1815, so was David, spending his last years in Brussels.

Paul Delvaux (1897–1994)

Delvaux, who studied, worked, and taught in Brussels, became famous for his surrealistic paintings of nude women, often wandering through weirdly lit landscapes. They cast long shadows, wandering bare-breasted among classical ruins. Some women grow roots.

• *Along with other Surrealist artists represented in this museum, such as Joan Miró, Salvador Dalí, Max Ernst, Yves Tanguy, and Roberto Matta, you'll see plenty of paintings by Magritte in the new René Magritte Museum.*

René Magritte (1898–1967)

Magritte paints real objects with photographic clarity, then jumbles them together in new and provocative ways.

Magritte had his own private reserve of symbolic images. You'll see clouds, blue sky, windows, the female torso, men in bowler hats, rocks, and castles arranged side by side as if they should mean something. People morph into animals or inanimate objects. The juxtaposition short-circuits your brain only when you try to make sense of it.

Magritte also trained and worked in Brussels. Though he's world-famous now, it took decades before his peculiar brand of Surrealism caught on.

SLEEPING

Normal hotel prices are high in central Brussels. But if you arrive in July, August, or on a Friday or Saturday night any other time, the city's fancy business-class hotels rent rooms for half price, making them your best budget bet. Otherwise, you do have budget options. The modern hostels are especially good and rent double rooms. April, May, September, and October are very crowded, and finding a room without a reservation can be impossible.

Business Hotels with Summer Rates

The fancy hotels of Brussels (Db-€150–200) survive because of the business and diplomatic trade. But they're desperately empty in July and August (sometimes June, too) and on weekends (most Fri, Sat, and—to a lesser extent—Sun nights). Ask for a summer/weekend rate and you'll save about a third. If you go through the TI, you'll save up to two-thirds. Three-star hotels in the center abound with amazing summer rates—you can rent a double room with enough comforts to keep a diplomat happy, including a fancy breakfast, for about €60.

The TI assures me that every day in July and August, tons of business-class hotel rooms are on the push list; you'll get a big discount just by showing up at either TI (for same-day booking only). In July and August and on any Friday or Saturday—trust me—your best value is to arrive without a reservation, walk from the Central Station down to either TI, and let them book you a room within a few blocks. You cannot book these deals in advance. They are only for the bold who show up without a reservation. The later you arrive, the lower the prices drop (room-booking TI closes at 19:00 July–Aug, last booking at 18:30, see page 380).

If you're nervous about traveling without advance reservations, contact the TI by email (info@visitflanders.be) and ask which

Sleep Code

(€1 = about $1.40, country code: 32)
S = Single, **D** = Double/Twin, **T** = Triple, **Q** = Quad, **b** = bathroom, **s** = shower only. Everyone speaks English and accepts credit cards. Unless otherwise noted, breakfast is included.

To help you easily sort through these listings, I've divided the rooms into three categories, based on the price for a standard double room with bath:

$$$ Higher Priced—Most rooms €100 or more.
 $$ Moderately Priced—Most rooms between €80–100.
  $ Lower Priced—Most rooms €80 or less.

business-class hotels will have special rates during your visit. Ask for the cheapest three-star place near the Grand Place. Historically the Hotel Ibis Centre Ste. Catherine has double rooms with bath and breakfast for €50 through the summer.

These seasonal rates apply only to business-class hotels. Because of this, budget accommodations, which charge the same throughout the year, go from being a good value one day (say, a Thursday in October) to a bad value the next (a Friday in October).

Hotels near the Grand Place

$$$ Hotel Ibis off Grand Place is well-situated halfway between the Central Station and the Grand Place, the best of six Ibis locations in or near Brussels. It's a sprawling, modern hotel offering 184 quiet, simple, industrial-strength-yet-comfy rooms (Sb/Db-€145 Mon–Thu, €90–100 Fri–Sun and daily July–Aug, extra bed-€20, breakfast-€13, non-smoking rooms, air-con, elevator, Grasmarkt 100, tel. 02-514-1223, fax 02-514-5067, www.ibishotel.com, h1046@accor.com).

$$$ Hotel Le Dixseptième, a four-star luxury hotel ideally located a block below Central Station, is an expensive oasis in the heart of town. Prim, proper, and peaceful, with chandeliers and squeaky hardwood floors, its 24 rooms come with all the comforts. Each is decorated with a different theme (Db-€200, Db suites-€270, extra bed-€30, 25 percent off Fri–Sat and daily July–Aug, see website for discounts, air-con, elevator, Rue de la Madeleine 25, tel. 02-517-1717, fax 02-502-6424, www.ledixseptieme.be, info@ledixseptieme.be).

$$$ Hotel La Madeleine, on the small square between Central Station and the Grand Place, rents 55 plain, dimly lit rooms. It has a great location and a friendly staff (S-€55; Ss-€78,

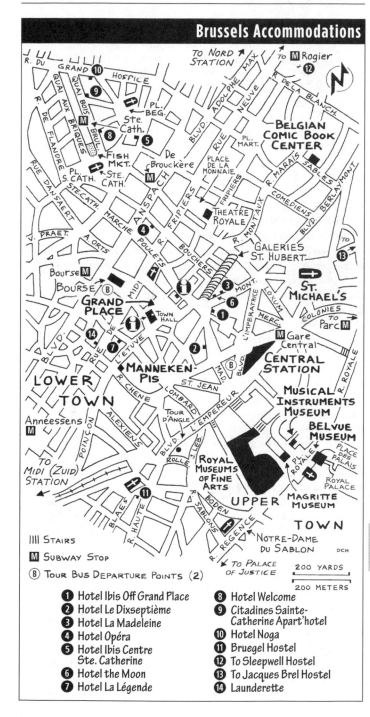

Brussels Accommodations

1. Hotel Ibis Off Grand Place
2. Hotel Le Dixseptième
3. Hotel La Madeleine
4. Hotel Opéra
5. Hotel Ibis Centre Ste. Catherine
6. Hotel the Moon
7. Hotel La Légende
8. Hotel Welcome
9. Citadines Sainte-Catherine Apart'hotel
10. Hotel Noga
11. Bruegel Hostel
12. To Sleepwell Hostel
13. To Jacques Brel Hostel
14. Launderette

IIII Stairs

M Subway Stop

B Tour Bus Departure Points (2)

200 YARDS
200 METERS

Sb-€102, Db-€112; "executive" rooms: Sb-€122, Db-€127, Tb-€137; 20 percent off Fri–Sat, 30 percent off July–Aug—see website for deals; family room for four available, request a quieter back room when you reserve, elevator, Wi-Fi, Rue de la Montagne 22, tel. 02-513-2973, fax 02-502-1350, www.hotel-la-madeleine.be, info @hotel-la-madeleine.be, Philippe).

$$$ Hotel Opéra, on a great, people-filled street near the Grand Place, is professional but standardized, with lots of street noise and 49 well-worn rooms (Sb-€82, Db-€105 or €85 in July–Aug, Tb-€135, Qb-€150, 10 percent less with this book, request quieter courtyard rooms, elevator, Wi-Fi, Rue Gretry 53, tel. 02-219-4343, fax 02-219-1720, www.hotel-opera.be, reception @hotel-opera.be).

$$ Hotel Ibis Centre Ste. Catherine is a big, impersonal, perfectly comfortable place with a great location that offers very deep discounts during its slow times only via the TI. Its double rooms, which are reasonable all year (Db-€80–100) rent for €50 with breakfast through the summer only when booked through the TI (Rue Joseph Plateau Straat 2 at Place Ste. Catherine, tel. 02-513-7620, fax 02-514-2214, www.ibishotel.com, h1454 @accor.com).

$$ Hotel the Moon is concrete and efficient, with 17 fresh, industrial-strength rooms and no public spaces. Although it has absolutely no character, you'll sleep fine and it's super–convenient, right in the old center (Sb-€50–70, Db-€60–90, Tb-€75–120, lower prices are for July–Aug, 10 percent discount with this book, Rue de la Montagne 4, tel. 02-508-1580, fax 02-508-1585, www. memon-hotels.be, info@hotelthemoon.com).

$$ Hotel La Légende rents 26 rooms with a dormitory ambience a block from the *Manneken-Pis* statue. Although it's on a busy road, it has a pleasant courtyard. The furnishings are basic, but the location and price are right and the rooms are comfortable enough (standard Db-€95, newer Db-€120, Tb-€145, Qb-€155, 30 percent off on weekends and July–Aug, elevator, Rue du Lombard 35, tel. 02-512-8290, fax 02-512-3493, www.hotellalegende.com, info @hotellalegende.com).

Hotels Around the Fish Market

The next three listings are a 10-minute walk from the intensity of the old center, near the Ste. Catherine Métro stop. This charming neighborhood, called "the village in Brussels," faces the canalside fish market and has many of the town's best restaurants.

$$$ Hotel Welcome, owned by an energetic bundle of hospitality named Meester Smeester, offers outrageously creative rooms, exuberantly decorated with artifacts he's picked up in his world travels. Each of the 16 rooms has a different geographic theme—

from India to Japan to Bali (Sb-€95, standard Db-€120, deluxe Db-€140, large suite-€210, much lower rates in Aug, special 20 percent off—even on discounted rates—with two-night stay and this book, elevator, Internet access and Wi-Fi, parking-€10, airport shuttle available, 23 Quai au Bois à Brûler, tel. 02-219-9546, fax 02-217-1887, www.brusselshotel.travel, info@hotelwelcome.com, run by Sophie and Michel Smeesters, plus Vincent and Natasha). Tour Michel's rooms on the Web.

$$$ Citadines Sainte-Catherine Apart'hotel, part of a Europe-wide chain, is a huge apartment-style hotel with modern, shipshape rooms. Choose from efficiency studios with fold-out double beds or two-room apartments with a bedroom and a fold-out couch in the living room. All 163 units come with a kitchen, stocked cupboards, a stereo, and everything you need to settle right in (one- or two-person studio-€125, €63 July–Aug; apartment for up to four people-€155, €105 July–Aug; 15 percent cheaper by the week, breakfast-€13, Wi-Fi, parking-€10, 51 Quai au Bois à Brûler, tel. 02-221-1411, fax 02-221-1599, www.citadines.com, stecatherine@citadines.com).

$$$ Hotel Noga feels extremely homey, with 19 rooms, a welcoming game room, and old photos of Belgian royalty lining the hallways. It's carefully run by Frederich Faucher and his son, Mourad (Sb-€90, Db-€110, Tb-€135, Qb-€160, all rooms about 20 percent off Fri–Sat and in Aug, 5 percent discount if you pay in cash, very quiet, non-smoking rooms, Rue du Beguinage 38, tel. 02-218-6763, fax 02-218-1603, www.nogahotel.com, info@noga hotel.com).

Hostels

Three classy and modern hostels—in buildings that could double as small, state-of-the-art, minimum-security prisons—are within a 10-minute walk of the Central Station. Each accepts people of all ages, serves cheap and hot meals, takes credit cards, and charges about the same price. All rates include breakfast and showers down the hall.

$ Bruegel Hostel, a fortress of cleanliness, is handiest and most comfortable. Of its many rooms, 22 are bunk-bed doubles (S-€31, D-€45, beds in quads or dorms-€18.60, nonmembers pay €3 extra per night, includes sheets and breakfast, open 7:00–13:00 & 14:00–1:00 in the morning, Rue de St. Esprit 2 midway between Midi and Central stations, behind Chapelle church, tel. 02-511-0436, fax 02-512-0711, www.vjh.be, brussel@vjh.be).

$ Sleepwell, surrounded by high-rise parking structures, is also comfortable (S-€41, D-€60, T-€85, dorm beds-€19–30, reduced rates for multi-night stays, includes breakfast, non-smoking, Internet access in lobby, Rue de Damier 23, tel. 02-218-5050, fax 02-218-1313, www.sleepwell.be, info@sleepwell.be).

$ Jacques Brel is a little farther out, but it's still a reasonable walk from everything (171 beds, S-€32, D-€46, dorm bed-€16–18, includes breakfast and sheets, no curfew, non-smoking rooms, laundry, Rue de la Sablonnière 30, tel. 02-218-0187, fax 02-217-2005, www.laj.be, brussels.brel@laj.be).

EATING

For many, the obvious eating tip in Brussels is simply to enjoy the Grand Place. My vote for northern Europe's grandest medieval square is lined with hardworking eateries that serve the predictable dishes to tourist crowds. Of course, you won't get the best quality or prices—but, after all, it's the Grand Place. Locals advise eating well elsewhere and enjoying a Grand Place perch for dessert or a drink. While many tourists congregate at the Rue des Bouchers, "Restaurant Row," consider a wander through the new emerging eating zone—gay, ethnic, and trendy—past the Bourse near Place Saint-Géry. Compare the ambience, check posted menus, and choose your favorite.

Brussels is known for both its high-quality, French-style cuisine and for multicultural variety. Seafood—fish, eel, shrimp, and oysters—is especially well-prepared here. As in France, if you ask for the *menu* (muh-noo) at a restaurant, you won't get a list of dishes; you'll get a fixed-price meal. *Menus*, which include three or four courses, are generally a good value if you're hungry. Ask for *la carte* (lah kart) if you want to see a printed menu and order à la carte, like the locals do. For more on Belgian cuisine, see page 366.

Mussels in Brussels

Mussels *(moules)* are available all over town. For an atmospheric cellar or a table right on the Grand Place, eat at **'t Kelderke.** Its one steamy vault under the square is always packed with both natives and tourists—a real Brussels fixture. It serves local specialties, including mussels (a splittable kilo bucket—just more than 2 pounds—for €20–22; daily 12:00–24:00, Thu–Sat until 2:00 in the morning, no reservations, Grand Place 15, tel. 02-513-7344). Also see Restaurant Chez Leon, next page.

Rue des Bouchers ("Restaurant Row")

Brussels' restaurant streets, two blocks north of the Grand Place, are touristy and notorious for aggressively sucking you in and ripping you off. But the area is an exhilarating spectacle and fun for at least a walk. Order carefully, understand the prices thoroughly, and watch your wallet.

Restaurant Chez Leon is a touristy mussels factory, slamming out piles of good, cheap buckets since 1893. It's big and welcoming, with busy green-aproned waiters offering a "Formula Leon" for €14.50—a light meal consisting of a small bucket of mussels, fries, and a beer. They also offer a €28.50 fixed-price meal that comes with a starter, a large bucket of mussels, fries, and beer (daily 12:00–23:00, kids under 12 eat free, Rue des Bouchers 18, tel. 02-511-1415). In the family portrait of Leon's brother Honoré (hanging in the corner), the wife actually looks like a mussel.

Aux Armes de Bruxelles is a venerable restaurant that has been serving reliably good food to locals in a dressy setting for generations. This is another food factory, with white-suited waiters serving an older clientele impressed by the restaurant's reputation. You'll pay a bit more for the formality (€24 fixed-price lunch, €35–46 fixed-price dinner, Tue–Sun 12:00–23:00, closed Mon, indoor seating only, Rue des Bouchers 13, tel. 02-511-5550).

Restaurant Vincent has you enter through the kitchen to enjoy their 1905-era ambience (€27.50 fixed-price meal, Mon–Sat 12:00–14:30 & 18:30–23:00, Sun 12:00–15:00 & 18:30–22:30, Rue des Dominicains 8–10, tel. 02-511-2607, Michel and Jacques).

Finer Dining

Restaurant de l'Ogenblik, a remarkably peaceful eddy just off the raging restaurant row, fills an early-20th-century space in the corner of an arcade. The dressy waiters serve well-presented, near-gourmet French cuisine (€24–27 plates, Mon–Sat 12:00–14:30 & 19:00–24:00, closed Sun, across from Restaurant Vincent—listed above—at Galerie des Princes 1, tel. 02-511-6151, Yves). A mussels-free zone, their rack of lamb with 10 vegetables is great.

Belga Queen Brasserie bills itself as a "wonderfood place." A huge, trendy, dressy brasserie filling a palatial former bank building, it's *the* spot for Brussels' beautiful people and visiting European diplomats. While a little more expensive than the alternatives, the "creative Belgian cuisine" is excellent, the service is sharp, and the experience is memorable—from the fries served in silver cones, to the double-decker platters of iced shellfish, to the transparent toilets stalls (which become opaque only after you nervously lock the door). The high-powered trendiness can make you feel a little gawky, but if you've got the money, this is a great splurge. Consider their €33 three-course, fixed-price meal with

Brussels Restaurants

1. 't Kelderke
2. Restaurant Chez Leon
3. Aux Armes de Bruxelles
4. Rest. Vincent & de l'Ogenblik
5. Belga Queen Brasserie
6. Le Mokafé
7. La Maison des Crêpes
8. Osteria a l'Ombra
9. Pitta Creta Grill
10. Panos Sandwiches
11. AD Delhaize Grocery
12. Super GB Grocery
13. Bij den Boer & Rest. Jacques
14. La Marie Joseph
15. Restaurant La Marée
16. Restaurant Le Pré Salé
17. La Villette Restaurant
18. A la Mort Subite Bar
19. Le Cirio Café
20. A la Bécasse Café
21. Fin de Siècle & Le Greenwich Bars

BRUSSELS EATING

matching beers (€20–30 entrées, €30–42 fixed-price meals, daily 12:00–14:30 & 19:00–24:00, call to reserve, two seatings: about 19:30 and 21:30, Rue Fosse-aux-Loups 32, tel. 02-217-2187). The vault downstairs is a plush cigar and cocktail lounge. For just a drink, grab a stool at the white-marble oyster bar.

More Eateries near the Grand Place

Le Mokafé is inexpensive but feels splurgy. It's in the quiet end of the elegant Galeries St. Hubert with great people-watching outdoor tables (€8 spaghetti, €10 salads, daily 8:00–24:00, Galerie du Roi 9, tel. 02-511-7870).

La Maison des Crêpes, a little eatery half a block south of the Bourse, looks underwhelming but serves delicious €8–10 crêpes (savory and sweet) and salads. It has a brown café ambience, and even though it's just a few steps away from the tourist bustle, it feels laid-back and local (good beers, fresh mint tea, sidewalk seating, daily 12:00–23:00, Rue du Midi 13).

Osteria a l'Ombra, a true Italian joint, is perfect for anyone needing a quality bowl of pasta with a fine glass of Italian wine. Across the lane from the TI and just a block off the Grand Place, it's pricey, but the woody bistro ambience and tasty food make it a good value. If you choose an entrée (about €15), your choice of pasta or salad is included in the price. While the ground-floor seating is fine, also consider sitting upstairs (Mon–Fri 12:00–15:00 & 18:30–23:30, Sat 18:30–23:30, closed Sun, Rue des Harengs 2, tel. 02-511-6710).

Cheap Eats on Grasmarkt: The Grasmarkt is lined with low-end eateries, especially fun on sunny days. To eat for less here, check out the **Pitta Creta Grill** (€3–4 pita sandwiches) or the **Panos** sandwich place.

Groceries: Two supermarkets are about a block from the Bourse and a few blocks from the Grand Place. **AD Delhaize** is at the intersection of Anspach and Marché-aux-Poulets (Mon–Sat 9:00–20:00, Fri until 21:00, Sun 9:00–18:00), and **Super GB** is half a block away at Halles and Marché-aux-Poulets (Mon–Sat 9:00–20:00, Fri until 21:00, closed Sun). **Mini-Markets** dot the city. Generally run by Pakistani and Indian immigrants, they are expensive but handy (open very late, drinks, groceries, phone cards).

Around the Sainte Catherine Fish Market

A 10-minute walk from the old center puts you in "the village within the city" area of Sainte Catherine (Métro: Ste. Catherine). The historic fish market here has spawned a tradition of fine restaurants specializing mostly in seafood. The old fish canal survives, and if you walk around it, you'll see plenty of enticing restaurants.

Make the circuit, considering these very good yet very different eating options.

Bij den Boer, a fun, noisy eatery popular with locals and tourists, feels like a traditional and very successful brasserie. The specialty: fish (€30 four-course fixed-price meal, Mon–Sat 12:00–14:30 & 18:00–22:30, closed Sun, Quai aux Briques 60, tel. 02-512-6122). Its neighbor, **Restaurant Jacques** (at #44, tel. 02-513-2762), also has a good reputation. You'll start things off with a free bowl of little gray shrimp as an appetizer.

La Marie Joseph, stylish and modern—both the food and the clientele—serves fancy fish and fries and earns raves from the natives (€25 plates, Tue–Sun 12:00–15:00 & 18:30–23:00, closed Mon, no reservations, Quai au Bois à Brûler 47, tel. 02-218-0596).

Restaurant La Marée is a classic local scene a couple of blocks away from the trendy canalside places. A non-touristy bistro with an open kitchen and an inviting menu, it specializes in mussels and seafood (closed Sun–Mon, near Rue du Marché aux Porcs at Rue de Flandre 99, tel. 02-511-0040).

Restaurant Le Pré Salé is noisy, high-energy, and family-friendly. A Brussels fixture for its traditional local cuisine, it fills a former butcher shop with happy eaters and a busy open kitchen (big, shareable €21 pots of mussels come with a salad, €15 meals, Wed–Sun 12:00–14:30 & 18:30–22:30, closed Mon–Tue, a block off the fish market at Rue de Flandre 20, tel. 02-513-6545).

La Villette Restaurant is a romantic, low-energy, seafood-free alternative, serving traditional Belgian cuisine: heavy, meaty stews and dishes with beer. It has a charming red-and-white-table-cloth interior and good outdoor seating facing a small square (€14 two-course fixed-price lunch, €15–18 meals, Mon–Fri 12:00–14:30 & 18:30–22:30, Sat 18:30–22:30 only, closed Sun, Rue du Vieux Marché-aux-Grains 3, tel. 02-512-7550, Agata).

Sampling Belgian Beer with Food and Ambience

Looking for a good spot to enjoy that famous Belgian beer? Brussels is full of atmospheric cafés to savor the local brew. The eateries lining the Grand Place are touristy, but the setting—plush old medieval guild halls fronting all that cobbled wonder—is hard to beat. I've listed three places a few minutes' walk off the square, all with a magical, old-time feel. If you'd like something to wash down with your beer, you can generally get a cold-meat plate, an open-face sandwich, or a salad.

All varieties of Belgian beer are available, but Brussels' most distinctive beers are *lambic*-based. Look for *lambic doux, lambic blanche, gueuze* (pronounced "kurrs"), and *faro*, as well as fruit-flavored *lambics*, such as *kriek* (cherry) and *framboise* (raspberry—

frambozen in Flemish). These beers look and taste more like a dry, somewhat bitter cider. The brewer doesn't add yeast—the beer ferments naturally from yeast found floating only in the marshy air around Brussels. For more on Belgian beer, see page 367.

A la Mort Subite, north of the restaurant streets, is a classic old bar that has retained its 1928 decor...and many of its 1928 customers (Mon–Sat 11:00–24:00, Sun 13:00–22:00, Rue Montagne-aux-Herbes Potagères 7, tel. 02-513-1318). Named after the "sudden death" playoff that workingmen used to end their lunchtime dice games, it still has an unpretentious, working-class feel. The decor is simple, with wood tables, grimy yellow wallpaper, and some-other-era garland trim. Tiny metal plates on the

walls mark spots where gas-powered flames once flickered—used by patrons to light their cigars. A typical lunch or snack here is a *tartine* (open-face sandwich, €5) spread with *fromage blanc* (cream cheese) or pressed meat. Eat it with one of the home-brewed, *lambic*-based beers. This is a good place to try the *kriek* (cherry-flavored) beer. The Bruxelloise claim it goes well with sandwiches.

At **Le Cirio,** across from the Bourse, the dark tables bear the skid marks of over a century's worth of beer steins (nightly 10:00–1:00 in the morning, Rue de la Bourse 18–20, tel. 02-512-1395).

A la Bécasse is lower profile than Le Cirio, with a simple wood-panel and wood-table decor that appeals to both poor students and lunching businessmen. The home-brewed *lambic doux* has been served in clay jars since 1825. It's just around the corner from Le Cirio, toward the Grand Place, hidden away at the end of a courtyard (Mon–Sat 10:00–24:00, Sun 11:00–24:00, Rue de Tabora 11, tel. 02-511-0006).

Two Humble Bars: The classics recommended above are famous among tourists and understandably so. The following local hangouts offer a more basic, neighborhood feel: **Fin de Siècle** is a youthful bohemian scene serving basic, no-pretense Belgian/French dishes for around €13 (daily from 18:00, Rue des Chartreux 9). The adjacent **Le Greenwich** is a chess bar with a rough, circa-1900 former elegance serving good beer and simpler plates—like spaghetti (closed Sun, Rue des Chartreux 7, tel. 02-511-4167).

TRANSPORTATION CONNECTIONS

Belgium

Belgium's train system is slick, efficient, and non-smoking. Consider these rail deals for traveling within the country (www .b-rail.be):

- **Youths** under age 26 can get a Go Pass: €46 for 10 rides anywhere in Belgium (www.gopass.be).
- **Seniors** (age 65-plus) can get a same-day round-trip ticket to anywhere in Belgium for €4 (weekdays: after 9:00; weekends: no restrictions mid-Sept–April, not valid May–mid-Sept).
- Those traveling on the **weekend** should request the weekend discount for round-trips (50 percent off, valid Fri after 19:00). Note that if you have a bike, you'll pay extra to bring it on the train (€5 one-way, €8 round-trip).

Bruges

Trains
From Bruges by Train to: Brussels (2/hr, usually at :31 and :57, 1 hr, €12.30), **Ghent** (2/hr, 40 min), **Ostende** (3/hr, 15 min), **Köln** (6/ day, 3.5 hrs, change at Brussels Midi), **Paris** (1/day direct, about 2/ hr via Brussels, 2.5 hrs on fast Thalys trains—it's best to book by 20:00 the day before), **Amsterdam** (hourly, 3.5–4 hrs, transfer at Antwerp Central or Brussels Midi; transfer can be timed closely— be alert and check with conductor), **Amsterdam's Schiphol Airport** (hourly, 3.5 hrs, transfer in Antwerp or Brussels,), **Haarlem** (1–2/hr, 3.5 hrs, requires transfer). Train info: tel. 050/302-424.

    Trains from London: Bruges is an ideal "Welcome to Europe" stop after London. Take the Eurostar train from London to Brussels (10/day, 2.5 hrs), then transfer, backtracking to Bruges

TRANS CONN BELGIUM

Belgian Train Lines

(2/hr, 1 hr, entire trip is covered by same Eurostar ticket; see Eurostar details on next page).

Brussels

Trains

Brussels has three train stations: Central, Midi, and Nord (described on page 381). Be sure you're clear on which station or stations your train uses.

From Brussels by Train to: Bruges (2/hr, 1 hr; from any of Brussels' train stations, catch Intercity train—direction: Ostende or Knokke-Blankenberge, €12.30), **Amsterdam** (stopping at Amsterdam's Schiphol Airport on the way, hourly, 2.75 hrs, from Central, Midi, or Nord—sometimes from just one station, but sometimes all three), **Haarlem** (hourly, 2.75 hrs, transfer in Rotterdam), **Berlin** (7/day, 7.5–9 hrs, from Midi, transfer in Köln; can also transfer to night train in Köln), **Frankfurt** (9/day, 3.5 hrs direct from Midi or 5.5 hrs with transfer in Köln from Midi), **Munich** (9/day, 7–8.5 hrs; from Midi and Nord, most transfer in

Köln or Frankfurt), **Rome** (3/day, 17 hrs; from Nord, transfer in Milan, Zürich, or Paris), **Paris** (fast Thalys trains zip to Paris 2/hr, 1.5 hrs, from Midi—it's best to book by 20:00 the day before, or risk limited availability on same day). When booking Thalys (and similar express) trains to or from Paris, Amsterdam, and Köln, even railpass-holders need to pay the supplement of €14.50 for second class or €20 for first class. The first-class supplement generally gets you a meal on board. Train info: tel. 02-528-2828 (long wait), www.thalys.com.

By Eurostar to/from London: Brussels and London are two and a half hours apart by Eurostar train (10/day). Fares are reasonable but complicated. Prices vary depending on how far ahead you reserve, whether you can live with restrictions, and whether you're eligible for any discounts (children, youths, seniors, and railpass holders all qualify). Rates are lowest for round-trips.

Fares can change without notice, but typically a **one-way, full-fare ticket** (with no restrictions on refundability) runs about $425 first-class and $310 second-class. Accepting more restrictions lowers the price substantially (figure $90–200 for second class, one-way), but these **cheaper seats** sell out quickly. Those traveling with a railpass that covers Belgium or Britain should look first at the **passholder** fare (about $90–160 for second-class, one-way Eurostar trips). Eurostar tickets between London and Brussels include travel to/from any Belgian city at no additional cost within 24 hours of the Brussels Eurostar arrival or departure (not valid on Thalys express trains). Just show the Eurostar ticket when boarding the other train(s).

You can check the latest fares and book tickets by phone or online in the US (order online at www.ricksteves.com/rail/euro star.htm, prices listed in dollars; or order by phone at US tel. 800-EUROSTAR) or in Belgium (www.eurostar.com, prices listed in euros; Belgian tel. 02-528-2828). While tickets are usually cheaper if purchased in the US, fares offered in Europe follow different discount rules—so it can be worth it to check www.eurostar.com before purchasing. If you buy from a US company, you'll pay for ticket delivery in the US. In Europe, you can buy your Eurostar ticket at any major train station in any country or

Eurostar Routes

ENGLAND
LONDON
AMSTERDAM
EBBS-FLEET
CALAIS FRÉTHUN
N · E · T · H.
ASHFORD
B · E · L · G.
LILLE
BRUSSELS
F · R · A · N · C · E
PARIS

50 MI
100 KM

—— EUROSTAR
- - - CHANNEL TUNNEL
····· OTHER RAIL

at any travel agency that handles train tickets (expect a booking fee).

Trains to London leave from platforms #1 and #2 at Brussels Midi. Arrive 30 minutes early to get your ticket validated and your luggage and passport checked by British authorities (similar to an airport check-in for an international flight).

By Bus to: London (cost can vary, but generally €35 one-way, €70 round-trip, about 9 hrs, Eurolines tel. 02-203-0707 in Brussels, www.eurolines.com).

Airports

Brussels Airport

The clear winner for getting to and from the airport (nine miles from downtown Brussels) is the Airport Express shuttle train that runs from Brussels Midi and Central stations (€2.90, 4/hr, 25 min, daily 6:00–23:00). If you're connecting the airport with Bruges, take this shuttle train and transfer in Brussels. For a taxi, figure on spending €40 between downtown Brussels and the airport. Airport info: tel. 0900-70000, www.brusselsairport.be.

Brussels Airlines flies cheaply between Brussels and Athens, Milan, Rome, Florence, Geneva, Nice, Lisbon, Barcelona, Madrid, and more (Belgian tel. 07-035-1111, www.brusselsairlines.com). Bmi british midland has inexpensive flights from Brussels to London and the British Isles (www.flybmi.com). Non-discount airlines, such as Lufthansa (www.lufthansa.com), Finnair (www.finnair.com), and Alitalia (www.alitalia.com), offer daily flights from Brussels Airport.

Brussels South Charleroi Airport

Discount airlines Ryanair (www.ryanair.com) and Wizz Air (www.wizzair.com) use this smaller airport, located about 30 miles from downtown Brussels in the town of Gosselies. The airport is connected to Brussels Central Station by shuttle bus (runs hourly, 60 min, last shuttle at 22:30, www.voyages-lelan.com) and by train (bus #A connects Charleroi Airport and Charleroi Station—2/hr, 18 min; Charleroi-Brussels trains go 2/hr, 60 min). Airport info: tel. 07-125-1211, www.charleroi-airport.com.

HISTORY

TWENTY CENTURIES IN SIX PAGES

A.D. 1–1300—Romans and Invasions

When Rome falls (c. 400), the Low Countries shatter into a patchwork of local dukedoms that are ravaged by Viking raids. Out of this poor, agricultural, and feudal landscape emerge three self-governing urban centers—Amsterdam, Bruges, and Brussels—each in a prime location for trade. Amsterdam and Bruges sit where rivers flow into the North Sea, while Brussels hugs a main trading highway.

Sights

- Amsterdam's Dam Square
- Exhibits in Amsterdam History Museum
- Haarlem's Market Square
- Bruges' original fort and church ruins
- Bruges' Basilica of the Holy Blood (1150)
- Brussels' St. Michael's Cathedral, model in the City Museum, and Tour d'Angle (tower) from city wall

1300–1500—Booming Trade Towns

Bruges, the midway port between North Sea and Mediterranean trade routes, becomes one of Europe's busiest and richest cities. Amsterdam augments its beer and herring trade with budding capitalism: banking, loans, and speculation in stock and futures.

Brussels sells waffles and beer to passing travelers. Politically, the Low Countries are united through marriage with the cultured empire of the Dukes of Burgundy.

Sights
- Churches: Amsterdam's Old Church (Oude Kerk) and New Church (Nieuwe Kerk), and Haarlem's Grote Kerk
- Amsterdam's Waag (in the Red Light District), the Mint Tower from the original city wall, and the wooden house at Begijnhof 34
- Bruges' bell tower, the Gothic Room in the City Hall, and the Church of Our Lady
- Flemish Primitive art (Van Eyck, Memling, Van der Weyden) in Bruges' Groeninge and Memling museums, and in Brussels' Royal Museums of Fine Arts of Belgium
- Brussels' Grand Place, medieval street Rue des Bouchers (Restaurant Row), and Notre-Dame du Sablon Church

1500s—Protestants vs. Catholics, Freedom-Fighters vs. Spanish Rulers

Protestantism spreads through the Low Countries, particularly in Holland (while Belgium remains more Catholic). Thanks to other

royal marriages, the Low Countries are ruled from afar by the very Catholic Habsburg family in Spain. In 1566, angry Protestants rise up against Spain and Catholicism, vandalizing Catholic churches and deposing Spanish governors. King Philip II of Spain sends troops to restore order and brutally punish the rebel-heretics, beginning the Eighty Years' War, also known as the Dutch War of Independence (1568–1648).

Sights
- Amsterdam's whitewashed, simply decorated, post-Iconoclasm churches
- Civic Guard portraits in Amsterdam History Museum
- Mementos of the Siege of Haarlem in Haarlem's Grote Kerk
- Brussels' tapestry designs

1600s—Holland's Golden Age

Holland gains its independence from the Habsburgs (officially in 1648), while Belgium languishes under Spanish rule. Amsterdam invents the global economy, as its hardy sailors ply the open seas, trading in Indonesian spices and South American sugar. Establishing colonies all over the world, they also conceive the African slave trade. Their nautical and capitalist skills combine to make Amsterdam the world's wealthiest city.

Sights

- Amsterdam's Rijksmuseum and Haarlem's Frans Hals Museum—paintings by Rembrandt, Hals, Vermeer, and Steen
- Old townhouses and gables in Amsterdam's Jordaan neighborhood and Red Light District
- Amsterdam's Begijnhof, Royal Palace, Westerkerk, and Rembrandt's House
- Brussels' *Manneken-Pis*
- Lace (popularity peaks c. 1700)

1700s—Elegant Decline

Holland and Belgium are both surpassed by the rise of superpowers France and England. Wars with those powers drain their economies and scuttle Holland's fleet. Still, they survive as bankers, small manufacturers, and craftsmen in luxury goods—but on a small scale fitting their geographical size. They hit rock-bottom in 1795, when French troops occupy the Low Countries (1795–1815), and Europe's powers subsequently saddle them with a monarchy.

Sights

- Amsterdam's Amstelkring Museum (hidden church), Willet-Holthuysen Museum (Herengracht Canal Mansion), and Jewish Historical Museum synagogue
- Brussels' Grand Place guildhalls

HISTORY

Islam and the Netherlands Today

The hottest hot-button issue in Amsterdam and the Netherlands today is the culture clash between secular, multicultural Netherlands and its recent Muslim immigrants. Many Muslims arrived in the last half of the 20th century after Indonesia (a Dutch colony) gained independence. Guest workers from Turkey and Morocco—drawn by economic incentives—swelled the ranks. Today, one in ten Amsterdammers is Muslim. The Muslim cultures have not meshed seamlessly with the Netherlands' Western, secular, and liberal culture. Here are several recent events that demonstrate how complex the issues are.

The Dutch are still haunted by a shameful episode concerning Muslims during the Bosnian War. In 1995, Dutch soldiers were stationed in Bosnia, charged by the UN with keeping peace during that region's troubled civil war. In July, the Dutch-protected town of Srebrenica was overrun by Bosnian Serbs. The 400 Dutch troops were outnumbered, and the UN gave them no logistical support. While Dutch soldiers huddled helplessly in their compound, the Serbs rounded up 8,000 Muslim men and boys and massacred them. In hindsight, there was little the soldiers could have done to prevent the atrocity, but it's still disturbing to the Dutch psyche.

In spring of 2002, a charismatic Dutch politician named Pim Fortuyn campaigned for Parliament on a strong anti-immigration platform. Like many Dutch, he was socially liberal (including being openly gay, pro-feminist, pro-drug, and pro-euthanasia) but was concerned that Islam posed a threat to Dutch tolerance. On May 6, Fortuyn was gunned down in

1800s—Revival

Though slow to join the Industrial Revolution, Holland picks up speed by century's end. A canal to the North Sea rejuvenates Amsterdam's port, railroads lace cities together, and Amsterdam hosts a World Exhibition. Belgium—having been placed under a Dutch king—revolts, gains its independence (1830), and picks its own king, a German this time. Wealth from its colony in Africa's Congo region helps rebuild Brussels in grand style.

Sights

- Amsterdam's Central Station, Rijksmuseum, and Magna Plaza
- Van Gogh paintings at the Van Gogh Museum
- Indonesian foods from the colonial era

a parking lot by a mentally troubled man who disagreed with his politics (though the assassin's full motives remain unclear). Dutch people were stunned by the violence, the kind of thing they thought only happened in America. Fortuyn's controversial legacy seems to be that his outspokenness broke taboos of political correctness and opened the floodgates of debate about these touchy issues.

On the morning of November 2, 2004, the great-grand-nephew of Vincent van Gogh was bicycling past Amsterdam's Oosterpark on his way to work. Theo van Gogh was a well-known filmmaker who'd recently released a controversial film about women and Islam. A Dutch citizen of Muslim descent shot Van Gogh, then stabbed a letter into his dead body threatening to harm the film's screenwriter as well.

The screenwriter for Van Gogh's film was Ayaan Hirsi Ali, who has become the most recent lightning rod for Western/Muslim controversy. Born a Muslim in Somalia, she emigrated to the Netherlands, where she became a member of Parliament and an outspoken critic of Islam and its treatment of women. (She also gained notoriety for gaining her citizenship under false pretenses.) Hirsi Ali currently lives with the threat of violence, under police protection provided by the Dutch government.

Whatever happened to peaceful, tolerant, quaint old Amsterdam? That's what the Dutch want to know. The Muslim immigration issue has forced the Dutch to confront a difficult paradox—how to be tolerant of what they perceive to be an intolerant culture.

- Brussels' Upper Town buildings and boulevards
- Brussels' Galeries Royales St. Hubert and BELvue Museum
- Chocolate

1900s–2000s—Invasions by Germans, Hippies, and Immigrants

Belgium is a major battleground in both World Wars. Holland, neutral in World War I, suffers brutal occupation under the Nazis in World War II. After the war, Brussels becomes the center of the budding movement toward European economic unity. In Amsterdam, postwar prosperity and a tolerant atmosphere in the 1960s and 1970s make it a global magnet for hippies, freaks, and your co-authors. In the 1970s and 1980s, Amsterdam and Brussels are flooded with

ANNE FRANK TAGEBUCH

immigrants from former colonies, causing friction but diversifying the population. Beginning in the 1990s, as Europe's nations have united to form the European Union, Brussels gradually became the de facto capital of this "United States of Europe." Facing an uncertain future today, the "Low Countries"—with much of their territory below sea level—keep a close watch on global warming and rising seas.

Sights

- Amsterdam's Beurs, Tuschinski Theater, and National Monument on Dam Square
- Amsterdam's Anne Frank House and Dutch Resistance Museum
- Amsterdam's Heineken Brewery, rock-and-roll clubs Paradiso and Melkweg, and the new "Stopera" opera house
- Haarlem's Corrie ten Boom House
- Paintings by René Magritte in Bruges' Groeninge Museum and in Brussels' Royal Museums of Fine Arts of Belgium
- Brussels' Atomium and European Parliament quarter

THE NETHERLANDS AND BELGIUM— A TIMELINE

57 B.C.	Julius Caesar invades the Low Countries, conquering local Batavian, Frisian, and Belgae tribes, beginning four centuries of Roman rule.
A.D. 406	Frankish tribes from Germany drive out the last Roman legions as Rome's Europe-wide empire collapses. Christian missionaries work to prevent the area from reverting to paganism.
c. 800	Charlemagne, born in Belgium, rules the Low Countries as part of a large northern European empire. After his death, his grandsons divide the kingdom and bicker among themselves.
c. 880–1000	Vikings rape and pillage during two centuries of raids in the Low Countries.
c. 900	The Low Countries are a patchwork of small dukedoms ruled by bishops and local counts (of Holland, Flanders, Brabant, and so on), who owe allegiance to greater kings in France, Germany, and England.
c. 1250	In Amsterdam, fishermen build a dike (dam) where the Amstel River flows into the North Sea, creating a prime trading port. Soon the town gains independence and trading privileges from the local count and bishop. Meanwhile,

Bruges becomes a major weaver of textiles, and Brussels becomes a minor trading town along the Germany–Bruges highway.

c. 1300 Italian and Portuguese sailors forge a coast-hugging trade route from the Mediterranean to the North Sea, with Bruges as the final stop.

1302 In Bruges, Flemish rebels drive out French rulers at the Battle of the Golden Spurs.

1345 Amsterdam experiences the Miracle of the Host, when a flame-resistant communion wafer causes miracles and attracts pilgrims.

1384 The discovery of a process to cure herring with salt makes Amsterdam a major fish exporter (to augment its thriving beer trade).

1384 Mary of Flanders marries Duke Philip the Bold of Burgundy, turning Holland and Belgium into part of a Burgundian empire that eventually stretches from Amsterdam to Switzerland.

c. 1400 Bruges is Europe's greatest trade city, the middleman between North and South.

1433 Burgundy's empire peaks when Duke Philip the Good takes over the titles of the local counts. His cultured court makes the Low Countries a center of art, literature, ideas, and pageantry.

1482 Mary of Burgundy, the last heir to the Burgundian throne, falls from a horse and dies. Her possessions (including Holland and Belgium) pass to her Austrian husband, Maximilian, and get swallowed up in his family's large Holy Roman Empire, ruled from Austria and later Spain.

1492 Columbus' voyage demonstrates the potential wealth of New World trade.

1517 The German Martin Luther's 95 theses inspire Protestantism, which becomes popular in the Low Countries (especially Holland). Later, refugees of religious persecution, including Calvinists and Anabaptists (such as the Amish and Mennonites), find a home in tolerant Amsterdam.

1519 King Charles V (1500–1558), the grandson of Mary of Burgundy and Maximilian, inherits all of his family's combined possessions. Charles rules Holland and Belgium, as well as Austria, Spain, Germany, Spain's New World colonies, and much more. A staunch Catholic, Charles battles rebellious Protestant princes.

1535 On Amsterdam's Dam Square, Anabaptist rebels are hanged, drawn, and quartered.

1540 Emperor Charles' son, Philip of Spain, invites the Inquisition to Spain.

1556 Philip II, based in Spain, succeeds his father as ruler of the Netherlands and intensifies the wars on Protestants (especially Calvinists).

1566 In a wave of anti-Catholic and anti-Spanish fury, extreme Protestants storm Catholic churches, vandalizing religious objects and converting the churches to Protestant (the Iconoclasm). Philip II sends soldiers to the Low Countries to establish order and punish rebels and heretics.

1568 Holland's Protestant counts rally around William "The Silent" of Orange, demanding freedom from Spanish Habsburg rule (the Beggars' Revolt). This begins 80 years of on-again-off-again war with Spain, called...the Eighty Years' War.

1572–1573 The Spanish conquer Haarlem after a long siege, but Haarlem's brave stand inspires other towns to carry on the fight.

1578 Amsterdam switches sides (the Alteration), joining the Protestant independence movement. Extreme Calvinists control the city for several decades, officially outlawing Catholic services. Within a few years, Spanish troops are driven south out of Holland, and future battles take place mostly on Belgian soil.

1580 Holland and Belgium go separate ways in the war. Holland's towns and nobles form a Protestant military alliance (the United Provinces) against Catholic Spain, while Belgium remains Catholic, with Brussels as the capital of Spanish Habsburg rule.

1585 Antwerp, northern Europe's greatest trading city (pop. 150,000), falls to Spanish troops. In the chaos, business plummets, and many Protestant merchants leave town. Industrious Amsterdam steps in to fill the vacuum of trade.

1588 Elizabeth I of England defeats the Spanish Armada (navy), breaking Spain's monopoly on overseas trade.

1602 The Dutch East India Company (VOC), a government-subsidized trading company, is formed, soon followed by the West India Company (1622). Together, they make Amsterdam (pop. 100,000) the center of a global trading empire, spawning Holland's Golden Age (c. 1600–1650).

1609 Henry Hudson's *Half Moon*, sailing for the Dutch East India Company, departs Amsterdam in search of a western passage to the Orient. Instead, Hudson finds the island of Manhattan, which soon becomes New Amsterdam (New York, 1625).

1616 Frans Hals paints the *St. George Civic Guards* (Frans Hals Museum, Haarlem).

1620 Pilgrims from England stop in Holland on their way to America.

1631 Rembrandt moves to Amsterdam, a wealthy city of 120,000 people, including René Descartes (1596–1650), plus many different religious sects and a thriving Jewish Quarter.

1637 After a decade of insanely lucrative trade in tulip bulbs ("tulip mania"), the market crashes.

1648 The Treaty of Munster (and the Treaty of Westphalia) officially ends the Eighty Years' War with Spain. The United Provinces (today's Netherlands) are now an independent nation.

1652–1654 Holland battles England over control of the seas. This is the first of three wars with England (also in 1665 and 1672) that sap Holland's wealth.

1672–1678 Louis XIV of France invades Holland and gets 15 miles from Amsterdam, but is finally stopped when the citizens open the Amstel locks and flood the city. After another draining war with France (1701–1713), England and France overtake Holland in overseas trade.

1689 Holland's William of Orange is invited by England's Parliament to replace the despot they'd deposed. He, ruling with wife Mary, becomes King William III of England.

1695 Louis XIV of France bombs and incinerates Brussels, punishing them for allying against him.

1776 The American Revolution inspires European democrats and worries nobles.

1787 Holland's budding democratic movement, the Patriots, is suppressed and exiled when Prussian troops invade Holland.

1789 The French Revolution begins.

1795   France, battling Europe's monarchs to keep their Revolution alive, invades and occupies Holland (establishing the "Batavian Republic," 1795–1806) and Belgium.

1806   Napoleon Bonaparte, who turned France's Revolution into a dictatorship, proclaims his brother, Louis Napoleon, to be King of Holland (1806–1810).

1815   After Napoleon's defeat at Waterloo (near Brussels), Europe's nobles decide that the Low Countries should be a monarchy, ruled jointly by a Dutch prince, who becomes King William I. (Today's Queen Beatrix is descended from him.)

1830   Belgium rebels against the Dutch-born king, becoming an independent country under King Leopold I.

1860   The novel *Max Havelaar,* by the Dutch writer Multatuli, exposes the dark side of Holland's repressive colonial rule in Indonesia.

1876   The North Sea Canal opens after 52 years of building, revitalizing Amsterdam's port. In the next decade, the city builds the Central Station, Rijksmuseum, and Concertgebouw, and hosts a World Exhibition (1883) that attracts three million visitors.

1881   King Leopold II of Belgium acquires Africa's Congo region, tapping its wealth to rebuild Brussels with broad boulevards and big marble buildings (Neoclassical style).

1914   In World War I, Holland remains neutral, while Belgium becomes the horrific battleground where Germany dukes it out with England and France—for example, at Ieper (Ypres in French).

1932   The Dutch Zuiderzee dike is completed, making the former arm of the North Sea into a freshwater lake (the IJsselmeer) and creating many square miles of reclaimed land.

1940–1945   Nazi Germany bombs Holland's Rotterdam and easily occupies the Netherlands and Belgium (1940). Belgium's king officially surrenders, while Holland's Queen Wilhelmina (1880–1962) flees to England. In Amsterdam, Anne Frank and her Jewish family go into hiding in an attempt to avoid arrest by the Nazis (1942–1944). Late in the war, Belgium is the site of Germany's last-gasp offensive, the Battle of the Bulge (1944–1945).

1945 Holland and Belgium are liberated by Allied troops.

1949 Indonesia gains its independence from Holland.

1953 Major floods in Holland kill almost 2,000 people, prompting more dams and storm barriers (the Delta Project, 1958–1997).

1957 Belgium and the Netherlands join the EEC (Common Market)—the forerunner of today's European Union—with headquarters in Brussels.

1960 The Benelux economic union between Belgium, the Netherlands, and Luxembourg—first proposed in 1944—becomes fully operational. After years of protests in the Belgian Congo, Belgium grants independence to the African nation.

1967 Amsterdam is Europe's center for hippies and the youth movement.

1975 Suriname (Dutch Guyana) gains its independence from Holland, and many emigrants flock to Holland.

1980 Queen Beatrix (b. 1938) becomes ruler of Holland.

1992 Belgium and the Netherlands sign the Treaty of Maastricht, which creates the European Union (EU).

1995 Floods in the Netherlands cause a billion dollars in damage.

2005 Dutch voters speak for all of Europe by voting for a referendum that slows the adoption of a European Constitution.

Today You arrive in Amsterdam, Bruges, and Brussels and make your own history.

APPENDIX

CONTENTS

RESOURCES

Tourist Information Offices

In the US

National tourist offices are a wealth of information. Before your trip, request or download any specific information you may want (such as city maps and schedules of upcoming festivals).

Netherlands Board of Tourism: www.holland.com, information@holland.com, tel. 212/370-7360. They no longer distribute printed material; all information is now available only on the Internet.

Belgian Tourist Office: www.visitbelgium.com, tel. 212/758-8130. Call or use the online form to request hotel and city guides; brochures for ABC lovers—antiques, beer, and chocolates; a map of Brussels; information on WWI and WWII battlefields; and a list of Jewish sights.

More Websites: Visit www.visitamsterdam.nl or www.amsterdamtourist.nl (Amsterdam Tourism Board's sites), www.amsterdam.nl (City of Amsterdam), and www.amsterdam museums.nl (exhibit info for 37 museums in Amsterdam).

In the Low Countries

The tourist information office is generally your best first stop in any new town (although Amsterdam's TIs are so crowded that you're better off visiting the airport TI or the TI in Haarlem). Have a list of questions ready, and pick up maps, brochures, and walking-tour information. Try to arrive before it closes or call ahead with critical questions. In this book, I'll refer to a tourist information office as a **TI.**

Most TIs offer English-speaking staff; a free map of the town; biking maps; listings of events, activities, and accommodations; bus and train schedules; and Internet access.

Resources from Rick Steves
Guidebooks and Online Updates

I've done my best to make sure that the information in this book is up-to-date, but things change. For the very latest, visit www.rick steves.com/update. Also at my website, you'll find a valuable list of reports and experiences—good and bad—from fellow travelers who have used this book (www.ricksteves.com/feedback).

This book is one of more than 30 titles in my series on European travel, which includes country guidebooks, city and regional guidebooks, and my budget-travel skills handbook, *Rick Steves' Europe Through the Back Door*. My phrase books—for German, French, Italian, Spanish, and Portuguese—are practical and budget-oriented. My other books are *Europe 101* (a crash course on art and history, newly expanded and in full color), *European Christmas* (on traditional and modern-day celebrations), and *Postcards from Europe* (a fun memoir of my travels). For a complete list of my books, see the inside of the last page of this book.

Public Television and Radio Shows

My TV series, *Rick Steves' Europe,* covers European destinations in 80 shows, including two shows on the Low Countries. My weekly public radio show, *Travel with Rick Steves,* features interviews with travel experts from around the world. All the TV scripts and radio shows (which are easy and free to download to an iPod or other MP3 player) are at www.ricksteves.com.

Begin Your Trip at www.ricksteves.com

At our travel website, you'll find a wealth of free information on European destinations, including fresh monthly news and helpful tips from thousands of fellow travelers.

Our **online Travel Store** offers travel bags and accessories specially designed by Rick Steves to help you travel smarter and lighter. These include Rick's popular carry-on bags (wheeled and rucksack versions), money belts, totes, toiletries kits, adapters, other accessories, and a wide selection of guidebooks, journals, planning maps, and DVDs.

Choosing the right **railpass** for your trip—amidst hundreds of options—can drive you nutty. We'll help you choose the best pass for your needs, plus give you a bunch of free extras.

Rick Steves' Europe Through the Back Door travel company offers **tours** with more than two dozen itineraries and 450 departures reaching the best destinations in this book...and beyond. We offer a 21-day tour of Europe that includes Amsterdam and Haarlem. You'll enjoy great guides, a fun bunch of travel partners (with small groups of generally around 26), and plenty of room to spread out in a big, comfy bus. You'll find European adventures to fit every vacation length. For all the details, and to get our Tour Catalog and a free Rick Steves Tour Experience DVD (filmed on location during an actual tour), visit www.ricksteves.com or call our Tour Department at 425-608-4217.

APPENDIX

Free Audiotours

If your travels take you beyond the Low Countries to France or Italy, you could take advantage of the free, self-guided audiotours we offer of the major sights in Paris, Florence, Rome, and Venice. The audiotours, produced by Rick Steves and Gene Openshaw (the co-author of seven books in the Rick Steves series, including this one) are available through iTunes and at www.ricksteves.com. Simply download them onto your computer and transfer them to your iPod or other MP3 player. (Remember to bring a Y-jack and extra set of ear buds for your travel partner.)

Maps

The black-and-white maps in this book, drawn by Dave Hoerlein, are concise and simple. Dave, who is well-traveled in the Low Countries, has designed the maps to help you quickly orient your-self and painlessly get to where you want to go. For more detail, consider buying a city map at any of the cities' TIs for a euro or two. Before you buy a map, look at it to make sure it has the level of detail you want.

Other Guidebooks

Especially if you'll be traveling beyond my recommended destina-tions, you may want some supplemental information. Considering the improvements that they'll make in your $4,000 vacation, $40 for extra maps and books is money well-spent. One budget tip can easily justify the price of an extra guidebook. Note that none of the following books are updated annually; check the publication date before you buy.

Historians like the green Michelin guides and the Cadogan series; both have individual books on all three cities—Amsterdam, Bruges, and Brussels. Others go for the well-illustrated Eyewitness guides (titles include *Amsterdam; Holland;* and *Brussels/Bruges/Ghent/Antwerp*). The Lonely Planet series (which has books on Amsterdam, the Netherlands, and Belgium & Luxembourg) is well researched and geared for a mature audience. Students and vagabonds enjoy *Let's Go: Amsterdam* (updated annually) for its coverage of hosteling, nightlife, and the student scene.

Recommended Books and Movies

To get the feel of the Netherlands and Belgium past and present, consider these books and films:

Non-Fiction

If you're interested in the WWII years in the Netherlands, read *The Diary of a Young Girl* (Anne Frank), *The Hiding Place* (Corrie ten Boom), and *A Bridge Too Far* (the story of the battle of Arnhem, by Cornelius Ryan).

Amsterdam (Mak) is an academic but engaging look at centuries of the city's history. Equally comprehensive is Simon Schama's *The Embarrassment of Riches: An Interpretation of Dutch Culture in the Golden Age*. Covering a similar timeframe, *Daily Life in Rembrandt's Holland* (Zumthor) focuses more on the everyday concerns of Dutch society in the 17th century.

Tulipmania (Dash) is about the Golden Age financial craze. Holland was at the center of the spice trade back when a pinch of cinnamon was worth its weight in gold. For engaging histories of these times, try *Spice: The History of a Temptation* (Turner) and *Nathaniel's Nutmeg: Or the True and Incredible Adventures of the Spice Trader Who Changed the Course of History* (Milton).

The Undutchables: An Observation of the Netherlands, Its Culture and Its Inhabitants (White and Boucke) is an irreverent guide to modern Dutch culture. *My 'Dam Life: Three Years in Holland* (Condon) is a humorous account of adventures in a low country.

Fans of Vincent may want to consider *Dear Theo: The Autobiography of Vincent van Gogh,* edited by Irving Stone. (Stone also wrote the fictional book about Van Gogh, *Lust for Life.*)

If you're visiting Belgium and have an interest in World War I, read Barbara Tuchman's Pulitzer Prize–winning book, *The Guns of August.* For a look at contemporary Belgium, try *A Tall Man in a Low Land* (Pearson).

Fiction

Set in 17th-century Holland, Alexandre Dumas' *The Black Tulip* tells a swashbuckling story of fortunes held in the balance. *Max Havelaar: Or the Coffee Auctions of the Dutch Trading Company* is another literary classic, in which the author, Multatuli, writes of the injustices of the Dutch colonial system in Indonesia.

For more modern reads, best sellers set in Holland include *Girl in Hyacinth Blue* (Vreeland), *Girl with a Pearl Earring* (Chevalier), *Tulip Fever* (Moggach), and *Confessions of an Ugly Stepsister* (Maguire). For Belgium, consider *Resistance* (Shreve) and *The Adventures of Tintin* (featuring a famous Belgian comic-book character, by Hergé).

Films

Vincent and Theo (1990) captures the relationship between the great artist and his brother. *Girl with a Pearl Earring* (2003) shows a fictionalized Vermeer in love with his servant in Delft.

The Diary of Anne Frank (1959) is a good version of Anne's story, which has been translated into film and theater many times. Paul Verhoeven's *Soldier of Orange* (1977) delves into the bleak WWII years (it's also a fine book). In *Black Book* (2006)—another Verhoeven film, which was filmed in Holland—a sexy blonde bombshell fights for the Dutch Resistance.

Set partially in the modern era, *Antonia's Line* (1995) tells the story of five generations of Dutch women. *Ocean's Twelve* (2004) has many scenes set in Amsterdam's Jordaan neighborhood. The dark and violent comedy *In Bruges* (2008) was filmed just where you'd think.

TELEPHONES, EMAIL, AND MAIL

Telephones

Smart travelers learn the phone system and use it daily to reserve or reconfirm rooms, get tourist information, reserve restaurants, confirm tour times, or phone home.

Types of Phones

You'll encounter various kinds of phones on your trip:

Card-operated phones, in which you insert a locally bought phone card into a public pay phone, are common in Europe.

Coin-operated phones, the original kind of pay phone (but now increasingly rare), require you to have enough change to complete your call.

Hotel room phones are sometimes cheap for local calls (confirm at the front desk first), but can be a rip-off for long-distance calls unless you use an international phone card (described below). However, incoming calls are free, making this a cheap way for friends and family to stay in touch, provided they have a good long-distance plan for calls to Europe.

American mobile phones work in Europe if they're GSM-enabled, tri-band or quad-band, and on a calling plan that includes international calls. They're convenient, but pricey. For example, with a T-Mobile phone, you'll pay $1 per minute for calls and about $0.35 for text messages.

European mobile phones run about $75–90 (for the most basic models) and come without contracts. These phones are loaded with prepaid calling time that you can recharge as you use up the minutes. As long as you're not "roaming" outside the phone's home country, incoming calls are free. If you're traveling to multiple countries within Europe, make sure the phone is electronically "unlocked," so that you can swap out its SIM card (a fingernail-sized chip that holds the phone's information) for a new one in

What Language Barrier?

People speak Dutch in Amsterdam, Flemish (virtually iden- tical to Dutch) in Bruges, and French in Brussels. But you'll find almost no language barrier in the Netherlands, as all well- educated folks, nearly all young people, and almost everyone in the tourist trade speak English. (When asked if they speak English, the Dutch reply, *"Natuurlijk"*—"naturally.") In tourist- friendly Bruges, you also won't encounter any difficulties with English. You will meet French-only speakers in Brussels, but it's generally a minor language barrier. Regardless, it's polite to use some Dutch (see page 471) or French pleasantries (see page 473).

other countries. For more information on mobile phones, see www .ricksteves.com/phones.

Using Phone Cards

Get a phone card for your calls. Prepaid phone cards come in two types: international and insertable (both described below).

Prepaid **international phone cards** are the cheapest way to make international calls from Europe (they also work for domestic calls).

Cards are sold at small newsstand kiosks and hole-in-the-wall long-distance shops. Some international phone cards work in mul- tiple countries—if traveling to both the Netherlands and Belgium, try to buy a card that will work in both places.

There are many different brands of cards, so ask the clerk which one has the best rates to the US. Some cards are recharge- able; you can call up the number on the card, give your credit-card number, and buy more time. Because cards are occasionally duds, avoid the high denominations.

You can use international phone cards from most phones, including your hotel-room phone (check to make sure that your phone is set on tone instead of pulse, and ask at the desk about hidden fees for toll-free calls).

To use a card, scratch off the back to reveal your code. After you dial the access phone number, the message tells you to enter your code and then dial the phone number you want to call. A voice may announce how much is left in your account before you dial. Usually you can select English, but if the prompts are in Dutch or French, experiment: Dial your code, followed by the pound sign (#), then the number, then pound again, and so on, until it works.

To call the US, see "Dialing Internationally," page 461. To

make calls within the Netherlands and Belgium, dial the area code plus the local number; when using an international phone card, the area code must be dialed even if you're calling across the street.

To make numerous, successive calls with an international phone card without having to redial the long access number each time, press the keys (see instructions on card) that allow you to launch directly into your next call. Remember that you don't need the actual card to use a card account, so it's shareable. You can write down the access number and code in your notebook and share it with friends. If you have a still-lively card at the end of your trip, give it to another traveler.

Insertable phone cards are a convenient way to pay for calls from public pay phones. Buy these cards at TIs, tobacco shops, post offices, and train stations. The price of the call (local or international) is automatically deducted while you talk. They are sold in several denominations starting at about €5. Calling the US with one of these phone cards is reasonable (about 2–3 min per euro), but more expensive than using an international phone card. Each European country has its own insertable phone card—so your Dutch card won't work in a Belgian phone. Be aware that with the prevalence of mobile phones, public phones (especially the type that accepts phone cards) are getting harder to find. To use an insertable phone card, simply take the phone off the hook, insert the prepaid card, wait for a dial tone, and dial away.

Using Hotel-Room Phones, VoIP, or US Calling Cards

The phone in your **hotel room** is convenient but expensive (unless you use an international phone card, described above). While incoming calls (made by folks back home) can be the cheapest way to keep in touch, charges for *outgoing* calls, especially international ones, can be a very unpleasant surprise. Before you dial, get a clear explanation from the hotel staff of the charges, even for local and (supposedly) toll-free calls. I find hotel room phones handy for making local calls.

If your family has an inexpensive way to call Europe, either through a long-distance plan or prepaid calling card, have them call you in your hotel room. Give them a list of your hotels' phone numbers before you go. Then, as you travel, send them an email or mobile-phone text message, or make a quick pay-phone call, to set up a time for them to give you a ring.

If you're traveling with a laptop, consider trying **VoIP (Voice over Internet Protocol).** With VoIP, two computers act as the phones, allowing for a free Internet-based call. The major providers are Skype (www.skype.com) and Google Talk (www.google.com/talk).

US Calling Cards (such as the ones offered by AT&T, MCI, or Sprint) are the worst option. You'll nearly always save a lot of money by paying with a phone card (see previous page).

How to Dial

Calling from the US to Europe, or vice versa, is simple—once you break the code. The European calling chart on the next page will walk you through it.

Dialing Domestic Calls

The Netherlands, like much of the US, uses an area-code dialing system. If you're dialing within an area code, you just dial the local number to be connected; but if you're calling outside your area code, you have to dial both the area code (which starts with a 0) and the local number. For example, the number of a recommended hotel in Haarlem is 023/532-4530. To call it within Haarlem, dial 532-4530. To call it from Amsterdam, dial 023/532-4530.

Belgium uses a direct-dial system (no area codes). To call anywhere within Belgium, you always dial a nine-digit number.

Dialing Internationally

To make an international call, follow these steps:

Dial the international access code (00 if you're calling from Europe, 011 from the US or Canada).

Then dial the country code of the country you're calling (31 for the Netherlands, 32 for Belgium, or 1 for the US or Canada).

Then dial the area code (without its initial 0) and the local number.

For example, to call the recommended Haarlem hotel from the US, dial 011 (the US international access code), 31 (the Netherlands' country code), 23 (Haarlem's area code without the initial 0), and 532-4530. To call a recommended hotel in Bruges (which has the phone number 050-444-444) from the US, dial 011 (the US international access code), 32 (Belgium's country code), and 50-444-444 (the phone number without its initial zero).

To call my office in Edmonds, Washington, from the Netherlands or from Belgium, I dial 00 (Europe's international access code), 1 (the US country code), 425 (Edmonds' area code), and 771-8303.

Useful Phone Numbers
Embassies/Consulates in the Netherlands
US Embassies and Consulates: Amsterdam—tel. 020/575-5309 during office hours, otherwise in case of emergency call after-duty officer at tel. 070/310-2209 (Museumplein 19, http://amsterdam .usconsulate.gov). Consulate open for general services Mon–Fri

European Calling Chart

Just smile and dial, using this key:
AC = Area Code, LN = Local Number.

APPENDIX

European Country	Calling long distance within ...	Calling from the US or Canada to ...	Calling from a European country to ...
Austria	AC + LN	011 + 43 + AC (without the initial zero) + LN	00 + 43 + AC (without the initial zero) + LN
Belgium	LN	011 + 32 + LN (without initial zero)	00 + 32 + LN (without initial zero)
Bosnia-Herzegovina	AC + LN	011 + 387 + AC (without initial zero) + LN	00 + 387 + AC (without initial zero) + LN
Britain	AC + LN	011 + 44 + AC (without initial zero) + LN	00 + 44 + AC (without initial zero) + LN
Croatia	AC + LN	011 + 385 + AC (without initial zero) + LN	00 + 385 + AC (without initial zero) + LN
Czech Republic	LN	011 + 420 + LN	00 + 420 + LN
Denmark	LN	011 + 45 + LN	00 + 45 + LN
Estonia	LN	011 + 372 + LN	00 + 372 + LN
Finland	AC + LN	011 + 358 + AC (without initial zero) + LN	999 + 358 + AC (without initial zero) + LN
France	LN	011 + 33 + LN (without initial zero)	00 + 33 + LN (without initial zero)
Germany	AC + LN	011 + 49 + AC (without initial zero) + LN	00 + 49 + AC (without initial zero) + LN
Greece	LN	011 + 30 + LN	00 + 30 + LN
Hungary	06 + AC + LN	011 + 36 + AC + LN	00 + 36 + AC + LN
Ireland	AC + LN	011 + 353 + AC (without initial zero) + LN	00 + 353 + AC (without initial zero) + LN

European Country	Calling long distance within ...	Calling from the US or Canada to ...	Calling from a European country to ...
Italy	LN	011 + 39 + LN	00 + 39 + LN
Montenegro	AC + LN	011 + 382 + AC (without initial zero) + LN	00 + 382 + AC (without initial zero) + LN
Netherlands	AC + LN	011 + 31 + AC (without initial zero) + LN	00 + 31 + AC (without initial zero) + LN
Norway	LN	011 + 47 + LN	00 + 47 + LN
Poland	LN	011 + 48 + LN (without initial zero)	00 + 48 + LN (without initial zero)
Portugal	LN	011 + 351 + LN	00 + 351 + LN
Slovakia	AC + LN	011 + 421 + AC (without initial zero) + LN	00 + 421 + AC (without initial zero) + LN
Slovenia	AC + LN	011 + 386 + AC (without initial zero) + LN	00 + 386 + AC (without initial zero) + LN
Spain	LN	011 + 34 + LN	00 + 34 + LN
Sweden	AC + LN	011 + 46 + AC (without initial zero) + LN	00 + 46 + AC (without initial zero) + LN
Switzerland	LN	011 + 41 + LN (without initial zero)	00 + 41 + LN (without initial zero)
Turkey	AC (if no initial zero is included, add one) + LN	011 + 90 + AC (without initial zero) + LN	00 + 90 + AC (without initial zero) + LN

- The instructions above apply whether you're calling a land line or mobile phone.
- The international access codes (the first numbers you dial when making an international call) are 011 if you're calling from the US or Canada, or 00 if you're calling from virtually anywhere in Europe (except Finland, where it's 999).
- To call the US or Canada from Europe, dial 00, then 1 (the country code for the US and Canada), then the area code and number. In short, 00 + 1 + AC + LN = Hi, Mom!

8:30–11:30, afternoons for immigrant visas only, closed Sat–Sun.

The Hague—tel. 070/310-2209, visits by appointment only (Lange Voorhout 102, http://netherlands.usembassy.gov).

Canadian Embassy: The Hague—tel. 070/311-1600 (Sophialaan 7, Mon–Thu 8:30–12:30 & 13:15–17:30, Fri 8:30–13:00, closed Sat–Sun; consular services Mon–Thu 10:00–12:30 & 14:00–16:30, Fri 9:30–12:30, closed Sat–Sun; www.canada.nl).

Embassies/Consulates in Belgium

US Embassies and Consulates: Brussels—tel. 02-508-2111 (Boulevard du Régent 27, Mon–Fri 9:00–18:00, closed Sat–Sun, for after-hours emergencies, call and ask to be connected to the duty officer, http://belgium.usembassy.gov). Consulate is next door to embassy, at Boulevard du Régent 25, passport services Mon–Thu 13:30–15:30, Fri 9:00–11:00, closed Sat–Sun.

Canadian Embassy: Brussels—tel. 02-741-0611 (Avenue de Tervueren 2, Mon–Fri 9:00–12:30 & 13:30–17:00, closed Sat–Sun; consulate open Mon–Fri 9:00–12:00, afternoon by appointment only, www.ambassade-canada.be).

Emergency Numbers

Police, Ambulance, or Fire (Netherlands): 112
Police (Belgium): 101 or 112
Ambulance or Fire (Belgium): 100 or 112

Email and Mail

Email: Many travelers set up a free email account with Yahoo, Microsoft (Hotmail), or Google (Gmail). Internet cafés are easy to find in big cities. Look for the places listed in this book, or ask the local TI, computer store, or your hotelier.

Some hotels have a dedicated computer for guests' email needs. Small places with no guest computer or Wi-Fi are accustomed to letting clients (who've asked politely) sit at their desk for a few minutes just to check their email.

If you're traveling with a laptop, you'll find that Wi-Fi is gradually being installed in many hotels. Most are free, while others charge by the minute. Wi-Fi is also available for a minimal fee at Internet cafés and some post offices.

Mail: To arrange for mail delivery, reserve a few hotels along your route in advance, and give their addresses to friends. Allow 10 days for a letter to arrive. Phoning and emailing are so easy that I've dispensed with mail stops altogether.

HOLIDAYS AND FESTIVALS

Here's a partial list of festivals and public holidays in the Netherlands and Belgium.

Jan 1	New Year's Day
Feb	Carnival (Mardi Gras)
March–May	Keukenhof flower show, Lisse, Netherlands (www.keukenhof.nl)
Easter Weekend	Good Friday through Easter Monday (April 2–4 in 2010)
April	Flower Parade (April 24 in 2010, www.bloemencorso-bollenstreek.nl), Noordwijk to Haarlem, Netherlands
April 30	Queen's Day (Koninginnedag), birthday of the late Queen Mother Juliana, party in the streets of Amsterdam
May 1	Labor Day (some closures in Belgium)
May 4	Remembrance of WWII Dead (Dodenherdenking), Netherlands
May 5	Liberation Day (Bevrijdingsdag), Netherlands
May	Art Amsterdam—contemporary-art exhibition (May 26–30 in 2010, www.kunstrai.nl), Amsterdam
May	Procession of the Holy Blood in Bruges; Ascension in Netherlands and Belgium (both events May 13 in 2010)
May	Pentecost and Pentecost Monday (May 23–24 in 2010)
June	Holland Arts Festival (concerts, theater, etc., www.hollandfestival.nl), Amsterdam; Amsterdam Roots Festival—Oosterpark (ethnic food, music, world culture; www.amsterdamroots.nl)
Mid-June	Grachtenloop (June 18 in 2010; run around canals, www.grachtenloop.nl), Haarlem
Late June/early July	Ommegang Pageant (historic costumed parade to Grand Place; www.visitbelgium.com/mediaroom/Ommegang.htm), Brussels
Mid-July	North Sea Jazz Festival (July 11–13 in 2009, www.northseajazz.nl), The Hague

July 21	Belgian Independence Day (parades, fireworks)
Aug 15	Assumption Day, Procession in Bruges
Aug	Carpet of Flowers (celebrated only in even years), Brussels
Aug	Open-air spectacle staged on the canals, held every three years, next in 2011 (Reiefeesten, www.reiefeest.be), Bruges
Mid-Aug	Prinsengracht canal concert on barges (August 15–23 in 2009; music and other festivities, www.grachtenfestival.nl), Amsterdam
Mid-Aug	SAIL Amsterdam, held every five years (August 19–23 in 2010, tall ships and other historic boats, www.sail2010.nl), Amsterdam
Sept (first week)	Flower parade on canals, Aalsmeer to Amsterdam
Mid-Sept	Jordaan Festival—neighborhood street party (www.jordaanfestival.nl), Amsterdam
Sept or Oct	Yom Kippur (Sept 28 in 2009, Sept 18 in 2010, Jewish holiday, some closures, including Anne Frank House and Jewish Historical Museum in Amsterdam)
Nov 1	All Saints' Day
Nov 11	Armistice Day (banks closed), Belgium
Mid-Nov	Sinterklaas ("Santa Claus") procession, Amsterdam
Dec	"Winter Wonders" European Christmas Market (www.plaisirsdhiver.be), Brussels
Dec 5	St. Nicholas' Eve (Sinterklaasavond, when Sinterklaas and Zwarte Piet arrive), procession and presents
Dec 25	Christmas
Dec 26	"Second Day" of Christmas (Tweede Kerstdag), Netherlands

CONVERSIONS AND CLIMATE

Numbers and Stumblers

- Europeans write a few of their numbers differently than we do. 1 = 1, 4 = 4, 7 = 7.
- In Europe, dates appear as day/month/year, so Christmas is 25/12/10.
- Commas are decimal points and decimals commas. A dollar and a half is 1,50, and there are 5.280 feet in a mile.
- When counting with fingers, start with your thumb. If you hold up your first finger to request one item, you'll probably get two.
- What Americans call the second floor of a building is the first floor in Europe.
- On escalators and moving sidewalks, Europeans keep the left "lane" open for passing. Keep to the right.

Metric Conversions (approximate)

1 foot = 0.3 meter
1 yard = 0.9 meter
1 mile = 1.6 kilometers
1 centimeter = 0.4 inch
1 meter = 39.4 inches
1 kilometer = 0.62 mile

1 square yard = 0.8 square meter
1 square mile = 2.6 square kilometers
1 ounce = 28 grams
1 quart = 0.95 liter
1 kilogram = 2.2 pounds
32°F = 0°C

Climate

The first line is the average daily high; the second line, the average daily low. The third line shows the average number of days without rain. For more detailed weather statistics for destinations throughout the Low Countries (as well as the rest of the world), check www.worldclimate.com.

	J	F	M	A	M	J	J	A	S	O	N	D
Amsterdam												
	41°	42°	49°	55°	64°	70°	72°	71°	66°	56°	48°	41°
	30°	31°	35°	40°	45°	52°	55°	55°	51°	43°	37°	33°
	8	9	16	14	16	16	14	12	11	11	10	9
Brussels												
	41°	44°	51°	58°	65°	71°	73°	72°	69°	60°	48°	42°
	30°	32°	34°	40°	45°	53°	55°	55°	52°	45°	38°	32°
	9	11	14	12	15	15	13	12	15	13	10	11

Temperature Conversion: Fahrenheit and Celsius

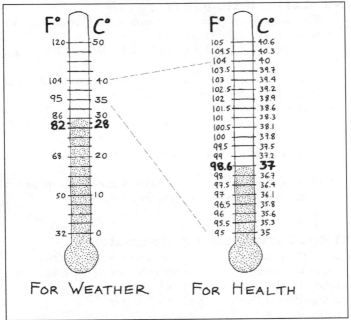

Europe takes its temperature using the Celsius scale, while we opt for Fahrenheit. For a rough conversion from Celsius to Fahrenheit, double the number and add 30. For weather, remember that 28°C is 82°F—perfect. For health, 37°C is just right.

Essential Packing Checklist

Whether you're traveling for five days or five weeks, here's what you'll need to bring. Remember to pack light to enjoy the sweet freedom of true mobility. Happy travels!

- ❑ 5 shirts
- ❑ 1 sweater or lightweight fleece jacket
- ❑ 2 pairs pants
- ❑ 1 pair shorts
- ❑ 1 swimsuit (women only—men can use shorts)
- ❑ 5 pairs underwear and socks
- ❑ 1 pair shoes
- ❑ 1 rain-proof jacket
- ❑ Tie or scarf
- ❑ Money belt
- ❑ Money—your mix of:
  - ❑ Debit card for ATM withdrawals
  - ❑ Credit card
  - ❑ Hard cash in US dollars
- ❑ Documents (and back-up photocopies)
- ❑ Passport
- ❑ Airplane ticket
- ❑ Driver's license
- ❑ Student ID and hostel card
- ❑ Railpass/car rental voucher
- ❑ Insurance details
- ❑ Daypack
- ❑ Sealable plastic baggies
- ❑ Camera and related gear
- ❑ Empty water bottle
- ❑ Wristwatch and alarm clock
- ❑ Earplugs
- ❑ First-aid kit
- ❑ Medicine (labeled)
- ❑ Extra glasses/contacts and prescriptions
- ❑ Sunscreen and sunglasses
- ❑ Toiletries kit
- ❑ Soap
- ❑ Laundry soap (if liquid and carry-on, limit to 3 oz.)
- ❑ Clothesline
- ❑ Small towel
- ❑ Sewing kit
- ❑ Travel information
- ❑ Necessary map(s)
- ❑ Address list (email and mailing addresses)
- ❑ Postcards and photos from home
- ❑ Notepad and pen
- ❑ Journal

Hotel Reservation

To: _____   _____
           hotel   *email or fax*

From: _____   _____
           name   *email or fax*

Today's date: _____ /_____ /_____
                  day   *month*   *year*

Dear Hotel _____ ,
Please make this reservation for me:

Name: _____

Total # of people: _____   # of rooms: _____   # of nights: _____

Arriving: _____ /_____ /_____   My time of arrival (24-hr clock): _____
              day *month* *year*   (I will telephone if I will be late)

Departing: ____ /____ /_____
                day   *month*   *year*

Room(s): Single____   Double ____   Twin ____   Triple ____   Quad____

With: Toilet ____   Shower ____   Bath ____   Sink only____

Special needs: View____   Quiet____   Cheapest ____   Ground Floor____

Please email or fax confirmation of my reservation, along with the type of room reserved and the price. Please also inform me of your cancellation policy. After I hear from you, I will quickly send my credit-card information as a deposit to hold the room. Thank you.

_____
Name

_____
Address

_____
City   *State*   *Zip Code*   *Country*

Before hoteliers can make your reservation, they want to know the information listed above. You can use this form as the basis for your email, or you can photocopy this page, fill in the information, and send it as a fax (also available online at www.ricksteves.com/reservation).

Dutch Survival Phrases

You won't need to learn Dutch, but knowing a few phrases can help if you're traveling off the beaten path. Taking a few moments to learn the pleasantries (such as please and thank you) will improve your connections with locals even in the bigger cities.

To pronounce the difficult Dutch "g" (indicated in phonetics by hhh) make a hard, guttural, clear-your-throat sound, similar to the "ch" in the Scottish word "loch."

Hello.	Hallo.	hol-LOH
Good day.	Dag.	dahhh
Good morning.	Goeiemorgen.	hhhoy-ah MOR-hhhen
Good afternoon.	Goeiemiddag.	hhhoy-ah MIT-tahk
Ma'am	Mevrouw	meh-frow
Sir	Meneer	men-ear
Yes	Ja	yah
No	Nee	nay
Please	Alstublieft	AHL-stoo-bleeft
Thank you.	Dank u wel.	dahnk yoo vehl
You're welcome.	Graag gedaan.	hhhrahhk hhkeh-dahn
Excuse me.	Pardon.	par-DOHN
Do you speak English?	Spreekt u Engels?	spraykt oo ENG-els
Okay.	Oké.	"okay"
Goodbye.	Tot ziens.	toht zeens
one / two	een / twee	ayn / t'vay
three / four	drie / vier	dree / feer
five / six	vijf / zes	fife / ses
seven / eight	zeven / acht	say-fen / ahkht
nine / ten	negen / tien	nay-hhhen / teen
What does it cost?	Wat kost?	vaht kost
I would like...	Ik wil graag...	ik vil hhhrahhhk
...a room.	...een kamer.	un kah-mer
...a ticket.	...een kaart.	un kart
...a bike.	...een fiets.	un feets
Where is...?	Waar is...?	vahr is
...the station	...het station	het sta-tsee-on
...the tourist info office	...de VVV	duh vay vay vay
left / right	links / rechts	links / rechts
open / closed	open / gesloten	"open" / hhhe-sloh-ten

In the Restaurant

The Dutch have an all-purpose word, alstublieft (AHL-stoo-bleeft), that means: "Please," or "Here you are," (if handing you something), or "Thanks," (if taking payment from you), or "You're welcome" (when handing you change). Here are other words that might come in handy at restaurants, particularly if you're day-tripping to small towns:

I would like...	Ik wil graag...	ik vil hhhrahhk
...a cup of coffee.	...kopje koffee.	kop-yeh "coffee"
non-smoking	niet-roken	neet roh-ken
smoking	roken	roh-ken
with / without	met / buiten	met / bow-ten
and / or	en / of	en / of
bread	brood	broht
salad	sla	slah
cheese	kaas	kahs
meat	vlees	flays
chicken	kip	kip
fish	vis	fis
egg	ei	eye
fruit	vrucht	frucht
pastries	gebak	hhhe-bak
I am vegetarian.	Ik ben vegetarish.	ik ben vay-hhhe-tah-rish
Tasty.	Lekker.	lek-ker
Enjoy!	Smakelijk!	smak-kuh-luk
Cheers!	Proost!	prohst

French Survival Phrases

When using the phonetics, try to nasalize the <u>n</u> sound.

Good day.	Bonjour.	boh<u>n</u>-zhoor
Mrs. / Mr.	Madame / Monsieur	mah-dahm / muhs-yur
Do you speak English?	Parlez-vous anglais?	par-lay-voo ah<u>n</u>-glay
Yes. / No.	Oui. / Non.	wee / noh<u>n</u>
I understand.	Je comprends.	zhuh koh<u>n</u>-prah<u>n</u>
I don't understand.	Je ne comprends pas.	zhuh nuh koh<u>n</u>-prah<u>n</u> pah
Please.	S'il vous plaît.	see voo play
Thank you.	Merci.	mehr-see
I'm sorry.	Désolé.	day-zoh-lay
Excuse me.	Pardon.	par-doh<u>n</u>
(No) problem.	(Pas de) problème.	(pah duh) proh-blehm
It's good.	C'est bon.	say boh<u>n</u>
Goodbye.	Au revoir.	oh vwahr
one / two	un / deux	uh<u>n</u> / duh
three / four	trois / quatre	twah / kah-truh
five / six	cinq / six	sa<u>n</u>k / sees
seven / eight	sept / huit	seht / weet
nine / ten	neuf / dix	nuhf / dees
How much is it?	Combien?	koh<u>n</u>-bee-a<u>n</u>
Write it?	Ecrivez?	ay-kree-vay
Is it free?	C'est gratuit?	say grah-twee
Included?	Inclus?	a<u>n</u>-klew
Where can I buy / find...?	Où puis-je acheter / trouver...?	oo pwee-zhuh ah-shuh-tay / troo-vay
I'd like / We'd like...	Je voudrais / Nous voudrions...	zhuh voo-dray / noo voo-dree-oh<u>n</u>
...a room.	...une chambre.	ewn shah<u>n</u>-bruh
...a ticket to ___.	...un billet pour ___.	uh<u>n</u> bee-yay poor
Is it possible?	C'est possible?	say poh-see-bluh
Where is...?	Où est...?	oo ay
...the train station	...la gare	lah gar
...the bus station	...la gare routière	lah gar root-yehr
...tourist information	...l'office du tourisme	loh-fees dew too-reez-muh
Where are the toilets?	Où sont les toilettes?	oo soh<u>n</u> lay twah-leht
men	hommes	ohm
women	dames	dahm
left / right	à gauche / à droite	ah gohsh / ah dwaht
straight	tout droit	too dwah
When does this open / close?	Ça ouvre / ferme à quelle heure?	sah oo-vruh / fehrm ah kehl ur
At what time?	À quelle heure?	ah kehl ur
Just a moment.	Un moment.	uh<u>n</u> moh-mah<u>n</u>
now / soon / later	maintenant / bientôt / plus tard	ma<u>n</u>-tuh-nah<u>n</u> / bee-a<u>n</u>-toh / plew tar
today / tomorrow	aujourd'hui / demain	oh-zhoor-dwee / duh-ma<u>n</u>

In the Restaurant

I'd like / We'd like...	**Je voudrais / Nous voudrions...**	zhuh voo-dray / noo voo-dree-oh<u>n</u>
...to reserve...	**...réserver...**	ray-zehr-vay
...a table for one / two.	**...une table pour un / deux.**	ewn tah-bluh poor uh<u>n</u> / duh
Non-smoking.	**Non fumeur.**	noh<u>n</u> few-mur
Is this seat free?	**C'est libre?**	say lee-bruh
The menu (in English), please.	**La carte (en anglais), s'il vous plaît.**	lah kart (ah<u>n</u> ah<u>n</u>-glay) see voo play
service (not) included	**service (non) compris**	sehr-vees (noh<u>n</u>) koh<u>n</u>-pree
to go	**à emporter**	ah ah<u>n</u>-por-tay
with / without	**avec / sans**	ah-vehk / sah<u>n</u>
and / or	**et / ou**	ay / oo
special of the day	**plat du jour**	plah dew zhoor
specialty of the house	**spécialité de la maison**	spay-see-ah-lee-tay duh lah may-zoh<u>n</u>
appetizers	**hors-d'oeuvre**	or-duh-vruh
first course (soup, salad)	**entrée**	ah<u>n</u>-tray
main course (meat, fish)	**plat principal**	plah pra<u>n</u>-see-pahl
bread	**pain**	pa<u>n</u>
cheese	**fromage**	froh-mahzh
sandwich	**sandwich**	sah<u>n</u>d-weech
soup	**soupe**	soop
salad	**salade**	sah-lahd
meat	**viande**	vee-ah<u>n</u>d
chicken	**poulet**	poo-lay
fish	**poisson**	pwah-soh<u>n</u>
seafood	**fruits de mer**	frwee duh mehr
fruit	**fruit**	frwee
vegetables	**légumes**	lay-gewm
dessert	**dessert**	duh-sehr
mineral water	**eau minérale**	oh mee-nay-rahl
tap water	**l'eau du robinet**	loh dew roh-bee-nay
milk	**lait**	lay
(orange) juice	**jus (d'orange)**	zhew (doh-rah<u>n</u>zh)
coffee	**café**	kah-fay
tea	**thé**	tay
wine	**vin**	va<u>n</u>
red / white	**rouge / blanc**	roozh / blah<u>n</u>
glass / bottle	**verre / bouteille**	vehr / boo-teh-ee
beer	**bière**	bee-ehr
Cheers!	**Santé!**	sah<u>n</u>-tay
More. / Another.	**Plus. / Un autre.**	plew / uh<u>n</u> oh-truh
The same.	**La même chose.**	lah mehm shohz
The bill, please.	**L'addition, s'il vous plaît.**	lah-dee-see-oh<u>n</u> see voo play
tip	**pourboire**	poor-bwar
Delicious!	**Délicieux!**	day-lee-see-uh

For more user-friendly French phrases, check out *Rick Steves' French Phrase Boo* *and Dictionary* or *Rick Steves' French, Italian & German Phrase Book*.

INDEX

Start your trip a

Free information and great gear t

▶ Plan Your Trip

Browse thousands of articles and a wealth of money-saving tips for planning your dream trip. You'll find up-to-date information on Europe's best destinations, packing smart, getting around, finding rooms, staying healthy, avoiding scams and more.

▶ Eurail Passes

Find out, step-by-step, if a rail pass makes sense for your trip—and how to avoid buying more than you need. Get a bunch of free extras!

▶ Graffiti Wall & Travelers' Helpline

Learn, ask, share—our online community of savvy travelers is a great resource for first-time travelers to Europe, as well as seasoned pros.

Rick Steves' Europe Through the Back Door, Inc

ricksteves.com

turn your travel dreams into affordable reality

▶ Free Audio Tours & Travel Newsletter

Get your nose out of this guidebook and focus on what you'll be seeing with Rick's free audio tours of the greatest sights in Paris, Rome, Florence and Venice.

Subscribe to our free *Travel News* e-newsletter, and get monthly articles from Rick on what's happening in Europe.

▶ Great Gear from Rick's Travel Store

Pack light and right—on a budget—with Rick's custom-designed carry-on bags, roll-aboards, day packs, travel accessories, guidebooks, journals, maps and DVDs of his TV shows.

Rick Steves

TRAVEL SKILLS
Europe Through the Back Door

EUROPE GUIDES
Best of Europe
Eastern Europe
Europe 101
European Christmas
Postcards from Europe

COUNTRY GUIDES
Croatia & Slovenia
England
France
Germany
Great Britain
Ireland
Italy
Portugal
Scandinavia
Spain
Switzerland

CITY & REGIONAL GUIDES
Amsterdam, Bruges & Brussels
Athens & The Peloponnese
Budapest
Florence & Tuscany
Istanbul
London
Paris
Prague & The Czech Republic
Provence & The French Riviera
Rome
Venice
Vienna, Salzburg & Tirol

PHRASE BOOKS & DICTIONARIES
French
French, Italian & German
German
Italian
Portuguese
Spanish

RICK STEVES' EUROPE DVDs
Austria & The Alps
Eastern Europe
England
Europe
France & Benelux
Germany & Scandinavia
Greece, Turkey, Israel & Egypt
Ireland & Scotland
Italy's Cities
Italy's Countryside
Rick Steves' European Christmas
Spain & Portugal
Travel Skills & "The Making Of"

PLANNING MAPS
Britain, Ireland & London
Europe
France & Paris
Germany, Austria & Switzerland
Ireland
Italy
Spain & Portugal

JOURNALS
Rick Steves' Pocket Travel Journal
Rick Steves' Travel Journal

NOW AVAILABLE

RICK STEVES APPS FOR THE iPHONE OR iPOD TOUCH

With these apps you can:

► Spin the compass icon to switch views between sights, hotels, and restaurant selections—and get details on cost, hours, address, and phone number.

► Tap any point on the screen to read Rick's detailed information, including history and suggested viewpoints.

► Get a deeper view into Rick's tours with audio and video segments.

Go to iTunes to download the following apps:

Rick Steves' Louvre Tour

Rick Steves' Historic Paris Walk

Rick Steves' Orsay Museum Tour

Rick Steves' Versailles

Rick Steves' Ancient Rome Tour

Rick Steves' St. Peter's Basilica Tour

Once downloaded, these apps are completely self-contained on your iPhone or iPod Touch, so you will not incur pricey roaming charges during use overseas.

Rick Steves books and DVDs are available at bookstores and through online booksellers.
Rick Steves guidebooks are published by Avalon Travel, a member of the Perseus Books Group.
Rick Steves apps are produced by Übermind, a boutique Seattle-based software consultancy firm.

CREDITS

Researcher
To help update this book, Rick relied on...

Cameron Hewitt

Cameron updated and expanded the Dutch day trips chapters: a week of windmills, wooden shoes, steam trains, black-and-white cows, and colorful cheese markets. Cameron, who writes and edits guidebooks for Rick Steves, lives in Seattle with his wife Shawna.

IMAGES

Location	Photographer
Netherlands full-page: Edam	Jennifer Hauseman
Amsterdam full-page: Amsterdam Canal	Cameron Hewitt
Haarlem full-page: Haarlem Hofje	Rick Steves
Belgium full-page: Belgium Canal	Dominic Bonuccelli
Bruges full-page: Belgium Canal	Dominic Bonuccelli
Brussels full-page: Brussels	Rick Steves

Rick Steves' Guidebook Series

Country Guides

Rick Steves' Best of Europe
Rick Steves' Croatia & Slovenia
Rick Steves' Eastern Europe
Rick Steves' England
Rick Steves' France
Rick Steves' Germany
Rick Steves' Great Britain
Rick Steves' Ireland
Rick Steves' Italy
Rick Steves' Portugal
Rick Steves' Scandinavia
Rick Steves' Spain
Rick Steves' Switzerland

City and Regional Guides

Rick Steves' Amsterdam, Bruges & Brussels
Rick Steves' Athens & the Peloponnese
Rick Steves' Budapest
Rick Steves' Florence & Tuscany
Rick Steves' Istanbul
Rick Steves' London
Rick Steves' Paris
Rick Steves' Prague & the Czech Republic
Rick Steves' Provence & the French Riviera
Rick Steves' Rome
Rick Steves' Venice
Rick Steves' Vienna, Salzburg & Tirol

Rick Steves' Phrase Books

French
French/Italian/German
German
Italian
Portuguese
Spanish

Other Books

Rick Steves' Europe 101: History and Art for the Traveler
Rick Steves' Europe Through the Back Door
Rick Steves' European Christmas
Rick Steves' Postcards from Europe

(Avalon Travel)

Avalon Travel
a member of the Perseus Books Group
1700 Fourth Street
Berkeley, CA 94710, USA

Printed in the U.S.A. by Worzalla
Third printing October 2009

Portions of this book were originally published in *Rick Steves' Mona Winks* © 2001, 1998,
1996, 1993, 1988 by Rick Steves and Gene Openshaw; and in *Rick Steves' France* © 2006,
2005, 2004, 2003, 2002 by Rick Steves and Steve Smith.

ISBN(13) 978-1-59880-103-3
ISSN 1543-012X

For the latest on Rick's lectures, books, tours, public radio show, and public television series,
contact Europe Through the Back Door, Box 2009, Edmonds, WA 98020, tel. 425/771-
8303, fax 425/771-0833, www.ricksteves.com, rick@ricksteves.com.

Europe Through the Back Door Senior Editor: Jennifer Madison Davis
ETBD Editors: Tom Griffin, Cathy McDonald, Sarah McCormic
ETBD Managing Editor: Risa Laib
Avalon Travel Senior Editor & Series Manager: Madhu Prasher
Avalon Travel Project Editor: Kelly Lydick
Research Assistance: Cameron Hewitt
Copy Editor: Judith Brown
Proofreader: Ellie Behrstock
Indexer: Claire Splan
Production & Typesetting: McGuire Barber Design
Cover Design: Kimberly Glyder Design
Maps and Graphics: David C. Hoerlein, Laura VanDeventer, Lauren Mills, Pat O'Connor,
Barb Geisler, Mike Morgenfeld
Photography: Rick Steves, Dominic Bonuccelli, Gene Openshaw, Jennifer Hauseman,
Laura VanDeventer, Bruce VanDeventer
Front matter color photos: p. i, Amsterdam at night, © Rick Steves; p. vii, Amsterdam
© Rick Steves
Cover Photo: Amsterdam canal © Rick Steves